Courts
of
Common Reason

~

Awakening the Spirit of 1776
To Form a More Perfect Union

A Handbook of Historical Evidence, Scientific Inquiry and Philosophical Analysis

Howard DeLong

BELCREST PRESS
2010

DeLong, Howard
Courts of common reason : awakening the spirit of 1776 to form a
more perfect union / Howard DeLong.
578 p. ; 23 cm.
Includes bibliographical references and index.
ISBN 978-0-615-32326-8
1. Democracy--Economics aspects--United States. 2. United
States--History--Revolution, 1775-1783--Historiography. 3. United
States--History--Revolution, 1775-1783--Influence. 4. United
States--Politics and government--Philosophy.
E209 .D45 2010

Second Printing

Published by

BELCREST PRESS
WEST HARTFORD, CT

*To David, Jamie, Chris, Casey
and the memory of Karen*

CONTENTS

Prologue. Updating an Old Proposal to New-Model America   1

Part I.   The Politics of Self-Knowledge   7

   1. The Ancient Background   8

   2. John Locke and the Spirit of 1776   30

   3. The Declaration: An Eighteenth-Century Betrayal   46

   4. The Declaration: A Twentieth-Century Betrayal   105

   5. The Constitution as a Revolutionary Document   121

   6. Courts of Common Reason   158

   7. Perfectionist Democracy and American Society   211

Part II.   The Economics of Honesty   235

   8. Economic Ignorance   236

   9. Economic Truth   250

   10. Economic Health   268

Part III.   The Philosophy of Aspiration   287

   11. The Epistemology of Aspiration   288

   12. The Ethics of Aspiration   308

   13. The Politics of Aspiration   347

   14. The Aesthetics of Aspiration   377

   15. The Metaphysics of Aspiration   418

   16. The Logic of Aspiration   444

   17. A New Order of the Ages   481

Epilogue. Posterity and American Revolutionary Ideals   515

References.   524

Acknowledgments.   562

Index.   564

Prologue

Updating an Old Proposal to New-Model America

> Yesterday the greatest Question was decided, which ever was debated in America, and a greater perhaps, never was or will be decided among Men. A Resolution was passed without one dissenting Colony 'that these united Colonies, are, and of right ought to be free and independent States, and as such, they have, and of Right ought to have full Power to make War, conclude Peace, establish Commerce, and to do all the other Acts and Things, which other States may rightfully do.' You will see in a few days a Declaration setting forth the Causes, which have impell'd Us to this mighty Revolution, and the Reasons which will justify it, in the Sight of God and Man. (Butterfield, Lyman 1963 2:27-8).
>
> John Adams to Abigail Adams, July 3, 1776.

On March 12, 1799, Thomas Jefferson declared that the "spirit of 1776 is not dead. It has only been slumbering"(1903 10:123). Jefferson's judgment is true of America today and the aim of this book is to help sound reveille. The phrase "spirit of 1776" referred not only to the resolve to abolish political ties to Great Britain (its rebellious aspect), but to create new governments of unprecedented excellence (its revolutionary aspect). Unlike all previous attempts elsewhere, these new governments would fit human nature, and would secure, among other rights, life, liberty and the pursuit of happiness. The state constitutions, the Articles of Confederation, the Constitution of 1787, and the Bill of Rights of 1791 were all part of this mighty revolution. Yet the generation of 1776 was not content. "It is pleasing to observe," John Jay noted in 1790, "that the present national government already affords advantages which the preceding one proved too feeble and ill-constructed to produce. How far it may be still distant from the degree of perfection to which it may possibly be carried, time only can decide"(1890 3:388). After more than two centuries, "time" has still not decided because, from the end of the revolutionary era to the present, politicians generally have not been concerned with reaching the highest degree of perfection in their craft that it is possible in practice to achieve. The spirit of 1776 remains in a slumber. Here we will imagine the spirit is awakened and with it the intense striving to complete the American revolution. We will consider in detail the changes needed to achieve and maintain that awakening.

I am acutely aware of how contrary this view of the American revolution is to most judgments of it made after the eighteenth century. As early as 1802 Noah Webster was in the spiritual slumber of which

Jefferson complained: "The real truth is, our revolutionary schemes were too visionary . . . and our hopes too sanguine"(1802 24-25). Webster's view continues to be the dominant interpretation and, when I started this book, I accepted it. I would have dismissed the preceding paragraph out of hand. I would have claimed that the intention to complete the American revolution is misconceived and utopian, that the path of political wisdom is lighted by those, such as the Founders, who reject visionary thinking and concentrate on what will work in practice, that seeking perfection in political matters courts disaster for humanity, that to even propose such an attempt betrays an ignorance of the totalitarian implications of such perfectionist thinkers as Plato or Marx. Perfectionist schemes of social design, such as those of the French revolution or Hitler, have led to such enormous human suffering that only the ignorant or the callous would propose another. An author advocating political perfection, I would have thought, was not just wrong but morally suspect.

I do not now deny the truth of these views in all respects. It is true that the American revolution cannot be completed in one sense of the word but, as we shall see, in two other important senses, it can be. It is also true that the Founders were intensely interested in what would work in practice, but that did not prevent them from aspiring to perfection in both the theory and practice of government. Finally, it is true that the pernicious influence of perfectionist thinkers has been very real, but the abominations associated with that influence, such as the Inquisition or the Gulag, were not due to perfectionism, but to the use of coercion and violence in the cause of a rigid, nonempirical fanaticism. In sharp contrast is the American ideal of a peaceful and empirical perfectionism, based on reason and persuasion, in the cause of humanity. These kinds of qualifications of the prevailing view are extremely important for, without them, the understanding of our past, and with it our knowledge of what to do in the present, is seriously compromised.

This book presents the evidence and argument needed to understand the American revolution as it was commonly understood in the eighteenth century. The revolution was then seen not merely in political terms but as the creation of a new kind of civilization, a civilization that would alter the basis of all aspects of human aspiration. I have tried to be thorough in my exposition, since anything less will not be persuasive, given the current weight of received opinion. I have quoted liberally from eighteenth-century American writers. I wanted the *dramatis personae* of the revolution to communicate the spirit of 1776 directly to the reader. By supplying the considerable testimony needed to understand their aspirations, this book is also intended to serve as a work of reference. Hence I have given many cross-references, as well as numerous references to relevant passages not quoted. Yet the aim is not just to convey information, but to provide the resources useful to a reader who wishes to develop a *habit* of thinking in American revolutionary terms, something I know from my own experience is not today so easy to do. Habits require repetition and some readers may find the quotations excessive, even annoying, and they can of course skip them if they choose. In my judgment, quotations justifying historical claims concerning ideas are much like proofs for mathematical theorems, or experiments for scientific hypotheses. They are valuable not merely for testimony but as one of the great joys of inquiry. It is common for mathematicians and scientists to redo proofs or experiments that they know well merely for pleasure. To achieve a more profound understanding, they may also demonstrate the same result with different proofs or experiments. Thus a mathematician might study a score of distinct proofs and applications of the Pythagorean theorem. So, for the same reasons, historians or philosophers of the American revolution may reread evidence, or deepen their understanding by studying a number of quotations establishing the same point. My hope is that readers will appreciate the book's variety and organization of evidence, and that its recurring themes will enable them to experience more deeply the excitement, the beauty, and the moral power of that revolution.

My intent, however, is go beyond establishing historical claims about how the American revolution was perceived by its creators. I wish, first, to show that, with refinements, the fundamental ideals of the American founding are the best principles on which government can be organized and, second, to illustrate how we should revise our political and economic practices to be consistent with those ideals. My account is not a prediction of what will happen, but an interpretation of what should happen, were we wholly faithful to our revolutionary heritage. Thus little attention is paid to political differences among the Founders, or changes in substance that one or another of them might have made over the course of a lifetime. The primary emphasis is on their common revolutionary spirit. That spirit was understood as guiding science as well as politics. The Founders believed that humans are capable of a general rationality that can be exhibited in mathematics, in the natural sciences (whether theoretical or practical), and in the moral sciences (such as politics or economics).

In Jefferson's words: "Science has liberated the ideas of those who read and reflect"(Cappon 1959 2:391). And science was seen as directly relevant to politics: "A republican government and science, mutually promote and support each other"(12) is the judgment of Phillips Payson from a 1778 sermon. Anyone who sees mathematics and science as cold and inhuman, or technology as primarily the cause of disasters, will have a hard time comprehending how the Founders understood their revolution. To explicate it, they made extensive use of analogies to mathematics and science, such as the parallel explanation of common law and Newtonian theory given by James Wilson (2007 1:568). It will help *our* understanding if we try to emulate them. Newton gave a perfectionist analysis that revolutionized our knowledge of the mathematical and physical world; Jefferson gave a perfectionist analysis that revolutionized our understanding of the moral and political world. Each revolution displays extraordinary ambition; to present either as modest is to misrepresent them. But that ambition was highly disciplined, for their analyses were grounded in reason, observation, experiment, and proof. The scientific spirit, which we associate with Newton, and the spirit of 1776, which we associate with Jefferson, are two aspects of the same phenomenon. The American revolution is the scientific revolution applied to the moral and political world; the scientific revolution is the American revolution applied to the natural world.

American perfectionist democracy is my name for a concrete but grand experiment that aims to test how close, in a contemporary setting, we can actually come to fulfilling the ideals of the American revolution. Three dimensions of American perfectionist democracy — political, economic, and philosophical — are articulated in the three parts of this book. The Founders' high ideals will be illustrated by showing how much we must still do to live up to them. James Madison once elaborated on a point of Jefferson as follows: "As the people are the only legitimate fountain of power, and it is from them that the constitutional charter, under which the several branches of government hold their power, is derived; it seems strictly consonant to the republican theory, to recur to the same original authority . . . whenever it may be necessary to . . . new-model the powers of government"(1962 10:461; cf. Iredell's comments in Elliot 1836 4:9). American perfectionist democracy is a proposal to new-model our governments by appealing — using twenty-first-century standards — to the *deliberate sense* or the *common reason* of the people. These terms, the first from Madison, the second from Jefferson, come from our revolutionary past but, as we shall see, discovering the reality to which they refer will significantly test the humanistic, mathematical, scientific, and technological resources of twenty-first-century America. This is perhaps surprising, but a good revolution, like a good book or good friend, means more as we come to understand it better. Trying to summarize many of the benefits of awakening the American revolutionary spirit is certainly a daunting task. Trying to describe all of them is an impossibility. As the Boston minister Samuel Thacher put it on July 4, 1796: "The advantages of the American Revolution cannot be compressed within the compass of a few pages. Its effects are not confined to one age or country. The human mind has received a stimulus, and attained an expansion which will extend its influence beyond calculation"(1796 22; cf. Ramsay 1779 2).

Part I

The Politics of Self-Knowledge

"*Cratylus*. And you, Socrates, appear to me to be an oracle, and to give answers much to my mind, whether you are inspired by Euthyphro, or whether some Muse may have long been an inhabitant of your breast, unconsciously to yourself.

"*Socrates*. Excellent Cratylus, I have long been wondering at my own wisdom; I cannot trust myself. And I think that I ought to stop and ask myself What am I saying? for there is nothing worse than self-deception — when the deceiver is always at home and always with you — it is quite terrible, and therefore I ought often to retrace my steps and endeavour to 'look fore and aft,' in the words of . . . Homer"(1937 1:217).

Plato

"For what is a man profited, if he shall gain the whole world, and lose his own soul?"(*Matthew* 16:26).

Jesus

"It is not safe to play with errour, and dress it up to ourselves or others in the shape of truth. The mind by degrees loses its natural relish of real solid truth, is reconciled insensibly to any thing that can be dressed up into any faint appearance of it; and if the fancy be allowed the place of judgment at first in sport, it afterwards comes by use to usurp it; and what is recommended by this flatterer (that studies but to please) is received for good"(1824 2:379).

John Locke

"A nation ought to know itself. . . . This duty of self-knowledge is of vast extent and of vast importance, in nations as well as in men"(2007 1:536).

James Wilson

"We think in America that it is necessary to introduce the people into every department of government as far as they are capable of exercising it; and that this is the only way to ensure a long-continued and honest administration of it's powers"(1950 15:283).

Thomas Jefferson

"While reason retains her rule, while men are as ready to receive as to give advice, and as willing to be convinced themselves, as to convince others, there are few political evils from which a free and enlightened people cannot deliver themselves"(1788 3).

John Jay

1

The Ancient Background

The ideals of the Declaration of Independence are well-known; unfortunately, what is well-known is not necessarily known well. Herein lies the difficulty of understanding the Declaration: Its familiarity obscures the significance of what it says. Many Americans see its meaning as rhetorical and patriotic, worthy of mention on the Fourth of July, but of no real contemporary significance. Others look to it as an affirmation of what they already believe and do. It confirms the *status quo* as being good or right. Still others use it as an indispensable document to understand eighteenth-century America. Here we study it in order to understand the American revolution, because its pithy and beautiful articulation of that revolution is why it remains today what it was from the beginning: a glorious monument for all humanity . We will try to learn from it, and will especially look for whatever might serve as a valid criticism of our present political theory and practice.

The Declaration presupposes a view of human nature that is a blend of parts of two traditions; one is religious and reaches back through Christianity to ancient Judaism, the other is secular and reaches back through the Romans to the ancient Greeks. (For a discussion of historical counterparts of fundamental American laws and political ideals that are even more ancient, see McGuire 1994; cf. below, page 494) By looking at these traditions we can gain the background needed to understand the Declaration's meaning.

We will begin with the religious tradition since it is older. In the eighteenth century the vast majority of Americans were Protestant Christians, and reverence for political authorities was part of their heritage. To justify that reverence, the command of Jesus to "Render to Caesar the things that are Caesar's . . ."(*Mark* 12:17) could easily be appealed to, as could the directives of St. Paul: "Let every soul be subject unto the higher powers. For there is no power but of God: the powers that be are ordained of God. Whosoever therefore resisteth the power, resisteth the ordinance of God; and they that resist shall receive to themselves damnation"(*Romans* 13:1). "Put them in mind to be subject to principalities and powers, to obey magistrates . . ."(*Titus* 3:1). "Submit yourselves to every ordinance of man for the Lord's sake: whether it be to the king, as supreme; Or unto governors

..."(1 *Peter* 2:13-14). Furthermore, the words of Martin Luther and John Calvin could be used to strengthen this ethos: In 1520 Luther stated that ". . . even when the government commits an injustice, as the King of Babylon did to the people of Israel, God wants the government obeyed, without treachery or deception"(1955 44:92; cf. *Jeremiah* 27:6-7, and *Baruch* 2:21, in the *Apocrypha*). In 1536 Calvin writes: "A very wicked man utterly unworthy of all honor, provided he has the public power in his hands, . . . should be held in the same reverence and esteem by his subjects, in so far as public obedience is concerned, in which they would hold the best of kings if he were given to them"(1960 2:1513; cf. 1518 and 1948 480).

In 1609 James I of England likewise interpreted the Bible as giving divine authority to existing political power:

> The State of MONARCHIE is the supremest thing vpon earth: For Kings are not onely Gods Lieutenants vpon earth, and sit vpon Gods throne, but euen by God himselfe they are called Gods. . . . Kings are iustly called Gods, for that they exercise a manner or resemblance of Diuine power vpon earth: For if you wil consider the Attributes to God, you shall see how they agree in the person of a King. God hath power to create, or destroy, make, or vnmake at his pleasure, to giue life, or send death, to iudge all, and to be iudged nor accomptable to none. . . . And the like power haue Kings . . . (1918 307-8; the Biblical reference to where kings are called gods is uncertain, but cf. *Psalms* 82:6-7 and *John* 10:34).

The colonial experience, however, was leading Americans away from the idea that kings or governments had divine sanction, or the right of arbitrary rule. It was moving them to believe that the sole *raison d'être* of government is the happiness of the people. By the late eighteenth century clergymen in America were using even the above-quoted passages from Paul as part of arguments for resistance to bad government (cf. Tucker, John 1771, Turner 1773, Hitchcock, Gad 1774 and West, Samuel 1776). Furthermore, ministers typically said there was "a striking resemblance between our own circumstances and those of the antient Israelites"(Cooper, Samuel 1780 2). Again, Oliver Noble said that "the Jews were the Lord's *covenant* people," but then he adds, "Are not the people of *America*, also God's covenant people?"(1775 19, 20). Or again, "It has often been remarked that the people of the United States come nearer to a parallel with Ancient Israel, than any other nation upon the globe. Hence, 'our American Israel,' is a term frequently used; and common consent allows it apt and proper"(Abbot, Abiel 1799 6; cf. also Jefferson 1903 3:383). Escaping from European "Egypts" under pharaohs such as James I, emigrants crossed the Red Sea (called the Atlantic Ocean), and came to the promised land (called America), which, under God, could become a new Jerusalem.

This identification with ancient Israel made it easier to take the Old Testament as authoritative when considering the proper role of government. That role was found by colonial ministers to be republican. For example, on May 31, 1775, Samuel Langdon, the president of Harvard, delivered a sermon in which he claimed that the "Jewish government, according to the original constitution which was divinely established, if considered merely in a civil view, was a perfect Republic"(1775 11, cf. also 1788). "Jewish government" was taken as a standard because its leaders "managed the public affairs according to the general voice" and in this they had God's approval. Monarchy, in contrast, was condemned by God:

> And let them who cry up *the divine right of Kings* consider, that the only form of government which had a proper claim to a divine establishment was so far from including the idea of a King, that it was a high crime for Israel to ask to be in this respect like other nations; and when they were gratified, it was as a just punishment of their folly, that they might feel the burdens of court pageantry, of which they were warned by a very striking description, than as a divine recommendation of kingly authority. Every nation, when able and agreed, has a right to set up over themselves any form of government which to them may appear most conductive to their common welfare. The civil Polity of Israel is doubtless an excellent general model, allowing for some peculiarities; at least, some principal laws and orders of it may be copied, to great advantage, in more modern establishments. (1775 12; cf. Shute 1768 12ff)

Here we have the Bible being employed to refute the divine right of kings. However, that authority could even be used to show government itself is dispensable. The Garden of Eden shows that human beings could live well without government, provided God's law was obeyed. The book of *Judges* describes a time when Israel had no government at all. It ends with the words: "In those days *there was* no king in Israel: every man did *that which was* right in his own eyes." Hence colonial Protestant piety raised the question: What form of government, *if any*, has divine sanction?

Liberty too was judged in religious terms. Thus, in 1774 Nathaniel Niles claimed that we can infer "that civil liberty is of great worth . . , from the conduct of God toward the Jewish nation"(1774 21). An example of that conduct is the story (alluded to by Langdon) of the elders of Israel coming to Samuel and saying: ". . . now make us a king to judge us like all the nations"(1 *Samuel* 8:5). Samuel was displeased and the Lord has him warn the people about the dangers of kings. This story was widely quoted in the eighteenth-century political debates. The historian David Ramsay, writing in 1789, observed:

> With the view of operating on the sentiments of a religious people, scripture was pressed into his service, and the powers, and even the name of a king was rendered odious in the eyes of numerous colonists who has read and studied the history of the Jews, as recorded in the Old Testament. The folly of that people in revolting from a government, instituted by Heaven itself, and the oppressions to which they were subjected in consequence of their lusting after kings to rule over them, afforded an excellent handle for prepossessing the colonists in favour of republican institutions, and prejudicing them against kingly government. (1789 1:338; cf. *Judges* 8:22-3, and *Hosea* 13:9-11 in addition to the Samuel story; also cf. Elliot 1836 2:225-6 and Paine 1945 1:10-12. In England that story had been used in political arguments by James Harrington (2003 26) and by Algernon Sidney (1990 126-7), both of whom were cited by Americans to justify their revolution.)

In large part, republican government had great appeal because of the breakdown of British and European class distinctions in colonial America. The belief in political equality came easily, and it led Americans to draw political consequences from the doctrine that, as descendants of Adam and Eve, we are all of the same stock and made in God's image (cf. Wilson 2007 1:387-8, 636-7). Thus Samuel Cooke's election sermon of May 30, 1770, claimed that the "first attention of the faithful ruler will be to the subjects of government in their specific nature; — He will not forget that he ruleth over men — Men, who are the same species with himself, and by nature equal — Men who are the offspring of God, and alike formed after his glorious image — Men of like passions and feelings with himself, and as men, in the sight of their common Creator of equal importance"(1770 13-14). Since no person is created with more worth than any other, impartiality is required for the attainment of justice, that is, equality before the law becomes a legal ideal. As the Lord says to Moses: "Ye shall do no unrighteousness in judgment: thou shalt not respect the person of the poor, nor honour the person of the mighty: but in righteousness shall thou judge thy neighbour"(*Leviticus* 19:15; cf. *Acts* 10:34, *Galacians* 3:28). This passage served as the inspiration for the oath that Supreme Court judges take: "I will administer justice without respect to persons, and do equal right to the poor and to the rich."

The Bible in general, and the Old Testament in particular, is not consistent in promoting the moral equality of all human beings. Nevertheless the contrast with Plato and Aristotle, the principal philosophers of our classical heritage, is worth noting. In the *Republic* (1955 106-7) Plato presents the myth that God mingles either gold, or silver, or brass and iron, in the substance of everyone, and a person's worth is determined by the worth of the metal. It is thus not surprising that Plato nowhere rejects slavery. Aristotle likewise maintains the inequality of human beings: ". . . some men are by nature free, and others slaves, and . . . for these latter slavery is both expedient and right"(1984 2:1991). He claims that hunting is "an art which we ought to practise against wild beasts and against men who, though intended by nature to be governed, will not submit; for war of such a kind is naturally just"(1984 2:1994). Aristotle's view that slavery could be justified by an appeal to nature had at most a minor influence on political theory in the eighteenth century. In any case, his view was probably a reaction to expressions of human equality by others. Thus Alcidamas states: "God has given all men their freedom; nature has made no man a slave"(2002 33). The sophist Antiphon writes: ". . . we are all by nature born the same in every way, both barbarians and Hellenes"(Freeman 1966 148; cf. Eratosthenes' view in Strabo 1917 1:249). Lycophron says that "the nobility of good birth is obscure, and its dignity a matter of words — the preference for it is a matter of opinion, and in truth there is no difference between the low-born and the well-born"(Aristotle 1984 2:2422). Again, a character in Euripides' *Ion* says, "Only one thing brings shame to slaves, the name. In all else a slave who is valiant is not at all inferior to free men"(1999 421). Expressions of equality can also be found in Roman civilization: "Kindly remember that he whom you call your slave sprang from the same stock, is smiled upon by the same skies, and on equal terms with yourself breathes, lives, and dies. It is just as possible for you to see in him a free-born man as for him to see in you a slave"(Seneca 1989 1:307).

Unfortunately Jefferson, the author of the immortal words "all men are created equal," became, and then remained, a practicing Aristotelian. He sought to recapture slaves who would not "submit." Here is an advertisement that he placed in the *Virginia Gazette* on September 7, 1769:

Run away from the subscriber in *Albemarle* a Mulatto slave called *Sandy* about 35 years of age, his stature is rather low, inclining to corpulence, and his complexion light; he is a shoemaker by trade, in which he uses his left hand principally, can do

coarse carpenters work, and is something of a horse jockey; he is greatly addicted
to drink, and when drunk is insolent and disorderly, in his conversation he swears
much, and his behavior is artful and knavish. He took with him a white horse,
much scarred with traces, of which it is expected he will endeavour to dispose; he
also carried his shoemakers tools, and will probably endeavour to get employment
that way. Whoever conveys the said slave to me in *Albemarle* shall have 40 s.
reward, if taken up within the county, 4 l. if elsewhere within the colony, and 10 l.
if in any other colony, from Thomas Jefferson. (1950 1:33; Jefferson also sold
slaves, cf. 24:410)

George Mason, author of the Virginia Declaration of Rights, and
George Washington, "the father of our country," placed similar
advertisements (Mason 1970 2:855-6 and Washington 1976 3:45).
Jefferson, Mason, and Washington were asking their compatriots to
violate the command expressed in *Deuteronomy* 23:15-6: "You shall
not give up to his master a slave who has escaped from his master to
you; he shall dwell with you, in your midst, in the place which he shall
choose within one of your towns, where it pleases him best; you shall
not oppress him."

If the Bible is accepted as authoritative, then life itself must be a
gift from God. In *Genesis* (2:7) we are told that "God formed man of
the dust of the ground, and breathed into his nostrils the breath of life,
and man became a living soul." He then made Eve from Adam's rib
and thus women likewise have life from God. But God did not stop at
life. As Jefferson said in 1774: "The god who gave us life, gave us
liberty at the same time"(1950 1:135). The assistance Israel got when
it fled from the Egyptians is a gift of God and from this gift arises a
positive duty to promote liberty. The Lord orders Moses to ". . .
proclaim liberty throughout *all* the land unto all the inhabitants thereof
. . ."(*Leviticus* 25:10); this passage was inscribed on the Liberty Bell
and was appealed to by abolitionists). Speaking of his people God
says substantially the same thing to Jeremiah: ". . . ye . . . had done
right in my sight, in proclaiming liberty every man to his neighbour
. . ." Among the consequences of violating this command are
pestilence, famine and death (*Jeremiah* 34:15-20). Just as "Thou shall
not kill"(*Exodus* 20:13) means that we violate God's law when we take
away his gift of life, so we likewise violate his law when we take away
the gift of liberty.

These grants of life and liberty are "unalienable," to use the
language of the Declaration. Jefferson's "original Rough draught" of
it used "inalienable" (1950 1:423), but no one today knows who made
the change or why. A check of four dictionaries published between
1773 and 1777 (Bailey 1773, Kenrick 1773, Ash 1775, and Perry

1777) reveals no consistent difference in their use. In any case, "unalienable" — we will stick to this term — had two senses. One sense referred to people *distributively* as individuals. This sense appears paradoxical in that unalienable rights may, in some circumstances, be rightfully alienated. Thus a person's unalienable right to liberty can legitimately be taken away as just punishment for a crime. What the distributive sense means is that a right may not be alienated to another by agreement or contract. The justification for this claim had been expressed by both Thomas Hobbes (1968 192) and John Locke (1988 353): the transfer of any right must aim at some good for the individual losing it. To say that a right is unalienable is to claim that there is no such good. "Among natural rights," the New Hampshire Constitution of 1784 declares, "some are in their very nature unalienable, because no equivalent can be given or received for them. Of this kind are the RIGHTS OF CONSCIENCE"(Thorpe 1909 2454; cf. also Whiting 1788 22 and Brutus 1787 2). Consider a present-day illustration. Imagine a tackle and a guard on a football team being charged, in court, with assault and battery against a halfback of the opposing team. The halfback testifies that during the game while he was peacefully carrying the ball toward the goal he was attacked. The judge rather sensibly rules that in virtue of the halfback's agreement to play football, the laws concerning assault and battery are suspended during the game. On the other hand, suppose the tackle and guard intentionally killed the halfback after he had agreed that they could try to do so during the game. In such a case, the judge could rule that the agreement is null, and appeal as far back as Grotius, who in 1620 said that, since the right to life is unalienable, "no one may pledge his life by contract"(1926 1:71, 73). Similarly, Grotius thought the right to a free life is unalienable (73). Locke (1988 284) and Montesquieu (1989 247-48) agreed, arguing that a contract to become a slave is void since because there is no good for which a reasonable person would make such an exchange. Note again that unalienable rights in the distributive sense are not absolute. Thus a democratic society might decide that an individual can legally contract to have life support removed under specified circumstances.

The second sense of "unalienable" applies to people *collectively*. Here rights are absolutes, they cannot *legitimately* be violated for any reason whatsoever. Slavery of black people in the eighteenth century and genocide in the twentieth century are examples of such violation. These are crimes against human nature whose ground is in "the Laws of Nature and of Nature's God." Governments that do not recognize such rights are illegitimate and may rightly be abolished by internal revolution or exterior force. The Biblical source for the idea that human beings have unalienable rights comes in part from the claim, referred to above by Cooke, that "God created man in his *own* image" (*Genesis* 1:27). The kingdom of God precedes all civil governments and provides the moral constraints within which any government must operate; in the words of John Dickinson: "We claim [the *rights essential to happiness*] from a higher source — from the King of Kings, and Lord of all the earth. They are not annexed to us by parchments and seals. They are created in us by the decrees of Providence, which establish the laws of our nature. They are born with us; exist with us; and cannot be taken from us by any human power, without taking our lives"(1766 4). "The sacred rights of mankind," Alexander Hamilton wrote in 1775, "are not to be rummaged for, among old parchments, or musty records. They are written, as with a sun beam, in the whole *volume* of human nature, by the hand of the divinity itself; and can never be erased or obscured by mortal power"(1961 1:122). Hamilton's words were probably inspired by the Bible, perhaps by that part of *Jeremiah* where the Lord says: ". . . I will make a new covenant with the house of Israel and the house of Judah . . . I will put my law within them, and I will write it upon their hearts; and I will be their God, and they shall be my people"(31:31, 33; cf. also *Romans* 2:12-16 and *Hebrews* 8:10 and 10:16). Jefferson's language is even closer to Jeremiah's: "Our Revolution . . . presented us an album on which we were free to write what we pleased. We had no occasion to search into musty records, to hunt up royal parchments, or to investigate the laws and institutions of a semi-barbarous ancestry. We appealed to those of nature, and found them engraved in our hearts" (1903 16:44; cf. also Adams, Samuel 1904 4:356, Madison 1900 6:164; in England, even the skeptical David Hume had referred to "ideas of primitive equality which are engraven in the hearts of all men"(1879 2:251). Gouverneur Morris, in a pamphlet "published according to a resolution of Congress," writes: "The great principle therefore is and ever will remain in force, that MEN ARE BY NATURE FREE. . . . it is conceded on all hands that the right to be free can never be alienated"(1779 1-2). When it is asked why the philosophical doctrine of unalienable rights was not seriously questioned in eighteenth-century America, the answer is that it was taken as axiomatic: if a government's taking the lives or liberty of a whole people is not wrong, what could be? If that is not contrary to morality and religion, what is? Indeed prophets such as Amos, Hosea, Micah, Isaiah, and Jeremiah were thought of as *political* revolutionaries. Thus their words could serve as justification of the divine "right" and "duty" of the people to "alter or abolish" government when it becomes destructive of its proper ends.

Francis Hutcheson, an Irish-Scottish philosopher, may have influenced American political theory, when he claimed in 1725 that "unalienable Rights are essential Limitations in all Governments"(1969 1:303). In any case, those limitations were everywhere inspired by Biblical stories. Thus God made a covenant with Noah that is universal: "I establish my covenant with you, that never again shall all flesh be cut off by the waters of a flood, and never again shall there be a flood to destroy the earth"(*Genesis* 9:11). God became a ruler bound by his own agreements: even he cannot commit worldwide genocide again. In fact, when he wished to destroy just Sodom and Gomorrah, Abraham objected: "Shall not the Judge of all the earth do right?"(*Genesis* 18:25). Moses likewise argues that God must obey his own moral laws:

> And the Lord said to Moses, "I have seen this people, and behold, it is a stiff-necked people; now therefore let me alone, that my wrath may burn hot against them and I may consume them; but of you I will make a great nation." But Moses besought the Lord his God, and said, "O Lord, why does thy wrath burn hot against thy people, whom thou hast brought forth out of the land of Egypt with great power and with a mighty hand? Why should the Egyptians say, 'With evil intent did he bring them forth, to slay them in the mountains, and to consume them from the face of the earth'? Turn from thy fierce wrath, and repent of this evil against thy people. Remember Abraham, Isaac, and Israel, thy servants, to whom thou didst swear by thine own self, and didst say to them, 'I will multiply your descendants as the stars of heaven, and all this land that I have promised I will give to your descendants, and they shall inherit it for ever.'" And the Lord repented of the evil which he thought to do to his people. (*Exodus* 32:9-14)

If the Lord can contemplate evil, and Moses can prevent it by arguing that God should not break his promise of an unalienable right to life for his people so, the revolutionists thought, how much more so are the American people justified in insisting — with force, if necessary — that governments keep their promises to respect unalienable rights?

Thus biblically inspired limitations were incorporated in political covenants from the Mayflower Compact to the Declaration and Constitution. The ways in which rulers ought to be limited becomes the theme of sermon after sermon given before and during the revolutionary era. The substance of the preaching was often very like that of the Declaration. In fact, the words themselves were sometimes remarkably close. Consider once again Langdon's 1775 sermon:

> Thanks be to God, that he has given us, as men, natural rights independent of all human laws whatever; and that these rights are recognized by the grand Charter of British Liberties. By the law of nature any body of people, destitute of order and government, may form themselves into a civil society according to their best prudence, and so provide for their common safety and advantage. When one form is found by the majority, not to answer the grand purpose in any tolerable degree, they may by common consent put an end to it, and set up another: only as all such great changes are attended with difficulty, and danger of confusion, they ought not to be attempted without urgent necessity, which will be determined always by the general voice of the wisest and best members of the community. If the great servants of the public forget their duty, betray their trust and sell their country, or make war against the most valuable rights and privileges of the people; reason and justice require that they should be discarded, and others appointed in their room, without any regard to formal resignations of their forfeited power. (23-4)

Such views were expressed most frequently toward the middle and end of the eighteenth century, but they were not unknown earlier. Thus, in 1717, John Wise (1652-1725) could write: "The first Humane Subject and Original of Civil Power is the People. For as they have a Power every Man over himself in a Natural State, so upon a Combination they can and do bequeath this Power unto others; and settle it according as their united discretion shall Determine. For that this is very plain, that when the Subject of Sovereign Power is quite Extinct, that Power returns to the People again. And when they are free, they may set up what species of Government they please . . ."(44). Much earlier in 1644, Roger Williams (1603-1683) made a similar statement (quoted below, page 30). In this conception the people are the final authority and, to express this idea, it was sometimes said that the voice of the people is the voice of God (cf. Machiavelli 1998 117-18) That is, just as there is no appeal in natural theology beyond the creator of nature (that is, "Nature's God"), so there is no appeal in republican politics beyond the creator of government (that is, the people, who are, so to say, government's god). Of course, the analogy can be pushed too far, and this was recognized in revolutionary times (see, for example, Parsons 1778 17).

Nevertheless it is worth noting that the same difficulties that arise in trying to respond to the voice of God also arise in trying to respond to the voice of the people. First, as Locke had argued, any claim of revelation from God must be carefully investigated to determine whether it is truly from God (1975 701). The criteria are experience and reason: "*Revelation* is natural *Reason* enlarged by a new set of Discoveries communicated by GOD immediately, which *Reason* vouches the Truth of, by the Testimony and Proofs it gives, that they come from GOD"(1975 698, cf 598). Americans generally accepted this doctrine. The "Word of Reason," Ebenezer Gay said, is the "Word of God": "The manifest Absurdity of any Doctrine, is a stronger Argument that it is not of God, than any other Evidence can be that it is. 'A Revelation must be agreable to the Nature of God, and Possibility of Things.' "(1759 11, 22; cf. Jefferson below, page 293 and 1903 14:197). As reason determines which prophets falsely claim to speak for God, so reason must determine which presidents, legislators, and judges falsely claim to speak for the people. Second, as Madison noted (cf. below, page 151) following Locke (1975 667, 692), even if a voice comes from God there is the question of whether it is understood correctly. The same difficulty arises with respect to the voice of the people.

Finally, according to the Bible, God has ethical limitations. He regrets his intentions: "And the Lord repented the evil which he thought to do to his people"(*Exodus* 32:14; cf. *Jonah* 3:10). And his actions: ". . . the Lord was sorry that he made man on earth, and it grieved him in his heart"(*Genesis* 6:5-6), ". . . the Lord repented that he had made Saul king over Israel"(1 *Samuel* 15:34). He deceives people: "Therefore God sends upon them a strong delusion, to make them believe what is false . . ."(2 *Thessalonians* 2:11; cf. *Isaiah* 5:10, *Mark* 4:10-12). "The Lord has put a lying spirit in the mouth of all these your prophets . . . "(1 *Kings* 22:23; cf. *Ezekiel* 14:9). "Ah, Lord God, surely thou hast utterly deceived this people and Jerusalem, . . . "(*Jeremiah* 4:10). He gives bad commandments: "I gave [the Jewish people] statutes that were not good and ordinances by which they could not have life"(*Ezekiel* 20:25; cf. Montesquieu 1989 322). He makes people economically unequal: "The Lord makes poor and makes rich"(1 *Samuel* 2:7). He interferes with good judgments which humans are likely to make: "I will harden his heart, so that he will not let the people go"(*Exodus* 4:21), "But they would not listen to the voice of their father; for it was the will of the Lord to slay them"(1 *Samuel* 2:25), "O Lord, why dost thou make us err from thy ways and harden our heart, so that we fear thee not?"(*Isaiah* 63:17). Note that the prayer of Jesus petitions, "Lead us not into temptation, but deliver us from evil"(*Matthew* 6:13). And the cause of that evil may be the Lord himself: "I make peace, and create evil"(*Isaiah* 45:7), "Is it not from the mouth of the Most High that good and evil come?"(*Lamentations* 3:38), "Does evil befall a city, unless the Lord has done it?"(*Amos* 3:6; cf. *Jeremiah* 18:11, 42:10). And he is brutal to those Hebrews who forget him: "I will be to them like a lion, like a leopard I will lurk beside the way. I will fall upon them like a bear robbed of her cubs, I will tear open their breast, and there I will devour them like a lion, as a wild beast would rend them"(*Hosea* 13:7-8). Yet, when faced with God's ethical limitations, humans are not always powerless, for they can reason with him: ("Come now, let us reason together, says the Lord . . . "(*Isaiah* 1:18)). As God chooses leaders who have the courage to challenge him with arguments when he either contemplates unjust acts (Abraham and Moses), or allows such acts (Job's unjust suffering (cf. 23:1-7)), so, according to our revolutionary heritage, we need leaders who will confront the American people whenever their ethical limitations lead them to favor immoral or mistaken policies. In Hamilton's words we need leaders who have the "courage and magnanimity enough to serve [the people] at the peril of their displeasure"(1961 4:608). Thus although the people are a leader's best guide on earth, as the faithful believe God is beyond it, in neither case should obedience be uncritical. The voice of the people, no less than the voice of God, may not, if it is to be a guide to action, demand deeds which our experience and reason tell us contradict that which is right. "Submission even to the *Deity*," Charles Chauncy declared, "ought always to be exercised under the conduct of reason and good sense"(1784 180). Nevertheless, God in Biblical theology, and the people in revolutionary ideology, are the final authorities, and if God demands immoral acts (say, to kill Isaac), or the people do (say, to steal Indian land), then a refusal to cooperate by the faithful, or by the political leader, is the only course for an upright person. God or the people must then directly commit their own abominations, and bear the responsibility for them.

Although it is beyond question that some of the fundamental ideas in the Declaration were Biblically inspired, the historical roots of others go back to the ancient Greeks. Their influence can be summed up in three words: reason, excellence, and happiness. Let us look at each. First, the importance of reason in Greek philosophy went well beyond the importance the Hebrews ascribed to it. The stipulation that reason must be satisfied before a proposition is worthy of belief is a Greek conception. The Greeks invented the idea of a logical proof, without a doubt one of the greatest intellectual achievements of all time. They believed that a capacity for reason distinguished human from animal nature, while superior reasoning ability distinguishes the best human beings. Lysias (*circa* 458 - 380 B.C.) thought that reasoning ability distinguished the Athenians, who, in contrast to other peoples, believed "humans should determine justice by means of law and persuade by using reason: they should be ruled by law and taught by reason, and their actions should serve both ends"(2000 31). Being reasonable, however, requires deliberation, which may involve a group, as in Socratic dialogues, where the aim is self-knowledge, or in legislatures, where the aim is wise laws. An individual, however, may also deliberate within himself. As Socrates put it: ". . . the soul when thinking appears to me to be just talking — asking questions of herself and answering them, affirming and denying . . . To form an opinion is to speak, and opinion is a word spoken, — I mean, to oneself and in silence, not aloud or to another . . ."(Plato 1937 2:193). In the same spirit Aristotle writes: ". . . demonstration is not addressed to external argument — but to argument in the soul . . ."(1984 1:124).

Protagoras, who Cynthia Farrar calls "the first democratic political theorist in the history of the world"(1990 77), emphasized deliberation when he claimed that there are two sides to every question. In making the strongest case for each side, the significance of the question is brought out and the basis for a good judgment is laid (63-4; cf. also Aristotle's remark below, page 164). For both Protagoras and the Founders, this reasoning process is a necessary part of any legitimate government. We are unsure exactly how Protagoras and other ancient democrats understood deliberative reason. However, in eighteenth-century America it consisted of four things: first, the introduction of conceptual clarity by paying careful attention to meaning, second, a consideration of what can be said for and against each alternative, third, a choice made in light of the preceding inquiry and, fourth, a determination to reassess the choice when new evidence or new considerations emerge. (My summary is meant to capture the spirit of Benjamin Franklin's "*Moral Algebra*"(1959 19:299-300, 1907 7:281-282; cf. Locke 1975 552)). Making decisions based on rational deliberation is what the people ought to practice in themselves, in juries, in town-meetings, and in judging their representatives. The representatives for their part ought to practice it in themselves, when framing laws or constitutions, or when judging whether their actions truly represent their constituents. Deliberative soul-searching is the foundation of self-knowledge and self-government; it is the only proper source of ethical and political action.

"It has been frequently remarked," Hamilton asserted in the opening paragraph of the *Federalist*, "that it seems to have been reserved to the people of this country, by their conduct and example, to decide the important question, whether societies of men are really capable or not, of establishing good government from ref[l]ection and choice, or whether they are forever destined to depend, for their political constitutions on accident and force"(1961 4:301; cf. Washington 1992 6:488, Paine 1945 1:29, Niles 1822 63 (John Jay); Ramsay 1779 2, DHRC 1976 2: 342, 353 362 (James Wilson), Madison 1962 11:172, and DHRC 1976 10:1498-99 (Madison)). Hamilton presupposes that the capacity for rational deliberation and action must be developed in the people themselves (1961 4:608). This presupposition was widespread. "Why should we be illuminated by reason," James Wilson asked in 1790, "were we only made to obey the impulse of irrational instinct? Why should we have the power of deliberating, and of balancing our determinations, if we were made to yield implicitly and unavoidably to the influence of first impressions? Of what service to us would reflection be, if, after reflection, we were to be carried away irresistibly by the force of blind and impetuous appetites?"(2007 1:504-5).

The belief that reason was a kind of natural revelation suggested to many eighteenth-century Americans that there were two non-Biblical sources for our knowledge of God. The first is the world of nature. According to the book of *Genesis*, God created the universe. Hence, as St. Paul points out, "ever since the creation of the world his invisible nature . . . has been clearly perceived in the things that have been made"(*Romans* 1:20). Religious interest has been the motivation of much scientific investigation — indeed without that interest the scientific revolution associated with Copernicus, Galileo, Kepler, and Newton might never have occurred. They all believed that the "heavens are telling the glory of God"(*Psalms* 19:1). So did the American naturalist John Bartram who wrote in a 1762 letter: "my head runs all upon ye works of god in nature[;] it is through that telescope I see god in his glory"(1992 579). The second non-Biblical source is the human spirit. If human beings, as *Genesis* tells us, are made in the image of God, then by studying the image one can learn about the reality. "The spirit of man is the lamp of the Lord, searching all his innermost parts"(*Proverbs* 20:27). This conception is adopted in a sermon of Nathanael Emmons: "The dignity of man appears from his bearing the *image* of his Maker. . . . His soul is a transcript of the *natural* perfections of the Deity. God is spirit, and so is the soul of man; God is intelligence and activity, and so is the soul of man. In a word, man is the living image of the living God . . . The truth is, rationality is the same in all intelligent beings. Reason is the same thing [*nota bene*] in God, in Angels, and in Men. As men therefore bear the *image* of God, in point of Rationality; so they possess all the *rational* powers and faculties, which bear any analogy to the divine intelligence . . ."(1787 7-8, 25). Each and every human being is an imperfect reflection of God, but imperfect in different ways. Imagine some object that could not be viewed directly, but only through a set of irregular mirrors each of which distorted the object's appearance in a different way. By knowing the laws of refraction and by carefully studying the various distorted images one could produce a knowledge of the object that was much less distorted than any of its many images. Each mirror would be vitally important in that rational reconstruction. In like manner God's will can be discovered by democratic procedures; in the physical sciences we can discover the character of God's intellect in nature, in virtuous republics we can discover the character of God's will in the people.

The Declaration's phrase "deriving their just powers from the consent of the governed" means that governmental powers must be authorized by the public. But it by no means follows that any derived power must be accepted. An unreasonable authorization — for example, one that could lead to the violation of unalienable rights — must be rejected even if correctly derived from the people's opinions. Jefferson emphasized this in his first inaugural address: "All, too, will bear in mind this sacred principle, that though the will of the majority is in all cases to prevail, that will, to be rightful, must be reasonable; that the minority possess their equal rights, which equal laws must protect, and to violate which would be oppression"(1903 3:318). The point is this: the will of the majority can be arbitrary (for example, by oppressing a minority). It is one of the purposes of republican government to thwart such majorities since they are not truly deliberative. Could even a deliberate majority be wrong? Yes, but just as a deliberate person would not arbitrarily cut off her arm, so a deliberate people would not purposely violate the rights of any part of body politic. In a mood favorable to deliberation, the intentions of the people are the most reliably good because they lack a motive to be otherwise. In the natural world, science protects against arbitrary belief; in the political world, democracy protects against arbitrary government.

The desire to correct errors, and the ability to do so, is of course one of the conditions for excellence. And the display of the passion for excellence is one of the great legacies of the ancient Greeks. They exhibited it in mathematics and science, art and literature, theater and athletics, history and philosophy. Thus Isocrates boasts: "our own country is able to bear and nurture men who are not only the most gifted in the world in the arts and in the powers of action and of speech, but are also above all others in valour and in virtue"(1928 2:151). This is a common observation about Greek aspirations, but it is not so common to observe that excellence is one of the founding ideals of American civilization. It was not sufficient for the Founders to produce an enduring government, it must also be an excellent government. Today we seem willing to settle for an economy and government that "works tolerably well." The idea that our political and economic institutions should work superbly well, when not completely forgotten, has been relegated to the status of a dangerous, unachievable, utopian dream. Yet, as we shall see, revolutionary leaders often used terms such as "excellence" or "perfection" when speaking of government, and it is a central theme of this book that we ought to revive that revolutionary ideal. A perfect government, as they saw it, is one that, better than any other alternative, produces those conditions that allow each citizen to achieve excellence in the art of living. That excellence constitutes the Aristotelian ideal of happiness.

According to Aristotle, "happiness [*eudaimonia*] is the realization and perfect exercise of excellence" (1984 2:2113). Happiness is the best state of a person or society. The pursuit of happiness is the pursuit of what is most valuable to have and to do, it is the pursuit of whatever enables a person to flourish as an excellent human being. That doctrine finds frequent expression in eighteenth-century America. In 1776, an anonymous author writes: "I take the essential benefit of civil liberty, wheresoever or in whatever degree it is found, to be, its tendency to put in motion and encourage the exertion of all human powers. It must therefore evidently improve the human mind, and bring with it, in highest perfection, all the advantages of the social state. It is the parent or the nurse of industry, opulence, knowledge, virtue, and heroism"(D***, F***, H*** 1776 167; the quotation is from a magazine edited by Thomas Paine). "Let man pursue his own perfection and happiness"(2007 1:503, cf. 523) proclaims James Wilson. "We have remarked," he says elsewhere, "that civil government is necessary to the perfection of society. We now remark that civil liberty is necessary to the perfection of civil government. Civil liberty is natural liberty itself, divested only of that part, which, placed in the government, produces more good and happiness to the community than if it had remained in the individual. Hence it follows, that civil liberty, while it resigns a part of natural liberty, retains the free and generous exercise of all the human faculties, so far as it is compatible with the public welfare"(DHRC 1976 2:358-9, cf. 346-7; cf. also Hume 1985 41 and Parsons 1778 8). John Adams argued that among the advantages of a free government is that it produces "a universal energy to the human character" and "gives full scope to all the faculties of man"(1850 4:288). Jefferson thought the exercise of human powers is so important that, on one occasion, he adds it to his famous trio of rights: ". . . our right to life, liberty, the use of our faculties, the pursuit of happiness, is not left to the feeble and sophistical investigations of reason, but is impressed on the sense of every man"(1903 15:124). Jefferson's meaning can perhaps be captured by subsuming all four rights under the phrase *human flourishing*, or equivalently, under the phrase *pursuit of happiness*, in the Aristotelian sense just described. Jefferson's reference to the "feeble and sophistical investigations of reason" is, I believe, an allusion to theologians and philosophers, the large majority of whom were hostile to democracy. He is denying that, without knowledge of these theologians and philosophers, ordinary people would be ignorant of their fundamental rights. On the other hand, reason, rightly conceived, is central to his conception of a free society. As he put it: ". . . in a republican nation, whose citizens are to be led by reason and persuasion, and not by force, the art of reasoning becomes of first importance"(1903 16:30; cf. also Franklin 1959 3:413-14). Human flourishing — "the exertion of all human powers" or "the free and generous exercise of all the human faculties" — is the essence of the pursuit of happiness and it is democratic government alone that can reliably protect *and* extend that right; it should "be so free as to restrain [man] in no moral right, and so firm as to protect him from every moral wrong"(Jefferson 1903 10:292). Hence civil liberty is more perfect than the "natural liberty" that preceded it; in contemporary terminology, Philadelphia freedom is more productive of human flourishing than Paleolithic freedom.

Happy persons may have external advantages such as friends, health, and wealth. Since they are fulfilling their own nature to the highest degree of excellence, they may gain internal advantages, such as frequent or regular feelings of great pleasure, contemplative tranquility, justified pride, and exuberance for life. Yet the degree to which any advantages are necessary may be quite small in some happy people. John Flavell's phrase — "In the pursuit of happiness, striving even to an Agony"(1669 20, 1709 20) — may be appropriately applied to some individuals. Francis Bacon speaks of a "wise and industrious sufferinge, which draweth, and contriueth vse and aduantage out of that which seemeth aduerse and contrary"(2000 147; cf Aristotle 1984 2:1739 and Adams (Cappon 1959 2:472-3)). On some occasions in some persons, melancholia may be appropriate for a morally prosperous life. But to all these things there are limits. "Those who say that the victim on the rack or the man who falls into great misfortune is happy if he is good, are," says Aristotle, "talking nonsense"(2:1823; cf. Diogenes Laertius 1925 2:645). Yet specifying the limits can be difficult, and thus it can be uncertain whether a person is happy in Aristotle's sense. The great-souled Lincoln is a case in point. Nevertheless the meaning of the unalienable right to the pursuit of happiness is clear: it is the right of an individual or a community to flourish in the highest possible degree of moral or political excellence; the person or society who consistently fails in such activity is hapless. A good society is one that protects the right of every individual to seek and maintain excellence in the art of living and, if that protection is itself excellent, the society will have achieved public happiness (also called "political happiness," "political prosperity," "social happiness," or "the general welfare."). It is assumed God or nature has so fashioned us that no person's rightful pursuit of happiness is ultimately inconsistent with any other person's rightful pursuit. If a wolf eats a lamb, the lamb's "happiness" is sacrificed; if the wolf makes peace with the lamb, *pace* Isaiah, the wolf starves. The essence of American optimism is the assumption that humans are not, in this respect, like wolves and lambs, that it is possible to design government and regulate society so that each person can pursue happiness — that is, exercise full and proper freedom to flourish as a human being — without preventing that pursuit for any other person. One person's pursuit cannot require any other to be "on the rack," or to fall into "great misfortunes."

This American optimism precedes the Founders by generations. "The End of all good Government," said John Wise in 1717, "is to Cultivate Humanity, and Promote the happiness of all, and the good of every Man in all his Rights, his Life, Liberty, Estate, Honour, etc. without injury or abuse done to any"(1958 61; cf. Jefferson's words: "Being myself a warm zealot for the attainment and enjoiment by all mankind of as much liberty as each may exercise without injury to the equal liberty of his fellow citizens"(1950 28:340)). It is this optimism that allows the pursuit of happiness to be an equalitarian idea; no person ought to be excluded by law or social customs from reaching the greatest level of flourishing that the individual has the capacity to achieve. This point was widely emphasized in the eighteenth century: "Heaven and happiness," William Bentley declared in 1790, "were not designed by God as the exclusive rights of learned priests, or ingenious doctors; they are the end which God has proposed for all mankind, and are therefore, by the same means, attainable by all men"(1790 8-9). Among the rights that all men have, according to George Mason's Virginia Declaration of Rights (June 1776), are "pursueing and obtaining happiness and safety"(below, page 50; cf. Adams 1850 4:220 and Madison, below, page 493). Thus the right of pursuit of happiness is not understood in the empty sense according to which the government guarantees the pursuit of happiness, but also creates or allows circumstances that make happiness itself unlikely or impossible to obtain. Government, as far as possible, ought to promote the conditions that would encourage its achievement by everyone. The actual achievement, however, is the responsibility of the individual. The political optimism of the American revolution has its counterpart in the natural philosophy of the Enlightenment. Adopting that philosophy, the scientist presupposes that through the use of reason the many and obvious observational conflicts can be resolved into a consistent set of natural laws. Adopting the philosophy of the American revolution, the politician likewise presupposes the many and obvious political conflicts can be resolved by framing and passing a consistent set of wise laws. Neither physical nature nor human nature is ultimately irrational or self-stultifying.

The pursuit of happiness is a Greek ethical ideal, not a Biblical one. In fact, the word "happiness" does not occur at all in the King James translation. But we must not conclude that this ideal must be understood in purely secular terms. Consider: "ye shall be unto me a kingdom of priests"(*Exodus* 19:6) and "ye shall be holy: for I the Lord your God am holy"(*Leviticus* 19:2). Both can be thought of as describing the ideal human condition of blessedness, where a human being need "but to do justly, and to love mercy, and to walk humbly with thy God"(*Micah* 6:8). Blessedness is religious happiness and thus includes developing one's talents and character in a morally and socially responsible way. Again, Plato claimed that "God ought to be the measure of all things . . . And he who would be dear to God must, as far as is possible, be like Him, and such as He is"(1937 2:488; cf. Aristotle 1984 2:1863-64). Elsewhere Plato says that we ought "to become like God, as far as this is possible: and to become like him, is to become holy, just, and wise"(178; cf. 1:871). Cicero maintains that "virtue exists in man and God alike, but in no other creature besides; virtue, however, is nothing else than Nature perfected and developed to its highest point; therefore there is a likeness between man and God"(1988 325). These classical conceptions are not far from the teaching of Jesus, "Be ye therefore perfect, even as your Father which is in heaven is perfect"(*Matthew* 5:48). For many eighteenth-century Americans, the Greek ideals of reason, excellence, and happiness receive their finest embodiment in Protestantism. "The precepts of Christianity," Thomas Reese tell us, "require us not to eradicate, but to govern and regulate our passions, in such a manner, as is most worthy of the dignity, and most conductive to the perfection and felicity of rational creatures. . . . . Let [the passions] be under the conduct of reason; give them the due tone; keep them within the bounds of moderation which Christianity prescribes, and they will invariably tend to social happiness"(1788 62).

It would nevertheless be a misconception to conclude that the colonists merely unified the Biblical and the classical views of human nature. *Some of the similarities between the colonists and the Biblical or Greek views may have been coincidental, or due to finding the same solutions to comparable problems.* Further, there is no one Biblical view, or one classical view, there are many. The colonists were quite selective. They rejected any classical claim that was inconsistent with republicanism. Thus, in a letter to John Adams, Jefferson disparaged Plato's *Republic*:

> I amused myself with reading seriously Plato's republic. I am wrong however in calling it amusement, for it was the heaviest task-work I ever went through. I had occasionally before taken up some of his other works, but scarcely ever had the patience to go through a whole dialogue. While wading thro the whimsies, the puerilities, and the unintelligible jargon of this work, I laid it down often to ask myself how it could have been that the world should have so long consented to give reputation to such nonsense as this? (Cappon 1959 2:432; cf. Jefferson 1892 9:143-4)

Adams, unlike Jefferson, did have some respect for the *Republic* (1850 4:448-463), but he was appalled that the work was filled with "astrological and mystical whimsies"(1850 4:449); he thought it must be "a bitter Satyre upon all Republican Government"(Cappon 1959 2:437). Turning to Aristotle, the colonists did not quote him to show that humans are created with unequal moral worth, or to maintain that slavery can be right. Similarly, classical stoicism was rejected as inappropriate for social life. Again, I will quote Thomas Reese: "Were it possible for men to bring themselves to that total insensibility, which was the pride and the boast of the Stoic, it would deprive them of a great part of that happiness which they derive from a reciprocal exchange of the kind affections and mutual offices of love, which constitutes one of the principal bonds, as well as chief felicities of social life"(1788 62).

Rejecting parts of the classical traditions was easy because they were pagan. But what about the Bible? Since it was believed to be a divinely inspired authority by a large majority of Americans, rejecting it out of hand was not possible. Yet straight-forward acceptance as a political authority was also not possible, since it contained many passages that contradicted the republican spirit (cf. below, page 468). During the revolutionary period they generally ignored or reinterpreted such passages. For example, although there were some Biblical appeals to justify slavery (see Gales 1834 2:1187, Johnston 1970 110-12, and Schmidt and Wilhelm 1973) they were few compared to the number of Biblically inspired attacks on the institution. Further, Christians refused to take the Bible literally wherever it contradicted their own reason and experience. Ebenezer Gay's words (quoted above, page 18) are a good example. Here is another. After remarking that St. Paul cites "a known Rule among Husbandmen: *But this I say, He that soweth sparingly, shall reap also sparingly: and he which soweth bountifully, shall reap also bountifully*," Jared Eliot cautions, "In the application of this Rule we are to be under the conduct of Reason, Use, Prudence & Discretion: We are not to cover the ground with Seed; for instead of having more increase we shall have less: But that we do not spare, but use such proportion of Seed as is found by Experience to be best"(1749 15-16; cf. 2 *Corinthians* 9:6). Americans applied the same sobriety to make their religion compatible with their political reason and political experience: "Let the pulpit resound with the doctrines and sentiments of religious liberty, . . ." John Adams declared in 1765, "Let us see delineated before us, the true map of man. Let us hear the dignity of his nature, and the noble rank he holds among the works of God! that consenting to slavery is a sacrilegious breach of trust, as offensive in the sight of God, as it is derogatory from our own honor or interest or happiness; and that God almighty has promulgated from heaven, liberty, peace, and good-will to man!"(1977 1:126). This attitude led to a republican principle of Biblical interpretation. It was expressed in a sermon delivered in 1773 by Charles Turner: "The scriptures cannot be rightly expounded, without explaining them in a manner friendly to the cause of freedom . . . "(38). With such a principle, the revolution is not only protected from opposition on religious grounds, religion itself becomes a passion that propels it. Biblical interpretations inconsistent with republican principles are considered incorrect, even perverse. Consequently it is not surprising to find Benjamin Rush asserting that "a Christian cannot fail of being a republican"(1786a 15) even though it apparently has the consequence that there were at most only a few Christians for the 1500 years following New Testament times. Gad Hitchcock was on the same page: "Liberty is the spirit and genius of the sacred writings; the great thing aimed at in them, is to make men free from sin; to deliver them out of bondage to their lusts, and procure and establish the moral freedom of their minds. . . . . As far as the liberty of mankind has been impaired, and their rights invaded, and oppression and tyranny have prevailed in any kingdom or nation on earth; so far has there been a repugnance to, and a departure from the true spirit of the holy scriptures. The religion of the Bible hath a regard to our benefit in both worlds [that is, civil and religious] "(1775 34). John Adams even called the Bible "the most republican book in the world"(Schutz and Adair 1966 76). I think he also referred to the adoption of a republican understanding of Christianity when, in 1818, he asked : ". . . what do we mean by the American Revolution? Do we mean the American war? The Revolution was effected before the war commenced. The Revolution was in the minds and hearts of the people; a change in their religious sentiments of their duties and obligations"(1850 10:282). Protestantism became Americanized, it became revolutionary in a republican sense. Luther's and Calvin's directives to submit before unjust government were cast aside. To understand the new attitude, suppose the people, using the republican principle to find Biblical passages to guide them, had turned to Paul's words, ". . . where the Spirit of the Lord is, there is freedom"(2 *Corinthians* 3:17) or to James' words, "But he who looks into the perfect law, the law of liberty, and perseveres, being no hearer that forgets but a doer that acts, he shall be blessed in his doing"(*James* 1:25). How could Americans, when contemplating "their duties and obligations" as good Christians, not actively oppose British threats to their liberty? "Resistance," declared the Provincial Congress of Massachusetts on February 9, 1775, "is so far from being criminal, that it becomes the christian and social duty of each individual"(JEPCM 1838 91; cf. Williams, Samuel 1775 12). Hence the political doctrines of the Declaration were given Biblical authority before it was written, and revolution itself was again and again fueled by religious fervor.

2

John Locke and the Spirit of 1776

The philosophical foundation for the Declaration received its classic statement in the philosophy of John Locke. Yet Locke did not originate many of the revolutionary ideas that eighteenth-century America adopted. Americans drew on a large variety of sources, many of whom Locke himself was indebted to, or who were in Locke's debt. This list would include the Bible, Plato, Aristotle, Polybius, Cicero, Plutarch, Aquinas, Machiavelli, Milton, Hooker, Coke, Grotius, Hobbes, Harrington, Sidney, Pufendorf, Bayle, Trenchard and Gordon, Montesquieu, Bolingbroke, Burlamaqui, Hutcheson, Kames, Reid, Hume, Adam Ferguson, and a host of rhetoricians and historians. A Puritan political tradition also preceded Locke. The extent to which that tradition directly influenced him is complex and not easily answered. For example, the Puritan Samuel Rutherford published *Lex, Rex* in 1644, when Locke was twelve years old. It contains such phrases as the following: "if all Men be born equally free (as I hope to prove)," "all are born alike and equal," "the people is to suffer much before they resume their power," "A man being created according to Gods image, he is *res sacra*, a sacred thing, and can no more by natures law be sold and bought than a religious and sacred thing dedicated to God"(1644 3, 43, 63, 91). Locke never refers to the work and there are significant differences between Locke's thought and Rutherford's. Nevertheless Locke was influenced by many of the same things that influenced the radical religious writers who preceded him, and, except for their general influence, he might not have reached his republican understanding of religious doctrines and duties.

In any case, many ministers in America considered themselves part of the Puritan tradition. It was their colonial experience, combined with that tradition, which sometimes led them to express ideas that were closer to Locke than any counterpart living in Britain. For example, also in 1644, Roger Williams, founder of the colony of Rhode Island, wrote:

> . . . the *Soveraigne, originall*, and *foundation* of *civill power* lies in the *people* . . . And if so, that a People may erect and establish what *forme* of *Government* seemes to them most meete for their *civill condition*: It is evident that such *Governments* as are by them erected and established have no more *power*, nor for no longer time, then the *civill power* or people consenting and agreeing shall betrust them with.

This is cleere not only in *Reason*, but in the experience of all *commonweales*, where the people are not deprived of their *naturall freedome* by the power of Tyrants. (1867 249-50)

Perhaps it was the colonial background, experienced directly by Williams, and known indirectly by Locke, that influenced them to express such similar ideas. In any event, that experience led a large number of ordinary people in America to assume the right of self-government as a matter of course. This is illustrated by the following story. In April 1894 Judge Mellen Chamberlain gave an address in which he related a conversation he had had in 1842 with Levi Preston, a ninety-one year old veteran of the battle at Concord.

"Captain Preston, why did you go to the Concord Fight, the 19th of April, 1775?" The old man, bowed beneath the weight of years, raised himself upright, and turning to me said: "Why did I go?" "Yes," I replied; "my histories tell me that you men of the Revolution took up arms against 'intolerable oppressions.' What were they?" "Oppressions? I didn't feel them." "What, were you not oppressed by the Stamp Act?" "I never saw one of those stamps, and always understood that Governor Bernard put them all in Castle William. I am certain I never paid a penny for one of them." "Well, what then about the tea-tax?" "Tea-tax! I never drank a drop of the stuff; the boys threw it all overboard." "Then I suppose you had been reading Harrington or Sidney and Locke about the eternal principles of liberty." "Never heard of 'em. We read only the Bible, the Catechism, Watts Psalms and Hymns, and the Almanack." "Well, then, what was the matter? and what did you mean in going to the fight?" "Young man, what we meant in going for those red-coats was this: we always had governed ourselves, and we always meant to. They didn't mean we should." (PCSMC 1982 189-90)

Even Thomas Paine, who ignited the call for independence, claims he "never read Locke," and, further, "the people of America, in conducting their revolution, learned nothing from Locke; nor was his name, or his work, ever mentioned during the revolution that I know of"(Aldridge 1953 377, 381). Locke also wrote the Constitution of Carolina in 1669 that includes the following provision: "Every freeman of Carolina shall have absolute power over his negro slaves"(1823 9:196; see also Farr 1986 for a discussion of Locke and slavery). John Adams called the Carolina Constitution a "signal absurdity"(1850 4:463), although in fairness to Locke there remains a question whether he was truly the author since he was acting as a secretary. Yet Locke neither protested these views at the time, nor renounced them later. Further, he was an investor in the Royal African Company and involved in the practice of African slavery in other ways. But these views and activities had no influence on American political doctrine during the Founding era.

Nevertheless Locke's philosophy was important for the American revolution. That importance was expressed by James Wilson in 1787. He said the "great and penetrating mind of Locke seems to be the only one that pointed towards even the theory of this great truth," namely, that "the supreme, absolute, and uncontrollable authority *remains* with the people"(DHRC 1976 2:472). Wilson believed that this theory was expressed in the Declaration, that the Declaration "is the broad basis on which our independence was placed," that the Constitution was constructed "on this same and certain solid foundation"(472-3). Note the Constitution's opening phrase: "WE, THE PEOPLE OF THE UNITED STATES . . . " Locke was of great importance to the American revolution because he had explicated a view of human nature on which the Declaration and Constitution were subsequently based. That view was articulated in his three most important works: *An Essay Concerning Human Understanding (1690), Two Treatises of Government (1690),* and *A Letter Concerning Toleration* (1689, followed by three others 1690, 1692, 1704). Further, Jefferson even borrowed Locke's phraseology extensively when composing the Declaration. All of the following parallels come from the second of Locke's *Two Treatises of Government* (1988):

Declaration of Independence	*Two Treatises of Government*
We hold these truths to be self-evident, that all men are created equal, . . .	This *equality* of *Men* by Nature, the Judicious [Richard] *Hooker* looks upon as so evident in it self, . . . (270)
	. . . all that share in the same common Nature, Faculties and Powers, are in Nature equal, and ought to partake in the same common Rights and Priviledges, . . . (190)
	. . . *all Men by Nature are equal* . . . (304).
. . . that they are endowed by their Creator with certain unalienable Rights, that among these are Life, Liberty, and the pursuit of Happiness. [Jefferson's original rough draft had said "all men are created equal & independant"(1950 423).]	The *State of Nature* has a Law of Nature to govern it, which obliges every one: And Reason, which is that Law, teaches all Mankind, who will but consult it, that being all equal and independent, no one ought to harm another in his Life, Health, Liberty, or Possessions. For Men being all the

Workmanship of one Omnipotent, and infinitely wise Maker; . . . (271; cf. *Ephesians* 2:10).

Men being . . . by Nature, all free, equal and independent, . . . (330)

. . . That to secure these rights, Governments are instituted among Men, deriving their just powers from the consent of the governed, . . . [cf. "since no Man can pretend an immediate Right from Heaven, all the Right that one more than another has to command, must be the Consent of the Governed"(Tindal 1697 4).]

. . . Government being for the Preservation of every Mans Right and Property, by preserving him from the Violence or Injury of others, is for the good of the Governed (209-10).

The *Liberty of Man, in Society*, is to be under no other Legislative Power, but that established, by consent . . . (283).

And thus that, which begins and actually *constitutes any Political Society*, is nothing but the consent of any number of Freemen capable of a majority to unite and incorporate into such a Society. And this is that, and that only, which did, or could give *beginning* to any *lawful Government* in the World (333).

That the *beginning of Politick Society* depends upon the consent of the Individuals, to joyn into and make one Society; who, when they are thus incorporated, might set up what form of Government they thought fit (337).

That whenever any Form of Government becomes destructive of these ends, it is the Right of the People to alter or abolish it, and to institute new Government, laying its foundation on such principles and organizing its Powers in such form, as to them shall seem most likely to effect their Safety and Happiness. [cf. Francis Hutcheson's words from 1747: "But the end of all civil power is acknowledged by all to be the safety and happiness of the whole body"(1969 4:302; cf. also Mason's words quoted below, pages 50 and 290). It should be remembered that in political contexts "safety" can have an

. . . yet the Legislative being only a Fiduciary Power to act for certain ends, there remains still *in the People a Supream Power* to remove or *alter the Legislative*, when they find the *Legislative* act contrary to the trust reposed in them. For all *Power given with trust* for the attaining an *end*, being limited by that end, whenever that *end* is manifestly neglected, or opposed, the *trust* must necessarily be *forfeited*, and the Power devolve into the hands of those that gave it, who may place it anew where they shall think best for their safety and security. And thus the *Community* perpetually *retains a Supream Power* of saving expanded meaning.   Thus when speaking of "*the safety of the people*" Hobbes says, "But by Safety here, is not meant a bare Preservation, but also all other Contentments of life, which every man by lawfull Industry, without danger, or hurt to the Commonwealth, shall acquire to himselfe"(1968 376).]

themselves from the attempts and designs of any Body, even their Legislators, whenever they shall be so foolish, or so wicked as to lay and carry on designs against the Liberties and Properties of the Subject (367).

. . . *when the Government is dissolved*, the People are at liberty to provide for themselves, by erecting a new Legislative, differing from the other, by the change of Persons, or Form, or both as they shall find it most for their safety and good (411).

Whensoever therefore the *Legislative* shall transgress this fundamental Rule of Society; and either by Ambition, Fear, Folly or Corruption, *endeavour to grasp* themselves, or *put into the hands of any other an Absolute Power* over the Lives, Liberties, and Estates of the People; By this breach of Trust they *forfeit the Power*, the People had put into their hands, for quite contrary ends, and it devolves to the People, who have a Right to resume their original Liberty, and, by the Establishment of a new Legislative (such as they shall think fit) provide for their own Safety and Security, which is the end for which they are in Society.   What I have said here concerning the Legislative, in general, holds true also concerning the *supreame Executor* . . . (412-13).

. . . the People have a Right to act as Supreme, and continue the legislative in themselves, or erect a new Form, or under the old form place it in new hands, as they think good (428). [cf. also Locke's words with Mason 1970 1:287.]

Prudence, indeed, will dictate that Governments long established should not be changed for light and transient Causes; and accordingly all experiences hath shewn, that mankind

For till the mischief be grown general and the ill designs of the Rulers become visible, or their attempts sensible to the greater part, the People, who are more disposed to are more disposed to suffer, while evils are sufferable, than to right themselves by abolishing the forms to which they are accustomed.

suffer, than right themselves by Resistance, are not apt to stir (417-18).

People are not so easily got out of their old Forms, as some are apt to suggest. They are hardly to be prevailed with to amend the acknowledg'd Faults, in the Frame they have been accustom'd to (414).

But when a long train of abuses and usurpations, pursuing invariably the same Object evinces a design to reduce them under absolute Despotism, it is their right, it is their Duty, to throw off such Government, and to provide new Guards for their future security. [The claim of duty in addition to right was common. For example, here are the words of Samuel West's sermon of May 29, 1776: " . . . resistance is not only allowable, but an indispensable duty in the case of intolerable tyranny and oppression"(42).]

. . . if a *long Train of Actings shew the Councils* all tending that way . . . (405).

But if a long train of Abuses, Prevarications, and Artifices, all tending the same way, make the design visible to the People, and they cannot but feel, what they lie under, and see, whither they are going; 'tis not to be wonder'd that they should then rouze themselves, and endeavour to put the rule into such hands, which may secure to them the ends for which Government was at first erected; . . . (415).

It is thus not surprising that Jefferson once said: "Locke's little book on government [that is, the *Second Treatise*] is perfect as far as it goes. Descending from theory to practice there is no better book than the Federalist"(1950 16:449; cf. also 1:77, 79). This suggests that Jefferson fully endorsed Locke's political theory and that he believed American government was based on it. Writing to Madison about the Declaration, Jefferson said that "Richard Henry Lee charged it as copied from Locke's treatise on government" (1892 10:267-268; the reference is to the grandson of the man (also named Richard Henry Lee) who introduced the resolution for independence on July 2, 1776). Lee wasn't alone in charging plagiarism (cf. C 1801 2)). Jefferson replied to the charge by saying, "whether I had gathered my ideas from reading or reflection I do not know. I know only that I turned to neither book nor pamphlet while writing it." This is possibly true, but it should be noted that Jefferson's claim was made forty-seven years after the fact, and the parallels between the *Second Treatise* and the Declaration are so close that it is likely that Jefferson's memory of it — whether conscious or unconscious — was decisive in the latter's composition. Jefferson's *A Bill Establishing Religious Freedom* (drawn in 1777) has numerous verbal echoes from Locke's *A Letter Concerning Toleration* (cf. Sandler 1960). Hence, Jefferson was heavily indebted to Locke for the two documents of which he was most proud.

It is repeatedly claimed that Jefferson's great contribution, which distinguishes him from Locke, is the phrase "pursuit of happiness," that Jefferson invented and substituted for "property" in Locke's "life, liberty, and property," thereby humanizing and universalizing Locke's theory. This claim is dead wrong. First, Locke never uses the specific phrase "life, liberty, and property" as such, whereas Jefferson does: "In no portion of the earth [that is, America] were life, liberty and property ever so securely held"(1903 16:334; cf. also 15:489 and 17:446). Further, Locke uses the phrase "pursuit of happiness" at least four times (1975 25, 260, 266, and 273). For both Locke and Jefferson, the right to the pursuit of happiness is part of the natural property of a human being, whereas the right to acquire property, in the sense of real estate or personal effects, is an essential component of the right to pursue happiness. Even Locke was not the first to employ that phrase (see, for example, Coleman 1643) and he is no better than the tenth author to adopt it. In any case, Locke used the phrase in articulating the core of his moral philosophy (a core that Jefferson fully accepted):

> As therefore the highest perfection of intellectual nature, lies in a careful and constant pursuit of true and solid happiness; so the care of our selves, that we mistake not imaginary for real happiness, is the necessary foundation of our *liberty*. The stronger ties, we have, to an unalterable pursuit of happiness in general, which is our greatest good, and which as such our desires always follow, the more are we free from any necessary determination of our *will* to any particular action, and from a necessary compliance with our desire, set upon any particular, and then appearing preferable good, till we have duly examin'd, whether it has a tendency to, or be inconsistent with our real happiness; and therefore till we are as much inform'd upon this enquiry, as the weight of the matter, and the nature of the case demands, we are by the necessity of preferring and pursuing true happiness as our greatest good, obliged to suspend the satisfaction of our desire in particular cases. (266; cf. Aristotle 2:1757; Jefferson expressed that "necessity" by using the phrase "eternally in pursuit of happiness, which keeps eternally before us"(1903 6:82)).

Locke believe that "Nature . . . has put into Man a desire of Happiness"(1975 67; cf. 1999 161 (1695)), and that ". . . God . . . by an inseparable connexion, joined Virtue and publick Happiness together"(69; cf. Washington's comment below, page 422 and

Jefferson 1903 16: 282, 19:210). For Locke, there is a direct connection among the ideas of nature, God, deliberation within the soul (above, page 20), moral perfection, and the pursuit of happiness. The same is true for William Wollaston, as expressed in his widely-read book, *The Religion of Nature Delineated (1725)*:

> And so, at last, natural religion is grounded upon this triple and strict alliance or union of *truth, happiness, and reason*; all in the same interest, and conspiring by the same methods, to advance and perfect human nature: and its truest definition is, *The pursuit of happiness by the practice of reason and truth*. (52)

William Blackstone, in his authoritative *Commentaries on the Laws of England* (1765-1769), also followed Locke and Wollaston in making the pursuit of happiness the central ethical and political imperative. He says that the creator

> graciously reduced the rule of obedience to this one paternal precept, "that man should pursue his own happiness." This is the foundation of what we call ethics, or natural law. . . . This law of nature, being co-eval with mankind and dictated by God himself, is of course superior in obligation to any other. It is binding over all the globe, in all countries, and at all times: no human laws are of any validity, if contrary to this; and such of them as are valid derive all their force, and all their authority, mediately or immediately, from this original. (1771 1:41).

Adding to the absurdity of honoring Jefferson for originating the phrase is the fact that Bernard Mandeville used it in 1710 (1), as did David Hume in 1742 and 1748 (1985 148, 176, 1955 33), and Samuel Johnson in 1759 (1990 129). The first sermon in *The Sermons of Mr Yorick* (1760-69) by Laurence Sterne, perhaps Jefferson's favorite author, begins: "The great pursuit of man is after happiness: it is the first and strongest desire of his nature . . . "(1927 5; Jefferson owned all the above works mentioned in this paragraph except Coleman and Johnson, although, it should be noted, he was critical of Wollaston, Hume, and Blackstone.) The exact phrase "pursuit of happiness" was also used in at least five works published in America before Jefferson (Flavell 1709 20, Davies 1751 15, W. W. 1753 1, Hopkins (1721-1803) 1770 7, Backus 1771 61 (quoting Locke)). An article in *The Virginia Gazette* (November 18, 1773) was called "*The Pursuit after* HAPPINESS"(PAH) and George Mason's Virginia Declaration of Rights (June 1776) spoke of "pursuing and obtaining happiness"(below, page 50). Thus it is wrong to give Jefferson credit for "pursuit of happiness" either as a phrase or as an ideal. It is thoroughly Lockean; indeed the concept, but not the phrase, goes back to Aristotle. Nevertheless Jefferson deserves lasting fame for introducing that ideal into what became the founding declaration of the United States of America.

Let us turn to the question of meaning. The word "pursuit" has two senses, both of which were intended by Locke and Jefferson. It can mean the "action of seeking, or striving to obtain, attain, or accomplish something." Or it can mean the "action of following or engaging in something, as a profession, business, recreation, etc; that which one engages in or follows"(OED 1989). Thus those entering medical school are pursuing medical knowledge that they do not yet have (first sense), whereas doctors pursue medicine by practicing it (second sense). Now recall Aristotle's definition of happiness (*eudaimonia*): "the realization and perfect exercise of excellence"(above, page 23). Conjoining these ideas, "the pursuit of Happiness" in the Declaration means trying to attain excellence in the art of living and, if that excellence is achieved, maintaining it as long as one shall live. This is the essence of American revolutionary virtue; in James Wilson's words (which echoes Locke's): "a high sense of moral excellence is approved above all other intellectual talents. This high sense of excellence is accompanied with a strong desire after it, and a keen relish for it"(2007 1:512). There is no implication that one must do the impossible by developing all of one's talents to the utmost, nor is it implied that those who fail to achieve happiness have fewer rights. Furthermore, the content of the happy life may vary; neither Locke nor the American revolutionists would accept Aristotle's claim that "happiness . . . must be some form of contemplation"(1984 2:1863), although it may be so for some individuals, or it may even be necessary to achieve happiness for all individuals, without itself being happiness for many.

Accepting the centrality of the pursuit of happiness for morality, it follows that the most important discipline for a child to develop is the habit of resisting short-term temptations for the sake of long-term happiness. And this is what Locke maintained:

He that has not a Mastery over his Inclinations, he that knows not how to *resist* the Importunity of *present Pleasure or Pain*, for the sake of what Reason tells him is fit to be done, wants the true Principle of Vertue and Industry; and is in Danger never to be good for any thing. This Temper therefore, so contrary to unguided Nature, is to be got betimes; and this Habit, as the true Foundation of future Ability and Happiness, is to be wrought into the Mind, as early as may be, even from the first dawnings of any Knowledge, or Apprehension in Children; and so to be confirmed in them, by all the Care and Ways imaginable, by those who have the over-sight of their Education. (1989 147-8; cf. 107)

The habitual use of reason to determine the best course to take in the pursuit of happiness is, for Locke, the be-all and end-all of morality. (*Moral freedom* is perhaps the best phrase to denote this activity (cf. Gad Hitchcock's words above, page 29)). It would be hard to imagine Locke being any more explicit than he was on this issue.

Whatever necessity determines to the pursuit of real Bliss, the same necessity, with the same force establishes *suspence*, *deliberation*, and scrutiny of each successive desire, whether the satisfaction of it, does not interfere with our true happiness, and mislead us from it. This as seems to me is the great privilege of finite intellectual Beings; and I desire it may be well consider'd, whether the great inlet, and exercise of all the *liberty* Men have, are capable of, or can be useful to them, and that whereon depends the turn of their actions, does not lie in this, that they can *suspend* their desires, and stop them from determining their *wills* to any action, till they have duly and fairly *examin'd* the good and evil of it, as far forth as the weight of the thing requires [*nota bene*]. This we are able to do; and when we have done it, we have done our duty, and all that is in our power; and indeed all that needs. (1975 267)

For Locke, "*Reason* must be our last Judge and Guide in every Thing (1975 704; cf. 1999 14); its "right improvement, and exercise" is "the highest Perfection, that a Man can attain in this Life"(1989 186), it is that "which God hath given to be the Rule betwixt Man and Man, and the common bond whereby humane kind is united into one fellowship and societie"(1988 383). Thus a legitimate government is a device of reason used to check those actions of any individual, or group of individuals (including public officials), that interfere with the right of anyone to pursue a life of moral excellence. If it were "not for the corruption, and vitiousness of degenerate Men"(1988 352), says Locke, there would be no need for government. Madison makes Locke's point more explicitly: ". . . what is government itself but the greatest of all reflections on human nature? If men were angels no government would be necessary. . . . In framing a government which is to be administered by men over men, the great difficulty lies in this: You must first enable the government to control the governed; and in the next place, oblige it to control itself"(1962 10:477; cf. Brutus 1787 2 and Wilson 2007 1:452). Again, ". . . it is the reason of the public alone that ought to controul and regulate the government. The passions ought to be controuled and regulated by the government"(Madison 1962 10:463; cf. Adams 1850 6:246). The point is this. Communities, like individuals, know that in the future they may have weak moments and ought to prepare for that possibility. For example, just as a man might authorize friends to prevent him—with force if necessary—from driving home if he gets drunk at a party, so a people might likewise authorize the government to prevent the people—with force if necessary—from lynching a person who has not received a fair trial. "Democratic communities," Madison says, "may be unsteady, and be led to action by the impulse of the moment. — Like individuals they may be sensible of their own weakness, and may desire the counsels and checks of friends to guard them against the turbulency and weakness of unruly passions"(Farrand 1937 1:430). From this point of view, then, the formation of a legitimate government is an act of self-restraint required by the pursuit of happiness; it is meant to ensure the triumph, in political matters, of critical reason over irrational desire. Self-mastery is as important for nations as it is for individuals. Most people, I suppose, are reluctant to judge one person more moral than a second if the first's imagination is so dull as never to consider some immoral act, whereas the second considers it, knows she might yield to temptation, and uses her reason to arrange her life so that she never actually performs the act. Intellectual and artistic freedoms of free societies constantly stimulate the people's imaginations so they cannot count on a dull imagination to protect them from immorality. Government is needed, Hamilton argues, "because the passions of men will not conform to the dictates of reason and justice, without constraint"(1961 4:362). American government, then, was intended to achieve that conformity, to create, in Madison's words, "one paramount Empire of reason, benevolence and brotherly affection"(1962 14:139; cf. Webster 1787 6, and Reese above, page 27). Happiness, whether private or public, requires not the eradication of the passions, but their direction: "Men," says John Adams, "should endeavor at a *balance* of affections and appetites, under the monarchy of reason and conscience, within, as well as at a balance of power without"(1850 4:407).

The centrality of the concept of the pursuit of happiness in eighteenth-century America thus reflects its centrality in Locke's educational, ethical, and political philosophy. The pursuit of happiness is our "greatest good", it is our "great privilege", it is "the highest perfection of intellectual nature." For Locke and revolutionary Americans, the pursuit of public happiness is the highest calling that is open to a human being, even the most noble and gifted. Concern with the rights and welfare of others is part and parcel of the striving for moral excellence and the best that human life has to offer. Yet Locke and the Founders are often associated with an atomistic individualism that teaches an indifference to others and their fate. This claim will not bear examination. According to Locke, when a people leave a state of nature — that is, living without an impartial judge who has authority to settle disputes — it is not just due to the inconveniences of that state, but also because of "the love, and want of Society"(1988 334): "God having made Man such a Creature, that, in his own Judgment, it was not good for him to be alone [cf. *Genesis* 2:18], put him under strong Obligations of Necessity, Convenience, and Inclination to drive him into Society, as well as fitted him with Understanding and Language to continue and enjoy it"(318-19). (Jefferson, as usual, follows Locke: "We consider society as one of the natural wants with which man has been created . . . "(1903 14:487; cf. Smith, William 1755 9, Wilson 2007 1:638, DHRC 1976 2:344-5 and 356)). Further, Locke claims that part of our natural sociability includes strong social obligations: "Every one as he is *bound to preserve himself*, and not quit his Station wilfully; so by like reason when [his] own Preservation comes not in competition, ought [he], as much as [he] can, *to preserve the rest of Mankind*, and may not unless it be to do Justice on an Offender, take away, or impair the life, or what tends to the Preservation of the Life, Liberty, Health, Limb or Goods of another"(1988 271). Elsewhere Locke goes so far as to claim the duty to preserve mankind should "regulate our Religion [*nota bene*], Politics and Morality"(1989 180). For Locke, republican politics is the final arbiter; it leads him into a republican interpretation of the Bible and, with some exceptions, toward a complete toleration of religious diversity. Locke, unlike Marx, did not want to abolish religion, he wanted to make it reasonable; hence the title of his book: *The Reasonableness of Christianity* (1695).

Nor is Locke's defense of property inconsistent with having a strong social conscience. Thus he recommends that children be imbued with a habit of liberality: "Covetousness, and the desire of having in our possession, and under our Dominion, more than we have need of, being the root of all Evil, should be early and carefully weeded out, and the contrary Quality of a Readiness to impart to others, implanted"(1989 170). Locke's social conscience was influenced by the Old Testament (cf. *Leviticus* 19:9-10), and the commands of Jesus (cf. *Matthew* 19:16-22; *Mark* 10:17-22; *Luke* 18:18-24).

But we know God hath not left one Man so to the Mercy of another, that he may starve him if he please: God the Lord and Father of all, has given no one of his Children such a Property, in his peculiar Portion of the things of this World, but that he has given his needy Brother a Right to the Surplusage of his Goods; so that it cannot justly be denied him, when his pressing Wants call for it. And therefore no Man could ever have a just Power over the Life of another, by Right of property in Land or Possessions; since 'twould always be a Sin in any Man of Estate, to let his Brother perish for want of affording him Relief out of his Plenty. As *Justice* gives every Man a Title to the product of his honest Industry, and the fair Acquisitions of his Ancestors descended to him; so *Charity* gives every Man a Title to so much out of another's Plenty, as will keep him from extream want, where he has no means to subsist otherwise. . . . (1988 170)

Compare this passage with *Deuteronomy* 15:7-8: "If there is among you a poor man, one of your brethren, in any of your towns within your land which the Lord your God gives you, you shall not harden your heart or shut your hand against your poor brother, but you shall open your hand to him, and lend him sufficient for his need, whatever it may be." To illustrate his point, Locke imagines a man whose ship loaded with corn stops at a port where the population is near famine: "If he carry [the corn] away unless they will give him more than they are able, or extorts soe much from their present necessity as not to leave them the means of subsistence afterwards he offends against the common rule of Charity as a man and if they perish any of them by reason of his extorsion is noe doubt guilty of murder. . . . He is soe far from being permitted to gain to that degree, that he is bound to be at some losse and impart of his owne to save an other from perishing"(1991 2:499). Nor is such charity limited to the realm of private morality for, in another place, Locke says that "only common Charity teaches, that those should be most taken care of by the Law, who are least capable of taking care for themselves"(1991 1:220). Hence for Locke, whenever property rights go beyond need, they are to that degree limited by the human rights of others, since those in "extream want" have a "Right" or a "Title" to the excess property of others (provided they have no other means of relieving that want). Or to be more exact, since Locke uses "property" in the wider sense of "Lives, Liberties and Estates"(1988 350, cf. 323, 383), our property rights in goods or estates are limited by property rights in life and liberty (cf. 170). Our right to property in the narrow sense is acquired by mixing our labor with it — for instance, we hunt and kill a rabbit in the wild — but property in our lives, liberties, and pursuits of happiness, is God-given, neither labor nor anything else is needed to earn it.

Unfortunately, in practice, Locke was willing to accept a society in which the poor were treated with a callousness that made a life of excellence highly insecure, if not impossible. Thus he believes there should be laws that require the poor to carry passes and, among other things, that "all men begging in maritime counties without passes, that are maimed or above fifty years of age . . . shall be sent to the next house of correction, there to be kept at hard labour for three years"(Bourne 1876 2:380). Poor children over three should be forced to work. If they refuse, they should be deprived of food. It is a pity that Locke, whose epistemology committed him to relying on experience, did not live for a period of time with the poor, experience their world, and consider their rights, before writing these heartless words. He might then not have written them. But he did, and thus should be strongly condemned by his own (and our) moral standards.

Fortunately, the Founders were influenced by Locke's theory of property, not his specific claims with regard to the poor. For example, Jefferson is emphatic in his insistence that property rights in the narrow sense must be restricted by human rights:

> Whenever, there is in any country, uncultivated lands and unemployed poor, it is clear that the laws of property have been so far extended as to violate natural right. The earth is given as a common stock for man to labour and live on. If, for the encouragement of industry we allow it to be appropriated, we must take care that other employment be furnished to those excluded from the appropriation. If we do not the fundamental right to labour the earth returns to the unemployed. (1950 8:682; cf. Locke 1988 286, 291; *Psalm* 115:16)

Hence "the right to labour" transcends the property right in estates.

Madison held similar views. He distinguishes between a "larger and juster meaning" of property in which "a man has property in his opinions and the free communication of them" from a narrow sense in which "a man's land, or merchandize, or money is called his property". He then goes on to say:

> That is not a just government nor is property secure under it, where arbitrary restrictions, exemptions, and monopolies deny to part of its citizens that free use of their faculties, and free choice of their occupations, which not only constitute their property in the general sense of the word; but are the means of acquiring property strictly so called. . . . If the United States mean to obtain or deserve the full praise due to wise and just governments, they will equally respect the rights of property, and the property in rights: they will rival the government that most

sacredly guards the former; and by repelling its example in violating the latter, will make themselves a pattern to that and all other governments. (1900 6:101-103)

James Wilson at the federal convention also denied that property (in the narrow sense) was "the sole or the primary object of Governt. & Society"; rather, "the cultivation & improvement of the human mind was the most noble object"(Farrand 1937 1:604).

To sum up, for Locke and the Founders, the pursuit of happiness was understood to be a moral ideal. God or nature has given us a general desire for happiness. This desire is an essential part of being human. However, our particular desires cannot always be trusted, because sometimes their satisfaction does not really contribute to happiness, and sometimes their satisfaction is incompatible with happiness. It is our duty as rational human beings to aspire to "the highest perfection of intellectual nature," which is to judge wisely what will bring us the "true happiness" that is our greatest good. Hence if one asks what is the most important function of government, the answer can only be: to secure the right to pursue happiness for each and every individual, a condition called public happiness. All other pursuits — such as the pursuit of wealth — must be regulated in accordance with this fundamental right and duty. And one would expect that anyone who held this view would place great emphasis — as did Locke and the Founders — on moral education. For that kind of education teaches a person what humankind has so far learned about the nature of true happiness, and how it can best be pursued. It instills the *habits* necessary to live an excellent life where "we mistake not imaginary for real happiness." If such education is universal, it promotes virtue in individuals and thereby, through an "inseparable connexion," public happiness. Virtue in individuals is thus the foundation of good government. Locke would surely have agreed with Madison: "To suppose that any form of government will secure liberty or happiness without any virtue in the people, is a chimerical idea"(1962 11:163; cf. Machiavelli 1998 49, Harrington, James 2003 35). In a similar vein, Adams claimed that "public Virtue is the only Foundation of Republics"(below, page 319; cf. 3:399-400, Cappon 1959 2:550; cf. also the comments of Samuel Adams (1904 3:305), Franklin (1907 9:569), and Wilson (2007 1:289-90)). These claims, it should be noted, are Aristotelian: "A city can be excellent only when the citizens who have a share in the government are excellent, and in our state all the citizens share in government" (1984 2:2114). To conclude, Locke's philosophy articulated the view of human nature and the proper function of government that is presupposed in the Declaration. The Founders' great contribution was to lead a revolution and then create a constitutional structure which embodied that philosophy.

3

The Declaration: An Eighteenth-Century Betrayal

The Declaration presupposes that the people make a compact among themselves whereby they become subject to the laws of a government, which they create, so that each can secure the right to pursue happiness, and any other right necessary for that one. Yet laws under just governments do more than provide that security. As Locke wrote:

> For *Law*, in its true Notion, is not so much the Limitation, as *the direction of a free and intelligent Agent* to his proper Interest, and prescribes no farther than is for the general Good of those under that Law. Could they be happier without it, the *Law*, as an useless thing would of it self vanish; and that ill deserves the Name of Confinement which hedges us in only from Bogs and Precipices. So that, however it may be mistaken, *the end of Law* is not to abolish or restrain, but *to preserve and enlarge Freedom* . . . (1988 305-6; cf. Cicero 1988 383, 385, Wilson, James 2007 2:1056, DHRC 1976 2:345 and 356-7)

Thus, for example, laws forbidding the power to legally contract oneself into slavery, or laws prohibiting the choice to not educate one's own children, or laws denying the freedom to drive on the left side of the road, are no "Confinement," rather they function "*to preserve and enlarge Freedom.*" Anarchistic libertarianism is rejected because some freedoms must be limited in order to enlarge freedom overall; these limitations are required for the greatest human flourishing. Government itself is justified by this criterion; it is entirely subordinate to the people's good. In the words of David Ramsay: "The far famed social compact between the people and their rulers, did not apply to the United States. The sovereignty was in the people"(1789 1:355-56; cf. Madison 1962 14: 191 and various state constitutions, for example, Massachusetts (Thorpe 1909 3:1889-90), New Hampshire (4:2455), Pennsylvania (5:3082), Vermont (6:3740)). In the American sense, to use Paine's words, "a constitution is a thing *antecedent* to a government, and a government is only the creature of a constitution. The constitution of a country is not the act of its government, but of the people constituting a government."(1945 1:278; cf. 375, 381). If a government fails to secure and enhance their right to pursue happiness, the people can justly move to revolution, provided lesser forms of protest fail. This democratic ideal provides a moral sanction for slave revolts. Slavery is a species of totalitarian government, a form of social organization where the government claims the right of absolute control over the governed. No totalitarian government can possibly be just. As James Wilson put it, slavery "is repugnant to the principles of natural law, that such a state should subsist in any social system"(2007 2:1077). Just governing powers must always be limited by the rights of life, liberty, and the pursuit of happiness. It is ironic that leaders of slave revolts, such as Gabriel Prosser, Denmark Vesey, and Nat Turner, as well as their followers, were all faithful to the Declaration, while Washington, Jefferson, and Madison, as slaveholders, betrayed it. In the *Federalist* Madison refers to "an unhappy species of population abounding in some of the states, who during the calm of regular government are sunk below the level of men; but who in the tempestuous scenes of civil violence may emerge into the human character"(1962 10:415). Gabriel Prosser, Denmark Vesey, and Nat Turner emerged into human character when they revolted, they were exercising their *duty* of revolution as asserted in the Declaration, any less response to continuing gross oppression is an unnatural, morally wrong, acceptance of a condition "below the level of men"(cf. Adams 1977 1:126). Slaves who revolted could rightly compare themselves to Washington. Thus Robert Sutcliff reports:

> In the afternoon [of March 25, 1804] I passed by a field in which several poor slaves had lately been executed, on the charge of having an intention to rise against their masters. A lawyer who was present at their trials at Richmond, informed me that on one of them being asked, what he had to say to the court on his defence, he replied, in a manly tone of voice: 'I have nothing more to offer than what General Washington would have had to offer, had he been taken by the British and put to trial by them. I have adventured my life in endeavouring to obtain the liberty of my countrymen, and am a willing sacrifice in their cause: and I beg, as a favour, that I may be immediately let to execution. I know that you have pre-determined to shed my blood, why then all this mockery of a trial. (1812 50).

Again, revolutionary black slaves could easily be inspired by the language of revolutionary white freemen. Here, for example, is what Congress said when, in 1775, it declared the justification for armed resistance: "Honor, justice, and humanity forbid us tamely to surrender that freedom which we received from our gallant ancestors, and which our innocent posterity have a right to receive from us. We cannot endure the infamy and guilt of resigning succeeding generations to that wretchedness which inevitably awaits them, if we basely entail hereditary bondage upon them"(DRUC 1775 7).

Critics of the Declaration have sometimes complained that the phrase "all men" was intended, by those who signed it, to apply only to white men, and that blacks were definitely not included. Under this interpretation, the Founders only *seem* to be hypocrites. A revolt by black slaves could not be justified on the basis of the Declaration, because only white men have that right. Consider the argument that might today be given by a defender of this interpretation:

> It is notorious [the defense might begin] that the creators or discoverers of something often fail to understand fully the significance of what they have done. Columbus did not understand he had discovered a new world. Girolamo Saccheri (1667-1733) did not understand he had discovered non-Euclidean geometry. What is true in exploration, or in mathematics, holds also in politics. Thus the Founders did not appreciate the possibility that "all men" might apply to anyone other than white males. It is probable that they did not pay careful attention to the meaning of their own words since they considered the document, at the time it was signed, to be unimportant. Thus on July 2, 1776, when the members of Congress passed Richard Henry Lee's resolution proclaiming independence, their main interest was in securing foreign aid. What we today call the Declaration of Independence was a justification of their July 2nd action; it was not clearly conceived as the foundational document of a new nation. The casual way in which it came to be signed and the shabby treatment which the original document received (in contrast to the Constitution) illustrate the low regard it commanded. Thus, the charge of hypocrisy holds only in a formal, ahistorical sense. Put in a historical context, the charge is substantially false.

What can be made of this argument? It is undeniable that some of the Founders did not initially appreciate the importance of the Declaration. Yet they believed their actions toward gaining independence were momentous. Recall, for example, the words of John Adams to Abigail quoted at the beginning of the Prologue. Further, some of the Founders immediately foresaw the role the Declaration could have. For example, on July 5, 1776, John Hancock wrote to the New Jersey Convention, enclosed the Declaration "in Obedience to the Command of Congress," and spoke of the "important Consequences resulting to the American States from this Declaration of Independence, considered as the Ground & Foundation of a future

Government"(Smith, Paul 1976 4:392; cf. also 396). July 4, 1776, has traditionally and correctly been taken as the birth day of America although the resolution for independence was passed two days earlier. The latter date was chosen, I believe, because what made the American revolution uniquely important in the eyes of its participants was not the insurrection, for which there were many precedents, but the unprecedented commitment to universal moral ideals to which, as they said, "we mutually pledge to each other our Lives, our Fortunes, and our sacred Honor." It is this commitment which transformed the rebellion of the 2nd of July into the revolution of the 4th of July. "The Declaration of Independence," said an anonymous writer in 1790, "is not to be celebrated, merely as affecting the separation of one country from the jurisdiction of another: but as being the result of a rational discussion and definition of the rights of man, and the end of civil government; and as opening the fairest prospect of political happiness, that ever smiled upon our world"(BTDM 1790 3). "The independence of America," Thomas Paine wrote in 1792, "considered merely as a separation from England, would have been a matter but of little importance, had it not been accompanied by a revolution in the principles and practise of government"(1945 1:354).

Thus from the beginning the Founders understood the unique importance of what they were doing. For the first time since Adam, they were basing a rebellion on universal moral and political principles that were part of "the Laws of Nature and of Nature's God." Had someone proposed replacing "all men" in the Declaration by "all property-owning white men" or "all men except negroes" it would, I believe, have been rejected by Congress. Consider what happened in Virginia. In May of 1776 George Mason composed a draft of the Virginia Declaration of Rights that began with the following paragraph: "That all Men are born equally free and independant, and have certain inherent natural Rights, of which they can not by any Compact, deprive or divest their Posterity; among which are the Enjoyment of Life and Liberty, with the Means of acquiring and possessing Property, and pursueing and obtaining Happiness and Safety"(1970 1:277). Objections were raised to this declaration. As Thomas Ludwell Lee wrote to his brother, Richard Henry:

> I enclose you by last post a copy of our declaration of rights nearly as it came thro the committee. It has since been reported to the Convention & we have ever since been stumbling at the threshold, . . . I will tell you plainly that a certain set of Aristocrates, for we have such monsters here, finding that their execrable system cannot be reared on such foundations, have to this time kept us at bay on the first

line, which declares all men to be born equally free and independant. A number of
absurd, or unmeaning alterations have been proposed. The words as they stand are
approved by a very great majority, yet by a thousand masterly fetches &
stratagems the business has been so delayed that the first clause stands yet
unassented to by the Convention. (Miller, Helen 1975 149)

In response to the objections, the paragraph was changed to: "That
all men are by nature equally free and independent, and have certain
inherent rights, of which, when they enter into a state of society, they
cannot, by any compact, deprive or divest their posterity; namely, the
enjoyment of life and liberty, with the means of acquiring and
possessing property, and pursuing and obtaining happiness and
safety"(Mason 1970 1:287). These word changes are indeed
"unmeaning alterations," for if blacks are "by nature equally free and
independent," there can be no justification for keeping them as chattel
slaves either in a state of nature or under government. It does not
matter whether their slavery had been created by compact or force.
Noah Webster uses religious language to make this point: "That
freedom is a sacred right of every man whatever be his color, who has
not forfeited it by some violation of municipal law, is a truth
established by God himself in the very creation of human beings. No
time, no circumstance, no human power or policy can change the
nature of this truth, nor repeal the fundamental laws of society by
which every man's right to liberty is guaranteed"(1793 33). Since
such views were widely accepted it was not possible even in Virginia
to get a change in a declaration of rights that would explicitly exempt
blacks from its reach. Another example of the reluctance to exclude
blacks is New Jersey, a state in which slaveholding was legal. In June
of 1778 New Jersey objected to the Ninth article of the Articles of
Confederation that referred to "white Inhabitants" because such
reference was inconsistent with the Declaration of Independence (see
DHRC 1976 1:116). Rhode Island was even more explicit. A 1784
act intended to eliminate slavery begins:

Whereas, all men are entitled to life, liberty, and the pursuit of happiness, and
the holding mankind in a state of slavery, as private property, which has gradually
obtained by unrestrained custom and the permission of the laws, is repugnant to
this principle, and subversive of the happiness of mankind, the great end of all
civil government, — Be it therefore enacted by this General Assembly, and by the
authority thereof it is enacted, that no person or persons, whether negroes,
mulattoes, or others, who shall be born within the limits of this state, on or after
the first day of March, A. D, 1784, shall be deemed or considered as servants for
life, or slaves . . . (RSRI 1865 7)

Throughout the Founding era there were few public, or even private, defenses of black slavery compared to the exceedingly large number of denunciations of it (examples of defense can be found in Gales 1834 2:1450-1474, and in the references given above, page 28). Below are a substantial sample of quotations taken from letters or published works that demonstrate that *slavery was understood to be utterly inconsistent with the moral, political, and religious principles proclaimed again and again and again in eighteenth-century America, principles that were at the heart of the American revolution and expressed in the Declaration of Independence.* These wonderful and mostly forgotten passages can help us to understand anew the moral power of that revolution.

1764   "The Colonists are by the law of nature free born, as indeed all men are, white or black. No better reasons can be given, for enslaving those of any color than such as baron Montesquieu has humorously given, as the foundation of that cruel slavery exercised over the poor Ethiopians; which threatens one day to reduce both Europe and America to the ignorance and barbarity of the darkest ages. Does it follow that tis right to enslave a man because he is black? Will short curl'd hair like wool, instead of christian hair, as tis called by those, whose hearts are as hard as the nether millstone, help the argument? Can any logical inference in favor of slavery, be drawn from a flat nose, a long or a short face. Nothing better can be said in favor of a trade, that is the most shocking violation of the law of nature, has a direct tendency to diminish the idea of the inestimable value of liberty, and makes every dealer in it a tyrant . . ."(Otis 1764 29; in *The Spirit of the Laws*, Montesquieu said that "it is impossible for us to assume that these people [that is, the negroes] are men because if we assume they were men one would begin to believe that we ourselves were not Christians"(250). Benjamin Rush said that Montesquieu gives "the ridicule it deserves" to the argument that the color of negroes "subjects them to, or qualifies them for slavery"(1773 3).)

1767   Arthur Lee in the *Virginia Gazette*: "Now, as freedom is unquestionably the birth-right of all mankind, of Africans as well as Europeans, to keep the former in a State of Slavery is a constant violation of that right, and therefore of Justice"(MacMaster 1972 154).

". . . how many of those who distinguish themselves as the Advocates of Liberty, remain insensible and inatttentive to the Treatment of Thousands and Tens of Thousands of our Fellow-Men, who, from Motives of Avarice, and the inexorable Decree of Tyrant Custom, are at this very Time kept in the most deplorable State of Slavery . . . "(Benezet 1767 1).

1770   "Let the time more than suffice, wherein we, the patrons of liberty, have dishonored the christian name, — and degraded human nature, nearly to a level with the beasts that perish. Ethiopia has long stretched out her hands to us — Let not sordid gain, acquired by the merchandize of slaves, and the souls of men — harden our hearts against her piteous moan"(Cooke 1770 42).

1774   "Blush ye pretended votaries for freedom! ye trifling patriots! who are making
a vain parade of being advocates for the liberties of mankind, who are thus making
a mockery of your profession by trampling on the sacred natural rights and
privileges of *Africans* . . ."(Allen, John 1774 27).

". . . let us either cease to enslave our fellow-men, or else let us cease to
complain of those that would enslave us"(Niles, Nathaniel 1774 38).

"The meanest slave hath a soul as good by nature as your's, and possibly by
grace it is better. A dark complection may cover a fair and beautiful mind. Every
soul is beautiful, that resembles the moral character of the blessed God, who is the
standard of perfection"(Eliot, Andrew 1774 50).

"Among the innumerable evils that abound among us, I look upon the
oppression, bondage and slavery, exercised upon our poor brethren the Africans to
be a God provoking and a wrath procuring sin. I call them brethren, because God
has told us in his word, that he has made of one blood all nations that dwell on the
earth. They are as free by nature as we, or any other people; have a natural right to
liberty and freedom as much as we . . ."(Colman 1774 4).

Abigail Adams to her husband: "I wish most sincerely that there was not a
Slave in the province. It allways appeared a most iniquitious Scheme to me —
fight ourselfs for what we are daily robbing and plundering from those who have as
good a right to freedom as we have. You know my mind on this
Subject"(Butterfield, Lyman 1963 1:162).

1775   The people of the district of Darien, Georgia, through their representatives
stated the following: ". . . we hereby declare our disapprobation and abhorrence of
the unnatural practice of Slavery in *America*, . . . a practice founded in injustice and
cruelty, and highly dangerous to our liberties, (as well as our lives,) debasing part
of our fellow-creatures below men, and corrupting the virtue and morals of the rest;
and in laying the basis of that liberty we contend for . . . upon a very wrong
foundation"(AA 1837 1135).

"[African people belong] to the same common Father, and have an equal claim
to the same common Savior of mankind with ourselves, and consequently to the
same privileges and freedom"(Byrnes, Daniel 1775 1).

"When, O when shall the happy day come, that Americans shall be
consistently engaged in the cause of liberty, and a final end be put to the cruel
slavery of our fellow men"(Hart 1775 20).

"So monstrous is the making and keeping them slaves at all, abstracted from
the barbarous usage they suffer, and the many evils attending the practice; as
selling husbands away from wives, children from parents, and from each other, in
violation of sacred and natural ties; and opening the way for adulteries, incests,
and many shocking consequences, for all of which the guilty masters must answer
to the final Judge. If the slavery of the parents be unjust, much more is their
children's; if the parents were justly slaves, yet the children are born free; this is
the natural, perfect right of all mankind; . . . Certainly one may, with as much
reason and decency, plead for murder, robbery, lewdness, and barbarity, as for this
practice"(Paine 1945 2:18).

1776   "The Virginians begin their Declaration of Rights with saying, 'that *all* men are born equally and independent, and have certain inherent rights, of which they cannot, by any compact, deprive themselves or their posterity; among which are the enjoyment of life and *liberty*.' The Congress declare that they 'hold these truths to be self-evident, that all men are created *equal*, that they are endowed by their Creator with certain *unalienable rights*, that among these are life, *liberty* and the pursuit of happiness.' The Continent has rang with affirmations of the like import. If these, Gentlemen, are our genuine sentiments, and we are not provoking the Deity, by acting hypocritically to serve a turn, let us apply earnestly and heartily to the extirpation of slavery from among ourselves"(William Gordon as quoted in Moore, George 1866 176).

Thomas Hutchinson, the loyalist governor of Massachusetts, wrote a pamphlet against the Declaration, ". . . I could wish to ask the Delegates of Maryland, Virginia, and the Carolinas, how their Constituents justify the depriving more than an hundred thousand Africans of their rights to liberty, and the *pursuit of happiness*, and in some degree of their lives, if these rights are so absolutely unalienable . . ."(1766 9-10; thus the enemies, as well as the friends of the revolution, recognized that the Declaration included blacks as men).

1777   The Vermont Constitution: "THAT all men are born equally free and independent, and have certain natural, inherent and unalienable rights, amongst which are the enjoying and defending life and liberty; acquiring, possessing and protecting property, and pursuing and obtaining happiness and safety. Therefore, no male person, born in this country, or brought from over sea, ought to be holden by law, to serve any person, as a servant, slave or apprentice, after he arrives to the age of twenty-one years, nor female, in like manner, after she arrives to the age of eighteen years, unless they are bound by their own consent, after they arrive to such age, or bound by law, for the payment of debts, damages, fines, costs, or the like"(Thorpe 1909 6:2739-40).

This is a formal application to the Massachusetts House of Representatives: "The petition of A Great Number of Blackes detained in a State of slavery in the Bowels of a free & Christian Country Humbly shuwith that your Petitioners apprehend that they have in Common with all other men a Natural and Unaliable Right to that freedom which the Grat Parent of the Unavers hath Bestowed equalley on all menkind and which they have Never forfuted by any Compact or agreement whatever. . . . A Life of Slavery Like that of your petioners Deprived of Every social privilege of Every thing Requiset to Render Life Tolable is far worse then Nonexistance. . . . Every Principle from which Amarica has Acted in the Cours of their unhappy Deficultes with Great Briton Pleads Stronger than A thousand arguments in favowrs of your petioners"(MA n. d. 212, 132; cf. MHSC 1877 436-7).

1778   "Slavery, in whatever point of light it is considered, is repugnant to the feelings of nature, and inconsistent with the original rights of man. It ought therefore to be stigmatized for being unnatural; and detested for being unjust. 'Tis an outrage to providence, and an affront offered to divine Majesty, who has given to man his own peculiar image. — That the Americans, after considering the subject in this light — after making the most manly of all possible exertions in defence of liberty — after publishing to the world the principle upon which they contended, viz. 'that all men are by nature and of right ought to be free,' should still retain in subjection a numerous tribe of the human race, merely for their own private use and emolument, is, of all things, the strongest inconsistency, the deepest reflexion on our conduct, and the most abandoned apostacy that ever took place, since the Almighty fiat spoke into existence this habitable world. So flagitious a violation can never escape the notice of a just Creator, whose vengence may be now on the wing, to disseminate and hurl the arrows of destruction"(Othello 1788 415).

1779   This is from an application addressed to the New Hampshire House of Representatives: "The petition of the subscribers, natives of Africa, now forcibly detained in slavery in said state most humbly *sheweth,* That the *God* of nature gave them life and freedom, upon the terms of the most perfect equality with other men; That freedom is an inherent right of the human species, not to be surrendered, but by consent, for the sake of social life; That private or public tyranny and slavery are alike detestable to minds conscious of the equal dignity of human nature; That in power and authority of individuals, derived solely from a principle of coertion, against the will of individuals, and to dispose of their persons and properties, consists the completest idea of private and political slavery; That all men being ameniable to the Deity for the ill-improvement of the blessings of His Providence, they hold themselves in duty bound strenuously to exert every faculty of their minds to obtain that blessing of freedom, which they are justly entitled to from that donation of the beneficent Creator; That through ignorance and brutish violence of their native countrymen, and by the sinister designs of others (who ought to have taught them better), and by the avarice of both, they, while but children, and incapable of self-defence, whose infancy might have prompted protection, were seized, imprisoned, and transported from their native country, where (though ignorance and unchristianity prevailed) they were born free, to a country, where (though knowledge, Christianity and freedom are their boast) they are compelled and their posterity to drag on their lives in miserable servitude: Thus, often is the parent's cheek wet for the loss of a child, torn by the cruel hand of violence from her aching bosom; Thus, often and in vain is the infant's sigh for the nurturing care of its bereaved parent, and thus do the ties of nature and blood become victims to cherish the vanity and luxury of a fellow mortal. Can this be right? Forbid it gracious Heaven"(Hammond 1889 63).

1783   After quoting from the Declaration of Independence David Cooper said: "We need not now turn over the libraries of Europe for authorities to prove that blacks are born equally free with whites; it is declared and recorded as the sense of America . . ."(1783 13).

1784   A conference of Methodists, meeting in Virginia, declared: "We are deeply conscious of the Impropriety of making new Terms of Communion for a religious Society already established, excepting on the most pressing Occasion: and such we esteem the Practice of holding our Fellow-Creatures in Slavery. We view it as contrary to the Golden Law of God on which hang all the Law and the Prophets, and the unalienable Rights of Mankind, as well as every Principle of the Revolution, to hold in the deepest Debasement, in a more abject Slavery than is perhaps to be found in any Part of the World except America, so many Souls that are all capable of the Image of God"(PCSM 1904 374).

1786   "To the Honourable Legislature of the State of Virginia. The petition of the undersigned electors of the said state, Humbly sheweth that your petitioners are clerly and fully persuaded that liberty is the birthright of all mankind, the right of every rational creature without exception who has not forfeited that right to the laws of his country, that the body of negroes in this state have been robbed of that right without any such forfeiture, and therefore ought in justice to have that right restored. That the glorious and ever memorable revolution can be justified on no other principle but doth plead with greater force for the emancipation of our slaves in proportion as the oppression exercised over them exceeds the oppression formerly exercised by Great Britain over these states. . . . "(Johnston 1970 106).

1787   Samuel Hopkins, a signer of the Declaration of Independence, writes: "It was repeatedly declared in Congress, as the language and sentiment of all these States, and by other public bodies of men, 'that we hold these truths to be self-evident, that *all men* are created *equal*: That they are endowed by their Creator with certain *unalienable rights*: That among these are *life, liberty*, and the pursuit of happiness.' 'That all men are born *equally free* and *independent*, and have certain natural, inherent, and *unalienable* rights, among which are the defending and enjoying *life* and *liberty*, acquiring, possessing, and protecting *property*, and pursuing and obtaining happiness and safety.' . . . The Africans, and the blacks in servitude among us, were really as much included in these assertions as ourselves; and their right, *unalienable right* to liberty, and to procure and possess property, is as much asserted as ours, if they be *men*. And if we have not allowed them to enjoy these unalienable rights, but violently deprived them of liberty and property, and are still taking, as far as in our power, all liberty and property from the nations in Africa, we are guilty of a ridiculous, wicked contradiction and inconsistence; and practically authorize any nation or people, who have power to do it, to make us their slaves"((1721-1803) 1787 1; cf. Countryman 1787 2, CPS 1788 21, and Dana 1791 28).

1788   "For by nature [the freeman and the slave] both possess an equal degree of dignity; their natural rights are the same — Slavery may deprive a man of the use of his rights and dignity, but it cannot deprive him of his title to them. The freeman should . . . not entertain any ideas of self-superiority"(Brissot de Warville 1788 68).

In April 16, 1788, Consider Arms, Malichi Maynard, and Samuel Field from Massachusetts, objecting to the proposed federal Constitution, made this statement: "If we could once make it our own case, we should soon discover what distress & anxiety, what poignant feelings it would produce in our own breasts, to have our infants torn from the bosoms of their tender mothers — indeed our children of all ages, from infancy to manhood, arrested from us by a banditti of lawless ruffians, in defiance of all the laws of humanity, and carried to a country far distant, without any hopes of their return — attended likewise with the cutting reflection, that they were likely to undergo all those indignities, those miseries, which are the usual concomitants of slavery. Indeed when we consider the depredations committed in Africa, the cruelties exercised towards the poor captivated inhabitants of that country on their passage to this — crowded by droves into the holds of ships, suffering what might naturally be expected would result from scanty provisions, and inelastic infectious air, and after their arrival, drove like brutes from market to market, *branded* on their naked *bodies* with *hot irons*, with the initial letters of their masters names — fed upon the entrails of beasts like swine in the slaughter-yard of a butcher; and many other barbarities, of which we have documents well authenticated: then put to the hardest of labour, and to perform the vilest of drudges — their master (or rather *usurpers*) by far less kind and benevolent to them, than to their horses and their hounds. We say, when we consider these things (the recollection of which gives us pain) conscience applauds the decision we have made [that is, to vote against ratification]. . . . "(DHRC 1976 17:47-8).

1789   Speech by William Pinkney in the House of Delegates of Maryland: "It will not do . . . to talk like philosophers, and act like unrelenting tyrants; to be perpetually sermonizing it with liberty for our text, and actual oppression for our commentary. . . . is the encouragement of civil slavery, by legislative acts, correspondent with the principle of a democracy? Call that principle what you will, the love of *equality*, as defined by some; of liberty, as understood by others; such conduct is manifestly in violation of it. . . . these shackled wretches are men as well as we are, sprung from the same common parent, and endued with equal faculties of mind and body. . . . Born with hearts as susceptible of virtuous impressions as our own, and with minds as capable of benefiting by improvement, they are in all respects our equals by nature . . ."(1790 8, 9-10, 15-16, 16-17; note the favorable reference to democracy which, it is often said, is only denounced in the eighteenth century (cf. below, pages 481-483).)

Jonathan Parker of Virginia "hoped Congress would do all that lay in their power to restore to human nature its privleges, and, if possible, wipe off the stigma under which America labored. The inconsistency in our principles, with which we are justly charged, should be done away, that we may show, by our actions, the pure beneficence of the doctrine we hold out to the world in our Declaration of Independence" (Gales 1834 1:351; cf. Baldwin 1788 15-16).

1790   The Constitution of the Virginia Society for Promoting the Abolition of Slavery from *The Virginia Gazette, and Petersburg Intelligencer* : " *[The Lord] created mankind of every nation, language, and colour, equally free; and, that slavery in all its forms, in all its degrees, is an outrageous violation, and an odious degradation of human nature: That it is inconsistent with the precepts of the Gospel, of 'doing to others, as we would they should do unto us;' and that it is not only a moral, but a political evil, which tends wherever it prevails, to deprave the morals of the people, weaken the bands of society, and discourage trades and manufactures, and rather promotes arbitrary power, than secures the full rights and liberties of mankind*"(VGPI 1790).

1791   "It is a principle, the truth of which hath in this country been generally, if not universally acknowledged, ever since the commencement of the late war, *that all men are born equally free.* If this be true, the Africans are by nature equally entitled to freedom as we are; and therefore we have no more right to enslave, or afford aid to enslave them, than they have to do the same to us"(Edwards 1791 5).

1792   "In America, a slave is a standing monument of the tyranny and inconsistency of human governments. His is declared by the united voice of America, to be by nature free . . ."(Rice 1792 14).

1793   "God hath created mankind after his own image, and granted to them liberty and independence; and if varieties may be found in their structure and colour, these are only to be attributed to the nature of their diet and habits, as also of the soil and climate they may inhabit, and serve as flimsy pretexts for enslaving them. . . . . What! shall a people, who flew to arms with the valour of Roman Citizens, when encroachments were made upon their liberties, by the invasion of foreign powers, now basely descend to cherish the seed and propagate the growth of that evil, which they boldly fought to eradicate. To the eternal infamy of our country this will be handed down to posterity, written with the blood of African innocence"(Buchanan 1793 7, 12).

1795   Two petitions were sent to the Virginia legislature that contained 538 signatures. Here is a sample from one of them: "Your petitioners regret that several states in the American union where those inalienable rights of human nature to life, liberty and the pursuit of happiness have been so clearly defined and successfully asserted should in contradiction thereto, and contrary to the divine command of "doing to others, as they would they should do unto them" suffer under sanction of law, so large a number of their fellowmen to remain in a state of abject slavery at a time too, when the living spirit of liberty seems to be diffusing itself through the world. "(Johnston 1970 108; for a petition presented to the Connecticut legislature, see DHNPUS 1969 10-12; for petitions presented to Congress, see MPCUS 1792 and Schweninger 1998).

This long list — which could easily be greatly extended (cf. Bruns 1977) — is more than enough to show the falsity of the claim that Americans generally understood the Declaration (and similar public statements) to apply only to whites. It is ironic that such a claim — which is often expressed by radical or Marxist writers — was asserted by Chief Justice Taney in the infamous 1857 Dred Scott decision:

The general words [in the Declaration of Independence] would seem to embrace the whole human family, and if they were used in a similar instrument at this day, would be so understood. But it is too clear for dispute, that the enslaved African race were not intended to be included, . . . for if the language, as understood in that day, would embrace them, the conduct of the distinguished men who framed the Declaration of Independence would have been utterly and flagrantly inconsistent with the principles they asserted; and instead of the sympathy of mankind, to which they so confidently appealed, they would have deserved and received universal rebuke and reprobation. Yet the men who framed this Declaration were great men — high in literary acquirements — high in their sense of honor, and incapable of asserting principles inconsistent with those on which they were acting. (60 U. S. 393, 410)

Not only is this claim about the meaning of the Declaration ludicrous, none of the many declarations of equality and freedom in the entire revolutionary period excluded blacks. Hence some slaveholders hesitated to issue such declarations. For example, in the debate on the ratification of the federal Constitution in South Carolina, Charles Cotesworth Pinckney suggested a reason that "weighed particularly, with the members from this state, against the insertion of a bill of rights. Such bills generally begin with declaring that all men are by nature born free. Now, we should make that declaration with a very bad grace, when a large part of our property consists in men who are actually born slaves"(Elliot 1836 4:316; of course, they already acted in that "bad grace" when representatives of the state signed the Declaration of Independence, and then their pledge made with their "sacred honor" led to no action toward ending slavery). The issue is not whether blacks are men — note that Pinckney calls them "men." The issue is hypocrisy. It is equally ludicrous for Taney to claim that because the Founders were great men, "high in literary acquirements — high in their sense of honor," that they were "incapable of asserting principles inconsistent with those on which they were acting." Even a modest knowledge of history is sufficient to show that literary or political greatness are not always exhibited in conjunction with moral integrity. The Founders were men of high integrity in many respects but for most of them that integrity did not include the subjects of blacks or slavery. This was especially true of southern leaders. For example, Patrick Henry explicitly acknowledged his weakness of will and continuing hypocrisy. When questioned about his slaves he replied: "I am drawn along by y^e. general inconvenience of living without them, I will not, I cannot justify it. However culpable my Conduct, I will so far pay my devoir to Virtue, as to own the excellence & rectitude of her Precepts, & to lament my want of conforming to them"(Meade 1957 300; y^e. = the). Henry even used the image of the slave with great rhetorical effect in his famous "give me liberty or give me death" speech. An eyewitness reports: "When he said, 'Is life so dear, or peace so sweet, as to be purchased at the price of chains and slavery?" he stood in the attitude of a condemned galley slave, loaded with fetters, awaiting his doom. His form was bowed; his wrists were crossed; his manacles were almost visible as he stood like an embodiment of helplessness and agony. After a solemn pause, he raised his eyes and chained hands towards heaven, and prayed, in words and tones which thrilled every heart, 'Forbid it, Almighty God!' "(Tyler 1887 130). One wonders if Henry ever recognized a kindred spirit when he heard of a slave either escaping to freedom, or dying in the attempt. The wonder ceases, however, when one learns that neither while living nor in his will did Henry ever free a slave, and that "They'll free your niggers!"(Grigsby 1890 157) are words he used in arguing against ratification of the Constitution.

Nevertheless the word "hypocrisy" does not adequately describe the phenomenon as it existed in the minds of many revolutionary leaders. Few people can remain hypocrites about principles that they frequently and strongly assert in public. Instead, over time they slip into self-deception. Self-deception is a kind of internal hypocrisy, a self-misrepresentation, and it was described in eighteenth-century America as a principal source of social and political evils. Thus, Thomas Paine said: "It is impossible to calculate the moral mischief, if I may so express it, that mental lying has produced in society. When a man has so far corrupted and prostituted the chastity of his mind as to subscribe his professional belief to things he does not believe he has prepared himself for the commission of every other crime"(1945 1:464-65). John Adams is equally emphatic: "There is nothing in the science of human nature, more curious, or that deserves a critical attention from every order of men, so much, as that principle, which moral writers have distinguished by the name of *self-deceit*. This principle is the spurious offspring of *self-love*; and is perhaps the source of far the greatest, and worst part of the vices and calamities among mankind"(1977 1:78; cf. 1961 2:54). Adams does not mean, I think, to condemn all kinds of self-love, but only its "spurious offspring." I believe he would have agreed with what his friend Richard Price wrote in 1787: "*Reasonable and calm* self-love, as well as the *love of mankind*, is entirely a virtuous principle. They are both parts of the idea of virtue. Where this is greatest, there will be the most ardent and active benevolence, and likewise the greatest degree of true prudence, the highest concern about bettering ourselves to the utmost, and the most effectual and constant pursuit of happiness and perfection, in opposition to whatever hindrances and temptations to neglect them may be thrown in our way"(1948 193; cf. Butler 1896 2:25 and Aristotle 1984 2:1846-48). Notice the blend of Christian elements — Jesus' commands to "love your neighbor as yourself" (which makes no sense unless you love yourself) and "be ye therefore perfect, even as your Father which is in heaven is perfect" — with Greek ideals of "bettering ourselves to the utmost" in a "constant pursuit of happiness." According to this conception, neither self-hate, nor self-neglecting, nor self-indifference, nor irrational self-love, will support human excellence. In the words of Joseph Butler from 1726: "if we will act conformably to the economy of man's nature, reasonable self-love must govern"(1896 2:62).

One of the "moral writers" to whom Adams referred may have been Adam Smith. At least in 1759 Smith discussed self-deceit, and said something very similar to Adams:

> The opinion which we entertain of our own character depends entirely on our judgments concerning our past conduct. It is so disagreeable to think ill of ourselves, that we often purposely turn away our view from those circumstances which might render that judgment unfavorable. He is a bold surgeon, they say, whose hand does not tremble when he performs an operation upon his own person; and he is often equally bold who does not hesitate to pull off the mysterious veil of self-delusion, which covers from his view the deformities of his own conduct. . . . This self-deceit, this fatal weakness of mankind, is the source of half the disorders of human life. If we saw ourselves in the light in which others see us, or in which they would see us if they knew all, a reformation would generally be unavoidable. We could not otherwise endure the sight"(1982 158-9). [This quotation is from *The Theory of Moral Sentiments*, from which Adams quoted at great length in 1790 (1850 6:257-62).]

Others whom Adams might have read include Daniel Dyke (1642); Joseph Butler (1896 2:168-84, 317-38); Laurence Sterne (1927 37-47), and Samuel Johnson (1969 1:151-57; 1978 107-15). The idea of self-deception goes back at least as far as Socrates (see quotation above on page 7) and Demosthenes (1998 53). The literature on self-deception is now very large. (See, for example, Martin, Mike 1985, 1986 and McLaughlin and Rorty 1988. I found Stephen Darwall's essay in the latter especially insightful and have been influenced by it.) Throughout this book "self-deception" is used as a category of criticism of moral character; it does not refer to other kinds or uses of self-deception that may be necessary or beneficial for such things as great achievement (cf. Smith, Adam 1982 405), artistic enjoyment, romantic love, devotion to political ideals, or recovery from severe illness or trauma. Just as a knife can be used for life-saving surgery or murder, so self-deception can be used for noble or ignoble ends. Thus a noble person might deliberately forget personal slights and other pettinesses. Lying to ourselves, just as lying to others, can at least on some occasions be justified, even be praiseworthy.

Self-deception can also be trivial, as in those people who cannot regularly arrive in time for their appointments without keeping their watches five or ten minutes fast.

Suppose you were writing a novel about a colonial rebellion in which the revolutionists owned slaves, or tolerated slavery, and they continually complained about taxes on tea in terms of slavery, using language so general that it "Pleads Stronger than A thousand arguments"(above, page 53) in favor of a rebellion by their own slaves, a quest for freedom that the revolutionists conspire to prevent. I do not believe such a story can be made plausible without invoking the phenomenon of self-deception. In any case, it provides an excellent explanation of the moral paralysis that prevented clear thought and effective action against slavery by the Founders. It is sometimes said that self-deception is impossible, for how can a person fail to see through the deception? This view is plausible if deception is always direct, but deception can be indirect and it comes in many varieties. For instance, consider a subordinate A and her boss B. A hears about a document that B would eventually read and that might (she isn't sure) reflect badly on herself. She finds and destroys the document because she doesn't want his opinion of her to go down. We could say that "A intended to deceive B by destroying the document," even if A did not read it. The deception is successful if the document actually reflected badly on herself. Let us start again. This time A hears about a document that might reflect badly on herself in an incident in which A was involved many years ago. A remembers the incident, but does not specifically remember anything bad. She doesn't want her opinion of herself go down. If she finds and destroys the document without reading it, we can say "A intended to deceive A by destroying the document." The deception is successful if it actually reflected badly on herself. There is no paradox here, just a refusal to examine relevant evidence. Again, suppose a boy doesn't want his mother to ask about how well he did in a school test. So he diverts the attention of the mother whenever she seems to be thinking about the subject. The diversion of attention is an artful deception. Yet such artfulness can exist completely within the theater of a single mind.

Self-deception involves tampering with the normal modes of securing and evaluating evidence. It is initially a kind of selective attention. It becomes a category of moral criticism when the reason for the selection is the fear of confronting the flaws in one's own character, a fear that leads to a willful and cultivated ignorance of that character. Self-deceivers become dishonest with themselves in order to make their true self stealthy; it thus becomes invisible to the radar of their own judgment.   Self-deception is thus different from the *weakness-of-will* hypocrisy that Patrick Henry expressed, since he was honest enough to admit his moral flaw. The dishonesty in self-deception has two levels: First, there is *avoidance* self-deception, where self-deceivers avoid thinking about an issue that would make clear the gulf between their lives and their own moral standards. It is a sin of omission; when the subject comes into their head they focus their attention on something else, and they avoid people and situations that would compel them to deal with it. They know just enough to dread the pain of knowing more; so they gerrymander the country of their own potential experience into a district safe for their self-esteem. As the avoidance becomes habitual, the capacity to initiate inquiry into issues outside their safe district is compromised, and becomes virtually impossible as the habit becomes ingrained. The corruption of their character is revealed whenever occasions arise in which they are forced to face such issues. Then, they give some excuse — with no analysis as to whether the excuse is justified — and as quickly as possible get on to another subject. If action is required, they procrastinate, and if action finally comes, it is weak and indecisive.

An even more serious defect is the second stage: *rationalizing* self-deception. It is a sin of commission; here self-deceivers hide their moral flaws behind a bodyguard of sophistical arguments. In legitimate ethical deliberation the strongest arguments on either side of an issue are considered, and perceived truth or rightness are the guiding principles in making a judgment. In rationalizing self-deception, selective attention is used so that arguments on one side, however weak are accepted, whereas arguments on the other side, however strong, are ignored or dismissed (cf. Francis Bacon's description at 2004 83-4). Here judgment is impervious to reason or conscience, truth or rightness becomes imperceptible, and judgment is guided by vanity. To protect their self-image rationalizing self-deceivers interfere with the mechanism of evidence and the process of reasoning. By undermining the power of their moral self-judgment to be negative, they no longer have to be guided by it. They would rather be dupes of their own cowardice than face the contradiction between their professed principles and their action. They thus undermine that intellectual integrity which is a crucial element in the maintenance of moral decency.

For examples of self-deception, consider Washington and Jefferson. Washington was the foremost political figure of the revolution, as Jefferson was its most famous philosophical advocate.

According to their repeated assertions, the war was fought over the issue of liberty. Hence the existence of slavery in America, in Virginia, and in their own households was an unpleasant and embarrassing fact. How did they deal with it? Washington avoided the subject. For example, here are several examples of criticisms in print from 1788 and a 1797 letter sent directly to Washington:

> We cannot think the noble general, has the same ideas with ourselves, with regard to the rules of right and wrong. We cannot think, he acts a very consistent part, or did through the whole of the contest with Great Britain: who, notwithstanding he wielded the sword in defence of American liberty, yet at the same time was, and is to this day, living upon the labours of several hundreds of miserable Africans, as free born as himself. . . . (Yeomanry 1788 4; cf. DHRC 1976 17:52-3)
>
> Every considerate person must know [the Constitution] to be against their principles, as one must suppose it to be against the principles of all the sincere professors of christianity, to raise a man [Washington] to a throne, in opposition to a lawful government, who notoriously holds negroes in slavery without any design of liberating them, and who sells them, when his necessities urge him to do it, as if they were beasts. (DHRC 1976 16:532; cf. 6:1354]
>
> You are a republican, an advocate for the disemination of knowledge and for universal justice — where then are the arguments by which this shameless dereliction of principle can be supported . . . You took arms in defence of the rights of man — your negroes are men — Where then are the rights of your negroes? . . . consider the force of an example like yours, consider how many of the sable race may now be pining in bondage, merely forsooth, because the president of the united states, who has the character of a wise and good man, does not see cause to discontinue the long established practice . . . are you sure that the unwillingness which you have shown to liberate your negroes, does not proceed from some lurking pecuniary considerations . . . (Rushton 1797 10, 12-13, 14, 23; Pleasants in 1785 (Washington 1992 3:449-51)) and Jasper Dwight in 1796 also wrote strongly critical letters to Washington.)

Washington never answered such censures of his integrity and morality. But, in the theater of his mind, did he ever confront the issues that these criticisms raise? We cannot know for sure, but in 1794 he wrote Robert Morris: "With respect to the other species of property [that is, human slaves], concerning which you ask my opinion, I shall frankly declare to you that I do not like to even think, much less talk of it"(1931 34:47). This is an expression of avoidance self-deception. When the revolutionary war was beginning, Washington argued that the "time is now near at hand which will probably determine, whether Americans are to be, Freemen, or Slaves"(1931 5:211); he asserted that "the crisis is arrived when we must assert our rights, or submit to every imposition, that can be heaped upon us, till custom and use make us as tame and abject slaves, as the blacks we rule over with such arbitrary sway"(3:242). Since Washington thought his own cause of freedom was just, and worthy of great risk to his own life, should he not also have to think the cause of the slaves to be even more so? In 1775 Levi Hart said that "The Egyptian bondage was a state of liberty and ease compared with the condition of these unhappy sufferers [that is, victims of the slave trade]"(18). In 1796 the Virginian St. George Tucker wrote that slavery was "ten thousand times more cruel than the utmost extremity of those grievances and oppressions, of which we complained"(10). Earlier the Quaker David Cooper, when speaking of "the treatment we have received from Britain," said that it is "no more to be equalled, with ours to negroes, than a barley corn is to the globe we inhabit"(1783 5; cf. Hume 1985 383.). Yet, for Washington, the condition of black slaves, was never a "crisis."

In a "Circular to the States" on June 14, 1783, Washington wrote: "With this conviction of the importance of the present crisis, silence in me would be a crime; I will therefore speak . . . the language of freedom and sincerity, without disguise"(1783 14). But Washington never considers his own silence on slavery a "crime" nor, on this subject, does he speak "the language of freedom and sincerity, without disguise." Instead the energetic and forceful hero of the revolution becomes tame and morally abject. In 1784 when he was asked if he would sign an antislavery petition to be given in the Virginia legislature he refused, saying that he would write a letter provided that the legislature actually took it up (1976 4:145-6). But the legislature was not going on the road to abolition without an energetic fight. Washington's active intervention might not have made a difference, but his passivity certainly helped defeat the antislavery forces. Until late in life, Washington, through selective attention, could believe that it was the legislators' responsibility to abolish slavery and, if they failed to act, his own moral principles required no action with regard his own slaves, much less a leadership responsibility in seeking antislavery legislation. His avoidance self-deception apparently gerrymandered the moral power of abolitionism out of his consciousness and this gerrymandering destroyed his integrity. Hence he could both be a slaveholder and think of himself as a champion of liberty for blacks, he could be by far the most powerful leader in America and think the responsibility for initiating action on abolition fell on other shoulders. So 1793, when the Fugitive Slave Law came before him for his "official decision," he signed it. In practice, as Gary Nash pointed out in his book *Race and Revolution*, the Act "gave virtual hunting licenses to southern agents intent on seizing free blacks in northern cities"(1990 77; cf. Finkelman 1990 417). Given the atmosphere of political self-deceit, it is not surprising that the word "slave" was left out of the Act (PAS 1789 104, cf. Finkelman 1990 420), as it had earlier been left out of the Constitution. America's race war was born within the duplicitous consciousness of its founding leaders.

Inaction attended Washington's private acts as well. On February 5, 1783 Lafayette wrote to Washington suggesting that they "Unite in Purchasing a Small Estate Where We May try the Experiment to free the Negroes, and Use them only as tenants. Such an Example as Yours Might Render it a General Practice, and if we Succeed in America, I Will Cheerfully Devote a part of My time to Render the Method fascionable in the West Indias"(1976 5:91-2). Washington replied: "I shall be happy to join you in so laudable a work; but will defer going into a detail of the business till I have the pleasure of seeing you"(121). Not surprisingly nothing comes of this collaboration, nor does Washington act on his own. Lafayette, however, did act on his own and three years later wrote Washington that he bought a "plantation in the Colony of Cayenne and am going to free my Negroes in order to make that experiment which you know is my hobby-horse"(1976 309; cf. Adams 1850 8:277). Washington, rather characteristically, approved of Lafayette's action but did not offer to join in by sending his own slaves, or even to lend his name to the endeavor. Washington adds: "Would to God a like spirit would diffuse itself generally into the minds of the people of this country; but I despair of seeing it"(1931 28:424). One wonders if Washington ever had the moral courage to reflect on the implications of the following thought: "If a like spirit diffused itself in my soul, I would join Lafayette, or act alone. I am doing neither." In any case, the experiment apparently worked until Lafayette was arrested in the French revolution (Gillard 1934).

On November 23, 1794, Washington wrote Alexander Spotswood: "Were it not then, that I am principled agt. selling negros, as you would do cattle in the market, I would not, in twelve months from this date, be possessed of one, as a slave"(1931 34:47; cf. 33:358). Yet in 1796, when Washington was President and in Philadephia, his wife's slave, Oney Judge, ran away. After learning that Judge was in New Hampshire, he wrote to Joseph Whipple:

. . . however well disposed I might be to gradual abolition, or even to an entire emancipation of that description of People . . . it would neither be politic or just to reward *unfaithfulness* [Was Washington faithful to his master, George III?] . . . If she will return to her former service without obliging me to use compulsory means to effect it her late conduct will be forgiven by her Mistress . . . If she will not you would oblige me, by resorting to such measures as are proper to put her on board a Vessel bound either to Alexandria or the Federal City. . . . I do not mean however, by this request, that such violent measures should be used as would excite a mob or riot, which might be the case if she has adherents. or even uneasy Sensations in the Minds of well disposed Citizens; rather than either of these should happen I would forgo her Services altogether, and the example also which is of infinite more importance. (1931 35:297-8)

On another occasion when Washington was worried that some of his slaves might use the law to gain their freedom in Philadelphia, he wrote to Tobias Lear: "If upon taking good advise it is found expedient to send them back to Virginia, I wish to have it accomplished under pretext that may deceive both them and [*nota bene*] the Public"(1987 8:85). The proposed actions to Whipple and Lear were both illegal. Washington also sold slaves, who ran away or challenged his authority, to very harsh owners in the West Indies (1931 2:437 and 32:366). In a letter to Robert Morris Washington counted it as a "misfortune" to have "slaves as attendants." Yet he protests that "slaves who are happy and contented with their masters" are "seduced to leave them" by Quakers. Of course, such seduction would be very difficult or impossible if the blacks were genuinely "happy" with their slavery. In the same letter he stated: "I can only say that there is not a man living who wishes more sincerely than I do, to see a plan adopted for the abolition of [slavery]; but there is one proper and effectual mode by which it can be accomplished, and that is by Legislative authority . . ."(1931 28:408). Are we to believe that Washington is as sincere as Quakers and others who publicly challenged the slave interest when he did not? When Quakers visited him in March of 1790 concerning proposals for ending the slave trade presented to Congress, he declined to express his opinion because "it was matter which might come before me for official decision"(1976 6:47). But, as before, it was improbable that abolitionist legislation would ever come before him without his energetic advocacy. The Quaker proposals drowned in political self-deceit (for details, see the fine account in Ellis 2000 81-119). One history of their petitions noted: "The Senate Journal's account for the day departed radically from the customary format by omitting any reference to the object of the petitions. In addition, it demeaned the petitioning organizations by referring to them generically rather than by their names"(PHNOD 1998 316). Tabling without any action was the final method of Congressional evasion. Nevertheless Washington was pleased: "The Memorial of the Quakers (& a very mal-apropos one it was) has at length been put to sleep . . ."; he believed it was "not only an ill-judged piece of business, but occasioned a great waste of time"(1987 5: 288, 525). One wonders, with regard to slavery, what Washington would have thought apropos, well-judged, and a good use of time.

Here is the great psychological payoff of self-deception; Washington can believe false but flattering things about himself. As color conceals the mortal danger of a tiger to the inattentive, so flattery masks the moral danger of self-deception to the unmindful (cf. John Mason's words below, page 221). It is thus, in Adams' words, "the spurious offspring of self-love." When Washington's rights were threatened, he became a revolutionary, he was not willing to wait for legislative authority to protect those rights; he was ready to defy legislative authority, and overthrow it by force. On slavery, however, he could simultaneously wish, with utmost sincerity, to end slavery by "Legislative authority," yet be against the deliberations that might create such authority. With regard to the natural rights of blacks, he became a servile subject of legislatures, and was willing to wait for their action all his life if necessary. Only in his will did he act, when he would not have the inconvenience of living without them, when he would not have to suffer obloquy from the southern aristocracy by freeing them. When it came to blacks Washington was unwilling to risk any part of his enormous popularity, or any part of his very substantial wealth, or any part of his political career, for the sake of their unalienable right to liberty. Thus Washington, whose physical courage made him seem superhuman, disgraces himself when confronted with the reality of his own slaves. After all, if it be fitting and proper, without specific legislative authority, to emancipate them after death, why would it not be fitting and proper, without specific legislative authority, to emancipate them during life? For a contrasting example, consider General Horatio Gates. In 1790, on his Virginia plantation, Gates "summoned his numerous family of slaves about him, and amid their tears of affection and gratitude, GAVE THEM THEIR FREEDOM, in a manner so judicious, as not only to secure them the inestimable blessings of liberty, but to prevent the ill consequences of a too precipitate and indiscriminate emancipation"(BTEM 1790 30; cf. Brissot de Warville 1964 241 and Patterson, Samuel 1941 368). Washington could have imitated his comrade-in-arms. He was president at the time and at the height of his prestige and influence. Today we can easily see that he was the person best situated to be a role model for other slaveholders, to make apropos proposals to legislatures, and to set Virginia as well as the country on the road to abolition. This was also recognized at the time. Thus in 1791 Brissot de Warville says of Washington: "It would undoubtedly be fitting that such a lofty, pure, and disinterested soul be the one to make the first step in the abolition of slavery in Virginia"(1964 238; cf. the comments of Gordon (1784) and Pleasants (1785) in Washington 1992 2:64, 3:450). Yet Washington's moral cowardice prevented him from taking the "first step," from acting on the noble political principles to which he devoted his life. It is no wonder that he did not like to think about the subject!

Nevertheless, on occasion he did think about emancipating his own slaves, especially late in his career. He determined to free them all in his will, the only Founder to do so (among those who had a substantial number of slaves). When he acted, it was in the face of practical and legal difficulties, as well as strong opposition within his own household. In contrast, Jefferson freed only a few but he, unlike Washington, *began* by not only thinking about slavery, but acting on his thoughts. As a member of the Virginia House of Burgesses in 1769, Jefferson sought to make it easier for slaveholders to manumit their slaves. Then, in 1770 he defended a slave in court: "Under the law of nature, all men are born free, every one comes into the world with a right to his own person, which includes the liberty of moving and using it at his own will. This is what is called personal liberty, and it is given him by the author of nature, because necessary for his own sustenance. The reducing the mother to servitude was a violation of the laws of nature . . . "(1892 1:376; cf. Locke 1988 394). Again, when composing the Declaration in 1776, he asserted that blacks are men. George III, he charged,

has waged cruel war against human nature itself, violating it's most sacred rights of life & liberty in the persons of a distant people who never offended him, captivating & carrying them into slavery in another hemisphere, or to incur miserable death in their transportation thither. this piratical warfare, the opprobrium of infidel powers, is the warfare of the CHRISTIAN king of Great Britain. determined to keep open a market where MEN should be bought & sold, he has prostituted his negative for suppressing every legislative attempt to prohibit or to restrain this execrable commerce: and that this assemblage of horrors might want no fact of distinguished die, he is now exciting those very people to rise in arms among us, and to purchase that liberty of which *he* has deprived them, by murdering the people upon whom *he* also obtruded them; thus paying off former crimes committed against the *liberties* of one people, with crimes which he urges them to commit against the *lives* of another. (1950 1:426)

Unfortunately, Jefferson's efforts were in vain: the House of Burgesses defeated the proposal to make manumission easier, his defense of the slave was thrown out of court, and the paragraph in the Declaration was deleted by Congress out of deference to South Carolina and Georgia.

We cannot but cheer such abolitionist acts that are fully in tune with the spirit of the American revolution. Unfortunately Jefferson was neither persistent nor consistent. By keeping large numbers of slaves his whole life, by buying and selling them, Jefferson illustrated in his own person the moral blindness that he ascribed to "the CHRISTIAN king of Great Britain." He lost whatever sympathy he had for them. For example, in 1791 the slave revolt began in Saint Domingue, now Haiti. Referring to it, Theodore Dwight asked: "Who . . . can charge the negroes with injustice, or cruelty, when 'they rise in all the vigour of insulted nature,' and avenge their wrongs? What American will not admire their exertions, to accomplish their own deliverance?"(1794 23; cf. Rice 1792 13-14). One answer, unfortunately, is Thomas Jefferson, who had no sympathy for the revolt and, like George III, actually encouraged slavery by doing what he could to help put down the uprising (Cohen 1969 520, 522; Finkelman 1998 149-52). (Ironically, that revolt made possible the signal achievement of Jefferson's presidency, namely, the Louisiana Purchase.) Another answer is President Washington, who, when requested by the French for aid to put down the insurrection, gave it, while "sincerely regretting . . . the cause which has given rise to this application"(1931 31:375). Elsewhere Washington wrote: "Lamentable! to see such a spirit of revolt among the Blacks"(31:453). Both men were apparently oblivious to the simple moral honesty expressed in a Boston newspaper in 1791 by Abraham Bishop: "I speak the words of truth and soberness, in saying that the blacks are now fighting in a just cause — My assertion, that they are entitled to freedom, is founded on the American Declaration of Independence. . . . for we did not say, all *white* men are *free*, but *all men* are free"(Matthewson 1982 153). And he points out American inconsistency: "The blacks are still enslaved within the United States. The Indians are driven into the society of savage beasts, and we glory in the equal rights of men, provided that *we white men can enjoy the whole of them*"(151).

Although Jefferson thought of himself as sympathetic to blacks that sympathy was seldom revealed after 1776. Writing to Henri Grégoire (February 25, 1809), he said: "Be assured that no person living wishes more sincerely than I do, to see a complete refutation of the doubts I have myself entertained and expressed on the grade of understanding allotted to them by nature, and to find that in this respect they are on a par with ourselves" (1892 9:246). Jefferson never tried to refute those doubts, but others tried to show that blacks were intellectually equal, some by collecting their literature, some by educating them, some by conducting experiments. For example, Benjamin Rush reports on the case of Thomas Fuller. Fuller was a "negro slave of 70 years old," living in Virginia, and had "marks of the weakness of old age," such as some memory loss. Nevertheless "on being asked, how many seconds a man lived, who is 70 years, 17 days, and 12 hours old, he answered in a minute and a half, 2,210,500,800." When someone told him the answer was wrong he pointed out correctly that the person forgot the leap years. He was able to solve even harder problems (1789 120). In 1791 Brissot de Warville wrote: "These examples [that is, of Fuller and a negro doctor] prove beyond a doubt that mental capacity of Negroes is equal to any task, and that all they need is education and freedom"(1964 237). James M'Henry's account (August 8, 1791) of Fuller concludes: "I consider this negro as a fresh proof that the powers of the mind are disconnected with the colour of the skin"(1792 186). In 1763 Franklin reports visiting a negro school: "I was on the whole much pleas'd, and from what I then saw, have conceiv'd a higher Opinion of the natural Capacities of the black Race, than I had ever before entertained. Their Apprehension seems as quick, their Memory as strong, and their Docility in every Respect equal to that of white Children"(1969 10:396). In 1774 he wrote Condorcet that negroes were "not deficient in natural Understanding, but they have not the Advantage of Education"(396). Hamilton too believed that "their natural faculties are probably as good as ours"(1961 2:19). Thomas Branagan, a former slave-trader who had seen blacks in Africa, both on the coast and in the interior, strongly defended their intelligence (1804 100-10). But the capacity for equal intelligence was not considered enough for immediate and universal emancipation; it was widely believed that abolition, to be successful, required educating slaves (for example, see Franklin 1907 10:66-8 and Humphrey 1924 484).

Jefferson, who was so fond of experiments and so interested in education, could have experimented by trying to educate his slaves, so they would be ready to fully enjoy freedom when it came. There is no evidence he ever tried although at least once he apparently expressed that intention. In January 26, 1788 he wrote from Paris: ". . . I am decided on my final return to America to try this experiment. I shall endeavor to import as many Germans as I have grown slaves. I will settle them and my slaves on farms of 50 acres each, intermingled. . . . Their children shall be brought up, as others are, in habits of property and foresight, and I have no doubt but that they will be good citizens. Some of their fathers will be so; others I suppose will need government"(1950 14:492-3). When Jefferson actually returned to Monticello on December 23, 1789, his daughter Martha reports that the slaves "collected in crowds around [Jefferson's carriage] and almost drew it up the mountain by hand. The shouting had been sufficiently obstreperous before but the moment it arrived at the top it reached the climax. When the door of the carriage was opened they received him in their hands and feet some blubbering and crying others laughing. It seemed impossible to satisfy their anxiety to touch and kiss the very earth which bore him"(1950 16:167). By allowing others to debase themselves before him, Jefferson debased himself. It is worth noting the sharp contrast between Jefferson and Lincoln. When Lincoln entered Richmond, at the close of the Civil War, he encountered a dozen negroes at the landing. "Their leader, an old man, sprang forward exclaiming: 'Bless de Lord, dere is de great Messiah!' and he fell on his knees before the President, his comrades following his example. The President was much embarrassed. 'Don't kneel to me,' he said, 'kneel to God only, and thank Him for the liberty you will hereafter enjoy.' "(Porter 1886 798). It has been said that Lincoln had a strong racial bias against blacks but, even if that be granted, there is this great difference: Jefferson allowed his racial prejudices to overwhelm the political principles he expressed in the Declaration whereas, in the end, it was Lincoln's honest dedication to those principles that overcame his personal biases.

Jefferson's view of blacks can be illuminated by an observation of Benjamin Rush published in 1773:

I need hardly say any thing in favour of the Intellects of the Negroes, or of their capacities for virtue and happiness, although these have been supposed, by some, to be inferior to those of the inhabitants of Europe. The accounts travellers give us of their ingenuity, humanity, and strong attachment to their parents, relations, friends and country, show us that they are equal to the Europeans, when we allow for the diversity of temper and genius which is occasioned by climate. We have

many well-attested anecdotes of as sublime and disinterested virtue among them as
ever adorned a Roman or a Christian character. (1773 1-2)

Rush uses "happiness" here in the sense that Jefferson would use it
three years later in the Declaration: a life of moral excellence. It would
be pointless to argue that negroes can't be happy in the sense of
contentment, since no one claimed they couldn't be comfortable. In
the words of Aristotle: "Any chance person — even a slave — can
enjoy the bodily pleasures no less than the best man; but no one
assigns to a slave a share in happiness — unless he assigns to him a
share in human life"(1984 2:1860). Rush assigned that share,
Jefferson did not. Jefferson adopted the view was that although
blacks are men, they are of an inferior race, incapable of excellence in
the art of living, incapable of happiness in the Aristotelian sense. Of
course, Jefferson still believed they could be happy in the contentment
sense. Thus in a 1787 letter Jefferson writes: "Nor would I willingly
sell the slaves as long as there remains any prospect of paying my
debts with their labour. In this I am governed solely by views to their
happiness . . ."(1950 2:640; note that this claim is ludicrous if
"happiness" is taken in the Aristotelian sense). Jefferson thought,
perhaps rightly, that other slaveholders were generally more harsh than
he. But he also believed that the mixture of whites and blacks
"produces a degradation to which no lover of his country, no lover of
excellence in the human character can innocently consent"(1892
9:478). It is a degradation because whites, but not blacks or mulattos,
are capable of "excellence in the human character," are capable of
Aristotelian happiness.

If Jefferson had been faithful to the principles of the Declaration,
he would have been committed to creating a society based on equal
rights among individuals of whatever race, with liberty and justice for
all. In the eighteenth century no one knew whether such a multiracial
society was possible; but no one knew it was impossible either. One
can certainly understand, although not justify, Jefferson's failure to act.
To do so he would have had to educate his slaves, give them freedom,
greatly reduce his standard of living, and antagonize many of his
friends. Furthermore, the emancipation of all slaves in Virginia would
have caused new social problems. To solve them would have greatly
challenged the wisdom and imagination of the legislators, and the cost
would have been substantial. "It may be objected," David Cooper
argued in 1783, "that there are many difficulties to be guarded against
in setting of negroes free, and that, were they all to be freed at once,
they would be in a worse condition than at present. I admit that there

is some weight in these objections; but are not these difficulties of our own creating? And must the innocent continue to suffer because we have involved ourselves in difficulties?"(15; cf. Franklin 1907 10:66-68) "Yes, they must suffer," Jefferson said in effect. He was the principal articulator of the spirit of 1776 and, if he really wanted to express that spirit in his life, he had no choice: he had to take all the risks and challenges of freeing his own slaves, he had to try to bring about a general emancipation, he had to work for the great goal that John Jay expressed in 1785: "I wish to see all unjust and all unnecessary discrimination everywhere abolished, and that the time may soon come when all our inhabitants of every colour and denomination shall be free and equal partakers of our political liberty"(1890 3:140; cf. 1975 1:823).

In sharp contrast to Jay, and during a time when almost everything written in America about blacks was in their defense, Jefferson attacks them and descends into a deep abyss of rationalizing self-deception. In 1780-81, less than five years after the Declaration, he composed *Notes on the State of Virginia* (first published in 1785) in which he claims, among other things, that color *is* important, that blacks are not as beautiful as whites, that they have an inferior form and hair, that the male "Oran-ootan" prefers black women to a female of its own kind, that blacks give off "a very strong and disagreeable odour," that "their griefs are transient," that their imagination is "dull, tasteless and anomalous," that he could not find a black who had "uttered a thought above the level of plain narration," that they are incapable of poetry and geometry, that the "improvement of the blacks in body and mind, in the first instance of their mixture with the whites, has been observed by every one, and proves [*nota bene*] that their inferiority is not the effect of their condition of life"(138-43). These claims were not credible in Jefferson's own lifetime. A 1786 antislavery petition to the Virginia legislature maintained that "the argument drawn from the difference of hair, features, and colour is so beneath the man of sense, much more the Christian, that we would not insult the Honourable Assembly by enlarging upon them"(above, page 55). Jefferson's felt no qualms about "enlarging" on this issue and insulting his readers. In 1786, David Ramsay, the slaveholding historian from South Carolina, wrote Jefferson complaining that he [Jefferson] had "depressed the negroes too low"(Jefferson 1950 9:441). In 1787, an anonymous reviewer of the *Notes* said that Jefferson's reasons for not incorporating blacks into the state are "inconsistent with truth and repugnant to the feelings of human nature"(RNSV 1787 379). When Benjamin Banneker arrived in Washington to help survey and lay it out, the *Georgetown Weekly Ledger* (March 12, 1791) referred to him as "an Ethiopian, whose abilities, as a surveyor and astronomer, clearly prove that Mr. Jefferson's concluding that race of men were void of mental endowments, was without foundation"(Kaplan 1973 116). (Ironically, Banneker was appointed by Jefferson himself, in his capacity as Secretary of State, on the recommendation of Andrew Elliot, who was in charge of the survey.) In 1792 Gilbert Imlay, a man who was born in New Jersey and spent most of his life in Kentucky, published a book in which he said: "I have been ashamed, in reading Mr. Jefferson's book, to see, from one of the most enlightened and benevolent of my countrymen, the disgraceful prejudices he entertains against the unfortunate negroes"(1797 222). He subjects Jefferson's view to strong criticism (221-31). In 1796 Duc de La Rochefoucauld-Liancourt, a French visitor to Monticello, reported that Jefferson had not changed the views he expressed in the *Notes*, and he "adds so many conditions to render [emancipation] practicable, that it is thus reduced to the impossible"(Stanton, Lucia 1993 174). In 1814 Jefferson said that "there is nothing I would not sacrifice to a practicable plan of abolishing every vestige of this moral and political depravity"(1903 14:184), and in 1820 he repeated this claim, adding that to refer to slaves as "property" is to misname the relationship (15:249). Yet what Jefferson meant by "practicable" could not in the nature of the case be had. He meant a proposal that would have the support of almost all whites, would preserve Virginia society and the union of the states, and would banish blacks, whether slaves or free. In 1797 Edward Rushton accursed Jefferson of using a "subterfuge" when he attempted "to show that the negroes are an inferior order of being"(1797 7-8). In 1800 William Linn published a pamphlet in which he attacked Jefferson from a conservative Christian perspective. He charged: "You have degraded the blacks from the ranks which God hath given them in the scale of being! You have advanced the strongest argument for their state of slavery! You have insulted human nature!"(Linn 1800 13). Clement Clarke Moore, of *The Night Before Christmas* fame, owned slaves and didn't disapprove of slavery. Yet, in 1804, he charges that Jefferson wrongly "debases the negro"(21) and objects to the orangutan story. He goes on: "Among the numerous opportunities which Mr. Jefferson must have had of observing the dispositions of these unfortunate people, did he never discover in any instance a nobleness of spirit, and delicate sense of honour, not exceeded by any hero of history or romance? Or did he always see through the fallacious medium of a darling theory?"(23).

In 1804 Oliver Oldschool gave Jefferson's book a highly negative review, and took him to task for his view on blacks in general, and for his orangutan comment in particular. In the second edition of his *Essay on the Causes of the Variety of Complexion and Figure in the Human Species* (1810), Samuel Smith dismisses Jefferson's characterizations of blacks in the *Notes* as hardly worth attention: "These remarks upon the genius [character] of the African negro appear to me to have so little foundation in true philosophy that few observations will be necessary to refute them"(1810 267).

Unconvincing as Jefferson's claims were at the time, they are even more unconvincing from our contemporary perspective. Consider the claim about orangutans, which was then a general term for apes but principally referred to chimpanzees. (Orangutans, in our usage of the term, are not native to Africa.) We know that in Africa there were stories of "leopard men" or "lion men" who dressed up in leopard or lion skins and, by witchcraft, claimed to actually become leopards or lions. This superstition may have originally been created to enhance the social power of shamans because it allow them to flout morality — for example, to become cannibals — without suffering the usual consequences since, if the shaman really becomes a leopard or lion, no cannibalism takes place. Similarly the stories of "chimpanzee men" may have been a superstitious cover that allowed shamans to rape women. If these speculations are correct, it would be natural for slave traders, to use these stories to help dehumanize blacks in the eyes of whites and thereby reduce opposition to African slavery. In America such motivations may have been the principal reason why educated slave owners, like Jefferson, accepted (or feigned acceptance) of what would otherwise be rejected out of hand. John Gardner Kemeys, a Jamaican planter who accepts the orangutan claim, rather candidly explains its role in justifying slavery (1785 60-68). In a book published in London in 1774, Edward Long claims that "the oran-outang and some races of black men are very nearly allied, is, I think, more than probable"(2:365). But even this defender of slavery, unlike Jefferson says "some," and distances himself from the stories about "oran-outangs" and black women by saying they are "averred"(2:360). In response to my query, Jane Goodall confirmed (in a letter dated December 18, 1993) that there isn't anything that chimpanzees might actually do that could be reasonably interpreted as raping women. Slavery existed for thousands of years without racial myths. Racial myths were a technique of moral disengagement, born in an environment where individuals were unable to live by their own moral standards, and were loathe to admit that fact. The myths facilitated escape from self-condemnation by proud leaders, from whom they spread to others, and were subsequently taught to children. American racism is thus a product of enlightenment figures whose pride exceeded their integrity and moral courage.   Clear and honest thinking requires that one gives the strongest arguments one can on both sides of an issue, and then impartially use one's reason to choose the better alternative. Jefferson set very high standards for believing blacks were capable of doing poetry and geometry, and very low standards for believing the orangutan story. The most radiant mind in America is made stupid by self-deceit; Jefferson becomes a paradigm of rationalizing self-deception.

The mechanism by which Jefferson undermined his own reason was perhaps described by Locke before Jefferson ever lived: "It is not safe to play with errour, and dress it up to ourselves or others in the shape of truth. The mind by degrees loses its natural relish of real solid truth, is reconciled insensibly to any thing that can be dressed up into any faint appearance of it; and if the fancy be allowed the place of judgment at first in sport, it afterwards comes by use to usurp it; and what is recommended by this flatterer (that studies but to please) is received for good"(above, page 7). Jefferson played with falsehood, initially perhaps with the intention of making his beloved Virginia look better to foreigners, but he ended up believing his lies because, borrowing language from Lady Macbeth, he could not bear to live a coward in his own esteem. The ethics of belief requires that the greater the importance of a knowledge claim, or the greater the costs of being wrong, the greater the price we should pay before believing it. That price requires more care in the definition of terms, in the formulation of arguments, in a higher quality and quantity of evidence, and so on. The claim that one race is inferior to another is of enormous importance and the costs of being wrong are horrendous. Yet the case that Jefferson makes for this belief is again and again and again declared flimsy by his own contemporaries.

Further, in addition to an ethics of belief, there is an ethics of expression. It requires that we weigh the moral risks of expressing something, even if what we express is true. To voluntarily identify a child as a Jew to a Gestapo agent is a violation of the ethics of expression. The claim that one race is inferior to another is, unless there are extensive safeguards in its articulation, a violation of the ethics of expression. Those safeguards might include great care in which possible weaknesses of the argument for the claim are pointed out, an explicit statement of the kind of evidence that might be discovered in the future that would qualify or contradict the claim, a vigorous defense of rights that might be threatened by the claim, and a forthright attempt to prevent the claim from inflaming passions contrary to reason and justice. Jefferson was himself aware of the ethics of expression when he claims to hesitate drawing a "conclusion [that] would degrade a whole race of men from the rank in the scale of beings which their Creator may perhaps have given them"(1972 143). But since the context violates the rule — as in the injunction: *Don't verb nouns* — Jefferson's claim cannot be taken seriously. His pose is transparent. In his lifetime his description of blacks was correctly seen as evidence of bad character. An anonymous book called *Letters from Virginia* devotes an entire chapter to severely criticizing Jefferson, including his "allusion to the obscene fable of the Oranootan"(LFV 1816 76). The book asserts that ". . . there is no just excuse for [Jefferson's] remarks. I am afraid, indeed, that his opinion is but too popular here, as I have heard several masters ready to justify their severity to these poor wretches, by alleging, that they are an inferior race, created only to be slaves. What a horrible doctrine . . . and what a pity that any gentleman of Mr. J's reputation for talents, should lend it the countenance of his name"(73; cf. Hall, Francis 1819 333). The gross flouting of the ethics of belief and expression that Jefferson exhibits in the *Notes on the State of Virginia* deserves our contempt. But it equally deserves our astonishment. For Jefferson concludes, "I advance it therefore as a suspicion only, that the blacks, whether originally a distinct race, or made distinct by time and circumstances, are inferior to the whites in the endowments both of body and mind"(1972 143; a few pages earlier he stated their inferiority was proved (above, page 73)). This claim betrays the corruption of Jefferson's thinking. For example, if a person believes *all right angles are equal* is self-evident, this means she cannot imagine, much less seriously suspect, that right angles come in different sizes. Similarly, if Jefferson believes *all men are created equal* is self-evident, then he should not suspect that there is a race of grossly inferior human beings. In his mind even free blacks did not have equal rights with free whites. Sometimes transcendent intellectual brilliance does not result in clear thinking; sometimes good reasoning requires good character. It is as if the Declaration and the *Notes* were written by two different men, but since they were written by the same man we can only conclude they were written by a person lacking basic moral integrity.

This view was expressed directly to Jefferson. In the *Notes* Jefferson had opined: "I think one [that is, a black] could scarcely be found capable of tracing and comprehending the investigations of Euclid"(1972 139). A decade later, in 1791, he received a letter from a mathematician, Benjamin Banneker, who described himself as "of the African race, and in that colour which is natural to them of the deepest dye"(1950 22:50). He enclosed an almanac he had written that demonstrated sophisticated ability in geometry. Jefferson replied to Banneker the self-flattering but false claim that "no body wishes more than I do to see such proofs as you exhibit, that nature has given to our black brethren, talents equal to those of the other colours of men"(97). He sent Banneker's almanac to Condorcet, who was the Secretary of the Academy of Sciences in Paris, and stated "I have seen very elegant solutions of Geometrical problems by him and would like to see more examples to prove that the lack of manifest talents in blacks is merely the effect of their degraded condition, and not proceeding from any difference in the structure of the parts on which intellect depends"(99). So far so good, although one cannot but reflect that Jefferson might have better helped blacks by circulating the almanac among his friends who held political power in Virginia, instead of just sending it to Condorcet, who was a strong abolitionist. (For example, in "Rules for the *Society of the Friends of Negroes*" Condorcet writes ". . . the action of keeping a man as a slave is always immoral"(1994 356).) In any case, Jefferson's private opinion of Banneker was not favorable, as is revealed in a letter to Joel Barlow: "We know he had spherical trigonometry enough to make almanacs, but not without the suspicion of aid from Ellicott, who was a neighbor and friend, and never missed an opportunity of puffing him. I have a long letter from Banneker, which shows him to have had a mind of very common stature indeed"(1903 12:322). Jefferson deprecates Banneker's talents because the existence of even one talented, pure African undermined Jefferson's perception of blacks, a perception necessary to support his euphemized self-image as a consistent champion of universal liberty and equality. B a n n e k e r ' s   l e tt e r directly challenged that self-image. Referring to the revolutionary war Banneker said:

> This, Sir, was a time in which you clearly saw into the injustice of a State of Slavery, and in which you had just apprehensions of the horrors of its condition, it was now Sir, that your abhorrence thereof was so excited, that you publickly held forth this true and invaluable doctrine, which is worthy to be recorded and remember'd in all Succeeding ages: "We hold these truths to be Self evident, that all men are created equal, and that they are endowed by their creator with certain unalienable rights, that among these are life, liberty, and the pursuit of

happiness." Here, Sir, was a time in which your tender feelings for your selves had engaged you thus to declare, you were then impressed with proper ideas of the great valuation of liberty, and the free possession of those blessings to which you were entitled by nature, but Sir how pitiable is it to reflect, that altho you were so fully convinced of the benevolence of the Father of mankind, and of his equal and impartial distribution of those rights and privileges which he had conferred upon them, that you should at the Same time counteract his mercies, in detaining by fraud and violence so numerous a part of my brethren under groaning captivity and cruel oppression, that you should at the Same time be found guilty of that most criminal act, which you professedly detested in others, with respect to yourselves. (Jefferson 1950 22:51)

Jefferson could not deny the obvious truth of Banneker's claims, so he disparaged him. Just as obvious to us is Jefferson's continued to use of selective attention to protect his self-esteem. Thus he writes to Barlow that "it was impossible for doubt to have been more tenderly or hesitatingly expressed than that was in the Notes of Virginia"(1903 12:322), a observation that evidently referred to the above "suspicion only" statement. But that description of his own mental condition, in the context of the brutal characterization he gives of blacks, can only be read as sarcastic understatement. It is hardly plausible that the authors of the avalanche of antislavery literature that appeared in revolutionary times would have agreed that Jefferson's doubts were "tenderly or hesitatingly expressed." Should we? For example, in Jefferson's time, George Buchanan, John Gabriel Stedman, Voltaire, Thomas Branagan, Thomas Clarkson, Johann Blumenbach, Gilbert Imlay, Benjamin Rush, Henri Grégoire, Samuel Stanhope Smith, and George Washington could praise the work of Phillis Wheatley, the black poet (Buchanan 1793 10; Blumenbach 1865 310; Stedman 1988 516-20; Wheatley 1989 29-32;). What does Jefferson say? "The compositions published under her name are below the dignity of criticism"(1972 140). Again, Jefferson states: "It will be right to make great allowances for the difference of condition, of education, of conversation, of the sphere in which they move"(139). But Jefferson far from making "great allowances," when faced with evidence contrary to his view of blacks, introduces doubts about the evidence itself. Thus about Banneker, he has "suspicion of aid from Ellicott," about Ignatius Sancho, he raises doubts that Sancho's letters are "genuine," or at least unamended by whites, and he describes Wheatley's work as "compositions published under her name." Jefferson does argue in a letter to Grégoire that "whatever be their degree of talent it is no measure of their rights. Because Sir Isaac Newton was superior to others in understanding, he was not therefore lord of the person or property of others"(1903 12:255). Yet Jefferson elsewhere belittles Grégoire's efforts to show that blacks are intellectually capable and admits that his letter to Grégoire was "a very soft answer"(1903 12:322). Put in context *we* have the suspicion that Jefferson did not really believe the wonderful Newton statement when applied to blacks. Again, consider Jefferson's stirring prophecy: "Nothing is more certainly written in the book of fate than that these people are to be free." It would seem that these words deserve to be immortalized, and they were in fact put on the Jefferson Memorial in Washington, D. C. But out of context they mislead the public. A devotion to honesty and the Declaration requires that they be removed, because Jefferson continues: "Nor is it less certain that the two races, equally free, cannot live in the same government"(1903 1:72-3). Jefferson thus raises the level of certainty of his parochial and speculative racial prejudice to that of a universal self-evident truth.

The glorious Declaration of American Independence was composed by Jefferson and its authority depended, as Jefferson later rightly claimed, "on the harmonizing sentiments of the day"(1903 16:118). Yet within five years he was composing the infamous *Notes on the State of Virginia,* which contained what deserves to be called the Declaration of American Racism, whose authority rested on divisive prejudices of the day, prejudices that Jefferson was the first American — perhaps even the first human being — to collect, summarize, and express. Among the most divisive of these prejudices was the fear of a posterity of mulattos. Jefferson asks: "Will not a lover of natural history then, one who views the gradations in all the races of animals with the eye of philosophy, excuse an effort to keep those in the department of man as distinct as nature has formed them? This unfortunate difference of colour, and perhaps of faculty, is a powerful obstacle to the emancipation of these people"(1972 143). David Rice also had the fear of a posterity of mulattos but, unlike Jefferson, faced them honestly. As he wrote in 1792: "To plead this, as a reason for the continuation of slavery, is to plead the fear that we should disgrace ourselves, as a reason why we should do injustice to others: to plead that we may continue in guilt, for fear the features and complexion of our posterity should be spoiled." Rice argues that a posterity of mulattos is a "mathematical certainty" due to the sexual behavior of masters. "Thus this evil is coming upon us in a way much more disgraceful, and unnatural, than intermarriages." He recognizes that the fear (his own as well as that of others) is "a prejudice of education"(1792 26-27). Further, the impression Jefferson gives that the "natural history" of his day supports his portrayal of blacks is doubtful. These are the words of an anonymous author from May of 1788; remarkably they express a view that is today held by evolutionary biologists: "The negro of Africa is a branch of the same stock with the European, whether English or French, a Spaniard or a Portuguese. . . . From the united authority of able naturalists, there is not a doubt but man and the Owran-Outang are of distinct and widely-separated species"(AM 1788 392-3; cf. the words of George Buchanan above, page 57). Jefferson rightly thought of himself as a "lover of natural history," but it is rationalizing self-deception to believe that such love was an obstacle to embracing emancipation, since it is beyond question that slavery greatly promoted sexual unions between whites and blacks, even at Monticello, probably even by Jefferson himself. Elijah Fletcher was a graduate of the University of Vermont and soon to be President of the New Glasgow Academy in Clifford, Virginia. In 1811, he visited Monticello and gave his opinion of Jefferson:

> I learnt he was but little esteemed by his neighbers. Republicans as well as federalists in his own County dislike him and tell many anecdotes much to his disgrace—I confess I never had a very exalted opinion of his moral conduct—but from the information I gained of his neighbors, who must best know him—I have a much poorer one—The story of black Sal is no farce—That he cohabits with her and has a number of children by her is a sacred truth—and the worst of it is, he keeps the same children slaves—an unnatural crime which is very common in these parts— (Jefferson 2004 3:610)

Gordon-Reed 1999 and the *National Genealogical Society Quarterly* (NGSQ 2001) give a thorough review of the evidence that supports the suspicion that Jefferson had children by his slave Sally Hemings. Whatever be the truth in this matter, John Adams is certainly correct that such a suspicion "is a natural and almost unavoidable consequence of that foul Contagion in the human Character, Negro-Slavery"(1954 Reel 118 185). Even in ancient times, when race was not an issue, there were strong condemnations of masters having sex with their female slaves (Musonius Rufus 1947 87-9). Jefferson, however, is silent about this common practice which, by his own theory of racial purity, he should vigorously denounce.

By choosing to play with falsehood Jefferson impaired his intellect and, consequently, paralyzed his will. Hence, for him, as for Washington, vigorous action becomes impossible. He saw the dangers to himself and his country: "It is high time we should foresee the bloody scenes which our children certainly, and possibly ourselves (south of Potommac), have to wade through, and try to avert them"(1892 6:349-50). Jefferson was also prescient: "But if something is not done, and soon done, we shall be the murderers of our own children"(1892 7:168; cf. Cappon 1959 2:570). Yet he could not act. "It is part of the American character to consider nothing as desperate: to surmount every difficulty by resolution and contrivance"(1950 11:251). These were Jefferson's words in the context of another topic, but where was Jefferson's "American character" with regard to slavery? Why did he not find a way to free his slaves in a responsible manner (as many others had done)? Why did he not use his superb intellect and unmatched literary talent to propose and propagate reasonable means for ending the institution of slavery? Why did he not do scores of things that someone of his imagination and gifts could easily conceive? The answer is that to take such a course, he would first have had to admit to himself the enormously painful idea that, by the ethical and political standards for whose articulation he was justly famous, and to which he had pledged his life, his fortune, and his sacred honor, by those standards he had been a tyrant and a depraved man, and that the Virginia society that he loved, and the lavish Monticello lifestyle that he enjoyed, were both founded on a moral abomination.

This abomination was enforced by torture. Alexander Hewatt, who was born in Scotland but lived in Charleston, South Carolina from 1763 to 1775, gives a description of a common one:

> It would rouze the anguish and indignation of a humane person to stand by while a puny overseer chastises . . . slaves, and behold with what piercing stripes he furrows the back of an able negro, whose greatness of soul will not suffer him to complain, and whose whole strength could crush his tormentor to atoms. The unmerciful whip with which they are chastised is made of cow-skin, hardened, twisted, and tapering, which brings the blood with every blow, and leaves a scar on their naked back which they carry to their grave. . . . Can it be deemed wonderful [that is, surprising], that such unhappy creatures should now and then be tempted to assert the rights of nature? (1779 2:96-7)

Jame Hubbard was one of those slaves who asserted the "rights of nature." In 1805 Hubbard escaped from Monticello, but was captured and returned. In 1810 he escaped once more and Jefferson hired Isham Chisolm to catch him. Chisolm failed but, when given an extra twenty-five dollars to try again, he succeeded. Hubbard was brought back in chains and, as Jefferson describes it, "I had him severely

flogged in the presence of his old companions, and committed to jail
. . ."(1976 35 [2004 4:620]; see also 1997 2:1275). Thomas Day's
observation from 1776 seems especially relevant: "If there be an object
truly ridiculous in nature, it is an American patriot, signing resolutions
of independency with the one hand, and with the other brandishing a
whip over his affrighted slaves"(1784 7). Or consider what a black
slave from Woodbury, New Jersey, named Abraham Johnstone wrote
on the day before his execution:

> Even the patriotic who stood forth the champions of liberty, and in asserting
> the natural rights of all mankind, used the most perswasive eloquence the
> most powerful rhetoric and the choicest language the rich treasury of words
> could afford, those who undauntedly stood forth day by day the advocates of
> liberty, at night would be cruel rigid and inexorable tyrants.   How
> preposterously absurd must an impartial observer think the man whom he sees
> one moment declaring with the most incredible volubility in favour of natural
> rights and general freedom, and the next moment with his own hands for some
> very trivial offence inflicting the cruel ignominious stripes of slavery and
> riveting it's shackles — (1797 11)

Suppose Hubbard had gotten free while being prepared for flogging,
and in the scuffle he had killed both the flogger and Jefferson
(assuming, for the moment, that Jefferson was present), then by
Lockean and Jeffersonian standards Hubbard's actions would be
wholly justified and admirable. Even Hobbes said that slaves "may
break their bonds, or the prison; and kill, or carry away captive their
Master, justly"(1968 254). We might reflect how little human nature
seems to vary. In Africa, talented and powerful men create a belief in
magical powers ("chimpanzee men" are chimpanzees) so that they can
use it, among other things, as a justification for raping women; in
America, the talented and powerful Jefferson helps create a belief in
racism (blacks are grossly inferior humans) so that he can use it,
among other things, as a justification for torturing Hubbard. In each
case, feeble excuses — the skin of an animal or the dark skin of a
human — become effective in the context of gross superstitions.
Protected by a racist mentality that corrupts the government of
Virginia, Jefferson become a natural law criminal without fear of
prosecution by the state; protected by self-deceit that corrupts the
government of his own character, he can live with that criminality
without fear of recognition by his own moral sense. Hubbard's
actions, in contrast, make him a natural law hero, for at enormous risk,
he rejects Jefferson's superstition, he rejects Jefferson's treatment of
him as being "below the level of men," he declares his independence

of Jefferson's tyrannical fiefdom, he becomes an American revolutionist. Jefferson knew that Hubbard would "never again serve any man as a slave. The moment he is out of jail and his irons off he will be off himself"(35). So Jefferson decided to sell Hubbard, but Hubbard ran away for the final time. The moral contrast between the two men is astounding. Hubbard, by great misfortune, was born into slavery, but wants nothing from Jefferson except his freedom. Jefferson, who was favored by fortune with a universal genius and substantial wealth, decides he must be master of Hubbard, even if that requires torture. And it is unlikely that violence and threats of violence — Hubbard was flogged "in the presence of his old companions" — was limited to males. Thus Jefferson says, "I consider a woman who brings a child every two years as more profitable than the best man of the farm, what she produces is an addition to the capital, while his labors disappear in mere consumption"(46). But what if a female slave would resist being treated like a sow or mare, what if she would resist becoming what Jefferson called a "breeding woman"(43)? What then? Fear deliberately instilled in blacks — whether slaves or not — was the America's own Reign of Terror.

Slavery's corrupting influence on both the morals of slaveholders and the politics of government was clearly recognized by masters themselves. George Mason spoke of slavery as

> that slow Poison, which is daily contaminating the Minds & Morals of our People. Every Gentlemen here is born a petty Tyrant. Practiced in Acts of Despotism & Cruelty, we become callous to the Dictates of Humanity, & all the finer feelings of the Soul. Taught to regard a part of our own Species in the most abject & contemptible Degree below us, we lose that Idea of the Dignity of Man, which the Hand of Nature had implanted in us, for great & useful purposes. Habituated from our Infancy to trample upon the Rights of Human Nature, every generous, every liberal Sentiment, if not extinguished, is enfeebled in our Minds. And in such an infernal School are to be educated our future Legislatures & Rulers. (1970 1:173; cf. Mason's comments in Farrand 1937 2:270)

Jefferson also recognized the moral danger to masters:

> There must doubtless be an unhappy influence on the manners of our people produced by the existence of slavery among us. The whole commerce between master and slave is a perpetual exercise of the most boisterous passions, the most unremitting despotism on the one part, and degrading submission on the other. Our children see this, and learn to imitate it . . . . The parent storms, the child looks on, catches the lineaments of wrath, puts on the same airs in the circle of smaller slaves, gives a loose to his worst of passions, and thus nursed, educated,

and daily exercised in tyranny, cannot but be stamped by it with odious peculiarities. The man must be a prodigy who can retain his manners and morals undepraved by such circumstances. (1972 162)

It was a great misfortune for himself, and a transcendently greater one for America, that Jefferson, who was a prodigy in almost every other way, never recognized that he was no prodigy in this respect. At least there is no evidence that he imagined his judgments about blacks might have been distorted by the "unhappy influence" of living amongst slaves; or that he even considered he might have been depraved by slavery when he schemed to engender terror in his slaves, when he directed that runaway slaves be hunted down, when, giving "loose to his worst of passions," he ordered Hubbard flogged. An item in Benjamin Rush's *Commonplace Book* is relevant here: "This day a German Physician, Dr. Seger of South Carolina . . . dined with me. He had lived five years in Charleston. When he went there, he said, his head was stuffed with morality and Christianity, and that he could not bear to see a negro corrected, but that now he could bear to flay one of them alive"(1948 219-20). Jefferson lived almost his whole life in a environment that included slaves. We ought to learn from Jefferson's example, by introducing habits and practices that would force us to recognize those elements in our environment that might be corrupting our judgment, our manners, our morals.

Of course, Jefferson also recognized that slavery corrupts the slave. Using the concept of moral sense derived from Francis Hutcheson and David Hume, Jefferson writes: "A man's moral sense must be unusually strong, if slavery does not make him a thief. He who is permitted by law to have no property of his own, can with difficulty conceive that property is founded in any thing but force"(1950 14:492; cf. Franklin 1959 229). For Jefferson, and the Founders in general, both absolute power *and* absolute powerlessness corrupt. The rights of persons and the rights of property are intended to give each individual enough power to pursue a flourishing life, but this power must be so structured that it cannot be used to nullify the power of any other individual to be engaged in the same pursuit. Archaeological evidence at Monticello shows that the slaves' weekly food ration required "much supplement out of the slaves' own gardens, and probably enhancement from gifts or pilfered food from the main house"; further, the sanitation was dismal (Kelso 1986 32). It is likely, however, that these conditions were typical of plantations in Virginia. On the other hand, the "mildest form of slavery, if there be such a form, looking at the chattel principle as the definition of slavery, is comparatively the worst form"(1849 v). This judgment of James W. C. Pennington (1807-70) comes from his autobiographical slave narrative. After describing some terrifying examples of slaves with "mild" masters, he concludes, "Talk not then about kind and christian masters. They are not masters of the system. The system is master of them . . . "(vii). Jefferson does not appear to be an exception. It is sometimes said that Jefferson, by the standards of Virginia shareholders, treated his slaves well. This may be true enough *provided that the slave accepted slavery*. But woe to the slave that "should now and then be tempted to assert the rights of nature"! Such an assertion could turn a Thomas Jefferson, the eloquent defender of "rights of nature", into a Simon Legree. The most destructive lies of humanity often begin during corrupt internal dialogues within talented and powerful persons. As Paine pointed out, "mental lying" prepares one for the "commission of every other crime"(above, page 59). In Jefferson's case, his mental lying disabled his moral judgment and thus prepared him to use terror and torture to counteract actions that were in full harmony with his own moral and political principles.

Jefferson thus became unable on a political level to empathize with the plight of blacks as human beings. For example, it is hard to imagine that anyone in eighteenth-century America would deny that a mother has a natural right to raise her own children. Yet one of Jefferson's fanciful schemes for emancipation would violate this right. He comments: "The separation of infants from their mothers, too, would produce some scruples of humanity. But this would be straining at a gnat, and swallowing a camel"(1903 16:13). He seems here to be entirely incapable of clear thought. What would he have said if his daughter Patsy, while still an infant, had been taken from Martha and him? Yet did Martha and he have any natural rights that black parents did not possess? Would he have been impressed if the perpetrators had given an explanation for Patsy's separation by saying that it was necessary to solve some social problems of the ruling class and that Jefferson's people too would eventually benefit? Jefferson's personal callousness is revealed when, in his will, he authorizes freedom for five slaves, but neglects freeing their wives, children, and relatives (NGSQ 2001 185). The wife and children of one of these slaves, Joseph Fossett, are later separated and sold; Fossett had to spend ten years trying to unite his family (Finkelman 1994 223). In addition, Jefferson makes the absurd claim, although Madison also believes it (1900 9:25), that it is in the slaves' interest for slavery to spread, "their diffusion over a greater surface would make them individually happier, and proportionally facilitate the accomplishment of their emancipation, by dividing the burthen, on a greater number of coadjutors"(1903 10:158; cf. 15:301). This assertion contradicts his wish made years earlier to prevent "this abominable crime from spreading itself over the new country"(1950 10:58; cf. Thomas Pickering's words from 1785 in Ernst 1968 54). Lincoln, by the way, makes mincemeat of diffusion arguments in his last debate with Douglas (1953 3:313). Jefferson's thoughts about blacks, and his heartless disregard of their thought or feelings, are so repugnant because they are so dishonest, they had so much to do with protecting his vanity and so little to do with recognizing human realities, and applying his own ethical and political principles to those realities. In speaking of self-deceit, Laurence Sterne gives a description that ironically applies to Jefferson himself: "a man may be guilty of very bad and dishonest actions, and yet reflect so little, or so partially, upon what he has done, as to keep his conscience free, not only from guilt, but even the remotest suspicions that he is the man, which in truth he is, and what the tenor and evidence of his life demonstrate"(1927 42-3). The fact that Sterne writes this is ironic because it was Jefferson's judgment that "the writings of Sterne . . . form the best course of morality that ever was written"(1950 12:15).

If we wish to know the truth about Jefferson's moral character, we must compare the content of his statements on blacks and slavery with those of other eighteenth-century Americans, we must compare his words and acts for abolition with his words and acts for the slave interest, and we must look at him not only through his own eyes but also, as best we can, through the eyes of Sandy, Benjamin Banneker, Jame Hubbard, and Joseph Fosset. Slavery caused a civil war in Jefferson's soul, a war whose battles we cannot directly view but whose outcome is known: The South won. He was willing to have Virginia secede from the union rather than for it to give up to the Federal government its "right" to be a slave state (1950 31:174). It is almost impossible to study this great man and not be jealous of his colossal and wide-ranging talents; but who would want such talents, or the fame they brought, if the price were a rot in one's character comparable to that of Jefferson's self-deceit?

Again and again those who today defend Jefferson's character claim that harsh criticism of it depends on importing contemporary moral standards into the eighteenth century. In a balanced account, it is argued, using standards of his time, Jefferson's moral character will survive intact. Yet the standards that warrant severe criticism can easily be found even in the mouths of Jefferson's fellow slaveholders.

Consider the justification that the Virginian Richard Randolph gives in his will (he died in 1797), when he frees the slaves he inherited:

> . . . to exculpate myself to those, who may perchance think or hear of me after death, from the black crime which might otherwise be imputed to me of voluntarily holding the above mentioned miserable beings in the same state of abject slavery in which I found them on receiving my patrimony at lawful age; to impress my children with just horror at a crime so enormous and indelible; to conjure them, in the last words of a fond father, never to participate in it in any the remotest degree, however sanctioned by laws (framed by the tyrants themselves who oppress them), or supported by false reasoning; used always to veil the sordid views of avarice and the lust of power . . . (Bruce 1922 104)

By these standards, we, who think of Jefferson after his death, should harshly condemn him both for holding slaves and for putting his own children in a situation which, as Jefferson himself recognized, corrupts their character. There is no need to import anachronistic criticism. Jefferson once proposed an amendment to a Virginia "bill concerning slaves" that gave "freedom to all [slaves] born after a certain day." We cheer. Unfortunately the sentence continues, "and deportation at a proper age"(1892 1:68). The bill itself, which Jefferson wrote and Madison presented, also contained provisions that were even more heartless than the existing code, such as the extraordinary provision that negroes who voluntarily came into Virginia "shall be out of the protection of the laws"(1950 2:471; recall the charge that Jefferson made against George III in the Declaration: "He has abdicated Government here, by declaring us out of his Protection and waging War against us."). By Jefferson's provision, a free negro who entered Virginia could be enslaved, tortured, raped, or murdered without legal consequence. But by the philosophy of the American revolution, no human being within a state, under any circumstances whatsoever, can "be out of the protection of the laws." The rule of law always holds, and that rule entails that no human law can be contrary to "the Laws of Nature and of Nature's God."(cf. below, page 136). Jefferson believed the self-flattering thought that his proposals were rejected because the "public mind would not yet bear the proposition"(1892 1:68) of emancipation. If by "public mind" Jefferson means the legislators, there was no doubt truth to this claim. Yet there is no evidence he ever considered the self-critical thought that his proposals were rejected because they were too cruel. But this is what happened. Julian Boyd, the distinguished first editor of the Jefferson *Papers*, points out that Jefferson's slavery bill "was far less liberal even than the legislature would accept, preserving as it did some of the harshest and most inhumane features of the colonial slave code. These the legislature of 1785 would not tolerate"(1950 2:473). Adams was writing in general but his words apply to Jefferson:

> There is not in human nature a more wonderful phænomenon; nor in the whole theory of it, a more intricate speculation, than the *shiftings, turnings, windings*, and *evasions* of a guilty conscience. Such is our unalterable moral constitution, that an internal inclination to do wrong, is criminal; and a wicked thought, stains the mind with guilt, and makes it tingle with pain. Hence it comes to pass that the guilty mind, can never bear to think that its guilt is known to God or man, no, nor to itself. (1977 2:257)

I have often wondered if my appraisal of Jefferson is too harsh, perhaps even the product of a self-righteous moralism, so easy to adopt when the critic is not faced with moral dilemmas. At such times I am reminded of Jefferson's words about the possibility a slave revolt: "The Almighty has no attribute which can take side with us in such a contest"(1972 163). But what attributes could we have today which, while consistent with honesty and decency, which would allow us to side with Jefferson? "The god who gave us life, gave us liberty at the same time"(above, page 13), Jefferson said in defense of his own freedom. But what would such a god today consider an appropriate amount and intensity of indignation toward Jefferson? Jefferson pledged his "sacred honor" to support the Declaration, then mostly gave it mouth-honor. Speaking for the representatives and himself, he appealed "to the Supreme Judge of the World for the rectitude of our Intentions." Again, what would such a Judge consider fitting and proper criticisms of the rectitude of Jefferson's own intentions with regard to blacks or slavery? It is hard to believe that the human authors of the eighteenth-century abolitionist literature, from which I have quoted so liberally, and those who acted on their abolitionist sentiments, would be less harsh than I have been. But let's consider things that Jefferson could not know, such as the formation of the Confederacy. These are the words of Alexander H. Stephens, its Vice President, from a speech given in Savannah, Georgia, on March 21, 1861: "Our new government is founded . . . upon the great truth, that the negro is not equal to the white man; that slavery — subordination to the superior race — is his natural and normal condition. This, our government, is the first, in the history of the world, based upon this great physical, philosophical, and moral truth"(1886 721; cf. Calhoun 1999 533 and Aristotle: "from the hour of their birth, some are marked out for subjection, others for rule"(1984 2:1990)). Compare these words with the testimony of Augustus John Foster, a British diplomat who visited Monticello in 1807. Foster reported that Jefferson stated Banneker knew mathematics but his letters were "very childish and trivial"; that Jefferson said probably "little good" would come from the abolition of slavery; that Jefferson believed emancipation "was an English hobby, and that the English are apt to ride their hobbies to death"; that Jefferson "appeared to think that we should only render the Negroes' fate more miserable by our perseverance in endeavouring to abolish the trade." Not surprisingly Foster objected to "Mr. Jefferson's prejudices"(1954 148-9).

The spread of these prejudices greatly contributed to the Civil War, the various failures of Reconstruction, the creation of the Ku Klux Klan, the persistence of lynching, and the admiration that believers in the master race had for the race of masters. Hermann Rauschning reports Hitler as saying: "The beginnings of a great new social order based on the principle of slavery and inequality were destroyed by [the American Civil] war, and with them also the embryo of a future truly great America that would not have been ruled by a corrupt caste of tradesmen, but by a real *Herren*-class that would have swept away all the falsities of liberty and equality"(1940 76). Even at the turn of the twenty-first century the view was not yet dead that blacks are condemned by their race to be inferior human beings. Jefferson did not create racism, but what he did do was to use his awesome literary talents to succinctly express its artful form, grounded in self-deception, that allows an otherwise good person to be racist without a bad conscience. He became the greatest eighteenth-century propagandist of negro inferiority, not only in America, but in the entire world. In 1829, David Walker, a black living in Boston, wrote, "Mr. Jefferson's remarks respecting us, have sunk deep into the hearts of millions of whites, and never will be removed this side of eternity"(Walker 2000 30). Allowing for hyperbole, these words have proven prophetic. The contemptuous view of blacks that Jefferson held continued far into the twentieth century. Consider the criminal case against Charles Edward Bledsoe on October 13, 1941 in Mobile, Alabama. The US attorney, Francis H. Inge, summarizes the facts: "Indictment in four counts charges two separate instances in which by force, intimidation and threats, defendant Bledsoe held certain individuals to a condition of peonage . . ." (Inge 1941 50-745; Daniel 1989 Reel 25 [0408] 50-745; cf. Blackmon 2008 377). The individuals were black and Bledsoe pleaded guilty. His previous criminal record included shooting and cutting, carrying a gun and impersonating a police officer, and assaulting his former wife with intent to kill (for which he served nine years). Yet so scornful was the federal court of the rights of blacks that Bledsoe's punishment was merely a fine of one hundred dollars and six months probation (in lieu of six months of incarceration). Jefferson wanted the federal government to be incapable of ending slavery; in his words, the power "to regulate the condition of the different descriptions of men composing a State," is "the exclusive right of every State, which nothing in the Constitution has taken from them and given to the General Government"(1903 15:250). Jefferson's interpretation of federal power is not convincing (cf. below, pages 130-141), but even if it were, the legitimate power of the several states could not extend to hereditary slavery, for that violates the "Laws of Nature and of Nature's God." Nevertheless, in a stunning example of doublethink, Jefferson believed both that the Declaration was correct and that the states had a legitimate power to protect hereditary slavery. This Jeffersonian doublethink lived on in various states until the middle of the twentieth century (cf. Daniel 1972, 1989 and Blackmon 2008). Again, more than one hundred and seventy-five years after Jefferson composed his *Notes,* two of the most distinguished historians the United States has produced, Samuel Eliot Morison and Henry Steele Commager, in a widely used textbook, ignored the abundant abolitionist literature opposing Jefferson, including Walker's *Appeal to the Coloured Citizens of the World* (1829), and adopted Jefferson's prejudices: "As for Sambo, whose wrongs moved the abolitionists to wrath and tears, there is some reason to believe that he suffered less than any other class in the South from its 'peculiar institution.' The majority of slaves were adequately fed, well cared for, and apparently happy. . . . . If we overlook the original sin of the slave trade, there was much to be said for slavery as transition from a primitive to a more mature culture"(1956 1:537, 539). One shudders to think what would have been said if the "much to be said" had been said. Evidently, knowing the past does not by itself protect one from the repetition of even its grossest errors, in this case errors repeatedly exposed in the eighteenth century. Thus Jonathan Edwards, hardly an obscure figure, says: "The arguments that have been urged against the slave-trade, are with little variation applicable to the holding of slaves"(1791 24). For Edwards and many other eighteenth-century Americans, even if "we overlook the original sin of the slave trade," there is still nothing to be said in favor of slavery. Again, in June of 1958 Mildred Jeter and Richard Loving were arrested in Virginia for violating the state law against interracial marriages. On January 6, 1959 they were found guilty. Judge Leon Bazile's decision included the following: "Almighty God created the races white, black, yellow, malay and red, and he placed them on separate continents. And but for the interference with his arrangement there would be no cause for such marriages. The fact that he separated the races shows that he did not intend for the races to mix"(388 U. S. 3). Compare this sentiment with Jefferson's: "Will not a lover of natural history then, one who views the gradations in all the races of animals with the eye of philosophy, excuse an effort to keep those in the department of man as distinct as nature has formed them?"(above, page 80). The Supreme Court of Virginia upheld Bazile's decision, but it was finally overturned by the U. S. Supreme Court on June 12, 1967 (388 U. S. 1-13; see Newbeck 2004 for details on the case). Virginia was then one of sixteen states with laws against interracial marriage. Yet it wasn't until November 2000 that Alabama removed the following sentence from its Constitution: "The legislature shall never pass any law to authorize or legalize any marriage between any white person and a negro, or descendant of a negro"(Article IV, Section 102; SOUTH 2000 B15). So long has it taken for a Jeffersonian racism to be expunged from American constitutions and laws, which even by that year continued, to some extent, to live in our culture.

All these considerations forced me into an extreme, uncomfortable, even painful, ambivalence: Dr. Jekyll Jefferson's immense contributions to the American revolution continue to inspire my awe and enormous gratitude; yet Mr. Hyde Jefferson's betrayal of that revolution by his treachery toward blacks destroyed my respect for his moral character. I found myself in sympathy with Abigail Adams when, infuriated by Jefferson's mendacity and actions with respect to her husband, wrote in a letter to him: "Affection still lingers in the Bosom, even after esteem has taken flight"(Cappon 1959 1:281). Jefferson, the great champion of reason in human affairs, chose to degrade his reason in his own affairs, rather than use it to clearly see moral truths about blacks and slavery in the United States, in Virginia, in Monticello, perhaps even in his bedroom there; hence he could not use his superb intellect to honestly ponder what those truths required of him, or his state, or his country. One might think that Jefferson, who seemed to understand everything in a flash, found himself and his fellow slaveholders to be an unsolvable riddle. For he said: "What a stupendous, what an incomprehensible machine is man! Who can endure toil, famine, stripes, imprisonment, or death itself in the vindication of his own liberty, and the next moment be deaf to all those motives whose power supported him thro' his trial, and inflict on his fellow man a bondage, one hour of which is fraught with more misery than ages of that which he rose in rebellion to oppose"(1950 10:63). Yet the meaning of these words for Jefferson is very difficult to interpret in a straightforward manner since they were intended to be published under another man's name in France. With this anonymity and distance he writes other things he does not believe; for example, he strongly defends the Society of the Cincinnati, which he personally detests (cf. 6). So in this context Jefferson's words may not reveal that he had any real understanding of himself, nor any sincere contrition for the gross moral contradiction in personal and professional life. It is often said that Jefferson hated slavery but, if so, that feeling was not the genuine hatred of the teetotaler who completely abstains from alcohol because she detests the thing-in-itself; rather Jefferson's hatred was the counterfeit hatred of the drunkard who claims he really hates drinking when, in fact, he enjoys the thing-in-itself, hating only some of its effects, even while denying that he is an alcoholic. Jefferson hatred of slavery's effects did not prevent him from enjoying the thing-in-itself, the life of the petty tyrant, even while saying "the rights of human nature [are] deeply wounded by this infamous practice"(1950 1:130), even while calling it a "great political and moral evil"(1972 87), even while believing "nobody wishes more ardently to see an abolition not only of the trade but of the condition of slavery: and certainly nobody will be more willing to encounter every sacrifice for that object . . ."(1950 12:578; cf. 1903 14:184). Given what we know of Jefferson's life, if such flattering self-appraisals are not evidence of gross self-deceit, it is hard to know would count as evidence.

It might be said that Washington and Jefferson had other pressing demands in the cause of freedom, that there were great practical difficulties in any abolition scheme, that the political power of the slaveholders raised the possibility that any strong action against slavery would end in civil war and the dismemberment of the union. (For a sober assessment of the substantial impediments to abolition as seen by a white southerner in 1795, see MHSC 1877 405-412.) There is some truth here, although they could certainly have acted with regard to their own slaves, and it is not plausible to assume that if they had said or done anything more against slavery than they actually did, the union would have dissolved. Nevertheless, Washington and Jefferson did not have it within their power to create a just multiracial society in Virginia, much less in the United States. However, *moral criticism of their self-knowledge is not directly a criticism of their failure to speak and act, but of their greatly diminished ability to speak and act, should an opportunity arise, because they perverted their own minds and character.* In Shakespeare's words, they were "over-proud and under-honest." They portrayed themselves as friendly to the cause of blacks, and quite willing to sacrifice their own advantages from slavery, if only the right occasion arose. Other motives that seem so plausible to us — political ambition, economic convenience (their slaves allowed them both to live grandly), the fear of ostracism by their fellow slaveholders — are not mentioned. Without self-deceit, how else could these men, so full of talent, power, and honor, preside over one of the great crimes against humanity, the first such crime, I believe, to be so recognized? In the minds of Washington and Jefferson the responsibility for slavery was always somewhere else, such as the legislature or the public mind. Are we to believe that Washington thought of himself as a political tyrant over free blacks after signing the Fugitive Slave Law, and a personal tyrant over his black slaves after selling some for insubordination? Did he think that either tyranny exhibited a callousness and moral cowardice utterly inconsistent with his own sense justice and honor? "I have sworn upon the altar of God, eternal hostility against every form of tyranny over the mind of man"(1903 10:175), Jefferson wrote to Benjamin Rush. But did he ever show any hostility to the artful lies, the falsehoods, the specious reasoning that tyrannized his own thinking on blacks and slavery? "I tremble for my country when I reflect that God is just"(1972 163) he said, but, on the day he had Hubbard flogged, did he tremble for himself with the thought God is just and that he, Thomas Jefferson, was personally responsible for "a long train of abuses and usurpations" against "the Laws of Nature and of Nature's God"? Did he tremble for himself during the time when he had Sandy, Jame Hubbard, or Joe hunted down like wild animals? In 1806, Jefferson explains in a letter that Joe ran away "without the least word of difference with any body, & indeed having never in his life recieved a blow from any one," as if some such reason is necessary to one who believes that the "god who gave us life, gave us liberty at the same time"(above, page 13). He adds "I must beg of you [Joseph Daugherty] to use all possible diligence in searching for him in Washington & Georgetown"(1976 22-23). Jefferson was President at the time. The first sentence of the letter is thus no surprise: "In the first place say not a word on the subject of this letter but to mr Perry, the person who delivers it to you." During

Jefferson's lifetime at least forty of his slaves escaped. Brissot de Warville's 1791 judgment still seems correct: "The strongest obstacle to abolition is in the character, inclinations, and habits of Virginians. They like to live off the sweat of their slaves, to hunt, and to display their wealth without having to do any work. This way of life would change were there no longer any slaves . . . "(1964 231).

In the draft of the Declaration Jefferson accused George III of waging "cruel war against human nature itself" by making slaves of Africans (above, page 68). He believed a "truly republican" government cannot tolerate slavery (1903 1:73; cf. Wilson 2007 2:1077). He declared that "republican is the only form of government which is not eternally at open or secret war with the rights of mankind"(1950 16:225) and that "a bill of rights is what the people are entitled to against every government on earth, general or particular, and what no just government should refuse, or rest on inference"(1950 12:440, cf. 571). Hence, in 1792, when it was Jefferson's duty as Secretary of State to officially inform the states about the successful passage of the Bill of Rights, we might expect that he would use this occasion to write a magnificent letter with soaring rhetoric celebrating this glorious achievement as of the highest importance not only for America, but for all of humanity. Had he done so, it is likely the letter might rival even the Declaration of Independence in the fame that posterity could rightly bestow upon it. Yet such a letter would also call attention to the contradiction between the Bill of Rights and the existence of slavery in the United States. In my judgment, it was Jefferson's fear of facing that contradiction, whether in his private life or his public career, that led him to pass up this supremely great opportunity — great as defined by own political philosophy — and write the following remarkable letter that I quote in full (1792 355-6):

To the Governors of the several States.
Philadelphia March 1 1792.

Sir

I have the honor to send you herein enclosed, two copies duly authenticated, of an Act concerning certain fisheries of the United States, and for the regulation and government of the fishermen employed therein; also of an Act to establish the post office and post roads within the United States; also the ratifications, by three fourths of the Legislatures of the several States, of certain articles in addition to and amendment of the Constitution of the United States, proposed by Congress to the said Legislatures, and of being with sentiments of the most perfect respect, your Excellency's &.

Th: Jefferson

In 1785 Jefferson said that he looked "to the rising generation, and not to the one now in power," to abolish slavery in Virginia (1950 8:184). Yet in 1814 when a member of that rising generation, Edward Coles, asked Jefferson to "put into complete practice those hallowed principles contained in that renowned Declaration," he refused (MHS 1900 1:200). Jefferson argued that Coles was wrong to leave Virginia and free his slaves in a place where that was legal (1892 9:477-79). Coles urged Jefferson to institute a plan for the gradual abolition of slavery. "This difficult task could be less exceptionably, and more successfully performed by the revered fathers of all our political and social blessings than by any succeeding statesman; and would seem to come with peculiar propriety and force from those whose valor, wisdom, and virtue have done so much in meliorating the condition of mankind"(MHS 1900 1:200). This argument looks as good today as when Coles wrote it, and the story of the trials and difficulties Coles took to free his slaves is inspiring (Ketcham 1960). His example is yet another refutation of the claim that Washington and Jefferson did all they could regarding abolition, given the circumstances of their time and place. On this issue they were political magicians who, through sleights of mind, diverted their own attention from their responsibilities, and the public's from its true happiness. There is here a stench about Washington, and a greater one about Jefferson, that cannot be sweetened by all the perfumes of military or intellectual or political genius.

The stench extends to others but in different degrees. Some had no slaves but trafficked in them. Referring to the deletion of the clause on slavery from the Declaration, Jefferson said: "the clause . . . reprobating the enslaving the inhabitants of Africa, was struck out in complaisance to South Carolina & Georgia, who had never attempted to restrain the importation of slaves, and who on the contrary still wished to continue it. our Northern brethren also I believe felt a little tender . . . under those censures; for tho' their people have very few slaves themselves yet they had been pretty considerable carriers of them to others"(1950 1:314-5; cf. Rutledge's comments at Farrand 1937 2:364, 373). Among those who had the greatest political power, the profit motive *and* the low esteem in which blacks were often held, helps explain, but in no way justifies, the fact that northerners joined southerners in being unwilling to give slavery the hard thought and the persistent concern it required. Even John Adams seemed incapable of seeing blacks as he saw whites, as bearers of God given-natural rights, much less did he see himself as violating those rights by his acts, by his silence, by his cooperation with the slave interest. In 1785 he said that his philosophical opposition to the slave trade would not prevent him from doing everything he could to get blacks returned that were in British hands as a result of the war (1785 GLC00024). (Hamilton thought bringing free blacks in British hands back into slavery was "as *odious* and *immoral* a thing as can be conceived"(1961 18:519)). In 1795 Adams said: "the rise and progress of slavery . . . is a subject to which I have never paid any very particular attention . . ."(MHSC 1877 401). Why not, one wonders, he was, and was famous for, being a great champion of unalienable rights. In 1801 he signed a bill that in effect made the Federal City into a southern state by having Virginia and Maryland laws apply there (PSLUSA 1845 103-4). In the same year he said that the use of slaves, which he thought was "fast diminishing," was not as important as "many other evils in our country"(1850 9:92). By 1819 he said "negro Slavery is an evil of Colossal Magnitude"(Reel 124 22). In 1820 he speculated that "the calamities which slavery is likely to produce in this Country"(42) could include the extermination of the blacks (42), and "disunion."(44). Yet he said "I shall read no more upon the subject of Slavery in Missouri"(44). In 1821 he wrote to Jefferson: "I have been so terrified with this Phenomenon that I constantly said in former times to the Southern Gentlemen, I cannot comprehend this object; I must leave it to you. I will vote for forceing no measure against your judgements"(Cappon 1959 2:571). Politically, slavery became the great repression of the Founders, a repression for which America has paid dearly, because the return of the repressed was our Civil War, and a set of racial troubles that continued even into the twenty-first century.

It is worth noting what it was possible for the Founders to have done. First, as far as possible, they could have refused personally to benefit from the institution of slavery. Madison expressed such an intention in 1785 (1962 8:328), but did not act on it. Although it was easier for him than a southerner, John Adams nevertheless deserves credit in this matter. As he put it in 1819: "I have, through my whole life, held the practice of slavery in such abhorrence, that I have never owned a negro or any other slave [*nota bene*], though I have lived for many years in times, when the practice was not disgraceful, when the best men in my vicinity thought it not inconsistent with their character, and when it has cost me thousands of dollars for the labor and subsistence of free men, which I might have saved when they were very cheap"(1850 10:380; cf. 9:92). (Unfortunately, as we have just seen, Adams did not allow that "abhorrence" to challenge the slave interest.) Washington, Jefferson, and Madison accumulated much of their wealth through slavery, and they kept that wealth. In contrast, many people emancipated their slaves in the years following the Declaration of Independence. For example, Moses Bloomfield did so publicly in Woodbridge township, New Jersey, on July 4, 1783. (He was the father of Joseph Bloomfield, who was to become Governor of New Jersey (Nelson, William 1916 32-38).) A platform was erected that Dr. Bloomfield climbed

> followed by his fourteen slaves, male and female, seven taking their stations on his right, and seven on his left. Being thus arranged, he advanced somewhat in front of his slaves and addressed the multitude on the subject of slavery and its evils, and in conclusion pointing to those on his right and left. "As a nation," says he "we are free and independent — all men are created equal, — and why should these, my fellow citizens — my equals be held in bondage? From this day they are emancipated, and I here declare them free and absolved from all servitude to me, or my posterity." (NAS 1841 102; in 1783, free blacks were citizens in New Jersey, and their color would not legally prevent them from voting.).

What a spectacle it would have been, what an example for their fellow slaveholders, had the moral courage of Washington, Jefferson, and Madison equaled that of Moses Bloomfield. It is easy to imagine that even the Gettysburg Address would not have exceeded in fame or importance the eloquent speech that any of them might have made in manumitting their slaves. If that occurred, perhaps, the Gettysburg Address would have been unnecessary. But it was not to be. If Washington had taught his slaves to read and write, freed them even late in life (rather than in his will), saying that he, as a man of honor and believing in freedom, could no longer countenance slavery, it might have had no important immediate effect. Yet later it might have led Virginia to join the Union rather than the Confederacy, or at least led Robert E. Lee to do so. The difference for our country might have been enormous but, again, it was not to be. Nevertheless, in Virginia during the Founding era there were a substantial number of manumissions under the influence of natural-rights philosophy. Jefferson himself (1950 14: 492; cf. 8:342-343) mentions Joseph Mayo whose 1780 will freed about 200 slaves. Consider what was said by some Virginian masters upon freeing their slaves: "freedom is the natural right of all men, agreeable to the Declaration of the Bill of Rights," "God created all men equally free," "being deeply conscious of the impropriety of Negro slavery ," "freedom is the natural right of all men, and . . . no law moral or divine hath given me a right to or property in the person of my fellow creatures," "liberty is the natural condition of all mankind"(Jackson, Luther 1930 282-4 and Russell, John 1913 56). Yet all these statements put together could not have had the political impact that Washington or Jefferson or Madison could have had, if any one of them had freed his slaves and made a speech that included the words: "All men, black and white, are created equal." Perhaps this would have been sufficient to prevent the Dred Scott decision. It might even have been prevented, if Adams, when president, had conspicuously said that slavery was inconsistent with the Declaration of Independence. In 1791 Robert Carter, a prominent tobacco farmer and the largest slaveholder in Virginia, declared that "Slavery is contrary to the true Principles of Religion and Justice" and ordered that all his slaves — about four to five hundred of them! — be set free (Morton 1941 260; see also Zwelling 1986 631). This was to be carried out in a prudent fashion: gradually, according to law, and with attention paid to keeping families together. Unfortunately this heroic act had little influence. In contrast, Washington, Jefferson and Madison, who might have had great influence, continued to hold large numbers of slaves and, while they lived, Mount Vernon, Monticello, and Montpelier remained important islands in an archipelago of southern slave labor camps.

Second, Washington, Adams, Jefferson, and Madison, could have used the Presidency to combat the institution of slavery. Yet during their combined administrations it was greatly strengthened and we could hardly say, "it was strengthened despite their imaginative, subtle, and determined opposition." None of these Presidents even spoke out against the utter cruelties that black slaves often received. Here, for example, is a Virginia law passed in 1748:

> . . . that where any slave shall be notoriously guilty of going abroad in the night, or running away, and laying out, and cannot be reclaimed from such disorderly courses, by the common methods of punishment, it shall be lawful for the county court, upon complaint, and proof thereof to them made, by the owner of such slave, to order and direct such punishment, by dismembering, or any other way, not touching life, as such court shall think fit: and if such slave shall die by means of such dismembering, no forfeiture, or punishment, shall be thereby incurred. (Henig 1819 6:111)

These harsh realities did not disappear as the revolution began; they continued despite some efforts in southern states to end them. In 1778 Benjamin West, on a visit from Massachusetts, gives the following description of the situation of blacks in South Carolina:

And yet a man will shoot a Negro with as little emotion as he shoots a hare, several instances of which have come within my knowledge since I've been here. They have also a brief way of trying Negros for capital crimes. The court consists of one justice and two freeholders, who order the Negro before them at any place, try him, and hang him up immediately. But there would perhaps be but few Negros prosecuted were it not from interested motives, for when a Negro is hanged by authority the government pay his master his full value, which if he shoots him he loses; this brings many to the gallows who would otherwise receive their pass to the other world from the musket of their masters. (1963 33)

Of course private executions occurred. For example, in 1782 Crèvecoeur was walking in the woods in North Carolina. He came across a cage hanging in a tree surrounded by birds. He scares off the birds and sees a black man inside. He relates that:

. . . the birds had already picked out his eyes, his cheek bones were bare; his arms had been attacked in several places, and his body seemed covered with a multitude of wounds. From the edges of the hollow sockets and from the lacerations with which he was disfigured, the blood slowly dropped, and tinged the ground beneath. No sooner were the birds flown, than swarms of insects covered the whole body of this unfortunate wretch, eager to feed on his mangled flesh and to drink his blood. . . . The living spectre, though deprived of his eyes, could still distinctly hear, and in his uncouth dialect begged me to give him some water to allay his thirst. . . . A shell ready fixed to a pole, which had been used by some negroes, presented itself to me; filled it with water, and with trembling hands I guided it to the quivering lips of the wretched sufferer. Urged by the irresistible power of thirst, he endeavoured to meet it, as he instinctively guessed its approach by the noise it made in passing through the bars of the cage. "Tanke, you white man, tanke you, pute some poison and give me." "How long have you been hanging there?" I asked him. "Two days, and me no die; the birds, the birds; aaah me!" (1926 172-73; see Johnston 1970 85-6 for another example of gross torture of a black slave).

On October 29, 1785 the following advertisement appeared in a North Carolina newspaper:

Ten silver dollars reward will be paid for apprehending and delivering to me my man Moses, who ran away this morning; or I will give five times that sum to any person who will make due proof of his *being killed*, and never ask a question to know by whom it was done. (Weld 1839 155)

Robert Sutcliff reported an 1806 case in Delaware of a slave boy falsely accused of stealing. He describes the boy's death by torture after which he comments: ". . . such was the protection which that

State afforded these oppressed fellow-creatures, that the master escaped punishment, as is commonly the case on occasions of murder committed by the whites on their black slaves"(1812 178). In spite of such realities, there were no political leaders who would say: ". . . silence in me would be a crime; I will therefore speak . . . the language of freedom and sincerity, without disguise," to use again Washington's words with regard to the actions of the British (above, page 64). When Jefferson was asked to subscribe to an antislavery work in 1805, he refused saying: "I have most carefully avoided every public act or manifestation on that subject [slavery]"(1892 8:352). Nor did his policy change between 1805 his death in 1826. Yet it was not politically impossible for leaders in Virginia to associate themselves with abolition. As David Brion Davis has pointed out, "In 1789, Beverley Randolph, then governor of Virginia, sent copies of Virginia slave laws to the Pennsylvania Abolition Society, adding that 'it will always give me pleasure to give any aid in my Power to forward the humane & benevolent Designs of the Philadelphia Society.' James Wood, also while presiding as governor of Virginia, served as vice-president of the Virginia Abolition Society"(1975 170; Wood was governor from 1796 to 1799 and in 1801 became president of the Society.). Ambition, fear of condemnation by slaveholders, the desire for the conveniences that slavery brought them, can easily explain Washington's and Jefferson's fear of being associated with abolition, but there are no reasons of humanity or morality to justify it. One wonders what either would have done if, at the beginning of their second term, someone had written a play about them and the blacks comparable to the portrayal of Pius XII and the Jews, found in Rolf Hochhuth's *The Deputy*. In any case, Jefferson's claim that his motive in remaining silent was to help blacks is preposterous. Would blacks in general (let alone the man in the cage or the slave boy) have objected if he had publicly and frequently expressed abolitionist sentiment? Can anyone really believe blacks were helped by the self-imposed silence of the most eloquent voice in America? In the mind's ear, Jefferson's "sounds of silence" policy loudly and clearly reverberates as: "I am a self-deceiver."

Finally, Washington, Adams, Jefferson and Madison could have tried to protect the rights of free blacks, and of slaveholders who wanted to emancipate their slaves. As a member of the Virginia House of Burgesses in 1769, Jefferson did just that. He sought unsuccessfully to make it easier for slaveholders to manumit their slaves. Had he received the support and applause of Virginia's leaders, I believe he would have continued his abolitionist efforts. Yet he did not like to stand alone. Thus as a schoolboy Jefferson wanted changes in a curriculum and induced a friend to make the proposals to the headmaster. When the friend was reprimanded Jefferson remained silent. Similarly, Jefferson got a cousin to make the 1769 proposal and remained silent while his cousin received most of the vituperation. If only Jefferson had kept his abolitionist sentiments when he gained real political power. Thus he had a chance to prevent slavery in the Federal City, and in all or most of the Louisiana Purchase, but he did not do so (see Miller, John 1977 4-5, 132, 142-44, 209). As noted, Washington signed the Fugitive Slave Law that made it common for free blacks to be kidnapped in one state for sale as slaves in another. Yet the Constitution says that the "citizens of each state shall be entitled to all privileges and immunities of citizens in the several states"(Article IV, Section 2). Again, in 1806, while Jefferson was President, Virginia passed a law requiring free blacks to leave the state within one year. Although republican rights were thus violated, Jefferson did not act to guarantee a republican form of government in Virginia (as the Constitution requires). He could be in favor of freedom for blacks in Africa, or Massachusetts, or the Northwest Territory, or could contemplate freeing his own slaves when he was in Paris, but it became thoroughly repugnant for him to envision the possibility of living amongst free blacks in Virginia. If the slaves were freed, he claimed, "all the whites south of the Potomac and Ohio must evacuate their States, and most fortunate those who can do it first"(1892 10:177).

Nevertheless it was certainly possible for whites to defend the *political* rights of free blacks in eighteenth-century America. For example, in 1778 a proposed constitution for the state of Massachusetts was sent to the various towns for approval. It was rejected. One of the reasons was Article V that denied "Negroes, Indians and molattoes" the right to vote (CFGSM 1778 7). Town after town objected to Article V. The town of Spencer gave the following reason: "we Concieve that the Depriving of any men or Set of men for the Sole Cause of Colour from giving there votes for a Representative, to be an Infringment upon the Rights of Mankind . . ."(MA n. d. 160:7). Georgetown sarcastically said it rejected the Article because "a Man being born in Afraca, India or ancient America or even being much Sun burnt deprived him of having a Vote . . ."(MA n. d. 156:407). The towns of Hardwick, Sutton, Boothbay, Blanford, Shelburne, Westminister, Rochester, Douglass all argued for the rights of blacks. (See MA n. d. 156:329, 348, 370, 414, 419;

160:17; 277:444, 89). Two years later the town of Hardwick objected to the statement that "All men are born free and equal" in the revised Constitution "lest it should be misconstrued hereafter, in such a manner as to exclude blacks." The town's proposed amendment (passed 68 to 10) was: "All men, whites and blacks, are born free and equal"(Paige 1883 116; cf. MHSC 1835 203).

We can conclude that, on the subject of rights for black Americans, the Founders were far behind many other Americans, mainly because they succumbed to self-deception. It is interesting to see how Leo Tolstoy's brilliant portrayal of that phenomenon — in *The Death of Ivan Ilych* — illuminates the way in which emotion subverts conscious judgment:

> Ivan Ilych saw that he was dying, and he was in continual despair. In the depth of his heart he knew he was dying, but not only was he not accustomed to the thought, he simply did not and could not grasp it. The syllogism he had learnt from Kiezewetter's Logic: 'Caius is a man, men are mortal, therefore Caius is mortal,' had always seemed to him correct as applied to Caius, but certainly not as applied to himself. That Caius — man in the abstract — was mortal, was perfectly correct, but he was not Caius, not an abstract man, but a creature quite, quite separate from all the others. (1964 131-2).

Just as Ivan believes that "all men are mortal" in the abstract but cannot face the implications for his own person, so most Founders could hold that "all men are created equal" in the abstract but could not, with regard to blacks and slavery, face the implications for their own private lives and public careers. To the question, "What did they know and when did they know it?" the answer is: They knew blacks were human, they knew in the depths of their hearts that slavery was an abomination, and they knew these things from before the start of the revolutionary war. To their credit they did not argue in favor of slavery as an institution in their public speeches or private letters. Yet again and again when faced with opportunities to redeem their integrity by reducing the gross contradiction between their ideals and the reality of slavery, they refused to face the issue forthrightly but, if they thought about it at all, put any decision off to the indefinite future. It is an insult to their age and a libel to their high moral standards and enormous talents, to give them a figurative pat on the head by saying: "Now, now, you could not have done much better." Were they presently looking at America from an afterlife I believe they would condemn themselves in language at least as strong and certainly more eloquent than I have used (cf. Jefferson 1892 9:477); they "could not otherwise endure the sight."

Yet our purpose here is not just to understand the past, but to learn from it. If persons of the stature of Washington and Jefferson could be caught in shameful hypocrisies and self-deceptions, and if these corruptions, shared as they were by so many others, brought national calamity, one would have expected that great efforts would have been made to reduce the probability of such hypocrisy and self-deception in the future, both in our political leaders and in the people at large. Yet, even into the twenty-first century, little has been done. What can be done is a topic that will be taken up again and again in the pages that follow. Here we will emphasize that merely because the philosophy of the American revolution was composed by men who were often hypocritical and self-deceptive regarding blacks and slavery, we cannot argue that the ideas expressed in that philosophy are tainted. Such an argument commits the abusive form of the logical fallacy called *argumentum ad hominem*. The Founders' political philosophy transcended their personal faults. Martin Luther King, Jr. challenged the Jeffersonian legacy that color is morally and politically important: "I have a dream my four little children will one day live in a nation when they will be not be judged by the color of their skin but by the content of their character"(1986 219). In the articulation of that dream, King followed Benjamin Banneker (above, page 78), David Walker (2000 78-9), and Frederick Douglass (1979 2:359-88) by appealing to Jefferson's magnificent Declaration, since it provided a moral standard with which to condemn slavery and racism, a standard that Americans frequently, publicly, and proudly profess.

4

The Declaration: A Twentieth-Century Betrayal

The political problems of self-deception did not end in the eighteenth century. To support this claim, we will consider a twentieth-century betrayal of the ideals of the American revolution in which self-deception was a prominent element. The betrayal concerns a decision made near the end of World War II to return Soviet refugees to their homeland forcibly in spite of the fact that our leaders knew the ghastly fate that awaited these people. This policy applied to men, women, and children, combatants and noncombatants alike. It was a policy that preceded Yalta, was sealed by a secret agreement there (on February 11, 1945) and continued into 1947. Altogether over two million people were sent back by American and British soldiers — a very large number against their will. Yet, with few exceptions, the topic is not mentioned, much less discussed, in the memoirs of those responsible for the policy

Let us consider some examples of that policy. At Fort Dix, New Jersey in June of 1945 there were 154 Soviet prisoners. They had been captured by the Germans and, by death threats, compelled to serve in Hitler's army, although some were willing to oppose Stalin's tyranny. They had surrendered to the Americans, but only after being told that they would not be returned to the Soviet Union against their will. American officials knew that they would be grossly mistreated or shot if they were repatriated. Earlier these Soviets had been forced by American soldiers with submachine guns to board a Soviet ship in Seattle, Washington. Although unarmed, they put up such resistance that they were sent to Fort Dix. At Fort Dix some of the Soviets repeatedly attempted to kill themselves. In spite of stupendous efforts by American authorities to prevent suicides some succeeded, and all of them seemed willing to do so. They wanted to be shot by Americans rather than be sent home. Through the use of fraud and enormous force they were put on a Soviet boat for a second time. Again, they put up strong resistance and succeeded in damaging the ship's engines. Back to Fort Dix they went. On the third try, the army succeeded by putting barbiturates in their coffee and in a sleeplike state they were taken to still another Soviet ship and their dreadful fate.

Such scenes took place again and again. At Platting, Germany, in February of 1946, the American army used lies, deception, clubs, and machine guns to turn over more than fifteen hundred Russians to the

Soviet authorities. Again, a great effort was made to prevent suicides but nevertheless some succeeded because they had taken the precaution of sewing razor blades into their coats. Here is an account by one of the Russians:

> Many of us were barefoot and clad only in our underwear, though some had managed to snatch up a blanket. Any dawdler received a rain of blows from the soldiers' sticks. Many of us had to stand in six degrees of frost from 6 am until four o'clock that evening. We were in small groups surrounded by guards, two for every prisoner. They began shouting people's names out from lists and dividing us into two groups. Each of the groups was told, "Don't worry, you're only going to be moved to another part of the camp. It's the other group that's being sent to the Soviet Union."

After being forcibly put on trucks "the prisoners, who were sitting down or lying on the bottom of the truck, could not see where they were being taken. It was only by the length of the journey that they realized they were going outside the camp, and only at the railway stations, when they saw the bars on the carriage windows, that they realized they were doomed"(Bethell 1974 193). This description does not seem notably different from the methods used by the SS in their roundup of Jews. William Sloane Coffin, Jr., who later became a renowned minister, was in a position to warn some Soviets on the evening before repatriation. His description is painfully honest:

> For a while I thought I was going to be physically ill. Several times I turned to the [Soviet] commandant sitting next to me. It would have been easy to tip him off. There was still time. The camp was minimally guarded. Once outside the men could tear up their identity cards, get other clothes. It was doubtful that the Americans would try hard to round them up. Yet I couldn't bring myself to do it. It was not that I was afraid of being court-martialed; the commandant probably wouldn't give me away. But I too had my orders. (1977 76)

Even at Dachau, the location of the infamous Nazi concentration camp, a similar event occurred. Here is the description given on January 28, 1946, by Parker Buhrman who was on the staff of the United States Political Advisor for Germany:

> Conforming to agreements with the Soviets, an attempt was made to entrain 399 former Russian soldiers who had been captured in German uniform, from the assembly center at Dachau on Saturday, January 19. All of these men refused to entrain. They begged to be shot. They resisted entrainment by taking off their clothing and refusing to leave their quarters. It was necessary to use tear gas and some force to drive them out. Tear gas forced them out of the building into the

snow where those who had cut and stabbed themselves fell exhausted and bleeding in the snow. Nine men hanged themselves and one had stabbed himself to death and one other who had stabbed himself subsequently died; while 20 others are still in the hospital from self-inflicted wounds. The entrainment was finally effected of 368 men who were sent off accompanied by a Russian liaison officer on a train carrying American guards. Six men escaped enroute. A number of men in the group claimed they were not Russians. This, after preliminary investigation by the local military authorities, was brought to the attention of the Russian liaison officer, as a result of which eleven men were returned by the Russians as not of Soviet nationality. The story of this group of former Russian soldiers is that after their capture they were given the option by the Germans of starvation or joining labor battalions. They joined labor battalions and were subsequently transferred as a group into the German Army without their having any choice in the matter. This story conforms to the claims which were made by former Russian soldiers who were captured in German uniform and who were imprisoned in the United States. All of these men apparently firmly believe that they will be executed on their return to Russia. The fact that so many attempted to commit suicide is an indication of the unfortunate plight in which they find themselves"(FRUS 1969 141-2; See also McLaughlin, Kathleen 1946 25).

This report was forwarded to Secretary of State Byrnes who was responsible for the policy. That policy assumed that the Soviet Union was more than a necessary ally in the war against Germany, that Soviets in German uniform were likely to be Nazi sympathizers, that securing the Soviet's good will beyond the war was so important as to require a blindness to the harsh reality of what American troops were actually doing. For our actions implicitly assumed that there existed a kind of International Fugitive Slave Law that American officials were somehow morally obliged to obey. Those officials, knowing that the Soviet soldiers *were* slaves of others, treated them *as* slaves of Americans. They became chattel, runaway animals, who were merely being returned to Stalin, their rightful owner. The soldiers' own thoughts and desires had nothing to do with what happened to them; they had no rights that Americans were bound to respect.

In September of 1983 a description of another harrowing incident was given by Professor R. R. Davison of Texas A & M University. Like Coffin's it is noteworthy for its outstanding integrity because Davison does not diminish his part in one of these grim scenes that took place at Kempton, Germany, in August 1945. At the time he was nineteen years old. Davison comments:

We were battle-hardened veterans but most of us were in our late teens and twenties; yet we knew, even in 1945, that Stalin would probably kill these people. How then could our leaders, including Truman, not have known, or worse not have cared, especially in view of the trials about to begin at Nuremberg. . . . We willingly obeyed orders. No one complained. I remember no expressions of guilt. The terrible truth is that we had had a good time. A few months later at Nuremberg I guarded SS troops who were being used in work details around the Palace of Justice during the war crime trials. Most of them were very young, about my age. They had been drafted into the SS, but they were being punished for obeying orders. (1983 31)

The Nuremberg trials were made possible by an agreement signed by the United States, France, Great Britain, and the Soviet Union in London on August 8, 1945. (Note the date was contemporaneous with the events at Kempton and before those at Platting and Dachau.) This agreement established the charter of the international military tribunal. After signing, Robert H. Jackson, the United States representative and later chief prosecutor at Nuremberg, made a statement: "The definitions under which we will try the Germans are general definitions. They impose liability upon war-making statesmen of all countries alike"(DSB 1945 227). Let us look at some of the definitions from the charter. War crimes include "ill-treatment, or deportation to slave labor or for any other purpose of civilian population of or in occupied territory"; crimes against humanity include "deportation, and other inhumane acts committed against any civilian population" and "persecutions on political, racial or religious grounds"(DSB 1945 224). The charter explicitly states that the "official position of defendants, whether as heads of state or responsible officials in government departments, shall not be considered as freeing them from responsibility," nor shall a defendant be free from responsibility if he "acted pursuant to order of his government or of a superior"(224). By these standards, Roosevelt, Truman, and Eisenhower, in addition to many lesser officials, could be accused of war crimes and crimes against humanity. The British actions were just as disgraceful, and such leaders as Winston Churchill, Anthony Eden, and Harold Macmillan were likewise culpable. In this matter British and American troops became tools of the Soviet army and secret police. Of course, British and American leaders are not in the same category with Hitler and Stalin. They are not even close. The Korean war, for example, was extended under both Truman and Eisenhower because of a refusal to engage in forced repatriation of displaced persons and prisoners of war. (See DSB 1952 328 and Eisenhower 1953 21). Yet such facts do not excuse the disgraceful and disastrous policies during and after World War II. Nikolai Tolstoy writes that "the full story of the Russian prisoners in

1941-5 will reveal the extent of a tragedy which, in both the numbers involved and the depths of suffering experienced, is fully comparable to Nazi treatment of the Jews"(1977 22). If this is an exaggeration, it is not a misleading one. (My account of American involvement with Soviet displaced persons is mainly indebted to Epstein 1973; Elliott 1973, 1982; Bethell 1974; Nikolai Tolstoy 1977, 1982; and Moore, Jason 2000.)

Let us ask how decent and high-ranking American officials could participate in this abomination. It was completely against American political principles formulated in the Founding era. Thus, in 1770, Benjamin Franklin asserted that "The Right of Migration is common to all Men, a natural Right"(1959 17:400). Three years later he put the point this way: "God has given to the Beasts of the Forest and to the Birds of the Air a Right when their Subsistence fails in one Country, to migrate into another, where they can get a more comfortable Living; and shall Man be denied a Privilege enjoyed by Brutes . . . ?"(1959 20:527). A year later Jefferson likewise referred to "a right, which nature has given to all men, of departing from the country in which chance, not choice has placed them, [and] of going in quest of new habitations"(1950 1:121) and in 1806 he repeated his sentiment with greater emphasis: "I hold the right of expatriation to be inherent in every man by the laws of nature, and incapable of being rightfully taken from him even by the united will of every other person in the nation. If the laws have provided no particular mode by which the right of expatriation may be exercised, the individual may do it by any effectual and unequivocal act or declaration"(1892 8:458 (if only Jefferson had been willing to apply this abstract principle to escaping slaves); cf. 1903 15:124 and 19:236; cf. also Samuel Adams' words, below, page 208, and Bland 1766 9-10). In the 1790s James Wilson affirmed the same right, citing Cicero and Locke among other authorities, in a discussion that concludes by referring to the Constitution of Pennsylvania, which asserts that "emigration from the state shall not be prohibited"(2007 1:641-44; cf. Cicero 1958 2:665 and Locke 1988 347). The point is this: if you are in the majority you have a natural right to change the government, if you are in the minority, you have a natural right to leave. This latter right, so central to American political history and theory, had little effect on those responsible for the forced repatriation of Soviet citizens. What did have an effect were the lies the American government told the American people about "Uncle Joe" Stalin and the nature of the government he headed. Roosevelt, for example, approved of, and probably encouraged, the making of *Mission to Moscow* (1943), a

Warner Brothers film that glorified Stalinist Russia (Culbert 1980 16-17; Koppes and Black 1987 190-93). He suggested that Soviet citizens had freedom of religion comparable to ours (1950 401-2). When he was asked at a news conference on December 17, 1943, for his personal impressions of Stalin at the Teheran Conference, he answered;: "Well, the actual fact of meeting him lived up to my highest expectations. We had many excellent talks"(1950a 549). A week later in a "fireside chat" to the American people he said: "To use an American and somewhat ungrammatical colloquialism, I may say that I 'got along fine' with Marshall Stalin. He is a man who combines a tremendous, relentless determination with a stalwart good humor. I believe he is truly representative of the heart and soul of Russia; and I believe that we are going to get along very well with him and the Russian people — very well indeed"(558). On March 8, 1944, he said that "we are now working, since the last meeting in Teheran, in really good cooperation with the Russians. And I think the Russians are perfectly friendly; they aren't trying to gobble up all the rest of Europe or the world"(1950b 99). Roosevelt was repeatedly warned about Stalin and he knew that he was a tyrant of the worst sort (1941 93). So are not Paine's words relevant and worth quoting again? "When a man has so far corrupted and prostituted the chastity of his mind as to subscribe his professional belief to things he does not believe he has prepared himself for the commission of every other crime"(above, page 59). Roosevelt saw himself, and wanted to be seen, as the great war leader of the unified Allies, as the man whose ultimate aim was to achieve four freedoms: freedom of speech and expression, freedom of every person to worship God in his own way, freedom from want, and freedom from fear. There is some truth to Roosevelt's view of himself, but there is also truth that he, like Jefferson, was a deeply self-deceptive man, whose lack of clear, honest thinking about Stalin led him to delude the American people, led him to initiate policies that caused calamity for millions of refugees, led him to disgrace the country he led.

Roosevelt might be defended by saying that he was trying, in a desperate situation, to hold the needed alliance of the Soviets and Americans together. But he seemed oblivious to the danger that deceptions often slip into self-deceptions, which thereafter can become necessary to carry out policy. Nicholas Bethell, in his book *The Last Secret: The Delivery to Stalin of Over Two Million Russians by Britain and the United States*, writes about an incident that took place shortly before D-day: "The British and American governments . . .

found themselves, not for the first time in the war, obliged to accept as the truth something which the Soviet authorities had told them and which was false, and which all three sides knew to be false"(1974 29). Over time the policy of forced repatriation became more and more difficult to reverse. The Founders refused to face squarely the contradiction between slavery and American political principles because to do so would have created great political problems (What are we going to do with hundreds of thousands of freed slaves?) and would have revealed — to themselves and to others — their own past crimes of commission and omission with regard to slavery. It might have made cooperation between the states difficult or impossible. Similarly American officials during and after World War II refused to face squarely the contradiction between forced repatriation of Soviets and American political principles. To do so would have created great political problems (What are we going to do with two million displaced Soviets?) and would have revealed — to themselves and to others — the lies told about Stalin and the Soviet Union by many American intellectuals and government officials during the 1930s and 1940s. It might have made cooperation between the Soviet Union and the United States more difficult or impossible. In the eighteenth century truths about slavery were repressed in order to protect the self-image of those responsible, in the twentieth century, with the same motive, truths about forced repatriation received similar treatment. As Mark Elliott has pointed out: "A surprising number of sources, including memoirs, the press, and some government publications, evade the fact or flatly deny that the United States once subjected ordinary Soviet citizens to forced repatriation . . . "(1973 270). Elliott gives extensive evidence for the truth of this claim, but it is not that surprising. It is an illustration of Nietzsche's epigram: " 'I have done that,' says my memory. 'I cannot have done that,' says my pride, and remains inexorable. Eventually — memory yields"(1966 80).

We can now see why American authorities made such enormous efforts to prevent suicides of Soviets being repatriated. It certainly could be argued that if the Soviets are going back to torture, concentration camps, and brutal deaths, why not let them commit suicide? Indeed, why not provide them with a painless means of doing so, since such deaths were no doubt preferable to what was in store for them? The reply is, of course, that to act in this fashion would make clearer the very painful truth: that with regard to the forced repatriation of Soviet citizens during and after World War II, American leaders and many lesser officials were committing war crimes and crimes against humanity. To have allowed a large number of suicides would have called public attention to Stalin's murderous regime, to Roosevelt's deceitful portrayal of him, to the many acts of our military contrary to the American values so loudly proclaimed in our war propaganda. Instead there was a coverup; even in the 1970s, Julius Epstein, Nicholas Bethell, and Nikolai Tolstoy ran into official obstructionism that made their research efforts more difficult.

In 1775 Samuel Johnson asked: "How is it that we hear the loudest yelps for liberty among the drivers of negroes?"(1977 454) The answer is that such yelps drown out the cries for freedom of their own slaves and that such yelps promote self-deceit. Hence there were a lot of yelps against forced repatriation by those responsible for it. "In mid-1947," James Byrnes declared, "we had in our zone in Germany approximately 573,000 displaced persons. We support them and will not force them to return to the countries of their origin as long as there is reason to believe they would be punished for political reasons"(1947 168; cf. 1958 379). He writes this in a book called *Speaking Frankly*. Yet, as Secretary of State, he was the senior civilian official (under Truman) in charge of the terrible events at Fort Dix and Dachau. Needless to say those events are not "frankly" discussed. Truman himself was quite a yelper. In a speech on April 5, 1947, he said:

> We know that as long as we remain free, the spirit of Thomas Jefferson lives in America. His spirit is the spirit of freedom. We are heartened by the knowledge that the light he kindled a century and a half ago shines today in the United States. It shines even more strongly than in his time. What was then an untried faith is now a living reality. But we know that no class, no party, no nation, has a monopoly on Jefferson's principles. Out of the silence of oppressed peoples, out of the despair of those who have lost freedom, there comes to us an expression of longing. Repeated again and again, in many tongues, from many directions, it is a plea of men, women and children for the freedom that Thomas Jefferson proclaimed as an inalienable right. (1947 51)

Unfortunately, the demons in Jefferson also lived on in Truman, because it was his policies that denied freedom to countless thousands who, so to say, came to him with "an expression of longing." He also had the demons of Roosevelt. Thus, in 1948, recollecting the Potsdam Conference of 1945, Truman said: "I got very well acquainted with Joe Stalin, and I like old Joe! He is a decent fellow. But Joe is a prisoner of the Politburo. He can't do what he wants to do"(1964 329).

Now let us consider the yelps of George C. Marshall. On May 20, 1947, Marshall, then Secretary of State, declared: "It is the fixed policy of the United States Government to oppose any forced repatriation of displaced persons"(1947a 1085). He added that with regard to the current repatriation program: "Any coercion of displaced persons under our jurisdiction would not be tolerated. No instances of coercion has been brought to our attention. . . . " Not quite two months later he was speaking of "persons born in areas now subject to Soviet governmental authority." He said: ". . . it is against American tradition to compel these persons, who are now under our authority, to return against their wills . . . "(1947 195). Yet Marshall was one of the principal officials who grossly violated that "American tradition" during World War II. "As Chief of Staff during the war years," he says, "I naturally followed the subject [of displaced persons] very closely"(194). The actual policy under Marshall during the time he was Chief of Staff is correctly described in an official army history: "Individuals identified by the Soviet repatriation representatives as Soviet citizens were subject to repatriation without regard to their personal wishes"(Floyd 1947 68; see also Epstein 1970 209-10; 1973 x, 2, 38 and Elliott 1982 112). Even Soviet Jews were not exempt (Floyd 1947 73).

The practice of forced repatriation was made more palatable because the Soviets had British and American citizens under their control and Stalin was ready, willing, and able to use them to blackmail Allies. (For the sad story, see Sanders, Sauter, and Kirkwood's *Soldiers of Misfortune: Washington's Secret Betrayal of American POWs in the Soviet Union*, 1992). The truth is that the Allies were in a severe moral dilemma, so that any policy would, to some extent, involve them in either abandoning Allied POWs or forcibly returning some Soviet refugees. But no one who looks at the record can believe that the dilemma was faced with clear thinking and deep soul-searching, much less that it produced clever and imaginative Allied actions that were the least repugnant among those practically available. The does not seem to have been any great moral anxiety, any visceral dread, any overwhelming sense of sin. The subject is seldom mentioned, even less discussed. Self-deceit of the avoidance type apparently protected Allied leaders against those decidedly uncomfortable emotions.

It is sometimes claimed that the Yalta agreement explicitly authorized force. It did not. For the same reason the word "slave" was left out of the Constitution and the Fugitive Slave Law of 1793 (above, page 65), the word "forced" was left out of the Yalta agreement. It is doubtful that Roosevelt or Churchill would have signed it had forced repatriation been explicit. But even if it had been explicit, the moral dilemma remained. The Yalta agreement could not *legitimately* require mass forced repatriation because, by the political principles under which America was founded, any agreement is void if it violates collective unalienable rights (above, page14). In addition, by the principles of Nuremberg, an appeal to an international agreement is no more an excuse for crimes against humanity than is an appeal to national laws. The policy of forced repatriation was actually in place before Yalta. On December 20, 1944 Secretary of State Edward Stettinius said, in a top secret document, that the "policy adopted by the United States Government . . . is that all claimants to Soviet nationality will be released to the Soviet Government irrespective of whether they wish to be so released"(FRUS 1966 1272). At Yalta, Stettinius received a telegram from Joseph Grew, the Acting Secretary of State in Washington. Grew urged Stettinius to raise issues having to do with the protections of the Geneva Convention of 1929 and, further, the question of "Soviet citizens in the United States not prisoners of war whose cases the Attorney General feels should be dealt with on the basis of traditional American policy of asylum"(FRUS 1955 697). From Yalta, on February 9, 1945, Stettinius answered: "The consensus here is that it would be unwise to include questions relative to the protection of the Geneva Convention and to Soviet citizens in the U.S. . . . "(757). It is no wonder Stettinius found a consensus. For if the protections of the Geneva Convention had been raised it would have made clear that the United States had already violated those protections and that Roosevelt, Stettinius, and Marshall were directly responsible. Had that issue been pressed with Stalin, or had it been made very clear that the Roosevelt administration intended to act "on the basis of traditional American policy of asylum," then it is very probable that Roosevelt's "grand alliance" would have crumbled, and no agreement at all would have been reached. In 1949 Stettinius published a book called *Roosevelt and the Russians: The Yalta Conference*. It begins: "A deep respect for the memory of President Roosevelt and an unshaken faith in the rightness of his foreign policy have impelled me to write this book about the Yalta Conference." The topics of forced repatriation, the Geneva Convention of 1929, and the American policy of asylum are not discussed. The most candid expression of general allied policy that I have found comes from across the water by Harold Macmillan in his diary on May 13, 1945: "Among the surrendered Germans are about 40,000 Cossacks and 'White' Russians, with their wives and children. To hand them over to the Russians is condemning them to slavery, torture and probably death. To refuse, is deeply to offend the Russians, and incidentally break the Yalta agreement. We decided to hand them over"(1984 757; see also Horne 1988).

Finally, let us consider the yelps of Eisenhower from his book *Crusade in Europe* that was published in 1948:

> The truly unfortunate were those who, for one reason or another, no longer had homes or were "persecutees" who dared not return home for fear of persecution. The terror felt by this last group was impressed on us by a number of suicides among individuals who preferred to die rather than return to their native lands. In some instances those may have been traitors who rightly feared the punishment they knew to be in store for them. But in many other cases they belonged to the oppressed classes and saw death as a far less terrifying thing than renewed persecution. The Allies had, on the political level, worked out formulas for distinguishing between displaced persons who were to be returned to their own countries and those who were to be cared for by the occupying powers. These policies and agreements we first tried to apply without deviation, but we quickly saw that their rigid application would often violate the fundamental humanitarian principles we espoused. Thereafter we gave any who objected to return the benefit of the doubt. (1948 439)

Since forced repatriation began in 1944 and continued until 1947, a period during which Eisenhower was Supreme Allied Commander in Europe or (after November 1945) the Chairman of the Joint Chiefs of Staff, one might want to question the word "quickly." In fact, Eisenhower was a formulator of the forced repatriation policy in the first place. Here are two statements from official army histories on displaced persons in Europe: First, the "general terms of the [Yalta] agreement, as related to displaced persons, constituted a reiteration [*nota bene*] of the terms set down by Supreme Headquarters in its long-range planning"(Floyd 1947 15). Second, "although the Yalta Agreement did not contain any categorical statement that Soviet citizens should be repatriated regardless of their personal wishes, it was so interpreted by the Joint Chiefs of Staff"(RRRLPW 1947 64).

Now let us consider "the benefit of the doubt." On December 20, 1945, the War Department sent a memorandum to Joseph McNarney, the Commanding General of the United States Forces in Europe. On April 19, 1946, he replied by telegram as follows:

> Your [memorandum] in certain instances requires forcible repatriation of "persons who were both citizens of and actually within the Soviet Union on 1 Sept. 1939". Repatriation boards, having had recourse only to American Law and procedures in absence of any other, decided against repatriation of several hundred cases on basis

the individuals were not citizens, having been denied one or more of such right of citizenship as the right to vote, to bear arms, etc., or having been members of persecuted groups, etc. Urgently request legal opinion as to whether such loss or deprivation of any single right of citizenship as encountered herein or otherwise, is considered deprivation of citizenship, thus rendering the individual non-repatriable by force. (FRUS 1969 154)

The "several hundred" were Kulaks, White Russians, and dissenters. On June 7, 1946 the Joint Chiefs of Staff (remember Eisenhower was chairman at the time) transmitted the following reply that they had "received from the State, War and Navy Departments":

Since the political system in force in the Soviet Union is basically different from that applying in the United States, and the questions of what rights a Soviet citizen has are matters which concern the Soviet Government solely, the question does not arise in interpreting the directive regarding repatriation of Soviet citizens whether an individual should be considered as having lost his Soviet citizenship because he was deprived of certain rights which under American law would cause him to lose his American citizenship. American rules of citizenship do not apply to Soviet citizens and it is not a proper function of American officials to attempt to determine whether Soviet citizenship has been lost in individual cases through denial of civil rights. Question of citizenship of Kulaks, White Russians who opposed the 1917 revolution but continued to reside in the Soviet Union, and dissenters . . . who are otherwise subject to forcible repatriation under the terms of the basic directive is one for determination of Soviet authorities only. The only criteria to be applied in interpreting the directive are the following: 1. That the individual was a Soviet citizen under Soviet interpretation of Soviet law and was domiciled in the USSR on 1 September 1939; 2. That in cases of doubt the Soviet authorities declare that they continue to consider such person to be a Soviet citizen today, and specifically request his repatriation. (170)

Hence what we have is that in 1948 Eisenhower publicly claims that following "fundamental humanitarian principles" the "benefit of the doubt" was given to the "truly unfortunate . . . who dared not return home for fear of persecution," whereas in 1946 Eisenhower had secretly transmitted the order that "cases of doubt" be given not to the "truly unfortunate" but to "Soviet authorities." What we have is Eisenhower ordering the commanding American general in Europe to apply, not *American* standards of individual rights (that are universal: all individuals have rights of life, liberty, and the pursuit of happiness), but *Soviet* standards of governmental powers (that are totalitarian: no individual has any right that the Soviet government must respect). Eisenhower wanted to, and often did, violate the Geneva convention

(Moore, Jason 2000 385). (The occupation was also incredibly harsh in other respects (MacDonogh 2007).) In fairness, it must be pointed out that Eisenhower had tremendous practical problems of governance that might have led to substantial social, political, and military problems (perhaps even war) had he allowed the refugees to remain. Further, under the American system of government, the military *should* generally follow civilian authority. Yet Eisenhower seemed unable to rise above practical problems and loyalty by at least recognizing he was a leader in a colossal humanitarian tragedy. If there were other high officials who in fact recognized the depth of that tragedy, they were unwilling to expose the reality that was contrary to the Declaration of Independence, the Bill of Rights, the traditional American practiced of asylum, the Geneva convention of 1929 (which the United States supposedly accepted during World War II), and, after August 8, 1945, the Charter of the International Military Tribunal.

Although the vast majority of Soviet citizens were subject to forced repatriation, U.S. policy explicitly provided that Soviet citizens "charged by the Soviet Union with having voluntarily rendered aid and comfort to the enemy" would be "repatriated without regard to their personal wishes and by force if necessary"(Floyd 1947 114-5). American officials knew that by Soviet standards you were either dead or a deserter; the Soviet " 'Decree No. 270' of 1942 declares a prisoner captured alive by the enemy is ipso facto a traitor"(Dallin and Nicolaevsky 1947 283; cf. also FRUS 1967 1097-8). They knew that the displaced Soviets contained many more "enemies of Stalin" than "friends of Hitler." By cooperating with Stalin they were silencing the voices of those who could, by direct experience, tell the truth about the nature of his regime. In *The Gulag Archipelago*, Solzhenitsyn talks about the repatriated Soviets. He writes:

> That spring of 1945 was, in our prisons, predominantly the spring of the Russian *prisoners of war.* They passed through the prisons of the Soviet Union in vast dense gray shoals like ocean herring" (1974 237). In their own countries Roosevelt and Churchill are honored as embodiments of statesmanlike wisdom. To us, in our Russian prison conversation, their consistent shortsightedness and stupidity stood out as astonishingly obvious. . . . what was the military or political sense in their surrendering to destruction at Stalin's hands hundreds of thousands of armed Soviet citizens determined not to surrender? (259)

According to the Declaration of Independence, Soviet citizens had a right *and* a duty to overthrow the absolute despotism of Stalin precisely because he systematically denied the people of Russia their unalienable rights. By these standards, Stalin could not, as Roosevelt claimed, be "truly representative of the heart and soul of Russia," and hence America could not both "get along very well with him and the Russian people"(above, page 110). Yet claiming to represent America, Roosevelt and Stettinius, Truman and Byrnes, Marshall and Eisenhower, all chose to join Stalin in his war against the Soviet people. On this issue moral detachment reigned, the Declaration counted for nothing, the spirit of 1776 was in a deep coma. There is no evidence that any of these men ever recognized that they were party to one of the greatest crimes of the twentieth century and that they bore direct responsibility for it. They lacked the integrity to see the gross contradiction between their actions and their professed American ideals, and so their accounts of their part in these crimes are suppressed or sugar-coated; their self-deceit allowed pride to triumph over memory.

One can hardly correct mistakes if one does not recognize them as mistakes. Hence it is likely that the lack of candor by World War II's military and political leaders made more probable other sickening events on an individual scale. Here is an example. On November 23, 1970 a Lithuanian seaman, Simas Kudirka, jumped from a Soviet fishing ship, the *Sovetskaya Litva*, to the U.S. Coast Guard cutter *Vigilant*. The ships were in U.S. territorial waters and were moored together to hold discussions on Soviet fishing off the New England coast. About eight hours later the Captain of the *Vigilant*, Ralph Eustis, was ordered to return the seaman forcibly. Not wanting to have his men do the evil deed, Eustis allowed six Russians to board. Here is an eye witness report:

The six Russians were allowed to go to the room where Kudirka was placed. A fight ensued and cries were heard by all of us from the room where the Russians had entered to get Kudirka. The door was temporarily opened, and I heard cries of "help, help," and saw Kudirka being beaten by the Assistant Soviet Commander. His face was bloody and his shirt torn off: Somehow, Kudirka managed to escape the room, ran on deck, and still shouting "help, help," disappeared from sight on the upper deck. Somebody shouted, "he jumped, he jumped," and at that time the *Vigilant* started its engines and snapped its lines from the *Sovetskaya Litva*. The Russian sailors continued searching the U.S. ship. They found Kudirka hiding, overpowered him, tied him with ropes and blankets, and beat him violently. At midnight, somebody ordered a United States lifeboat lowered and several U.S. seamen accompanied the six Russians and Kudirka to the Soviet ship. When the U.S. sailors returned, they said that Kudirka had been beaten savagely and that he was either unconscious or dead when he was taken aboard the Russian ship. They said he had been kicked repeatedly. After the Soviet ship raised its anchor, we followed it out of United States territorial waters. On the way back to port, Captain Eustis asked all of us to keep the matter quiet. (ADLSSK 1971 32-3).

Kudirka survived, received a sentence of ten years, and was subjected to vicious treatment by his jailers. However, Lithuanian Americans discovered that Kudirka's mother was an American citizen. They put pressure on the State Department, who in turn put pressure on the Soviet government, and, after serving four years, Kudirka was allowed to come to the United States (for details of his inspiring story, see Kudirka and Eichel 1987). Kudirka perfectly expressed the principle involved in his ship experience: "The real tragedy is that I, as a Lithuanian, was seen by the American government as the legal property of Brezhnev, the heir to Stalin, who had to be returned"(94). That coercive returning, authorized by American officials without even considering whether Kudirka had any valid claim to be protected, shows that the International Fugitive Slave mentality lived on. The decision might have been different had American leaders been forthright in the 1950s and 1960s about the forced repatriation of Soviet and East European citizens during the 1940s. Perhaps many other violations of the Geneva convention by the United States government since World War II would also have been mitigated or prevented.

Given the enormous evil that self-deceit makes possible, even in otherwise decent individuals, the design of political institutions and practices that would minimize it is of crucial moral importance. It is still common for American political leaders to say things that they know to be false and that often most of their audience knows to be false. Our present election practices discourage those with outstanding integrity from even running for office. Nevertheless, some do but face continual pressure to be dishonest. We have a politics of deception and self-deception, a politics that attracts and even creates deceivers and self-deceivers. For thousands of years slavery was so common as to be thought a natural and intrinsic part of human civilization. Almost no one considered the possibility of restructuring the political process so as to make such an evil unlikely or impossible. Yet, when it was finally considered, a restructuring successfully solved the problem. Today deceit and self-deceit is a daily political occurrence, as slavery earlier was, that it is most often thought to be inherent to politics itself, as slavery was earlier thought to be inherent in civilization. Hence, little thought is given to the problem of creating a politics characterized by high standards of honesty and integrity.

Yet if, as John Adams claimed, self-deceit "is perhaps the source of far the greatest, and worst part of the vices and calamities among mankind," should not the creation of a politics of self-knowledge be of highest priority?

5

The Constitution as a Revolutionary Document

The Declaration precedes the Constitution both historically and logically. The Declaration holds that government is a device to protect and promote rights that the people already have; the Constitution is the compact through which the people created such a government, and pledged their allegiance to it in exchange for the protection and enhancement of their rights. Sovereignty is entirely invested in the people. This is asserted in the Preamble: "WE, THE PEOPLE . . . do ordain and establish this Constitution for the United States of America." Madison pointed out that the Articles of Confederation have been "derived from the dependent derivative authority of the Legislatures of the States; whereas [the Constitution] is derived from the superior power of the people"(DHRC 1976 9:996; cf. Madison 1962 14:218). In adopting the Constitution the people are exercising their right, asserted in the Declaration, "to institute new Government, laying its Foundation on such Principles, and organizing its Powers in such Form, as to them shall seem most likely to effect their Safety and Happiness." The Constitution is a compact meant to embody the Declaration's ethical and political ideals in a tangible political foundation for American government (cf. Madison 1962 10:377, Wilson's comments above, page 32, and Jay's in Dallas 1790 2:470-71). By its operation the spirit of 1776 could be given a more secure life, protected from those who would violate it, and awakened in those in whom it is asleep. Unfortunately, the subsequent actions of politicians, and the subsequent interpretations of the Constitution by judges, often betrayed that spirit.

For example, the Constitution's Preamble explicitly states that one of its purposes is to "secure the Blessings of Liberty to ourselves and our Posterity." Hence circumlocutions were used when trying to refer to slaves, so as to veil hypocrisy and contradiction while promoting deception. Benjamin Gale, speaking to a town meeting in Killingworth, Connecticut, in 1787, asked: "Why all this sly cunning and artful mode of expression unless to cover from your observation and notice that *Negroes* was intended by the word persons, . . . used on this occasion, lest it should frighten people who may have some tender feelings and a just sense of the rights of human nature"(DHRC 1976 3:425; cf. 2:667 and 19:253). Or, as Luther Martin put it in 1788, the Founders "anxiously sought to avoid the admission of expressions which might be odious in the ears of Americans, although they were willing to admit into their system those *things* which the *expressions* signified"(55). In 1819, John Jay explained that "the word slaves was avoided, probably on account of the existing toleration of slavery, and of its discordancy with the principles of the Revolution; and from a consciousness of its being repugnant to . . . the Declaration of Independence . . ."(1890 4:431). As we have seen, the belief that "all men are created equal" included blacks was expressed again and again in the eighteenth century. It is sometimes claimed that slaves were not citizens, and had no representation at the Constitutional Convention, their slavery, while morally repugnant, was politically correct. But it is far from clear that the American people as a whole, or just white male Americans, would have agreed that slaves were not citizens. Even Jefferson refers to slaves as citizens (1972 162-3). In any case, the claim is irrelevant since, by the standards of the Declaration, the collective right of blacks to liberty is absolutely unalienable. This right exists before, during, and after any human compact or government; it is a right to which they are entitled by "the Laws of Nature and of Nature's God." Hence both black and white Americans could quite properly oppose slavery, using natural rights arguments in general, and quoting the Declaration in particular.

Further, republican government was widely understood as being compatible with natural rights (cf. Jefferson's comments above, page 95), and thus incompatible with slavery. Luther Martin writes: ". . . *slavery* is *inconsistent* with the *genius* of *republicanism*, and has a tendency to *destroy* those *principles* on which it is *supported*, as it *lessens the sense* of the *equal rights* of *mankind*, and habituates us to *tyranny* and *oppression*"(1788 58; cf. Farrand 1937 2:364). In 1795, James Sullivan argued that, to eradicate slavery, the children of slaves must be educated at the same schools and in the same manner as white children. He then says: "There is an objection to this, which embraces all my feelings; that is, that it will tend to a mixture of blood, which I now abhor; but yet, as I feel, I fear that I am not a pure Republican, delighting in the equal rights of the human race"(MHSC 1877 414). (Note the presupposition, a "pure Republican" must oppose slavery, Jim Crow, and racism.) In 1798 the Virginian David Barrow published a "Circular Letter" that states: "The Author, from a conviction of the iniquity, and a discovery of the inconsistancy of hereditary slavery, with a republican form of government, manumitted his slaves in the year 1784"(Allen, Carlos 1963 445). John Adams' definition of a republic is likewise incompatible with slavery: "a government, in which all men, rich and poor, magistrates and subjects, officers and people, masters and servants, the first citizen and the last, are equally subject to the laws"(1850 5:453). Since the Constitution is the foundation of a republican government, it isn't surprising that there are various passages in it that are incompatible with slavery. For example, the Fifth Amendment states that no person shall "be deprived of life, liberty, or property, without due process of law," but blacks were so deprived. As Hamilton points out in another connection, that the "words '*due process*' have a precise technical import, and are only applicable to the process and proceedings of the courts of justice; they can never be referred to an act of legislature"(1961 4:35).

It is almost always claimed that the protections in the Bill of Rights originally applied only to federal power. For the moment, but only for the moment, let us accept this claim. There remains the question of slavery on federal lands. On July 16, 1790, Congress accepted the land for a capital in which laws would remain the same "until Congress shall otherwise by law provide"(Gales 1834 2:2293). Under Article I, Section 8, Congress has the power to "exercise exclusive legislation in all cases whatsoever, over" the nation's capital. On December 15, 1791 the Bill of Rights became part of the Constitution, and those rights are certainly inconsistent with a racial or hereditary slavery, which is thus unconstitutional on all federal lands, including Washington, D. C. For example, the First and Fifth Amendments are inconsistent with slavery, since slaves have no right to freedom of religion and speech, much less to peaceably assemble. Yet the slave trade was big business in Washington. In an 1816 speech in the Senate, Edmund Randolph of Virginia, a defender of slavery, gave an impassioned denunciation of the slave trade. This practice, he said

> was not surpassed for abomination in any part of the earth; for in no part of it, not even excepting the rivers on the coast of Africa, was there so great and so infamous a slave market as in the metropolis, in the very Seat of Government of this nation, which prided itself on freedom. . . . it was not necessary . . . that this city should be made a depot of slaves, who were bought either from cruel masters or kidnapped; and of those who were kidnapped, he said there were two kinds — slaves stolen from their masters, and free persons, stolen, as he might say, from themselves. (DPCUS 1854 1115-16).

A more detailed account is given by Jesse Torrey, based on his 1815 visit to Washington. Torrey's book — *A Portraiture of Domestic Slavery in the United States* — describes the large slave auctions, slaves in chains driven through the streets, suicides by blacks to avoid their fate, the sale of kidnapped free blacks and, in general, the incredible hardship that blacks suffered.

Now let us see how Madison — often called the "Father of the Constitution" — handled the issue of slavery. In April of 1787 Madison made a brilliant analysis of the "Vices of the Political System of the United States." There he states that slavery and a republican government are irreconcilable, or to use his exact words, "where slavery exists, the republican Theory becomes . . . fallacious"(1962 9:351). Yet when he was president Madison saw what Randolph and Torrey described. Madison's abolitionist-minded friend Edward Coles remarks that they

> frequently talked unreservedly about the enslavement of the Negroes . . . On occasions of seeing gangs of Negroes, some in irons, on their way to a southern market, I have taken the liberty to jeer him, by congratulating him, as the Chief of our great Republic, that he was not then accompanyed by a Foreign Minister, & thus saved the deep mortification of witnessing such a revolting sight in the presence of a representative of a nation, less boastful perhaps of its regard for the rights of man, but more observant of them. (Ketcham 1960 52)

Even with such jeers Madison did not act, he did not "preserve, protect and defend the constitution of the United States"(Article 2, Section 1), he did not "take care that the laws be faithfully executed"(Article 2, Section 3). His great intellect, with its subtle sense of right and wrong, was disabled. It is hardly credible that Madison would have been so passive if free blacks in Washington had started a lively trade in white slaves. Nor can it be claimed that slaves are not persons. Not only does this contradict the normal sense of the word "person," it violates the Constitution in an Orwellian fashion. This can be seen through the parable of

The Madisonian Logician

> On one occasion while he was President Mr. Madison was asked by a Washington resident if he would answer a few questions one of his slaves had about the Constitution. The President, always polite, agreed.
>
> "Sir, who is referred to by 'other Persons' in Article I, Section 2?"
>
> "That means you, and other slaves like you," the President responded.
>
> "Sir, and who is referred to as 'Persons' in Article I, Section 9?"
>
> "Again, that means the slaves."
>
> "Sir, and who is referred to by 'Person held to Service' in Article IV, Section 2?"

"The answer is the same."

"Well, sir, I then suppose that when the Fifth Amendment says 'No person shall . . . be deprived   of . . . liberty . . . without due process of law' I am being referred to."

"Oh no!"

Clear and forthright expression undermines self-deception; self-deceivers must make use of evasion, ambiguity, vagueness, circumlocution, and lies to protect the truth from being exposed to themselves or anyone else. In the Constitutional Convention Madison said it was "wrong to admit in the constitution the idea that there could be property in men. The reason of duties did not hold, as slaves are not like merchandise, consumed &c"(Farrand 1937 2:417). But slaves *were* like merchandise, bought and sold, and consumed in the sense in which tables or chairs were consumed — that is, used until worn out. A slave was not, as Madison maintained in the *Federalist*, "protected . . . in his life and in his limbs, against the violence of all others, even the master of his labour and his liberty:(1962 10:500). Normally Madison was a precise thinker with a fine command of English. When he composed the Fifth Amendment why did he not say, for example, "no white person" or "no free person? The answer I think can be found by considering Madison's own example of unjust power, which he gave in a masterful speech at the Convention: "We have seen the mere distinction of colour made in the most enlightened period of time, a ground of the most oppressive dominion ever exercised by man over man"(1962 10:33). Had he written "no white person" in the Bill of Rights it would have become more obvious to himself and to others, that in submitting the Bill for whites only, he would be actively contributing to "the most oppressive dominion ever exercised by man over man."

How did Madison think of himself in this regard? How should we think of him? Writing from Pennsylvania to his father in 1783, Madison betrays his attitude when he describes his motivation in determining the fate of a slave:

On a view of all circumstances I have judged it most prudent not to force Billey back to Va. even if could be done; and have accordingly taken measures for his final separation from me. I am persuaded his mind is too thoroughly tainted [*nota bene*] to be a fit companion for fellow slaves in Virga. The laws here do not admit of his being sold for more than 7 years. I do not expect to get near the worth of him; but cannot think of punishing him by transportation merely for coveting that liberty for which we have paid the price of so much blood, and have

proclaimed so often to be the right, & worthy the pursuit, of every human being.
(1962 7:304)

This letter again shows that Madison understood that the many declarations of liberty proclaimed in eighteenth-century America applied to blacks since they are human. It also shows some of Madison's decency, but decency is a much diminished virtue when it is not united with an honest self-image. Such an image would require Madison to think and act on the simple truth that "he who would *be* no slave, must consent to *have* no slave"(the words are Lincoln's (1953 3:376)). A few years before Madison penned this letter, John Cooper wrote a strongly-worded, antislavery essay in which he described honesty and slavekeeping:

> If we are determined not to emancipate our slaves, but to hold them still in bondage, let us alter our language upon the subject of tyranny; let us no longer speak of it as a thing in its own nature detestable, because in so doing . . . we shall condemn ourselves. But let us rather declare to the world, that tyranny is a thing we are not principled against, but that we are resolved not to be slaves, because we ourselves mean to be tyrants. . . . Whatever colouring slavekeeping may receive from interested individuals who wish to keep it on foot, there is something in its nature so universally odious, that we meet with but few of the slavekeepers themselves that are willing to be thought tyrants; . . . they cannot bear to be deemed what they really are; for nothing is more clear, than that he who keeps a slave is a tyrant"(1780 2).

Madison, like many other southern leaders, could not bear to think of himself as a tyrant, but it is hard to imagine that Billey had such difficulty. Nor should we.

Nevertheless Madison was capable of an honest analysis of slavery in the abstract. Here is an example from his notes: "In proportion as slavery prevails in a State, the Government, however democratic in name, must be aristocratic in fact. The power lies in a part instead of the whole; in the hands of property, not of numbers. All the antient popular governments, were for this reason aristocracies. The majority were slaves. . . . The Southern States of America, are on the same principle aristocracies."(1962 14:163). Now let us turn to the speech in which Madison proposed amending the Constitution with a bill of rights: "I wish . . . that those who have been friendly to the adoption of this constitution, may have the opportunity of proving to those who were opposed to it, that they were as sincerely devoted to liberty and a republican government, as those who charged them with wishing the adoption of this Constitution in order to lay the foundation of an aristocracy or despotism"(1962 12:198). But such a proof would require something that Madison was not prepared to give, namely, a commitment to apply the Bill of Rights to everyone, including blacks. Madison's lack of integrity is stunning. For example, the Fugitive Slave Law of 1793 (which he supported) is manifestly inconsistent with the restraints on federal power in the Bill of Rights (which he composed). Likewise, since that Law prevents the states from protecting the natural rights of fugitive slaves, it is clearly contrary to the Constitutional requirement, which Madison help to draft, that the "United States shall guarantee to every state in this union a Republican form of government." By his own standards, no state can have an aristocratic government (as the southern states in fact did); hence, when he was a legislator or when he was President, he had a responsibility to speak and act. Yet Madison did neither, since self-deceit blinded his mind's eye to his own moral rot. Gouverneur Morris rightly worried that, if Madison carried Pennsylvania in the election of 1812, the southern states "may for a dozen or fifteen years exercise the privilege of . . . whipping negroes, and brawling about the inborn inalienable rights of man"(1888 2:542-3).

In 1790, when some Quakers, with Franklin's endorsement, petitioned Congress to put an end to the slave trade, Madison acted quickly and effectively to head off possible federal action by silencing debate, for he knew, in the words of Frederick Douglass, that "slavery and prejudice cannot endure discussion (1950 1:115; cf. Madison 1865 1:60). Again, in 1797, when the subscribers of a petition to Congress complained that they, as free blacks, were under the greatest threat of being re-enslaved, Madison spoke and callously voted against even giving them a hearing (Gales 1834 6:2015-2024): "If they are slaves, the Constitution gives them no hope of being heard here"(2020). "Why not?" we may ask. How does Madison reconcile this statement with what he elsewhere called the "republican spirit of the Constitution"(1962 14:322)? In the *Federalist* Madison claimed that representatives in the new government would "most likely" have "enlightened views and virtuous sentiments"(1962 10:269). Yet, in this matter, his words and actions were neither enlightened nor virtuous. Here was a opportunity to do something about the gross injustice of free blacks being kidnapped and enslaved, an occasion to consider ways to ensure the new capital would be slave free, perhaps even an opening debate how southern, slave-based aristocracies might be peaceably transformed into republican governments. There is nothing in the Constitution that would have prevented such debates, or even the passage of antislavery measures. Madison rightly claimed that a "prudent regard to the maxim that honesty is the best policy is found by experience to be as little regarded by bodies of men as by individuals"(1962 10:33; cf. 213, 9:355). But this judgment applied to Madison himself when he became a leader in creating, on the federal level, a highly successful politics of self-deception (of the avoidance type). In the cause of slave interests, he organized a faction, which according to his justly famous analysis in *Federalist* No.10, is "a number of citizens, whether amounting to a majority or minority of the whole, who are united and actuated by some common impulse of passion, or of interest, adverse to the rights of other citizens, or to the permanent and aggregate interests of the community"(1962 10:264). What, by either eighteenth-century standards or our own, could be more "adverse . . . to the permanent and aggregate interests of the community" than the gross evil of hereditary slavery, and of governments that enforce and promote it? Madison's description of the danger in representation seems to fit himself: "Men . . . of local prejudices . . . may by intrigue . . . betray the interests of the people"(268).   Elsewhere Madison argued that only a republican form of government "would be reconcileable. . . with the fundamental principles of the revolution"(10:377). Madison believed that all governments that are compatible with the universal principles of the Declaration are republican, that the Constitution is compatible, and that to further ensure that compatibility, it ought to contain a bill of rights. Without Madison's commitment to that "ought," it is unlikely there would be a Bill of Rights. With regard to his role in creating the Constitution and Bill of Rights, Dr. Jekyll Madison is rightfully owed posterity's great admiration and appreciation, but it is equally true that Mr. Hyde Madison, who used his enormous talents to defend the slave interest and state aristocracies, is rightfully owed posterity's great censure and condemnation.

Madison thought it was "wrong to admit in the constitution the idea that there could be property in men," but he willingly admitted that ugly idea into his mind, heart, and soul. It is thus not surprising that Madison, like Jefferson, put such conditions on abolition as to render it impossible: "A general emancipation of slaves ought to be 1. gradual. 2. equitable, & satisfactory to the individuals immediately concerned. 3. consistent with the existing & durable prejudices of the nation"(1900 8:439). Such is the power of self-deceit that it allows the most subtle political mind in America to put forward this fantasy as serious, which is so out of touch with the reality of slavery, so out of touch with the strong aristocratic prejudices shared by himself and so many of his fellow petty tyrants. In 1791, when Madison is asked by Robert Pleasants for help with a petition "declaring the Children of Slaves to be born after the passing of such Act, to be free at the usual Ages of Eighteen and twenty one Years"(1962 14:30), he refuses, explaining that "those from whom I derive my public station are known by me to be greatly interested in that species of property . . . I might be chargeable at least with want of candour, if not of fidelity, were I to make use of a situation in which their confidence has placed me, to become a volunteer in giving a public wound, as they would deem it, to an interest on which they set so great a value"(91). But, if Madison never volunteers to give that "public wound," is not he justly chargeable with a want of honesty about his political principles, with a want of moral courage and honor, with a want of fidelity to his own portrait of the wise legislator, who, even in the face of a feverish factions, is always coolly faithful to republican principles? How can a republican legitimately represent a property right of his constituents if they have no right to that so-called property? Like that judgment of Brissot de Warville about Washington (above, page 68), or the proposal Coles made to Jefferson (above, page 96), Pleasants makes a suggestion to Madison that seems as wise today as when it was made: "would it not then be Noble in thee, and others, who fill the first stations, and are favored with abilities & influence, to espouse the cause of the injured, the ignorant, and the helpless . . . "(1962 14:91). Writing to Madison on January 8, 1832, Coles said that "distinguished for good feeling, and pure principles, is it not the more incumbent on you to act a part to your slaves which shall be in unison with both. It seems to me repugnant to the distinctive & characteristic traits of your character — nay pardon me for saying, it would be a blot and stigma on your otherwise spotless escutcheon, not to restore your slaves that liberty & those rights which you have been through life so zealous and able a champion"(1927 37). Like Jefferson, but unlike Washington, Madison did not emancipate his slaves at death.

"Hypocrisy," declares La Rochefoucauld's fine epigram, "is the homage that vice pays to virtue"(1778 69). This observation applies equally well to the "internal hypocrisy" of self-deceit. If internal hypocrisy led the Founders to write a virtuous Constitution and Bill of Rights that nowhere named the vice of slavery, why should those free of that hypocrisy be obliged to find it there? As Frederick Douglass observed on July 7, 1863: "I hold that the Federal Government was never, in its essence, anything but an anti-slavery government. Abolish slavery tomorrow, and not a sentence or syllable of the Constitution need be altered. It was purposely so framed as to give no claim, no sanction to the claim, of property in men"(1950 3.365; cf. Madison's words above, pages 125, 128). To understand the Constitution in the spirit of 1776 is to understand it as a antislavery document. Of course, in the eighteenth century it wasn't generally thought of in that way, but history shows that revolutionary work is often initially misunderstood, at least in some important way, even by its innovators, even for a long time thereafter. For example, Poincaré started what we today call the science of chaos, which is arguably as important as relativity and quantum mechanics, but that importance was hardly recognized until three-quarters of a century later in the 1960s and 70s. Poincaré himself did not see the significance of his discovery because of his *intellectual* repugnance to the idea that there were deterministic, physical systems whose future was unpredictable. Madison understood the Constitution as well as, or better, than any of his contemporaries, yet he did not see that, given the republican principles of the American revolution, it had to be consistently interpreted as making slavery illegal in every state and territory, and on all federal property. His failure was surely rooted in his *moral* repugnance to the idea of a free and equal interracial society. The proslavery interpretation of the Constitution was wrong from the beginning, but that was not fully grasped until Civil War times, and then only by a small minority. To appreciate the Constitution anew in an American revolutionary sense, let us conduct a thought experiment by imagining that in 1792 the question of the legality of slavery in the Federal City came before the Supreme Court, with an outcome that could be described as follows:

Like the Constitution itself, the decision was unexpected and astonishing. Like the delegates to Federal Convention, the justices went well beyond what many thought they were charged to do. New standards of legal excellence were set, in the collection of evidence, in the quality of argument, in persuasive eloquence. For the first time there was just one ruling signed by all justices, instead of separate opinions. After briefly giving an antislavery judgment on the case at hand, the justices gave an expansive and principled defense of their decision. It began with a masterful survey of antislavery thought in European history that ended with a commentary on the 1772 British *Somerset* ruling outlawing slavery in Britain (see Wiecek 1975). The antislavery nature of the American revolution was then stressed: First, by giving an extensive selection of its abolitionist literature (above, pages 51-

57) and, second, by demonstrating the inconsistency of slavery with the Declaration of Independence, which they claimed fully authorized a rebellion by the slaves. The justices then referred to the *Federalist* where "it is admitted, that if the laws were to restore the rights which have been taken away, the negroes could no longer be refused an equal share of representation with the other inhabitants"(Madison 1962 10:501). The justices objected: "This statement, put into the mouth of 'one of our Southern brethren,' is a falsehood; the laws cannot restore what they are powerless to take away. The only understanding of law consistent with our revolution, and with reason, is that laws may not violate natural freedom. This doctrine was proclaimed by Mr. Samuel Adams: 'the Right to Freedom being *the Gift of God Almighty*, it is not in the Power of Man to alienate this Gift'(VPFITB 1772 7; cf. Adams, Samuel 1904 2:355 and Webster, above, page 50). It was proclaimed by Mr. Jefferson: 'The god who gave us life, gave us liberty at the same time: the hand of force may destroy, but cannot disjoin them"(above, page 13). It was proclaimed by Congress: 'The great principle therefore is and ever will remain in force, that MEN ARE BY NATURE FREE. . . . it is conceded on all hands that the right to be free can never be alienated'(above, page 15). Hence it would be contradictory and grossly hypocritical for white Americans to boldly, publicly, and frequently appeal to a universal, God-given freedom that is absolutely unalienable in response to *threatened* despotism by Britain, and then to tolerate *actual* slavery of black Americans by themselves. [cf. John Marshall's words: "The [revolutionary] war was a war of principle, against a system hostile to political liberty, from which oppression was to be dreaded, not against actual oppression"(2000 299).] We have militarily defeated the spirit of domination in the British with respect to ourselves, we must now morally defeat that spirit in ourselves with respect to slaves. If we do not *peacefully* help the slaves now, we must surely face violent insurrections and civil wars in the future. We note with great pleasure the formation of Anti-Slavery Societies in America: first in Pennsylvania (1775, renamed in 1787), then New York (1785), then Delaware (1788), then Maryland (1789), then Rhode Island (1789), then Connecticut (1790), and then Virginia (1790). The members of these societies consist of very respectable gentlemen, including, John Jay, Gouverneur Morris, Alexander Hamilton, George Clinton, Benjamin Franklin, Benjamin Rush, and Ezra Stiles. Any consistent patriot of the American revolution, any lover of freedom

and humanity, would certainly want all America to become an Anti-Slavery Society, for the dreadful alternative is that of committing 'high treason against the *majesty of human nature*'(D***, F***, H*** 1776 158)."

Turning to the Constitution, the justices quoted Patrick Henry who, when objecting to the lack of a bill of rights in the Constitution, had said of religious liberty: "This sacred right ought not to depend on constructive logical reasoning"(DHRC 1976 10:1213; cf. 1328-30). The justices agreed, and said that, as the lack of explicitness renders religious freedom insecure because it makes it easier for corrupt governors to invade that liberty (a Constitutional insecurity relieved by the First Amendment), so the same lack also renders slavery insecure because it makes it easier for virtuous governors to weaken or abolish it. "If slavery did not exist in America, would any candid person agree that its introduction today is compatible with the Constitution, which does not even mention it? The ambiguity, vagueness, and other limitations of language will almost guarantee that it is possible to find slavery in the document using unsound principles of interpretation; however, *no sound principles can produce it.*" As ground for their claim the justices quoted legal authorities. First, Edward Coke: "When the construction of any act is left to the law, the law, which abhorreth injury and wrong will never so construe it, as it shall work a wrong"(1670 42a; cf. 149b); "*Nota*, the rehearsal or preamble of the statute is a good mean to find out the meaning of the statute, and as it were a key to open the understanding thereof"(79a; cf. Locke 2006 379; Morris, Gouverneur 1888 2:573-4). The justices declared that slavery was a great wrong incompatible with the Preamble, and that the people's intentions, as they are there explicitly and grandly declared, are superior to any *inferred* claims elsewhere in the document, even if such inferences were correct (which the justices did not grant). With sarcastic wit the justices said that those who maintain slavery is in the Constitution believe that God created a new class of human beings who are individually persons in the United States but are collectively not people in the United States, that they believed that the children of masters and female slaves cannot be posterity because Jupiter is the real father, that they believed that best way to fulfill the people's intentions to form a "more perfect Union" and "establish Justice" was to maintain a large and growing class of Negro enemies within the country's borders. They again cited Coke, "for when an Act of Parliament is against Common right and reason, or repugnant, or impossible to be performed, the Common Law will controll it, and adjudge such Act to be void"(2003 1:275; cf. 1670 140b). They quoted John Milton: "Our Liberty is not *Caesar's*; 'tis a Blessing we have received from God himself; 'tis what we are born to; to lay this down at *Caesar's* feet, which we derive not from him, which we are not beholden to him for, were an unworthy Action, and a degrading of our very Nature. . . . . Being therefore peculiarly God's own, and consequently things that are to be given to him; we are intirely free by Nature, and cannot without the greatest Sacrilege imaginable be reduced into a Condition of Slavery to any Man . . . "(1692 56). Next William Blackstone was cited: "This law of nature [that man should pursue his own happiness], being co-eval with mankind and dictated by God himself is of course superior in obligation to any other. It is binding over all the globe, in all countries, and at all times: no human laws are of any validity, if contrary to this"(above, page 37).They next noted that Grotius believed that the "Law of Nature is so unalterable, that God himself cannot change it. For tho' the Power of God be infinite, yet we may say, that there are some Things to which this infinite Power does not extend, because they cannot be expressed by Propositions that contain any Sense, but manifestly imply a Contradiction"(1738 11). "We can only conclude," the justices said, "that it would contradict the axioms of our revolution, it would be a depraved attempt to do what even the Lord of the universe cannot consistency do, it would be a corrupt principle of Constitutional interpretation supported by nothing but a malicious spirit of domination, were we to use *constructive logical reasoning* in an effort to put asunder the freedom and humanity that God himself hath joined together. The United States is founded on self-evident truth, not the self-evident falsehood that being born a slave is consistent with the natural or divine right of liberty. John Hancock proved to be a true prophet when, on July 5, 1776, he said the Declaration should be 'considered as the Ground & Foundation of a future Government'(above, page 48). That *Ground & Foundation* is found in the Ninth Amendment which states: 'The enumeration in the Constitution of certain rights, shall not be construed to deny or disparage others retained by the people.' It is self-evident that the rights retained by the people must include those rights which no human power can remove, such as the Declaration's unalienable rights of life, liberty, and the pursuit of happiness. These rights this Court would never, under any circumstances whatsoever, *deny or disparage*."

Moving on, the justices gave an antislavery interpretation to the phrase "Republican form of government" in the Guarantee clause, thoroughly rejecting Platonic or Roman senses of "republican" as made obsolete by the American revolution. (Their views were similar to those that Adams and Jefferson would later express (cf. above, page 27, and Cappon 1959 2:549-51)). Rather, they said, the only early model was Hebraic, and that in only a rough way. The justices gave arguments common in many sermons of the time emphasizing Old Testament themes of liberty and the voice of the people. They quoted Charles Crawford approvingly, who said that "we find that monarchy is reprobated in scripture, and that the Deity makes by the mouth of his prophet, a solemn protest to the Jews against the government of a king when they request that their republican form of government may be abolished"(1783 7-8). To now qualify as a republic, they declared, a government must be designed to insure the protection of unalienable rights, created by God or nature. They cited the *Federalist*: "The first question that offers itself is, whether the general form and aspect of the government be strictly republican. It is evident that no other form would be reconcilable with the genius of the people of America; with the fundamental principles of the Revolution; or with that honorable determination which animates every votary of freedom, to rest all our political experiments on the capacity of mankind for self-government. If the plan of the convention, therefore, be found to depart from the republican character, its advocates must abandon it as no longer defensible"(Madison 1962 10:377).

The justices acknowledged that if the Constitution sanctioned slavery in an explicit and clear expression, then a failure to amend would leave revolution as the only honorable course. Fortunately, they said, Publius is right, the Constitution is republican and defensible: They then considered three passages where it had been claimed that the Constitution sanctioned slavery by referring to it. In reference to the first (Article I, Section 2), they said: "We will not gratify those who hunger and thirst after arbitrary power by giving an aristocratic interpretation to 'other Persons' (that is, that such persons must be slaves) when a republican interpretation is so easily available — that is, that they are *resident aliens* and *Indians not taxed*. Hence there is here no unambiguous reference to slavery." The justices argued in detail that even if an ambiguity would allow slaves to be meant here, the ten amendments annul this understanding wherever the general government has authority, and the Guarantee clause annuls it wherever states have authority. The justices then considered a second passage (Article I, Section 9): It states that the "migration or importation of such persons as any of the states now existing shall think proper to admit, shall not be prohibited by the Congress prior to the year one thousand eight hundred and eight." The justices denied that this passage specifically refers to black slaves by citing the *Notes on the State of Virginia*, where Jefferson speaks of the "importation of white settlers"(1954 138). But then they supposed there was such a reference. "Since any amendment voids everything that both contradicts and precedes it, after the ten amendments had been adopted, the passage can only mean that Congress could not stop immigration of males or females, Jews or Turks, blacks or whites, or even indentured servants (provided their term is appropriately limited), into any state in the union. If Congress is forbidden to abridge freedom of religion, speech, press, peaceable assembly, and petitioning government to redress grievances by the First Amendment, and if these freedoms are put into the ten amendments to guarantee that the federal government be republican, then the inferior legislatures of the states, which the federal government guarantees to also be republican, cannot legitimately violate these restrictions. Hence all immigrants must have republican freedoms." Moving on the justices said it was an absurdity that a slave should be "delivered up on the claim of the party to whom . . . service or labour may be due"(Article IV, Section 2), noting that since any contract to be a slave is void (citing Hobbes 1968 192 and Locke 1988 353), slaves can't legally owe service or labor to masters. They said that slaves "have no obligation at all"(quoting Hobbes 1968 255), and concluded that no valid constructive logical reasoning could find a reference to slavery in the "delivered up" passage. The justices said "there are no words in the Constitution that become nugatory if slavery did not exist in America, nor are there any to authorize it; if the writers of the Constitution intended any of its passages to unambiguously refer to slavery, we can only say they completely failed. In any case, by republican theory, *any attempt to justify hereditary slavery in any way whatsoever has absolutely no standing in either morality or politics or law.* Let us here recur to the July 28th, 1764 letter of the Virginia Committee of Correspondence: 'We conceive that no Man or Body of Men, however invested wth power, have a Right to do anything that is contrary to Reason & Justice'(1905 12:13). Thus neither the President, nor Congress, nor this Court, nor any state, has authority to sanction slavery by birth, or by color, for nothing is more contrary to reason and justice. As there can be no hereditary kings in America, so there can be no hereditary slaves; both are contrary to the laws of human nature, both contrary to our sacred declaration that *all men are created equal*. It is a deceitful caricature, a mockery worthy of a buffoon, to include laws which flagrantly violate natural rights as part of one's devotion to the *rule of law*. James Otis, when he was helping to take our revolution from birth pangs to birth, rightly said that declarations of human law are completely subordinate to God: 'Should an act of parliament be against any of *his* natural laws, which are *immutably* true, *their* declaration would be contrary to eternal truth, equity and justice, and consequently void'(1764 47). A year later Blackstone said that if a human law were contrary to reason or divine law, judges should not 'pretend to make a new law, but to vindicate the old one from misrepresentation. For if it be found that the former decision is manifestly absurd or unjust, it is declared, not that such a sentence was *bad law*, but that it was *not law*'(1771 1:70). Laws that uphold the slavery of innocent persons are thus *not law*. Nor are Otis and Blackstone proclaiming a novel doctrine. Sophocles has *Antigone* say (cf. Dickinson 1774 107 and Sophocles 1886 153):

> I could never think
> A mortals law of power or strength sufficient
> To abrogate the unwritten law divine,
> Immutable, eternal, not like these
> Of yesterday, but made e'er time began.

Cicero himself said, 'those who formulated wicked and unjust statutes for nations . . . put into effect anything but "laws." It may thus be clear that in the very definition of the term "law" there inheres the idea and principle of choosing what is just and true'(1988 385). The great John Locke asserted that if the law reaches beyond 'the general Good of those under that Law,' then 'the *Law*, as an useless thing would of it self vanish'(above, page 46), vanish, that is, in the eyes of republicans, in the eyes of devotees of the rule of law, in the eyes of all friends of humanity. There is no obligation to submit to these so-called laws; rather, as our Declaration of Independence gloriously proclaims, there is a right *and* a duty to rebel, as abuses and usurpations extend into a long train. And who does not see if government is given the power to uphold slavery for blacks, it will have the power to uphold it for whites? The Constitution draws no distinction between white and black. 'Tell us, ye who can thus, cooly, reduce the impious principle of slavery, to a constitutional system: ye professed violators of liberties of mankind: where will ye stop? what security can you give, that, when there shall remain no more black people, ye will not enslave others, white as yourselves? when Africa is exhausted, will ye spare America?'(in 1788, by "Republicus"(DHRC 1976 8:450-1)). Any candid observer of America knows that some slavery of whites already exists in fact, although it is *indentured servitude* in name and so-called law. Slavery is insidious. It is absurd to believe that, since slaves were no part of the original compact and thus had no rights under it, a republican government in America could be compatible with slavery. For then any time a majority wanted to enslave a minority, the majority could dissolve the government, direct a military leader to enslave the minority, reconstitute the government but exclude the minority, and rightfully call it *republican.* What charm could a *republic* then have to a free and deliberate people setting up a government? No rational person would accept the rule of law where that law could authorize hereditary slavery, Herod's decree, or any other moral abomination. We agree with Mr. Rush: 'Nothing can be politically right, that is morally wrong; and no necessity can ever sanctify a law, that is contrary to equity. V i r t u e is the living principle of a republic'(1786 40). Thus even if the delegates in Philadelphia had made a secret agreement to interpret the Constitution as upholding an aristocratic evil they cowardly feared to name, it would greatly *dishonor* this Court to honor their intention (as if these men had the power to veto a law of God), and the people would have no obligation to submit to our decision if we did (as if we had such power). Who could be so stupid as to believe that courts should follow the intention of lawmakers if that intention is perspicuously contrary to the laws of nature and the laws of God? We agree with the Proclamation of the Great and General Court of the Colony of Massachusetts-Bay which said that since 'the Great Creator having never given to Men a Right to vest others with Authority over them, unlimited either in Duration or Degree,' it follows that whenever such power is exercised, magistrates 'become public Enemies, and ought to be resisted'(PGGC 1776 189). Let us now reassure all Americans that we are not subscribing to a belief in anarchy or lawlessness, *bad laws must be obeyed where republican freedoms exist, for these freedoms allow the bad laws to be peacefully repealed.* But where there are so-called laws that are indisputably contrary to the republican freedoms expressed in the Declaration, the Constitution, and its ten amendments, where these presumed laws uphold an hereditary slavery that gives black people no peaceful redress (their petitions having been ignored again and again in sundry state legislatures), this Court stands with the celebrated Algernon Sidney: '*That which is not just, is not Law; and that which is not Law, ought not to be obeyed*'(1990 380). We also agree with the Chief Justice William Cushing of Massachusetts when, in 1783, he said the American people reject the very idea of slavery (PMHS 294). As it is grotesque to think that a few minor differences of skin and hair from the European standard could justly deny the unalienable right of freedom given to humans by their Creator, so it is grotesque to think that a few minor ambiguities in the Constitution could justify slavery in this great land, for slavery is contrary to intentions of the people asserted in its Preamble, and contrary to the rights asserted in its amendments. The creator of the Constitution is the people; they ordained and established it; to find slavery there would be treason to them and treason to all that is revolutionary in the American revolution. Republican virtue demands that the Constitution be a faithful image of the people (cf. Harrington below, page 401). Are we to suppose that slavery is engraved on the soul of the American people? Is there anyone so witless as to think that the Constitution would have been ratified had the Preamble said it was the intention of the people to establish, continue, or condone slavery in America? Or that the amendments would have been approved if it said that its rights applied to everyone except those with a dark skin? All who find slavery anywhere in the Constitution are participating in a fraud, whether knowingly or unknowingly. We will not join this fraud; we preside over a Court of Justice, not a Court of Injustice that upholds a despotic power worthy of destruction by insurrection. It is not only our *right*, it is our *duty*, to reject any interpretation of the Constitution that destroys the sacred honor the virtuous have for the rule of law. We will relentlessly strive to secure the equal rights of all citizens, and we believe, with Mr. Jefferson (1972 162-3), Mr. Page (Gales 1834 1:1245), and Dr. Bloomfield (above, page 98) that slaves are citizens. (Page was the Lieutenant Governor of Virginia (1776-79), then one of its Congressional representatives (1789-1797), and then its Governor (1802-1805).) But even if they are not, was there ever be a more egregious case of inequity than that of hereditary slavery? Article III, Section 2, states that our 'power shall extend to all Cases, in Law and Equity, arising under this constitution.' Could there be a more pressing occasion to use that power in the cause of 'Law and Equity' than now?"

Next the justices turned to Christianity and, in republican fashion, quoted two strongly antislavery injunctions of Jesus: "Do unto others as you would have them do unto you" and "Inasmuch as ye have done *it* unto one of the least of these my brethren, ye have done *it* unto Me." "It is impossible to imagine," the Court declared, "that Jesus would ever own a slave; and if a Christian discovered that Jesus was his slave, he would surely free him. How can we, with the fate of hundreds of thousands of slaves hanging on our words, be good Christians and find for the slave interest? Since the Constitution expresses a reverence for Christ and America by first dating itself from Christ's birth, and then from America's birth, we do not believe it signified a continuation of chattel slavery that so glaringly violated the Golden Rule in the 1787th year of our Lord, and that so glaringly violated the 'Laws of Nature and Nature's God' during the 12th year of our Declaration." The justices concluded their religious comments by saying that they were protestant Christians, but they meant no insult to Catholics, Jews, Mohammedans, Hindoos, or any other religion, much less an establishment of Protestantism. Rather, they said, their religion made them friends of humanity, and they believed other religions could have a similar effect. They quoted Benjamin Franklin as saying: "In this business, the friends to humanity in every country are of one nation and religion"(Hoare 1820 251-2).

The decision concluded with a surprising and eloquent tribute to southern character and honor. It applauded George Mason for his Virginia Declaration of Rights, Jefferson for his Declaration, and Madison for his Bill of Rights. The Court further noted that although many delegates owned slaves they nevertheless signed the Declaration in which they pledged their "sacred honor" to the principle that all men have unalienable rights, they appealed "to the Supreme Judge of the world for the rectitude" of their intentions, and they relied "on the protection of Divine Providence." The Court said that southerners expressed the gratefulness of their hearts to Divine Providence, the rectitude of their intentions to the Supreme Judge, and the integrity of their character, by signing the Northwest Ordinance that outlawed slavery in that territory (Thorpe 1909 2:962), by passing a republican constitution that gave no authority to the idea of property in men, by adopting a Bill of Rights inconsistent with slavery. The justices noted that southerners were not political neophytes, they well knew they were rendering so-called "human property" insecure. The Court followed with a survey of, first, antislavery sentiments expressed by southerners; second, manumissions by plantation owners; third, provisions in southern state constitutions inconsistent with slavery; and fourth, acts by southern legislatures that weakened, or made less harsh, the institution of slavery. It ended by warmly commending "the College of William and Mary for awarding, just last year [1791], an honorary LL. D. to Granville Sharp, the greatest abolitionist who ever lived (Hoare 1820 254). Our ruling should be understood as an additional tribute to Sharp, and to many Americans who, by words or acts, actively opposed slavery in our great land. 'But whoso looketh into the perfect law of liberty, and continueth *therein*, he being not a forgetful hearer, but a doer of the work, this man shall be blessed in his deed'(*James* 1:25)." The justices concluded: "Locke's book on government begins: 'Slavery is so vile and miserable an Estate of Man, and so directly opposite to the generous Temper and Courage of our Nation; that 'tis hardly to be conceived, that an *Englishman* [Robert Filmer], much less a *Gentleman*, should plead for't'(1988 141). It is even harder to conceive that an *American,* much less the highest court of *American Justice*, should plead for it. This Court will forever be a palladium for the sacred liberties granted by the Laws of Nature and of Nature's God, it will do all in its power to help guarantee that each state be republican, it will begin *now* to fulfill the desire of a great American [Benjamin Rush]: 'The next Generation we hope, will behold and admire the finished TEMPLE OF AFRICAN LIBERTY IN AMERICA'(1773 6). But if our ruling is in vain, if the federal and state governments shamelessly fail to eradicate, and eradicate wisely, the practice of bondage among us, the United States will be seen as a vast theatre of hypocrisy and self-deceit, the American revolution living on only in infamy. And then, if slaves could speak with one voice, they would truly say of white Americans (echoing the language of Tacitus (1969 1:81)): 'They kidnap, they rape, they flog, this they falsely name a republic, and where they have crushed the human spirit so it can resist no more, they call it freedom.' Even if this Constitution remains in force for two or three centuries, we are confident that, even then, posterity will judge our understanding of the law to be correct, our reasoning to be sound, and our decision to be just. Done by the Unanimous Consent of the Justices of the Supreme Court on the Fourth of July in the Year of our Lord one thousand seven hundred and ninety two and on the Sixteenth Anniversary of the Independence of the United States of America." [My historical fiction was greatly influenced by pre-Civil-War antislavery readings of the Constitution of 1787 and 1791. These should be consulted for more details on antislavery interpretations. See Parrish 1806, Goodell 1845, Tiffany 1849, and especially Spooner 1860 (first edition 1845).] Let us now imagine what happened next. However much such a decision might have pleased the abolitionists, Washington and most members of Congress reacted with anger, consternation, and impeachment on their lips. Separation of powers was thrown to the winds: the Senate and House went into a secret session with Washington presiding. Guilt over the practice and toleration of slavery, the enormous fear that the Saint Domingue revolt would spread to the United States, an extreme uncertainty as to what to do, all these were prominently displayed in the declamations (which exhibited much acrimony and moral posturing). However, the turning point was honor, which can lead individuals to act even against their strongest interests. Among all, but especially among southerners, there was an incredibly intense and painful awareness that their honor as individuals, the honor of their states, and the honor of their infant country, were all at stake. The result was legislation to end slavery. Not wishing to start a Gracchi-type civil war, southern slave owners were very well rewarded with western land (mostly stolen from the Indians), as were northern speculators who took it off their hands at a discount. Let us end this thought experiment by supposing that, although there were substantial difficulties along the way (including fraud, violence, and much backsliding), the union survived, and so-called "legal" slavery ended on July 4, 1800.

If this scenario had actually occurred, would anyone today claim that the justices were good men but not good jurists? Or that the Constitution was a proslavery document,? Or that Court's decision to end slavery was morally right but legally wrong? It will be said with some justice that this republican scenario is implausible; but a thorough reading of the best historians of America, who write about the incredible changes that took place in the years from 1760 to 1791, will easily demonstrate that their truths are often stranger than my fiction. Of course, we could imagine other fictions, such as a Congressman giving a similar speech when the House considered the petition of the Quakers and Franklin, or a prominent European writing a pamphlet claiming Washington, Adams, Madison, and Jefferson, were all despots, full of hypocrisy, self-deceit, and moral cowardice, utterly devoid of honor or common decency. But whatever might have been possible, the Constitution did not constrain enlightened leaders anxious to end slavery; rather, it was the willingness of leaders to debase their own character by self-deceptive tricks that constrained their abolitionist thoughts, words, and deeds. "It is essential to the character of a free republic," Joel Barlow asserted in 1793, " . . . that no shadow of deception should ever be offered to the people; as it cannot fail to corrupt them"(below, page 235). Once self-deceit became a habit in the minds of leaders, that deception was "offered to the people," and it eventually metastasized throughout much of the population, the way regional accents in language begin with leaders, and then spread throughout the land. Their forked consciousness allowed the Founders to commit their "sacred honor" to the Declaration and be passive about slavery's existence in America, even in their own households, it allowed them to believe the absurdity that the Constitution was both republican and protected the slave interest, it allowed them to ignore antislavery applications of the Bill of Rights, even in Washington, D. C. , it allowed them to transform their own depravity into a national catastrophe. This catastrophe began with the introduction of a new principle into the administration of governments. That principle was racism, which over the years went from Jefferson's disingenuously expressed "suspicions" of negro inferiority to Judge Taney's belief that blacks "had no rights which the white man was bound to respect"(60 U. S. 393, 407). That principle meant that, for blacks, the Declaration became a tale told by an idiot, where the rights of life, liberty and the pursuit of happiness signify nothing. Racism in America was not genetic (Declaration), nor congenital (Constitution), but developmental (administrative). The leaders of the slave interest needed a racist administration of the Constitution to prevent the federal government from abolishing slavery. So they tried, and almost succeeded, in using federal power to impose slavery on all states and territories. Yet a racist interpretation of the Constitution was a moral, legal, and administrative abomination from the beginning; slave states or territories have no right to exist under the Constitution, even less to become independent states by the standards of the Declaration. If "domestic Violence" had overwhelmed Virginia due to a slave insurrection, and George Washington responded with an army (as he did in response to the Whiskey Rebellion) of over 12,500 men to the state's application for help, but surprisingly ordered it to side with the slaves, and he then forcibly reorganized Virginia's government into a republican form, he could scarcely be charged with an act inconsistent with the Declaration, and he would certainly be fulfilling the Federal government's obligation to guarantee a republican government for Virginia. Why would it be right for France to help America in its justified armed revolt against Britain, but wrong for the Federal government to help black Americans in their transcendently more justified armed revolt against Virginia? And we have Jefferson's words to describe the nature of republican government: "From the moment that to preserve our rights a change of government became necessary, no doubt could be entertained that a republican form was most consonant with reason, with right, with the freedom of man . . ."(1903 16:333). "Slavery," John Leland tell us, "in its best appearance, is a violent deprivation of the rights of nature, inconsistent with republican government . . . "(1791a 4). It is doubtful that a significantly better Constitution could have been agreed to in the eighteenth century than the one the Founders and Congress achieved by 1791; likewise, with regard to slavery, it is hard to imagine a worse understanding and administration of that Constitution than the Federal government generally followed before 1860. For example, in *Antelope* (23 U. S. 66 (1825)) a unanimous Supreme Court under John Marshall asserted that, although the slave trade was founded in force, and was contrary to the law of nature, the legality of the slave trade remained, until the offending slave trading nations themselves agreed to respect that law (120-123; see Noonan 1977 for background on the case). A more radical repudiation of the philosophy of the American revolution can hardly be conceived. Even today the spirit of 1776 remains in such a stupor that we are almost never expected, when explicating our eighteenth-century Constitution, to emulate the antislavery interpretation of virtuous republicans whose integrity, whose commitment to the rule of law, whose love of freedom, prevented them from finding slavery there; rather, we are nearly always asked to continue the fraudulent, proslavery interpretation created by the dog-whistle politics of artful aristocrats who, in order to give their despicable vice the pretext of legal standing, invented, and then propagated, a dishonest, racist innuendo to override the Constitution's strong and explicit republican character, a character that, paying homage to virtue, the aristocrats themselves repeatedly and rightly proclaimed.

Now let us consider the question of whether the Bill of Rights applies to the states in more detail. According to Article VI,

> This Constitution, and the laws of the United States which shall be made in pursuance thereof; and all treaties made, or which shall be made, under the authority of the United States, shall be the supreme law of the land; and the judges in every state shall be bound thereby, any thing in the constitution or laws of any state to the contrary not withstanding.

State judges appear "bound" by the Bill of Rights since those rights were, as Madison explicitly made clear when he proposed them, necessary for any government to be rightly considered republican. If, by the standards of the eighteenth century, the Bible, although it contains scores of passages contrary to the spirit of 1776 (below, page 468), can nevertheless be given an interpretation so that it becomes "the most republican book in the world" and "friendly to the cause of freedom"(above, page 28), then why could not the Constitution, whose language was specifically designed to be republican, was proclaimed to be republican by the Founders and its other champions, was amended by a Bill of Rights to make more explicit its republican character, was endowed with a guarantee that every state be republican, why could not political and judicial leaders interpret that document as republican, and therefore everywhere hostile to the cause of slavery? This refusal to be faithful to a republican interpretation was not derived from an understanding of what the deliberate sense of the majority of the people had intended when they authorized the Constitution and the Bill of Rights. It is hard to believe that if the leaders had given the matter hard thought, they would have concluded that a majority of the people, in a cool and reflective mood, would have claimed that the Declaration, which expressed the principles of the revolution, was compatible with slavery; or that the Constitution, which expressed the people's intention to "establish Justice," to "secure the Blessings of Liberty," to guarantee a republican government for each state, to protect all the rights expressed in the Bill of Rights, was also compatible with racial and hereditary slavery; or that the people wanted the federal government to have a capital with slaves and slave auctions, desired their society, under its living Constitution, to be a living lie. (Slaveholders represented a small minority of the adult white population in 1787, and slaveholders of any considerable number of slaves, represented a very tiny minority.) Nor could the leaders claim they were confined by legal precedents since British precedents included the antislavery *Somerset* (1772) ruling, and American precedents included juries consistently setting slaves free. In fact, the leaders were bound by no precedents, they created all precedents, and they could have established the precedent of interpreting the Constitution in the spirit of 1776. Instead the leaders anesthetized that spirit, embraced a racial ideology, and drained the Bill of Rights of the moral and political meaning that an honest devotion "to liberty and a Republican Government" would require. So it was that lovers of republican freedom won on the text, but mendacious protectors of slavery won on the interpretation and practice.

This is why the Guarantee clause of the Constitution guaranteed nothing. The word "republican" could be made empty by understanding it to mean "rule by more than one." Would a despotism headed by a king and queen of equal power then be a republic? With as much sense one might say that to be a republic a state must have a Platonic philosopher-king, or must be a tyranny, since Saint-Just in 1794 said that "what constitutes a republic is the total destruction of everything that stands in opposition to it"(1984 700; translation from Dunn 1999 91). The proslavery interpretation of the Constitution is a classic "bait and switch": the Constitution was sold under one meaning of "republican" and then interpreted as if the term was cognitively empty. To support the latter interpretation, it was claimed that the Guarantee clause presupposed that every state in 1787 was in fact republican. This argument is no more persuasive than claiming that the Declaration presupposed that, in 1776, there was no hereditary slavery in America. As Madison asked during the Federal Convention: "Was it to be supposed that republican liberty could long exist under the abuses of it practiced in <some of> the States"(Farrand 1937 1:134). What abuse of "republican liberty" could be greater than using that freedom to secure property in humans? Without the spirit of 1776, the Bill of Rights was nearly stillborn. For instance, the first part of the Fourth Amendment reads: "The right of the people to be secure in their persons, houses, papers, and effects, against unreasonable searches and seizures, shall not be violated, . . . " In the spirit of 1776 one would interpret this to mean "shall not be violated by the federal government, or any state or local government." A slumbering interpretation could read: "shall not be violated by the federal government. The right of violation is reserved to the state or local governments, should their laws allow it." This slumbering interpretation of the Bill of Rights triumphed by 1833 when, without argument, the Supreme Court held — in *Barron vs Baltimore* (7 Peters 243-251) — that the Fourth Amendment gave no protection to individuals so long as it was not the federal government that violated their rights. Did the judges really think that the people fought a revolution to rid themselves of British tyranny only to create a federal government that allowed for the antirepublican violation of property rights by the states? (cf. John Adams' understanding of "republican" below, page 283). The fact that some states acted contrary to various parts of the Bill of Rights at the time of its adoption made convenient the claim that the Bill of Rights did not apply to the states, for if it did, federal officials were faced with great difficulties. But if one believes that the "people through all the States are for republican forms, republican principles"(Jefferson 1903 10:164; cf. 9:378), if one believes "the intention of the people [ought to be preferred] to the intention of their agents"(Hamilton 1961 4:658), then what is merely convenient for federal officials to guarantee, seems unlikely to be the kind of protection the people intended when the federal government was agreed to. Or are we to believe that when the American people adopted the Constitution and Bill of Rights, they wanted the word "republican" in the Constitution, but not the republican reality in their capital, or in their states?

The argument that the Constitution of 1787 and the Bill of Rights of 1791 were and are revolutionary documents in the spirit of 1776 can be further be strengthened by giving a more detailed examination of the Ninth Amendment. (For even more detail see Patterson, Bennett 1955, and Barnett 1989). There is irony here for, until recently, almost all historians, constitutional scholars, and jurists have either denied that American citizens have any rights not enumerated in the Constitution, or disparaged those not listed by contrasting them with the "fundamental" ones that are. Yet the ethos of the Amendment was expressed by George Washington before it was even composed. In his official letter (September 17, 1787) submitting the Constitution to Congress, Washington said: "Individuals entering into society, must give up a share of liberty to preserve the rest. The magnitude of the sacrifice must depend as well on situation and circumstance, as on the object to be obtained. It is at all times difficult to draw with precision the line between those rights which must be surrendered, and those which may be reserved"(DHRC 1976 1:305). The point is that there are rights that the people have antecedent to government that government may not take away. The Ninth Amendment denies that these rights are all articulated in the Constitution.

Madison originally proposed it in answer to some common objections against incorporating a bill of rights into the Constitution. The Federalists had said that a bill of rights was unnecessary and dangerous. Here are the words of James Wilson, defending the Constitution at the Pennsylvania ratifying convention:

> . . . in delegating federal powers . . . the congressional authority is to be collected, not from tacit implication, but from the positive grant expressed in the instrument of union. Hence it is evident, that . . . everything which is not given, is reserved. This . . . will furnish an answer to those who think the omission of a bill of rights, a defect in the proposed Constitution: for it would have been superfluous and absurd to have stipulated with a federal body of our own creation, that we should enjoy those privileges, of which we are not divested either by the intention or the act, that has brought that body into existence. For instance, the liberty of the press, which has been a copious subject of declamation and opposition, what control can proceed from the federal government to shackle or destroy that sacred palladium of national freedom? If indeed, a power similar to that which has been granted for the regulation of commerce, had been granted to regulate literary publications, it would have been as necessary to stipulate that the liberty of the press should be preserved inviolate, as that the impost should be general in its operation. . . . In truth then, the proposed system possesses no influence whatever upon the press, and it would have been merely nugatory to have introduced a formal declaration upon the subject — nay, that very declaration might have been construed to imply that some degree of power was given, since we undertook to define its extent. (DHRC 1976 2:167-8; cf. 387-390. See also Jefferson 1950 12:440, Washington 1931 29:478, Elliot 4:166-67, and Webster 1790 45.)

Thomas Hartley, in the same debate, made the connection to the Declaration explicit:

> As soon as the independence of America was declared in the year 1776, from that instant all our natural rights were restored to us, and we were at liberty to adopt any form of government to which our views or our interests might incline us. This truth, expressly recognized by the act, declaring our independence, naturally produced another maxim, that whatever portion of those natural rights we did not transfer to the government was still reserved and retained by the people; for, if no power was delegated to the government, no right was resigned by the people; and if a part only of our national rights was delegated, is it not absurd to assert that we have relinquished the whole? Where then is the necessity of a formal declaration that those rights are still retained, of the resignation of which no evidence can possibly be produced? (DHRC 1976 2:430)

Alexander Hamilton in the *Federalist* argued likewise:

I go further, and affirm that bills of rights, in the sense and in the extent in which they are contended for, are not only unnecessary in the proposed constitution, but would even be dangerous. They would contain various exceptions to powers which are not granted; and on this very account, would afford a colourable pretext to claim more than were granted. For why declare that things shall not be done which there is no power to do? Why for instance, should it be said, that the liberty of the press shall not be restrained, when no power is given by which restrictions may be imposed? (1961 4:706; cf. also Pinckney's words in Farrand 1937 2:256 and Edmund Randolph's in DHRC 1976 9:1085)

The Anti-Federalists, however, had answers to such arguments. First, they argued that powers already given could interfere with rights that everyone wants to retain. Thus the Federal Farmer contends that

all parties apparently agree, that the freedom of the press is a fundamental right, and ought not to be restrained by any taxes, duties, or in any manner whatever. Why should not the people, in adopting a federal constitution, declare this, even if there are only doubts about it? But, say the advocates, all powers not given are reserved: — true; but the great question is, are not powers given, in the exercise of which this right may be destroyed? . . . By art. I sect. 8 congress will have power to lay and collect taxes, duties, imports and excise. . . . Printing, like all other business, must cease when taxed beyond its profits; and it appears to me, that a power to tax the press at discretion, is a power to destroy or restrain the freedom of it. (1788 151-2; cf. De Witt 1787 1)

Second, the Anti-Federalists argued that the Constitution explicitly protected some rights with respect to powers not given. Again, let me quote the Federal Farmer:

By article I, section 9, "No title of nobility shall be granted by congress" Was this clause omitted, what power would congress have to make titles of nobility? In what part of the constitution would they find it? The answer must be, that congress would have no such power — that people, by adopting the constitution, will not part with it. Why then by a negative clause, restrain congress from doing what it would have no power to do? (1788 146-7; cf. Brutus 1787 2 and Countryman 1787a 2)

The answer, according to the Federal Farmer, can only be that it was done "from very great caution." But why not exercise a similar caution with regard to other republican freedoms, such as the freedom of the press?

Finally, the Anti-Federalists said that there were other interpretations of the natural rights tradition that strongly spoke for the necessity of a bill of rights. Agrippa argued as follows:

> . . . all the power of government originally reside in the body of the people; and that when they appoint certain persons to administer the government, they delegate all the powers of government not expressly reserved. Hence it appears, that a constitution does not in itself imply any more than a declaration of the relation which the different parts of the government bear to each other, but does not in any degree imply security to the rights of individuals. This has been the uniform practice. In all doubtful cases the decision is in favour of the government. (1788 2)

Madison's political problem was clear. On the one hand, he believed that anyone who understood the true nature of the Constitution could see that a bill of rights was unnecessary. A listing of rights, therefore, was a danger since the list would be incomplete, and the very existence of the list might be interpreted as affirming the false view of government according to which it has all powers not expressly denied (see DHRC 1976 10:1502, 1507). On the other hand, Madison knew that this incorrect view had a substantial number of adherents and that sometime in the future the members of the government might — whether they really believed it or not — assume powers contrary to reserved rights, or use legitimate powers in such a way as to violate a reserved right. To alleviate this fear Madison proposed his bill of rights.

But how about the fears of those (including Madison himself) who saw the dangers of explicitly listing rights? In Congress, when proposing his bill of rights, Madison dealt directly with the problem:

> It has been objected also against a bill of rights, that, by enumerating particular exceptions to the grant of power, it would disparage those rights which were not placed in that enumeration, and it might follow by implication, that those rights which were not singled out, were intended to be assigned into the hands of the general government, and consequently insecure. This is one of the most plausible arguments I have ever heard urged against the admission of a bill of rights into this system; but, I conceive, that it may be guarded against. I have attempted it, as gentlemen may see by turning to the last clause of the 4th resolution. (1962 12:206)

That clause reads: "The exceptions here or elsewhere in the constitution, made in favor of particular rights, shall not be so construed as to diminish the just importance of other rights retained by the people; or as to enlarge the powers delegated by the constitution; but either as actual limitations of such powers, or as inserted merely for greater caution"(201-2). Evidently this is what Madison intended as the meaning of the Ninth Amendment. His purpose was to capture the substance of similar proposals that were suggested during the debates to adopt the Constitution in New York, Virginia, and North Carolina (see DHCUSA 1894 2:191, DHRC 1976 10:1555, Elliot 1836 4:246). Now consider the Tenth Amendment: "The powers not delegated to the United States by Constitution, nor prohibited by it to the states, are reserved to the states respectively, or to the people." The Ninth Amendment and the last phrase of the Tenth are intended to prevent the assumption that the listing of rights or powers elsewhere in the Constitution mean that the people have no other rights or powers than those listed, or that they have no other important rights or powers.

The Ninth and Tenth Amendments are in effect instructions on how to interpret the Constitution. The Federal Farmer, when lamenting the lack of a bill of rights, declared:

> It is said, that when the people make a constitution, and delegate powers, that all powers not delegated by them to those who govern, is reserved in the people; and that the people, in the present case, have reserved in themselves, and in their state governments every right and power not expressly given by the federal constitution to those who shall administer the national government. It is said, on the other hand, that the people, when they make a constitution, yield all power not expressly reserved to themselves. The truth is, in either case, it is mere matter of opinion, and men usually take either side of the argument, as will best answer their purposes. . . (1787 30).

The Ninth and Tenth Amendments were intended to take this out of the realm of opinion; to interpret the Constitution, readers may not "take either side of the argument as will best answer their purposes." Rather the Constitution should be interpreted in accordance with a revolutionary view of government expressed in the Declaration (cf. Wilson's words above, page 32). This means that the people have all rights prior to government, of which some are alienable. A specified number of these are given up to the government when it is formed, but the people can, whenever they wish, alter the government and take back some rights, or dissolve the government, and take back all rights. The people are sovereign; the powers of government are only held by their continuing grant. The view that the Declaration and the Constitution are philosophically at odds is thus incorrect.

Yet both documents seem unfinished: the Declaration asserts an indefinite number of unalienable rights, but identifies only some of them; the Constitution enumerates certain rights, but the Ninth Amendment asserts that the enumeration is incomplete. The question arises: why not list all the rights? Madison's answer is given in the *Federalist*:

> The use of words is to express ideas. Perspicuity therefore requires not only that the ideas should be distinctly formed, but that they should be expressed by words distinctly and exclusively appropriate to them. But no language is so copious as to supply words and phrases for every complex idea, or so correct as not to include many equivocally denoting different ideas. Hence it must happen, that however accurately objects may be discriminated in themselves, and however accurately the discrimination may be considered, the definition of them may be rendered inaccurate by the inaccuracy of the terms in which it is delivered. And this unavoidable inaccuracy must be greater or less, according to the complexity and novelty of the objects defined. When the Almighty himself condescends to address mankind in their own language, his meaning luminous as it must be, is rendered dim and doubtful by the cloudy medium through which it is communicated. (1962 10:362-3)

Let me try to interpret this passage by extending Madison's reference to traditional theology. In the Old Testament we find a prohibition against giving God a name, and a prohibition against a graven image. These prohibitions may have been meant to emphasize that, for the ancient Hebrews, God cannot be reduced to a name, a thing, an idol. Humans, made in his image, are likewise irreducible to a formula. It follows that any claims of a complete listing of rights would be highly problematical. That is why Madison suggested the Ninth Amendment. Writing to Jefferson on October 17, 1788, he said: ". . . there is great reason to fear that a positive declaration of some of the most essential rights could not be obtained in the requisite latitude. I am sure that the rights of Conscience in particular, if submitted to public definition would be narrowed much more than they are likely ever to be by an assumed power"(1962 11:297). Since Madison believed that words were inadequate to express some of our rights, and *a fortiori* all of them, they could not completely capture the essence of our humanity. This contrasts with the traditional logical doctrine that asserts that a definition is a phrase that captures the essence of whatever is being defined, as in the example, "Man is a rational animal." Madison was suggesting that a living people, like a living God in whose image the people are made, is not subject to such definition. Definitions in these cases are inherently incomplete; the rights and powers of the people in declarations or constitutions, or the properties and powers of God in theology, can at best be partially defined. As the only provisions in the Constitution that distinctly refer to rights or powers not listed, as the only provisions that explicitly reaffirm the doctrine of the Declaration that the people have rights and powers that are prior and independent of government, the Ninth and the Tenth Amendments are philosophically one of the most important parts of the Constitution. The Constitution, they declare, must be interpreted in the spirit of revolution — the American revolution.

Nevertheless, for more than a century and a half, their import was almost completely ignored, or treated as empty of significance. Thus Robert H. Jackson relates how "a lawyer friend asked me in a friendly way what I thought the Ninth Amendment to the Constitution meant. I vainly tried to recall what it was." Jackson goes on to say that he "couldn't recall it ever being used and that, after some research, the Ninth Amendment rights remained a 'mystery' to him"(1955 74-5). There is great irony here because Jackson had been both an associate justice of the Supreme Court and the chief U. S. prosecutor at Nuremberg. Those trials presupposed human rights exist independent of government, the view that the Ninth Amendment is meant to express. Among the rights referred to by that Amendment is the natural right of revolution expressed in the Declaration. Since Gabriel and his followers were completely denied peaceful means of redress of their oppression, when they when they attempted to rebel in 1800, their action had Constitutional authority under the Ninth Amendment, for certainly they had suffered a longer and worse "train of abuses and usurpations" under the American government than had white Americans under the British government. Jack Bowler, one of the leaders, said: "[W]e have as much right to fight for our liberty as any men"(Flournoy 1890 160). "The doctrine of non-resistance against arbitrary power, and oppression, is absurd, slavish, and destructive of the good and happiness of mankind"(Thorpe 1909 4:2455). This statement from the New Hampshire Constitution of 1784 explicitly affirms what is implicit in the federal Constitution.

Consider an analogy. In casualty insurance a distinction is made between an "all-risk" policy (which normally has a few listed exceptions) and a "named-peril" policy. The difference is where the burden of proof falls: In an all-risk policy it falls on the insurance company to prove that the loss was due to one of the few excluded risks named in the policy (for example, earthquake); in the named-peril policy it is up to the policy holder to prove that a loss was due to some named risk (for example, fire). Naturally the all-risk policy is of far higher quality. Suppose a person has an all-risk policy, but out of an excess of caution asks that some covered risks be named. The policy might state: "With the exception of earthquake damage, this policy covers all risks, including fire, theft, and water damage." Afterward the person has a claim due to wind damage, but the insurance company says that since it is not listed (that is, it is not fire, theft, or water damage) they will not pay. Would not the person justifiably feel swindled, since the three perils were clearly named for the sake of illustration, not for the sake of limiting coverage to those three? The first eight amendments were likewise named rights for the sake of illustration, yet historically have commonly been interpreted as limiting rights to those named.

For example, consider Article IV in the Articles of Confederation: "The people of each State shall have free ingress and regress to and from any other State"(Thorpe 1909 1:10). The Constitution does not list this right explicitly, although it is certain that the people did not intend to give up it when they, through their representatives, accepted the Constitution. So let us suppose at some later time a man, in court, claims the federal government, which prevented him from leaving a state, violated his Constitutional rights. Under an "all-risk" interpretation, it would be up to the government to prove that the people, after 1787, explicitly gave up this right they once had. This attempt would certainly fail and the man would be free to travel. However, under a "named-peril" conception of rights it would be up to the man to prove that some explicit right in the Constitution implies this right. And yet there might be no such valid deduction, with the consequence that the man's freedom to travel would be denied. With a "named-peril" conception of rights, the list of rights that the people enjoyed in, say, 1786, would have to be indefinitely long. It would have to include, to use Noah Webster's satirical example, "That Congress shall never restrain any inhabitant of America from eating and drinking, *at seasonable times,* or prevent his lying on his *left side,* in a long winter's night, or even on his back, when he is fatigued by lying on his *right*"(1790 149). The Ninth Amendment was intended to prevent such absurdities. Its general function was to round out the Bill of Rights so as to make it impossible for the government, even if acting in accordance with the body of the Constitution and the first eight amendments, to nevertheless find a way to undermine the pursuit of flourishing lives by some or all the people.

Hamilton's words have proven prophetic: "Bills of rights would contain various exceptions to powers which are not granted; and on this very account, would afford a colourable pretext to claim more than were granted." Here is an example. In 1942 a farmer with a modest piece of land was fined for growing wheat, for his own use, on his own land, with his own labor. The Supreme Court upheld the fine (317 U.S. 111). It was up to the man to show that some named Constitutional right was violated by the fine, which in the Court's judgment, he failed to do. The Court did note, however, that others benefitted from the regulation that prevented the man from growing his own wheat. It added: "The conflicts of economic interest between the regulated and those who advantage by it are wisely left under our system to resolution by the Congress under its more flexible and responsible legislative process"(129). The Court ignored the plausible possibility that sometimes Congress is not primarily "flexible and responsible" to the public as a whole but rather to those economic interest groups who "advantage" by the regulation. In fact, it completely washed its hands of any but the most narrow responsibility: ". . . with the wisdom, workability, or fairness, of the plan of regulation we have nothing to do"(129). This evasion of responsibility is a betrayal of one of the functions of judges as described by Hamilton in the *Federalist*: ". . . it is not with a view to infractions of the constitution only that the independence of the judges may be an essential safeguard against the effects of occasional ill humours in the society. These sometimes extend no farther than to the injury of the private rights of particular classes of citizens, by unjust and partial laws. Here also the firmness of the judicial magistracy is of vast importance . . ."(1961 4:661).

Let us suppose the wheat farmer had appealed to the Ninth Amendment. He could then have made the very plausible claim that in the late eighteenth century all Americans — both before and after the adoption of the Constitution — would have agreed that any person has the right to grow his own wheat for his own use on his own land. For example, in his *A Summary View of the Rights of British America* (1774), Jefferson objected to "certain . . . acts of the British parliament, by which they would prohibit us from manufacturing for our own use the articles we raise on our own lands with our own labor. . . . an American subject is forbidden to make a hat for himself of the fur which he has taken perhaps on his own soil. An instance of despotism to which no parallel can be produced in the most arbitrary ages of British history"(1950 1:124-5). Again, Noah Webster in defending the Constitution asks: "Do you not know that in this country almost every farmer is lord of his own soil? . . . The same laws which secure the property in land, secure to the owner the right of using it as he pleases"(1790 149-50). Elsewhere he said that the "right of a farmer and mechanic to the exclusive enjoyment and right of disposal of what they *make* or *produce*, is never questioned"(1843 175). The wheat farmer could argue that from the eighteenth century to 1942 the American people never indicated they intended to give up that right to the federal government. Of course, the farmer could have added that Congress along the way might have taken action implying that intention, but Congress is only acting to "advantage" those who gain by the regulations, they were not genuinely acting in the name of the people. In the actual case, the Court quoted approvingly an earlier judgment: "The power of Congress over interstate commerce is plenary and complete in itself, may be exercised to its utmost extent, and acknowledges no limitations other than are prescribed in the Constitution"(317 U.S. 124; cf. 315 U.S. 119). But the Ninth Amendment, as part of the Constitution and subsequent to the commerce clause, limits the uses that Congress can make of that clause. Yet so complete had been the neglect of the Ninth Amendment that even victims of the government failed to appeal to it. In fairness to the Court, it must be said that it has sometimes gone out of its way to prevent injustice by stretching the meaning of words in one of the listed rights. This is unfortunate because it gratuitously abuses the language of the Constitution when, without such abuse, the Court could appeal to the Ninth Amendment. Note that under an "all-risk" interpretation, judges do not invent rights; rather rights are created either by God or nature, or they are invented by the people. For instance, if an individual or individuals claim a right in court that is not explicitly affirmed in the Constitution, a right that the government disputes, the government must give evidence that a majority of the citizens in a calm and deliberate mood either recognize no such right, or they recognize it, but reaffirm that they had given it up. The Court then gives its judgment as to whether the government has proved its case. Fulfilling this eighteenth-century conception of virtuous government will, as we shall see, substantially test the intellectual, moral, and political character of twenty-first century America. In sum, the Ninth Amendment is an instruction to read the Constitution as embodying the superior "all-risk" conception of rights, but what courts have too often delivered is a inferior "named-peril" conception.

The "all-risk" understanding is required because the Constitution is in the service of an independent and sovereign people. It is thus to them that we must turn for its ultimate meaning, not to its written image. The people may, of course, consult experts. But whatever the experts say, it is the people that must ultimately choose, and that choice may not always be right. One should not confuse an authoritative decision and a right decision. The distinction is implicit in the conception of either individual or political autonomy. Suppose a woman is trying to decide between buying camera A or camera B and asks an expert for advice. Let us suppose that the expert gives numerous cogent arguments for buying camera A. Further let us suppose that if the woman were to buy camera A, she would be much more satisfied than with camera B. All this does not prevent it from being true that the woman has the authority (it being her money) to decide on camera B, and the expert's being right does not give the expert the authority to make the decision. The buyer has a right to make the choice, even if that choice will prove mistaken.

Similarly an independent people have ultimate authority in political matters (it being their country), but that does not mean they will necessarily choose rightly. To quote Jefferson's words again: "All . . . will bear in mind this sacred principle, that though the will of the majority is in all cases to prevail, that will, to be rightful, must be reasonable"(above, page 22). Yet although the people may make mistakes, they often are more reasonable than political authorities. For example, slavery was legal in Massachusetts in 1773. Nevertheless in October of that year, Caesar Hendrick, a black, sued Richard Greenleaf, for holding him in slavery. He asked for fifty pounds in damages. The jury ruled in his favor and he was awarded eighteen pounds and costs. (Coffin, Joshua 1845 339; see Adams 1850 2:200, Allen, John 1774 28, Nelson, William Edward 1975 101-2 and Kaplan 1973 216 for references to other such cases.) The people, whenever they had a chance to deliberate, opposed slavery. As John Adams wrote in 1795: "I never knew a jury, by a verdict, to determine a negro to be a slave. They always found them free"(MHSC 1877 402; see also Coffin, Joshua 1845 339 and Jeremy Belnap's comments at MHSC 1835 202). The Supreme Court, to put it mildly, does not have a similar record. The historical roots of the idea that the people have better judgment than the few goes back to Aristotle. While recognizing the imperfection of individuals, he argued for the importance of each citizen in determination of social policy:

> For the many, of whom each individual is not a good man, when they meet together may be better than the few good, if regarded not individually but collectively, just as a feast to which many contribute is better than a dinner provided out of a single purse. For each individual among the many has a share of excellence and practical wisdom, and when they meet together, just as they become

in a manner one man, who has many feet, and hands, and senses, so too with regard to their character and thought. . . . Again, the many are more incorruptible than the few; they are like the greater quantity of water which is less easily corrupted than a little. The individual is liable to be overcome by anger or by some other passion, and then his judgement is necessarily perverted; but it is hardly to be supposed that a great number of persons would all get into a passion and go wrong at the same moment. (1984 2:2033, 2:2041. See also 2:2034, 2:2367, Thucydides 1928 3:257, and Machiavelli 1998 117-18.)

In a well-run democracy each person's "share of excellence and practical wisdom" can be brought to bear on decisions and thereby prevent the corruption that is so common when decisions are made by only a few, however intelligent or talented. Since it is the least likely to be corrupted, the voice of the people, provided it is reasonable, ought to be the foundation of public policy. Nevertheless the qualification of being "reasonable" is crucial, for when Aristotle says "it is hardly to be supposed that a great number of persons would all get into a passion and go wrong at the same moment," he is obviously in error as the phenomena of groupthink or lynch mobs illustrate. But, then, how can each person's "share of excellence and practical wisdom" be discovered and then made part of an effective public policy?

6

Courts of Common Reason

Let us suppose, at least provisionally, that the philosophy presupposed by the Declaration and the Constitution (including its Bill of Rights) is correct. What, then, ought we to do to better embody that philosophy in our political practice? The essential difficulty is to ensure that the rulers, first, *know* what the people, after adequate reflection, want; second, are *competent* to do it; and, third, are *willing* to do it. The Founders were acutely aware of the failures of past forms of government. The history of ancient Athens made clear to them that when the people are assembled they are often incapable, or unwilling, to govern responsibly. Here the Founders agreed with Cicero who claimed that "Greece, which once was so notable for its resources, its power, its glory, fell because of this defect alone — the undue freedom and irresponsibility of its assemblies. Untried men, without experience in any affairs and ignorant, took their places in the assembly and then they undertook useless wars, then they put factious men in charge of the state, then they drove most deserving citizens out of the country"(1937 383, 385; cf. Harrington, James 2003 37-8). A pure democracy was unacceptable because it becomes a mobocracy (Cicero 1988 222-3). On the other hand, government of the one or the few tends easily to corruption and tyranny.

The best procedure to secure our rights, the Founders decided, is to have the people choose — sometimes quite indirectly — the most wise and public-spirited citizens to be their representatives in running the government. This conception can be found in both the Bible and ancient Greece (below, page 491). From within the government, there would be numerous checks against abuse of power, and from without, there would be periodic elections to determine who, in the judgment of the people, could best represent them. Leaders, however, are not always expected, at any given moment, to do what the people want. Madison puts the point this way: "As the cool and deliberate sense of the community ought in all governments, and actually will [*nota bene*] in all free governments ultimately prevail over the views of its rulers; so there are particular moments in public affairs, when the people stimulated by some irregular passion, or some illicit advantage, or misled by the artful misrepresentations of interested men, may call for measures which they themselves will afterwards be the most ready to lament and condemn." In such circumstances, the rulers ought "to suspend the blow meditated by the people against themselves."(1962 10:546; cf. also Madison's comments (Farrand 1937 1:421-2) during the Constitutional Convention). The rulers Madison is talking about are Senators, and it is of course open to debate whether the Senate has proved itself to be a worthy institution for correcting the follies of the people. In any case, for Madison rulers should know the "cool and deliberate sense" of the people, and by careful use of reason embody that sense in the laws of the land — often better than the people could themselves. That is the essence of virtuous political talent. In the same vein, Hamilton writes: "The republican principle demands, that the deliberate sense of the community should govern the conduct of those to whom they entrust the management of their affairs . . . "(1961 4:608). If a population is homogeneous and small, if the political issues few and simple, then the rulers, from evidence of their own reflection, might reasonably find that sense. But, even in eighteenth-century America, it was understood that introspection, however conscientious, will produce outcomes significantly different from those of the population as a whole. Madison observed in his notes of the Federal Convention that "if the opinions of the people were to be our guide, it wd. be difficult to say what course we ought to take. No member of the Convention could say what the opinions of his Constituents were at this time; much less could he say what they would like if possessed of the information & lights possessed by the members here . . ."(Farrand 1937 1:215; cf. 431).

So what could be done? In 1656 James Harrington argued that the legislature should be "so constituted as can never contract any other interest than that of the whole people"(2003 24). Following this idea, one option of the Founders was to make the legislature, in our language, statistically representative with respect to profession. That would greatly reduce the possibility that it would act contrary to the public happiness. The Federal Farmer claimed that a "fair representation" would "allow professional men, merchants, traders, farmers, mechanics, etc., to bring a just proportion of their best informed men respectively into the legislature"(1788 11). Yet the Founders agreed with Hamilton that this option was "altogether visionary"(1961 4:479); there are too many professions and free elections would not produce such outcomes. Elective representation is incompatible with statistical representation. Consequently a legal model was adopted: as a lawyer represents a client so government officials represent the people. In the words of John Adams: "Rulers are no more than attorneys, agents and trustees for the people"(1977 1:121; cf. Locke 1988 366-67, 371). When an individual chooses a lawyer who is both competent and willing to be a legal representative, there is no necessity that the lawyer be like the client in personality, or of the same social class. What is crucial is that the lawyer know, and be responsive to, the interest of the client. The same reasoning holds for legislatures; as George Mason put it in 1788, "To make representation real and actual, the number of Representatives ought to be adequate; they ought to mix with the people, think as they think, feel as they feel, ought to be perfectly amenable to them, and thoroughly acquainted with their interest and condition"(DHRC 1976 9:938; cf. Elliot 1836 2:245, and ARDM 1787 14). In this conception public policy ought to be determined not by introspection, but by evidence gained through mixing and acquaintance with the citizens. But how should elected officials gather that evidence today? The conversation they can have with their respective constituents is likely to be an unreliable or inadequate source. The size and complexity of their constituencies, combined with time restraints, ensures this. The political and financial power of special interest groups introduces further distortions. And ordinary polls hardly reveal the "cool and deliberate sense of the community" that should "ultimately prevail over the views of its rulers." Most citizens have not even have thought about many of the issues, much less reflected long and hard to determine their best judgment. What government officials need to know is: What would the American people think if they had the information, interest, time, and ability to consider political issues in a truly deliberative fashion?

We can take a step toward the answer by asking: What are the informed values of the American people? An informed value is not one that is necessarily "right" or "true." It refers to the way in which a person comes to hold it. A person's values are *informed* if the person first, has carefully considered the pros and cons of her values; second, has had extensive exposure to those who hold and argue for values contrary to hers; and third, has a strong commitment to retest her values in light of new experiences, or new arguments for rejected values. *Mutatis mutandis* we can also speak of *considered* judgments or *responsible* decisions. If we could discover the informed values, considered judgments, and responsible decisions of the American people, we would discover "the cool and deliberate sense of the community" that "actually will in all free governments ultimately prevail over the views of its rulers."

Since that discovery would be the deliberative reason of the American people, it might seem that problem of finding it could be solved by appealing to the reason's universality. If honest and diligent representatives would only use their deliberative reason to make decisions, then the decisions would match the deliberative reason of the people. Unfortunately deliberative reason is not always universal in the requisite sense. "When men exercise their reason coolly and freely, on a variety of distinct questions," Madison points out, "they inevitably fall into different opinions on some of them. When they are governed by a common passion their opinions, if they are so to be called, will be the same"(1962 10:472). Madison had no answer to the question of how the reason of the public, which he believed should ultimately prevail, could even be known, let alone triumph, on those occasions when it was different from the reason of the rulers. However, Jefferson did. In a letter to John Adams, he proposed that Virginia be divided into small political units called wards: "A general call of ward-meetings . . . on the same day thro' the state would at any time produce the genuine sense of the people on any required point, and would enable the state to act in mass, as your people have so often done, and with so much effect, by their town meetings"(Cappon 1959 2:390). Wards were the institutional means through which the "common reason of society" (1892 10:44) could remedy the ineptitude and corruption that seem so characteristic of political life. Throughout this book, Madison's "deliberate sense" and Jefferson's "common reason" will be treated as synonymous.

Jefferson's idea was far ahead of its time. To reduce his scheme to practicality, he would need a host of disciplines (such as mathematical logic, programming, and sampling theory) and a host of technologies (such as computers and telecommunications) that did not then exist. The proposal is one of the earliest ever made for a direct democracy in which the people do not gather together; only their views, so to say, are assembled into a collective decision. It is a recommendation for democracy at a distance; literally, a teledemocracy. Jefferson was trying to devise a mechanism that would reliably express the common reason of society — the ultimate political authority — and thereby enable the people to identify and destroy the power of politicians who are unfaithful to that reason. That such a mechanism could be designed and actually incorporated into the ordinary politics of free societies is, in my judgment, one of the most important and original ideas in the history of political philosophy. In spite of Jefferson's reputation as one of the greatest democrats of all time, in spite of his enthusiastic advocacy in calling wards the "most admirable of all human contrivances in government"(1903 14:454), his idea has received relatively little attention either as a theory or as a practical proposal for political reform.

Let us give it the attention it deserves. A long line of thinkers beginning with Socrates has emphasized the importance of deliberation as a means of overcoming ignorance and self-deceit; it is the foundation of an ethics of self-knowledge, the basis of all autonomous morality. A country that aims to be both autonomous and moral must likewise use deliberation to overcome social ignorance and public self-deceptions; it must create a politics of self-knowledge. That politics contrasts sharply with those chilling conceptions of social design — beginning with Plato — in which schemes are imposed on the people, or certain classes of people. Instead it requires institutions through which an autonomous people can search their own hearts and minds, and then impose on themselves, as an autonomous person can, the outcomes of their own reasoning. Through this examination of their national character, the people could collectively become their own philosopher-king. Democratic autonomy cannot be achieved without deliberative soul-searching among the people; it is the foundation of political excellence in a free society; in eighteenth-century terms, it is the foundation of public happiness. "Know thyself," John Adams declared, "is as useful a precept to nations as to men"(1850 4:393; cf. James Wilson's similar remark above, page 7).

Let us imagine how we might new-model our government so that its operation would be determined by a politics of self-knowledge. This politics would require that governmental policies and action perfectly reflect the "common reason of society." The goal of achieving such fidelity could be called *American perfectionist democracy*. It would be a "hi-fi government" aiming to realize such continuing excellence as to be a paradigm for any country that strives toward the ideals of equality, liberty, and human flourishing. Such was the hope in the Founding era: Athens "was the wonder of the ancient world" said Paine, whereas America "is becoming the admiration and model of the present"(1945 1:372; cf. Jefferson 1950 31:53).

The new-modelling problem is initially epistemological, namely, to devise a method of reliably identifying the common reason of society on any political issue. Let us consider the kind of commitment that is necessary to secure such knowledge, *without claiming that every detail considered is likewise necessary*. We will begin with a thought experiment. Imagine that the President successfully calls on Congress to create an Agency for Public Choice; that is, an institution whose goal is to provide accurate information about the informed values, considered judgments, and responsible decisions of the American people. After an initial period of organization and experimentation, the Agency, we will suppose, chooses a substantial random sample of the people — say, for the sake of illustration, 1/10 of 1% of the adult population, or about 240,000 people. The aim would be to embody John Adams' idea of a "Representative Assembly," that "should be in miniature, an exact portrait of the people at large. It should think, feel, reason, and act like them"(1977 4:86, cf 2:283 and Harrington, James 2003 24, 273). In contemporary language, the group should be a statistically valid representation so that there will be an extremely high probability that the group's decisions would match what the population as a whole would decide. Hence, if there are x% of women in the general population, we should expect x% in the group; if Californians represent y% of the population, Californians should be y% of the group; if there are z% of the population who earn less than $12,000 a year, then there ought to be z% of such individuals in the group, and so forth. (Of course, by chance alone our expectations will not always be exactly fulfilled.) The Agency would try to create an environment so favorable to deliberative reason as to reach the highest achievable precision in reporting the cool and deliberate sense of the American people. For a few issues — such as declaring war or revising the Constitution — the entire group might participate, but only a randomly chosen subset would normally be involved in dealing with a specific issue. Each of the members of the group might serve a relatively long time (say, seven years with overlapping terms) or a relatively short time (say, no longer, on average, than trial juries usually do). Experience could determine what works best for various kinds of questions. In any case, jurors would be paid and their responses periodically made public.

All this would take a large capital investment. But if one wants to reduce the cost of anything — raw materials, goods, services — large capital investments are frequently necessary. Our present political procedures for value resolution are often needlessly crude, inefficient, and inappropriate. We should try to greatly reduce the cost of value conflicts by resolving them with greater speed, accuracy, and authority. That speed, accuracy, and authority requires a controlled setting. For example, to test the economic worth of anything we must put it into the environment of a fair market; to prove a person is legally guilty requires the environment of a fair trial. In like manner, the deliberate sense of the community can only reliably be revealed in a special kind of environment.

How should this environment be designed? It should be very different from the "town-meetings" of the sort that Ross Perot, Bill Clinton, or Hillary Clinton conducted. They were not founded on statistically valid samples of the people, and were often directed toward influencing, rather than discovering, the views of the people. Such meetings do not provide an appropriate environment for people to deliberate among themselves, much less to demonstrate where their considered judgments differ from those of their rulers. Nor should the environment be what has been called "electronic democracy," that is, a continuing systematic poll (by use of electronic means) of whatever people's opinions happen to be on the various issues. Radio talk shows, interactive television, and the Internet can be as fertile a ground for producing mobs as the village green. Safeguards are here missing, and thus there is great risk of the kind of corrupt democracy that the Founders took great pains to avoid. In the eighteenth century, slow communications gave some protection against corruption: "In large Districts," Madison claimed, "there will be no Danger of Demagogues"(Farrand 1937 1:56; cf. 133; cf. Aristotle 1984 2:2057; Wilson 2007 2:850). Since modern communications has wiped out that safeguard, it is necessary to provide new protections to secure the public happiness. What is needed is an environment comparable to a well-run courtroom, which is designed to prevent hasty and uninformed decisions controlled by emotions that undermine truth or justice. Let us call such an environment a *court of common reason*. The representative group of people that the Agency for Public Choice selects will be called an *advisory jury*. Their job is to deliberate and answer political questions submitted to them. Their answers will help guide the President, members of Congress, federal judges, and other governmental employees in the performance of their duties.

Any issue given to the advisory jury would be presented in the context of arguments made in behalf of conflicting points of view. "We must be able," Aristotle says, "to employ persuasion, just as deduction can be employed, on the opposite sides of a question, not in order that we may in practice employ it in both ways (for we must not make people believe what is wrong), but in order that we may see clearly what the facts are, and that, if another man argues unfairly, we on our part may be able to confute him"(1984 2:2154). Politics, like natural science, is a disputational, and often an adversarial, activity. Preferences, values, and perceptions of truth become informed by this competitive activity; the stronger and more extensive the competition, the more informed are the dispositions. Hence, as in ordinary courtrooms, the advisory jury would hear opposing arguments, whose presentation is governed by fair and impartial rules. This competition will help ensure that the jury's decisions are a product of critical reason. Let us suppose that, before listening to arguments and deliberating, the jury is randomly divided into subjuries, each consisting of twelve people. Every subjury will have its own "jury room," which might be actual or virtual (using video-conferencing or tele-immersion). That isolation from other subjuries will help protect against the dangers of groupthink or mob decision that are often found in large gatherings. As Madison warned: "In all very numerous assemblies, of whatever characters composed, passion never fails to wrest the sceptre from reason. Had every Athenian citizen been a Socrates, every Athenian assembly would still have been a mob"(1962 10:505; cf. Hume 1985 523, Hamilton 4:538, Wilson 2007 2:851 and John Jay in Washington 1992 4:502).

A decision of a subjury will count only if the decision is unanimous. As in a trial jury, the requirement of unanimity promotes the goal of a considered judgment, since each may have to convince others so that his or her point of view will prevail. The decision of the entire advisory jury is determined by a plurality of the decisions of those subjuries that achieve unanimity. For example, suppose an advisory jury of 12,000 people is divided into 1,000 subjuries. On a given question the total of the subjuries might be 487 affirmative, 301 negative and 212 undecided (unanimity not being achieved in those subjuries). Hence the advice to governmental officials is affirmative. If 10 percent of the subjuries are negative and the rest undecided, the advice is weakly negative; if 85 percent of the subjuries are affirmative, the advice is strongly affirmative. A Court of Common Reason thus measures the *strength*, as well as the *nature*, of the people's advice. The probability of a subjury being unanimous can be increased by posing a number of questions at once. Political compromise can then be achieved by vote trading: "I will vote with you on the second question, if you will vote with me on the third." The Court's design and operation would continuously be self-correcting, as experience teaches what works and what does not. Furthermore, decisions would not be determined for all time, but would be periodically revisited, so that a point of view that fails on one occasion may triumph at a later time, when the people's considered judgments have changed. State and local courts could likewise be established.

This advisory jury system is thus a generalization of the ordinary trial jury system, in that facts about American considered judgments in general are discovered, instead of merely facts applying to a particular case, such as the guilt of a specific defendant. The size of the advisory jury can be enlarged merely to increase civic participation, if that is desirable in a particular deliberation. Or the size can be split to increase efficiency. Critics who claim that direct democracy must be inefficient overlook this simple point: just as creating superfast computers requires parallel processing, where a number of computations are carried out by different microprocessors at the same time, so the efficient determination of the common reason of society requires parallel deliberation, where different groups of subjuries deliberate on different aspects of that reason at the same time. For example, a 12,000-member advisory jury could decide ten questions simultaneously by being randomly split into ten equal groups of 1,200 jurors, where each group (consisting of 100 subjuries) could, in the same time frame, answer a separate question.

Some words about terminology. "Agency for Public Choice" is chosen to suggest that a bureau of the government provides the administrative support through which the *public* makes a choice. The eighteenth-century phrase "common reason of society" (Jefferson 1892 10:44) is meant to have a gentle echo in the phrase "court of common reason." Each part of the latter is intended to suggest something. First, "court" implies the controlled setting typical of a courtroom with unbiased rules governing the presentation of evidence and arguments. Second, "common" means the procedures of decision would be structured, using statistically valid subsets of the people, so as to be identical to what the people as a whole would, after due reflection, decide. Third, "reason" would serve as a reminder that the aim, as in an ordinary trial jury, is to have choices be made on the basis of a deliberative, and critical, reason. An ordinary trial jury is not supposed to decide as the community would decide ("lynch him"), but rather, as the community would decide, in a reasonable and deliberative temper, after hearing all the evidence and arguments relevant to the case. The use of upper case in "Court of Common Reason" is meant to follow established usage where a specific court in the judicial branch of government is being referred to ("Court of Common Pleas"), whereas "court of common reason" is a more general term that refers to function ("court of law"). Further, judges at present have a virtually unrestricted power to appoint advisory juries in trials (where there is no right to a jury) *and* they are just as free to disregard the jury's findings. The function of the advisory jury is to let the judge know what the community's considered judgment would be in a particular case. My use of the term "advisory jury," requires that it be a statistically valid representation that is unlike its usual use in courts of law (for details on the latter. see PPAJ 1987). However, the function remains the same, since the jury gives advice, and public officials are under no legal obligation to follow its findings. In eighteenth-century terminology, the institution is "republican," not purely "democratic." Naturally the institution might in various ways become more purely "democratic" — that is, the results would have direct consequences — if it becomes the people's considered judgment to make it so, and legislators subsequently agree.

The questions and problems that might come before advisory juries are almost endless: What kinds of taxes should the government impose? What constitutes malpractice liability for a practicing physician? What types of advertising are misleading? What should legislators earn? What ought the government require for safety in trains, planes, cars, or the environment in general? What penalties should there be for various criminal offenses? What constitutes "cruel and unusual punishments"? How much of our public resources should go into the exploration of space? What criteria should be used for legal immigration? To what degree should the government control guns and other weapons? When is eminent domain justified, and what is a fair determination of the price? What should be in the public — or private — sector? What sort of zeal is proper, and what improper, for prosecution and defense lawyers? What kinds of information can be kept secret from the public, and for how long? Under what conditions, if any, should abortion, infanticide, assisted suicide, or euthanasia be allowed? What is the social cost of smoking? Under what conditions, and in what way, should victims of crime be compensated? What criteria should be used in determining citizenship? What rights do suspected foreign terrorists have? How should the shape of congressional districts be determined? Are names given for legislation, such as "Fair Trade Act" or "Patriot Act," appropriate? How long should a copyright last? What are appropriate questions on a census? Who should receive a Presidential pardon?

Second-order questions could be used to reduce the likelihood that answers would be successfully manipulated by factions. Juries that answer these questions could be called *metajuries*. For example, a metajury could decide what issues are important enough to justify the time and expense of a deliberative decision by an advisory jury. After an issue has been chosen, a second metajury could be asked to approve the questions to be put to the advisory jury, who could then deliberate and decide the issue. Even those given the responsibility for presenting one or another side of an issue could often be determined by a competition rather than appointed by an authority. Consider a simplified example. Suppose there are seven applicants who want to present one side of an issue. Imagine that the Agency for Public Choice randomly chooses a twelve-hundred-person metajury, which is then randomly divided into one hundred subjuries. After all the applicants make their presentations, the subjuries discuss the relative persuasiveness of the seven proposals, and finally there is a secret vote — this time individually, not by subjuries — to determine the most persuasive candidate. Refinements of such a procedure could help achieve the aim of choosing proponents to argue before advisory jurors who have been *proven* the most persuasive for each side of an issue.

Random procedures should also be employed to reduce manipulation, as well as help regulate the operation of courts of common reason. Since their use in political contexts is often overlooked, a little background is appropriate. Although random procedures were initially used sacredly to discern the will of the gods or God (Plato 1937 2:519-20; *Proverbs* 16.33, *1 Samuel* 10:20-24, *Acts* 1:23-6), they were employed secularly for social choice at least as early as 487 B.C. in ancient Greece (Larson 1949 171, Plato 1955 282 and Aristotle 1984 2:2091, 2:2173). The ancient Hebrews may also have used them in a secular fashion: "The lot puts an end to disputes and decides between powerful contenders"(*Proverbs* 18:18). And this use is alive today in the House of Representatives, where members of equal seniority draw lots to determine office suites. Random methods have been extensively employed in American democracy, for example, in determining the winner of an election in the case of ties (Pennsylvania), the order of candidates on the ballot (California), the placement of party columns on the ballot (Idaho), the sample of names on petitions to be checked for validity (Florida), the selection of jurors (Connecticut), the order of simultaneously filed petitions (Illinois), the choice of which judge is to preside over a particular trial (New York), and the issuance of hunting permits (Minnesota). On a national level, the resolution of which of the first two senators from Alaska should be senior was settled by the toss of a silver dollar, and then another toss resolved who should first draw lots to decide the length of the terms. There are numerous reasons why random techniques are employed by democracies: promoting freedom by enlarging the pool of those who participate in governance, avoiding additional compulsory taxation by using voluntary lotteries, thwarting corruption and undermining political intrigue, supplying an unbiased means of deciding tied elections, settling disputes that might otherwise go on interminably, and providing a decision procedure when every other method would be viewed as unfair or would threaten democratic equality, as in issuing hunting permits or in drafting young men. A lottery in these latter cases achieves fairness and equality precisely because its outcome is arbitrary. Lotteries can also allow us to escape paradox. For example, in the voting paradox — where one-third of voters prefers A to B, and B to C; one-third prefers B to C and C to A; and one-third prefers C to A and A to B — the outcome is that a two-thirds of the voters prefer A to B, B to C and C to A. Randomly choosing the winner is the equitable solution. In general, the Court of Common Reason must determine where and when random methods should be used to promote public happiness in the body politic; and metajuries must likewise determine where they should be used in the Court's own procedures to frustrate those who would manipulate outcomes. Without integrity, politics, like science, is useless or dangerous.

It cannot be validly objected that the members of the advisory jury lack the knowledge to deal with issues that might reasonably be presented to them. Initially, a trial jury also lacks knowledge. The purpose of a fair trial is to make the jury knowledgeable — indeed, some trials take as long as a year to present the evidence on which the jury bases its decision. Much of this evidence is technical, such as that concerning the intricacies of the economic structure of an industry (in an antitrust trial) or the testimony of a physiologist (in a murder trial). The advisory jury would thus not decide questions of, say, malpractice liability for physicians *in vacuo*. On the contrary, the existing law would be carefully explained to the jury by judges. Furthermore, the clash of interests would be exhibited before them: lawyers representing victims could argue that present procedures are cruel, that they result in inadequate compensation, that doctors are very often sloppy or incompetent, and they could illustrate this in case after case. The members of the medical profession could argue that the number of malpractice suits is preposterous, that forcing doctors and nurses to look at every patient as a legal adversary results in many unnecessary tests, that the cost of malpractice insurance is pushing medical expenses out of sight, that unrelenting litigation is making the profession unattractive to the next generation. And they could illustrate this in case after case. Consumer groups could also give their arguments. And so on. The advisory jury could then decide hypothetical case after hypothetical case of malpractice, in a context where the clashes between insurance costs, on the one hand, and the plight of victims with their traditional legal rights to sue, on the other hand, are continually highlighted. If jurors set rewards too high they would know that their own insurance expenses (whether direct or indirect) would rise to amounts they deem unaffordable, if they set them too low they would know that victims (perhaps including themselves) would be left with inadequate funds, and little recourse against malpractice. On the basis of these advisory judgments, legislators could devise laws that best embody the informed values of the public on malpractice; judges and trial juries could be guided in making awards to victims; insurance companies could more accurately price their insurance; and victims could know when they were getting a fair deal according to the standards of the American people.

One plausible interpretation of the oldest law codes know to us — such as those associated with the names of Ur-Nammu, Shulgi, Lipit-Ishtar, and Hammurabi — is that they are not law codes in our sense; rather, they are declarations of what ideal justice is for many cases, and those cases should serve as guides to whomever makes judicial decisions. If this interpretation is correct, then, one could rightfully see the above use of hypothetical cases as an updating of a four-thousand-year-old practice, since judges and trial juries would be guided by the hypothetical cases. However, there is this difference, the cases for the Mesopotamians derive from the authority of the gods, whereas for us the cases derive from the authority of the people. The latter authority allows us to create an *evidence-based* politics that is *self-correcting*. In science, evidence is not restricted to experiences of everyday life, but includes precise observation, sophisticated equipment, and the use of computers in analysis of data (whose collection may depend on extensive historical research, as in evolutionary medicine). Experiments to ascertain the informed values and considered judgments of the American people would be similar. Determination in the face of difficulties must prevail if we are to create an impartial environment through which the deliberate sense of the community can be discovered. And once informed values and considered judgments are determined, great ingenuity will still be needed to find the best laws embodying those values and judgments. Even it were possible to automate the collection of evidence, and the formulation of laws, as is now possible in science, at least in some cases, it would take very substantial human work to pull this off in a practical way. Hence government officials would not be mere puppets; their work will be at least as difficult as the work of engineers, for the activity of politicians being guided by the deliberate choices of the people is comparable to the work of engineers being guided by the nature of the materials that they employ. Both activities require systematic observation and experiment, the use of technology, and an unflagging creativity; they require the discipline of persistent, hard, and often tedious or frustrating work. The physical experiments to test whether there is or was life on Mars were expensive, with thousands of hours of planning preceding any given experiment. The political experiments of American perfectionist democracy will have equally demanding requirements.

The thesis of Oliver Wendell Holmes, Jr. , "that the best test of truth is the power of the thought to get itself accepted in the competition of the market"(250 U.S. 616, 630 [1919]) can be properly applied to politics provided that the "market" has customers who are statistically representative of the people as a whole, that the relevant contentions are fairly heard, that there is adequate time for deliberation and reflection, and so forth. In this sense a command polity is no more necessary than a command economy. A court of common reason is an institution of distributed intelligence, a democratic marketplace whose values are not monetary, but moral and political. There is no abstract standard to determine whether the flavor of carrots or peaches has more aesthetic value, but an ordinary marketplace gives a concrete standard to compare, at a given time and place, their *economic* value. Similarly, one cannot compare abstractly the commercial claim to exploit a piece of government property for coal versus the conservationist claim that the land ought not to be disturbed. Yet a court of common reason enables us to compare concretely the *political* value of these claims at a given time and place. This comparison will involve not only a consideration of unanimous subjuries on each side of the question but, in addition, the pattern of vote trading used to get the unanimity when there is more than one issue presented at a given time. In fact the rules that govern vote trading should be specifically designed to reflect the complexity of agreement and disagreement among the participants. Votes on one issue could be traded for votes on another, but votes could not be exchanged for anything else (for example, money). Just as the law ought not to recognize contracts regarding slavery (because they violate the unalienable right of political freedom), so the procedures of a court of common reason ought not allow one to sell one's voting power for money (because this would violate the unalienable right of political equality). With such restrictions, an analysis of the pattern of vote trading will allow the strength of political interest in various topics to be measured. For example, if a person is willing to trade votes on any question for a vote on a particular one, then it is reasonable to conclude that the voter thinks that question is the most important being considered. Of course, *outside the jury room anonymity would be preserved*, but the pattern of vote trading could be recorded, processed by computers, and analyzed. For instance, on a given question it would be known, say, that eight people voted yes and one person voted yes four times (having traded votes three times on other questions to get that power). A minority should be able to control public policy on a given issue *provided that* the majority (on that issue) is willing to give them that power in exchange for the votes on other issues that are less important to that minority. Courts of Common Reason are the brain scanners of the body politic; they put information into the laser-sharp focus that is required to develop true excellence in democratic government. A politics of self-knowledge is thus an information science; it allows us to create a knowledge-based polity to complement our knowledge-based economy.

A skeptic might object that such standards are too exacting, that one should always keep in mind Aristotle's dictum that "it is the mark of an educated man to look for precision in each class of things just so far as the nature of the subject admits"(1984 2:1730). This is excellent advice, but how much precision does a subject allow? For example, natural science has achieved much more precision than Aristotle believed was possible (cf. Aristotle's words below, page 420). One can only know the limits of precision by vigorously and imaginatively testing those limits until bounds become evident. Even then, one should recognize that those bounds may be only temporary. The degree of precision possible for republican government — resting as it does on the "cool and deliberate sense of the community" — has increased greatly since the eighteenth century; the present limits of precision have scarcely been tested, much less reached. Aristotle's maxim should help us avoid a false exactitude, not serve as a balm for the unimaginative, or an excuse for the lazy to neglect attempts at greater precision than have hitherto been possible.

The skeptic might raise another objection by claiming that a court of common reason is impossible to construct. For example, the best known result in social choice theory (cf. Sen 1987) is Kenneth Arrow's theorem (cf. 1967 and 1987), which shows, according to the economist Paul Samuelson, that a "perfect democracy" is a "logical self-contradiction" (1966 4:938; see also 4:935-6, 3: 409-12, and Gardner 1974 120.). The philosopher Robert Paul Wolff states that Arrow has proven that inconsistency "infects virtually every method of social choice which can lay a reasonable claim to being called 'democratic'(1970 63). In my judgment such claims are refutable (see DeLong 1991), provided that one is very careful in analyzing the technical argument, in order to judge what has actually been proved, as against the claims so often made for the proof. Such an analysis shows, I believe, that the theorem has no serious implications for public policy. As Gordon Tullock put it: ". . . as far as I can see, almost all students in the field, including Arrow himself, simply disregarded his proof when they turned to policy matters"(1979 27).

The skeptic might also claim that there are insurmountable practical problems in trying to construct courts of common reason. We lack completely adequate models for group decision involving ordinary voting, and we are in even worse shape with regard to group decision founded on the deliberate sense of the people. Furthermore, there are psychological problems of how to motivate citizens to participate, and political problems in getting Congress to authorize the necessary research and tests. Yet any revolutionary undertaking in human affairs generates skeptics — sometimes very knowledgeable skeptics — who charge that the undertaking is either impossible or impractical. For example, ENIAC, the breakthrough device that marked the beginning of the computer industry in this country, was largely and actively opposed by members of the scientific elite, including Vannevar Bush of MIT and George Robert Stibitz of Bell Labs. Even after ENIAC was operational—it completed its first major computation in December of 1945—there were plenty of distinguished skeptics. As late as 1947, for example, Howard Aiken of Harvard reportedly said that "there will never be enough problems, enough work for more than one or two of these computers"(Stern, Nancy 1981 111). American democracy likewise produced its own distinguished skeptics. Jeremy Bentham thought the American revolutionists had "out done the utmost extravagance of /all former/ fanatics"(1968 1:341-43); he believed the Declaration of Independence to be "a hodge-podge of confusion and absurdity"(1859 10:63). Nor was Bentham alone. Even though the Constitution had already been in force for over forty years, Hegel, perhaps misled by a tradition that includes Plato, Montesquieu, and Rousseau, denied that the example of America "proves that republican states are possible on a large scale"(1975 169, slavery was here not an issue).

The source of these skeptical errors is a failure of self-examination—the skeptics do not see that their experience and convictions might cripple their imagination as to the feasibility or

importance of some major new undertaking. Francis Bacon pointed
out that "Men's anticipations of the new are fashioned on the model of
the old. The old governs their imagination. Yet this is a completely
fallacious pattern of thought. There is no universal law that
discoveries fetched up from the source and fount of things must flow
down to us along familiar channels"(Farrington 1964 96). ENIAC
involved such a novel blend of so many disciplines—mathematical
logic, physics, chemistry, electronics, and so forth—that the skeptics
were in no position to claim either that it would not work or, if it did
work, that it would not be useful. In retrospect, their comments seem
quite foolish. The same holds true for the formation of the American
government, which involved novelties of geography, constitutional
conventions, written constitutions, explicit bills of rights, federalism,
and so forth. Could Bentham have been more wrong in calling
American revolutionists "fanatics"? Or Hegel more wrong about the
possibility of large republican states? Distrust of uncritical skepticism
is as wise as distrust of uncritical belief. Particularly when faced with
a fundamentally new undertaking, it is important to ask in what respect
one's own experience and education might be misleading. Suppose
that in 1950 a group of scientists wrote a joint paper whose purpose
was to describe a trip to the moon. They would realize that their
description could not be accurate because a detailed description would
depend on future experiments and theoretical results that they could
not anticipate. What they could do is to say something like this: "The
critics of a manned moon mission complain that it is not possible, that
it is not hardheaded science, that the technology is a pie-in-the-sky.
This criticism is cheap because although the critics may be right, *they
are in no position to know the true difficulty of the problems*. They
may also be wrong. Our claim is not that the description we have
given of the moon trip is accurate in detail. Rather the purpose of the
description is to create a *program* to encourage the investments, the
theoretical work, and the experiments that are needed to test whether
the trip is feasible." These same considerations apply to courts of
common reason. *The description of courts of common reason given
here is a first approximation that ought to be revised in light of
extensive experiments and theoretical reflection.* We neither know
enough to declare that such courts are impossible or impractical, nor
enough to produce an exact description of versions that would work
well. A court of common reason involves such a fresh blend of logic,
philosophy, political science, rhetoric, psychology, social choice
theory, law, statistics, and so forth, that it is difficult to justify initial

skepticism with solid evidence and reasoning. Possible paradigm shifts can seldom be predicted ahead of time, even by the most knowledgeable. My favorite illustration of this point comes from a speech given by Wilbur Wright on November 5, 1908: "I confess that, in 1901, I said to my brother Orville that men would not fly for fifty years. Two years later, we ourselves were making flights"(2001 2:934-35). The only way to find out whether a revolutionary technology—such as an airplane, a computer, or a court of common reason—is actually possible is to make imaginative, persistent attempts to create and use it. Here the risk of complete failure is always high. The reason we should nevertheless take that risk is democratic integrity, for if we do not create institutions that will reliably reveal "the cool and deliberate sense of the community," we cannot be sure that the reason of the public will "ultimately prevail over the views of its rulers." Hence we can never achieve that continuing democratic excellence which alone would redeem the political ideals of the American revolution.

In the latter half of the seventeenth century Newton worked out a theory of artificial satellites, but it was not until 300 years later that we had the disciplines and technology to produce a sophisticated embodiment of his theory. In the same period John Locke worked out a theory of government. A hundred years later the American revolutionists tried to embody Locke's theory in their governments. Jefferson's ward proposal was intended to further improve that embodiment. Unfortunately, his proposal was incomplete, not much more than a sketch. However, we now have the disciplines and technology to bring about its refined fulfillment. Of course, as in the development of space exploration by the National Aeronautics and Space Administration, prudence would dictate extreme care; any actual political use of a Court of Common Reason would be preceded by feasibility studies, extensive testing on experimental groups, and actual trials with small and then large organizations, such as churches or unions. Politically one could then go from the small to the large, from villages to towns to counties to states to the national government. This plan would have to deal with many unknowns. Thus it may be that creating reasonable rules for voting in a court of common reason is like creating projections of a global map of the earth onto a flat piece of paper. Every way of doing it distorts something. But this does not mean that for any particular purpose there is not a good projection — only that there is no universally satisfactory projection. The Founders themselves chose a number of ways of electing officials, one for members of the House, another for Senators, another for the

President. It is possible that the best democratic decision might involve multiple kinds of voting with totals arrived at in different ways. We also need experiments, for example, to determine the optimal size of subjuries for a given purpose, or to learn how to overcome psychological problems concerning the capacity of people for jury work, such as the arrangements that will best ensure the views of shy people are fairly represented. Again, what kinds of instructions should be given to advisory juries? How, in practice, can the passions that interfere with deliberative reason, such as racial, sexual, or ethnic prejudice, be minimized or checked, while at the same time strengthening the passions that support it, such as those for honesty, truth, and justice? The quality of a jury's deliberation depends on a spirit of high morale and seriousness. How can this spirit be created and maintained? Would a looser structure sometimes work better than the one I have described for courts of common reason? Again, suppose each of three people have a strong preference for one restaurant, but each falsely believes the other two want to go to another restaurant; consequently, out of polite deference, each fails to mention their own desire, and they all end up, each secretly unhappy, at the second restaurant. In this case, the "public happiness" would require expressing a "selfish" desire. So how, in courts of common reason, can expression and discretion, self-love and patriotism, be put into that exquisite balance that will best promote the public happiness?

In general, then, it does not take much imagination to see that extensive empirical and theoretical work should be performed before any serious political decision is made using courts of common reason. Nevertheless is it not about time that we use America's enormously powerful scientific and managerial capabilities, not just for defense, or space exploration, or commercial development, but for strengthening the democratic process itself? The resources available are enormous. In addition to large numbers of colleges and universities, there are many other organizations that have the necessary expertise such as IBM, Microsoft, Google, A. C. Nielsen, the American Institute of Public Opinion (Gallup), the Educational Testing Service, the American Bar Association, the Library of Congress, and the Census Bureau. This expertise would enable protocols to be created for various elements in courts of common reason: protocols for honesty (How do you minimize the harmful effects from falsification of preferences? (cf. Kuran 1995)), protocols for intelligence (How do you organize jurors to maximize their collective intelligence?), protocols for preparation (What kind of experiences should be provided, and what kind of tests must be passed, before an advisory jury be deemed ready for its job?), protocols for passion (How, in practice, can those feelings and emotions favorable to deliberation in the cause of public happiness be increased?), protocols for independent confirmation (How can different schemes of voting, differently phrased questions, different representative sets of jurors, be best used to increase confidence in the results?), protocols for dealing with errors (How can one make the courts self-correcting?), and so on. Protocols for interpretation of results might even be added, such as using the technique of "hiding the answer"(Glanz 2000) to undermine biased analyses. All these protocols and many more would have to be produced so that results would be persuasive to a skeptical world.

In this effort we might get help from nature itself. Thus just as it was found that studying dolphins is useful in designing a submarine, or snake fangs in designing a hypodermic needle, or geckos and mussels in designing adhesive tape, so perhaps studying such things as brains, self-regulating ecological systems, or synthetic biological creatures might be useful in designing self-government. Such biomimicry might extend to evolution itself. Darwin believed he found the "simple way by which species become exquisitely adapted to various ends"(1987a 2). Let us reflect on this "simple way" with regard to a worry of John Adams: "A perfect constitution of government is so delicate an instrument that I fear no nation will ever have an ear sufficiently exquisite to keep it always in tune"(1954 Reel 124 215). Since evolution, whether natural, or simulated on a computer, can produce objects of transcendent beauty, subtlety, economy, and functionality, might it not be prudent to use Darwin's "simple way" to design that exquisite ear to regulate our political and social lives? That is, we could create a fierce competition among ideas in the Court of Common Reason in order to prevent the ruthless competition among people that has been so characteristic of human history and prehistory. Let me illustrate using a simplified thought experiment. Suppose that public policy must be decided on topic X. X might be taxation, or welfare, or drugs. Now imagine that eight individuals or organizations each submit a different proposed policy for X to the Court of Common Reason. After discussing all the proposals, the jurors vote and reject one of them in the first round (the functional equivalent of "natural selection"). Now the sponsors of the remaining seven proposals examine what has been accepted and rejected, and then they may modify their proposals, if they wish, for submission to the second round (the functional equivalent of "descent with modification"). The process continues for six more rounds when there will be just one surviving proposal, the political outcome of successive designs generated through intelligent variation by proposers, and successive choices generated through deliberate selection by the people. (Biological outcomes, *in sharp contrast*, are the produced by successive designs generated through random variation and natural selection.) The authors of the winning proposal would be handsomely rewarded, and their proposal would become the advisory jury's recommendation for the public policy on X. In principle, there is no need for a special creation of policy by a political authority whenever this *democratic evolutionary paradigm* is available to the people. It really is a kind of a "genetic algorithm" for humans analogous in effect to genetic algorithms for computers. In the paradigm, the selection is always democratic, but the creation of variations need not be (as in our example where the proposers were not necessarily democratically chosen or organized). The democratic evolutionary paradigm might be especially useful on issues where the people are quite passionate and divided, such as abortion, or which American history textbook to adopt in a school district. Just as biological evolution in nature produces highly surprising but successful animals (for instance, the platypus), so the democratic evolutionary paradigm, assuming it could be rendered practical, might generate astonishing social policy that nevertheless has informed and overwhelming support. For services and physical things, the superiority of a well-designed marketplace rests with its superiority in creating and distributing economic information, which itself creates the conditions for continual innovation; well-designed courts of common reason have the same superiority in the moral and political realm. The opportunities to enhance public happiness by creating evolutionary arenas favorable to entrepreneurial democrats seems limitless.

Again, we might try to copy natural evolution by having new and favorable ideas spread throughout an advisory jury the way a new and favorable gene spreads through successive generations of living things. New ideas would be thought of as "mutations," and most of them would quickly perish in the intense competition. But occasionally one will prove robust enough to spread throughout the advisory jury. To illustrate again with a simplistic example, suppose there are nine people — A, B, C, D, E, F, G, H, I — in an advisory jury, where each subjury has three persons. They are given a tricky mathematical problem where only one juror (out of the nine) has a correct analysis of the problem. Now imagine that we shuffle jurors so that in four rounds of deliberating every person could deliberate with every other person and yet never deliberate with any person twice: First round (ABC, DEF, GHI), second (ADG, BEH, CFI), third (AEI, BDI, CDH), fourth (AFH, BFG, CGE). The one juror's correct analysis could thus spread (propagation of the favorable "gene") before the final vote, which would now be unanimous and right (3-0), instead of having a majority of wrong subjuries (2-1), had there been no deliberating rounds. Note that increasing the diversity of jurors makes it more likely that a favorable idea will arise. Of course, whether any idea is really favorable for public happiness only subsequent experience can determine. It is certainly worth investigating whether the idea of biological evolution and its mathematics, as applied to plants and animals, may be relevant to the idea of democratic evolution and its mathematics, as applied in courts of common reason.

In practice there will be many complications compared to my idealized evolutionary examples. How could a large number of proposals be handled in an actual case where there are constraints of time and money? How could parallel deliberations speed up the process? What are the optimal number of alternatives to offer subjurors, so they do not become frustrated by too few choices, or overwhelmed by too many? There may be jurors who are sterile (right, but incapable of convincing anyone else), or dogmatic (no discussion will change their minds), or amenable (always trying to vote with the majority), or rebellious (always creating or trying to vote with the minority), or apathetic (whose votes approximate randomness), or true deliberators (whose final judgment is determined by their own deliberate sense). Recognizing these and other complications, the problem is to devise arrangements that would work well in actual applications. Traditionally, deliberation itself was a requirement meant to kill off unfavorable ideas, as were the additional requirements of being cool and unanimous. Our attempt here is to refine those requirements by combining them with a democratic selection applied to successive intelligent designs. (Perhaps one might even apply the democratic evolutionary paradigm to itself and thereby generate more realistic democratic procedures for political purposes.) In nature the evolutionary principle is mindless and brutal, in courts of common reason it is mindful and caring; *ideas* are subjected to a repeated, evolutionary competition so that only the fittest survives, fittest, that is, at promoting the flourishing of a free and independent people. That is why a politics of self-knowledge is necessary, for a people, in order to be free and independent, must ultimately control all government. Yet to do that, they need, through deliberative soul-searching, to know their own minds, feelings, and humanity. Then, by constantly improving their deliberative skill, and the arrangements used to express their deliberate sense, they create the conditions for that continuing political excellence that alone can reliably protect the human animal against itself.

The Agency for Public Choice could increase civility in American life by providing a peaceful and rational environment for settling political controversies. This conception should not be confused with that form of participatory democracy, in which every citizen is involved in every decision. Besides being a colossal waste of time and money, participatory democracy, in this sense, is not a good form of government; it is comparable to having all decisions about the body be conscious so that, for example, deciding to exercise would require a further conscious choice to produce adrenalin. One should not become a slave to politics. If the government is efficient and responsive, all the things necessary for a decision of the advisory jury to be carried out will be forthcoming. In an ideal democratic society the people would participate in government only to the extent that such participation is a good for them, but that participation, whether small or large, would also be sufficient for public policy to be in harmony with their informed values. Unlike many participatory proposals, American perfectionist democracy would relentlessly give efficiency a high priority so as not to undermine the pursuit of happiness of the people in other respects.

For example, after much experience, it might often be possible to estimate when the deliberate sense of the people is going to differ from their pre-deliberate sense. In cases where the probability of difference is small, ordinary polls or futures markets, such as the Iowa Electronic Markets, might indirectly, but reliably, reveal their deliberate sense. It might also be possible in some cases to simulate deliberation on computers. Thus, jurors could answer a large number of questions about themselves with, of course, strict safeguards to protect privacy. Included could be carefully chosen hypothetical questions concerning legal or political issues. Then their answers could be used to generate a computing *virtual twin* for each juror. Evolutionary programs might be developed that would simulate deliberation among virtual jurors so that, for some questions, it might be possible to predict accurately what the deliberate sense of the people would be without the people actually deliberating. Computer simulations would thus greatly augment our moral powers when united with courts of common reason. If this approach were successful over many (but not necessarily all) issues, it might be possible to formulate a (partial) mathematical model of the changing legal or political character of the American people. (For example, perhaps eventually 90% of legal issues, whether for crimes or suits, could be satisfactorily be resolved using virtual trials.) Here we would be using highly efficient means that were inconceivable before the invention of computers and simulation software. We would be engineering a hybrid democracy that combines virtual, digital democracy, using computer simulations, with an actual, analog democracy, using human deliberations. We could say: "As the virtual people calculate and the actual people deliberate, so the legal and political world will be." This is a paraphrase of Leibniz: "As God calculates and thinks, so the universe will be"(1960 7:191, my translation). I paraphrased Leibniz here to show that hybrid democracy would be fully consistent with the revolutionary idea that, provided they do not violate universal morality, the people rightfully have God-like authority in establishing and maintaining the state. The "people in mass," Jefferson said, "are inherently independent of all but moral law"(1903 15:214). Perhaps over the years we could learn how to indirectly determine the common reason of society with less effort and more good effects than initially could reasonably have been thought possible. Of course, it would be up to the people to periodically decide, in actual second-order decisions by metajuries, what first-order decisions should be virtual, what actual, and eventually, what decisions, if any, should be dictatorial, rather than merely advisory. Nevertheless these speculations at least show the conclusion that *government based on courts of common reason must be inefficient* can at present only be derived by an argument from ignorance. Without an effort comparable to that put into the development of the airplane or the computer — both of which were also called inefficient, even impossible — we cannot with plausibility declare that Jefferson's idea of wards, adopted to the science and technology of the twenty-first century, must be a failure in practice. With that effort, the adaptation might be so successful as to become that century's defining technology.

Jefferson was himself well aware that public service should have limits:

> It were contrary to feeling & indeed ridiculous to suppose that a man has less right in himself than one of his neighbors or indeed all of them put together. This would be slavery & not that liberty which the bill of rights has made inviolable and for the preservation of which our government has been charged. Nothing

could so completely divest us of that liberty as the establishment of the opinion that the state has a *perpetual* right to the services of all it's members. (1892 3:58-9)

Hence the amount of time it is reasonable to ask people to spend on jury duty would be determined by the people themselves through metajuries. These are the limits within which designers must work. Who says we cannot be as clever at saving human energy in making deliberative decisions, as nature has been in saving psychic energy in the brain, or we have been in saving physical energy by using robots? In general, the Court of Common Reason is meant to be have an evolutionary design so that new empirical or theoretical knowledge will lead to improvements in its operation.

No democrat could be against finding out the informed preferences of the people if that could be achieved with little effort or cost. The argument, like the ones about getting moon rocks or sending a manned mission to Mars, is really about practicality, and the use of resources. In any age bad governments are an evil, in an age capable of sophisticated military technology they can become substantial threats to humanity as a whole. Hence the creation of viable courts of common reason is as urgent as any present large-scale scientific initiative. The problems of their construction ought to inspire us to produce ingenious solutions, rather than serve as an excuse for inaction. Nevertheless, there is something bold and extravagant in the very attempt to produce responsible decisions on such a scale, and in such detail. But is this goal any more bold than trying to create a theory of everything (TOE) in physics, or are the difficulties any more extravagant than those associated with space travel? Jefferson, given the meager resources available in his time, conceived of the possibility of finding "the genuine sense of the people on any required point"(above, page 161). Should we not be able to imagine that same possibility, given the enormous resources at our disposal? In his first inaugural address Lincoln said: "A majority, held in restraint by constitutional checks, and limitations, and always changing easily, with deliberate changes of popular opinions and sentiments, is the only true sovereign of a free people"(1953 4:268). But, without courts of common reason, or their functional equivalent, "deliberate changes of popular opinions and sentiments" will even today be inscrutable on most issues, unnecessarily compromising the sovereignty of the people.

The Court of Common Reason will be working well when it is not uncommon for there to be, through civil and reasoned debate, a triumph of some point of view over that initially preferred. The description given in Madison's notes on the Constitutional Convention ought, in this regard, to apply to the members of the advisory jury: "Disinterestedness & candor demonstrated by mutual concessions, & frequent changes of opinion . . . Few who did not change in the progress of discussions the opinions on important points which they carried into the Convention . . . Few who, at the close of the Convention, were not ready to admit this change as the enlightening effect of the discussions "(Farrand 1937 3:455). The system of advisory subjuries should be designed as far as possible to promote the "enlightening effect of the discussion," that is, a desire for a jointly agreed upon answer that is the result of listening and learning from other members of the subjury. This is, of course, a republican virtue *par excellence*. The Court will be an exhibition of value conflict and resolution. It should reveal the common sense, empathy, and humanity of the American people. Perhaps by studying the Court we could better understand the passions for truth, equality, and justice, and how best to overcome prejudice, faction, and fanaticism. Any democratic government needs procedures for finding out the values and judgments of the people so that it may be truly representative. Elected officials already have numerous ways: ordinary polling, listening to complaints of citizens, weekend trips to visit constituents, hearings on special topics, and the like. Yet these relatively easy methods do not enable officials to reliably know the informed values and considered judgments of the citizens in the detail necessary for true political excellence. Such knowledge requires courts of common reason that should be designed, as far as possible, to embody every epistemological virtue and to be shorn of every epistemological vice. Democrats cannot take their epistemological ease.

Plato believed that with a little observation and some empathy, he could know what the planets — which he thought of as alive — "want to do"(1957 112). Of course, Plato was naive: we now know that knowledge of the planets is enormously expensive; it requires the cooperative efforts of thousands of individuals from many disciplines (physics, astronomy, geology, etc.) as well as a sophisticated technology (telescopes, spectroscopes, rockets, etc.). We are as naive about the American people, as Plato was about the planets, if we think we can know what the American people really want by a little observation and a little empathy. If we wish to know their informed values and considered judgments, if we wish to know what responsible decisions they would make on some issue, we need courts of common reason whose design and operation would also require the cooperative

efforts of thousands of individuals from many disciplines. There is
no easy or inexpensive way to know those values or judgments, any
more than there is an easy or inexpensive way to know whether there
is, or was, life on Mars. The Mariner mission and the Viking probe
made possible the first detailed photographs of Mars; similarly, courts
of common reason can make possible the first detailed "photographs"
of the distributed intelligence and character of the American people.

In fact, courts of common reason might reveal unexpected
possibilities for knowledge. Photography, for example, was invented
to duplicate vision, but it eventually extended vision by the use of slow
motion, time-lapse exposures, stroboscopic lighting, infrared
illumination, and so forth. Some photographs do not reveal light but
temperature, as in computer enhanced pictures from satellites showing
various surface temperatures of the earth. Photographs of ourselves
as children, or of the earth from outer space, have helped change the
sense we have of ourselves. Imaginative use of courts of common
reason might have similar effects. Consider racism in America.
Suppose an advisory jury is formed consisting of people of one race.
Operating as usual, the jury answers a number of political questions.
In the same time frame, a second advisory jury is formed consisting of
people of a different race. The members answer the same questions.
A set of issues on which the two races differ is thereby identified.
Then the two advisory juries are merged into one hybrid jury, where
each subjury consists of six people from the first group and six from
the second. The issues on which the two races differ are then
presented simultaneously, and compromises are made via vote trading
within each subjury. The decisions of the hybrid jury, if approved by
the Court of Common Reason, and Congress, would resolve the
political issues for a given time in the same sense in which an ordinary
election resolves who will serve for a given time. Hybrid juries would
help create a "more perfect Union." After all the centuries of conflict
between the races, or between the sexes or social classes, would it not
be prudent and wise to collect solid evidence as to where, after due
deliberation and reflection, these groups actually differ from one
another, and then let the members of the groups themselves, rather
than their leaders, make any necessary compromises? Of course, all
this is expensive but suppose, for the sake of argument, that many
years ago a hybrid jury in Los Angeles had been set up that cost a
substantial sum to construct and maintain. If, as a result, there were no
riots following the Rodney King decision, or subsequent bitterness
about it, might not such sums be rightly judged to have been well

spent? Another example: The speed and maneuverability of planes in dogfights can be boosted by purposely introducing some instabilities that are then directly managed by computers to ensure the safety of the flight; analogously, the agility of the federal government in crises might be increased by purposely allowing violation of some laws or entrenched practices that could then be directly managed by courts of common reason to ensure the rights of the people are maintained. Perhaps in time courts of common reason will have advantages that at present we cannot even imagine, much less exploit (cf. Bacon's words at 2004 65 (2)). None of the early pioneers in computers thought they would be used for word processing,, guiding rockets, or the Internet.

Jefferson believed that through wards "the voice of the whole people would be . . . fairly, fully, and peaceably expressed, discussed, and decided by the common reason of the society"(1892 10:44). The wards, among other things, were meant to ensure that representatives of the people actually represented them. In Jefferson's words:

> [Wards] will be pure and elementary republics, the sum of all which, taken together, compose the State, and will make of the whole a true democracy as to the business of the wards, which is that of nearest and daily concern. The affairs of the larger sections, of counties, of States, and of the Union, not admitting personal transaction by the people, will be delegated to agents elected by themselves; and representation will thus be substituted, where personal action becomes impracticable. Yet, even over these representative organs, should they become corrupt and perverted, the division into wards constituting the people, in their wards, a regularly organized power, enables them by that organization to crush, regularly and peaceably, the usurpations of their unfaithful agents, and rescues them from the dreadful necessity of doing it insurrectionally. In this way we shall be as republican as a large society can be; and secure the continuance of purity in our government, by the salutary, peaceable, and regular control of the people. No other depositories of power have ever yet been found, which did not end in converting to their own profit the earnings of those committed to their charge. (1892 10:45)

In this spirit, consider how courts of common reason might make Senators more responsible to the people. Near the end of a Senator's term, a state advisory jury would hear arguments for and against the job he or she was doing. The jury would give a considered judgment as to what the Senator was doing well and what poorly. Then the jury would make an overall evaluation of his or her term of office. In particular, the state jury could see videos of previous campaigns, determine the degree to which promises had been kept, and judge how well the Senator had represented the long-range interests of the people. The jury would then answer the question: Has this person, openly or secretly, betrayed the public trust? If the answer is "yes," then, mimicking part of the Athenian practice of ostracism, the person would be ineligible to be a future candidate for any public office whatsoever. In this era of high infidelity to the public trust, do not the people need, more than ever, an institution that, on a deliberative basis, can "crush, regularly and peaceably, the usurpations of their unfaithful agents"? A constant possibility of political ostracism might bring more rectitude to public affairs than all the rules of ethics or term limits that have ever been, or will be, proposed. Further, a federal Court of Common Reason could also review the Senator's term. It could answer the question: Has the Senator's zeal for representing the interest of the state led him or her to violate the national interest? Again, the threat of ostracism would put an end to pork, indeed, federal reviews of this sort, would give an on-going, operational definition of pork.

By fully exploiting the advisory jury, the political art is likely to be transformed in a way that can be made clear by an analogy. In times past, physicians — however talented and well-intentioned — were severely handicapped because (among other things) their diagnostic techniques were crude and they very often had only vague information about the state of the body. The advent of blood analysis, biopsies, x-rays, echocardiography, CT, MRI, and PET scans, transformed medicine, enabling physicians to diagnose and often cure disease with hitherto unheard-of success. Perhaps our political leaders could likewise have hitherto unheard-of success in moderating or eliminating injustice, were their knowledge of the body politic greatly improved. It has been commonplace for Americans, when traveling to some foreign undeveloped country, to marvel at the way tradition inhibits the application of scientific means to improve their lives. A visitor to this country might possess the same wonderment with regard to our failure to know the common reason of society. This refusal to fully exploit science and technology to improve our political knowledge is as foolish as the refusal to use it to improve medical knowledge. A crude dentistry caused George Washington to suffer greatly, but we do not have to likewise suffer. Washington also suffered from a crude politics: It is only rarely that he could find out what the people truly wanted. Thus, near the end of his life he said: ". . . it always has been, and will continue to be, my earnest desire to learn, and to comply, as far as is consistent, with the public sentiment; but it is on *great* occasions *only*, and after time has been given for cool and deliberate reflection, that the *real* voice of the people can be known"(1931 35:31-2). Today political leaders are in the same position as Washington: they can reliably know the "*real* voice of the people" only on infrequent occasions. But we have much less excuse for our ignorance: as science and technology enables us to do things medically that were closed to the Founders (John Adams also had embarrassingly bad teeth), so the growth of knowledge since the eighteenth century might enable us to routinely decipher the "*real* voice of the people." The Court of Common Reason is a political technology that uses representative government in the statistical sense (that is, the jurors' choices mirror what the people as a whole would choose) to enhance representative government in the agent sense (that is, elected officials who try to act in the interests of the people). With the Court, legislators could better design the political shoe because they would know with much greater accuracy the size and shape of the political foot, and where, for a given shoe, it is likely to pinch. "The excellence of every government," Jefferson states, "is its adaptation to the state of those to be governed by it"(1892 10:22; cf. 15:101; cf. Montesquieu 1989 8; Hamilton 1961 22:404). The Court makes possible the achievement of Jefferson's ergonomic government to a new and higher degree of excellence appropriate to the twenty-first century. Avoidance self-deception would be impossible, and rationalizing self-deception would be made less likely, by the deliberative structure of the Court, a structure that emphasizes honesty, integrity, reason, empathy, and self-knowledge.

For a state to fulfill its function, Aristotle tells us, "there must be a power of deciding what is for the public interest"(1984 2:2108). American perfectionist democracy gives us, for the first time in human history, a reliable way of defining — and redefining — the meaning of that phrase. For instance, the Court could limit the power of special interest groups that lobby Congress. Typically each group claims that its proposed legislation is in the public interest. Many of these claims are no doubt false, but which ones are, in fact, true? An appropriate advisory jury would enable legislators to get an authoritative answer and thus be in a better position to resist unjustified political pressure. We must exercise care here. The phrase "public interest" is often used to create the illusion of unity, or as a synonym for what the speaker approves. The phrase has a legitimate use, but the reality to which it refers is complex. For example, just as a person has an interest in some things and none in others, so the public interest admits of degrees: it is strong in some areas (say, terrorism) and absent in others (say, whether I write with my right or left hand).

Furthermore, there are many "publics" (ethnic groups, college students, union members, farmers, stockholders, welfare recipients, etc.) that are often at odds, and their interest is subject to change — sometimes to rapid change. A detailed and dynamic description of the public interest is perhaps as difficult and involved as a detailed and dynamic description of the earth's weather and climate. The Court of Common Reason is an institution specifically designed to deal with this enormous complexity.

We should note that decisions of the Court of Common Reason are not at all comparable to Rousseau's *general will*. That will "cannot pass judgment on either a man or a fact"(1978 63). The advisory juries can. The general will is "always right"(61). Advisory juries can make mistakes. The common reason of society is meticulously evidence-based and operationally defined, the general will is not. Furthermore, Rousseau's political theory is very far from that presupposed by the American revolution. Rousseau claims that one must totally alienate "all" rights to join a social contract (53), that the "social compact gives the body politic absolute power over all its members"(62), that "the people cannot be represented in the legislative power"(103), that "the instant a people chooses representatives, it is no longer free"(103), that censorship is necessary (123-24), that printing ought to be banned (1964 61), that one cannot be "a good citizen or a faithful subject" if one denies belief in God and an afterlife (1978 130-1), that "the larger the State grows, the less freedom there is"(80), that "one should forbid with care any machine and any invention that can shorten labor, spare manpower, and produce the same effect with less difficulty"(143). Finally, consider the contrasting attitudes toward humanity between American intellectual leaders and Rousseau: Adams says, "Let us see delineated before us, the true map of man. Let us hear the dignity of his nature, and the noble rank he holds among the works of God"(above, page 28). Jefferson says, "I am among those who think well of the human character generally" and James Wilson says, "It is the glorious destiny of man to be always progressive"(both below, page 287). But Rousseau says, "I have no liking for the world. . . . . Mankind disgusts me"(Boswell 1953 223-4). Thus, to apply the term "general will," which is embedded Rousseau's protototalitarian ethos, to the decisions of the Court of Common Reason, which is embedded in spirit of 1776, is to display gross misunderstanding.

We now turn to a paradox that has puzzled so many. How is it possible that we can create such magnificence in science and technology while we create such ugliness in politics? Who would not be pleased to have been the first to discover relativity, or the genetic code? Who would not be pleased to have invented the pocket calculator, or xerography? On the other hand, what sensitive and thoughtful individual would not be embarrassed to have been responsible for our tax laws? Or our insurance regulations? Or our penal codes? What made the theory of relativity or the pocket calculator possible was a revolution in science and technology that began in earnest in the sixteenth century. That revolution consisted in a spreading belief that observation, and reflection thereon, were not enough to determine the truth about nature. As Francis Bacon put it, "the nature of things shows itself more openly under the vexations of art than in its natural freedom"(2004 39). To understand nature, one must approach it with questions, and then create an artificial environment in which nature is "forced" to yield answers. This artificial environment is called an experiment, and without experiments we could not have created our magnificent science and technology. Today, we need a Jeffersonian revolution in politics equivalent to the Baconian revolution in science. At present we empathize with the American people, the way Plato did with the planets. Or we consult the experts about them, the way that Scholastics consulted the ancient texts. Or we poll them. But we seldom experiment to find out their deliberate sense, and we never, never experiment to find it out at the greatest level of exactitude possible in the twenty-first century. Until we systematically do the latter, we will not have excellence in politics comparable to the excellence we have achieved in science and technology. As the scientist needs experiments in a laboratory to discover the true laws of nature, so the politician needs experiments in courts of common reason to discover the best laws for society.

Our scientific practice is superior to our legal practice. If we wish to develop empirical knowledge, we must deal with *hypothetical* cases: If gravity were the only force acting on a falling body, what would happen? If the acceleration could be measured, what would its numerical value be? Galileo devised experiments to "force" nature to answer such questions and thereby was able to understand the acceleration of falling objects precisely, and in a hitherto unrealized general fashion. Of course, a leaf falling in air, for example, does not obey Galileo's equation (since other forces are involved). Nevertheless knowledge of the hypothetical cases concerning gravity is an indispensable component of understanding the falling leaf. Similarly, to achieve excellence in democracy comparable to that achieved in science, one must ask hypothetical questions and try to answer them experimentally. For example, in actual cases of medical malpractice, the unknowns can be difficult, if not impossible, to know: What actually occurred? What were the motivations of the people involved? To what extent was the outcome of an honest error? And so forth. Experiments in the Court of Common Reason could focus on hypothetical cases that would isolate the various factors. Thus an advisory jury might be presented with two hypothetical cases that are identical except that in the first there is an honest error, and the second there is irresponsible negligence. After considering a variety of such cases, an advisory jury could choose, using a democratic evolutionary paradigm, a scheme of fines and punishments for malpractice that they judged was fair and just overall. The job of the trial jury would then be to decide, after hearing prosecution and defense arguments, which hypothetical case was closest to the actual case before them. Understanding the hypothetical case, and considering actual case in its terms, the trial jurors would be in a better position to achieve a higher degree of precision in their job of representing all of the people. Trial juries are often criticized for the amounts they award (both large and small), and their decisions frequently overturned, but no great effort has been expended on changing the trial system to increase the probability that awards will be made in accordance with the informed values of the American people.   Drawing on the outcome of experiments in the Court of Common Reason dealing with hypothetical cases, trial juries could operate with more ease and justice, judges could have authoritative guidance in sentencing, and the district attorneys could plea bargain (or not) with greater assurance that they were upholding the public trust. In a sense what we are talking about is a new birth of common law based not on precedents set by judges, but on precedents set by the people. The earlier and traditional sense was well expressed by Edward Coke: "For reason is the life of the Law, nay the common Law it selfe is nothing else but reason, which is to be understood of an Artificial perfection of reason, gotten by long study, observation, and experience, and not of every mans natural reason, for Nemo nascitur artifex [No person is born an expert.]."(1670 97b). The new sense of common law also requires an "Artificial perfection of reason," but not the reason of the "grave and learned men" that Coke had in mind, but the common reason of the people that Jefferson had in mind (cf. also the words of Marcus Aurelius below, page 510). Trial juries would thus be limited by the precedents set by the Court of Common Reason, which would represent the highest artificial perfection of common reason achievable at a given time. However, the Court itself, as a statistically valid representation of all the people, would be free to change those precedents any time its members judged a modification to be favorable for the public happiness.

The derivation of the just powers of government from the authority of the people is comparable to the derivation of the laws of nature from the authority of observed phenomena. In natural science the derivation consists in the creative process of devising hypotheses, imagining thought experiments, testing by actual observation and demonstration, discarding, revising or refining the hypotheses, testing again, and having results independently verified. This process continues until a theory is arrived at that is aesthetically satisfying, accounts for experience, and provides a framework for the discovery of new scientific truths. The theory can later be upset by fresh reflections, the introduction of novel aesthetic standards, observations or experiments, and the creation of a more fruitful framework to discover new truths. The determination of the just powers of government, or the best laws for society, consists of the same creative process except that the experiments are carried out in courts of common reason, and the requirement of independent verifications is even more important because there will inevitably be, relative to natural science, more self-deception protecting favored theories, and more manipulation of outcomes using junk (political) science.

The testing to determine the best laws ought to come both before and after a given law becomes operational. Consider the latter case with regard to criminal law. Americans already have a testing mechanism; it is called *jury nullification*. This is the power of the trial jury to judge both the facts and the law itself. Historically, this power reaches back to the ancient Athenians. The main idea is contained in Aristotle's *Rhetoric*:

> . . . let us take laws and see how they are to be used in persuasion and dissuasion, in accusation and defence. If the written law tells against our case, clearly we must appeal to the universal law and to equity as being more just. We must argue that the juror's oath 'I will give my verdict according to my honest opinion' means that one will not simply follow the letter of the written law. . . . We shall argue that justice indeed is true and profitable, but that sham justice is not, and consequently the written law is not, because it does not fulfill the function of law. . . . Or [we shall argue] that the better man will follow and abide by the unwritten law in preference to the written. (1984 2:2190; cf. Thucydides 1928 1:325)

The political philosophy of the American revolution was based on the appeal to universal unwritten laws. Nullification should occur whenever the people, speaking through a jury, judged that the written law was contrary to the unwritten law contained in their minds and hearts. Nullification was defended by a variety of revolutionary leaders, among them John Adams (1850 2:253-5), Hamilton (Johnson, William 1812 345), John Jay (Dallas 1790 3:4), Jefferson (1892 3:236, 15:283; 1972 130), Theophilus Parsons (Elliot 1836 2:94) and James Wilson (2007 2:1000, 1203). (See Conrad 1998 for a general survey of jury nullification.) Trial juries have often used this power to good effect. Thus slave laws in the eighteenth and nineteenth century, and prohibition laws in the twentieth, were frequently nullified by juries who refused to convict, even in cases with overwhelming evidence of guilt. (One wonders how many refugees would have been sent back to the Soviet Union after World War II if, in each case, an American jury would first have had to agree to the use of force.) The nullification power is important in American political theory because it allows juries — appealing to their own deliberate conscience — to put limits on laws that they deem tyrannical or unjust or unfair, either generally or in the particular application before them. It thus belongs to those powers of the people (such as voting leaders out of office) that are designed to encourage intermediate steps between acquiescence, on the one hand, and armed revolt, on the other.

However, respect for, and use of, jury nullification has diminished during the nineteenth and twentieth centuries for a number of reasons. First, the power could be abused, as when some all white juries, in the face of convincing evidence, refused to convict whites who committed crimes against blacks. Second, the inconsistent application of a law resulted when one jury would nullify a law, and another would not, in very similar cases. Finally, frequent use of jury nullification could make a mockery of the law. In response to such abuses judges have generally tried, in effect, to deny the right of nullification by juries by keeping them ignorant of their power. Yet abuse alone doesn't seem a sufficient reason to deny power. After all, police, prosecutors, and judges sometimes abuse their power to, respectively, not enforce, not prosecute, or not allow a case to go forward, and these facts are not sufficient reason to take away their powers. Further, whenever the power of nullification is carefully explained to jurors, they do not generally abuse it. But some critics go further and argue that although juries have the power to nullify they do not have the right. This objection is answered by Alexander Hamilton: "All the cases agree that the jury have the *power* to decide the law as well as the fact; and if the law gives them the power, it gives them the *right* also. Power and right are convertible terms, when the law authorizes the doing of an act which shall be final, and for the doing of which the agent is not responsible"(Johnson, William 1812 345; cf. Hobbes 1968 328.) Nevertheless, a trial is not a well-designed institution for the *political* task of eliciting the people's judgment about the nullification of laws. In contrast, a Court of Common Reason is such an institution, since it would allow the people to decide in a responsible way whether they approve of existing laws. As a trial jury can nullify a particular application of a law, so the people, speaking through the Court of Common Reason, should ultimately be able to nullify the law itself whenever it is contrary to their sense of right and justice (cf. the ancient Athenian practice as described in Aeschines 1919 337, 339).

If members of Congress were committed to evidence-based democracy, the Court of Common Reason could guide them in formulating new laws. The idea here goes back to James Harrington who in 1656 said that the "commonwealth consisteth of the senate proposing, the people resolving, and the magistracy executing"(2003 25). Let us see how the people could resolve Congressional proposals. Today engineers use Computer Aided Design (CAD), for example, to put a proposed airplane through multiple tests that simulate the stresses to which it will be subjected, all before the airplane is created. Legislators, considered as legal engineers, could do the same thing. Before they pass a new law, they could use the data bank from the Court of Common Reason to test whether it is the optimum way of achieving the legislative goal. Hence members of Congress could know, with greater precision than is possible today, what stresses the new laws would cause and what stresses they would reduce. In fact, only through courts of common reason can the politically relevant notion of "stress" be accurately defined. The aim of simulation is to raise the probability that an actual flight, or an actual proposal written into law, will be beautifully successful. In both cases designs could be modified to reduce unintended consequences. An ultimate goal in industry is the automated factory. In politics an ultimate goal is automated government, where changes in the informed values of the people would automatically generate a new set of proposed laws that Congress, for its part, could try to improve. Then the people would be asked to confirm the result. This is meant to be a twenty-first adaptation of Harrington's idea that "Democracy . . . consists of such laws as the people, with the advice of their council, or of the senate, shall choose or have chosen"(2003 288). We would thus have *a new kind of automation that is not ultimately controlled by the mindless calculations of mechanical robots, but by the soul-searching deliberations of autonomous humans.* American perfectionist democracy would thus allow our legal clothing to be regularly changed and with a better fit than our present system. There would be little need for nullification by trial juries. Perhaps the concept of a "friendly" law will arise on the analogy with a "friendly" computer program. We are sometimes dazzled by the ease of use, and intuitive feel, of the products of physical science. Perfectionist democracy creates the possibility of having the same reaction with regard to legal products. At the very least, we could ensure that when a person starts a business, writes a will, buys a house, fills out a tax form, applies for welfare or a passport, and so forth, it would be as friendly as possible. Courts of common reason could create, as it were, a proprioceptive sense in the body politic, a sense that would continually undermine alienation by maintaining an exact ergonomic relation between the people and their government.

We can thus go far beyond what it was possible to conceive in the eighteenth century. Thus John Adams states, "The systems of legislators are experiments made on human life and manners, society and government. Zoroaster, Confucius, Mithras, Odin, Thor, Mahomet, Lycurgus, Solon, Romulus, and a thousand others, may be compared to philosophers making experiments on the elements"(1850 4:297; cf. 8:370). Here is a eighteenth-century conception of legislation as a science, where legislative efforts are seen as experiments, and wise legislators base their experiments on careful observation of all human history so as not to repeat past mistakes. "Unhappily," Adams begins the next sentence, "political experiments cannot be made in a laboratory, nor determined in a few hours. The operation once begun, runs over whole quarters of the globe, and is not finished in many thousands of years." Democratic simulations on computers allow us to do what Adams could not imagine, namely, to use courts of common reason to conduct "political experiments . . . in a laboratory," experiments whose outcome could perhaps sometimes be "determined in a few hours."

In 1651, Thomas Hobbes, one of the originators of political science, claimed that "all *Automata* [including the state] . . . have an artificiall life" and that the laws of the state are a kind of "artificiall *Reason.*" The computer revolution has given Hobbes' language an enhanced meaning that he could not have anticipated. Thus, when he speaks of "artificiall life" we can think of artificial life created by computers (cf. Steven Levy's *Artificial Life: A Report from the Frontier Where Computers Meet Biology* (1992)); or when Hobbes calls the state an "Artificiall Man"(1968 81) we can think of designing this artificial person to have a constantly improving artificial intelligence (AI). In any case, Hobbes' conception was not forgotten in eighteenth-century America. There was this difference, that for Hobbes the artificial person was embodied in the monarch, whereas in America the embodiment was in the people. To quote James Wilson: "In free states, the people form an artificial person or body politick, the highest and noblest that can be known. They form that moral person, which [is] . . . a complete body of free natural persons, united together for their common benefit; as having an understanding and a will; as deliberating, and resolving, and acting; as possessed of interests which it ought to manage; as enjoying rights which it ought to maintain; and as lying under obligations which it ought to perform. To this moral person, we assign, by way of eminence, the dignified appellation of *state*"(2007 2:831; cf. 534, where Wilson makes clear the state is a virtual person, not real in the sense an individual human is; cf. also Wilson's words below, page 235, Jefferson 1903 1:480,16:263, and Madison 1900 9:572). Given this structural similarity between the real individual we call a person, and the virtual individual we call a state, the description Locke gives for the pursuit of individual happiness (above, page 36) applies, *mutatis mutandis*, to the pursuit of public happiness. Those states that are successful in that pursuit achieve it through the exercise of their moral freedom, again, as described for the individual by Locke (above, page 39). Thus the principal problem in creating a democracy is to ensure that this artificial person has an intelligence and disposition that, under conditions of moral freedom, will forever be dedicated to perfecting the pursuit of public happiness. Designing this artificial person, and creating an artificial evolution to control changes in its powers and character, represents a greater challenge for the AI community than designing robots that can run our factories, or clean our homes. Such robots ought to be thought of as a technological triumph, but they will not bring us happiness if we must live under poorly crafted laws, and a government in disharmony with the people in their calm and reflective moods. The American revolution will be awakened when we use methods that ensure that legislation, as passed, is consistent with the informed values of the people, and that it will remain in force only as long as it keeps their considered consent. Our challenge is to achieve a twenty-first-century level of excellence in striving toward the eighteenth-century ideal of "Governments . . . deriving their just powers from the consent of the governed."

One step toward meeting that challenge is to exploit a theorem first proved in 1785 by Condorcet. (Unfortunately neither Jefferson, nor anyone else in America during Jefferson's lifetime, explicitly refers to the theorem although he and Madison may have known of it.) The Condorcet jury theorem, as it is now called, states that, if each voter independently and sincerely answers a question (such as a yes-no or multiple-choice question), and if the probability that any vote has a property (such as *being negative,* or *being a vote for truth)* that is the same for all voters and is between 50% and a 100%, then, as the size of the group increases, the probability that the group's majority vote has that property approaches certainty. For example, if the probability that each vote has the property of *being Republican* is 80%, then as the size of the voting group increases, the probability that the majority of votes will be Republican approaches 100%; in fact, it there are only thirteen voters, the probability that the majority of votes will be Republican is greater than 99%. The Condorcet jury theorem is really an application of the binomial theorem, and thus its mathematics is not especially difficult. However, the size of the multiplications and additions is so large, that it can take a powerful computer to give an exact answer to questions that a reasonable democrat might ask. On the other hand, there is an intuitive explanation that makes the theorem plausible without a mathematical proof. Suppose elementary students are given a yes-no mathematical question, such as "Is 31 a prime number?" Suppose they work independently, put their answers on a piece of paper, and then, one by one, "cast their ballots" in a box. For each student suppose the chance of *being right* (the property in question) is 6 out of 10. Then as the number of "votes" in the box increase, we could say with greater and greater confidence that the ratio of right answers to the total number of "ballots" in the box will be close to 6/10. But this means that we could say with greater and greater confidence that the majority of "votes" in the box is right. (For ease of illustration, all examples of the theorem in this book will assume the ideal requirements of the theorem apply. A fuller account, as it might apply to real life applications, would have to deal with generalizations, and with relaxation of some of the theorem's conditions; see Grofman and Owen 1986, DTPI 1989, Berend and Paroush 1998.)

Now consider an application of the theorem to courts of common reason. Suppose that IQ measures intelligence, and the intelligence of each jury member is 100. Suppose further that we measure the jury's *collective* intelligence using an IQ test, where the answers are determined by majority vote on each question. Our aim is to devise a scheme (based on many experiments) that would consistently allow the jury to exhibit a collective intelligence much greater than 100. This would answer critics who say the people are not intelligent enough for political deliberation. Let us call a subjury *competent* if, whenever it is unanimous, its answer is more likely to be true than a random device. Aristotle said that "men have a sufficient natural instinct for what is true, and usually do arrive at the truth"(1984 2154). The assumption here is much more limited; it is that under conditions very favorable to deliberation, with an adequate number of independent, unanimous subjuries, the majority of them is better than a random device on all questions relevant to public happiness. Hence if, on a given issue, we have an advisory jury of competent subjuries who answer questions independently (one of the purposes of isolating subjuries), the theorem tells us that the probability of the advisory jury giving a right answer approaches certainty as the number of unanimous subjuries increases. The purpose of hearing opposing views, and then deliberating, is to increase the likelihood of competent subjuries. It sometimes even happens that deliberation might allow a right answer to be reached where, prior to deliberation, every juror was wrong . A dramatic illustration of the latter possibility is given in the classic 1957 movie *Twelve Angry Men*. In it, each member of the jury initially believed the evidence eliminated reasonable doubt of guilt but, because one juror wanted to deliberate, the jury eventually came to a contrary, and correct, judgment. Surprisingly, even when unanimous subjuries barely achieve competence above 50%, it still may be practical to attain collective competence close to 100%. For example, by the mathematics of the theorem, if the probability that each unanimous subjury is right is 51%, and if there are 13,627 unanimous subjuries, then the probability that a majority of them is right is greater than 99%. Note, however, with the same number of unanimous subjuries, if the probability that each is wrong is 51%, then, the probability that a majority of the them is wrong is greater than 99%. In other words, near-incompetence by subjuries (51% chance of being right) rather quickly yields near-collective perfection (less that 1% chance of being wrong), whereas near-competence (49% chance of being right) rather quickly leads near-collective imperfection (greater than 99% chance of being wrong). The mere 2% difference of subjury competence leads to the highly likely collective difference of true and false, right and wrong, intelligent and foolish. Hence it is of crucial importance to increase the competence of subjuries — by general education, by the structure of courts of common reason, by initial instructions given to jurors, by endless testing — in order that the collective proficiency of the advisory jury be made as high as possible.

One great advantage of jurors over legislators is that the former, unlike the latter, seldom have a temptation to be corrupt. The reason was expressed four hundred years ago by Francis Bacon: "Marvel not if the vulgar speak truer than the great, for they speak safer"(1860 9:160). Although advisory juries will almost never be inferior in motive to legislatures, it is also true that legislators will often exceed jurors in "information & lights"(Madison's phrase, above, page 159). Our goal is to constantly improve the "information & lights" of subjuries, until the quality of the collective decisions of the Court of Common Reason exceeds, or at least equals, that of legislatures. Although increases in size will indefinitely increase the collective competence of advisory juries if competence after deliberation by subjuries is attained, knowing that that competence is attained is difficult. Fulfilling democratic optimism based on the Condorcet jury theorem, like fulfilling scientific optimism in general, requires hard work, relentless experiment, and theoretical reflection. In my judgment, deliberative competence in politics can be understood by studying deliberations in areas where a correct answer is well-defined, such as crossword puzzles, detective stories, predictions of the future events, logic, medicine, engineering and the like. The experience of devising successful systems for a variety of topics in which correct answers are known, could then be used in devising systems for political questions, where answers are often controversial. By *successful* I mean cases in which the knowledge and talents of each individual in a subjury may be unlikely to get the correct answer, but where the probability that unanimous judgment, after deliberation, is right would be better than chance. The greater the divergence between individual and collective achievement, the greater the success of the deliberative system. The fact that political decisions often involve judgments of preference or value does not mean that these judgments are not subject to deliberative reason. For example, an initial preference to lynch a person without a fair trial could be examined by considering whether the following factual proposition is true: *if the person is lynched without a fair trial, then public happiness in the longer term will be increased.* If the common reason of society judges that proposition to be false, then the starting preference ought not to be fulfilled, *even if the preference remains.*

Hence the decisions of society should be "controuled by subjecting the will of the society to the reason of society"(Madison 1962 14:207). Courts of common reason are devices to help insure that subjection; they give many opportunities to measure and increase the quality of collective decisions. How? Well, we verify that computers are sound by having them calculate the decimal expansion of π, because the decimals are already known to an accuracy of billions of digits. Similarly, exercises in critical thinking, where answers are known, could verify that advisory juries have the collective intelligence that is necessary to deliberate on political questions. For example, imagine an advisory jury where each subjury is given instructions in critical thinking, and then practices on questions with well-defined answers until some level of deliberating competence — call it x — is reached. Next the subjuries take up a series of questions concerning political issues. After answering the political questions, each of the subjuries in the majority again achieves level x of deliberating competence on questions with well-defined answers. We could then assert that the answers given for the political issues had been authenticated by a *sandwich* of deliberative competence at level x. If we could make successful attempts to forever increase the quality of collective reason of advisory juries in practice, we could justly say that the Court of Common Reason embodies Wilson's "moral person, which [is] . . . a complete body of free natural persons, united together for their common benefit; as having an understanding and a will; as deliberating, and resolving, and acting." Hence we could use the Court to explore in detail the long-term aspirations of the American people, in effect, we could create the first fully authoritative expression of the American dream. Then short-term decisions about public policy could then be judged by the degree to which they contributed to fulfilling that dream.

It is a melancholy reflection that, after all these years, the theory has not been sufficiently developed, nor the experiments performed, for creating American perfectionist democracy. There is a large body of scholars concerned with reason, but few with common reason. Hence my design for courts of common reason certainly contains much guesswork because the tests necessary to create successful "deliberator software" have not been carried out. Creating such software will be a sophisticated and arduous undertaking. For example, imagine an experiment in which a large number of people take a written test in which they each answer a thousand questions. On the basis of this test and psychological profiles of the subjects, a mock advisory jury is formed where, unbeknownst to the participants, each subjury contains eleven arrogant know-it-alls, plus one very shy person. The jury is given a question from the test (though disguised so as not to make that obvious), to which each shy person earlier gave the right answer, and each arrogant know-it-all the wrong one. What procedures would maximize the probability that the deliberative decision of the advisory jury would be correct? One procedure might require that, after the question is posed, each subjury break into six pairs for discussion, and then into four triads, before everyone discusses the issue together. That way the shy person might have a better chance of ultimately prevailing, as she would initially have only one arrogant know-it-all to convince.

Again, imagine that a mock advisory jury is given a question, which, unbeknownst to them, each member had answered incorrectly in a preliminary, individual test. What software would maximize the chances of the jury getting the right answer? One approach might require a minimum of an hour's discussion (even where everyone is agreed), and then require, not just an answer, but an argument for that answer. Consider the voting scheme that I suggested for courts of common reason (above, page 165). It has the following consequence: Suppose an advisory jury of 12,000 people is divided into 1,000 subjuries; one subjury unanimously votes no, and the other 999 each vote 11 to 1 yes. My scheme would give the social decision as (weakly) negative (1 negative, 999 undecided) although, it might be said, the probability is much stronger that the correct answer is yes. Yet such reasoning assumes that the probability of each individual's being right is greater than chance, whereas mine only makes the weaker assumption that the probability of unanimous subjuries' being right after deliberation is greater than chance. Note the analogy to science: Widespread belief among scientists doesn't by itself make a belief scientific; only the persuasiveness of good arguments and evidence for the belief does. On the other hand, the holdouts may merely be fanatics, who are incapable of being persuaded no matter what is said. The best scheme to deal with this problem cannot be determined without extensive empirical evidence. In general, the intellectual challenges of writing software for deliberating juries are considerable. That software would have to specify the best instructions to give jurors beforehand, the best voting scheme (or schemes) for any size subjury (say, from 2 to 24), the best size of the advisory jury for a given purpose (say, from 12 to 12 million), the minimum probability, in a given case, for a subjury being right after deliberation on questions with known answers (say, 51% to 99%).

Beta tests of the software would have to consistently work under mock, but realistic, conditions before they are used in any actual court of common reason.

It might be objected that juries could generally only answer slowly compared to a single individual. Even if that were true for easy problems, it wouldn't follow that it is true for difficult ones. (It is slower to use a computer to multiply two single-digit numbers, but not to multiply two thousand-digit numbers.) Imagine, for instance, that a hundred thousand advisory juries exist, some large, some small, and some consisting just of gymnasts, others just of mathematicians whose area of expertise is sampling theory, others just of ten-year old girls with cancer, others just of healthy 100-year old males, and so forth. The aim would be to have a very large canopy of human endowments available if they are needed to save time or money or get information. We would be here creating a synthetic politics, on the analogy of synthetic biology, engineering political life the way we engineer biological life. What would emerge as killer applications? Consider the social problems relating to health care. Would it be possible to organize a set of such advisory juries, all operating at once, to solve these problems better and faster than any single human, or small groups of humans, could do, no matter how intelligent or talented? Can human beings, properly organized, become superdeliberators capable of superthoughts? Again, just as computer programmers use artificial evolution to solve software problems, which the programmers sometimes don't understand why the resulting software works, so artificial evolution might also be useful in creating successful deliberator software that the software engineers might not fully understand. Should such an approach prove fruitful, we could create an artificial superintelligence in the service of an artificial will that is completely devoted to securing the right to the pursuit of happiness for every human being. The joke has it that computers can save the world — if we can only find the right program. But perhaps it is no joke to say that our future public happiness will depend on creating successful deliberator software that would reveal, accurately and regularly, the distributive intelligence and sensibility of the public. We could then banish forever the brutal leviathans of tyranny and the clumsy (and therefore sometimes brutal) leviathans of the democracies that have so far been created. Should not such speculations excite our wonder?

Cynicism about the collective intelligence of the American people may be understandable, but it is certainly paradoxical. In biology, the human brain is presented as the most sophisticated and complicated thing in all nature, with enormous flexibility and awesome powers well beyond our complete understanding; but in political science, ordinary people — who possess these wonderful brains — are presented as forever unwilling or incapable of the collective deliberative reason that excellent self-government requires. We know that comparing a microprocessor to a human brain is like comparing a candle to the sun. Yet we are willing to spend billions of dollars to create massively parallel computing that combines a million or more microprocessors, but we do not even think of creating massively parallel deliberation that combines a million or more autonomous humans. Distributed computing gains our attention and dollars, but not distributed deliberation. We experiment with computational neural networks to govern robots, but do not experiment with deliberate "neural" networks to govern ourselves. We treat microprocessors with respect, optimistically confident that we will eventually make them collectively intelligent. We treat ordinary humans in their civic capacity with disrespect, cynically convinced that they are incapable of being collectively intelligent. We believe in things mechanical, but not in humans autonomous. Our colleges and universities have rightfully created departments of computer science in response to the enormous demand to understand and improve computation by machines, but they have not created departments of deliberator science since there is no similar demand to understand and improve deliberation by humans. In 1788 Enos Hitchcock could speak with pride that America produced a "revolution by reasoning"(11), but we cannot make a similar boast using our own standards of reason, deliberation, and representation. Why should our intelligence technology only apply to robots? Should we not here exhibit our "American character" as described by Jefferson: "It is part of the American character to consider nothing as desperate: to surmount every difficulty by resolution and contrivance"(above, page 82). Yet even in small ways we seldom try. Thus, in 1991, on the two-hundredth anniversary of the birth of Charles Babbage, probably the person who first understood the concept of a computer, a half million dollars was spent to construct his Difference Engine No. 2, which demonstrated that his ideas on calculation actually worked in practice (Swade 1993); yet, in 1993, on the two-hundred and fiftieth anniversary of the birth of Jefferson, perhaps the person who first proposed that a direct democracy does not require that the people assemble *en masse*, there was no money spent to show that Jefferson's ideas on direct democracy actually worked in practice.

The crucial problems of politics concern decisions about abstract values that may be incommensurable. Nevertheless they can be politically resolved, for a given time and place, by informed and deliberate choices made in the minds and hearts of the people. These soul-searching choices might bring to light hypocrisies and self-deceptions whose exposure would create a new integrity in American politics. John Milton once said that "when God gave [Adam] reason, he gave him freedom to choose, for reason is but choosing"(1644 17). Reason is surely more than choosing, since choosing informed by reason requires a careful consideration of facts and what can be said for and against each alternative choice. The great political failure of the intellectual elite in this country is its failure to design the institutions through which the American people can make choices informed by reason. To claim that the unexamined life is not worth living is surely an exaggeration, but it is no exaggeration to claim that the best political system is based on deliberative soul-searching by the people. A politics of self-knowledge is a necessary condition for the greatest possible excellence in self-government.

It is thus an unalienable duty of the people to maintain the kind of autonomy that qualifies them to exercise ultimate political authority. As our forefathers' practices revealed that they were sometimes willing to let "white males with property" be what they knew was a crude and wrong approximation to "all men," so we are often willing to let "public opinion polls and elections" be what we know is a crude and wrong approximation to "consent." "Consent" requires that we ask under conditions that allow an informed answer to be given. It does not mean "consensus" in the sense of "general agreement." *Consent only requires a majority, and there is a great deal of difference between saying that a deliberate majority decides an issue authoritatively for the American people, and saying that there is a consensus on the issue.* A consensus exists only in unanimous or near unanimous votes, a state of affairs that the Court of Common Reason will not always — and perhaps only occasionally — achieve. If consensus is not achieved at a particular time there still has to be some policy or other. What should it be? Jefferson tells us: "The first principle of republicanism is, that the *lex majoris partis* is the fundamental law of every society of individuals of equal rights; to consider the will of the society enounced by the majority of a single vote, as sacred as if unanimous, is the first of all lessons in importance, yet the last which is thoroughly learnt"(1903 15:127. cf. 3:60, Locke 1988 332, and Madison 1900 570). That principle is not forgotten here: The decision of a deliberate majority of the Court of Common

Reason holds even if it is by only one subjury (just as a one-vote majority is sufficient to elect a candidate for a full term); and it should continue to hold until the Court again takes up the issue. Madison thought that "the more extensive a country, the more insignificant is each individual in his own eyes. This may be unfavorable to liberty"(1962 14:170). Since Courts of Common Reason (whether federal, state, or local) are a tiny minority of the population, since preliminary investigation could eliminate most topics where there is apt to be a strong deliberate majority, since unpredictability of outcome could be further achieved by painstaking care in framing unbiased questions and in allowing vote trading, the likely result would be frequent instances of small majorities in the Courts, which would undermine the perceived insignificance of each juror in her own eyes, and this may be favorable to liberty.

American political principles require that courts of common reason (or their functional equivalent) be created in the twentieth-first century just as those same principles required the abolition of slavery in the eighteenth-century. The reasons that can be given against creating courts are like those given against abolition: Abolishing slavery or creating courts of common reason is at best a speculation that should be avoided in practice. It is inconvenient to free the slaves, and it is likewise inconvenient to consult the people. Many powerful people profit from slavery, so nothing can be done. Many powerful special interest groups profit from our present deceptive — and self-deceptive — politics, so nothing can be done. The claim that it would be dangerous to free the slaves (you never know what freed slaves will do) is matched by the claim that it is dangerous to seek the informed consent of the people (you never know what a truly autonomous people will decide). Looking back on the Founding era it is easy for us to underestimate the great political and economic problems that abolition would have brought about. But the point is that the Founders did not use their enormous political talent to *try* to solve these problems. Instead they used the slaves' admittedly wretched condition (created by the slaveholders themselves) as an excuse to do little or nothing. Today we use the ignorance of the American people about their constitutional and civil rights as an excuse to do little or nothing, but is this any more believable than the excuse that slaves lacked the manners to be free? In the eighteenth century, a fidelity to the philosophy of the American revolution as expressed in the Declaration, the Constitution, and the Bill of Rights left no choice, the slave system had to be destroyed. By Jefferson's political standards an emancipation could only come about by appealing to the most incorruptible political power on earth — the people. This would have meant making extensive and imaginative use of wards since other representatives of the people — congressmen, senators, presidents, and judges — were generally hostile, indifferent, or unreliable when it came to protecting the natural rights of blacks. To quote John Adams again, "I never knew a jury, by a verdict, to determine a negro to be a slave. They always found them free"(above, page 156). Adams was talking about Massachusetts but white people in the South were often not hostile to educating slaves, or freeing them, or marrying blacks. This is shown by the fact that legislators felt it necessary to pass laws against doing such things. Thus Jefferson could have suggested that slavery in Virginia might be eliminated using his ward idea. Western Virginia was hostile to the slave interests and this fact could have been exploited. Unfortunately, on this issue, Jefferson never even proposed acting on his own brilliant political insight.

But how about ourselves? Consider again the revolutionary maxim of Madison: "the cool and deliberate sense of the community ought in all governments, and actually will in all free governments ultimately prevail over the views of its rulers"(above, page158). We cannot be faithful to that maxim and also deny that it is impossible to create a practical mechanism to discover that deliberate sense. A Court of Common Reason might be impractical in the sense that it might not work well for a number of years. Virginia society might not have "worked well" if all slaves had been freed in the eighteenth century, but it is reasonable to believe that it would have recovered. It certainly would not have declined as rapidly as it did with slavery. Courts of common reason would be expensive and might cause all kinds of sticky problems that do not now exist. But we might decline rapidly without them. To call for courts of common reason opens one to the charge of being an idealistic dreamer, as did the call for freeing the slaves in the eighteenth century. But however speculative the idea might be, our political principles require them and no one can now know they must be impractical. *What is impractical can often become quite practical through an energetic and persistent application of imagination, intelligence, and money.* (The difference between the ENIAC, America's first electronic computing device, and a contemporary computer is a good illustration of this point, and remember that computers sometimes caused problems, they did not always merely solve them.) It takes only a moment's reflection to see that slavery is inconsistent with the Declaration; it takes not much more time to see that if our government rests on the cool and deliberate sense of the people, there must be some means of regularly and accurately determining what that sense is regarding any political issue. Again, how practical was the institution of slavery if, as Jefferson correctly believed, it would lead to civil war? And how practical are the present political practices if, as many believe, we are at continual risk of moral and political catastrophes? If courts of common reason could be made practical, they would be as revolutionary in morality and politics as computers have been in the science and business. Must cynicism, fear of new problems, and a lack of imagination, forever prevent any constructive action in this direction?

With the institution of a viable Court of Common Reason, the Ninth Amendment (above, page 133) could finally gain its rightful place in American political practice. Until 1964, the Amendment played almost no role in Supreme Court cases. One reason is the difficulty in making definite the unstated rights. Thus in 1964, Justice Goldberg, in his concurring opinion, tried to find Ninth Amendment rights in the "traditions and [collective] conscience of our people."(*Griswold vs Connecticut*, 381 U.S. 493). Dissenting, Justice Black argued that one cannot avoid using "personal and private notions" in discussing those rights. He noted sarcastically: "Our Court certainly has no machinery with which to take a Gallup Poll. And the scientific miracles of this age have not yet produced a gadget which the Court can use to determine what traditions are rooted in the '[collective] conscience of our people'."(519). The Court of Common Reason is such a "scientific miracle," since it could give authoritative advice as to what rights the people have under the Ninth Amendment. In *United States v. Darby* (312 U.S. 100, 124) the Supreme Court asserted that the Tenth Amendment "states but a truism that all is retained which has not been surrendered." Stewart, dissenting from *Griswold*, claimed that the Ninth is also such a truism (529). Well, suppose it is. It does not follow that the Ninth is thereby unimportant. "$x + 0 = x$" is a truism, but it is hardly unimportant since it is an independent axiom of arithmetic, that is, it is not derivable from the other axioms. It is a truism that all truisms are true, and if the Ninth is true, there *exist* rights, which cannot be disparaged, that are not listed in the Constitution. What are they? The answer, according to our revolutionary principles, is that they are whatever non-listed rights the people, after soul-searching deliberation, say are needed or desirable for their pursuit of happiness. Any American government — federal, state, or local — that fails to protect these rights should be altered or abolished.

In the eighteenth century there certainly were people who understood that the Declaration's clause "to alter or abolish" needs an operational definition. For example, during the debates on the ratification of the Constitution in Pennsylvania, John Smilie put the case for the bill of rights in these words:

> . . . the supreme authority naturally rests in the people, but does it follow that therefore a declaration of rights would be superfluous? Because the people have a right to alter or abolish government, can it therefore be inferred that every step taken to secure that right would be superfluous and nugatory? The truth is that unless some criterion is established by which it could be easily and constitutionally ascertained how far our governors may proceed, and by which it might appear when they transgress their jurisdiction, this idea of altering and abolishing government is mere sound without substance. . . . . So loosely, so inaccurately are the powers which are enumerated in this Constitution defined, that it will be impossible, without a test of that kind [that is, a bill of rights], to ascertain the limits of authority, and to declare when government has degenerated into oppression. In that event the contest will arise between the people and the rulers: "You have exceeded the powers of your office, you have oppressed us," will be the language of the suffering citizen. The answer of the governments will be short: "We have not exceeded our power; you have no test by which you can prove it." Hence . . . it will be impracticable to stop the progress of tyranny . . . (DHRC 1976 2:385, 392)

The Constitution without amendment explicitly affirmed some rights. For example, rights with regard to *habeas corpus*, trials for crimes, and no *ex post facto* laws. Hamilton went so far in the *Federalist* as to claim that the entire Constitution is a bill of rights (1961 4:708). The first eight amendments of the Constitution were added to make explicit some of the rights that the people did not want to give up. The Ninth and Tenth Amendments was added to ensure that the people have all the rights and powers that were not expressly given up, and that these rights and powers require their expressed consent to be abridged or taken away. Hence the government — if it is to fulfill its function — must keep abreast of any changes in the considered judgments of the people about their rights. As James Wilson put it: "To every suggestion concerning a bill of rights, the citizens of the United States may always say, WE reserve the right to do what we please"(DHRC 1976 2:389). The great epistemological problem for American democracy is how to determine, regularly and accurately, what the people, after due deliberation, "please." What can be used as a criterion? Jefferson's system of wards is an old proposal, and the Court of Common Reason a new one, for an institution whose normal operation would provide a "criterion . . . by which it could be easily and constitutionally ascertained how far our governors may proceed." Without such a criterion, Ninth Amendment rights will continue to be insecure because they will either be ignored, or denied, or depend on inadequately justified inference by Supreme Court judges.

We can now see the Ninth Amendment was not an afterthought of the American revolution. It was part of it. On November 20, 1772, at a town meeting in Boston, Samuel Adams, declared: "All men have a Right to remain in a State of Nature as long as they please: And in Case of intollerable Oppression, civil or religious, to leave the Society they belong to, and enter into another. When Men enter into Society, it is by voluntary Consent; and they have a Right to demand and insist upon the Performance of such Conditions and previous Limitations as form an equitable *original Compact*. Every natural Right, not expressly given up, or from the Nature of a social Compact necessarily ceded, remains"(VPFITB 1772 2-3; cf. Adams, Samuel 1904 2:351-2). Natural rights are not created by compacts: ". . . all the great rights which man never mean, nor ever ought, to lose, should be *guaranteed*, not *granted*, by the Constitution . . . "(FL 1776 22). The anonymous author is referring to any constitution of a free society. The revolution's purpose was to establish in practice the view of man and government implicit in the 1772 and 1776 quotations. The revolutionists believed the war threw them into a state of nature: As Patrick Henry declared on September 6, 1774: "Fleets and Armies and the present State of Things shew that Government is dissolved. . . . We are in a State of Nature"(Adams 1961 2:124). On January 21, 1775, John Adams wrote to a friend in London: "The state of this province is a great curiosity . . . Four hundred thousand people are in a state of nature, and yet as still and peaceable at present as ever they were when government was in full vigour"(1977 2:215, cf. 191, 1961 2:240, and Hartley's words above, page 147). The Great and General Court of the Colony of Massachusetts-Bay proclaimed that "Mankind has seen a Phænomenon, without Example in the political World, a large and populous Colony, subsisting in great Decency and Order, for more than a Year, under . . . a Suspension of Government"(PGGC 1776 190). Notice that both the description of Adams and the Massachusetts Court contradicts Hobbes' assertion that "the state of nature is a state of war"(1998 108) as well as the claim, often made, that the state of nature is pre-historical, or merely theoretical. The people of Massachusetts were following Locke: "Men living together according to reason, without a common Superior on Earth, with Authority to judge between them, is *properly the State of Nature.*"(1988 280-1). The people of America were starting anew: ". . . the declaration of independency made the antecedent form of government to be of necessity null and void; and by that act the people of the different colonies slid back into a state of nature"(from a 1777 circular letter, Chase 1928 431). However, the Declaration did more than that; it laid down the founding principles of future governments in America (cf. above, page 48). The Articles of Confederation and the Constitution were subsequent compacts whose purpose was to re-establish government according to Lockean standards. The Constitution specified the rights voluntarily given up (see Washington's comments in his official letter closing the Constitutional Convention, above, page 146). All other rights from a state of nature remain, whether seemingly trivial (the right to wear a hat) or important (the right to worship or not). Of course, these rights do not include anything that violates universal morality; rather, they are consistent with "Men living together according to reason"(in Locke's language), or are part of "the Laws of Nature and of Nature's God"(in Jefferson's words). For example, suppose a young healthy person in a state of nature changes from hunting large to small game merely to starve his old neighbor who is capable of hunting only small game. This is artful murder and any equivalent under government could not be claimed as a Ninth Amendment right.

The protection of all rights not ceded to government — whether listed or not in the Constitution — is a central purpose of the American government. The Ninth Amendment was composed in the spirit of 1776, and it must be understood in that spirit. Our lack of revolutionary fervor is so complete that no branch of the government — or to my knowledge no person or organization — has even tried to find out in detail what the considered judgments of the American people are with regard to the unlisted rights that the government ought to respect. In *Roe v. Wade* Justice Douglas listed some examples of Ninth Amendment rights: "First is the autonomous control over the development and expression of one's intellect, interests, tastes, and personality . . . Second is freedom of choice in the basic decisions of one's life respecting marriage, divorce, procreation, contraception, and the upbringing of children . . . Third is the freedom to care for one's health and person, freedom from bodily restraint or compulsion, freedom to walk, stroll or loaf . . ."(410 U.S. 113). However, Douglas' examples need the imprimatur of the American people.

Because we lack such a proof mechanism, Ninth Amendment rights are generally denied or disparaged by presidents, legislators, and judges. Yet if we wish to live up to our revolutionary ideals, we have no choice but to transcend the written Constitution and, on a continuing basis, secure rights not listed. Hence we need not seek very far to answer the question: Why, after more than two centuries, have we failed to achieve public happiness? The answer is: Because we have not made good on the promise of consent. And making good on consent means creating a politics of self-knowledge — there is no other way.

7

Perfectionist Democracy and American Society

The Founding era in America produced an incredible outpouring of political geniuses — Franklin, Washington, Samuel and John Adams, Jefferson, Hamilton, Madison, Wilson, and many more. With a population a hundred times larger, and the ability to draw on the political talent of women, blacks, and native Americans, many would doubt we do as well, much less produce a hundred times as many master politicians as the late eighteenth century did. The reason, in my judgment, is not that such geniuses are unavailable but, rather, that present conditions of public service often make leadership an unattractive goal to individuals who combine ability, virtue, and a powerful aspiration for excellence. For the highly talented and ambitious white male seeking fame or power, the private sector in the Founding era was no match for public service. Today, art or architecture, computer science or biochemistry, business or medicine, and a hundred other occupations generally appear more attractive than politics. If we want an excellent political and economic system, we must make leadership is government as tempting as possible; we must change the ways in which leaders are chosen, and the conditions under which they work.

Consider the difference in attitude often found between private companies and government. Edwin Land of Polaroid and Steven Jobs of Apple both made it clear that, under their leadership, their companies did not strive to make what consumers wanted; instead they made what consumers would want if they had enough imagination to know such things were possible. The commercial world is filled with products — such as telephones or pacemakers or personal computers — which consumers wanted only after they were created. In contrast, the services government provides are seldom imaginative in this way. But they could be so. For example, the most desirable set of laws concerning some specific government service would no doubt be the simplest that are in harmony with the informed values of the people. But assuming a Court of Common Reason is possible, there will likely be problems in dealing with a mass of confusing data from the Court concerning that service. Yet the scientist is often presented with a similar situation. The astronomer Johannes Kepler, for instance, had a mass of confusing data from the work of Tycho Brahe, and fashioned them into his three beautiful laws of planetary motion. He presented scientists of the time with a simplicity they wanted, without necessarily knowing they wanted it. Similarly a legislative Kepler could fashion a beautiful set of laws concerning the specific government service from a mass of confusing data. If the advisory jurors of the Court were surprised and delighted with that set, they could, if they wished, reward the legislator with money, prestige, honors, and fame well beyond that which is available in the private sector.

Thus it might be possible to change the predominant psychological type of the politician. Being a politician today is as frustrating as being an investigator of nature before the scientific method developed. In pre-Baconian inquiry, the investigation of nature was often conceived as the mastery of soul (the investigator's) over another soul (the spirit in nature). Hence, magic was a key element, and one had to turn to magicians to understand and control the natural world. But that understanding and control was unnecessarily limited because magicians lacked the appropriate science and technology. What magicians understood, and to some degree controlled, was human emotion. In the minds of many today, politics is the mastery of many souls (the people) by a single soul (the politician). Hence, they believe, we must turn to the charismatic leaders — political magicians — to understand and control the political world. But the knowledge politicians have is often unnecessarily limited by the lack of an appropriate science and technology. What politicians do understand, and to some degree control, is human emotion. Nevertheless, as the scientific revolution changed the predominant psychological type of the investigator of nature from magician to scientist, so courts of common reason could change the predominant psychological type of the politician from charismatic figure to political scientist. Of course, some politicians might still be charismatic (as are some scientists), but what would be decisive for their career and fame would be verified fidelity to the common reason of society (as verified fidelity to nature is for the scientist). Until our method of choosing politicians consistently results in the winners having a proven, higher fidelity than any of their competitors, representative democracy will continue to discourage us, and it will be seen as merely the best of a bad lot of methods for organizing the governance of humankind.

Let us conduct, then, a thought experiment to illustrate a better system of choosing a President. Imagine the candidates are put in a competition to test their knowledge of what the people want. We assume arrangements are made for being a candidate that are satisfactory to the Court of Common Reason. Suppose there are twelve issues (chosen by metajuries) and that the first one concerns welfare. Each candidate will be given the results of what advisory juries have suggested for a large number of hypothetical welfare cases. The candidate will then formulate laws (legislative function), administrative practices (executive function), and fair procedures for resolving disputes (judicial function) that he or she believes will best embody the will of people on this subject. Candidates could use their own staff to assist them in taking these tests. This would increase the probability that a candidate, if elected president, would take a staff into the White House that is highly knowledgeable about the informed values of the American people.

After completing their proposals, the candidates would be ranked by a democratic evolutionary paradigm (above, page 178). The jurors would listen to what could be said for and against each candidates's proposal, deliberate, and reject one of them. The remaining candidates could then modify their proposals for the second round. This process would continue until there was just one proposal left. (That proposal might not be what the people initially wanted; but what they wanted once their imagination was stimulated by the election process itself.) There would thus be a ranking of candidates on the subject of welfare. The next five tests would be the same, except on different subjects. The last six tests would differ from the first six in only one respect: They would be on topics not yet presented to the Court of Common Reason. Thus candidates would have to exhibit their judgment as to what they think the people would want done in these areas. For example, the subject might be the sentencing of convicted criminals for a federal crime. They would aim to match what the people would say. Subsequently a national advisory jury would be asked the same questions (in ignorance of the candidates' replies). Candidates could then be ranked on how well they predicted the people's considered judgments. Getting the highest rank would prove that the candidate was best able to see things from the considered perspective of the American people.

Combining the scores of the twelve tests, the hundred highest ranking candidates would be tested in a Presidential simulator. Consider an analogy between the President, as captain of the ship of state, and a pilot, as captain of a jumbo jet. A person, however intelligent or talented, does not become the pilot of a jumbo jet by getting into the cockpit with an experienced pilot and taking off. This would be both a dangerous and an expensive way to learn. Rather he or she has to go through six steps: First, a good education must be obtained with an emphasis in mathematics, science, and engineering. Second, a substantial amount of time must be logged flying smaller airplanes with a high degree of demonstrated competence. Third, a rigorous series of tests about the jumbo jet and its operating procedures must likewise be passed. Fourth, an equally rigorous series of tests in a jumbo jet simulator must be passed. The simulators, which consist of a movable cockpit and computer generated displays, have a high degree of verisimilitude. Learning by a simulator is faster, cheaper, safer and in general much better than learning on an actual plane. Fifth, a substantial amount of time must be spent as a copilot. Sixth, even after one becomes a pilot, new written and simulator tests must be passed every six months.

When a large number of people (for example, pilots) achieve excellence in a complex task, extensive practice or simulations must be used. What makes a simulator feasible is a highly accurate definition of success and failure. A court of common reason makes political simulators possible by providing that accurate definition. Competence as a politician may still not be as precisely measurable as competence as a pilot, depending as it does on interpersonal relationships, but this does not mean that a useful simulator could not be constructed. A presidential simulator, for example, could be a mock oval office, where information coming from the "outside world" would be created and the "president" would have to act and react as he or she saw fit. A substantial number of possible political challenges could be presented and the performance of the "president" could be evaluated in a evolutionary fashion by advisory juries. Airplane simulators are so good that pilots can say: "Flying a plane is hardly any different from using a simulator." We would want our presidential simulator to be so good that Presidents leaving office would regularly say: "Being President is hardly any different from using a simulator." Hence, unlike our present system, the excellence needed to be elected President, would be just what is needed to be an excellent President.

Of course, building such a simulator would be enormously difficult. But, supposing it were possible, would it not be worth it? For if a simulator for the presidency could be built, so could one for supreme court justices, congressmen, ambassadors, and so forth. It would be an essential technique by which we achieve excellence in government. With that kind of practice, candidates could acquire the *habits* necessary to do the right thing instinctively, according to the deliberate standards of the people. It seems to me that we are more justified in saying today that a presidential simulator is possible than someone in 1950 would have been in claiming that a manned trip to the moon is feasible. After all, some kinds of management and political simulations already exist. Further, one would not start by trying to build a presidential simulator. Rather one would start by simulating the simplest political job one could find. Succeeding there, one would proceed to more complex simulations. There seems to be nothing inherently implausible about this attempt. If we are willing to create virtual sports for the sake of private enjoyment, why not create virtual politics for the sake of public happiness? Creating virtual politics would take great determination, daring and intellectual energy, but the task of completing the American revolution is not for the lethargic. In any case, is it unreasonable to ask that if politicians are going to represent us, that they ought not to represent our whims or casual opinions, but only our informed values or considered judgments; and that, before representing us, they must give a convincing demonstration they not only know those values or judgments, but can embody them into their acts of governing with a high degree of excellence? It is sad that we conduct our political life as if the advantages of simulation are intrinsically impossible for politicians, as if there can be no criteria for virtual success and failure — as if any combination of "excellence" and "politics" is an oxymoron. Were simulators never used in the training and testing of airline pilots, flying would be much more expensive and dangerous. Is it any wonder that government is so expensive, or that the competence and character of our leaders is so often problematical?

Using the results of the Presidential simulator tests, let us assume that an advisory jury has reduced the number of candidates to seven. The primaries could then reduce the number of candidates as follows. The fifty states would be divided into five groups of ten in such a way that the difference between the population of the largest and smallest group is a minimum. Similarly for the second largest and second smallest group. The five groups are then ordered by a random device. The first group of ten states will have a presidential primary on the first Tuesday in May. They are presented with the seven candidates and each voter votes for all the candidates of whom he or she approves, that is, the voter could approve of one or two or . . . or seven candidates. This is called *approval voting* (see Brams and Fishburn 1983 for details). (Approval voting is not without its critics, but it is the best voting system known to me for this particular situation. See Saari and Van Newenhizen 1988, 1988a for criticism, and Brams, Fishburn, and Merrill 1988, 1988a for a defense). Normally the candidate wins who gets the largest number of votes. Here we use a variant in which the candidate with the least number of votes is eliminated. On the first Tuesday in June the second group of states would have a primary with the remaining six candidates. This procedure continues through September, after which only two candidates would remain. Next each would choose a Vice-Presidential running mate from high ranking Presidential candidates. These candidates would then stand for election, or campaign for it, as they chose.

Of course this thought experiment is fanciful. But that does not mean that a practical proposal in the same spirit is impossible. If there is something to marvel in all this, it is not the novelty of repeatedly testing politicians, but the crude and haphazard methods we presently use. We go to great lengths to ensure our pilots are well-trained and continually tested, but even the most foolish or evil pilot of a commercial airliner could normally endanger only a few thousand people. Yet we do not adequately test those who pilot a ship of state that involves the safety of hundreds of millions, even billions, of people. Our ultimate aim is not mere competence; what we want in a politician — especially a President — is a political excellence that plays with the edge of what is humanly possible in politics, as the Olympic champion plays with the edge of what is humanly possible in sports. That requires objective criteria of achievement, widespread participation, and enormous prestige for success. The Olympics possess these factors, as does being CEO of a large corporation, where the criterion is a long string of substantial increases in earnings per share. What is lacking for the politician — and what hinders political excellence — is an objective criterion, which is precisely what tests using the Court of Common Reason would supply.

These tests would allow representation to meet the standards of the American revolution. Perhaps John Adams put those standards in the strongest terms:

> And liberty cannot be preserved without a general knowledge among the people, who have a right from the frame of their nature, to knowledge, as their great Creator who does nothing in vain, has given them understandings, and a desire to know — but besides this they have a right, an indisputable, unalienable, indefeasible divine right to that most dreaded, and envied kind of knowledge, I mean of the characters and conduct of their rulers. (1977 1:121; cf. Adams, Samuel 1904 3:237)

Using courts of common reason to impose the highest contemporary epistemological standards on "that most dreaded, and envied kind of knowledge," we could create a large set of excellent politicians, perhaps more than a hundred times as large as what the eighteenth century produced.

The Court of Common Reason could also be used to provide the necessary incentive for excellence in all employees of the government. For example, consider a governmental agency that has some definite budget. The Court could recommend a specific bonus to employees if they exceed their goals, or if they meet them at significantly less cost. The Court could harmonize the bureaucratic mind and the deliberate sense of the people. One might, for example, form a court of common reason consisting only of agency employees to see how their informed values might differ from the population at large. To resolve any differences a hybrid court might be set up with each subjury consisting of six employees and six persons drawn from the general population. Using this data, standards could be set so that those employees who did not live up to them could be replaced, and those that did could be paid very well. Successful leaders of the agency could gain great prestige. Of course, efficiency is not the only consideration and the jury might sacrifice some efficiency for the sake of other values. The crucial point is this: The Court would enable explicit and detailed goals to be set, making excellence as measurable thing as it is in sports or business.

Naturally, it is not enough to make excellence possible; it must be made actual. In 1789, Alexander Hamilton noted that "great revolutions . . . serve to bring to light talents and virtues which might otherwise have languished in obscurity or only shot forth a few scattered and wondering rays" (1961 5:348). Writing in the same year, David Ramsay observed that the American revolution

> gave occasion for the display of abilities which, but for that event, would have been lost to the world. . . . It seemed as if the war not only required, but created talents. Men whose minds were warmed with the love of liberty; and whose abilities were improved by daily exercise, and sharpened with a laudable ambition to serve their distressed country, spoke, wrote, and acted, with an energy far surpassing all expectations which could be reasonably founded on their previous acquirements. (1789 2:315-316)

America was born in a revolutionary fervor when conditions were conducive to the production of political genius. Today we foolishly subscribe to the accidental theory of political genius, hoping it will somehow appear when needed. We should give up that pious hope and, using courts of common reason, design nationwide political contests — accompanied by inducements of great honor, fame and the excitement of competition — to not only discover but *create* superb talents in the service of public happiness. Designing such a process may be more difficult than organizing the Olympics to produce athletic talent, or designing a fair marketplace to produce business ability, but it is hardly beyond human power and imagination.

It would be wrong to think of the Agency for Public Choice as a sufficient guarantee against bad government because it both lets politicians know the informed values of the people and provides better ways of testing political leaders. The only sure protection is the political education of the people. "I know no safe depository of the ultimate powers of the society," Jefferson observed, "but the people themselves; and if we think them not enlightened enough to exercise their control with a wholesome discretion, the remedy is not to take it from them, but to inform their discretion by education. This is the true corrective of abuses of constitutional power"(1903 15:278; cf. 483). Let us consider what a Jeffersonian education might mean today. "We hold these truths to be self-evident," the Declaration states, which means, that we, who have a strong moral sense, who have experienced political freedom, who have reflected on that experience, can see that "all men are created equal" is self-evident, and we "hold" it to be so. To say axioms are self-evident means that "no explanation can make them plainer"(Jefferson 1903 15:470; cf. Hamilton 1961 4:413). But attention and reflection are needed. For example, Andrew Eliot in a 1771 sermon given in Boston said: "We may be ignorant of self-evident truths, if we do not attend to them . . ."(1771 xxx). This follows Locke who argued that one needs reflection to see the self-evidence of some propositions (1975 599). But reflection depends on having, or knowing about, the experience or ideas one reflects on. For example, the postulate that "all right angles are equal" may be "self-evident" to someone who has experience in Euclidean geometry, and has reflected upon it. Those without that experience or reflection may not find it so. The same holds in politics. Thus in 1774 John Hancock said: "Security to the persons and properties of the governed is so obviously the design and end of civil government, that to attempt a logical proof of it, would be like burning tapers at noon-day, to assist the sun in enlightening the world"(1774 6). To most inhabitants of colonial America such security was "self-evident," but that does not mean it was "self-evident" to all humans throughout history. What is self-evident is not necessarily *immediately* obvious, for example, the induction axiom in arithmetic. Worldwide, most humans in the eighteenth-century were ignorant of the possibility of government that protects "property" in the extended Lockean sense which includes "Lives, Liberties and Estates"(above, page 42).

This kind of ignorance extends to many people in contemporary America who are unaware of their Declaration and Constitutional rights, or they are careless about them, or they deny them altogether. To remedy this ignorance one could begin by creating structural protection against outcomes that make future self-government difficult or impossible. To see how, consider an analogy. Imagine a thimble of water at 70° that we wish to cool to 50°. We have a glass thermometer that is at 60°. The attempt to measure the water's present temperature will disturb the reality we wish to know (since the thermometer will cool the water as it is measuring its temperature), but it will disturb that temperature in the direction that we want it to take. Let us call this a positive effect of the process of knowledge. A thermometer at 80° would produce a negative effect. Positive and negative effects also occur in obtaining political knowledge. In general there is no way to find out the informed values and considered judgments of the American people except by interfering with the political reality one seeks to know. Yet by carefully designing the environment in which people would respond, the Agency could ensure that this process of knowledge would be positive for the values of the American revolution. For instance, the experience could make it more likely that former jurors, compared to the general population, would presuppose that all human beings begin with equal moral worth. To bring this about, the opening passages of the Declaration could be read before major sets of questions are presented to the advisory jury. The jury could be told that the purpose of these questions is to find out in detail what the just powers of the American government ought to be, and what the people want to alter or abolish. The Bill of Rights could also be read. Consider Madison's description of the intended effect of the Bill: "The political truths declared in that solemn manner acquire by degrees the character of fundamental maxims of free Government, and as they become incorporated with the national sentiment, counteract the impulses of interest and passion"(1962 11:298-9; cf. Federal Farmer 1788 144-5). Thus the experience of serving in the Court of Common Reason could again make self-evident the "fundamental maxims of free Government"; it could teach old things anew by helping participants appropriate to the present moment our glorious Declaration, Constitution, and Bill of Rights.

In a letter to his wife Abigail on July 3, 1776, John Adams described how the American revolution itself was authorized by widespread deliberation:

> Time has been given for the whole People, maturely to consider the great Question of Independence and to ripen their Judgments, dissipate their Fears, and allure their Hopes, by discussing it in News Papers and Pamphletts, by debating it, in Assemblies, Conventions, Committees of Safety and Inspection, in Town and County Meetings, as well as in private Conversations, so that the whole People in every Colony of the 13, have now adopted it, as their own Act. (Butterfield, Lyman 1963 2:30; a similar observation is made by James Wilson about the Constitution in 2007 1:287).

But where did the people get the competence and spirit to carry on this deliberative soul-searching? Elsewhere Adams named four institutions — the towns, schools, congregations, militia — and said that the "consequences" of them "have been, that the inhabitants [of New England], having acquired from their infancy the habit of discussing, of deliberating, and of judging public affairs, it was in these assemblies of towns or districts that the sentiments of the people were formed in the first place, and their resolutions were taken from the beginning to the end of the disputes and the war with Great Britain"(1850 5:495).

One could emulate the colonial experience by using courts of common reason from "infancy" to recreate the spirit of the American revolution. From as early on as possible, students could get practice in both giving and judging persuasive argument, by regularly participating in subjuries, initially dealing with school issues, but later with local, state, national, and international politics. "We do not extol it too highly when we attribute as much to the power of eloquence as to the sword in bringing about the American revolution" said Benjamin Rush (1786a 29). "Eloquence is the child of a free State," David Ramsay declared, "in this form of government, as public measures are determined by a majority of votes, arguments enforced by the arts of perswasion must evermore be crowned with success. The rising patriot therefore, who wishes the happiness of his country, will cultivate the art of public speaking"(1779 1; cf. Adams 1850 249). Both observations are true enough and very important; but it must also be understood that this art can be used by the demagogue as well as the statesman. In Madison's words, "It should seem that Caesar excell'd Cicero in the Art of Persuasion"(1962 1:21). Hence a free society should have institutions whose consequences would give the people the power to detect that persuasive eloquence which makes private gain appear to be the public good (cf. Wilson 2007 1:538). If reason is to rule, the people must be able to detect its counterfeits. Students therefore should gain familiarity with cognitive illusions and the phenomenology of human credulity, by getting practice in avoiding logical and statistical fallacies, in distinguishing scientists from cranks, and doctors from quacks, in studying auditory, visual, and tactile illusions (including the wonderful use magicians make of them), in learning how experts identify art forgeries, in recognizing the means by which demagogues practice their deceptions, in identifying the characteristics of catastrophic ideologies — such as fascism, communism, racism, fanaticism, and terrorism — that proved capable of corrupting or endangering so many people for so long. They should understand that "I cannot tell a lie" is as much a fault when listening or reading as it is a virtue when speaking or writing. But perhaps the most important virtue to be instilled is the internal one of being able to recognize the tricks the mind uses to protect against unwanted criticism, whether internal or external. If students are to gain a genuine self-mastery free from toxic self-deceit, they must, in addition to the art of persuasion, learn the art of being persuaded by reason. Hobbes displayed the art when he first came across the Pythagorean theorem: "He was forty yeares old before he looked on Geometry, which happened accidentally, . . . , Euclid's *Elements* lay open, and 'twas the 47th Element liber I. He read the Proposition. 'By G—' sayd he, 'this is impossible.' So he reads the Demonstration of it, which referred him back to such a Proposition: which proposition he read: that referred him back to another which he also read, and sic deincips [slowly but surely], that at last he was demonstratively convinced of that trueth. This made him in love with Geometry"(Aubrey 2000 427-8). The art of being persuaded by reason consists in the ability to recognize or generate sound arguments, combined with the willingness to accept and abide by them, even if that means going against one's initial strong beliefs, or swallowing one's pride, or giving up a cherished goal, or modifying a strong habit. The awesome powers of critical thinking that Jefferson and Madison possessed were utterly worthless to protect them from great disgrace in our eyes, because they depraved their own consciousness, rendering impotent those awesome powers whenever they framed judgments about blacks and slavery; they wronged the right of the Declaration in their personal and professional lives; they ceased to be *freemen of deliberate reason* and became *slaves of base passion.* "Before we let our Thoughts judge of Things," John Mason said in 1789, "we must set Reason to judge our Thoughts; for they are not always in a proper Condition to execute that Office. We do not believe the Character which a Man gives us of another, unless we have a good Opinion of his own; so neither should we believe the Verdict which the Mind pronounces, till we first examine whether it be impartial and unbiased; whether it be in a proper Temper to judge, and have proper Lights to judge by. The Want of this previous *Act of Self-Judgment*, is the Cause of much Self Deception and false Judgment"(115). Jefferson and Madison were evidently incapable of that "previous *Act of Self-Judgment*." In eating, *the lack of the self-control to use and follow reason* has destructive consequences for the well-being of the body, such as diabetes, which can lead to gangrene; in believing, that lack has similar consequences for the mind. Sadly, "gangrene in the mind," which afflicts extraordinary as well as ordinary talents, is seldom recognized as a great educational challenge, namely, to figure out how to instill a life-long habit in children and young people to use their reason to decide correctly whether their own minds, or those of others, "be in a proper Temper to judge, and have proper Lights to judge by." The great task of achieving and maintaining moral and political excellence in a democratic society must ultimately rest on the success of this educational challenge. Because humor can be an important defense against toxic self-deception, might it not be wise to have high school students annually use a democratic evolutionary paradigm to pick the best comedies, written by themselves, that mock that self-deceit in teenagers and adults alike? Since human minds that are incapable of honest self-evaluation can be the greatest of all weapons of mass destruction — "When I think about it," Hitler told Himmler, "I realize that I'm extraordinarily humane"(1976 193)) — we cannot start too early, or be too careful, or be too persistent, in protecting ourselves against this threat. (The issues in this paragraph are many. For a survey of some of them, see "Practical Rationality," "Rational Beliefs," "Rationality of Belief," "Theories of Common-Sense Reasonings"(Craig 1998), as well as *Inevitable Illusions; How Mistakes of Reason Rule Our Minds* (Piattelli-Palmarini 1994).)

As a thought experiment concerning that challenge, imagine there are a million students who have to vote on the correct answer (among ten given answers) to a very difficult mathematical problem. They are not allowed to communicate, but they may abstain. However, each has perfect self-knowledge and only one student knows he knows the correct answer. So all abstain except that student. Hence collective decision is right by a vote of one to zero. This idea suggests that we ought to explore practically how to use self-knowledge to improve the quality of collective decisions. Here are some things to try: Expose students to problems that illustrate the pitfalls of the untutored reason; do it year after year with greater and greater subtlety so they gain the habit of not making a knowledge claim until certain conditions are met. Experiment with different schemes to find out which ones results in the best use of self-knowledge to improve the quality of collective decision, where students have a x% chance of getting the right answer when they believe they know it, a y% chance of being getting the right answer when they believe they do not know it, and a z% chance of getting the right answer when they are unsure. Use competition within and among schools to get students to increase their x and y through better self-knowledge, and increase their z by learning how best to deal with uncertainty.

The conception of a democracy being described here was perhaps first articulated by Pericles:

> . . . we Athenians decide public questions for ourselves or at least endeavour to arrive at a sound understanding of them, in the belief that it is not debate that is a hindrance to action, but rather not to be instructed by debate before the time comes for action. For in truth we have this point also of superiority over other men, to be most daring in action and yet at the same time most given to reflection upon the ventures we mean to undertake . . . (Thucydides 1928 1:329)

Our contemporary knowledge and technology gives us the opportunity to greatly surpass the Athenians in deeds thoroughly supported by debate and reflection. For example, in schools, children could be prepared by social games that are specifically designed to get them to recognize, and correct, even subtle intellectual or affective delusions that undermine sound thought, whether typically exhibited by individuals or groups. Perhaps such games could turn the most apathetic pupils into devotees, because they would force students to continually dance on the edge of frustration and success. The aim is to get them to perceive, by direct experience, that if they would internalize this social experience of deliberative reason, they would be developing the critical *and* self-critical consciousness necessary for their own good judgment, without which they would not be able to felicitously pursue either their own, or the public, happiness. Again, the idea here is Athenian:

> . . . the power to speak well is taken as the surest index of a sound understanding, the outward image of a good and faithful soul. With this faculty we both contend

against others on matters which are open to dispute and seek light for ourselves on things which are unknown; for the same arguments which we use in persuading others when we speak in public, we employ also when we deliberate in our own thoughts; and, while we call eloquent those who are able to speak before a crowd, we regard as sage those who most skilfully debate their problems in their own minds. (Isocrates 1929 327, 329)

Hence when advisory juries of students give their considered judgment on some of the same issues presented to state or national Courts of Common Reason, they would be gaining the habit of making responsible decisions based on honest and regular dialogue, both in social discourse and in the theater of their own minds. By increasing their own skills for political freedom, they would simultaneously increase them for personal freedom, enabling them to better cultivate their own individuality and humanity. In time they would not only understand, but directly feel, the necessity of free speech and free dialogue for the integrity of their decisions, and thus the importance of the First Amendment in American society. They would come to see that as the best science is produced where there is free speech and association among scientists, so the best politics is produced where there is free speech and association among the people. As jurors in courts of common reason they could instill in themselves the demeanor necessary for genuine democratic debate; they would directly perceive, in the words of Adam Smith, that "good temper and moderation of contending factions seems to be the most essential circumstance in the publick morals of a free people"(1981 2:775; ct. Plutarch 1927 1:427). By cultivating the habits of civility that are necessary for the flourishing of American perfectionist democracy, the students would be simultaneously cultivating the private morals that are necessary for the greatest flourishing of their own lives.

John Adams once said that the "five Pillars of Aristocracy, are Beauty, Wealth, Birth, Genius and Virtues. Any one of the three first, can at any time over bear one or both of the two last"(Cappon 1959 2:371). Students could study the historical background of Adams' statement and reflect on its implications for their own voting behavior. They could study the mathematics of public happiness, including such things as the Condorcet jury theorem, voting paradoxes, sampling theory, and how to reduce manipulation of democratic outcomes. They could learn to recognize toxic self-deceit in political leaders. They could also play games that would simulate both the ways in which political leaders betray the public trust, and the various means the people can use "to crush, regularly and peaceably, the usurpations of their unfaithful agents"(Jefferson, above, page 185). Conversely they could be taught to recognize political virtue (as defined by the Court of Common Reason) and the means the people can use to entice the best into serving. They could periodically be asked what knowledge and skills they need to participate in an advisory jury. Deliberating on their answers, they would teach themselves the importance of their own education. By frequently being forced to choose among competing values in a subjury, students would gain experience in the discipline of deliberative soul-searching, so that as adults they would be prepared to make fateful, yet responsible, political decisions, or thoughtful decisions as jurors in trials. Yet their own personal development would not be neglected, for by engaging their mind and spirit in creating a politics of self-knowledge, they would be learning how to cultivate an ethics of self-knowledge to promote their own happiness. As the American revolution in the eighteenth century created those talents that enabled the United States to be invented, so our educational system should rouse those talents that will allow it to forever flourish. That means practice, practice, practice. In the freest societies, an education designed to prepare an individual for a flourishing life, and an education designed to promote public happiness, are mutually supportive. Courts of common reason, we can conclude, are an indispensable part of an education that prepares citizens for excellence in self-government; they enable participants to learn directly the nature of free society, and to acquire the manners and habits necessary to prosper in one.

It was a change in the minds of the people that John Adams saw as the essence of the American revolution: "What do We Mean by the Revolution? The War? That was no part [*nota bene*] of the Revolution. It was only An Effect and Consequence of it. The Revolution was in the Minds of the People, and this was effected from 1760 to 1775, in the course of fifteen Years before a drop of blood was drawn at Lexington" (Cappon 1959 2:455; see also 1850 10:180, 182-4). Thomas Paine made a similar observation: "Our style and manner of thinking have undergone a revolution more extraordinary than the political revolution of the country. We see with other eyes; we hear with other ears; and think with other thoughts, than those we formerly used" (1945 2:243). The American revolution was a transformation of the human spirit made possible by the colonial experience of the revolutionaries. Our aim is to design education in general, and advisory jury duty in particular, so that the experience of them will be even better than the colonial experience was at awakening the American revolution in the "Minds of the People."

"Where then is our republicanism to be found?" Jefferson once asked. "Not in our constitution certainly, but merely in the spirit of the people. That would oblige even a despot to govern us republicanly"(1892 10:39). Of course, no one would suggest actually making a despot President. But one could simulate such a possibility. The game of "Despotism" could be played by students to find out the most likely ways in which despots might arise in America, and what could be done to prevent them. (Lincoln, by the way, thought despots were a real possibility (cf. 1953 1:114).) James Wilson recommended that we "introduce, into the very form of government, such particular checks and controls, as to make it advantageous even for bad men to act for the publick good"(2007 1:695-6; cf. Hume 1985 15-16). John Adams said that "it would be impossible to prove that a republic cannot exist even among highwaymen, by setting one rogue to watch another; and the knaves themselves may in time be made honest men by the struggle"(1850 6:219). Simulation after simulation could be devised to find out how to reduce the bad effects that typically result from the wickedness, hypocrisy, and self-deceit of political leaders. Totalitarians all want freedom for themselves, but slavery for every other citizen. Those who desire limited government must be prepared to disobey authority and the law under certain circumstances. For example, crimes against humanity by leaders are only possible if subordinates obey. Experiments in the Court of Common Reason could make clear the circumstances under which the people want members of the armed services, other governmental employees, and private citizens to disobey military and political leaders. These circumstances could be taught in school and widely publicized. "A revolution principle", James Wilson argued, "certainly is, and certainly should be taught as a principle of the constitution of the United States, and of every State in the Union. This revolution principle — that, the sovereign power residing in the people; they may change their constitution and government whenever they please — is not a principle of discord, rancour, or war: it is a principle of melioration, contentment, and peace"(2007 1:443). The goal would be to so infuse the revolution principle into the spirit of the American people that it "would oblige even a despot to govern us republicanly." The idea that one can actively resist unjust rulers was of course a commonplace during the revolutionary era (see, for example, Howard 1773 33-4, Hitchcock, Gad 1774 26-7, West, Samuel 1776 27, Parsons 1778 12-

3). Jefferson expressed it as an aphorism: "Rebellion to Tyrants is Obedience to God"(1950 1:494-7; cf. 1903 15:415). He liked this motto so much that he put it on his personal seal when he was Secretary of State (see Patterson and Dougall 1976 505). (When he did that, one wonders whether he reflected that if his own slaves rebelled against his petty tyranny, they would be obedient to God.). Although the formulation was probably Franklin's (see Jefferson 1950 1:677-79 and Patterson and Dougall 1976 14), the idea and some of the language can be found in Locke's *Second Treatise*: "Where it is plain, that shaking off a Power, which force, and not Right hath set over any one, though it hath the Name of *Rebellion*, yet is no Offence before God, but is that, which he allows and countenances . . ."(1988 396-97; cf. Isocrates: "those who take the lives of despots are given the highest rewards by their fellow-citizens"(1928 2:95, 97). To know when and how the people want governmental, or any other authority, defied and, if those circumstances occur, to act on that knowledge with great precision — these are among the skills of freedom. Were such republican virtues mastered by the people, it would be impossible for our government to commit crimes against humanity, such as using bogus laws to protect the slave interest, or forcibly returning millions of Soviet refugees after World War II.

Simulation games dealing with the character of leaders should not be limited to "Despotism." "Incompetence" and "Deception," among others, might also be fruitful. Other games could deal with weaknesses in the people themselves, such as "Mobs," "Collective Self-Deception," and "Groupthink." Still others, such as "Terrorism," could teach participants how to identify terrorists, and how to confront their threats with the least compromise of our traditional rights. "Have we not already seen," Hamilton asks, "enough of the fallacy and extravagance of those idle theories which have amused us with promises of an exemption from the imperfections, the weaknesses, and the evils incident to society in every shape?"(1961 4:316). The fact that we cannot eliminate "the imperfections, the weaknesses, and the evils" does not mean that we are necessarily helpless in reducing them, or diminishing their bad effects. We may live in an ethical and political imperfect world, but we do not have to leave it as imperfect as we find it. Contemporary game theory and simulation games, for example, give us the opportunity, if we would only seize it, to tackle ethics and politics with much greater effectiveness and precision than in the past.

The agency that operates the Court of Common Reason could grow in importance to become a Department of Public Choice and, finally, a Fourth branch of the government. This branch might be called the *deliberative* branch since it is deliberation by the public that uncovers facts about their collective choices. The operation of the deliberative branch, like the operation of the present government according to the Constitution, ought to be positive for the values of the American revolution. We certainly do not want to move in a direction that is both more participatory *and* more tyrannical. Hence the deliberative branch could give advice on political questions but initially would have no power to act on that advice. The other branches that could act would be under no legal obligation to do so. Nevertheless government officials would presumably try to follow the advice unless, to use Madison's words again, they believe it is one of those instances in which the people are "stimulated by some irregular passion, or some illicit advantage, or misled by the artful misrepresentations of interested men," that is, it is an instance in which the people go against reason in the pursuit of public happiness. In such circumstances, the rulers ought "to suspend the blow meditated by the people against themselves."(above, page 158).

The power to have questions considered or reconsidered by the advisory jury would have to be carefully controlled since the advisory jury's time and patience is limited. The executive, legislative, and judicial branches would need such power, and others would also need some access, such as the community of scholars. Disputes about what questions to take up, or the allocation of time to them, could be resolved by the judicial branch based on second-order advice from metajuries within the Court of Common Reason itself. Nevertheless the metajurors in the Court will *ultimately* have to decide what constitutes fair access, and the general means by which questions can come before the Court. Ways should be developed so that widespread and deep issues (by the jurors' own determination) could be decided. If a prior decision occasions regret, a study could be made (*al la* investigations of pilot error in airplanes) to see if a change of procedures might make less likely similar decisions in the future. Further, jurors must not only be respondents but on occasion actors, where they set their own agenda and monitor their own progress. Their creative potential ought to be effectively utilized in the evolution of policies that govern American society. The Court of Common Reason could then become a laboratory of the American spirit, and a self-governing people could fashion themselves in a way that reflects their sense of goodness and excellence. As a result of the consumer movement a new attitude emerged in the evaluation of the safety of consumer products. Previously it was solely the fault of irresponsible parents who left a bottle of medicine where a child could reach it, or it was the "nut behind the wheel" who was solely responsible for automobile accidents. The new morality of consumerism — reflecting a keener appreciation of the value of human life — requires consumer products be designed so as to minimize the dangers of both using *and* misusing them. This same attitude must prevail in the plan for the Court of Common Reason: we should anticipate the ways in which things can go wrong, and try to forestall or minimize that possibility by careful design.

Courts of common reason could also have many military applications, especially useful in the new kinds of warfare that are common today. For example, suicide bombers have been a difficult military problem. Well, in ancient Miletus many young women started to hang themselves and nothing relatives or friends said or did could stop the hysteria. Finally, "on the advice of a man of sense, an ordinance was proposed that the women who hanged themselves should be carried naked through the market-place to their burial"(Plutarch 1927 3:509). "The advice was followed; and had its desired effect: for the dread of the ignominy, that would attend their bodies after death, rivetted them to a life; which the horrors of death itself could not effect"(Polyænus 1974 361). Perhaps the military could reduce or eliminate suicide bombings if they accepted the advice of a court of common reason, specifically organized to find realistic, contemporary equivalents of being "carried naked through the market-place." The jurors could consist of historians, professors of religion, logicians, psychologists, military interrogators, political scientists, failed but cooperative suicide bombers, and so forth.   A second example: we know that the most accomplished players of the game of defend the king that we call *chess* can be defeated by a team of chess players, programmers, and computers. Would it not be wise to investigate whether the most accomplished players of the game of defend the secrets that we call *interrogation of enemy combatants* could be defeated, without coming close to torture, by a team of interrogators, programmers, and courts of common reason? Tests could be run on every enemy-combatant prisoner who is going to be released by telling them a secret and promising the longer they succeed in keeping it, the more money he or she will receive on release. A final military example: the best combination of weapons to develop for future warfare could be determined, using a democratic evolutionary paradigm, with advisory juries of the most varied sort, and hybrid juries to resolve differences. Whenever the advice eventually proved to be poor, tests would be run to see where the methods that were followed could be improved.

The idea of a court of common reason is not limited to use by a government. Many large private organizations such as churches, corporations, and unions, are run on democratic principles and might benefit by creating a court. Thus we can imagine entrepreneurs setting up private choice corporations that would organize advisory juries for various clients. Consider consumer products. Advisory juries could evaluate them in a context in which manufacturers could explain and defend their products, critics could point out limitations, users could describe their good and bad experiences with them environmentalists and consumer activists could also plead their case, and so forth. This having been done, an individual, by paying a fee to the private choice corporation, could find out the considered judgment about the product by, say, fifty persons on the advisory jury most like him or her (in age, sex, income, job type, etc.). Of course, we already do this kind of thing when we consult a neighbor or a consumer magazine. However, these means can be crude compared to what is technically possible, and often the emphasis is on hasty opinion rather than considered judgment. Private advisory juries could increase our freedom by increasing the number and depth of our rewarding experiences and, thereby, help promote our pursuit of happiness. Of course, people would be under no obligation whatsoever to use the advice they paid for.

Other uses of private choice corporations easily suggest themselves. The directors and executives of a large corporation, such as Walmart, should be faithful to the informed values and considered judgments of its stockholders. To do this they must know what those values and judgments are. Hence imagine that Walmart hires a private choice corporation to form a special advisory jury consisting exclusively of its stockholders. (We are here referring to ultimate stockholders: if a church owned x% of Walmart, then the special advisory jury would have (at least) x% of its members from the members of that church.) One could then determine the informed values and considered judgments of the stockholders on a wide variety of topics, such as dividend policy, executive compensation, trade with totalitarian countries, and the like. Hence one could help ensure that large corporations are controlled by the common reason of their stockholders, a control which is absent today since no one knows what that reason is. Similar comments could apply, *mutatis mutandis*, to large unions, churches, and charities.

If courts of common reason could be made cheap enough, they would have an indefinitely large number of uses. Thus private choice corporations could be used by foundations to set up special courts consisting only of scientists whose responses would influence the allocation of grants. Or they could test new methods of improving the efficiency of the Court of Common Reason. Or special interest groups who lobby before Congress could use them to demonstrate that their proposals are in fact also in the general interest of the American people, not merely the special interest of their group. Again, since courts of common reason are intended to be a self-conscious and efficient use of distributive intelligence, one wonders if a group of scientists could use them to solve difficult scientific problems more easily and quickly than by employing ordinary methods of journals, scientific conferences, informal contacts, and the like. For example, could they be used in the war against cancer? Computers were first employed for military purposes, but they were based on completely general logical principles, so that if a problem could be solved by any machine whatsoever, it could be solved by a machine based on those principles. Perhaps time and experience will eventually show that courts of common reason, although first used for political purposes, are based on completely general principles of human reasoning and thus, if humans can solve a problem at all, they can solve it using courts of common reason.

Finally, private choice corporations could also be employed to serve as a check against governmental power. The Agency for Public Choice is a governmental agency and we can imagine that, through incompetence or knavery, it would refuse to consider some issue important to the American people. Then private groups could pay to have a private choice corporation create a national advisory jury to deal with that issue. Imagine that the issue concerns a right, and that three-quarters of its subjuries call for its protection. Assume that the procedures of the corporation are of such high quality that it is not reasonable to doubt that its results represent the deliberate sense of the people. Then the right would be a Constitutional right by an appeal to the Ninth Amendment just as if it had been explicitly written into the Constitution. By checking the power of the Agency for Public Choice, private choice corporations could help ensure that James Wilson's revolutionary ideal would be a living reality: "To every suggestion concerning a bill of rights, the citizens of the United States may always say, WE reserve the right to do what we please"(above, page 207).

The first dimension of American perfectionist democracy is the restructuring of government so that it will operate according to the informed values and considered judgments of the people. As American society was computerized in the last half of the twentieth century, it should be "deliberized" in the first half of the twenty-first. The history of statehood has been a history of increasing explicitness. In the beginning, there were no doubt leaders who made decisions with only their own judgment and power as its basis. Then came oral traditions, then published laws, then written constitutions (as in ancient Athens), then constitutional conventions and bills of rights (as in America's state and federal constitutions). Finally, by using twenty-first century techniques to embody Jefferson's ward proposal, the grand contract among the people in forming their government would be made explicit in full detail, and both the structure of the government and its administration would be continually derived from the authority of the people.

To summarize, American perfectionist democracy is part of an unfinished revolution to fulfill political ideals formulated centuries ago. Whether on the level of political theory, or on the practical level of the politician, the fundamental mistake of our political life today is a failure to recognize the importance of designing institutions that would make it possible to know the common reason of society to the highest degree of precision presently possible. Without such institutions we cannot meet the great intellectual and moral challenge of the American revolution. Ignoring this challenge, many of our political scientists and politicians pay homage to public opinion as revealed, for example, in polls or referendums. Yet public opinion is often a fusion of ignorance and passion that can be a serious threat to individual rights. The extreme paradigm of that fusion is the lynch mob although there are, of course, many lesser violations. A perennial and correct complaint is that our government is inefficient and badly managed. New administrations, therefore, routinely promise to rectify this by introducing new managers, by reorganizing departments, and so forth. Yet all these risk mediocrity or worse — and for the simplest of reasons. In order to have good management, specific objectives or goals need to be set. But without detailed knowledge of the deliberate sense of the people, this cannot be done *authoritatively*. Government officials are forced to rely on what are, for the most part, educated guesses. An old joke has it that government officials are bureaucrats or political hacks if one disapproves of them, and public servants or statesmen if one approves. The advisory jury enables us to make good on the joke, that is, it enables us to accurately distinguish these two groups. Of every power that governmental officials exercise, we can — with the Court of Common Reason — authoritatively answer the questions: Is it a just power? Is it properly used? We sometimes require zero-based budgeting for financial reasons; what we need now is zero-based planning for political reasons. This is the purpose of the first dimension of American perfectionist democracy: the transformation of a politics of public opinion dominated by mediocrity into a politics of self-knowledge dominated by excellence. Suetonius remarks that Augustus Caesar "could justly boast that he found [Rome] built of . . . brick and left it in marble"(1944 1:167). We need a leader who could justly boast that, upon entering office, Americans were apathetic about excellence in self-government; but upon leaving, they were consumed with a soul-searching desire to achieve it. In the words of John Adams, ". . . it is the Part of a great Politician to make the Character of his People; to extinguish among them, the Follies and Vices that he sees, and to create in them the Virtues and Abilities which he sees wanting"(1977 3:398).

Part II

The Economics of Honesty

"A Wit's a feather, and a Chief a rod;
An honest Man's the noblest work of God"(1970 151).

Alexander Pope

". . . the acquisition of wealth [is] finally possible only under certain moral conditions of society, of which quite the first [is] a belief in the existence, and even, for practical purposes, in the attainability of honesty. Without venturing to pronounce — since on such a matter human judgment is by no means conclusive — what is, or is not, the noblest of God's works, we may yet admit so much of Pope's assertion as that an honest man is among His best works presently visible, and, as things stand, a somewhat rare one; but not an incredible or miraculous work; still less an abnormal one. Honesty is not a disturbing force which deranges the orbits of economy; but a consistent and commanding force, by obedience to which — and by no other obedience — those orbits can continue clear of chaos. It is true, I have sometimes heard Pope condemned for the lowness, instead of the height, of his standard: — 'Honesty is indeed a respectable virtue; but how much higher may men attain! Shall nothing more be asked of us than that we be honest?' For the present, good friends, nothing"(1903 17:19-20).

John Ruskin

"Is a toast asked? 'The *United States*,' instead of the 'People of the *United States*,' is the toast given. This is not politically correct. The toast is meant to present to view the *first* great object in the *Union*: It presents only the second: It presents only the *artificial* person, instead of the *natural* persons, who spoke it into existence. A State I cheerfully fully admit, is the noblest work of *Man*: But, *Man himself*, free and honest, is, I speak as to this world, the noblest work of God"(Dallas 1790 2:462-3).

James Wilson

"A man can do no greater wrong than by telling lies to a popular assembly; for, where the political system is based upon speeches, how can it be safely administered if the speeches are false?"(1926 364-5).

Demosthenes

". . honesty is the first chapter in the book of wisdom"(1903 15:180). "The whole art of government consists in the art of being honest"(1950 1:134).

Thomas Jefferson

"A sacred regard to Truth is among the first and most essential Virtues of a public Man"(MHS 1917 2:209).

John Adams

"It is essential to the character of a free republic, that every thing should be reduced to the standard of reason; that men and laws should depend on their own intrinsic merit, and that no shadow of deception should ever be offered to the people; as it cannot fail to corrupt them; and pave the way to oppression"(1793 50-1).

Joel Barlow

8

Economic Ignorance

What kind of economy would be appropriate for a society that is guided solely by the philosophy of the American revolution? The answer is this: *it must be a economy where the only limitations on the freedom of markets that produce economic values are those limitations generated by the freedom of markets that produce moral and political values.* More specifically, the only prohibitions (such as *no child prostitution*) or regulations (such as *package foods must list ingredients*) that apply in an economy operating under a government, compared to an economy operating without a government, are those authorized by courts of common reason. For Jefferson, honesty is an indispensable condition of any just government, whether political or economic, but beyond that he is open to experiment and unwilling to impose *a priori* conditions: "for in so complicated a science as political economy, no one axiom can be laid down as wise and expedient for all times and circumstances . . . "(1892 10:10). Madison, for his part, makes unmistakably clear that the pursuit of happiness, in the moral sense, limits economic rights concerning ownership of land and things:

> There is no maxim in my opinion, which is more liable to be misapplied, and which therefore more needs elucidation than the current one that the interest of the majority is the political standard of right and wrong. Taking the word 'interest' as synonymous with 'Ultimate happiness,' in which sense it is qualified with every necessary moral ingredient, the proposition is no doubt true. But taking it in the popular sense, as referring to immediate augmentation of property and wealth, nothing can be more false. (1962 9:141; cf. 1900 6:101-103)

Since the Court of Common Reason is specifically designed to generate authoritative decisions about the "Ultimate happiness" of the majority, "qualified with every necessary moral ingredient," decisions of the Court would define the rights of property in its economic sense. Hence, it might seem, from the point of view of the philosophy of the American revolution, that little can be said on questions of economics until these decisions have been made. That is to some degree true, and it explains why the economic section of this book is shorter and less detailed than the other parts. Yet what can be said is worth expressing because moral requirements foreclose the possibility that any economic system might be appropriate. In particular, we can ask how the people might reasonably judge whether our economic structures and practices are the best presently obtainable arrangements for the pursuit of their happiness.

To explore this issue, we will be more concerned with metaeconomic than economic issues. The distinction can be made clear by using an analogy. A college football coach normally deals with first-order questions. Who is the best running back on the opposing team? Who generally controls the opposition's plays — the coach or the quarterback? What is the best strategy for winning? And so forth. First-order questions are, so to say, *within* the game, whereas second-order questions are *about* it. The latter concern the structure, setting, and value of the game. Should tests for illegal drugs be given to players? Should freshman be allowed to play on the varsity team? How well does the football program fit in with the overall purposes of the college of which it is a part? And so forth. Economics is primarily, but not exclusively, concerned with first-order questions. What were the principal factors influencing the price of coal in the past decade? Is a city's wage tax fair to commuters? Metaeconomic questions are second-order questions about economics itself. What criteria should be used for determining whether an economic practice is appropriate for a free society? What is the correct relation of economics to other disciplines? What is the conception of economics as it is presently understood by some school of economists?

Metaeconomic issues can undermine the legitimacy of exclusively focusing on first-order questions. Suppose, for example, that in 1825 there had been a group of American economists who spent all their time studying the economics of slavery, taking up such topics as the best technique for renting slaves so that slave owners could pay off their debts. When challenged about their probity they answered: "Slavery has widespread acceptance. We are economists, not moralists. If it is wrong, let the moralists denounce it. We are only trying to understand the economics of it, so that it may be made more efficient." To this there is a simple retort: "The fact that you are economists does not exempt you from moral responsibilities. There is a moral responsibility in the very decision to investigate one question rather than another." This is an extreme example but it illustrates why economics should not operate in a metaeconomic vacuum.

If we take metaeconomic issues seriously we should ask: How should the economy be structured so as to maximize the knowledge that a self-governing people can have of it? Here we must reflect on economic epistemology. We can take a hint from physical knowledge. Starting with Bacon and Galileo at least, physicists have not merely observed nature, but have devised experiments because, to quote Bacon again, "the nature of things betrays itself more readily under the vexations of art than in its natural freedom"(above, page 189). Physicists actively pursue the secrets of nature with their own questions and methodology, and they "force" nature to answer. Similarly as economic epistemologists we must ask: can we, by the "vexations of art," so arrange economic practices and institutions that the economic facts of life readily betray themselves to the American people? Our assumption is the Baconian one that "human knowledge and power come to the same thing"(2004 65) and that when the people know, they will have the power to wisely control their own economic life. *Economic truths exist in a context we create, and the way in which we create that context can decisively influence how well, if at all, those economic truths can become known.* It is not a criticism of chess that it is a difficult game to analyze — that very fact makes it an attractive intellectual challenge to its devotees. But there is no reason whatever to design economic institutions so that it becomes more difficult than necessary to know economic truths. Imagine a game of football in which the point value of each touchdown is determined by the sum of the heartbeats of the players and spectators during the minute after the touchdown. Since the score is determined by statistical methods (the average heartbeat of spectators is determined by sampling) and since the definition of spectator is vague (spectators are continually coming and going, paying attention or not, etc.), definite answers to the question "What is the score of the game?" may often be lacking. Hence there are arguments that never end so that years later many disagreements still exist as to who "really" won many games.

Like such games, economic practices and institutions are frequently so organized as to make analysis needlessly difficult. The people do not know the "scores," even though everyone agrees on the importance of knowing them. Framers of economic practices and institutions set them up for a wide variety of motives — such as solving labor disputes, increasing investment, raising revenue, redistributing income — but in so doing, they often forgot the important issue of providing a reliable way for the people to know, and control, what was created. Economic arrangements should be devised so that the people can correctly judge, whether a given exchange of theirs is fair and, second, whether the economic claims of companies, or unions, or politicians, are true. Naturally the extent to which such epistemological friendliness is possible is uncertain, but it is not uncertain that free societies aiming at economic and political excellence should continually try to perfect whatever friendliness has been achieved.

To reach that goal one must begin with a careful definition and use of economic terms. As Hobbes puts it: "Seeing then that *truth* consisteth in the right ordering of names in our affirmations, a man that seeketh precise truth, had need to remember what every name he uses stands for; and to place it accordingly; or else he will find himself entangled in the words, as a bird in lime-twiggs; the more he struggles, the more belimed"(1968 105; cf. Adams 1850 10:377). Someone could immediately object that most economists do carefully define and use their terms. Yet economists in a democracy should define basic terms such as "money," "inflation," and "debt," in such a way that the ordinary citizen can understand and correctly use them. This important goal is largely ignored. How can the economic government of our country be derived from the consent of the governed, when the governed cannot even comprehend the terms in which that government is described? Economic realities are directly related to the beliefs — whether true or false — of the people, and those beliefs are decisively influenced by the terms in which economic realities are understood. The public language of economics must be taken seriously.

This language is frequently confused and corrupted, not because the language of the public is inevitably debased, but because a substantial number of our economic practices and institutions conceal, rather than reveal, economic truth. They allow for the abuse of language which then results in political or economic deception. Consider the word "inflation." The public is encouraged to believe that the Consumer Price Index is an objective, politically neutral, measure of inflation. This belief is naive. For example, the Index is supposedly a measure of price changes. If a price is to serve its function of accurately measuring economic value, then the exchange must be both voluntary and free from dishonesty. It is not a true price if someone uses a weapon to force an exchange for less money than would otherwise be required, nor is it a true price if there is deception in the exchange (receiving a fake, rather than a real, diamond). It follows that the Consumer Price Index in an environment of price controls (say, in World War II) is not comparable to the Index without controls. Yet during World War II the main political function of the Index was to minimize labor disputes and maximize support for the war. As it was put in the *Report of the President's Committee on the Cost of Living* in 1944: "The lessened comfort of traveling, reduced delivery and laundry services, the use of cuts of meat of lower grade, are examples of quality deterioration, that we accept as necessary under war conditions"(RPCCL 1945 105). Such quality deterioration "operated to keep the index down"(150). Even the disappearance from the market of such things as new cars or refrigerators — their "prices," so to say, had become infinite — caused no upward movement in the Index. Instead prices were invented out of whole cloth — it was assumed that their prices would change the way other available things in the Index changed. One wonders how far this manipulation would be pushed: If famine were to strike this country and food became unavailable, would the food component of the index be estimated on the basis of changes in prices of cars and refrigerators (assuming they were available)? In any case, the manipulation of the Consumer Price Index which took place during World War II was intended to deceive the people. It thus undermined the democracy the war was intended to protect.

Nor has such manipulation stopped with World War II. When pollution equipment was first required to be put on cars, the government decided that this was an improvement in "quality." Thus the increased cost of a car due to the equipment would not result in an increase in the Index. As a result the contribution of environmental control to inflation was hidden by governmental fiat, a decision to the political advantage of the car manufacturers (they are not contributing to inflation by price increases) and politicians (they are not contributing to inflation by requiring pollution devices). Economic awareness suffers, however, by hiding the degree to which price stability and environmental control — both "good" things — are incompatible. If we really want to know that degree, the question must be tested in a Court of Common Reason where both the kind of environmental equipment that the people want, and the extent to which such equipment represents an improvement in quality, can be authoritatively resolved.

In his book *On the Accuracy of Economic Observations*, Oskar Morgenstern has pointed out how distorted economic data are, the very data which form the basis of decisions by government officials, businessmen, politicians, and economists. He states that "we must carefully distinguish between what we think we know and what we really do and can know"(1963 vii). His theme is that we really know relatively little. One of the reasons for this is that the terms in which we try to understand and organize our economic life are epistemologically unfriendly. In my judgment, this unfriendliness is a principal cause of many failures in good judgment by scholars, business, and political leaders, as well as the people at large.

Let us imagine that years ago a woman started her car in gear and was horrified when the car crushed her husband's legs against the garage wall. Having mechanical ability she creates and patents a device that prevents a car not in neutral from being started. Such a device could be installed by manufacturers out of fear (otherwise they might be sued), out of legal necessity (the law requires it), out of economic advantage or social conscience (manufacturers think the public wants or should have it). The device protects drivers against a failure of a good habit (that is, engaging the clutch when starting). Now let us ask: what devices could protect the public against their failures of good habits of thought? Public officials, so far as I can tell, generally ignore this question. Consider the Federal Reserve. The people who design and run it assume little responsibility for the errors that ordinary people might commit when using money, or when thinking about the banking system. Yet, by the standards of American democracy, such fallacious thinking by the public ought to be considered a problem of the first importance.

To understand the kind of conceptual quicksand one is up against in trying to comprehend the Federal Reserve, let us consider a problem that illuminates the danger: If we agree to call Bob by the name Bill, and Bill by the name John, and John by the name Bob, and if, further, Bob is half the age of John but twice the age of Bill, then if John, who misnames everyone in a completely different way than indicated, says "Bob is 48" and if Bill hearing this, and thinking the original misnaming operation is in effect, says "It then follows that John is the oldest," is he reasoning correctly? The difficulty of this problem centers on misnaming and ambiguities. Even if we somehow solve it, it is not clear whether we should follow the original misnaming convention in our answer. The public language of our monetary system is likewise confusing. Fallacies of reasoning that exist because of ambiguities of meaning, or ambiguities of grammar, are very difficult to escape. One must always be on guard against them. Try this experiment. Take a half-dozen books on elementary logic or critical reasoning and read the sections on definitions and fallacies. Then ask: How painstaking and shrewdly have names and definitions in our monetary system been chosen in order, as much as possible, to *anticipate and discourage* fallacies of reasoning which might be committed not only by politicians or economists but, more importantly, by ordinary citizens who use money and patronize banks? Our monetary system is sometimes portrayed as a paradigm of an economically sophisticated institution. Yet from a logical point of view it appears to be pre-Aristotelian, from a political point of view, pre-Lockean.

Consider an analogy to illustrate how the system undermines contracts. Chris and Casey, 10-year-old twins, decide to play three games of ping pong, with the loser having to cut the grass. Since they often fight about the score, they agree that their father will keep score and tell them when the match is over. During the course of the games both Chris and Casey pay no attention to the score and never know it till the end of a game. While the second game is going on, the father, noticing the fun his children are having, decides to raise the winning score from 21 to 26 points. During the final game, again for their benefit, he raises the winning score from 26 to 31 points. After the games are over the following is the result:

	Chris		Casey
First Game	21		19
Second Game	19	(during game)	21
	24		26
Third Game	19	(during game)	21
	21	(during game)	26
	31		29

When they find out the results, each child believes the other should cut the grass. Casey argues that she did not lose since she won the second and third games (each by 21-19) using their understanding of the word "game" before they started (that is, the standards of the first game). Further, by the standards of the second game she also won the second and third games (26-24 and 26-21, respectively). Chris, however, argues that he won the first and third games as defined by the father (21-19 and 31-29, respectively) and, further, that he won the most points (76-74). The father, despite his good intentions, has made the word "loser" equivocal, which results in needless conflict. He was "pre-Aristotelian" in that he ignored fallacies of ambiguity, and "pre-Lockean" in that he did not consult his children about the change in the meaning of the word "game."

Similarly if, during the course of a private agreement, a monetary authority enlarges the money supply by a trillion percent, or by five percent, the authority undermines the integrity of the contract. Honesty becomes more difficult. If I borrow $1000 from a friend at no interest, and the money supply then doubles, am I honest if I merely return $1000? Perhaps I should return the amount of money which would purchase the same goods as $1000 would purchase when I borrowed it. But what specific goods are we talking about, the ones the friend would actually buy, or some general basket of them? Further there are ambiguities due to changes in quality. On the other hand, I only promised to give back $1000, not what $1000 might buy. In sum, without clear and fixed terms, not only is economic knowledge made more difficult, so is morality.

Let us imagine an economy which is honest; that is, one where the economic language is not misleading, and the data not distorted. Of course, a completely honest economy is impossible but, for an economy as for a person, there are degrees of honesty. We ought to ask how we can make the economy as honest as possible at some given time. If, as Jefferson says, "the whole art of government consists in the art of being honest"(above, page 235), then economic government ought to reduce economic deception as far as possible for the governed. For example, economists are wont to distinguish between real and nominal increases (or decreases) in buying power, or taxes, or whatever. Can we design an economy where the real and the nominal values — the true prices and the apparent prices — are identical or nearly so?

The quest for honesty must begin with an accurate measure, and that measure is money. Unfortunately, the design of our banking system encourages the public to confuse what they generally mean by money (currency and coins) with bank "deposits." Of course, they are not the same. A nationwide run on banks would prove to the depositor in a most painful way that the figures on a monthly bank statement refer almost entirely to debt — that is, private loan agreements or public bonds — and not to money understood as currency and coins. If these agreements or bonds are not convertible into currency, the depositor is out of luck. Of course, in such an extreme situation the Federal Reserve would doubtless create large amounts of new paper money. But then the depositor is cheated anyway because it is only depreciated currency that can be withdrawn. Money has in fact been given a variety of different definitions by the Federal Reserve. Our public economic language is debased — the more we struggle, the more we are belimed. If we wish the public to think more correctly and precisely, we must design institutions that make it more difficult to confuse the concepts of money and debt.

The Federal Reserve appears structured to perpetuate this confusion, a confusion which undermines the public's economic knowledge for the sake of powerful economic or political elites.

Consider a conception of money, and a monetary system, that would better serve the interests of a free people. Of course this is a speculation since free peoples must themselves ultimately decide what serves their interests through courts of common reason. However, the speculation will illustrate the kind of issues involved in creating an honest economy. One common view of money is influenced by utilitarian or pragmatic philosophy: money is a mere convenience that facilitates exchange. According to this view, the definition and supply of money might be manipulated by monetary authorities as seems most suitable for this purpose. Yet such manipulation also facilitates deception of the people. Money is certainly convenient, but it is not a mere convenience. The essential purpose of money can best be understood by using an extended analogy. Consider the role of mathematics in our understanding of nature. Although some ancient Greeks, such as Pythagoras, thought mathematics to be essential in understanding the world, and others, such as Archimedes, made extensive applications of mathematics, the dominant Greek view depreciated its role in physics. This view began to wane in the Middle Ages. Here is what Roger Bacon said in 1267:

> the acquisition of [mathematics] is the beginning of our knowledge. . . . . By means of [mathematics] all other sciences must be known and verified. . . . . For the things of this world cannot be made known without a knowledge of mathematics. . . . . it is plain . . . that celestial things are known by means of mathematics, and that a way is prepared by it to things that are lower. . . . Nothing within the power of things can be known without the power of geometry. . . . In like manner the other parts of mathematics are necessary. (1928 1:123, 125, 128, 129-30)

After the Middle Ages the idea of mathematization of physical knowledge gained strength. About 1500 Leonardo da Vinci said: "No human investigation can be termed true science if it is not capable of mathematical demonstration"(1964 127). In 1620 Francis Bacon asserted that the "investigation of nature turns out best when physics is given definition by mathematics"(2004 213). Earlier (1605) he said: "many parts of Nature can neither be inuented [discovered] with sufficient subtiltie, nor demostrated with sufficient perspicuitie, nor accommodated vnto vse with sufficient dexteritie, without the aide and interueyning [intervention] of the Mathematicks"(2000 88). With even greater emphasis, perhaps, Galileo tried to resurrect the Pythagorean belief that the physical world is inherently mathematical. "Philosophy," he said in 1623, "is written in that grand book — I mean the universe — which stands continually open to our gaze, but it cannot be understood unless one first learns to comprehend the language and interpret the characters in which it is written. It is written in the language of mathematics, and its characters are triangles, circles and other geometrical figures, without which it is humanly impossible to understand a single word of it . . ."(1960 183-4; see also Clavelin 1974 434). Although nature should be interpreted mathematically, it is far from obvious what that interpretation should be. Experiments, therefore, are devised to reveal *exactly* what mathematical structure — out of indefinitely many possible structures — the world has. Even though understanding nature as mathematical is now commonplace, care must still be taken. Experiments *per se* will not reveal that nature has a mathematical structure — that is a presupposition that guides the construction of the experiment. Aristotle, for example, did not conduct experiments to find mathematical structures implicit in the physical world because he did not presuppose that there are such structures (cf. his words below, page 420). But we do. Hence when we are told by the Pythagoreans that number is the essence of things, or by the Bible that God "hast arranged all things by measure and number and weight"(*Wisdom of Solomon* 11:20), or by Galileo that the book of nature is written in the language of mathematics, we are not being told a fact about the world like "ravens are black" or the "sun is gaseous"; rather we are being told that if we wish to understand nature we can only do so by initially presupposing that its essential structure is mathematical. That presupposition, unlike "ravens are black" or the "sun is gaseous," regulates how science is conducted. For example, if a scientist tries to find equations appropriate to some phenomenon and fails, she does not conclude there are no equations; rather, she concludes she is not clever enough. By organizing his inquires into nature according to the presupposition that nature is intrinsically mathematical, and by convincing others to do the same, Galileo became a revolutionary figure in the history of science.

Money is an application of this Pythagorean, Biblical, and Galilean view to the world of exchange. Money is as necessary to understand the exchanges among human beings, as geometrical figures (or numerical equations) are necessary to understand the motion of the planets. Monetary units are created by fiat out of nothing, like the units of score in a game. These measures of value are invested in certain physical objects. John Locke once said that we "put an *imaginary* value upon gold and silver"(1824 4:22). We use gold and silver as objective indications of imaginary measures of economic values as we use a tennis scoreboard as objective indications of imaginary measures of game values. If people were honest enough, and if their memories were good enough, tangible money would be as unnecessary as writing down (or even announcing) the score of a friendly game of tennis. The creation of money is the creation of a mathematical measure of value in the game of economic knowledge.

It is by social agreement that the original imaginary measure, whether in tennis or economics, becomes a real measure. By this agreement gold, silver, paper, or whatever, can become measures of economic values, something in which one can believe. "I have faith in the dollar" is an irrational faith apart from a powerful social commitment that will support that dollar. This social commitment, if made by a government, can make money legal tender, that is, it may be given to pay debts, and may not be refused by creditors. (Legally then a person is not culpable if she merely repays a $1000 debt after a trillion per cent inflation, although morally she may be so.) The central purpose of money, from a metaeconomic point of view, is not the convenience function of facilitating exchange, but the epistemological function of understanding exchange. The latter begins with the presupposition that the grand book of exchange is written in the language of mathematics, and its characters are natural numbers, integers, rationals, and other kinds of numerical objects. By the "vexations of art" we can create an experiment concerning values that we call the marketplace. If it is correctly designed, we can determine the price of goods and services and thus compare their exchange value. It is this knowledge which allows precise and rational economic planning by individuals, business, or government. To the degree that the marketplace distorts instead of revealing economic values, it interferes with knowledge, and thereby reduces our power and freedom. In a democratic society, an economic system is a thing for free and fair exchange.

According to Mach's principle, the local inertial properties of matter (say, water rising around the inside of a spinning bucket) are due to the influence of the distant stars. Likewise, the local forces determining the value of an exchange are decisively influenced by the distant monetary authority (who controls the creation of money). Once the epistemological function of money is understood, it is clear that that authority should define money as exactly and clearly as possible, so it can become as accurate a measure of exchange values as our technology will allow. As in the case of any other standard of measurement — such as a meter or a kilogram — the definition of a monetary unit should remain absolutely fixed if it is to be a precise measure.

At various times and places a great variety of things have been used for money: cattle, reindeer, oxen, slaves, whales' or dogs' teeth, stones, feathers, shells, coconuts, fur, sugar, grain, almonds, rice, butter, rum, tobacco, iron, copper, bronze, silver, gold, salt, leather, beads, kettle drums, arrows, gambling chips, cannons, lipsticks, and mahogany logs. The arbitrariness of what is chosen for money is further illustrated by the story of an ancient Chinese ruler, whose government was in desperate financial straits due to counterfeiting:

> The Emperor, always ready to try a new experiment, now attempted to grapple with this currency crisis, though his first efforts were far from successful. In the imperial park at Ch'ang An the Emperor had a white stag, a very rare beast, which had no fellow in the empire. On the advice of a minister, the Emperor had this animal killed, and made a kind of treasury note out of its skin, which he believed could not be copied. These pieces of skin were a foot square, and were made with a fringed border and decorated with a pattern. Each piece was assigned the arbitrary value of 400,000 copper coins. The princes, when they came to pay their respects to the throne, were compelled to buy one of these pieces of skin for cash, and present their gifts to the Emperor upon it. This precaution insured the circulation of the 'White Stag Notes'. (Fitzgerald 1935 164-5)

Notice that the Federal government's requirement of dollars for payment of (coercive) taxes likewise ensures the circulation of Federal Reserve Notes (quite apart from any other reason).

Suppose we abstract from the substance of all the things which have served as money. Like the Cheshire cat, which disappears and leaves only its grin behind, the irrelevant substances of money disappear and we are left with quantity. The definition of a monetary unit is determined by how *many* other monetary units there are, that is, the unit is a certain fraction of the total money supply. In mathematics the name *rational number* is used to indicate a number denoted by a fraction, the word "rational" being derived from the word "ratio." Examples of positive rationals are 1/2, 5/1, 41/3, 17/91, and so forth. The definition of a monetary unit derives from its rationality; if the unit is one out of a trillion units, then its meaning can be expressed as one-trillionth. Money which is part of a fixed, unchanging money supply can thus be called *rational money*. It is the rationality of money which enables it to be an accurate measure, just as it is the rationality of a centimeter (as 1/100 of a fixed meter) that enables it to be an accurate measure. And if a fixed meter is necessary to precisely measure physical changes (say, the difference in length between the same bar of iron when cold and when hot), so a fixed money supply is necessary to precisely measure economic changes (say, the difference in the cost of coal one month and the next).

Hence what is important for the dollar is not that it keeps its value over time with respect to a given good, or even a set of goods, such as that used in the Consumer Price Index; what is important is that it keeps its *meaning*. An honest dollar — that is, one that keeps its meaning — is a rational dollar. In an honest economy prices must go up and down to reflect accurately the changes in supply and demand. The measure of those changes, however, should not change over time, any more than the measure of distance, such as a meter, should change over time. Of course, a new definition can be given if it leads to a more accurate fixed standard. For example, an early definition of a meter — the distance between two scratches on a rigid noncorrosive platinum-iridium bar at 0° C., located in Sèvres, France — was changed in 1960 to 1,650,763.73 wave lengths of the orange and red light from the isotope krypton 86 measured in a vacuum. In 1983 it was again redefined as the distance light travels in a vacuum in one-299,792,458th of a second. Further refinements might continue to occur from time to time. Similarly a new definition should be given to the dollar if it could ensure a more accurate standard of rationality for the money supply. Such changes should not serve either as a cover for reducing the percentage of the money supply that any money holder has, nor for confusing language, but only, as in the case of the meter, to make existing language more precise than had hitherto been possible. Once the nature of money as a measure in the quest for economic knowledge is understood, great efforts should be made toward using the most advanced technological means and the stabilizing effects of well-established institutions to ensure that the money supply varies as little as is humanly possible. Rational money should become a national economic goal. We should make imaginative changes in our economic institutions so that the definition of the money supply is neither vague, nor ambiguous, nor is the amount of money subject to change. In his *Foundations of Mechanical Accuracy*, Wayne R. Moore states: "It was not until 1960, when light waves were chosen as the fundamental standard, that the unit of length was finally related to some unchanging phenomenon in nature. This standard of measurement realizes a long sought-after goal of metrologists — the agreement on an immutable standard"(1970 98). Once rational money becomes an "immutable standard" of economic metrologists, we might speculate that it would take a good deal of time, ingenuity, and determination to reach it. But would it be wise to choose such a standard?

9

Economic Truth

According to the ideals of American perfectionist democracy, the economy ought to be designed to promote good judgments by the people, not only in ordinary transactions as they pursue private happiness, but also in the Court of Common Reason, as they pursue public happiness. Excellence in self-government requires excellence in maintaining conditions of honesty and integrity, because to the degree that the people are deceived, the aspiration for self-government is compromised. Let us now look at the issue of promoting economic honesty by contrasting rational money with Federal Reserve money.

We can begin with an objection against the former: "A growing economy needs a growing money supply; thus rational money would promote economic stagnation." One might as well say that although 360° may be enough to measure a given circle, one needs a larger number of degrees to measure a larger circle. For a certain purpose more divisions might be needed to measure a larger circle (say, by measuring to the nearest minute instead of to the nearest degree). Similarly, finer divisions may be needed in a growing economy because a penny buys too much, or because the people wish to keep wages stable on average. If so, new money could be issued to holders of old money at some fixed ratio so that each money holder would have the same percentage of the new money supply as he or she previously held of the old. This system is akin to a stock dividend or split. After a money dividend or split, all previous contracts are appropriately adjusted, and thus no contracting party is better or worse off. The significance of a money dividend or split would, like its stock counterpart, be entirely the convenience in buying and selling, and what follows from that convenience. If this is all "increasing the money supply" means, there is nothing wrong with it. (Of course, any proposed money split (or reverse split) would need the advice of the "stockholders" in the United States, that is, its citizens speaking through the Court of Common Reason.) To illustrate this monetary system, imagine that the day a girl is born she is given $100. Over the years the money is not invested or spent, but is kept in cash, and she collects and saves any money dividends from it that she might receive. On her hundredth birthday the $100, plus its accumulated dividends, represents the exact same percentage of the money supply that it had on the day of her birth. All Lockeans, all American revolutionists, would certainly cheer this monetary government, since it protected the right of property so precisely for an entire century.

Unfortunately, they cannot cheer the Federal Reserve. In its language "increasing the money supply" means not only "increasing the money supply", but *decreasing* the percentage of the money supply that present money holders happen to have. It represents a loss of one's property and can be compared to the government printing a writer's copyrighted book without permission or compensation to the author. The theft is not of a physical object, but economic value is nevertheless unjustly lost. The way in which the Federal Reserve increases the "money supply" is likewise unjust, and it is certainly arguable that it violates the Fifth Amendment, according to which no person can be deprived of property "without due process of law; nor shall private property be taken for public use without just compensation." (cf. John Adams' interpretation of the meaning of "republic" below, page 283). Let us recall again Hamilton's claim that the "words 'due process' have a precise technical import, and are only applicable to the process and proceedings of the courts of justice; they can never be referred to an act of legislature"(above, page 123). By the standards of the Fifth Amendment, the federal government may publish a writer's copyrighted book without her permission provided that a federal court agrees both that it is necessary for the public welfare and that the writer receives just compensation. By the same standards the federal government may publish more money without permission of money holders provided that a federal court agrees both that there is a sufficiently strong public interest in doing so, and that money holders receive just compensation (say, government land).

Now consider what actually happens when the "money supply" is increased by the Federal Reserve. According to virtually everyone's analysis, such increases make some people relatively worse off than they otherwise would have been. For example, the poor who save their money (and thus hold a high percentage of cash compared to their net worth) are hurt disproportionally. Imagine that instead of increasing the "money supply," the government directly and openly confiscated money in a size and distribution pattern equal to what would have been effected by the increase in "money supply." Suppose that the government justified the confiscation by explaining that the members of the Federal Reserve Board thought it would be good for the economy. Surely there would be a violation of the Fifth Amendment. There is likewise a violation when the "money supply" is increased. To think otherwise would be analogous to claiming that if officials of the government confiscated unsold copies of a writer's book, the Fifth

Amendment would apply, but if they merely violated the copyright by printing copies, then the Amendment would not apply. What would we think if every citizen were an author, but the government reprinted some books without compensation (say, those by impoverished authors), but did not reprint others (say, those by affluent authors)? Or to use another illustration: would not a stockholder justly feel cheated if a company issued a 5% stock dividend, but sent her new shares to someone else? The case is no different when there is there is a 5% increase in the money supply.

It is sometimes claimed that increasing the "money supply" is really a hidden tax. Benjamin Franklin and John Adams, for example, thought of it in this way (1907 9:234;1977 5:273). Although the government under the Constitution has a legitimate power to tax, it does not follow that it may use deceptive language and deceptive means to effect that levy. To call a tax "increasing the money supply" is a governmental deception. Plato in his *Republic* suggests that "the rulers of the State . . . in their dealings . . . with their own citizens, may be allowed to lie for the public good"(1937 1:651; cf. 721). But our country, unlike Plato's polis, is founded on the consent of the governed, a standard which is incompatible with the deceptive language and structure of the Federal Reserve.

Historically, modern fractional reserve banking began with a simple case of dishonesty. For the sake of brevity, let me simplify. Long ago goldsmiths were often asked to store gold for safekeeping. They did this for a fee. No problem so far. However, they also noted that, ordinarily, not all depositors wanted their gold at the same time. Hence they could lend some of the gold at interest, keeping only a portion on hand for depositors who might want to withdraw their money in the meantime. The word "embezzle" means: "To divert to one's own use (money, etc.) in violation of trust or official duty"(OED 1989). The smiths were embezzlers. Had they been honest they would have separated these two functions: the safekeeping of gold for which the smith would receive a custodial fee, and the lending of gold at interest, for which the smith would receive a brokerage fee. The smiths could then allow customers to choose whether they wanted their gold stored or invested. But such honesty was not as profitable as embezzling. Here perhaps is the origin of the type of dishonesty that continues today, only now it is the government which embezzles. The profit to the government from expanding the "money supply" is, morally speaking, similar to private counterfeiting, since both are theft by deception and both undermine fair exchange.

"Nothing appears more surprizing to those, who consider human affairs with a philosophical eye," David Hume once observed,

> than the easiness with which the many are governed by the few; and the implicit submission, with which men resign their own sentiments and passions to those of their rulers. When we inquire by what means this wonder is effected, we shall find, that, as FORCE is always on the side of the governed, the governors have nothing to support them but opinion. It is therefore, on opinion only that government is founded; and this maxim extends to the most despotic and most military governments, as well as to the most free and most popular. (1985 32; cf. Hamilton 1961 5: 37 and La Boétie's earlier remarks (1988 41-42))

Hence, any government that has a monopoly on the means through which opinion is formed is a potential or actual despotism. Since it is one of the central aims of democracy that the collective opinion on which political power is grounded be *true* opinion, we should expect that those who run the Federal Reserve would have a fierce determination to define and use words in a way that misleads the governed as little as possible. Yet in practice the Federal Reserve creates unnecessary vagueness and ambiguity: debt which is not debt, money which is not money, deposits which are not deposits. If those who run the Federal Reserve were genuinely frank, they could do no better than apologize to William Henry Vanderbilt and exclaim: "The public language be damned!"

The reason for this obfuscation is the antidemocratic nature of the Federal Reserve System itself. Political despots cannot, typically and regularly, tell the truth without undermining the false opinions on which their power is based. They would be destroyed by a series of frank admissions such as: "Today I am going to steal ten million from the public treasury for my own use." Similarly our monetary authorities cannot honestly admit that what they are doing is a kind of Platonic paternalism, such as: "This year we are going to print money to finance the Vietnam war that cannot be financed by taxation since we believe the people would not agree to be taxed at that rate and for that purpose. We freely admit we take economic value from many people by our activities. We freely admit that we interfere with the decisions of individuals to spend, save, or invest. We do it for their own good." Franklin explains the fraudulent character of inflation better than I ever could: "This Currency as we manage it is a wonderful Machine. It performs its Office when we issue it; it pays & clothes Troops, & provides Victuals & Ammunition; and when we are oblig'd to issue a Quantity excessive, it pays itself off by depreciation"(1959 29:356). To be legitimate, the economic power of governments must be authorized by the people themselves, speaking through courts of common reason, or equivalent institutions. But no such authority has ever been sought. Even apart from such a test, a genuine concern for meticulous honesty would undermine the way in which the Federal Reserve has functioned. Our biggest monetary problem is not — as is often claimed — to determine the optimum rate of monetary growth; rather, it is the structural dishonesty of the banking system itself, and the resulting debasement of our public economic language, which is analogous to the debasement of political language by despotic governments.

The depth and extent of the 1929 stock market crash, and the subsequent depression, has been widely blamed on the incompetence of the Federal Reserve Board. It has also been said, that the Board was not incompetent; rather, it abused its power. Such criticisms often miss the important point that the Federal Reserve System itself is the abuse; it is built not just on a mistake, but on a vice founded on ambiguities. What we need instead is a National Monetary Institute of Standards and Technology which would create a money supply that would not be confused with anything else (such as private or public debt) and which would devise techniques to ensure that our money is rational. Although our money supply is not clearly defined, the Federal Reserve appears to follow the policy of random money, where the decisions concerning the size of the supply are guided by the accidental ups and downs of the economy. Over time such a policy undermines the dollar as a measure of economic value; that is, it undermines its essential epistemological function. If such an arbitrary convention were used in physics, the same difficulty would appear:

> Thus, to give an example which [the analytic philosopher] Moritz Schlick used in his lectures, the pulse beat of the Dalai Lama might be chosen as the standard clock; but — apart from its enormous technical inconvenience — this convention would have the consequence that the speed of all physical processes would depend on the state of health of the Dalai Lama; thus, e.g., whenever the latter had a fever and showed what, by customary standards, is called a fast pulse, then such events as one rotation of the earth about its axis or the fall of a rock from a given height would take up more temporal units — and would therefore be said to take place more slowly — than when the Dalai Lama was in good health. This would establish remarkable laws connecting the state of health of the Dalai Lama with all events in the universe — and this by instantaneous action at a distance; but it would preclude the possibility of establishing any laws of the simplicity, scope, and degree of confirmation exhibited by Galileo's, Kepler's, and Newton's laws. (1952 73-4)

The point of this quotation from the philosopher Carl Hempel applies equally well in economics. There are no doubt some "remarkable laws" connecting the decisions of the Federal Reserve's Board of Governors — possibly even the health of its chairman — with various events in the economy. But the policy of random money — "apart from its enormous technical inconvenience" — precludes "the possibility of establishing any laws of the simplicity, scope, and degree of confirmation exhibited by Galileo's, Kepler's, and Newton's laws." It is debatable that such monetary laws exist in economics, but it is surely foolish to choose monetary standards which rule out their discovery if they do exist. Proposals for random money are, to various degrees, like the idea of basing a unit of time on the Dalai Lama's heartbeat: it can be done, but at the cost of such complication that a monetary theory that is clear to ordinary people, which is what excellent self-government requires, becomes virtually impossible.

Somewhat better than random money is the suggestion that the money supply should increase at a fixed rate. Although this proposal gives greater stability, it also introduces gratuitous complications. Suppose that, instead of platinum-iridium, the International Kilogram at Sèvres had been made out of a radioactive material which caused a loss of mass at a fixed rate each year. Would not such a standard make measurement of weight gratuitously difficult? Money based on a steadily increasing money supply could be called *radioactive money*, since the ratio of any fixed amount of money to the entire money supply would be steadily decreasing. The kind of money one has — random, radioactive, or rational — is not independent of the economic knowledge one has. *Rational money is a condition for the most reliable economic knowledge* is thus a metaeconomic, not an economic, claim. One does not need to await new physical knowledge to know that a radioactive International Kilogram is inappropriate, nor do we need new economic knowledge to reject a policy of radioactive money. Logical coherence and precise speech demand consistency in meaning, and this would not be the case with either a radioactive International Kilogram or radioactive money. Monetarism in this sense rests on a metaeconomic mistake. No one would seriously suggest that we solve the weight problem of Americans by having the National Institute of Standards and Technology decree that henceforth there shall be 17 ounces to the (newly defined) pound, thereby decreasing everyone's weight by about 6% when measured in pounds. Nor would anyone seriously suggest that we continually increase the number of meters in a kilometer to deal with the "problems" of an expanding universe. It is just as foolish to change monetary standards to deal with the problems of an expanding economy.

A gold standard is likewise not a good way to structure a monetary system. A monetary unit is nothing in and of itself. Monetary units are pure fictions. As fictions they need no "backing" of gold or anything else. As noted (above, page 245), monetary units are indispensable in helping us understand changes in economic values. It is just as foolish to ask for "real" money (gold), over and above that paper money created by monetary authorities, as it is to ask for "real" points in a tennis game over and above those fictitious points which we carry in our heads as we play. The points in tennis are nothing in and of themselves; what gives them meaning is the relative way in which they change during a game. Likewise, monetary values only become meaningful in the context of economic games. What we should expect when we go to the monetary authority with a dollar bill is not gold, but an assurance of its rationality. Hence if there are a trillion monetary units called dollars, a dollar bill should be marked not just "One Dollar", but also "One-trillionth of the Dollar Supply. Guaranteed by the United States Government." What the government cannot do is to guarantee a constant ratio between the relative value of the "cost of living" and the dollar. Assuming free exchange, a worldwide decade of bad weather would raise the cost of food no matter what the government, or all world governments together, would do. Further, the "cost of living" depends on how people want to live, something mainly beyond governmental control in a free society. An honest government, like an honest person, is modest in with promises, since modesty increases the probability that promises can and will be redeemed. An honest artist can guarantee that only fifty genuine signed and numbered copies of a work were, or will be, made; she cannot in general guarantee how valuable each will be. Neither can the American government guarantee how valuable a dollar will be; but it can guarantee a fixed number of genuine signed and numbered copies.

Thus the "backing" paper money needs is a stable government that is conscientious about its public language, a government that is relentless and imaginative in reducing counterfeiting, a government that accepts its own money in payment of taxes. The process of going to the trouble and expense to find buried gold in its natural state, then refine it and bury it in Fort Knox and other places, is evidence of a pervasive misunderstanding. It makes gold into a fetish — a modern equivalent of the idolatry of the Golden Calf. Some people believe that having paper dollars convertible into gold at a fixed exchange ratio is the best way to ensure a fixed money supply because gold in practice is hard to find and very expensive to create. This claim is theoretically dubious, since at any time more gold might be discovered or produced, and in such great supply as to completely undermine the monetary system. Empirically it is foolish, for it gives power at our expense to those countries that can find or create new gold. Thus, Russia, for example, would, in effect, be given the opportunity to counterfeit our currency. It would be no different if we had only paper currency and allowed certain individuals or countries to counterfeit otherwise rational money. Money based on the gold standard is a form of Russian roulette. It opens our monetary system to an unnecessary risk, namely, that some person, corporation, or country will find, or be able to create cheaply, great quantities of gold.

The conception of rational money does not imply that the amount of loans available to borrowers would be fixed. In a banking system based on a careful and precise definition of terms, there would be a sharp distinction between money and debt. A deposit would be money held by banks for safekeeping. A fee would be charged for this custodial service, and larger fees would apply if checking privileges on that money were desired. In a completely separate operation, banks would also sell shares in a mutual fund based on their loan portfolios. These shares have the advantage of producing income but at the cost of some increase in risk. Banks could offer — for a fee — to provide checking privileges on these portfolios and could guarantee, using their own resources and insurance, the par value of the shares. Customers of the bank could then decide how much of their money they wished to deposit and how much to invest in the mutual fund. The investment nature of what we normally and misleadingly call a "deposit" would be clear, as would be the banker's twin role as a custodian of money on the one hand, and a broker in a mutual fund on the other. The amount of money available for loans would be influenced by such factors as the interest rate offered to the public, the quality of the loan portfolio, the ability of the various banks, using their own resources, to maintain par value on their mutual fund shares, and the quality of their insurance. (In each case, these factors would be expressed, at the time of deposit or purchase, in the most consumer friendly way possible.) The control of the amount of money available for bank loans would thus rest with the customers of banks in their response to the competition among banks. Note that the savings and loan scandal of the 1980s and 1990s would have been unlikely if this system had been in force. Even if it did occur, the holders of the various bank mutual funds would have lost value in their shares, but the public would not be required to make up the loss any more than the public is required to make up losses in a stock when a scandal depreciates its value. The depositors would, of course, be unaffected.

This proposal is not simply a call for 100% reserves, but an attempt to make the whole business of banking as honest and transparent as possible. Our present banking system is deceptive to the average user of its service; it violates "truth in packaging," a violation which should not be taken lightly. Those who think it is unimportant to design a banking system where the economic realities are obvious to its customers betray an antidemocratic bias, as if the judgments — and misjudgments — of the people are of little concern. Yet, as noted, the Federal Reserve has shown little interest in what ordinary people think. For example, no surveys are regularly made to determine what people believe is happening when they use a bank. Such surveys could be used to see where misconceptions exist and what can be done to eliminate them by way of redesign, language simplification, or advertising. As the Founders felt little need to consider the opinions of women or blacks or Indians in their deliberations, so the Governors of the Federal Reserve feel little need to consider the opinions, much less the considered judgments, of ordinary people in formulating their policies. It is as if they believe that a scrupulously honest and democratic controlled monetary system is beyond human imagination and virtue.

If we wish to eliminate, or at least reduce, common misconceptions due to the deceptive structure of the Federal Reserve System, the best way, I think, is to raise, and try to answer, philosophical questions about the System. Let me list some of them:

1. *Questions of logic.* Among the concepts of money, private debt, and public debt there are obvious differences. Yet the structure and operation of the Federal Reserve increases the possibility of confusion among them. Could a monetary system be designed that carefully keeps these three separate, so that when the people think about them, whether in their roles as consumers or citizens, their errors of reasoning are reduced to a minimum?

2. *Questions of epistemology.* Can a practical monetary system be designed so that it increases, to the maximum extent possible, the ability of people to understand it? Further, could the dollar be defined so as to minimize any contribution to the difficulty that consumers may have in knowing that they are, or are not, getting a fair deal?

3. *Questions of ethics.* Suppose a person or group interferes with the private contracts of others, where those contracts are both legal and ethical. We would normally consider this to be wrong, but our monetary authorities create exactly that kind of interference when they expand the "money supply." They undermine, for example, an annuity contract between a person and an insurance company. Can our monetary system be redesigned to avoid this continuing unethical practice? Just as the First Amendment protects speech from interference by political authorities, could we have a monetary system which would protect the freedom to save, invest, or spend from interference by monetary authorities?

4. *Questions of politics.* At present the smooth operation of our monetary system depends on the good intentions and the good judgment of a small group of people, two conditions we cannot always count on. Could a monetary system be devised whereby it would be checked whenever it was contrary to the deliberate sense of the people? Further, if the "money supply" is expanded under present conditions, there is a transfer of economic value from various classes of individuals to other classes. This transfer is unjust since, in general, the people who lose economic value do not deserve to lose it. Is it possible to design a good monetary system that avoids this injustice?

5. *Questions of aesthetics.* The Federal Reserve System has numerous definitions of money. In the philosophy of science there is a regulative maxim of thought called the principle of parsimony which states that a plurality of definitions, assumptions, and entities are not to be accepted unless they can be shown to be necessary. Could we do with fewer definitions of money — preferably just one? In general, can we design a good monetary system which has a beautiful conceptual simplicity?

Such philosophical questions are seldom raised, let alone energetically pressed. To make clear why they are important, let me again use a football analogy. Imagine that in a league of liberal arts colleges, football gets "out of hand." There are many unqualified students admitted solely to play the game; there are illicit payments to superior players; drug use is common, as are payoffs to corrupt referees. Imagine a coach who, although innocent of these activities, ignores them. Such a coach could be challenged by the following argument: "This football league exists in the context of a group of colleges devoted to humane learning. It is an evasion of responsibility to pay attention only to the content of the game and none to the integrity of its setting. Unless you sacrifice some of your coaching time to ensure that integrity, your coaching will be in vain — even if you produce winning teams." The Federal Reserve, I believe, could be transformed if analogous metaeconomic questions were not so often ignored, or quickly dismissed. Is it justifiable to spend so much time and effort on how to manage the national debt, or on the velocity of money, and so little on metaeconomic or philosophical questions? Sometimes in human affairs an initial and seemingly small dishonesty grows and by degrees becomes a tangled web, so embedded with institutional patterns of thought and action that its rectification requires an enormous upheaval. The eradication of the moral and political dishonesty of slavery and Jim Crow was worth the upheaval; the same is true of the institutionalization of the original dishonesty of the goldsmiths by the Federal Reserve. Yet even with the grave threats to our financial system that began in 1929 or 2007 there were only a few voices suggesting that we make the financial system, both in its theory and practice, not only meticulously honest, but so designed that it would also appear meticulously honest to the average person. It is as if the idea of *democratic honesty* were unknown.

Let me summarize the argument so far. A much debated question is: in a democracy what should be the most important goal for those who design and manage our economic institutions? Is it eliminating inflation? Or avoiding a recession? Or reducing unemployment? Or increasing the growth rate? The answer is: none of these. The first and most important goal ought to be the creation of an honest economy; that is, an economy whose organization is not deceptive to ordinary people, and where the countervailing powers in society are so arranged that distortions in economic transactions are reduced to a minimum. In general, some of our economic practices are objectionable because people, in addition to often being deceived in individual transactions, are also systematically deceived by the misleading structure of economic institutions. One of the purposes of an economic system in a free society is to make transparent the monetary values of the people in the marketplace. The marketplace distorts these values where language is corrupted (for example, by a policy of random money), where there is coercion (for example, price controls), or fraud (for example, false or misleading advertising). The marketplace is an experiment in the monetary values of consumers, and it ought to be designed to reveal the truth about those values. In general, a society which interferes with free exchanges of ideas is impoverished morally, and a society which interferes with free exchanges of property is impoverished financially. To create conditions in which accurate monetary measures of the people's economic values are possible is *ipso facto* to create one of the conditions of economic freedom.

A society, even a complex one, that does not value individual freedom does not need money. The economic historian Paul Einzig, speaking of the Incan civilization before the Spanish conquest, states that

> practically all authorities agree that the Peruvians had no knowledge of money. Although the country was exceptionally rich in gold and silver, these metals were not used either as a medium of exchange or as a store of value, but only for purposes of decoration. There was no need for any means of payment of even a standard of value, for the simple reason that every phase of the economic activities of the population was regulated by the State authority. The life of the people was planned from cradle to grave. (1966 335)

In contrast, a free society requires an economic marketplace in which the distinction between *formal* and *material* control is generally maintained. The referees of a football game have formal control of the game. They see to it that the game is played according to the rules, and they settle any disputes which arise. However, they do not interfere in the game itself in a material way by, for example, helping one player or one team. Otherwise the game would be unfair, it could make the announced score meaningless, and the true score impossible to know. A government that wanted an honest economy would not interfere with prices or wages or other material aspects of the marketplace. It would take this attitude as a matter of principle, the way an official in a game avoids, as a matter of principle, materially interfering in the game. Insofar as possible, economic exchanges ought, first, to be voluntary exchanges among participants who are in a position to know the relevant facts that might affect their participation in those exchanges and, second, ought to take place in a marketplace whose structure does not distort economic value. Using a large number of hypothetical cases, advisory juries could determine what scrupulous honesty requires each side to know in economic exchanges. The law could then embody these judgments. For example, in applying for a mortgage from a bank, it might be required that the borrower be told that, say, past experience has shown fifty-eight out of a hundred people borrowing that amount of money, with the borrower's credit capacity, lost their homes through foreclosure. On the other hand, if a borrower were warned of the risk, in language that has been approved by the Court of Common Reason, there would be no legal obstacle from getting any loan the borrower could obtain.

Furthermore, the same kind of requirements could apply if the bank attempted to sell, say, a thousand mortgages to some other financial institution. If we were to dramatize our Economy, so we could heed her soliloquies, conversation, and activities, we would be amazed by her talents and accomplishments, but would also be so appalled by her deceptions and self-deceptions as to greatly fear that we were watching a tragedy. Yet the playwrights of this immense drama do not seem to recognize the principal flaw in Economy's character, much less develop the plot and write the lines that would reform that character.

Consider the time between the beginning of economic decline in 2007 to the passage of the bailout on October 3, 2008. The decline was often referred to as the *subprime debacle,* but there is nothing wrong with subprime loans *per se,* which after all can be mutually rewarding. The problem was a *subhonest economy.* Yet there were no proposals that we solve the disaster by developing an economy and polity that operated through "regular control by the people," even though, as Jefferson says, no "other depositories of power have ever yet been found, which did not end in converting to their own profit the earnings of those committed to their charge"(above, page 185). We claim to be the greatest democracy the world has ever known, but the reality is often indistinguishable from an oligarchy, or at best, an elected oligarchy. Jeffersonian wards, or their contemporary functional equivalent, are not live options, even in crises. So we do not ask the people, what *their* standards of honesty are, or the kind of banking system *they* would trust, or the sort of economic arrangements *they* think would best contribute to public happiness. Is it reasonable to assume that a majority of the people, in a cool and deliberate mood, would approve a domino-structured economy, where risky behavior by a few could make the property of the majority insecure? Or one where the imprudent, if very lucky, can enjoy all the benefits of their imprudence but, if their luck follows probability, the prudent must pay?

In Aeschylus' play *The Suppliants,* fifty women ask the king of Argos to decide an excruciatingly difficult moral dilemma in their favor. He answers: "If the whole community risks infection, the people must find a cure together. I can promise nothing until I share the counsel of all my citizens." The women object: "You are the citizens, you are the state!" He replies: "Do not ask me to judge. I have said it before: although the power is mine, I will not act without the people"(1991 21-2). After the people make a decision in the women's favor, the women rejoice: "The people of this city: may they guard their rights without flinching and govern with forethought for the common good"(36). These sentiments come from ancient Athenian drama, but their principle is at the core of the American revolution. If the leaders of our political economy would adopt that principle, they could revolutionize our society by instituting a two-market solution to the great goal of perfecting the pursuit of public happiness: The first market is economic, which defines our property in things; the second is political, which defines our property in rights. Their guiding creed would become: *Free economic exchanges of money, products, and services by consumers in places of business, and free political exchanges of ideas, arguments, and votes by citizens in courts of common reason, constitute two markets that, operating with meticulous honesty and in a symbiotic relationship, can be, and ought to be, the secure foundation of our political economy in the twenty-first century.* Let me explain by using an analogy to complex numbers, which are so common in mathematics, science, and engineering. Complex numbers are a union of two components, neither of which can be reduced to the other. This complexity was first proposed because, by extending the concept of number beyond simple real numbers, certain algebraic problems that previously had no solution could be solved. Similarly, we are facing many social problems for which there is no simple market solution. We must extend the concept of market beyond consumers to citizens, developing a self-organizing complex of two markets, in which neither component — Thomas Jefferson, Inc. or Adam Smith, Inc. — can be reduced to the other. In short, if we wish to be revolutionary in the American sense, we must create *complex markets*, for those are the only infrastructures capable of attaining that revolution's great-souled aspiration: A perpetually improving union of material and moral prosperity. Consequently, the above simple model of restricting governmental interference in free economic exchanges to that of form only, will need modification. "Ultimate happiness . . . qualified with every necessary moral ingredient" should distort economic values in a material way (Madison above, page 236); that is, the distortion ought to occur if the people judge it to be required as they try to "guard their rights without flinching and govern with forethought for the common good." We put limits on free speech when it is a present danger, say, for a patron to falsely yell "Fire!" in a crowded theater; in like manner, we should, as the people may dictate, put limits on the freedom of individuals to invest (no financing of Hit Men, Inc.), or to spend (no buying sex from children), or to promote (no cigarette advertising), or to prevent innovation (no group of patent holders can collectively obstruct the development of the airplane (as almost happened)), and so on. In addition, it is certainly the political right of a free people to create monopolies, although it may not be wise. Madison's caution still applies: "Monoplies tho' in certain cases useful ought to be granted with caution, and guarded with strictness agst abuse"(1946 551). Suppose a utility is granted a monopoly in a state with the stipulation that its prices are to be regulated. For the people to have ultimate power, regulation should be controlled by the Court of Common Reason for that state. Thus the state advisory jury could hear arguments of stockholders, customers, consumer advocates, economists, and so forth, before giving its judgment on prices. Furthermore, the jury could periodically reconsider the grant of monopoly power to confirm that the common reason of society continues to authorize it. In sum, only a politically free market of courts of common reason, or their equivalent, has the moral power *and* subtlety necessary to structure a truly free economy, for a free economy is made for the people, not the people for a free economy.

Hence even if all the earlier arguments about rational money are unsound, as I suspect many readers believe, and the best arrangement is to keep the Federal Reserve, it would still be desirable for its Governors to seek advice of the people, speaking through the Court of Common Reason. In fact, thousands of randomly distributed and deliberating jurors would likely have a collective knowledge of the economy superior to that of the Board. As in a ordinary trial, the people could hear the experts, deliberate using their own experience, and then make a decision on the growth of the money supply. We would then expect the Governors to heed the advice of the people, unless the people, to use Madison's words yet again, are "stimulated by some irregular passion, or some illicit advantage, or misled by the artful misrepresentations of interested men"(above, page 158).

America's principal economic mistake is its failure to make the economy as honest as it is possible to be. As a result we do not know, and cannot know, all the truth about ourselves that it is possible to know. The price of many things has been distorted in *ad hoc* ways; for example, milk, medicine, or education. The difficulty or impossibility of knowing the truth behind all this unnecessary distortion has consequences. Few would deny, for example, that many of America's energy problems in the 1970s were due to dishonest pricing, or that the stock market's problems soon after the turn of the century were due to dishonest reporting (by both companies and research analysts). Indeed perhaps dishonesty in general is the principal source of those widespread economic misjudgments by consumers, CEOs, labor leaders, and government officials which lead to recessions and depressions. A typical analysis of these misjudgments would conclude that their causes are rooted in our failure to know the future. But perhaps accurate knowledge of the past and present would be sufficient to reduce or eliminate them. Suppose a scientist were allowed to experiment, but only with an apparatus which significantly and randomly distorted the outcome of the experiment. Would the scientist not be justified in being pessimistic about what could be learned? A central problem for the experimental scientist is to design experiments which reveal the truth about nature with as little distortion as possible. Likewise, a central problem for economists is to design the marketplace so that it becomes a series of experiments that reveals the truth about the economic values held by the American people.

Let me give an example of dishonest pricing. I was at a party where a lawyer was lamenting the way in which everyone looked to government for subsidies or welfare. In contrast, he always paid his own way. I asked where he went to law school. His answer: the University of Connecticut. In subsequent conversation he admitted that, by going to a public law school, he had received a large subsidy from the government, much larger than some of the welfare recipients he had been complaining about. Dishonesty in pricing — in this case, the pricing of a law school education — led to self-deception. The lawyer had an unjustified belief about his achievements (that is, he believed he paid the full price for everything he got) and this false belief contributed to a disdain for welfare recipients. Honest pricing would require, say, that a student's bill for law school clearly indicate the amount of government subsidy that he or she received. If we are to have superb economic self-government, it is crucial that our economy not be deceptive or contribute to self-deception. Again, it has been common in both the state and federal budgets to keep some public obligations and expenditures off-budget in order to deceive voters. Such governmental deceptions are clearly inconsistent with the ethos of American democracy, as are corporate deceptions such as those of Enron or WorldCom. Making our economy more honest is relatively easy, but making it as honest as is humanly possible is the work of generations. Creating an economics of honesty, and embodying it into our economic practices is the second dimension of American perfectionist democracy.

But what should happen if the people themselves call for dishonest economic policies? Consider an analogy. Suppose a woman is in a quandary because she must apparently choose to be honest, or give up one of her other closely-held values — say, kindness. What is the moral responsibility of a friend to whom she goes for advice? Surely it is to use all his ingenuity to suggest ways in which she can be both honest and kind. And if there are no such ways, then it is to suggest ways to minimize the dishonesty or unkindness. Furthermore, he could make suggestions as to how to avoid such situations in the future. Of course, an honest person might sometimes be forced to lie for moral reasons — say, to protect the life of a child. Yet it is part of the honesty of honest people to be as adept as possible in avoiding situations that encourage or require lying, at least where morality allows such avoidance. Now the moral responsibility of the democratic economist is similar to that of the friend. Cases where one must have "lying" prices for genuine moral reasons should be meticulously justified, that "must" should not reflect a failure of imagination or determination. In a generally honest economy, as in a genuine honest person, there is less need to be dishonest. As lying by the individual may — and often does — lead to more lies, so a dishonest price (say, for oil) may lead to other dishonest prices (say, for electricity or plastic whose manufacture is dependent on the oil). But suppose that the people call for dishonest pricing, say they want the government to ration gasoline because they fear extraordinary increases in price over the next several years. It is then the responsibility of the economist not only to emphasize the evils of rationing (such as the corruption it breeds, the bureaucracies it spawns, the compromising of the property rights of owners of gasoline, the spread of dishonest prices to other products), but also to devise new economic structures which are both honest and can relieve the fears of the people. For example, the institution of a retail futures market for gasoline would be honest. A person could buy a future from an oil company for 1000 gallons of gas to be delivered two years hence at a given price. This market could provide capital for new storage facilities and give the companies additional opportunities for profit. More importantly, consumers would know exactly what it truly costs to reduce their present fears of a runaway increase, a cost that is hidden by ordinary rationing. Thus the lack of a market mechanism for the transfer of risk — the purpose of a future — gives unnecessary political force to the call for rationing power by the government. Perhaps an eloquent defense of futures in the Court of Common Reason would prevent the rationing. If not, there would still be an advantage. For if a people accept "lying" prices when they are unnecessary for their happiness, they are making a mistake, and the subsequent recognition and correction of that mistake represents an enhancement of self-government. A people willing and capable of regularly correcting their own mistakes deserve to called self-governing, truly worthy of the exalted names *sovereign, free, independent, autonomous.*

10

Economic Health

Transforming our economy so that it becomes superbly honest is no easy task, but it doesn't appear to be impossible. Let me sketch how the Court of Common Reason might be used in six areas toward the creation of economic health. My hope is that this will be sufficient to suggest how it might be used in cases not mentioned. As with the description of the Court of Common Reason, the point is not that everything has to be precisely as described. Since the results in the Court might undermine some or all my suggestions, my discussion is necessarily speculative. Nevertheless I believe it is worthwhile to consider the kind of arrangements which might constitute economic health in the context of a politics of self-knowledge.

Taxation. There are a large number of different kinds of taxes: income taxes, excise taxes, property taxes, corporate taxes, wealth taxes, and so forth. What kinds a democracy should have, and their rate, ought to be determined by experiments in Courts of Common Reason. These experiments could also determine the relationship between those taxes. For example, as revenue requirements go up and down it might be the case that, in the judgment of the people, each kind of tax should not go up or down proportionally, but that the relationship should change relative to economic times. Thus it might be their judgment that in good economic times a wealth tax should be negligible, but should become substantial if conditions deteriorate. Eventually a single tax index could be created that would incorporate all such subtleties. Its purpose would be democratic control. Once formed, it would allow the people to give periodic advice to Congress as to what the tax index should be. Presumably Congress would generally take the advice unless the members believed that it was one of those times in which they must have, in Hamilton's words, the "courage and magnanimity enough to serve [the people] at the peril of their displeasure"(above, page 19). In such cases Congress should act contrary to the people's wishes. Even so, Congress must later test the arguments that determined its action against contrary points of view in the Court. If the effort fails, then members of Congress should either resign or capitulate since, "in matters of common sense, the few must yield to the many, when local and temporary prejudices are removed"(2002 461). These words from 1785 come from the Scottish philosopher Thomas Reid, who may have been one of the sources of Madison's view that the cool and deliberate sense of the people is the definitive standard to which any free government must forever be faithful.

That fidelity requires continuing experiments in Courts of Common Reason in order to know what kind of taxes a free people should have. But in the absence of such experiments, let us speculate that they would choose a tax system which makes the epistemological problem central; that is, they would require the real and apparent taxes to be as close as possible by minimizing hidden, and therefore often deceptive, taxes. Further, we suppose that the people would want a tax system which does not distort prices unless morally necessary. Although taxation must cause economic pressure, distortion of prices can be reduced by making that pressure as uniform as possible. Increase the interior and exterior air pressure on a balloon greatly, but let that increased pressure be uniformly exerted on all surfaces, and the balloon will not be distorted. Our goal, within the limits set by the Court of Common Reason, would be to apply the economic pressure of taxation uniformly, in the sense that no informed individual or institution would be tempted to commit or not commit economic acts that are both legal and moral *because* of the tax system. The aim would be to have no *tax* incentives — or disincentives. Of course, this ideal of a neutral tax is impossible to reach, but there are degrees of neutrality and I am supposing the people would choose the highest degree that is practically possible at a given time.

It is certainly a common judgment that our income tax code has become substantially arbitrary and too complex. At various times, if you were a member of the unmarried class, the tax law treated you differently than if you were married; if you were a farmer you were treated differently than if you were a merchant; if you were blind you were treated differently than if you had cystic fibrosis; if you received your income through municipal bonds you were treated differently than if you earned money working in a factory, and so on. And these distinctions are frequently changed. Is it any wonder that we have a large class of well-paid tax-avoidance lawyers? The evils of frequent changes in law were long ago pointed out by Madison:

> Another effect of public instability is the unreasonable advantage it gives to the sagacious, the enterprising and the moneyed few, over the industrious and uninformed mass of the people. Every new regulation concerning commerce or revenue; or in any manner affecting the value of the different species of property, presents a new harvest to those who watch the change and can trace its consequences; a harvest reared not by themselves but by the toils and cares of the

great body of their fellow citizens. This is a state of things in which it may be said with some truth that laws are made for the *few* not for the *many*. (1962 10:539-40)

Madisonian standards could be achieved in taxes by having the Court of Common Reason periodically confirm that, in the judgment of the advisory jury, our tax laws give no "unreasonable advantage" to the "enterprising and moneyed few . . . over the industrious and uninformed mass of the people."

The unnecessary complexity of our tax system encourages deception, and consequently violates a fundamental principle of the American revolution: "It is essential to the character of a free republic," Joel Barlow declared in 1793, " . . . that no shadow of deception ever should be offered to the people"(above, page 235). Simplicity is one important way to reduce deception. But what kind of simplicity would have this effect? Initially single-seater airplanes were simple, but difficult to control, whereas today they are relatively simple to control, but complex. Airplanes and tax systems should both strive for simplicity, but only a simplicity which satisfies ergonomics, and that simplicity might require great complexity in design. What we want is a tax system that, on the one hand, satisfies the demands of fairness and justice (according to the deliberate sense of the people) and, on the other, is simple for the people to understand and control. Such a purpose would have to deal with many subtleties. For example, a rich woman, through the charity deduction, might think of herself as more generous than she actually is. Although the deduction causes her self-deception, it would be for the people to decide the extent to which such self-deceptions are harmful or not, and how far they undermine or promote public happiness.

As generations of physicists have striven for a single theory of forces that satisfies experiments, so it might also take generations of political economists to achieve a tax index which satisfies experiments in Courts of Common Reason. In the eighteenth century the rallying cry was: *Taxation without representation is tyranny.* However, the twentieth century demonstrated that taxation, with representation by elected officials, is a relentlessly unstable, arbitrary, and devious scholasticism. Were the spirit of 1776 to awaken, the new rallying cry would be: *Taxation with statistical representation is freedom.* That is, if the ultimate control of taxation were given to a statistical representation of the people in their cool and reflective moments, their choices would be a transparent exercise of American political freedom, according to which the people themselves have to decide what kind and amount of taxes would best suit their pursuit of public happiness.

Government subsidies. An honest economy could reward productive virtues very exactly, but that does not mean that productive values must always prevail. Economic values must compete with the noneconomic values; as noted, a free society cannot tolerate a free market in hired assassins. There are a large number of ways in which the people might wish to modify the outcome of their own economy. Consider government subsides. Government subsidies to such groups as churches, farmers, hospitals, and oil companies are often hidden and complex. But they should, like taxes, be designed so that each and every one of them is both as transparent and as simple as possible, given the people's informed values. For example, experiments in the Court of Common Reason might reveal that the people want subsidies to farmers to vary depending on the conditions in the economy, whereas they would put no such restriction on subsidies to medical education. Experiments with a large number of hypothetical subsidies would allow for the creation of a subsidy index similar to the tax index. This would enhance democratic control because subsidies would exist, and only in the amount, that the people think is necessary or desirable. Of course, the people might even decide to be ignorant of some subsidies. Thus they might decide that religious freedom is so precious that the exact subsidy rate should remain uncalculated by the government, the way parents might think it wrong to keep an exact accounting of what is spent on each child.

The ancient code of Hammurabi was a government of persons; that is, it distinguished three classes — the aristocracy, commoners, and slaves — and people were treated differently depending on their class. Would not any distinction among the people, where one individual received a subsidy and another did not, bring back these morally objectionable distinctions? Not necessarily. What is objectionable about both Hammurabi's code and our present laws concerning subsidies or taxes is not the division into classes, but the moral arbitrariness of the divisions. Some distinctions are justified: it is not morally arbitrary to distinguish between an unfortunate, destitute person who needs continuing and expensive medical care from one who is not destitute or unhealthy. As argued above (page 178), Courts of Common Reason should use a democratic evolutionary paradigm of ideas to protect ourselves from a natural Darwinian process. Using courts to create an index of government subsidy is no doubt difficult, but it is hardly hopeless. What is hopeless are our impractical attempts to create economic welfare schemes without knowledge of the people's informed values and in disregard of questions of honesty. In general, hidden subsidies are as wrong as hidden taxes. Both of them interfere with our judgment of reality, undermine self-knowledge, and frustrate the aspiration for excellence in self-government. Nevertheless the ban on hiddenness is not absolute, a people, like a individual, may, on occasion, choose to be ignorant, or self-deceptive, for morally justifiable reasons.

Government penalties. Consider the classic problem of what to do about the polluting smokestack in a factory town. In the past. companies have considered the air to be a free means of waste disposal. This assumption can have a distorting effect on the price of whatever is produced: either it is lower than it ought to be, or the profit margin is greater. If the factory also produces solid industrial wastes which have to be disposed of on private property there is no similar distortion of price or profit. (For the sake of the illustration, I am assuming that the solid wastes are environmentally harmless.) The price of the factory's goods would have to reflect the cost to the company of disposing of that waste. The same should hold for airborne wastes, but without courts of common reason there is no good way to determine what the government should charge the company for polluting the air. With them there is a clear answer. In the context of arguments about the competing values of aesthetics, health, jobs, and social need for the product, the advisory jury could determine whether the company should be forced to eliminate the smokestack, be allowed free use of the air, or be charged such and such a fee. Assuming the government enacted laws embodying those values, the price of the factory's goods would then be honest, because it would accurately reflect the social cost, if any, of the pollution. The fees the American people might charge for polluting should also apply to the government itself. Thus a military base's smokestack ought to be treated by the same procedure as the polluting factory. Without this pollution fee, the true cost of the military base, and thus of government itself, would be unknown.

We might speculate that, as far as is practicable, pollution fees would go to those who bear the extra costs caused by the smokestack. One scheme might give it to those most directly affected in proportion to how much they are affected. Thus, for example, if the pollution caused a small increase in the incidence of cancer, some of the money might go into cancer research and some to subsidize the higher medical insurance that people pay by living in the town. This would have the effect of educating both the public about pollution and those responsible for it. If the fees were quite high, perhaps the best way for the company management to increase earnings would be to reduce or eliminate the pollution. Hence there would be a continuing incentive to stop polluting. On the other hand, the people could not in general charge arbitrarily high fees for polluting without causing the country's industry to collapse. But where to draw the line involves value judgments, and those judgments can only rightly be discovered by making "an appeal to the deliberate understanding of our fellow citizens"(the phrase is Jefferson's (1903 15:302)). Using courts of common reason for regularly and systematically determining social costs could become one of their most important functions.

Similar arguments should apply to "internal pollution," such as that associated with cigarettes or liquor. These social costs should be determined by the advisory jury in response to claims of benefits and harms that are associated with the products. For example, after hearing arguments by interested parties on the pleasures and dangers of smoking, the advisory jury might decide to impose a fee of x cents per pack. Suppose this becomes law. Now imagine some company creates a brand of cigarettes that contains a new substance, and this substance severs the connection, that is, henceforth smokers of that brand and nonsmokers get diseases at equal rates. Then the Court of Common Reason might recommend the elimination of the fee. This is the difference between a company's social cost fees and its taxes: the former, unlike the latter, would be reduced or abolished as the special harm to society of their products is reduced or eliminated. If x were a significant percentage of the price, and if no other company has a like product, the president of the company could be a simultaneous hero to the users, to the medical profession, to consumer groups, to the stockholders, and to the American people (who, after all, removed the fee). Of course, this example is fanciful as described, but the point is sound. The Court of Common Reason would allow social costs to be accurately determined, and it could give incentives to companies by lowering fees when those costs are reduced. Free enterprise could thus enter the arena of social problems on an unprecedented scale, because entrepreneurs would have a greater opportunity to compete for the favor of the American people in their role as citizens, and not only in their role as consumers.

Monopoly and antitrust. Image a very large corporation that dominates a major industry. Call it "ABC." From ABC's point of view, it cannot satisfy its critics: if it sets prices higher than the competition, it is gouging the public; if equal to the competition, it is conspiring with rivals; if lower than the competition, it is trying to drive them out of business. On the other hand, critics complain that ABC is so powerful that the antitrust laws are never applied. Others maintain that no company can indefinitely dominate a major industry and that eventually another corporation (domestic or foreign) will displace ABC. Still others say that even if this is true, such power is dangerous in the meantime, or if ABC somehow fails, the government might have to bail it out. What then should be done? Clearly any department of government — such as Commerce or Agriculture — should do what is in the public interest — nothing more and nothing less. A private individual or small firm must obey the law, but is by no means obligated to follow the public interest. It might be in the public interest for a person to become a physician rather than a hobo. It might be in the public interest for a small firm to make medical instruments rather than bubblegum. But neither the person nor the firm is legally obligated to do so. Indeed a population where everyone acted in the public interest — at least as narrowly defined — might be too docile to preserve freedom, especially when that freedom was seriously challenged.

The Court of Common Reason might decide that ABC has the same freedom as an individual or small firm. On the other hand, it might decide that, if ABC had the same freedom, there would be a threat to public happiness and thus it should operate under the watchful eye of an advisory jury chosen by the Agency for Public Choice. Each year after hearing arguments of the Justice Department, management, stockholders, union members, and so forth concerning threats to the public interest (even the threat of failure), the advisory jury could express its considered judgment. If it were a negative judgment the relevant regulatory agency of the government could subject it to more regulation, or impose a penalty. The latter could then fall on the individuals involved, whether officers, union officials, or stockholders. It would naturally be up to juries to decide which individuals were "involved." In general, it is unlikely that penalties would be arbitrarily severe or lenient because in either case society itself would suffer. Having an advisory jury review ABC's actions would also have advantages for the company. Thus ABC could pay a private choice corporation to form a jury whose answers could be used in planning, so that any future penalty could probably be avoided or reduced. By being continually judged by standards that are proven to be representative of the informed values of the American people, the company would gain protection from arbitrary or outmoded regulations.

This system also has a great moral advantage over present practices in which punishments fall on the innocent and guilty alike.

In a successful antitrust action innocent employees often lose their jobs, and innocent stockholders, their money. The issue is similar to that involved in the choice between confederation or federalism in the Founding era. As Alexander Hamilton put it in the *Federalist*: "The great and radical vice in the construction of the existing Confederation is in the principle of LEGISLATION for STATES or GOVERNMENTS, in the CORPORATE or COLLECTIVE CAPACITIES and as contradistinguished from the INDIVIDUALS of whom they consist"(1961 4:359). The experience of the United Nations certainly shows the checkered career of punishment for states. A like history applies to the punishment of corporations in their collective capacities for antitrust violations. The Court of Common Reason could ensure that, as far as possible, the innocent in antitrust suits would be protected and punishments would fall just on those individuals who are responsible. On the other hand, the Court could also impose the punishment on the corporate entity, whenever it rejected Hamilton's argument in an particular case.

Suppose, however, ABC is so successful that it becomes a potential threat to individual rights, or to honesty in the economy. Imagine also that, in the judgment of the Court of Common Reason, this happened — without the corporation violating either the law or the public interest. Management, we will assume, is both extremely talented and extremely lucky. How should ABC be treated? In my judgment, the government, if authorized by the Court of Common Reason, should break up the corporation but pay the shareholders for any financial loss that that breakup might entail. After all, they are innocent and the Fifth Amendment protections of property would apply. It is sometimes very difficult to split up a large corporation into viable parts. But that problem is here minimized. Corporate managements would know long in advance that if they keep growing they might have to split up; and if they make judicious use of private choice corporations, they would have a good idea when and how they might be so ordered. Hence over a period of years they could either make plans to be broken up, or change corporate policy to avoid that eventuality (for example by selling divisions). Naturally this would depend on their judgment about which course would be most favorable to their stockholders. Similar things could be said about companies that get so large that it is widely assumed they are "too big to fail." The Court would have to decide if this is true and, if so, what to do if failure comes. In general, problems of monopoly, antitrust, and size should make it clear that it is neither small nor large that is beautiful in a democracy; rather any size is beautiful that is within the boundaries set by the informed values of the people.

National debt. The ideal of an honest economy requires that a national debt be very carefully handled. For a national debt can ease the way for deceit by government officials. We can see this by understanding the relation of national debt to money. When a lender exchanges money for a promissory note, two things are lost: relative safety and liquidity. The lender loses safety because there is always the chance the money will not be returned or that the repaid money will not be as valuable as the money lent. Liquidity is lost because a promissory note is not as easily exchanged as money is for goods and services. It is for this double loss that interest is paid. The rate of interest is influenced by the judgment of the lender about the "safety" of the borrower, the quality of the money likely to be received on repayment, the length of the loan, and competition among lenders. If a state government is believed uncomfortably close to bankruptcy, then the rate of interest will be very high. On the other hand, the federal government can always, in one sense, pay off loans, that is, it can pay by printing more money. This power is a continual enticement for federal politicians to undermine the integrity of the currency whenever it suits their purposes. Further, that integrity can be compromised even if dollars are not actually printed. Suppose that the federal government's entire large debt is in notes which mature in one day, with the government refinancing its debt every day. Although called "debt" these notes would be functionally equivalent to money. What is true of these one-day bonds is also true to a lesser extent of longer duration bonds, for as they mature their liquidity increases to become virtually equal to that of money. The confusion of money and debt — so convenient for the governors who wish to manipulate the governed — is encouraged. David Hume made a classic statement of this phenomenon:

> It is very tempting to a minister to employ such an expedient [that is, the opening of the public treasure], as enables him to make a great figure during his administration, without overburthening the people with taxes, or exciting any immediate clamours against himself. The practice, therefore, of contracting debt will almost infallibly be abused, in every government. It would scarcely be more imprudent to give a prodigal son a credit in every banker's shop in London, than to empower a statesman to draw bills, in this manner, upon posterity. (1985 352, cf. 636).

Hume's point has been further verified by several hundred more years of experience. Consequently if we want to ensure that the powers of government actually do derive from the consent of the governed, a more direct control of the national debt by the people is necessary. Otherwise over time the public will almost certainly be manipulated again and again by public officials.

For example, in 1781 Hamilton claimed that a

> national debt if it is not excessive will be to us a national blessing; it will be a powerful cement of our union. It will also create a necessity for keeping up taxation to a degree which without being oppressive, will be a spur to industry; remote as we are from Europe and shall be from danger, it were otherwise to be feard our popular maxims would incline us to too great parsimony and indulgence. We labour less now than any civilized nation in Europe, and a habit of labour in the people is as essential to the health and vigor of their minds and bodies as it is conducive to the welfare of the State. We ought not to Suffer our self-love to deceive us in a comparison, upon these points. (1961 2:635)

Hamilton's "cement" argument had already been made by Paine in *Common Sense* (1776): "No nation ought to be without a debt. A national debt is a national bond . . ."(1945 1:32). As might be expected Jefferson and Madison disagreed with Hamilton, and even Hamilton elsewhere is quite cautious about creating a national debt (see, respectively, 1950 23:408, 1962 13:148, 1961 6:106, 18:102-3). What we should note here is that Hamilton's argument reveals that, from the beginning of American government, politicians were tempted to use the national debt as a means to control the people. If Hamilton thinks the American people too parsimonious and too indulgent, he can quite rightfully use his considerable powers of eloquence to convince them of the errors of their ways. In particular, he can argue that they need the debt as a device to protect themselves from their own vices. Persuasion and reason are legitimate. If these do not work then the American people's right to be parsimonious and indulgent must be respected. Not to do so violates their liberty, including the freedom to make their own mistakes. Our economic institutions should increase the control the people have over their own lives — they should not undermine political freedom. Yet the flourishing of various forms of Keynesian economics in the twentieth century shows that our public morality had not improved, for Keynesian economics makes manipulation of the people through deficit financing an essential feature of its structure. This holds both for totalitarian Keynesians (such as Hitler) and democratic ones (such as Roosevelt and Reagan). Lest my reference to Hitler be thought unfair to Keynes let me quote from the Preface to the German edition of *The General Theory of Employment, Interest and Money*, dated September 7, 1936:

"Nevertheless the theory of output as a whole, which is what the following book purports to provide, is much more easily adapted to the conditions of a totalitarian state, than is the theory of the production and distribution of a given output produced under conditions of free competition and a large measure of laissez-faire"(1973 7:xxvi).

Some economists argue that America's national debt puts an economic burden on posterity, while others deny it. Whatever the merits of either side, the economic burden (even if it exists) is not so important as the moral burden which increases the chances of deceit and self-deception. By passing on to our children a government that lives off a very large debt, we pass on to them a government that they are less likely to control and, to that degree, a government which is more likely to interfere with their unalienable right to the pursuit of happiness. In spite of these risks there may be occasions when they are worth taking. For example, the Louisiana Purchase was financed with public borrowing. Jefferson had to make a reversal. In 1798 Jefferson argued for "taking from the federal government the power of borrowing"(1892 7:310) and then just five years later he had no choice but to borrow money to achieve the crowning glory of his presidency. Assuming he correctly judged the common reason of society, borrowing for that purpose was justified by Lockean *"Prerogative,"* which is "*nothing but the Power of doing publick good without a Rule*"(1988 378). That is, the people might have thought that buying the land was a public good and that using deficit financing was also justified because they believed borrowing transferred some of the tax burden to the next generation (who were going to benefit from great enlargement of the United States). In contemporary terms, the purchase was a capital budget item, not a recurring expense. Jefferson was thus wrong to make an absolute constitutional restriction on borrowing, indeed this example illustrates once again his own dictum that in political economy "no one axiom can be laid down as wise and expedient, for all time and circumstances"(above, page 236). Nevertheless since the case for the integrity of the currency is strong, one might speculate the people would always place the burden of the argument on those who wish to have the government borrow.

Capitalism and socialism. Should an industry, such as the railroads, be owned by the government? The way in which such questions ought to be answered can be made clear by an analogy. In the dispute between Galileo and the Church over whether the earth moved, we tend to think that Galileo was right because he argued for motion, and that the Church was wrong. But this is not what made Galileo right. What make him right was the means he used to answer the question, namely, observation, experiment, and proof. In fact, from the perspective of Einstein's General Theory of Relativity, all motion is relative, so in a sense Galileo and the Church were both right and both wrong. In the physical world defined by the General Theory we cannot answer the question "Does the earth move?" unless we have answered the prior question "What is the frame of reference?" In the political world defined by the American revolution we cannot answer the question "Should the railroads be owned by the government?" unless we have answered the prior question: "What is the considered judgment of the people?" If the people lack the power to make decisions concerning capitalism and socialism, they can hardly be called free and independent. Thus to answer the question whether it is a just power of government to own and operate the railroads, we have to *prove* that that power can be derived from the informed consent of the people. Depending on that derivation it is possible that at one time America should be socialist in this respect, and at another time, capitalist. American revolutionary philosophy requires that the choices regarding economic policies be founded on evidence derived from the public's considered judgments. Yet, to my knowledge, none of the schools of economics — whether libertarian, conservative, liberal, socialist, or communist — have shown much interest in the observations and experiments on the grand scale which is necessary to know those judgments. In practice, what generally happens is that one side says: "We believe in the market, we believe in the market, we believe in the market," but when this side gains political power, it does not create a *market of ideas, arguments, and votes* to determine how they should govern; whereas the other side says: "We believe in democracy, we believe in democracy, we believe in democracy," but when this side gains political power, it does not create a democracy based on the *people's deliberate voice* to determine how they should govern. In neither case is integrity of thought achieved, the credos become pretexts for economic or political power, not a description of action that should be taken when that power is attained.

It was one of the conceits of Marx, Lenin, Stalin, Mao and their followers that communism is revolutionary as compared to the reactionary doctrine of democratic capitalism. But their theory disrespects the dignity of the people and their ultimate right to decide. In contrast, the truly revolutionary Declaration of Independence requires that the people arrange the political economy "as to them shall seem most likely to effect their Safety and Happiness." In 1800, a

New York attorney, Tunis Wortman, argued for the rights for citizens to look into such matters: "Politics is a subject of universal concern: it relates to objects of public utility. We are equally interested in supporting the genuine principles of Social Security and Happiness. We are entitled to investigate every question which concerns the Public Prosperity. We are equally entitled to communicate the result of our enquiry and deliberation"(145-6). Although we have not yet created courts of common reason that would allow the people to authoritatively state the "genuine principles of Social Security and Happiness," it is nevertheless possible to speculate. Consider poverty. John Adams claimed that "the condition of the labouring poor in most countries, that of fishermen particularly of the Northern states is as . . . abject as that of slaves." Adams thought the difference between those poor and slaves was "imaginary"(Jefferson 1950 1:321). Since a central purpose of the revolution was to avoid "slavery" to Great Britain, it can hardly have been thought right to substitute that "slavery" for "slavery" to poverty. It certainly seems plausible that the American people as a whole, after due deliberation, would want to relieve the slave level of poverty within their midst, perhaps directly by government, or indirectly by creating laws that make private charitable organizations flourish to such an extent that public intervention would be unnecessary.

Yet whatever their decision, a self-governing people must continually strive to maintain the conditions of responsible choice and, *when these conditions prevail*, they not only have a right, but a duty, to choose capitalism or socialism or some mixture as they wish, even though in so doing they may make wrong choices. Naturally they also have the right to correct their choices any time they recognize them as wrong. Maintaining the conditions for responsible choice by the people is the essence of political liberty, so that both *extreme* socialism (in the sense that the government owns each citizen's toothbrush and underwear) and *extreme* capitalism (in the sense that private citizens have a right to own atomic bombs) would threaten responsible choice by the people, and thus could not secure political freedom. In this sense, all good economic government is of the mixed sort, and that is how the Founders saw it. For example, Madison said: "The more thorough the examination of the question, which relates to the encouragement of domestic manufactures, the more true policy . . . will be found to lie between the extremes of doing nothing and prescribing everything; between admitting no exception to the rule of *'laissez faire*,' and converting the exceptions into the rule"(1865 4:12;

cf. 1962 12:71-2; 1865 428-9). Hamilton agrees: "*Industry will succeed and prosper in proportion as it is left to the exertions of individual enterprise.* This favorite dogma, when taken as a general rule, is true; but as an exclusive one, it is false, and leads to error in the administration of public affairs. In matters of industry, human enterprize ought, doubtless, to be left free in the main, not fettered by too much regulation; but practical politicians know that it may be beneficially stimulated by prudent aids and encouragements on the part of Government"(1961 25:467). The computer and the Internet, both first created by Defense Department funds, are contemporary examples of enterprise being "beneficially stimulated by prudent aids and encouragements on the part of Government." One can sum up these views by saying that *laissez faire* is the default position — that is, the Ninth Amendment applies — in free societies. Any qualification of that principle would have to be justified by showing that it is the people's considered judgment that that qualification will increase their happiness. They would surely judge, for example,that *laissez faire* cannot be extended to include "property in men." When the conditions of responsible choice prevail, an independent people, no less than an independent person, must make and be accountable for their own choices: if the choice be wrong they must live with the consequences as far as is necessary and correct the error as far as is possible, whereas if the choice be wise, they have the right to enjoy the benefits of its own wisdom.

We are now in a position to understand economic health. It is analogous to bodily health. Even though they have a compromised immunological system it is possible to raise apparently healthy mice in a completely germ-free environment. But when they are put in an ordinary environment they die. This example suggests that a healthy body is not one free of disease-bearing germs, but rather one which can best resist the disease germs it contains, or might reasonably encounter. Economic health is likewise not the absence of economic problems, but the presence of adequate procedures for solving the problems. Advocates of *laissez faire* would renounce any governmental solutions since they fear the incompetence or wickedness of the bureaucrats who lay down the rules for the economy. Advocates of governmental controls would abandon the freedom of the marketplace since they fear the incompetence or wickedness of the people who run corporations and unions. What we need, instead, is a well-designed economic system that is honest and democratically controlled even if some of the people who run it, and some of the leaders of corporations and unions, are incompetent or wicked. It was an exhibition of the strength of our political system that it could survive Watergate — a situation in which many with great power were either incompetent or wicked. We need to increase this sort of strength in our economic system. In America we have a number of important economic practices which allow and even encourage an arbitrary exercise of power, unrestrained by the deliberate sense of the people. In its place we ought to design an economy which is, to borrow Lincoln's phrase, of the people, by the people, and for the people.

An American economic revolution, on the model of the revolution of 1776, would throw off the fetters of the oligarchic elements in our economy. To know precisely what the people want to alter or abolish in their economic government we need the first and second dimensions of American perfectionist democracy: a politics of self-knowledge and an economics of honesty. And if this seems a daring experiment, let us remember that there is no way to be true to the Declaration without being so. If we wish to design a beautiful and superbly functioning economic system, we must redeem our political ideals. Those ideals require a revolutionary morality which is not merely one of duty, but also one of soaring aspiration, comparable to Aristotle's great-souled man, who is consumed by a desire to achieve "greatness in every excellence"(1984 2:1773). America must be a great-souled country. Such an aspiration, if pursued with intelligence, honesty, and integrity, can rightly justify that national pride without which the achievement of greatness is unlikely or impossible. "A good opinion of ourselves" Thomas Paine maintained, "is . . . absolutely necessary in public life, and of the utmost importance in supporting national character"(1945 1:124). The American dream is a society that unites equality, liberty, justice, and wealth. The word "wealth" comes from a root which means well-being, and it connotes secure riches. That was the typical understanding in the eighteenth century: ". . . all men have a right to whatever *property* they can acquire by the laws of a free country; and the principle on which this is founded is the common good of mankind"(MEG 1768 1). Let us call wealth (or property) *democratic* if it has been gained and held by means that are approved by the considered judgment of the people. For example, wealth in slaves is not democratic because individuals are self-owned and cannot alienate themselves; nor is stolen property or property protected by an illegal tax haven democratic because that property is not acquired or kept by means the people would approve. Increases in democratic wealth or property create like increases in individual opportunity. A person can pursue happiness by aspiring, economically speaking, to very little, as in the nomadic life in a desert, or in a severely ascetic life. Wealth gives one the chance for success in spite of great aspirations: A person is wealthy who, through education, advertising, travel and the like, is thoroughly aware of what life has to offer, and has the ability to fulfill his or her aspirations — at least so far as they are dependent on economic power. Wealth increases the significance of freedom, poverty decreases it. The stimulation of morale — of *joie de vivre* — is one of the functions of freedom: you engage in whatever engages you. But freedom is compromised without the wealth that is necessary to do and become what one decides. Wealth allows a person lacking charisma, or religious authority, or political influence, or physical might, to control the actions of others — so long as he or she meets their price. The pursuit of democratic wealth is not a shallow pursuit; it is an essential ingredient of freedom, for by increasing the democratic wealth of individuals we continue to increase the value of freedom. Private property provides strong motives to create and protect resources needed for perfecting the pursuit of happiness. As Aristotle said, "that which is common to the greatest number has the least care bestowed upon it"(1984 2:2002; cf. Wilson 2007 1:396). Nevertheless the tragedy of the commons can be avoided if the people would decide what property should be common for the sake of their own happiness, and, wanting that happiness, would also authorize the fines and taxes needed for its excellent care. Three cheers, then, for a country where all property is democratic, because that property is likely to efficiently contribute to happiness, whether that happiness is individual or social.

Jefferson believed that "a right to property is founded in our natural wants"(1903 14:490; cf. 7:23). Madison said that the "personal right to acquire property, which is a natural right, gives to property, when acquired, a right to protection, as a social right"(1865 4:51; cf. Dallas 1790 2:310-13). Adams found property to be part of

the true and only true definition of a republic. The word *res*, every one knows, signified in the Roman language wealth, riches, property . . . *Res populi*, and the original meaning of the word *republic* could be no other than a government in which the property of the people predominated and governed; and it had more relation to property than liberty. It signified a government, in which the property of the public, or people, and of every one of them, was secured and protected by law. This idea, indeed, implies liberty; because property cannot be secure unless the man be at liberty to acquire, use, or part with it, at his discretion, and unless he have his personal liberty of life and limb, motion and rest, for that purpose. It implies, moreover, that the property and liberty of all men, not merely of a majority, should be safe; for the people, or public, comprehends more than a majority, it comprehends all and every individual . . . (1850 5:453-54; cf. 6:8-9)

In the eighteenth century, republican freedom of property implied political freedom, and political freedom implied republican freedom of property. The qualification *republican* meant that all limitations on freedom of property have the informed approval of the people. This is what *democratic* means, or should mean, today. Hence Madison's words apply to our concept of democratic wealth or property: "That is not a just government nor is property secure under it, where arbitrary restrictions, exemptions, and monopolies deny to part of its citizens that free use of their faculties, and free choice of their occupations, which not only constitute their property in the general sense of the word; but are the means of acquiring property strictly so called"(above, page 43). Another term that could be used here is *commonwealth*, which is a country where the definition of property (for example, no property in men), and the just means by which it can be acquired or maintained, is determined by the common reason of the people.

If an individual voluntarily chooses to be poor, that is, of course, the individual's right. It might be noted, however, that sometimes when this is done, the individuals are religious authorities, or they are charismatic, even conspicuous nonconsumers, or they live in rich communities surrounded by rich friends, and thus their voluntary poverty is, in practice, not so severe. For any individual, the benefits of stifling the pursuit of wealth (for instance, it gave Socrates more time for philosophical conversation) must be weighed against the benefits of being wealthy (such as increasing the freedom to engage in expensive activities). The people likewise have to consider economic tradeoffs in making choices about public policy. Nevertheless public happiness is well served where the median individual — or even better, where the median individual in each decile — has substantial and growing democratic wealth. For example, wealth can enlarge the freedom to know, including the knowledge of how to make the best choices in the pursuit of individual or public happiness. The joke has it that anyone who doesn't believe money brings happiness, doesn't know how to shop. Joke it might be, but there is truth in it, and the idea applies to the wealth of nations as well (cf. Hamilton 1961 5:42). It seems doubtful that there exists even one country which uses its wealth so wisely that no other pattern of spending would better support the pursuit of public happiness. "Wealth as a whole," Aristotle writes, "consists in using things rather than in owning them; it is really the activity — that is, the use — of property that constitutes wealth"(1984 2:2164; cf. Thucydides 1928 1:327). That activity is greatly promoted, as Hamilton, emphasizes, by diversity:

> It is a just observation, that minds of the strongest and most active powers for their proper objects fall below mediocrity and labour without effect, if confined to uncongenial pursuits. And it is thence to be inferred, that the results of human exertion may be immensely increased by diversifying its objects. When all the different kinds of industry obtain in a community, each individual can find his proper element, and can call into activity the whole vigour of his nature. And the community is benefitted by the services of its respective members, in the manner, in which each can serve it with most effect. (1961 10:255; cf. Hume 1985 270).

America is star-spangled with talent. To maintain and enlarge that talent, the country must have a dynamic economy that continually increases the democratic wealth of individuals. How many talk about a knowledge economy, but how few recognize that it requires a self-knowledge polity in order to be efficient in using wealth to promote happiness. Contrary to its reputation, republican virtue creates and preserves wealth. Leonard Woods (from his commencement address at Harvard) states that a "spirit of liberty kindles republican virtue; and republican virtue is the only sure road to national wealth and happiness"(1796 5). In an independence oration, Benjamin Hichborn says that Americans "have nothing to fear from the profusion of wealth which is tendered to us by the generous hand of commerce. . . . . while we feel the influence of those virtuous principles which produced the Revolution, we must be independent, rich and happy"(1784 19). A republican society that adopts a politics of self-knowledge, then, will not only secure riches by making the protection of democratic wealth an inviolable trust (cf. Jefferson 1903 14:466), it will be able to continually expand that wealth without being corrupted, without undermining its ability to shop wisely. Those who advocate giving up the pursuit of affluence compromise to a large degree the pursuit of excellence which is intrinsic to the meaning of public happiness. The American revolution was, is, and forever will be, a very expensive proposition.

To sum up, by studying the philosophical foundations of economic knowledge and democratic control, we can see that the solutions to our economic problems are as simple to state as they are difficult to analyze and implement: Make the economy honest; give free reign to economic activities unless restrained or prohibited by the considered judgments of the people; aim to forever increase democratic wealth, and thereby forever increase the freedom of, and the value of freedom to, the American people.   Once these philosophical goals have been set, economic inquiry must focus on working out in technical detail concepts merely sketched here, such as complex markets, rational money, or comprehensive tax and subsidy indexes.   Enduring solutions to our economic problems elude us principally because the designers and administrators of our economic institutions ignore or betray the humane and liberating parts of our philosophical heritage: for example, the Socratic belief that honesty with oneself and others is the beginning of right living, the Aristotelian claim that the people as a whole are less likely to be corrupted than any minority, the Baconian belief that knowledge is power and depends on the careful use of words, and the Madisonian belief that the free governments should act according to the deliberate sense of the community.   Nietzsche remarks that Socrates neglected art, a neglect which led, at the very end of his life in prison, to an apparition repeatedly coming to him in a dream and saying: "Socrates, practice music"(1967 92-3; cf. Plato 1937 1:444).   Were that apparition to see our political economy, it would repeatedly appear and say: "Political economists, practice philosophy — the philosophy of the American revolution."

Part III

The Philosophy of Aspiration

"We are born with faculties and powers capable almost of any thing, such at least as would carry us farther than can easily be imagined: but it is only the exercise of those powers, which gives us ability and skill in any thing, and leads us towards perfection."(1824 2:331; cf. 1975 652).

John Locke

"I am among those who think well of the human character generally. I consider man as formed for society, and endowed by nature with those dispositions which fit him for society. I believe also . . . that his mind is perfectible to a degree of which we cannot as yet form any conception"(1950 31:127).

Thomas Jefferson

"That we should have more and better things before us, than all that we have yet acquired or enjoyed, is unquestionably a most desirable state. . . . It is the glorious destiny of man to be always progressive"(2007 1:523-4).

James Wilson

"I regard utility as the ultimate appeal on all ethical questions; but it must be utility in the largest sense, grounded on the permanent interests of man as a progressive being"(1978 10).

John Stuart Mill

"I think I may, without injury to humane Perfection, be confident, that our Knowledge would never reach to all we might desire to know concerning those *Ideas* we have; nor be able to surmount all the Difficulties, and resolve all the Questions [that] might arise concerning any of them"(1975 540).

John Locke

"The worth of a man does not consist in the truth he possesses, or he thinks he possesses, but in the pains he has taken to attain that truth. For his powers are extended not through possession but through the search for truth. In this alone his ever growing perfection consists. Possession makes him lazy, indolent, proud. If God held all truth in his right hand and in his left the everlasting striving after truth, so that I should always and everlastingly be mistaken, and said to me, 'Choose', with humility I would pick on the left hand and say, 'Father, grant me that. Absolute truth is for thee alone.' " (1956 42-3).

Gotthold Ephraim Lessing

"Perfect happiness I believe was never intended by the deity to be the lot of any of his creatures in this world; but that he has very much put in our power the nearness of our approaches to it, is what I as stedfastly believe"(1950 1:10).

Thomas Jefferson

"Happy country! May thy happiness be perpetual!"(2007 1:293).

James Wilson

11

The Epistemology of Aspiration

The political aspects of the American revolution cannot be thoroughly understood without understanding the philosophy that guided it. The central philosophical presupposition is that dignity is innate in human nature and that from this assumption certain political principles follow. One is that the people are superior to their government. In the words of James Wilson, "A *State*; useful and valuable as the contrivance is, is the *inferior* contrivance of *man*, and from his *native* dignity derives all its *acquired* importance"(Dallas 1790 2:455). Since the idea that humans have dignity has historical roots in both Biblical and Greco-Roman sources, it is not surprising that this claim received its classic expression in the Italian Renaissance. These are the words of Giovanni Pico della Mirandola from an "Oration" that was probably written in 1486: "Beasts as soon as they are born . . . bring with them from their mother's womb all they will ever possess. Spiritual beings, either from the beginning or soon thereafter, become what they are to be for ever and ever. On man when he came into life the Father conferred the seeds of all kinds and the germs of every way of life. Whatever seeds each man cultivates will grow to maturity and bear in him their own fruit." Pico has God address Adam:

> Thou, constrained by no limits, in accordance with thine own free will, in whose hand We have placed thee, shalt ordain for thyself the limits of thy nature. . . . We have made thee neither of heaven nor of earth, neither mortal nor immortal, so that with freedom of choice and with honor, as though the maker and molder of thyself, thou mayest fashion thyself in whatever shape thou shalt prefer. Thou shalt have the power to degenerate into the lower forms of life, which are brutish. Thou shalt have the power, out of thy soul's judgment, to be reborn into the higher forms, which are divine. (1948 225).

Locke adopts this view. After giving an example of human depravity, he writes: "Thus far can the busie mind of Man carry him to a Brutality below the level of Beasts, when he quits his reason, which places him almost equal to Angels"(1988 182; cf. *Psalms* 8:4-5). For Locke there is no original sin or original virtue, just an original desire for happiness that will lead to sin or virtue, to the degree that we quit, or do not quit, our reason. Americans adopted this conception politically, which meant that a rigorous pursuit of common reason is the only foundation for a felicitous pursuit of public happiness.

The claim that dignity characterizes human nature is thus not inconsistent with the commission of atrocities such as slavery, Auschwitz, Kolyma, or the killing fields. It is the power to choose between depravity and virtue, to be responsible for own's choice and character, that is central. If humans were merely depraved, self-government would be impossible; if they were only virtuous, the police powers of government would be unnecessary. In the words of Madison: "As there is a certain degree of depravity in mankind which requires a certain degree of circumspection and distrust: so there are other qualities in human nature, which justify a certain portion of esteem and confidence. Republican government presupposes the existence of these qualities in a higher degree than any other form"(1962 10:507-8; cf. Madison 1962 10:477, Hamilton 1961 4:637, Locke 1988 352, and Smith, Adam 1982 9). Nevertheless it is wrong to assume that the virtues required for republican government must necessarily be on display beforehand. It is possible to impose republican government and thereby create republican virtues in the people. Germany and Japan immediately after World War II may serve as rough examples. "The best republics will be virtuous, and have been so," John Adams said, "but we may hazard a conjecture, that the virtues have been the effect of the well ordered constitution, rather than the cause"(1850 6:219; cf. Rush 1951 1:265). Two anonymous essays published in 1787 express hope for such good effects from the new federal Constitution:

> It is in vain to expect a national trait in our characters, or a similitude of habits, but as the effect of a national efficient government — Virtue or good habits are the result of good laws — and from the excellent American Constitution those *habits* will be induced, that lead to those *exertions*, *manufactures* and *enterprises*, which will give a scope to the American genius . . . (FTC 1787 30)
>
> I would ask . . . if civil *habits* are antecedent, and prior to civil institutions? Would a wise legislator who was about to form a system of government, for a nation, in a state of nature, adapt his plan to the prevailing habits of such a people? No; his object would be, to introduce a code of laws that would *induce* those habits of civilization and order, which must result *from* good government. . . . . The proposed *Federal Constitution* is happily calculated to form us to a *national spirit*, and to diffuse those generous *federal* sentiments, without which, we never can be a happy and flourishing people. (BGCJ 1787 1)

Good governments can increase virtue among the people, but they also promote individual liberty, which allows for vices. So another principle is needed that was first clearly articulated, I believe, by Bernard Mandeville in 1724: "Private Vices by the dextrous

Management of a skilful Politician may be turned into Public Benefits"(1924 1:369). Republican politicians should be skillful in this sense but, unfortunately, the reverse of Mandeville's dictum is equally true; bad governments can turn private virtues, such as loyalty to one's own community, into public vices. Furthermore, when the government operates, say, to support invidious racial distinctions, it induces depraved habits that may lead many otherwise virtuous people to become racists, and to do so with a quiet conscience.

Suppose a man stops to buy some food on his way home from work. He knows if he also buys liquor he will get drunk after supper. So he does not buy it. After supper he craves a drink but the trouble of going out for liquor leads him to forgo it that evening. He thus regulates his passions (using laziness to defeat his craving for a drink) so as to bring about the best result (not drinking after supper). The decision not to buy the drink, when he had an easy opportunity but no strong desire, is an example of reason controlling desire. The capacity for such rational self-government within the individual is one of the "other qualities" to which Madison refers, and which Locke believes should become habitual in everyone (1824 2:400-1). Civil persons use reason to regulate their passions, habits, and behavior so that, on the one hand, they will not become slaves to self-destructive emotions or appetites while, on the other hand, they will be able to pursue their own happiness without violating the rights of others. They are dexterous managers of their own thoughts and behaviors. Republican government ought to encourage such self-mastery for the sake of both private and public happiness.

In the eighteenth century it was presupposed that a civil people is like a civil person; that it is possible, *though far from easy*, to anticipate human defects and render them relatively harmless. "For WHO ARE A FREE PEOPLE?" John Dickinson asked in 1768. "Not *those*, over whom government is reasonably and equitably exercised [this was a traditional answer], but *those* [and here Dickinson gives the new American answer], who live under a government so *constitutionally checked and controuled*, that proper provision is made against its being otherwise exercised"(1768 41). This American view assumes that through knowledge of history, direct experience, and rational deliberation, it is possible to introduce into the structure and operation of government the "proper provision" of self-restraint. In the words of George Mason's Virginia Declaration of Rights (June 12, 1776): "of all the various modes and forms of Government that is best which is capable of producing the greatest degree of happiness and safety, and is most effectually secured against the danger of mal-administration"(1970 1:287; cf. Adams 1850 6:117). It was "mal-administration." not its Constitution, that was the source of America's sordid racial history (above, page 142). Encouraging the widespread belief that all humans have dignity is meant to undermine such administration; every person deserves the respect that kings and queens traditionally got through inheritance. Of course, life contains many indignities, some of which are not allowed in public (defecation) and some that are (slovenly dress). Others are allowed (voluntary slavery) but are not legally recognized. Dignity and freedom may thus on occasion conflict, but it is for the people to decide, through courts of common reason, what tradeoffs to make for the sake of their own happiness.

When self-government is achieved, a crucial problem is to *choose* the goals to which a people may reasonably aspire. By definition, an independent people are not constrained by others; they can make themselves into what they become. But what should they make themselves into? The answer requires a philosophy of aspiration. My purpose is to sketch what such a philosophy might be, and how it could be translated from theory into practice. If we wish, so to say, "to be reborn into the higher forms" we must improve the forms of government to which we have been accustomed. We need to know, under present conditions, how to organize a society so that its members will intelligently and consistently strive to perfect public happiness. Philosophy has traditionally been divided into epistemology, ethics, politics, aesthetics, metaphysics, and logic. These divisions are convenient and will be used here to divide the discussion into chapters. However, the divisions overlap and the account in any one chapter must be understood in the context of the others. Let us then start with the epistemology of aspiration.

Epistemology begins in skepticism. If doubt were foreign to us, so would be the impulse to develop a theory of knowledge. The ability to be skeptical about a variety of propositions — especially those that are widely held — is one of the marks of disciplined intellect. It is especially difficult to entertain skeptical thoughts about one's most cherished beliefs, for that can take a substantial amount of intellectual imagination and moral courage. Nevertheless those who wish to be in charge of their own minds must practice skepticism as a runner must train — regularly and often. Yet skepticism has its limits. One cannot be skeptical of everything at once, although Descartes tried: "I would . . . undertake, once and for all," he says in his *First Meditation*, "to set aside all the opinions which I had previously accepted among my beliefs and start again from the very beginning"(1951 15). Descartes very quickly runs into difficulty. For example, his *Second Meditation* begins: "Yesterday's Meditation has filled my mind with so many doubts that it is no longer in my power to forget them"(20). Yet in the very next paragraph he writes: "I convince myself that nothing has ever existed of all that my deceitful memory recalls to me"(21). Note that if he now doubts that his earlier doubt ever existed, as his present deceitful memory claims, his argument falls apart. Descartes does not doubt his memory of Latin or French, nor is he skeptical that sentences in those languages really do have meaning. Indeed it seems to me that the soundness of Descartes' argument that he exists because he thinks, is itself as least as doubtful as the claim that "3 + 2 = 5," which he includes among doubtful things. This point was brought home to me by a dream I had years ago. I dreamt I was David Hume and said: "I think therefore I am." A wise guy in my dream objected: "It's Descartes, you dolt, who said that, not Hume!" Getting annoyed, I answered: "Listen here, I, David Hume, think, therefore it follows I exist. It doesn't matter what Descartes said." David Hume, the character in my dream, thought; yet he was mistaken about existing because he only was a figment of my imagination.

The self-stultifying quality of universal doubt can be illustrated by reflecting on the following claim: "I am full of self-doubt; well, at least I think I am; well, maybe not." It is legitimate to doubt as far as one can do so consistently, but no further. To avoid replacing inconsistent believing with inconsistent doubting, we need to adopt a "metaskepticism" through which we can be skeptical of skepticism. "A true sceptic," said David Hume, "will be diffident of his philosophical doubts, as well as of his philosophical conviction"(1968 273). Extreme skeptics must be extremely credulous of their own skepticism. The genuine critical thinker habitually keeps his skepticism and metaskepticism in a dynamic equilibrium. Claims of either belief or disbelief can be the result of such things as ignorance, illogic, arrogance, self-deceit, and the failure of imagination. We need reasonable belief, reasonable doubt, reasonable uncertainty. Knowledge is achieved in the dialectic between belief, disbelief, and uncertainty, one must forever be judging which has the stronger case. Reflecting on this idea gives us insight into the remarkable change between Protestantism, as it began, and the American Protestantism, which so influenced American democracy. Consider the contrast between Luther and Jefferson. Luther said: "Whoever wants to be a

Christian must be intent on silencing the voice of reason"(1955 23:99). Jefferson, who considered himself a "real Christian"(below, page 466), said "Your own reason is the only oracle given you by Heaven"(1892 4:432). This change came about because the Lutheran protest, which began against the Roman Catholic Church, inspired a Calvinist protest against both Luther and the Catholics, which inspired subsequent protests and so on until, in America especially, Protestantism became both protest and metaprotest. In the words of Edmund Burke from a speech in Parliament on March 22, 1775: "All protestantism, even the most cold and passive, is a sort of dissent. But the religion most prevalent in our Northern Colonies is a refinement on the principle of resistance; it is the dissidence of dissent, and the protestantism of the protestant religion. This religion, under a variety of denominations agreeing in nothing but in the communion of the spirit of liberty, is predominant in most of the Northern provinces . . ."(1981 3:121-2). It is thus not surprising to find John Adams, although a Protestant, attacking all religions, including Protestant ones:

> The priesthood have, in all ancient nations, nearly monopolized learning. Read over again all the accounts we have of Hindoos, Chaldeans, Persians, Greeks, Romans, Celts, Teutons, we shall find that priests had all the knowledge, and really governed mankind. Examine Mahometanism, trace Christianity from its first promulgation; knowledge has been almost exclusively confined to the clergy. And, since the Reformation, when or where has existed a Protestant or dissenting sect who would tolerate A FREE INQUIRY? The blackest billingsgate, the most ungentlemanly insolence, the most yahooish brutality is patiently endured, countenanced, propagated, and applauded. But touch a solemn truth in collision with a dogma of a sect, though capable of the clearest proof, and you will soon find you have disturbed a nest, and the hornets will swarm about your legs and hands, and fly into your face and eyes. (1850 6:517; cf. Cappon 1959 2:607-8))
>
> All the Protestant leaders were intolerant; and all the Protestant Dissenters too when they had the power. Even the settlers of Virginia and New-England. . . . The French Atheists, Deists, Philosophers in the late revolution were as intolerant as Christian Priests. What shall we say? human nature is intolerant whenever it has power. Trust power then without a Counterpoise to no church, to no sect, to no Party. Amen and Amen. (1954 Reel 118 270)

For Adams, religious feelings could be a great danger: "there is a germ of religion in human nature so strong that whenever an order of men can persuade the people by flattery or terror that they have salvation at their disposal, there can be no end to fraud, violence, or usurpation"(Schutz and Adair 1966 224). In the revolutionary era, American society was primarily the product of a large variety of

Protestant sects, while American government was the offspring of "the protestantism of the protestant religion," a metaprotestantism that repudiated laws "respecting an establishment of religion"(even protestant ones). Adams onetime spoke of "Protestans qui ne croyent rien ["Protestants who believe nothing"]" (Cappon 1959 2:339-40). He meant, I think, not Cartesian skeptics, but metaprotestants who are religiously agnostic. Collectively the American people were metaprotestants who saw within themselves a dangerous "germ of religion" that required self-restraint. On the one hand, public policy should be confined to what can be supported by reason and experience. On the other hand, governments should prevent lawbreaking in religious activities, but otherwise stay clear of them. Yet Americans went beyond the *laissez faire* of the spiritual life. Instead "the communion of the spirit of liberty" protected, tolerated, and encouraged all sects, whether Protestant or not, through tax exemption, as long as its members were peaceful and obeyed the law. This underwriting of a free market in religion, attracted foreign religious minorities, and encouraged domestic spiritual entrepreneurs, who created an abundance of new religions.

Countervailing exercises of skepticism against metaskepticism can also produce all kinds of *philosophical* speculations. Consider some skeptical ruminations for the place of humans in the universe. Perhaps our entire experience is mere virtual reality created by a culture so complex that we can understand nothing of it. (This is a contemporary version of the Platonic claim that we are the playthings of the gods(1937 2:425; cf. 558) or even, as is implied by the Book of *Job*, the playthings of Satan and God.) Or perhaps "selves" are a mere illusion in a completely material universe. Contrariwise, perhaps solipsism is true so that, except for one's self, everything in the universe has no more existence than the creatures of our daydreams. Indeed, solipsism is the right philosophy for the sleeping self but who, while dreaming, is smart enough to discover it? Yet even if the universe has a solid, independent existence it does not follow that we can know it. Imagine flipping a penny a large number of times. By chance some order might occasionally appear. For example, there might be a run of six heads in a row, or of heads and tails alternately for nine times in a row. Now suppose all physical objects are made of very small particles that move at random. We know from Ramsey theory that complete disorder is impossible, that a set of objects randomly placed will contain whatever orderly substructures we want, provided the set is large enough (see Graham and Spencer 1990). For example, if there are a large enough number of randomly distributed stars, then any shape or pattern — say, that of an American flag or the Declaration of Independence — will exist somewhere by accident. It is conceivable that all the order in the physical world is of this kind. Thus we might occupy a random universe where the seemingly stable order can instantly disappear at any time.

Even if we assume that the orderly substructure of nature will not disappear, chance can undermine our moral judgments. This point is illustrated by the parable of

The Moral Sad Sack

This is a tale of woe. It started promisingly enough. Larom Das was born into fortunate circumstances; he had a wonderful family that had substantial wealth. As he grew up everyone recognized and freely acknowledged that he was brighter than most, and more mature. However, he had this peculiarity: his efforts at good works either misfired or were ignored. As a boy, if he did something that required intellectual or athletic prowess, it was almost always observed and rewarded with at least a good word. On the other hand, if he did something that touched on moral conduct, then his good works were not recognized. Even worse, by chance, they were often misinterpreted as misdeeds.

When he was eight, for example, he bought some candy for a neighborhood girl who was mildly ill. The girl had a strong allergic reaction to the nuts in the candy. Everyone believed he well knew she was allergic to nuts, and had intended to create the allergic reaction. It was true that the previous night the allergy was discussed at the supper table; however, he had left at a crucial time to answer a call of nature. By chance everyone forgot his absence and no one believed his account. The reason for the disbelief is that the family had long experience with Larom's "lies." Actually he told the truth to a much greater degree than the average child, but unusual things kept happening to him and evidence for these events was almost always lacking. One evening, for example, Larom witnessed a burglary. A man in a Halloween costume opened a lower window of a neighbor's house and took $189.00. The thief left and cut across the Das' property. While doing so the thief mistakenly thought he saw someone in the woods behind the house, so he temporarily hid the money in a place that just happened to be Larom's outdoor playhouse. When the police came, as the result of Larom's call, there was no evidence of a burglary except the money in Larom's playhouse and the police, as well as everyone else, believed that Larom had stolen it.

Larom was also unfortunate in his personal relations. The neighborhood butcher, for example, was normally a friendly and open man. Larom was occasionally sent to his store on errands. By chance, whenever Larom was there, the butcher was having a bad day and took it out on Larom, or he misunderstood something Larom said and got very irritated, or some other unfortunate contingency occurred. As a result Larom was one of the few people the butcher disliked.

Many times Larom tried to ensure that people would recognize his generosity or other good deeds. But things backfired. After all was said and done, the deed would be recognized but quickly forgotten, or it would be remembered not so much for itself as for the lengths Larom went to have it remembered. People would think of him as someone who toots his own horn, or a doer of good deeds solely for selfish motives. Naturally Larom complained of his ill luck. His parents sent him to psychiatrist after psychiatrist. They called him a chronic paranoid — none took the time to check his stories. Larom's suggestion that perhaps some people were *justified* paranoids was taken as further evidence of his "paranoia." The older Larom got the more he longed to be loved and appreciated. However, as all his encounters with people were, by chance, unfortunate, he become quite antisocial. He tried to avoid contacts with anyone. He became a loner.

As an adult Larom got a good job. His talents brought him much success and recognition, in spite of the fact that he was widely disliked. Larom got little pleasure from his success — what he really wanted was to be recognized as the generous and kind person that he was. He took to reading but could find little that helped him. He read Plato's story of Gyges — a man who, by a magic ring, could make himself invisible. Gyges was thereby able to kill the king, marry the queen, commit misdeeds, but nevertheless have a wide reputation for justice. Larom reflected that he was a kind of reversed Gyges. Plato was stupid, he thought, to think a just man with an unjust man's reputation was better off than an unjust man with a just man's fame. He also read Mark Twain's "Aurelia's Unfortunate Young Man." This man was so highly accident prone that he became, over a period of time, a quadruple amputee. Larom thought of himself as a morally accident-prone human who had become a moral quadriplegic. He also read Kant, whom Larom judged to be a first-class idiot, teaching as he did that the only good thing is a good will. Larom thought that if he had the power, all human life — and with it all good will — would come to an end through the exercise of his own good will. Larom thought he would rather be — and the world would be better if he were — a kind of "inverse Larom," a person whose will was uniformly bad and evil, but who was so unlucky and clumsy that his actions harmed no one, and even benefitted large numbers of people. Everyone would be grateful, he slyly thought, if he became a paradigm of immoral turpitude, a man responsible for unprecedented travesties of injustice.

Although it brought him little comfort, Larom recognized his true situation. It was this. Almost everyone has occasions where, by chance, a good deed is unrecognized or, by bad luck, the deed leads to some recognizable evil. In a world with billions of people some will have this ill luck more than others. Larom correctly thought that he was by far the world's most unlucky person in this respect. In desperation Larom decided that if he tried to do wrong things then perhaps his luck would change. To his disappointment, but not to his surprise, his bad deeds were successful and understood as the product of venomous intentions.

His end befitted his life — the sort of thing one might expect from a third-class soap opera. In an act of genuine heroism he saved the lives of some children at the cost of his own. As usual the circumstances were such that his courage was not recognized, and he was wrongly believed responsible for the danger the children were in. His death was thought to be poetic justice for that particular "misdeed." He was missed by no one, and at his funeral, the speaker said he would make an exception to the usual rule — *De mortuis nil nisi bonum* — and catalog Larom's transgressions as a warning to others.

Incongruity is part of the very fabric of living in society. But only to a degree. One of the purposes of social arrangements, like one of the purposes of science and technology, is to reduce the role of chance and the arbitrary in order to gain some control over our own destiny. But that role cannot be entirely eliminated. In the past, theories of science, as well as those of social life, have often tried to weave the theoretical net absolutely tight, so that any disorder was mere appearance — something that would be explained or controlled in due time. The results of contemporary science and logic have undermined this view. Certainly quantum mechanics gives very strong evidence that disorder cannot be eliminated. The same holds true even with regard to parts of mathematics. Through the work of Löwenheim, Skolem, Gödel, Church, Turing, Kleene, Chaitin, and others, we learn that natural numbers have a gossamer structure that is more delicate than can be discerned by either the powers of our imagination, or our argumentation (see DeLong 1971, 2004). Thus Chaitin writes: "Number theory, the queen of mathematics, is infected with uncertainty and randomness!"(1987 68); "I can show that there are theorems connected with number theory that cannot be proved because when we ask the appropriate questions, we obtain results that are equivalent to the random toss of a coin"(1990 44). Randomness might even prevent all humans from knowing some aspect of the universe that is in fact knowable, but by chance, no one ever observes it; or our observations turn out, again by chance, to be systematically misleading.

The arbitrary is likewise so entangled in our social lives that it cannot be eliminated by any set of social arrangements, it is an unalienable part of human life. Preventing a Larom Das is beyond the limits of what a social order can do for the individual. Some disorder is fundamental. Each of us may be a Larom Das with respect to some feature of our lives. Someone is the most unlucky with respect to shameful temptations (that is, there is an opportunity to act whenever a weak moment appears), another finds herself perpetually in situations of moral ambiguity, another gets colds almost continuously, and so forth to more subtle properties. Small random events can make tremendous differences to success or failure in the pursuit of happiness. In history it is virtually certain that accounts of some past events will forever be wrong because of the accidental survival (or nonsurvival) of evidence that biases our interpretation. Even time travel would not eliminate it because of the enormity of the past. In 1620, Francis Bacon claimed that the "subtlety of nature far surpasses the subtlety of sense and intellect"(2004 67; cf. 73); and in 1815 John Adams wrote: "We are but Glow Worms, vainly conjecturing the Essence of the Sun and the Theory of Light. We are Ants, reasoning on the Influence of the Dog Starr"(1954 Reel 188 20). Perhaps Bacon's dictum and Adams' reflection applies to self-knowledge as well: human nature may be more subtle, and more grand than we can sense or conceive. If we put a major effort into finding and understanding the deliberate sense of the people, we might find the effort to be intellectually challenging and politically rewarding but, like randomness in number theory or quantum mechanics, extraordinarily baffling.

Metaskepticism nevertheless suggests that knowledge is to some degree possible both in principle and in fact. Doubt, like belief, requires justification. I need a stronger argument for doubting "3 + 2 = 5" than the very, very strong argument for affirming its truth,. Further, an acceptable hypothesis for our belief must be consistent with all, or almost all, the experience we have actually had or could reasonably have. The "almost all" allows for the possibility that we may discount some experience for theoretical reasons which includes the recognition that randomness may make our observations or experiments misleading. An acceptable hypothesis must also be inconsistent with some experiences we could have. For example, we might suppose we live in a thoroughly random universe, where our experience so far has been limited to random pockets of order. This view is consistent with any future set of experiences whatsoever. We reject this supposition not because it could not be true but because, if true, it seems impossible that we would be in a position to know it; we would have, so to say, no right of assertion. A similar statement could be made about universal determinism. The game of knowledge puts limitations on what we may reasonably assert. Within these limitations our aim is to produce responsible choices among relevant claims in mathematics or physics or history or politics or anything else.

Even religious beliefs can be judged by the standard of responsible choice, a point emphasized in the opening passage of 4 *Maccabees*:

The subject I am about to discuss is most philosophical, that is, whether devout reason is sovereign over the emotions. So it is right for me to advise you to pay earnest attention to philosophy. For the subject is essential to everyone who is seeking knowledge, and in addition it includes the praise of the highest virtue — I mean, of course, rational judgment.

Not only is reason praised, but religious experiments are even conducted in the Bible. Consider the story of Elijah on Mt. Carmel, which tells the story of a large-scale experiment concerning the authority of God:

And Elijah came near to all the people, and said, 'How long will you go limping with two different opinions? If the Lord is God, follow him; but if Baal then follow him.' And the people did not answer him a word. Then Elijah said to the people, 'I, even I only, am left a prophet of the Lord; but Baal's prophets are four hundred and fifty men. Let two bulls be given to us; and let them choose one bull for themselves, and cut it in pieces and lay it on the wood, but put no fire to it; and I will prepare the other bull and lay it on the wood, and put no fire to it. And you call on the name of your god and I will call on the name of the Lord; and the God who answers by fire, he is God.'

The priests of Baal try to get an answer for a long time, but nothing happens. Then Elijah calls and "the fire of the Lord" comes down (I *Kings* 18:21, 38). This experiment assumes that certain experiences are incompatible with a belief in Baal, or in God. When Baal did not answer by fire, but the Lord did, belief in Baal was discredited. (Of course, to be convincing by our standards, the meaning of "Baal" and"God" would have to be meticulously specified, and similar experiments would have to be repeated by skeptics, since fraud or unconscious error might have been present, assuming the event occurred at all.) Again, *Deuteronomy* 18:21-2 requires that a prediction from a prophet must come true, or he is not a prophet of the Lord. Hence even in ancient Israel it was sometimes recognized that the criteria for a religious belief to be considered true included reason, experiment, and successful prediction.

So how can we know what we should aspire to in politics? In the eighteenth century a traditional answer was that we should at least strive to obey the moral law. "The moral law is nature's law, whether given by an express external authority or not, and nature's law is the law of nature's God, and its obligation is universal and perpetual"(Mellen 1765 79). Eleven years later, this familiar conception was embodied in the Declaration of Independence, because it articulates an objective standard by which individuals and societies can be judged. Yet it is often assumed today that belief in such law is misguided, a fact that has contributed to the neglect of the Ninth Amendment. One argument for this conclusion goes as follows: The laws of physics represent true laws. If someone denies a law of physics, say that of gravity, and steps out a second-story window, he will find he is incapable of violating the law. So-called moral laws (the argument runs) are quite different. These are mere generalizations that are convenient for others to have you obey. Unlike true laws they can be violated at will. Lying, stealing, and murder are common. This is proof enough there is no moral law. In nature there are no crimes against worms, or chickens, or lions. Similarly, there are no crimes against humanity. It is no more right to be magnanimous than to practice genocide. Darwinian evolution destroys ethics. Hence (the argument concludes) a moral relativism, ultimately a moral nihilism, is the only rational point of view.

Perhaps the best way to counter this argument is to make an analogy — admittedly crude — between a simple game and human life. Consider tick-tack-toe. A analysis of the game reveals that there exists a non-losing strategy, but there does not exist a winning strategy. Players that make no mistakes will never lose, but neither will they win if their opponents make no mistakes. This existence or nonexistence of strategies in tick-tack-toe is just as certain as the existence of prime numbers greater than a thousand, or the nonexistence of even primes greater than two. A young boy might claim that there is a winning strategy and that he can find it by choosing moves as he goes along. He might deny the relevance of an analysis presented to him by an adult. Indeed he might even insist that the best way to choose moves is by the immediate feeling he gets of its rightness or wrongness. The answer to the boy is to agree that he is free to choose the best moves, but that immediate feelings are bad guides for those choices. Through the use of reason one can see that the nature of the game itself implies certain things. As soon as one recognizes the existence of the grid, X's, O's, and that there are good positions to be in toward the goal of winning (say, completing a move that gives two ways to get three-in-a-row) and bad positions to be in (say, having an opponent complete such a move), then the existence and nonexistence of certain strategies follows. It does not matter if the boy or any one else discovers these facts, they would hold anyway. Tick-tack-toe was thought up by humans, and we can certainly imagine human history without it. Yet once contemplated it necessarily follows that some strategies exist and some do not. Games provide a means of moving from "is" to "ought." The fact that this *is* a game of tick-tack-toe and the fact that each player *is* trying to win, implies that each player *ought* not let the opponent get two ways to achieve three-in-a-row. Hence from a set of facts ("*is*") a set of injunctions ("*ought*") follows. Note that the rules of tick-tack-toe can be correctly stated without using "ought" or a similar word.

The tick-tack-toe analogy suggests that once humans exist with a desire for happiness, there are better and worse positions to be in, and better or worse strategies to follow. Cicero says that "Law . . . is right reason applied to command and prohibition"(1988 345), but this sentiment applies just as well to strategic laws implicit in tick-tack-toe, or in the game of life. Of course, human life is a very different kind of game than tick-tack-toe. Leibniz was perhaps the first person to recognize what kind: "Games combining chance and skill give the best representation of human life"(1710 23, translation from Morgenstern 1973 2:264). Once life is understood as a game of chance, skill, and incomplete information, in the technical sense used in game theory, "oughts" follow for manners, morality, economics, or politics. Thus, just as the game of tick-tack-toe (the pursuit of three-in-a-row) has laws of nature (a player ought not let the opponent get two ways to achieve three-in-a-row), so the game of life (the pursuit of happiness) has laws of nature (when a long train of abuses and usurpations, pursuing invariably the same object evinces a design to reduce the people under absolute despotism, they ought to throw off such government). In either case, pursuit strategies exist whether or not we know them, or even try to know them, or whether we were created by God, aliens, evolution, or some other way. Knowing the source of the game of life is irrelevant to becoming a skilled player. It was part of the great genius of the Founders, part of their metaprotestantism, to see that special religious insight was neither required or desirable to achieve good government. Thus on January 1, 1787, John Adams, when considering the founding of American governments, wrote: "It will never be pretended that any person employed in that service had interviews with the gods, or were in any degree under the inspiration of Heaven, more than those at work upon ships or houses, or laboring in merchandise or agriculture; it will forever be acknowledged that these governments were contrived merely by the use of reason and the senses . . ."(1850 4:292). Game theory confirms that the kind of participation, cooperation, and teamwork necessary for free societies is possible without any appeal to religion. The creation of American governments, like the invention of Galilean and Newtonian science, was based on observation, experiments, reasoning, and organized scientific or political societies, not special revelation. Compare, for example, Adams' statement with Galileo's from 1615: "But I do not feel obliged to believe that same God who has endowed us with senses, reason, and intellect has intended to forgo their use and by some other means to give us knowledge which we can obtain by them"(1957 183).   On June 28, 1787, at the Constitutional Convention, Franklin made an impassioned plea "that henceforth prayers imploring the assistance of Heaven, and its blessings on our deliberations, be held in this Assembly every morning before we proceed to business . . . " The result? "The Convention, except three or four persons, thought Prayers unnecessary" and there were none (Farrand 1937 1:452). Elihu, an anonymous writer, sees the lack of religious language in the Constitution as a triumph: "The most shining part, the most brilliant circumstance in honour of the framers of the Constitution is their avoiding all appearance of craft, declining to dazzle even the superstitious, by a hint about grace or ghostly knowledge. They come to us in the plain language of common sense, and propose to our understanding a system of government, as the invention of mere human wisdom, no deity comes down to dictate it, not even a God appears in a dream to propose any part of it"(1788 3). This attitude — that legal and political action need not be underwritten by theological appeal — reaches back at least to Hugo Grotius who, in his *Law of War and Peace* (1625), wrote: "What we have been saying, would have a degree of validity even if we should concede that which cannot be conceded without the utmost wickedness, that there is no God, or that the affairs of men are of no concern to Him"(1913 2:13).

Over time this budding conception was developed in other directions by some who went well beyond Grotius. Thus Jefferson states: "The legitimate powers of government extend to such acts only as are injurious to others. But it does me no injury for my neighbour to say there are twenty gods, or no god"(1972 159; cf. Leland 1791 13, Nips 1794 10). Jefferson is here adopting Locke's phraseology: "If a *Roman Catholic* believe that to be really the body of Christ, which another man calls bread, he does no injury thereby to his neighbour"(1963 79). Yet Jefferson, like the Levellers, Robert Boyle, and Pierre Bayle before him, went beyond Locke who had claimed that "those are not at all to be tolerated who *deny the being of a God*"(93; cf. Jefferson 1950 1:548). Jefferson argued that it was not only possible for the atheist to be moral, but that "Diderot, D'Alembert, D'Holbach, Condorcet, are known to have been among the most virtuous of men"(1903 14:140). One did not need to be wicked to believe that God was unconcerned with men, or that he was a mere fiction. Hence it is wrong to claim that if there were no God, then morality would be abolished. One might as well argue that if God exists, some strategies are better than others in tick-tack-toe but, if he does not exist, then any strategy is as good as any other. Reason and experience tell us that whether one plays tick-tack-toe or pursues earthly happiness, some strategies are better than others, whether or not God exists.

The existence of strategies in the human game of living does not mean that everything that is not required is prohibited. For example, if we discover universal winning strategies in achieving excellence in the art of living there may be innumerable ways of fulfilling those strategies. The game of morality presents us with both required obligations and free choice. Of course, it may be that under some circumstances no strategies exist. For example, it can be shown that in certain games there are times when the best strategy is to have no strategy. (See Von Neuman, John 1959 26, and von Neuman and Morgenstern 1967 146.) Metareason, so to say, tells us not to use our reason, but to act randomly. The art of living well may, under certain circumstances, likewise require that we make random choices, that we act on whim. Yet this can hardly be general advice for all situations.

We can thus see that if one denies the existence of God, or the concept of a natural law as fixed by in human existence, the spirit of 1776 allows a game-theoretical approach, which requires no such entities. Imagine playing Tag. Here one person is "it" and must chase others; if he or she can tag one of the others, the tagged person becomes "it." Now "itness" is not a natural property of humans, it exists only in the context of a game, like "trump" in bridge, or "quarterback" in football. So skeptics may say with Hume: "Life is like a game: One may choose the game"(1985 178). However, the ethos of the American revolution does not allow any possible choice; rather, it requires that we choose moral and political games that presuppose the dignity of each human being. Each person is a bearer of rights, which we must respect, that is, nobody is a nobody. That respect does not imply esteem. Wicked people are human. But just as the game of Tag requires that we respond to a person who is "it" by running away, so the game of American politics requires that we respond to persons by respecting their dignity, and the rights and duties that follow from that dignity. In this game-theoretic approach, the property of having "dignity" requires no more reality than the property of being "it." According to animal psychologists, individual animals — such as dogs, lions, otters, or chimpanzees — require certain kinds of play in order to become and continue as excellent examples of their species. Experiments have shown that certain games especially contribute to their development, and that if these animals are deprived of these games, they become stunted in their psychic growth. Humans, likewise, are similarly affected if as children for example, they are deprived of their language games, or are taught they are by nature morally inferior. America is an experiment which seeks to demonstrate that human beings prosper best when they are part of a political community which has the "dignity" game as its basis: "The new [federal] Constitution is happily calculated not only to restore us to animation and vigour, but to diffuse a *national Spirit*, and inspire every man with sentiments of dignity, when he reflects that he is not merely the individual of a State, but a CITIZEN of AMERICA"(MFC 1787 30). Again, a John Adams tells us that a proper constitution, "introduces knowledge among the People, and inspires them with a conscious dignity; becoming Freemen. A general emulation takes place, which causes good humour, sociability, good manners, and good morals to be general"(1977 4:92). "Dignity" experiments require no more faith than animal psychologists have who investigate what kinds of games are optimal for chimpanzees or bonobos. Hence a person can think of dignity as merely a game-theoretic property invented by humans and still be an excellent economist, political scientist, politician, or patriot.

The question whether dignity or moral laws have more than a game-theoretic reality has a counterpart in the philosophy of mathematics. Some mathematicians believe numbers are mere artifacts of a symbol game. Others, probably most, believe numbers exist as abstract objects independent of human game playing, and properties of natural numbers, such as being prime, are real. The number theorist G. H. Hardy writes: "317 is a prime, not because we think so, or because our minds are shaped in one way rather than another, but *because it is so*, because mathematical reality is built that way"(1969 130). Again, Stephen Kleene, one of the giants of mathematical logic, writes: ". . . if we are not to adopt a mathematical nihilism, formally axiomatized mathematics [a mere symbol game] must not be the whole of mathematics. At some place there must be meaning, truth and falsity"(1967 193). The discipline of mathematics has prospered, and can continue to prosper, even though the fundamental nature of mathematical entities is contentious. American politics is similar where for some, dignity has only a game-theoretic reality. But for others it has an independent, real existence created by nature or God. The Founders thought of moral properties that way, they were, so to say, the political equivalents of Hardy and Kleene.

Locke, it should be noted, denied both that moral laws are innate and that they are all man-made. Speaking of them he says:

> I would not be here mistaken, as if, because I deny an innate Law, I thought there were none but positive Laws. There is a great deal of difference between an innate Law, and a Law of Nature; between something imprinted on our Minds in their very original, and something that we being ignorant of may attain to the knowledge of, by the use and due application of our natural Faculties. And I think they equally forsake the Truth, who running into the contrary extreams, either affirm an innate Law, or deny that there is a Law, knowable by the light of Nature, *i.e.*, without the help of positive Revelation." (1975 75; cf. Aristotle 1984 2187)

The games of tick-tack-toe or chess are not innate in us but are nevertheless games whose strategies for playing we "may attain to the knowledge of, by the use and due application of our natural Faculties." The "game" of life we are born into — we do not initially choose to play it. Furthermore, our choices are limited, for who being discontented with his or her lot in life, can choose to be a Shakespeare, or a lion, or a devil, or God? Both our powers and the limits of our powers must be discovered by reasoned inquiries, such as the natural and social sciences. The winning activity ("pursuing happiness felicitously") is not clearly defined, but must itself be investigated by independent inquiries (for example, neurology, psychology, history, and philosophy). Even so, there are better and worse ways of living that are, through the use of intelligence, open to discovery. The existence of ethical and political rules are either virtually or really imbedded in our humanity, whether or not we are products of a mindless evolution or a mindful design. An important part of ethics is the search for the best strategies to pursue happiness for the individual, just as an important part of politics is the search for the best strategies to pursue happiness for the public. "The city," Aristotle says, "is best governed which has the greatest opportunity of obtaining happiness . . . "(1984 2:2113). The goal of the American revolution is to create that "greatest opportunity," or, rather, to create in the public a perpetual and strong desire to transcend any achieved level of opportunity.

"This World," John Adams once declared, "is a Riddle and an Enigma"(Cappon 1959 2:376) and it still is. An ant hill or bee hive has an overall function that we assume the individual ants or bees do not appreciate. Humans are not ants or bees, but we are part of an earth and a universe that we do not fully understand. But let us suppose it is possible to discover answers, and an institute is created whose purpose is to investigate human nature and the universe, to understand human happiness and the best ways for humans to live, and to develop means to actualize those ways. Given the enormous complexity and difficulty of the assignment, we could immediately see that it might take decades or centuries to complete. Thus we would want a stable political system that could last indefinitely. It should emphasize education to provide the great variety of talents necessary for the project. We should also require an extremely efficient and productive economy to finance the expensive research. Furthermore, we would need a internal and external defense system to protect the entire operation. In short, it is not hard to see we would need something like the United States.

America is an Enlightenment idea. It is a kind of research program to experimentally test the proposition that the vocation of humankind is to recognize that we are jointly playing a game by living, a game whose point is to so organize ourselves that we may use reason to discover the laws of nature, the ideals of an excellent life, and the habits necessary or desirable to achieve that life. As Madison said in 1822:

> The American people owe it to themselves, and to the cause of free Government, to prove by their establishments for the advancement and diffusion of Knowledge, that their political Institutions, which are attracting observation from every quarter, and are respected as Models, by the new-born States in our own Hemisphere, are as favorable to the intellectual and moral improvement of Man as they are conformable to his individual & social Rights. What spectacle can be more edifying or more seasonable, than that of Liberty and Learning, each leaning on the other for their mutual & surest support? (1900 9:107-8; Payson 1778 12 and Howard 1780 43).

The aspiration for the "intellectual and moral improvement of Man" now requires an America in a more revolutionized form. This form would be created by American perfectionist democracy whose third dimension is the development of a philosophy of aspiration and its embodiment into the fabric of American society. With the institution of American perfectionist democracy the conditions would exist for the ultimate fulfillment of the original Enlightenment idea. It is commonplace to assume that the idea of America presupposes the use of reason to better the lot of the people. But to better the lot of the people presupposes that we know the meaning of "better." In a game with a well-defined goal, such as chess, it may be easy, at some point during a game, to determine which person has the best chance of winning. For other positions it might take enormous amounts of work and even that work might not yield an answer. When the goal itself is not fully determined — what exactly is human happiness? — the difficulties are multiplied. How then should we choose among the goals toward which we should aspire?

12

The Ethics of Aspiration

Let us imagine that it was our job to decide what objectives to set for a new unmanned satellite probe of Saturn's moon Titan. Since weight severely limits the number of things that can be investigated, the problem is to choose those objectives among the many available that will be the most scientifically fruitful. Our question is: What ought we to know in order to make a responsible decision? The answer is straightforward: we should have a very good grounding in mathematics, physics, biology, and astronomy, as well as the technology of rockets, satellites, radio telemetry, and so forth. In addition, we ought to have a thorough knowledge of past space exploration. To choose in ignorance of these subjects would be irresponsible; one must create an environment in which the pros and cons of each alternative are carefully weighed against what is known. A choice made in such an environment may be wrong, but it represents the most responsible decision possible. If we proceed in this way and come to believe that such-and-such a configuration of objectives is the best for the Titan probe, we have exhibited the epistemological virtues required by an ethics of belief based on reason.

Now suppose we want to exhibit these same virtues in choosing a configuration of goals for America. Since it is the people's job to do this, we can ask: what should they be trained in so they can choose their own goals responsibly? The answer is: the liberal arts. America is a be-all-you-can-be civilization, but it is through the liberal arts that one can learn what we can be, what human excellence is, and how we can transcend the past in our pursuit of private and public happiness. Thus, just as we need a professional community trained in science to judge whether something is a genetic disease, or a dinosaur bone, or a supernova, so we need a political community trained in the liberal arts to judge whether we have justice, or equality, or liberty. Today there is much uncertainty about the content of a liberal arts education as well as endless arguments about canons and curricula. Yet evidence is not collected. Courts of common reason give us this opportunity. After advisory juries have taken up some of the great political issues of our time, the participants could discuss the skills and knowledge they needed for that deliberation. An analysis of those discussions could determine the core of the curriculum in public schools. "The form of government we have assumed," Benjamin Rush tell us, "has created a new class of duties to every American. It becomes us, therefore, . . . to adapt our modes of teaching to the peculiar form of our government"(1786a 13). The "new class of duties" in the twentieth-first century ought to include participation in courts of common reason, so that we can perfect the pursuit of public happiness.

A politics of self-knowledge based on such courts thus requires a liberally-educated citizenry. That education has three goals: First, it should enable a person to appropriate the vast resources of human knowledge to the present moment. Let us listen to John Stuart Mill: "To have a general knowledge of a subject is to know only its leading truths, but to know these not superficially but thoroughly, so as to have a true conception of the subject in its great features; leaving the minor details to those who require them for the purposes of their special pursuit. There is no incompatibility between knowing a wide range of subjects up to this point, and some one subject with the completeness required by those who make it their principal occupation. It is this combination which gives an enlightened public: a body of cultivated intellects, each taught by its attainments in its own province what real knowledge is, and knowing enough of other subjects to be able to discern who are those that know them better"(1965 362). The trouble with learning from just one's own experience, and that of those we happen to meet, is that such experience is much too limited. We need to learn from the experiences of the most talented, honest, adventurous, creative, intelligent, sensitive, passionate and extraordinary individuals of all time. Then we will learn about human greatness, about outstanding integrity, about moral courage, about all the virtues that will increase our capacity and relish for excellence in the art of living.

Second, a liberal arts education should aim at identifying the philosophical basis of the intellectual and moral habits that anyone acquires by being born at a special time and place. It should foster an investigative spirit that results in a continuing and rigorous examination of that basis for our society, so as to be sure it is worthy of belief and commitment. Indoctrination has no place here, one needs to acquire the epistemological virtues of a demanding, but practical, ethics of belief *and* an ethics of unbelief. Consciousness must be both critical *and* self-critical. Hence honesty, integrity, observation, experiment, and the habit of making careful judgments should be instilled by education, along with the moral courage, if needed, to become subversive to the prejudices and superstitions that might exist at any particular time and place (cf. Locke 1975 82-3). We need to foster individual and social empathy, so as to understand those who are different from ourselves, whether within our own country, or in other cultures and civilizations. All these efforts will prepare the people, individually or collectively, for the soul-searching job of determining what kind of person, or what kind of civilization, is worthy of their aspirations.

Third, a liberal arts education should promote an unquenchable curiosity, wonder, and love of learning, so that self-education becomes a life-long habit. It should prepare us to become autodidacts in any new subject we might choose, and help us decide what it would be most fruitful to choose. The aim is to make us truly free persons. In the words of Locke: "The business of education . . . is not, as I think, to make [the young] perfect in any one of the sciences, but so to open and dispose their minds, as may best make them capable of any, when they shall apply themselves to it. If men are, for a long time, accustomed only to one sort or method of thoughts, their minds grow stiff in it, and do not readily turn to another. It is, therefore, to give them this freedom, that I think they should be made to look into all sorts of knowledge, and exercise their understandings in so wide a variety and stock of knowledge. But I do not propose it as a variety and stock of knowledge, but a variety and freedom of thinking; as an increase of the powers and activity of the mind, not as an enlargement of its possessions"(1824 2:356; cf. 1989 156, 249). To attain this variety, this freedom of thinking and learning, a liberal arts education must impart an internal system of checks and balances among the passions that is necessary for the most flourishing lives. By nature, we are born with great capacities but are dependent, ignorant, and generally talentless; through a liberal arts education inculcated to become second nature, we can exploit those capacities until we are reborn with the autonomy, knowledge, and aptitude to master the art of living well.

The achievement of the above three aims requires some training in ten areas of knowledge:

1. Abstract disciplines (logic, mathematics, computer science, game theory, . . .)
2. Natural sciences (physics, chemistry, biology, geology, . . .)
3. Social sciences (anthropology, geography, economics, sociology, psychology, linguistics, . . .)
4. Humanities (philosophy, literature, religion, history (including the history of art, mathematics, and science), . . .)
5. Language (reading, writing, rhetoric, foreign languages, . . .)

6. Arts (singing, dancing, acting, drawing, . . .)
7. Physical education (wellness, fitness, physiology, sports, . . .)
8. Professions (medicine, law, business, engineering, accounting, architecture, . . .)
9. Practical skills (civics, public speaking, household finance,. . .)
10. Practical wisdom (good judgment, self-knowledge, morality, manners, . . .)

The purpose of the last category is to learn how to make splendid use of one's own abilities and opportunities in the process of seeking an excellent life. Noah Webster, one of the founders of Amherst Academy (now Amherst College), said the Academy's duty to its students was "to enlighten their minds; to exalt their character; and to teach them the way to happiness and glory"(1820 8). "The first elements of morality," Jefferson said, must be to teach young people "how to work out their own greatest happiness"(1972 147; cf. Hobson 1799 11, Aristotle 1984 2:1800). The goal in studying the liberal arts is not to create dilettantes, but to instill that practical wisdom which will promote the continuing development of those good judgments and good manners essential for successful pursuits of happiness. In Locke's words: "The great Work of a *Governour* [of children] is to fashion the Carriage, and form the Mind; to settle in his Pupil good Habits, and the Principles of Vertue and Wisdom; to give him by little and little a view of Mankind; and work him into a love and imitation of what is Excellent and Praise-worthy; and in the Prosecution of it to give him Vigour, Activity, and Industry"(1989 156). A liberal arts education prepares the individual for independence, and the people for self-rule, it should implant whatever knowledge, habits, and passions are needed or desirable for a free person in a free society.

To be such a person requires excellent character. "For no one," Aristotle pointed out, "would maintain that he is happy who has not in him a particle of courage or temperance or justice or practical wisdom, who is afraid of every insect which flutters past him, and will commit any crime, however great, in order to gratify his lust for meat or drink, who will sacrifice his dearest friend for the sake of half a farthing, and is as feeble and false in mind as a child or a madman"(1984 2:2100; see Peterson and Seligman 2004 for a contemporary analysis of good character). Jefferson maintained that "some knowledge" of the sciences, which might seem remote from our everyday lives, is "necessary for our character as well as comfort"(1950 31:127). Yet the virtues needed for good character need qualifications, for a person can be brave in an evil cause, or truthful when it is pointlessly cruel, or rigorously just when mercy is called for. A liberal arts education should articulate those qualifications, acquaint us with the great variety of human flourishing, teach us the habits of self-knowledge needed to choose wisely among that variety, and arouse in us the passions to live by those choices.

Citizens so educated would be prepared for a politics of self-knowledge and an economics of honesty; they would be capable of achieving the highest excellence in self-government that is possible at a given time and place. Consider some examples of the worst political condition a people can be in: the Soviet Union under Stalin, Germany under Hitler, China under Mao, Cambodia under Pol Pot, Iran under Khomeini, Afghanistan under the Taliban, or North Korea under Kim Jong Il. To achieve their despotisms each government had to lie about history: persons became unpersons, events became nonevents, and known fictions were constantly reported as truths. The many local and national historical associations in America are important for they help ensure that no person or event becomes an unperson or nonevent in the Stalinist sense. Wise public policy must be based on knowledge of the historical truth — including those truths that are ugly, embarrassing, or inconvenient. "History," Locke points out, "is the great Mistress of Prudence and Civil Knowledge"(1989 237; cf. Adams 1850 6:118 and Franklin 1959 3:412). A knowledge of history is one of the conditions of excellence in self-government; it is a prerequisite for wise political decisions. In Jefferson's words: "History, by apprising [the people] of the past, will enable them to judge the future; it will avail them of the experience of other times and other nations; it will qualify them as judges of the actions and designs of men; it will enable them to know ambition under every disguise it may assume; and knowing it, to defeat its views"(1892 3:254; cf. Polybius 1922 1:3, 4:371). For example, if an advisory jury were going to give advice about public policy toward the American Indians, then the jury would need to know their history. As in a trial in which the jury hears eyewitness reports of the recent past so, in the Court of Common Reason, the jury would hear, among other testimony, the views of historians. Again, if the issue were abortion the jury would likewise hear historians, in addition to such experts as biologists, doctors, and ethicists. Naturally historians or experts might not agree among themselves but, as in a trial, it would be up to the jury to judge which expert views to accept; and it is a liberal arts education that should prepare the jurors to wisely make these kinds of judgments.

Literature and art, music and drama, should also have an essential part in a politics of self-knowledge. As far back as we know, humans have been dancers, singers, artists, and story tellers. These activities promoted both the enjoyment and understanding of life. It may be that there are some important, even defining, properties of ourselves and our world that only a few could understand in the form of science, but that almost any human can understand in artistic form. For example, suppose we had before us in linear sequence all the zeros and ones sent back from some space probe. The sequence would be meaningless, but when the same information was conveyed in the form of a photograph it would become understandable. Similarly, the arts might make something humanly meaningful where other ways fail.

Jefferson argued that an art form — fiction — is superior even to history and philosophy in moral education:

> A little attention however to the nature of the human mind evinces that the entertainments of fiction are useful as well as pleasant. That they are pleasant when well written, every person feels who reads. But wherein is its utility, asks the reverend sage, big with the notion that nothing can be useful but the learned lumber of Greek and Roman reading with which his head is stored? I answer, every thing is useful which contributes to fix us in the principles and practice of virtue. When any single act of charity or of gratitude, for instance, is presented either to our sight or imagination, we are deeply impressed with its beauty and feel a strong desire in ourselves of doing charitable and grateful acts also. On the contrary when we see or read of any atrocious deed, we are disgusted with it's deformity and conceive an abhorrence of vice. Now every emotion of this kind is an exercise of our virtuous dispositions; and dispositions of the mind, like limbs of the body, acquire strength by exercise. But exercise produces habit; and in the instance of which we speak, the exercise being of the moral feelings, produces a habit of thinking and acting virtuously. . . . a lively and lasting sense of filial duty is more effectually impressed on the mind of a son or daughter by reading King Lear, than by all the dry volumes of ethics and divinity that ever were written. (1950 1:76-7; cf. 31:308)

Jefferson's point is one that can be found among the poets themselves. Thus, in 1821, Percy Bysshe Shelley wrote:

> A man, to be greatly good, must put himself in the place of another and of many others; the pains and pleasures of his species must become his own. The great instrument of moral good is the imagination: and poetry administers to the effect by acting upon the cause. . . . Poetry strengthens the faculty which is the organ of the moral nature of man, in the same manner as exercise strengthens a limb. (1891 14)

Even music may be more than just pleasure. Marvin Minsky, one of the founders of artificial intelligence (AI), speculates that "maybe someday it will turn out that at least for some AI programs that the way for them to get better is to sort of play scenarios to them of problems that are not actually meaningful at all but force them to pay attention to certain kinds of control structures." He suggests that this sort of thing "is not so different from music"(1980 39). Thus it may be that certain kinds of music, in the right context, can not only be pleasant but also useful.   At least it seems possible that the great genius of Pythagoras, Galileo, Kepler, Jefferson, and Einstein was facilitated by their practicing music. Would the collective intelligence of jury members increase — say, in the wisdom they employ in making choices about aspirations — if music were in some way integrated into the practice of courts of common reason?   That music has important social functions is a frequent theme of musicians themselves.   For example, Dmitri Shostakovich states: "Music illuminates a person through and through, and it is also his last hope and final refuge. And even the half mad Stalin, a beast and a butcher, instinctively sensed that about music. That is why he feared and hated it"(1979 232). Other totalitarians, such as Hitler or the Taliban, have also restricted musical expression. So have authoritarians such as Plato, who says that "any musical innovation is full of danger to the whole State, and ought to be prohibited"(1937 1:687). In contrast, America has become — as it should forever be — a land of musical freedom.

The whole artistic realm must be an essential feature of our experience if we are to best achieve the virtues productive of a flourishing life. To fulfill the dictate "America, know thyself," to teach every American the skills of freedom, to ensure that we have a government that will protect our rights and respect our dignity, to do all these things American perfectionist democracy must rely not only on mathematicians, scientists, social scientists, historians, and philosophers, it must also rely on artists. In the words of the art critic Bernard Berenson: "All of the arts, poetry, music, ritual, the visual arts, the theatre, must singly and together create the most comprehensive art of all, a humanized society, and its masterpiece, the free man; free within and free without . . ."(1948 244). Since the American perfectionist ethos aims to make every citizen a "masterpiece," the arts must become an intrinsic part of our political experience. Their potentially great humane effect should not be left to chance.

This is especially true of leaders. In Jefferson's words, "those persons, whom nature hath endowed with genius and virtue, should be rendered by liberal education worthy to receive, and able to guard the sacred deposit of the rights and liberties of their fellow citizens, and that they should be called to that charge without regard to wealth, birth or other accidental condition or circumstance . . . "(1950 2:527). Yet care must be taken. Jefferson's and Madison's liberal education and their transcendent genius were together insufficient to prevent them from treachery to blacks, and a gross betrayal of the American revolution. Nor did the liberal education of so many of the British and American officials — who oversaw Soviet refugees after World War II — prevent them from participating in crimes against humanity. These great catastrophic failures by our leaders were fostered by an schooling that did not instill the virtues of intellectual integrity, moral courage, and social empathy. Hence it was not fully liberal. As self-deceivers, their own reason was compromised by their cowardice, they were not free within. Moral courage should thus be as strongly instilled in the education of citizens, as physical courage is in the training of Marines. We cannot be *the land of the free because we are the home of the brave* unless that bravery be both physical and moral. The eighteenth-century and the 1940s lacked the kind of poetry, fiction, and drama that would expose and counteract the corruption of the moral imagination. Perhaps it is not too much to say that had America in these periods been blessed with a Stowe or a Solzhenitsyn the calamities would have been greatly mitigated. If, with Jefferson, we genuinely swear "eternal hostility against every form of tyranny over the mind of man"(above, page 94), then we must cultivate ways to undermine internal tyrannies. The moral imagination of political leaders, as well as the people at large, must be continually stimulated, so that self-deceivers come to see what they do not want to see (say, the contradiction between their practice and their principles), come to feel what they have not felt (say, sympathy for the plight of the slave or the refugee), and come to act where they have never acted (say, publicly denouncing slavery or forced repatriation in order to stop it). Character counts in perfecting the pursuit of happiness.

In the contemporary world we can enlarge the meaning of "poetry, literature, and art" to include not only traditional compositions, but compositions in virtual reality and simulation games. Imagine the potential impact, for example, of a truly excellent simulation experience called *A Day in the Life of a Black in a Racist Society*. But, whether traditional or contemporary, such experiences can arouse feelings to counteract the passions that cloud the mind. In Locke's words, "When the fancy is bound by passion, I know of no way to set the mind free and at liberty, to prosecute what thoughts the man would make choice of, but to allay the present passion, or counterbalance it with another; which is an art to got by study, and acquaintance with the passions"(1824 2:400). John Adams likewise emphasizes opposing passions: "Men should endeavor at a *balance* of affections and appetites, under the monarchy of reason and conscience, within, as well as at a balance of power without"(above, page 40). A republican government should endeavor to supply the education and environment that encourages "acquaintance with the passions" along with "a *balance* of affections and appetites." In the eighteenth century the desirability of having theaters was controversial, but an argument for them was their power to invigorate republican sentiments: "A virtuous Theatre, combining every energy that can awake and excite [man's] ambition, will enlarge his views, correct his manners, and exalt his aims, to every great and noble pursuit, within the compass of human excellence!"(Bostonian 1792 32). We have systematic ways of insuring that the latest results of science and technology are incorporated into the production of goods and services of corporations, or into the requirements of the military — in fact these companies and the military often create the latest results. But we have no systematic ways of insuring that public policy is informed by that humane art which is productive of "a just equilibrium of all the passions," much less is there so strong a demand for that equilibrium as to create new artistic endeavors (the phrase is Jefferson's (Cappon 1959 2:467)). Isn't it strange and unreasonable that we lack a political institution to regularly incite such republican passions as intellectual integrity, moral courage, and social empathy, even though our history demonstrates that their lack was the cause of numerous social and political catastrophes?

Let there then be created, as part of American perfectionist democracy, a yearly Festival America — say, five days long — in which American values and culture are celebrated in music, in dance, in art, and in drama. The Festival, we may suppose, will be the finals in a nationwide competition for the best artistic productions. Its organization will be such as to emphasize the great diversity of American talent and sensibility. It could include comedies in which we laugh at our pretensions and self-deceptions, as well as dramas that explore the tragic faults of our national character. The Court of Common Reason would have an essential part in deciding which productions should be part of the Festival. It might be objected that such a procedure is inconsistent with the demand for excellence. But this is not so. We know that Athenian democracy and Athenian theater were born together and were thoroughly integrated, an integration that produced one of the greatest sequences of dramatic productions the world has ever known. We know this sequence was the result of a competition in a yearly festival, in which decisions about the plays were made by ordinary citizens who held one-year political terms. Aristotle, who could hardly be accused of ignoring or belittling excellence, declared that "the many are . . . better judges than a single man of music and poetry; for some understand one part, and some another, and among them they understand the whole"(1984 2:2033-34). If we want to strive toward excellence in American democracy we need to achieve a similar integration with American theater. We have copied the ancient Greeks by reintroducing the Olympics — an introduction that has regularly produced astounding athletic excellence. It is surely not beyond the ingenuity of Americans to copy, adapt, and improve upon the Athenian festival to regularly produce artistic works in the cause of public happiness.

Festival America could end on July 4th. The advisory jury could determine the prizes to be awarded to the artists on that day. Some of this civic art could become part of school curricula, perhaps some works would become American classics. Human beings apparently present us with a reality such that literal speech about them misses something essential; they seem to possess both "real" and "imaginary" components. It is one of the functions of a parent or teacher or friend or minister or psychologist to help us find the right metaphors for a good life. Festival America could generate the right metaphors for a free society; for the first time in its history, America's shattered soul could be made whole. If we want to form a "more perfect Union" as our Constitution declares, the nation needs a way to rebuild the infrastructure of its spiritual being, and give integrity to its political aspirations. To be civilized requires the arousal and exercise of refined emotions, including the moral (such as passions of love and empathy), the political (such as passions for liberty and justice), and the epistemological (such as passions for truth and reason). The arts are indispensable elements in refining that arousal and exercise. Of course, not all art produced in America should be directed toward Festival America, any more than all technology should be directed toward medicine. But just as our bodily life is more apt to be unhealthy if we do not fully integrate science into medicine, so our civic life is more apt to be unhappy if we do not fully integrate the humanities and the arts into our political dreams. Among those dreams none seems more important than uniting goodness with power, a goal no country has yet fully achieved. In his review of *Bury My Heart At Wounded Knee*, Geoffrey Wolff lamented:

> It falls to a journalist reviewing the books of our days to treat the dreadful almost as though it were commonplace. The books I review, week upon week, report the destruction of the land or the air; they detail the perversion of justice; they reveal national stupidities. None of them — not one — has saddened me and shamed me as this book has. Because the experience of reading it has made me realize for once and all that we really don't know who we are, or where we came from, or what we have done, or why. (1971 69)

If we want to stop the great litany of evils that our free press rightly and regularly exposes, if we want to "know who we are, or where we came from, or what we have done, or why," then we need to make the humanities and arts part of our personal ethics and public politics.

Let us thus suppose that after an advisory jury picked the winning art in Festival America, future advisory juries, as part of their preparation to make political decisions, spends, say, one-fourth of their working time experiencing that art. Participants in the Court of Common Reason would thus be in a better position to make their decisions wisely since their imagination — "the great instrument of moral good" — would be strengthened. For example, suppose in a given year one category in Festival America consisted of plays dealing with racism in America. Now during the course of the following year, when any jury considers problems relevant to racism, they do not deliberate and vote without seeing and discussing the winning plays. In this way the Court of Common Reason would exploit the great power of art toward the goal of increasing the likelihood that the members of the jury will make informed and humane judgments. Since problems concerning race can nowhere be solved but in the hearts and minds of the people, would it not be reasonable to construct an institution in which art, chosen by the people themselves, informs their deliberations, and perhaps transforms their hearts and minds? Here we have the opportunity to create a new class of systemic solutions to social problems, true moral and political antibiotics, not the mere antiseptics that have so far been used. In the kind of art they choose, in the way they conduct their deliberations, the people could use their common reason to overcome any base emotions they happen to have. Unfortunately, it is often assumed that they are incapable of such self-control, and devoid of the aspiration to achieve it.

Philosophers such as Plato (1937 2:217) and Locke (1975 659-61) have plausibly argued that soul-searching dialogue benefits the character. Courts of Common Reason should be designed so that, as much as possible, soul-searching for the sake of the public good will be experienced as a personal good by the individual juror. If the art and music entertains, as it educates and refines their emotions, jurors could become engrossed, and thus be better prepared to decide wisely among opposing political arguments. But preparation is not enough. The desire to serve must be strong. In the words of John Adams: "Public Virtue cannot exist in a Nation without private, and public Virtue is the only Foundation of Republics. There must be a possitive Passion for the public good, the public Interest, Honour, Power, and Glory, established in the Minds of the People, or there can be no Republican Government, nor any real Liberty"(1977 4:124). I believe Adams wanted the people to feel what he felt in May of 1776: "When I consider the great Events which are passed, and those greater which are rapidly advancing, and that I may have been instrumental of touching some Springs, and turning small Wheels, which have had and will have such Effects, I feel an Awe upon my Mind, which is not easily described"(Butterfield, Lyman 1963 410). Using advisory juries to decide great public questions should help instill that awe in the people at large, for Courts of Common Reason would be designed to have frequent close votes (above, page 204). Festival America should celebrate American ideals to intensify that awe, to intensify the "possitive Passion for the public good, the public Interest, Honour, Power, and Glory" to such an extent, that jurors would be willing, many even eager, to participate in advisory juries, despite the strenuous and at times upsetting character of that participation. In John Flavell's phrase (from 1669), they would be in "the pursuit of happiness, striving even to an Agony"(above, page 24).

As jurors struggle to make the best decisions in Festival America, as they directly understand and feel the influence of the arts in their deliberations, the importance of education in the arts would be more widely seen. We can even imagine that students could submit short stories, plays, songs, even games to the Festival, and the winners in student categories could be considered by local or state Courts of Common Reason for inclusion in textbooks or curricula. It might even be true that a large advisory jury of, say, eight-graders, could pick a superb collection of short stories (whether written by young people or adults), which would better instill a love of reading and learning in themselves than adults ever could. Might not the job, say, of picking the best short stories or plays about racism, also help eradicate it in their minds and hearts? In this context it is easy to think of other problems such as drugs, sexism, bullying, violence, alienation, where knowing the considered judgment of students might be necessary to solve social problems. If we really love our children, if we want them to flourish both as children and as later adults in a free society, they must become responsible for their own education, and thus we must, as early and as often as is reasonable, educated them to educate themselves. Why not regularly give them some power, such as choosing, for inclusion in future textbooks for younger students, the fifty works of art from five hundred that historians of art might deem appropriate, or the two or three proofs of the Pythagorean theorem that they judge most perspicacious from the many scores that have been devised? The great goal is to instill in students the practical wisdom to felicitously conduct their own lives, and by striving to answer questions about the education of the next generation of students, they will learn something about how to conduct their own education — what books to read, what videos to see, what proverbs to follow, what computer games to play, what life experiences to seek out. If we made maximum use of the ability of students to teach other students, we might be able to greatly increase the efficiency and quality of their education. Although students today are often subjected to manipulation using schemes distinguished by their stupidity and dishonesty (see Feynman 1997 288-302, Loewen 1996, Ravitch 2003), much remains uncertain about what genuinely are the best schemes. Here, as elsewhere, the proper procedure is to experiment, experiment, experiment.

Festival America also provides other opportunities, such as the chance to improve our language. In 1780 John Adams argued that language "influences not only the form of government, but the temper, the sentiments, and manners of the people"(1850 7:249). He thought we should develop institutions to improve English. Festival America could be one of those institutions. For example, in Middle English *Thou* was frequently a mark of inferiority, whereas *you* was often a mark of esteem (OED 1989). The linguist Otto Jespersen points out that because English has virtually eliminated this dualistic form in favor of *you*, it "has thus attained the only manner of address worthy of a nation that respects the elementary rights of each individual"(1968 223-24). By 2003, American speech was apparently even a factor causing a change in Japan, where "equality-minded parents no longer emphasize honorific language to their children, and most schools no longer expect children to use honorific language to their teachers. As a result, young Japanese . . . do not feel compelled to use it"(Onishi 3003 A1). Festival America could help make English — or whatever languages Americans choose to speak — even more suitable for a free people, not merely in matters of address, but in all respects. Consider linguistic sexism. If person says: "Suppose a lawyer is sued and he . . ." Where the context allows either male or female lawyers, the speaker is perhaps implicitly thinking, and getting the audience to think, in purely masculine terms. The Court of Common Reason could judge all the ways in which English is inappropriate to the character of a free people. It could call on the poets, dramatists and others to invent new ways of speaking, ways so attractive that productions written in those ways would become winners in Festival America, and so attractive that the American people would, over time, *freely* change their manner of speaking. If Americans say such things as: "in this pickle" or "neither here nor there" or "too much of a good thing" due to the influence of Shakespeare, why cannot they be likewise influenced by American poets to speak in a nonsexist way? Some of these "poets" might be otherwise ordinary people who enter the democratic evolutionary contest to find better ways of speaking for a free people. If sexism is really a structural issue, then it might not be solvable, or solvable quickly enough, by merely using traditional techniques, such as revising grammar books or school texts. Thus, just as it takes sophisticated techniques to remove lead from the body, so it may take sophisticated techniques, such as the creation of hybrid juries and Festival America, to remove sexism from the body politic. As the long-term solution for lead is to create an environment that makes it unlikely for lead to enter the body in the first place, so Festival America could help create an environment so that linguistic sexism is not a problem for the next generation. "Linguistic sexism" here refers to grammatical structures, idioms, and ambiguous terms (think of "men" meaning human), which encourage, according to the Court of Common Reason, invidious distinctions between the sexes. Of course, the Court might not find any objectionable language, or if it does, it might decide that it is inappropriate to take political or educational action. In order to make their judgments, however, advisory juries should learn something about the history of languages (including how various languages treat sexual distinctions) and achieve a certain level of group linguistic competence (where answers are well-defined) in preparation for their political deliberations.

Perceptions of one's own country can also be transformed through the study of the liberal arts. Consider Mexico. Mexico has large assets of oil and natural gas. But these "natural assets" are not quite natural: They were created by the science and technology developed in Europe and the United States. Without this scientific knowledge they would be worthless; there would be no demand for them and their existence would likely be unknown. This kind of argument is appreciated, but less often noticed is how the great cultural assets of the Mexican pyramids and ancient artifacts came to be seen as valuable. Cortez wished only to destroy the culture he found, and for centuries following him few valued the pyramids or other ancient art. It was through scholarship in the humanities and the arts that these objects came to be seen as valuable and, as the automobile made Mexican oil economically valuable, so tourism did for the Mexican pyramids. But the study of the humanities and arts brought about more than an economic asset: It created a new identity for the people of Mexico — the Olmec, Mayan, Teotihuacan, Astec, Toltec artifacts are not mere commodities, like oil, to be sold to the highest bidder. They are no longer the kinds of things Mexicans want to sell at all. The study of the humanities and the arts made these objects transcend the economic realm, it gave Mexicans a new pride, it made them more valuable to themselves. Turning to the United States, Festival America is meant to make the American people more valuable to themselves. In both ancient Athens and eighteenth-century America, slavery was, psychologically speaking, a spur to the democratic revolutionists, for a powerful reason to create their unique democratic institutions was to protect themselves against a slavery they could observe every day; the ideal citizen of Athens or the United States was understood to be the radical opposite of the slave. By celebrating our ideals, Festival America could regularly proclaim that we define ourselves as the radical opposite of the slavish condition of citizens in other times or other places, such as citizens under the Taliban, whose leaders despise life and art, freedom and music, the pursuit of happiness and the liberal arts. We should instill in citizens the truth that "liberty," as John Adams expressed it, "has no Enemy more dangerous than . . . a Prejudice [against liberal Education]"(1977 4:397; cf. Epictetus 1928 1: 213, 215). It is appalling that, by this standard, liberty today has so many domestic enemies. For example, in the eighteenth century slaveholders opposed liberally educating black slaves because they believed that slaves would start "thinking freedom." Is it progress that even into the twenty-first century so many join the slaveholders in opposing a liberal arts education for blacks because they falsely associate it with "thinking white"? Should we not say: "African

Americans have no enemy more dangerous than a prejudice against liberal education"?

When God ordered Moses to tell his people that they should be a "kingdom of priests"(*Exodus* 19:6) it probably implied that every person was important in God's eyes and therefore should at least be able to read, for importance and literacy were several of the distinguishing features of priests. Perhaps this view arose because Hebrews were a tiny minority in, or surrounded by, much larger cultures. In any case, a generalization of this idea is part of the ethos of the American revolution, where every person's importance is recognized by equal and unalienable rights, and where the identification and protection of those rights requires universal education in the liberal arts. Yet that education is often neglected today. One consequence is a weakening of the belief that trial juries are the best protectors of liberty; hence there is a disposition to limit their power, or even to abolish them altogether. In 1971 a labor contractor — Juan Vallejo Corona — was arrested near Yuba City. He was eventually accused of killing 25 men. His trial ran from September 11, 1972, to January 10, 1973. The jury took from January 11 to January 18 to find the defendant guilty. After the trial was over one of the jurors, Larry Gallipeo, said: "Being a juror was a terrible thing. I'm not smart and I'm not educated, and I don't know if it's right to put a person like me in that position of being judge. It was awful. I had to think like I've never thought before. I had to try and understand words like justice and truth . . ."(Villaseñor 1977 285). The intellectual elite of America should not appropriate to themselves the right to make such decisions. Rather they should use their ingenuity to create environments which increase the likelihood that even those who are not smart or educated will make responsible decisions as jurors and, from a longer term perspective, through public liberal arts education, make everyone intellectually, emotionally, and morally as smart as possible (cf. Jefferson's words, above, page 218). Jury duty on occasion may be dreadful, but all citizens should receive the kind of education that will prepare them for it.

Consider a historical parallel. In 1735, William Gooch, the Governor of Virginia, was asked by the Crown to justify a 1723 Virginia law that denied "free Negros & Mulattos of the priviledge of voting." He answered that the

Assembly thought it necessary . . . to fix a perpetual Brand upon Free-Negros & Mulattos by excluding them from that great Priviledge of a Freeman, well knowing they always did, and ever will, adhere to and favor the Slaves. And 'tis likewise said to have been done with design, which I must think a good one, to make the free-Negros sensible that a distinction ought to be made between their offspring and the Descendants of an Englishman, with whom they never were to be Accounted Equal. . . . the number of Free Negros & Mulattos entitled to the Priviledge of voting at Elections is so inconsiderable, that 'tis scarce worth while to take any Notice of them in this Particular, since by other Acts of Assembly now Subsisting they are disabled from being either jurymen or Witnesses in any Case whatsoever, and are as much excluded from being good and lawful Men, as Villains [feudal serfs or rustics] were of Old by the Laws of England. (Evans 1963 412-13)

This is an example of legislating immorality. The intent "to fix a perpetual Brand upon Free-Negros & Mulattos", "to make the free-Negros sensible that a distinction ought to be made between their offspring and the Descendants of an Englishman", to exclude them "from being good and lawful Men," all these helped create the environment that morally corrupted so many of the subsequent generations of Virginians. When Jefferson said those terrible things about blacks (above, page 73) what was he doing but trying to "fix a perpetual Brand upon" them? When Madison argued against hearing the petition of free blacks (above, page 127) what was he doing but trying to bar them "from being good and lawful Men"? To all suggestions that the slaves be freed and blacks and whites should be treated equally, slaveholders could always say: "Come, let us take you for a walk through a plantation. Then you will understand why negroes can never become responsible freemen." Yet the fault was not with the "reality of the negroes" but with the imagination and character of the slaveholders. Turning to ourselves, might not our cultural environment also contain elements that tend to corrupt our judgment? To all suggestions that everyone be given an excellent liberal arts education critics can always say: "Come, let us take you for a walk down Main Street." Yet the fault is in the imagination and character of the critics, not in the reality of the common person. Biologically speaking the common person possesses a brain that is awesomely powerful and supple. Larry Gallipeo's honest comments about himself are a searing indictment of our culture and educational practices. The change from Roman to Arabic numerals transformed long division from a difficult adult problem to a easy juvenile one. Similarly the change from hieroglyphics to alphabets greatly simplified writing. Who knows what could be successfully taught if we used all we know about how the brain learns (through our sight, sound, haptic structures, etc.), and fully exploited technology to optimize learning for each subject and each individual? "It is an axiom in my mind," Jefferson stated, "that our liberty can never be safe but in the hands of the people themselves, and that too of the people with a certain degree of instruction. This is the business of the state to effect . . . "(1950 9:151). Yet our states are failing to give that "degree of instruction" which would help the people to be excellent defenders of their own liberties, or to be excellent contributors to the common reason of society.

Perhaps the most important part of the education of each citizen is the part that creates a life-long habit of self-education. This applies collectively as well. One way of instilling that habit would be to structure Festival America so that, among the winners, will be art which, in the people's judgment, best exposes corruptions in American society. In eighteenth-century America even a large, eloquent abolitionist literature describing the gross sufferings of blacks, even the flagrant contradiction between America's ideals and actual bondage, even these were not enough to bring about the vigorous thought and action necessary for abolition. If the Founding era had a Festival *à la* Athens, if each year the greatest artistic talents would have taken for one of their subjects the reality of slavery in America, it certainly would have made the disgraceful actions of political leaders more difficult, and their failures more troubling to their conscience. Art could have been devised to attack the self-deceptions of the Founders, and the tricks they used to hide their own iniquity (such as Jefferson's deprecations of blacks and Madison's imposing political silence on slavery). It is unfortunate that Jefferson could not have seen a play called, *The Life and Times of a Breeding Woman*, written *à la* Stowe, or a production called, *One Day in the Life of Jame Hubbard*, written *à la* Solzhenitsyn; or that Washington or Madison could not attend a theater showing *Help, Help, But There Is No Help*, about the futile struggles of blacks to get justice from legislatures. Such drama might have awakened them from their deep moral slumber, it might have created in them a new sensibility that would have made it impossible for Jefferson to think in terms of breeding women at all, or to have any slave flogged, or have made it impossible for Washington or Madison to support the slave interest. Keeping slaves might have become too painful for them to bear. To quote Jefferson's words again: ". . . when we . . . read of any atrocious deed, we are disgusted with it's deformity and conceive an abhorrence of vice. Now every emotion of this kind is an exercise of our virtuous dispositions; and dispositions of the mind . . . acquire strength by exercise. But exercise produces habit; and in the instance of which we speak, the exercise being of the moral feelings, produces a habit of thinking and acting virtuously"(above, page 313). Literature, drama, and art can help prevent our reason from being compromised or overwhelmed by self-deceptions, they can increase the range and depth of emotions needed to "exercise . . . our virtuous dispositions," they can help make those dispositions a permanent part of our national character. Anyone who thinks Jefferson's words merely represent pious sentiments, or that literature has little real effect in the political world, might reflect on the remarkable role *Uncle Tom's Cabin* had in bringing about an end to slavery. Frederick Douglass, himself a runaway slave, states: "In the midst of these fugitive slave troubles came the book known as *Uncle Tom's Cabin*, a work of marvelous depth and power. Nothing could have better united the moral and human requirements of the hour. Its effect was amazing, instantaneous, and universal"(1962 282).

Festival America, in the context of a politics of self-knowledge, is intended to produce whatever best suits "the moral and human requirements of the hour." It is an act of republican virtue for the people to choose art which exposes unpleasant truths about themselves, to choose art which undermines collective self-deceptions. On occasion this might require substantial moral courage. Let us recur again to Adams' claim that self-deceit is "perhaps the source of far the greatest, and worst part of the vices and calamities among mankind"(above, page 59). Adams' judgment has continued to be vindicated as an important source of the misfortunes that have overtaken America. It is part of the purpose of Festival America to make impossible gross national self-deceit and to minimize its more subtle varieties. Of course, artists can use their talent for increasing destructive self-deceit; the art of Leni Riefenstahl, who lent her talents to Hitler, and Sergei Eisenstein, who lent his to Stalin, come to mind. As Adams reminds us, "Every one of the fine Arts from the earliest times has been inlisted in the service of Superstition and Despotism"(Cappon 1959 2:502-3). In Festival America it is the people's responsibility to deliberate and then distinguish such art from that which best contributes to their welfare. There is no hint whatsoever of censorship here; a free person can enjoy any kind of art she wishes — Adams includes "Homer and Milton Phidias and Raphael" — among those that support "the grossest Fictions." But it doesn't follow that any art that pleases an individual — even art exhibiting transcendent talent — will be seen by a soul-searching people as appropriate to prepare for their own fateful, political decisions. Rather, the people can choose art in Festival America to strengthen those emotions which their common reason approves, and which will protect them from the poetic injustice of any inhumane art that might undermine their character, liberties, or public happiness.

In a politically free country the external restrictions on an individual's pursuit of happiness are reduced to a practical minimum; in a morally free person the internal obstacles are likewise reduced. Both kinds of freedom are subject to degrees and both are complex; one can be politically free in one way but not another, one can be morally free in one way but not another. A successful liberal arts education will instill a deep, life-long devotion to secure and enlarge both political and moral freedom. Moral freedom, in my book, means the habitual exercise of reason in the pursuit of happiness, an idea articulated by Locke (see above, pages 36 to 39). It is reasonable to say that a person is born free in the political sense of freedom; it is a gift of society. However, a person cannot be born free in the moral sense. In that meaning we are all born dependent and ignorant, but we can become free through liberal education, whether formal or not; this freedom is not a *gift* of society, but an *achievement* of the individual. The goal of republican government is to create the best possible conditions favorable to that achievement. Without moral freedom the value of political freedom is reduced, if not made nugatory; as Joel Barlow remarked on July 4, 1787: "We have contended with the most powerful nation and subdued the bravest and best appointed armies; but now we have to contend with *ourselves*, and encounter passions and prejudices more powerful than armies and more dangerous to peace"(11). What is the use of having political freedom of conscience if you are not morally free to exercise that right? What is the use of an antislavery Constitution if authorities, overcome by a spirit of domination and racism, transform it by bogus interpretations into a proslavery document? "No man is free who is not master of himself," is a wonderful saying attributed to Epictetus (1928 2:477); and Locke takes up the same theme when he says, "he is certainly the most subjected, the most enslaved, who is so in his Understanding"(1975 711). The failure of Washington, Jefferson, Madison, Roosevelt, Truman, and Eisenhower to think and act in accordance with their principles is a stain on their character; they became — through self-deceit — their own jailers; by creating a psychic confinement imperceivable to their mind's eye, escape becomes unnecessary, indeed unthinkable. Their education did not sufficiently instill the habits necessary to make that stain improbable. As a result, self-deception on occasion overwhelmed their ability to maintain moral freedom, and because they were leaders, the political freedom of millions of others.

No country is securely safe or free if ignorance, prejudices, and passions make its leaders slaves to themselves. An anthropology of human felicity must pay as much attention to the moral ecology of the mind as it does to the political ecology of society; a truly free person is both morally free within and politically free without, a genuine masterpiece of the liberal arts. Let us call any psychic habit or activity that undermines moral freedom a *corruption of consciousness.* (I borrow this phrase from R. G. Collingwood (1958 215-21, 280-5, 336), who argued, as do I, that art is fundamental in combating that corruption; but I use the term in a wider sense than he does.) This corruption prepares us to be easily seduced by "*Idols* of the human mind"(2004 73), to use a phrase Bacon made famous, and these idols can make us as much of a slave or vassal as any tyrant or lord can.

We will miss half of the meaning of the American revolution, as most accounts of it do, if we limit our attention to the issues of avoiding external slavery and securing its radical opposite called political freedom; for the other half is avoiding internal slavery and securing its radical opposite called moral freedom. Let us listen to some eighteenth-century descriptions of internal slavery:

> Liberty is the spirit and genius of the sacred writings; the great thing aimed at in them, is to make men free from sin; to deliver them out of bondage to their lusts, and procure and establish the moral freedom of their minds. (Hitchcock, Gad, above, page 29; cf. also Cumings 1784:35-6 and Alison 1769 16)
>
> When a man goes beyond, or contrary to the law of nature and reason, he becomes the slave of base passions, and vile lusts, he introduces confusion and disorder into society, and brings misery and destruction upon himself. This therefore cannot be called a state of freedom, but a state of the vilest slavery, and the most dreadful bondage: The servants of sin and corruption are subjected to the worst kind of tyranny in the universe. Hence we conclude, that where licentiousness begins, liberty ends. (West, Samuel 1776 13).
>
> If the reason of the mind, man's immediate rule of conduct, is in bondage to corruption, he is verily the worst of slaves. (Payson 1778 16).
>
> But he is the man of freedom, in the most noble sense, who has the command of himself, who can rule his own spirit, command his own passions and appetites, keep under his body, and make reason the rule of his conduct — who fears God and walks uprightly, and orders his conservation aright. He that is master of himself is King. Bloody heroes conquer *others*, he subdues *himself*, a world greater and better than that without him. To take a city is now-a-days, a trifle. He that gets possession of the *world within* is greater than *Alexander.* For though a man may acquire universal empire, he may yet die a slave to his vanity and lust. (Mellen 1795 33]

If we wish to be true and complete American revolutionaries, we must cultivate both moral and political freedom; just as the common reason of the people should make them masters of their government, so their individual reason should make them masters of themselves, allowing each person to be "greater than *Alexander*." Consequently we must habitually oppose those feelings that can corrupt our consciousness. However, internal enemies of freedom are not limited to such feelings. For example, we appear naturally to have a very a difficult time judging probabilities. Even geniuses make elementary mistakes. For instance, speaking of a pair of dice, Leibniz claimed that "it is as feasible to throw a twelve as to throw an eleven"(1951 88). Yet it is only half as likely. Pascal and d'Alembert made comparable errors (Todhunter 1865 15; Schuh 1968 165). Paul Erdös, the most prolific mathematician of the twentieth century, misreasoned about a very simple probability problem and it took a great effort to convince him of his error (Hoffman, Paul 1998 249-256). We know we can overcome ordinary defects in probabilistic inference by reforming our intuitions to better conform with reason. But it has not been common for students to be taught how to recognize those defects, much less are they taught so young and so well and so often that in their actual everyday lives they habitually avoid them. This failure, so easily imbedded in a subhonest economy, was at the root of the financial breakdown that began in 2007. It was not only greed, for greed need not be united with ignorance or stupidity; their greed did not lead business leaders to gamble all their income at casinos, since they knew they would eventually lose. Yet they played business games they likewise had to eventually lose. Nevertheless, with the spirit of 1776 asleep, none of the bailout funds (October 3, 2008) went to secondary education to insure that no child was left behind in learning the history, philosophy, and pitfalls of probabilistic or statistical reasoning, nor did any of the funds go to the creation and advertising of games (*à la* Sudoku) so that the general public might be taught how treacherous such reasoning is, how treacherousness rapidly increases with each degree of increased complexity (or even subtle changes in initial conditions), and hence that uneasiness over the soundness of such reasonings should then likewise rapidly increase. For want of this elementary knowledge the prosperity of the country was lost. But beyond financial breakdowns such knowledge is important for, as Joseph Butler noted in 1736, "probability is the very guide to life"(1896 1:5; cf. Cicero 1951 15). If we would overcome this natural weakness of our own minds we would enlarge moral freedom and, thereby, not only help secure economic prosperity and political liberty; we would increase their worth. Similar things could be said, *mutatis mutantis*, about many other types of misreasoning that logicians and psychologists have identified, such as those associated with ambiguity, confabulation, or irrelevance. In general, the structure of Courts of Common Reason, the experiments used to refine that structure, the plays in Festival America, the requirement that every citizen receive a liberal arts education — all these together are aimed at preventing political and economic decisions that are the product of some corruption of consciousness. The stirring words marking the end of bodily slavery — *Free at last! Free at last! Thank God Almighty, we are free at last!* — will be equally appropriate when the public mind receives its emancipation. We need a new class of leaders who are abolitionists with respect to internal slavery, journalists who will not equivocate, excuse, or retreat, speakers who will be heard, educators who will teach, politicians who will act, until our civilization becomes, and forever remains, nothing but the offspring of the moral freedom of the American people.

Achieving that august goal will not be easy, because moral freedom has an indefinite number of internal enemies. Let us examine another enemy, one that is rooted not in moral cowardice, or in the instinctive tendencies of our own reasoning, but in our sociability. This enemy was correctly identified by the generation of 1776, but they failed to confront and defeat it. Consider some excerpts; first, from independence day addresses by George Clinton and then Thomas Day; and, second, from the writings of John Adams:

> Beware of the spirit of party: it may dissolve your union, dismember your empire, and render you the sport of ambition, and the cause of your destruction. (1798 12)
>
> Among those means, which are calculated to destroy a free government, none will be found more efficient than PARTY SPIRIT. It has long been said, and sanctioned by the authority of Heaven, that, "A HOUSE DIVIDED AGAINST ITSELF CANNOT STAND." (1798 7)
>
> While all other Sciences have advanced, that of Government is at a stand; little better understood; little better practiced now than 3 or 4 thousand Years ago. What is the Reason? I say Parties and Factions will not suffer, or permit improvements to be made. As soon as one Man hints at an improvement his Rival opposes it. No sooner has one Party discovered or invented an Amelioration of the Condition of Man or the order of Society, than the opposite Party, belies it, misconstrues it, misrepresents it, ridicules it, insults it, and persecutes it. (Cappon 1959 2:351) There is nothing which I dread so much as a division of the republic into two great parties, each arranged under its leader, and concerting measures in opposition to each other. This, in my humble apprehension, is to be

dreaded as the greatest political evil under our Constitution. (1850 9:511;cf. 1977 1:77)

These words have proven to be prophetic. Representative democracy, united with the spirit of party, becomes dysfunctional; excellent legislation is a rare event, while evils, even the most gross and catastrophic, are often strengthened. Such has been the influence of party, that the United States did not make slavery explicitly unconstitutional until there was a Civil War that risked its existence, and then it continued in various places even beyond World War II (cf. Daniel 1972, 1989 and Blackmon 2008). Nor was segregation or Jim Crow ended legislatively until there were widespread demonstrations, violence, and disconcerting judicial decisions. Nor, even by the turn of the twenty-first century, had Congress produced a system of taxes, or laws concerning health care, or a way for drawing political districts, that was not embarrassing; the party spirit continued to degrade politics.

Courts of Common Reason, as they have been described so far, would undermine the pernicious influence of party, but they could further reduce such influence by helping voters make political decisions that express their own unique individuality. Morally free citizens are the only secure foundation of politically free societies, but it will take very sophisticated technology for that freedom to receive precise political expression. Yet our voting procedures today are essentially the same as those used in eighteenth-century America, or even ancient Athens. As a result, it is difficult not to submit, by some significant degree, to party, to prejudice, to arbitrary choice. Let us imagine how we might create a technology to reduce that degree. Suppose a woman is faced with two issues on a state referendum, and one of two parties says to vote "yes" on the first and "no" on the second, while the second party says the opposite. Let us further suppose that, in her judgment, she has only enough time to investigate one issue. Now imagine that the woman is able to go to a computer, push a few buttons, and find out that of the hundred people most like herself in the state advisory jury (which had carefully investigated both issues), ninety-two approved of the first, but only fifty-two favored the second. She could thus know, with a high degree of probability, that if she took the time to carefully consider the first issue, she would approve it. (Of course, if she had the time and desire, she could have a summary of the reasons that, at greater length, would likely convince her.) On the other hand, the probability that she would approve the second is uncertain, so she herself would have to reflect in depth in order to know what her considered judgment would be. Notice that even if the woman deliberates about the second issue, there is always the possibility that if she thought longer, or read another article on it, and so forth, she might change her mind. Hence her direct knowledge of her true deliberate sense, like her indirect knowledge in the first case, is subject to probability. Nevertheless, by saving time investigating the first issue and using it to investigate the second, the woman would be more likely to express her true deliberate sense on both of them, than if she had used inadequate time to investigate both, or merely followed one of the parties. If we wish to have a superbly governed society, we must invest voting with the sophistication and subtlety which is necessary in order that it have the effect for which it was designed, namely, to ensure that government acts in harmony with the informed values and considered judgments of the people.

Let us call the Court of Common Reason a *public deliberator*, and use the name *private deliberator* for a court of common reason representing an organization — such as the shareholders of a company, or the members of a religious denomination. What the woman has been using could then be sensibly called a *personal deliberator*, analogous to a personal computer. Note that a personal computer allows the woman to give a considered judgment about the outcome of the calculations of her own mind without her actually calculating: "If I raised 2467 to the fifth power, what would I get?." Indeed, using a computer would be better than calculating herself, since it is less likely to make a mistake. Likewise, on the first issue, she could express the outcome of her deliberations without actually deliberating, perhaps even better than she could do herself since she might be more likely than the court to make mistakes in deliberating about that issue. This is not any different from a friend's convincing the woman to vote in a certain way because such a vote better express who she is. As the Court of Common Reason allows the American people to accurately express their own collective deliberate sense without the gross impracticality of having every adult American doing the deliberating, so a personal deliberator allows an individual to accurately express her own deliberate sense without the gross impracticality of deliberating on all the issues. Were we to invest as much intelligence and money to make responsible citizenship easier to achieve, as we have in making computers easier to use, perhaps the Founders' dream of an America consisting of citizens pursuing and obtaining individual happiness, under a government pursuing and obtaining the general happiness, would not seem so unrealistic.

The economics of responsible judgment has been given little attention by traditional philosophy, yet it is of immense importance and extends beyond political judgment. "I never submitted the whole system of my opinions," Jefferson maintained, "to the creed of any party of men whatever in religion, in philosophy, in politics, or in any thing else where I was capable of thinking for myself. Such an addiction is the last degradation of a free and moral agent"(1950 14:650). Since even this transcendent genius in the eighteenth century has to make a limitation — "where I was capable of thinking for myself" — how can an ordinary person, in the twenty-first century, faced with an exponentially greater number of issues "in religion, in philosophy, in politics," avoid "the last degradation of a free and moral agent"? The "addiction to party," a kind of permanent disposition to groupthink, seems unavoidable without using the technology of personal deliberators to determine what sweat equity we must put into our moral and political home, and what we can reasonably borrow from the deliberative banks of others like ourselves, or others like those we wish to become.

Self-knowledge, from a twenty-first-century perspective, appears so long, so difficult, and so expensive in opportunity costs, that it cannot be adequately achieved and maintained by talking to a few friends *à la* Socrates. Nor is it now any longer plausible, in the pursuit of self-knowledge, to exclude any part of the liberal arts. For example, the older Socrates believed physical inquiries to be irrelevant to his quest (Plato 1937 1:480-84). Yet our body is made out of matter and if we want to understand ourselves we need to know from science what it is and how it works. Erwin Schrödinger, author of the most famous equation in quantum mechanics, states that the "scope, aim and value" of science "is the same as that of any other branch of human knowledge. Nay, none of them alone, only the union of all of them, has any scope or value at all, and that is simply enough described: it is to obey the command of the Delphic deity, Γνῶθι σεαυτόν, get to know yourself"(1996 108). This view is old and was, if fact, central to American revolutionary thinking. This is how James Wilson expresses it:

"Know thou thyself," is an inscription peculiarly proper for the porch of the temple of science. The knowledge of human nature is of all human knowledge the most curious and the most important. To it all the other sciences have a relation; and though from it they may seem to diverge and ramify very widely, yet by one passage or another they still return. (2007 1:585)

To achieve and benefit from self-knowledge in contemporary terms, we should try to develop physical technologies such as "personal brain scanners," which would enable us to understand what is going on in our brain while having various thoughts or feelings; we could thus play games of brain solitaire, a kind of neurointrospection, that would greatly improve our chances of attaining human excellence. (Perhaps we could even become Shakespeares in the Delphic theater of our own minds.) We should also try to develop moral technologies, such as personal deliberators, which would enable individuals to know, with a certain degree of probability, the outcome of their own deliberations "in religion, in philosophy, in politics" without always taking the time and effort to deliberate. Just as an ordinary programmer with a personal computer can now easily solve many mathematical problems that in previous centuries could not be solved by the greatest mathematical geniuses, so perhaps someday an ordinary person, using a personal deliberator, could achieve a level of self-knowledge, self-mastery, and practical wisdom that previously could not reached by the greatest philosophical geniuses. The personal deliberator enhances our humanity; it is a personal assistant in the game of life, a technological aid in perfecting an individual's pursuit of happiness.

Consider a thought experiment. Imagine Martha, a ten-year-old girl. Of all ten-year-old girls on earth, a personal jury is formed of, say, the 96,000 most like her. (This would equal to 8000 subjuries.) "Like" here is understood to mean that each of the girls is at least as likely than any girl not in the jury to answer questions as Martha would. The jury would be a virtual answering twin of Martha at age ten and could be called MARTHA(10). MARTHA(D:10) would be a similar sized jury, composed of girls who are at least as likely as any girl not on that jury to answer questions as Martha would, after cool and deliberate reflection. MARTHA(10) is intended to duplicate Martha's answers as she is, MARTHA(D:10), her answers as she would be if she took the time and effort to be cool and deliberate. Now suppose ninety more D-juries, all of the same size, are formed of 11 year-olds, . . . , 100 year-olds, of those most likely to answer questions as Martha now does, after cool and deliberate reflection, when they were ten. Martha, we suppose, could pose questions to any of the juries, say, the deliberate nineteen year-olds, that is, MARTHA(D:19), or a group of them together, say, ten to twenty year-olds, that is, MARTHA(D:10-20). I will let MARTHA(D:10-100) be defined as Martha's personal deliberator (= MARTHA(D)) although there are, of course, other reasonable definitions. Answers given by personal deliberators will be determined by the majority vote of the unanimous subjuries. We will assume that the answers of a personal deliberator will be given to Martha by a virtual human — perhaps a realistic robot, a holographic image, or a controlled hallucination — so as to simulate an ordinary conversation. And just as Kasparov's computer opponents were modified whenever he played a new game, so Martha's deliberative archive is automatically enlarged anytime she talks to her deliberator. At times her deliberator would have to be reprogrammed, or new-modeled using other jury members, to continue to be her deliberate twin. On some questions, Martha would have to wait for an answer but, since the members of her personal juries are so like her, they could anticipate many questions — "What would I ask if I were Martha?" — deliberate before she asks them, create an archive, and thus give immediate responses to questions they anticipated. However, the deliberators need not be merely reactive. They could ask themselves what Martha should learn, what habits she should develop, what kind of experiences she should seek out, and so forth, in order to increase the probability she will have a long and happy life. They could discuss the answers to those questions based on their knowledge of the liberal arts and the enormous evidence they collectively possess of their own lives. The outcome of their votes will be the individualized, empirical morality that forms the basis of any advice they give to Martha. For example, imagine the Court of Common Reason picks out, say, the 5% happiest people in each age group among the members of her deliberator. Martha's education should aim at giving her whatever knowledge and exercise she needs to form habits of thought and action to achieve a comparable happiness every year of her life. It would be an *evidence-based* education that would determine in detail the virtues, manners, and habits she should adopt. Francis Bacon complained that "allowing [Aristotle's] Conclusion *that vertues and vices consist in habit*, he ought so much the more to haue taught the manner of superinducing [= displacing] that habite"(2000 151). Martha's education is a twenty-first-century adaptation of Aristotelian ethics and Baconian empiricism.

Martha and her deliberators could have private, even intimate, conversations. For example, suppose she asks about boys and sexuality. Anticipating this, the deliberators could debate the issues as to what she should, or should not, do, what books or videos with coming-of-age themes she should read or see, and so forth. The deliberators would even withhold advice wherever their evidence suggests that it is best for Martha to learn about that subject on her own. Every part of MARTHA(D)'s conversation would be based on extensive investigation and discussion so as to be able to give the best advice, in a timely fashion, and in a form most likely to be useful to Martha. MARTHA(D), then, is Martha's practically wise, but virtual, friend. Of course, Martha would be under no obligation whatsoever to take the advice and, as an identical twin will sometimes assert his or her individuality by, say, taking up the piano merely because the other twin takes up the violin, so Martha could reject advice merely to assert her individuality (or for any other reason). Metamoral education, so to speak, includes developing the ability and desire to critically examine the morality one is taught and, acquiring that autonomy, being willing to reject inappropriate advice. Nevertheless, the more Martha insists "I gotta be me," the more she will realize that she will be better able to express her unique humanity by using a personal deliberator, than if she made all decisions without such assistance. Knowing the common reason of her personal deliberators will help her gain uncommon practical wisdom. She would know where she should concentrate her education, how she could strengthen her reason, the means she could use to protect herself from corruptions of consciousness, and what are the best ways to overcome all other obstacles that might limit her chances for a life of excellence. In January of 1776 Washington wrote Joseph Reed: "At present, my time is so much taken up at my Desk, that I am obliged to neglect many other essential parts of my Duty; it is absolutely necessary therefore for me to have person's that can think for me, as well as execute Orders"(1985 3:173). In her war against everything that hinders the greatest possible success in the pursuit of happiness, a war as challenging as that facing Washington, Martha would also need, on occasion, personal deliberators to think and act for her. By using them she would be less likely to be miserable for years because of teenage angst, or less likely to have a mid-life crisis, or less likely to use up most of her life before finding her true calling.

If Martha is to achieve the utmost excellence in the art of living, she must pay close attention to the economy of moral decision, for the pursuit of happiness can hardly be felicitous if she gets bogged down in decision-making. On this subject she could listen to Elihu Palmer: "But awakened by the energy of thought, inspired by the American revolution, man will find it consistent with his inclination and his interest to examine all the moral relations of his nature, [and] to calculate with accuracy the effects of his own moral energies"(1797

27). Were Martha to fully exploit the powers of her personal deliberators, she could carry out that examination and calculation with much greater ease and accuracy than it would otherwise be possible to attain. The Court of Common Reason is a political technology which, because it efficiently uses statistical representatives, saves citizens time and effort in finding out their collective deliberate sense; its technological child — the personal deliberator — does the same for the individual. It is part of the wisdom of scientists to be a good judges of when to change their beliefs in the light of new evidence or arguments, and when to retain those beliefs because the new evidence is deceptive, or the new arguments unsound. A good person is similar, but when she judges the evidence and arguments to be reliable, she is ready, willing, and able to change her manners and habits; she is a true master of the psychology and ethics of everyday living. Thus the political and moral technology possible in the twenty-first century might enable individuals to achieve a scale of felicity in perfecting their pursuit of happiness hitherto unknown in the history of humanity; and that technology might even itself be susceptible to such rapid improvements as to be comparable to the advances made in computer technology in the last half of the twentieth century.

Let us now turn to Benjamin Franklin's reflections on moral improvement:

> It is said that the Persians in their ancient Constitution, had publick Schools in which Virtue was taught as a Liberal Art or Science; and it is certainly of more Consequence to a Man, that he has learnt to govern his Passions; in spite of Temptation to be just in his Dealings, to be Temperate in his Pleasures, to support himself with Fortitude under his Misfortunes, to behave with Prudence in all Affairs and in every Circumstance of Life; I say, it is of much more real Advantage to him to be thus qualified, than to be a Master of all the Arts and Sciences in the World beside. (1959 1:118; cf. 9:105, Xenophon 2001 23-28, and Locke 1989 155)

We could illustrate one of Franklin's examples with Jim Stockdale who certainly needed "to support himself with Fortitude under his Misfortunes." Stockdale, a naval pilot in the Vietnam war, became a prisoner for seven and a half years. He was severely tortured fifteen times, was in solitary for four years, and suffered many other deprivations. How did he endure? The title of one of the chapters from his book — *Thoughts of a Philosophical Fighter Pilot* — gives the answer: "Courage Under Fire: Testing Epictetus's Doctrines in a Laboratory of Human Behavior"(1995 185-201). Yet the Stoic philosophy that enabled Stockdale to survive and triumph might not necessarily be the most appropriate for Martha. For example, Abigail Adams, going through a particularly difficult period, said: "Neither the Morals of Epictetus or the Stoick phylosophy of the Ancients could avail to allay the Tumult of Grief excited by such a Succession of Distress" (Adams 1954 Reel 412 xxxv:176a). Christianity was the only "balm." Hence advice given by Martha's personal deliberator should be made in light of the actual experience of those members of the deliberator who best handled misfortune, combined with a thorough knowledge of developmental psychology and other liberal arts. As I understand Franklin's moral philosophy, he believes that teaching virtue is the most important part of education, that virtue should be taught as a liberal art, that, properly understood, virtue is a science based on evidence, experiments, proof, and that, as a science, virtue is capable of continual improvement. Franklin was well aware that the background assumptions of this morality are classical. He alluded to Xenophon; here are two further expressions of it, one Greek, one Roman:

> Neither by nature, then, nor contrary to nature do excellences arise in us; rather we are adapted by nature to receive them, and are made perfect by habit. (Aristotle 1984 2:1743).
>
> For nature does not bestow virtue; it is an art to become good. . . . . Virtue is not vouchsafed to a soul unless that soul has been trained and taught, and by unremitting practice brought to perfection. For the attainment of this boon, but not the possession of it, were we born; and even in the best of men, before you refine them by instruction, there is but the stuff of virtue, not virtue itself. (Seneca 1989 2:429, 431)

The first aim of public education, then, is to instill in students consistent dispositions — habits that become second-nature — both to act according to the voice of their practical wisdom and to relentlessly try to improve the quality of that voice. Practical wisdom is here understood as the capacity of the individual to make choices that will most likely result in a moral and flourishing life. The liberal arts ought to teach us how best to buy time and spend money for that pursuit; they ought to make a person *morally resourceful*, a condition achieved by Athenian citizens according to Pericles, since "each individual amongst us could in his own person, with the utmost grace and versatility, prove himself self-sufficient in the most varied forms of activity"(Thucydides 1928 1:331). That versatility would include developing that self-control which allows a continual adjustment of desires and habits so that one could, for example, be poor without discouragement, or be rich without corruption of character (cf Locke's words above, page 38). Practical wisdom requires that we achieve certain levels and kinds of self-knowledge to make those adjustments; for differences in character, talents, experiences, and luck mean that we cannot all be happy, despite Tolstoy, in the same way. For the classically-inspired American revolutionary, human nature is such that it is possible to devise laws and social arrangements, so that those who increase the flourishing of their own lives, will automatically increase public happiness.

Following this idea we assume that personal deliberators that operate within the bounds set by the Court of Common Reason are more reliable guides to individual happiness than those that do not. For example, there is nothing more important for general happiness than that individuals react with appropriate feeling and emotion, such as feeling horror at the torture of children, or joy when liberty triumphs over despotism. We suppose Martha's individual happiness will not be compromised if she feels such horror and joy, rather than the opposite. In general, we assume that if Martha's education as a child and young person instills feelings, emotions, and habits in her that promote the public happiness, her freedom as an adult to pursue individual happiness will not be compromised, she will not be false to herself. Within such restrictions that the Court of Common Reason could identify in detail, Martha's personal deliberator could suggest experiences, a kind of ongoing Festival Martha, to celebrate and teach those habits of mind and feeling that it believes are desirable both for Martha's private, and for the public, happiness.

Democratic government is greatly enhanced if the people are excellent judges of character, and thus students should be helped to achieve that excellence through courses in psychology, literature, history, and philosophy. ("Nothing doth more hurt in a State, than that Cunning Men passe for Wise," says Francis Bacon (2000a 72).) But that same excellence, exercised in choosing friends, associates, or a spouse, is just as important for the successful pursuit of individual happiness. Furthermore, students could gain experience in judging themselves where, without such training, some would almost always judge themselves positively, and some negatively. Using simulation after simulation they could be taught to judge their own cases, according to the standards of the American people, with a high degree of accuracy. They could directly understand that honesty and integrity are the only sure foundations of self-government, whether political or personal. Again, in the deliberate give-and-take struggle with their classmates to articulate the American dream for their generation, students would learn things directly useful to identifying and achieving their own dreams. They would be creating a commonwealth of learning. Civic learning for the sake of public happiness, and individual learning for the sake of personal happiness, appear to be in a reciprocal relationship; as Wilson remarks, "publick and private felicity will go hand in hand, and mutually assist each other in their progress"(2007 1:539; cf. Locke 1975 69). Perhaps the best way to embody this idea in the twenty-first century would be to construct [AMERICAN PEOPLE](D), that would allow anyone anywhere to have a simulated conversation with the American people expressing their deliberate sense. Given the opportunities here for domestic tranquility or world peace, it is hard to imagine overspending on this technology if it could be made practicable.

We really do not know as much as we could know about that practical wisdom which is founded in the liberal arts. An analogy may be useful here. We know a good deal in general about what sort of diet humans require, but the optimal diet for each person remains unknown, and it will take many years and billions of dollars to create the procedures to find out. Similarly, we know a good deal about what a free people require for happiness, but are ignorant of many important details that will take considerable time and money to discover. Given our physical nature, if we eat the wrong foods we compromise the health of our body; given our moral nature, if we feel the wrong emotions we compromise the happiness of our person. There are poisonous emotions as well as poisonous foods, and we ought to investigate, for example, how the happiest people deal with feelings of rage, or humiliation, or spite. Virtue taught as a "Liberal Art or Science" combined with deliberative technology should give us the evidence to identify the emotions that help us flourish, and Festival America should help us feel them under appropriate situations. In this way, for example, we could greatly reduce the risk of catastrophic failures in social empathy, such as the toleration of slavery, or the forced return of Soviet refugees after World War II. In 1787 an anonymous New Jersey essayist observed that "though the Athenians possessed but a small territory in Greece; yet by carrying the liberal arts & sciences to perfection, they compleated their own glory"(CDVALE 1787 49). We will not complete our own glory until we fully integrate the perfection of our liberal arts and sciences into American society.

My description of a liberal arts education is only a rough, first approximation that must be modified again and again in light of experiments in public, private, and personal deliberators. Secondary schools, colleges and universities could conduct and respond to those experiments so that educational inadequacies would be remedied in the next generation, or even sooner through adult education. For example, suppose, in a random fashion, that either of two versions of a play is shown individually to students on a video. The versions are identical except, say, the skin color of some of the actors are changed. The results reveal that students think one race has greater rights than the other, or make other invidious distinctions between them as judged by the Court of Common Reason. In response to this problem, a democratic evolutionary competition is held to find a set of plays or novels or critical thinking exercises or computer games, which tests show best strengthen the reason of students so that they become less likely to make or feel such morally unfounded distinctions. Using such techniques on a large variety of different issues, the best liberal education for a free people may be progressively defined and redefined as new evidence accumulates. The spirit of the American revolution, repeatedly proclaimed in Festival America, could energize each new generation to undergo the exhaustive and exhausting soul-searching needed to articulate and achieve the aspirations of a great-souled people; such a prospect would transform the earth; all lovers of humanity would want to be in that number when this new world is revealed.

.   The description I have given of a personal deliberator, however useful for expository purposes, is fanciful. I have put no limitations on the kinds of questions that could be asked, but every deliberator, like every computer, has limits. To be practical one could not insist that every girl in the deliberator be like Martha as far as is possible in every way, it would be more efficient to have a large number of small dedicated deliberators each capable of modeling Martha's deliberate sense in some very specific way, or on some very specific subject. The members of these dedicated deliberators would have to be like Martha collectively, but need not be so individually. If a collection of dedicated deliberators could create a practically useful MARTHA and MARTHA(D) then, since they need not cease to exist with Martha's death, we could get *some* of the benefits of Martha's judgment and character without Martha, and she could get kind of virtual immortality. (Perhaps here is a motive for the rich to fund the research necessary to create personal deliberators for themselves.) Contrariwise, once we have extensive experience with deliberators, it might be possible to create one for a dead person, thus achieving a virtual resurrection. (One wonders in what ways this would transform biography and history.) Perhaps someday a genius will come along who could precisely define a universal personal deliberator. If there is success in creating a personal deliberator for Martha we might expect that many efficiencies could be introduced so that it would be possible to simultaneously create deliberators for others, and eventually everyone. Maybe a relatively few dedicated deliberators might, through mix and match, be capable of creating a virtual twin for anyone. In any case, a *Jeffersonian* personal deliberator — that is, one that makes use of only eighteenth-century means — is probably too inefficient to be practical in every place where it would be desirable. Let us define a *Turing* personal deliberator to be one in which all the dedicated deliberators are computers. (Alan Turing gave the first theoretical definition of a computer in 1936 and believed computers could think.) Only the future will tell the extent to which such a deliberator is practically possible. At least initially, it seems likely that practicality will require a Jeffersonian-Turing hybrid in a symbiotic human-computer relation. We might even imagine that personal deliberators would eventually talk to each other via an Internet, since the best advice to give a single person is no doubt affected by the advice given to others. (One would expect that some of the techniques used in Wikipedia, Linux, blogs, or computer searches would be here applied to the moral life.) Note that even if a Turing personal deliberator becomes a practicality, it doesn't follow that it would always be desirable to use it. The fact that it may be possible to get a robot to look like me and walk precisely the way I do, does not mean that I should give up the pleasures of walking, and the benefits I get from the exercise of my body, nor does the existence of my Turing personal deliberator mean that I should give up the pleasures of deliberation, and the benefits I get from the exercise of my autonomy.

Twenty-four hundred years ago Hippocrates wrote: "Life is short, the Art long, opportunity fleeting, experience treacherous, judgment difficult"(1923 4:99). This aphorism is as appropriate to the human condition today as it has been since then. The aim of creating personal deliberators is to reduce the severity of these problems using twenty-first century technology. Further, personal deliberators appear to fit human nature, not only because the disposition to deliberate seems part of that nature, but also because the tendency to hear, or speak to, or to see virtual persons, seems just as much a part. Consider the daimon of Socrates; the imaginary friends of some children; the ghosts who scare them; the dream hallucinations of sleepers; the *ka,* saint, or god of those who pray; or the Christians who have a friend in Jesus, a person they have never actually met. Note also that it is a standard criticism of bad novels that the writer does not get us to "care" about fictional characters. In addition, consider the language used by humans who are devotees of ships, or cars, or planes. The capacity of humans to have virtual social relations with products of their own thought, or their own hands, seems intrinsic to their nature, a capacity perhaps made possible by mirror neurons. In any case, who would not like to have an intimate, if virtual, friend, capable of extraordinary conversation reflecting a thorough knowledge of the liberal arts, a conversation that would include highly individualized and wise advice on any problem whatsoever that might undermine felicity in the pursuit of one's own happiness? In a world where vice is so often greatly augmented by technology, the extreme case being weapons of mass destruction, would it not be prudent to arm republican virtue with the all the technology that twenty-first century liberal arts could supply? Facing widespread and deep doubt, entrepreneurs nevertheless became fabulously wealthy from the telegraph, the telephone, radio, xerography, the computer, and the Internet, because these technologies greatly reduced the cost of acquiring, copying, and manipulating information. Might there not be many fortunes to be made, probably in the face of similar deep doubt, if it were feasible to greatly reduce the cost of acquiring, copying, and manipulating information about ourselves as individuals? Or, of course, as pairs (say, in marriage), as triplets (say, in business partnerships), and so forth, to *n*-tuplets of individuals, where *n* might equal the population of a country? Entrepreneurs might make self-knowledge one of the great growth industries of the twenty-first century. If so, we should be acutely aware that such moral and political technologies, like other technologies, might bring their own problems, abuses, and dangers; consequently, exceptional efforts should be made to anticipate and minimize them.

To sum up: As safety and economy in contemporary travel requires replacing compasses based on magnetism with global positioning systems (GPS) based on satellites, so the pursuit of happiness in the contemporary world requires replacing *moral compasses* based on tradition with *ethical positioning systems* (EPS) based on deliberators. Today, with GPS technology, we can always know, as the ancients could not, exactly where we are on the earth; tomorrow, with EPS technology, we will be able to know, with much greater accuracy than is now possible, where we are ethically. The road to political happiness cannot be known without twenty-first-century precision in mapping the moral landscape formed by the common reason of the people. In 1974 Richard Feynman gave the commencement address at the California Institute of Technology. In it he spoke of

> a kind of scientific integrity, a principle of scientific thought that corresponds to a kind of utter honesty — a kind of leaning over backwards. For example, if you're doing an experiment, you should report everything that you think might make it invalid — not only what you think is right about it: other causes that could possibly explain your results; and things you thought of that you've eliminated by some other experiment, and how they worked — to make sure the other fellow can tell they have been eliminated. . . . But this long history of learning not to fool ourselves — of having utter scientific integrity — is, I'm sorry to say, something that we haven't specifically included in any particular course that I know of. We just hope you've caught on by osmosis. The first principle is that you must not fool yourself — and you are the easiest person to fool. . . . I'm talking about a specific, extra type of integrity that is not lying, but bending over backwards to show how you're maybe wrong, that you ought to have when acting as a scientist. (1999 209, 211-12)

If deliberators fulfill their function in the ethical and political world, they will operate with a standard of integrity that matches or exceeds what Feynman describes for science, they will everywhere be designed knowing that the "first principle is that you must not fool yourself — and you are the easiest person to fool." The goal of forming a "more perfect Union" would thus include fostering the personal integrity of each individual, not just promoting the political harmony among individuals, groups, and states. Elsewhere Feynman asks: "Is no one inspired by our present picture of the universe? This value of science remains unsung by singers; you are reduced to hearing not a song or poem, but an evening lecture about it. This is not yet a scientific age"(1989 244). By celebrating "our present picture of the universe" in drama, dance, music, and art, Festival America provides a chance to make the twenty-first century a progressive scientific age, an opportunity to thoroughly infuse our ethical, political, and economic lives with the habits of mind that produced the transcendent achievements of mathematics, the natural sciences, and their technologies. The only way to insure that those achievements will not be employed contrary to public happiness is through a political system impregnated with honesty, and controlled by a people educated in the liberal arts. But that honesty and education requires extensive experience in deliberative soul-searching, whether within the individual, or in schools, juries, legislatures, or other social groups. Such experience could ennoble the American people to produce a greater extent, variety, and depth of human excellence than under any previous system of government; it could generate the greatness of vision required to choose, from among many possible technological and social futures, the most worthy set of aspirations for America. A celebration of that set in Festival America would define our character and articulate our dreams; it would honor, not just our present picture of nature, but our present picture of ourselves. The people would sing the body politic, and glory in their rebirth as American revolutionaries.

When Athenian democracy was young, the Greeks, although badly outnumbered, defeated the Persians at Marathon (490 B.C.), at Salamis (480 B.C.), at Plataea (479 B.C.). In 472 B.C. Aeschylus won first prize in the Athenian Festival for his play *The Persians*. In it, the Persian Queen asks who is king of the Athenians. The answer: "Of no man are they called the slaves or vassals"(1996 129; cf. Euripides 1998 55). For the Athenian audience where many, like Aeschylus himself, were veterans, and where all had relatives, friends, or associates who died fighting the Persians, this may have been the most soul-stirring line of poetry they had ever heard; for it meant their democratic valor in war (cf. Herodotus 1998 332) had protected Athens from becoming a new Miletus, which had been destroyed in 494 B.C. after the Greek city revolted against Persian subjugation; it meant that they would never have to prostrate themselves, as the Persians had to do, before any monarch; it meant that they were free of all political oppressors, whether foreign or domestic; it meant their unique democratic freedom would henceforth *define* them as Athenians; it meant that the flourishing of that freedom would honor, as nothing else could, those who fought and died for Athens' sake. By the beginning of the twenty-first century Philadelphia freedom secured, enlarged, and perfected Athenian freedom in many, many ways, but it did not remove the idols of the mind that pervert human reason, such as the *hubris* and *ate* that were so important in the demise of Athenian democracy. Were Americans to fully utilize public, private, and personal deliberators in a rebirth of Philadelphia freedom, they would forge within themselves a new civic character, by developing a bend-over-backwards honesty, an unyielding moral courage, and a deliberate sense which together could subdue *hubris*, *ate*, addiction to party, toxic self-deception, xenophobia, natural but fallacious habits of thought, and any other quality of mind that compromises the pursuit of excellence in the art of living. After the display of unprecedented integrity, tenacity, and democratic valor in wrenching, soul-searching defeats of these enemies within — moral equivalents of Marathon, Salamis, and Plataea — perhaps a play in Festival America would identify these new, new Americans by the phrase: "Of no corruption of consciousness are they called the slaves or vassals."

13

The Politics of Aspiration

Reflecting on the possible development of American perfectionist democracy, it might not be too rash to entertain the thought, at least as a possibility, that it is now feasible, for the first time in human history, to have a society that is both large, powerful, and just. In view of the failures of all societies to achieve justice, and of endless attempts by philosophers to even define it, one's suspicions at such a thought must be greatly aroused. But perhaps these suspicions are no different, and no more justifiable, than the suspicions of those who doubted the possibility that fatal childhood diseases could largely be eradicated. The good intentions and intelligence of individual physicians alone did not make that achievement possible; a diverse, scientific community was needed as well. If we are to substantially eradicate injustice, the good intentions and intelligence of politicians or judges are not enough. A diverse, political community of liberally educated citizens will be required, which is one of the reasons why all citizens should be liberally educated.

But what is justice? Before turning to its meaning we should distinguish between its substantive and procedural aspects. In the search for truth there is a mutual interdependence between theory, on the one hand, and observation and experiment, on the other. The content of the theory determines which observations and experiments are worth making, while the results of the latter tend to confirm or refute the theory. Sometimes a theory is so firmly believed that contrary observations are ascribed to experimental error, and sometimes there is such confidence in certain experimental procedures that one contrary observation will lead to the overthrow of a theory. Continual adjustments are made in theory and practice until there are no known contradictions in the theory, and nor any repeatable observations contrary to it. At this point the theory is considered true until such time as new contradictions are found, or new contrary observations are made. The mutual interdependence between theory and practice is sometimes called a *dialectical relationship*. There is just such a relationship between the substantive and procedural aspects of justice. Substantive justice is whatever fulfills the definition of justice, whereas procedural justice refers to those practices that define justice operationally (for example, a trial by jury). It is by systematic exploitation of a dialectical relationship that justice, no less than scientific truth, can be achieved. Continual adjustments are made in theory and practice until there are no known contradictions in the theory, nor any repeatable observations contrary to it (for example, by the substantively innocent, according to theory, being found "guilty" in practice). At this point the theory of justice is considered true until such time as new contradictions are found, or new contrary observations are made.

We are now ready to look at the nature of justice. Traditionally three kinds of justice have been distinguished: retributive, distributive, and social. The hardest to define — and the most controversial — is social justice. We can understand it by first looking at the mathematical concept of a *fractal*. The term was coined by Benoit Mandelbrot and is explained in his books: *Fractals: Form, Chance, and Dimension* (1977) and *The Fractal Geometry of Nature* (1982). Fractals are mathematical objects that can have the property of self-similarity with respect to shape, not unlike the series of ever smaller images seen by a person between two mirrors. There is similarity under magnification. Only an ideal mathematical figure could possess exact scale invariance, that is, geometric self-similarity, down to an arbitrarily small scale. The images in two actual mirrors, for example, will not be precisely similar due to limits of resolution and imperfections in the reflecting surfaces. However, we can say that such images possess self-similarity within certain limits of scale. An object that possesses the property of self-similarity with respect to some quality (such as shape), but has that self-similarity only within certain limits of space and time, will be called *fractal-like*.

Some objects are fractal-like only in a statistical sense. Thus, imagine looking at a coastline from above the surface of the earth at successive heights of 100 miles, 90 miles, . . . , 10 miles, and 1 mile. In a statistical sense there is self-similarity with respect to shape, that is, by looking at the shape alone there would be no way to tell how high we are. Other examples of shapes that can have statistical self-similarity are mountains, craters on the moon, or the arrangement of stars in the sky. An auditory example is static on a radio: unlike a speech or music, if you record it and then speed up the tape, or slow it down, it is not distorted; it still sounds like static.

Now consider that there is a principle of minimum space and time that applies to the identity of objects or function (Collingwood 1960 17-27). This means is that below the minimum it no longer makes sense to apply some given concept. For example, it would seem that you could have any amount of water. Yet if one is speaking about an amount of space smaller than a molecule of water, the concept of water no longer applies, although that of hydrogen, or oxygen may still be relevant (depending on the size of the space). The principle of minimum space and time applies to fractal-like objects. For instance, consider the geographic problem of determining the length of a coastline between two coastal points A and B that are a thousand miles apart as measured in a straight line. Clearly the coastal distance is longer, but how much longer? A little reflection will show that the answer depends on the length of the measuring rod used. If the rod is ten miles long, the distance will be less than if it is one mile long. If the rod is only one yard in length, measurements around boulders would have to be taken. If the rod is reduced to a tenth of an inch, then it would be necessary to take measurements around small pebbles. And with the next wave the pattern of pebbles could change, so one could then speak of the length of the coastline only at an exact time of a given day, measured, say, to the millionth of a second. Here we have geographic nonsense; that is, there is a limit of both space and time below which "the concept of coastline ceases to belong to geography" (Mandelbrot 1977 44). Naturally it is up to geographers to determine that lower limit. Hence there is no definite answer to the question "How long is the coastline of Great Britain?" apart from a specification of the length of the measuring rod and the relevant time period. With such a specification two geographers working independently should get the same answer to the question within a certain margin of error.

Human activities also have a minimum space-and-time-threshold. We can take an hour-long walk or a ten-minute walk, but we cannot take a one-second walk. Similar remarks might be made about teaching a class, inciting a revolution, devising a theory, or taking a nap. An illustration of going below the space threshold for owning a piece of land can be found in a promotion by the Quaker Oats Company made in the1950s. It gave away "ownership" of one-inch-square pieces of the Yukon and then had potential legal problems when some of the children grew up and, as adults, claimed their land (Lublin 1974 1). Not to be outdone, speculators in the 1990s sold one-inch square pieces of American real estate to Chinese citizens. As one buyer griped: "What we bought is not a piece of land at all. . . . What we have is just a piece of paper. We can't even resell the land on our own. The only thing we can resell are the pieces of paper"(WuDunn 1993 1).

With this background social justice can be defined: *social justice in a society is the statistical similarity of all relevant groups with* respect to rightful pursuit of happiness. This definition gives the substantive meaning to the term. Procedurally, however, the meaning of "statistical similarity," "relevant group," or "rightful pursuit of happiness" must be forensically determined by the informed values and considered judgments of the people speaking through courts of common reason. For example, how alike do two groups have to be to be "statistically similar"? Or what is a "relevant group"? These are empirical questions that apply only for a given space and time. For example, the adjudication of a dispute between two children fighting over the most desirable space in the back seat of a car during an hour-long automobile trip with their parents is not a question of social justice. Both the time and the size of the group — each "group" has one person each — is too small. Again, the people might decide that, even if law-abiding citizens have greater opportunities for happiness than law-violating citizens (many of whom are imprisoned), there is no violation of social justice since these are not relevant groups in its determination. A life of crime is not a rightful pursuit of happiness.

Even though Aristotle did not have the concept of social justice, he did connect the ideas of justice and happiness: "so that in one sense we call those acts just that tend to produce and preserve happiness and its components for the political society"(1984 2:1782). Yet talking about an Aristotelian-type happiness in an hour is like talking about taking a one-second walk. On the other hand, Aristotle perhaps went too far in the other direction when he claimed, following Solon, that the proper time for measuring happiness was a "complete life"(1984 2:1735; cf. Sophocles 1994 483, Herodotus 1998 13-16, Plutarch 1914 1:483). Thus it seems to make good sense to say, "She had a flourishing life in the decade of the 1960s." Let us suppose, for the sake of illustration, that the Court of Common Reason decides that male and female are the only relevant groups and that a reasonable period is ten years. Further, suppose that, on average, randomly chosen females would, in the judgment of the Court, have equal opportunity for a flourishing life in the next decade as randomly chosen males. Then, if that prediction proves correct in the judgment of the Court, social justice would have prevailed (in an operational sense) for that decade.

Equality with regard to some property often necessitates inequality with respect to some other property. Thus if balls of iron, oak, and styrofoam are made equal in size they would be unequal in weight. If the state promises the equal protection of the right to life for each individual, then it cannot equally divide its resources in providing that protection. The witness who has been threatened by organized crime needs much more of the state's police resources than the average citizen. Equality of rights, therefore, may justly lead to inequality in the distribution of the means used to achieve that equality. What is true of individuals can also be true of groups. To equally protect the pursuit of happiness for certain minorities might require unequal use of the state's resources. What constitutes equality, and what means are legitimate to achieve it — indeed the entire content of social justice for a given place and time — rests on a politics of self-knowledge, without which social justice is incapable of an evidence-based, procedural definition.

Some thinkers deny that social justice makes any sense at all, while others have a permanent criticism of any society — it always fails at social justice. The situation is like the coastline of an island. The first kind says in effect that a coastline has no length since there is no definite answer as to its length, while the second always criticizes any distance as too short and then proposes smaller units of measurement. If the first kind of thinker prevails, it encourages an indifferent or callous attitude toward vulnerable groups; if the second, the relevant groups for social justice become smaller and smaller until they are individuals, and statistical similarity is interpreted so strictly that it becomes virtual identity. By the latter standard only a procrustean society of clones in a highly uniform environment would be socially just. With no means to set authoritative limits, the demand for social justice for vulnerable groups can lead to indefinitely large interference in the liberties of groups that are not vulnerable. Just as the community of geographers must have procedures to give an operational significance to the measurement of a coastline, so the political community must have procedures to give operational meaning to the measurement of social justice. The Court of Common Reason, by providing that meaning, makes it possible and reasonable to have the goal of social justice as an essential part of the pursuit of public happiness. In short, common reason is what operationally defines the common good.

The idea that the moral force of juries is the foundation of democratic justice can be found in ancient Greece. These are the words of Demosthenes when speaking to a jury:

> For if you would only examine and consider the question, what it is that gives you who serve on juries, such power and authority in all state-affairs, whether the State empanels two hundred of you or a thousand or any other number, you would find that it is not that you alone of the citizens are drawn up under arms, not that your

physical powers are at their best and strongest, not that you are in the earliest prime of manhood; it is due to no cause of that sort but simply to the strength of the laws. And what is the strength of the laws? If one of you is wronged and cries aloud, will the laws run up and be at his side to assist him? No; they are only written texts and incapable of such action. Wherein then resides their power? In yourselves, if only you support them and make them all-powerful to help him who needs them. So the laws are strong through you and you through the laws. Therefore you must help them as readily as any man would help himself if wronged; you must consider that you share in the wrongs done to the laws, by whomsoever they are found to be committed. (1935 150, 151).

Courts of Common Reason are meant to bring about the final triumph of this conception in America; that is, the moral force of the people, exercised through juries, must continually control the actual administration of the laws. "We think in America," said Jefferson, "that it is necessary to introduce the people into every department of government as far as they are capable of exercising it; and that this is the only way to ensure a long-continued and honest administration of it's powers"(above, page 7).

Keeping this conception in mind let us consider retributive and distributive justice. Both are concerned with desert, that is, with the assignment, respectively, of deserved punishments and deserved rewards. "Deserves" is used in the wide sense of the term, as when we say such things as: he deserves to be punished since he committed the crime, she deserves the money since she earned it, he deserves the inheritance since he is the only living relative, or she deserves the food because she is the only one who is starving. In practice, "deserve" must be defined by advisory juries that might decide, for example, that healthy persons with good educations deserve only whatever salary they can get in a free market, or that persons seriously retarded from birth deserve a certain income each month. Hence it will be up to the government to devise laws to ensure a free and honest market so the former get what they deserve, and to ensure that fallback public welfare is available whenever private welfare initiatives fail to deliver the monthly income that the latter deserves. America will be a retributively and distributively just society when each receives what is deserved according to the informed standards of the relevant community.

The quality of justice is one of the *identifying* characteristics of a political community; it is not merely *expressive* in the sense of transmitting an idea or feeling. A person who identifies herself as neat will continue to be neat even if she sees no one for the last thirty years of her life. A scientist wants *to be* right, a soldier wants *to be* brave, a person wants *to be* sane. The desire is existential, not merely expressive. Identification explains, I believe, why people vote in large elections; they would not be satisfied to merely express themselves as loyal democrats to others by going in a voting booth, and then secretly not voting since they believe their vote would not make any difference. Instead they want the pleasure and duty of acting in their American character, they want *to be* patriotic, which means, in the words of James Wilson, that "every citizen should consider the public happiness as depending on his single vote"(2007 1:292). Individuals frequently do not simply want to exist; they want exist as such-and-such, and they are often willing to pay a price — sometimes a substantial price — to achieve that end. Again, they want *to be* honest, not merely considered honest; they want *to be* praiseworthy, not merely praised; they want *to be* virtuous, not just seem so; they want *to be* happy, and not merely exude happiness (cf. Smith, Adam 1982 113-14). The same considerations hold true for a community. Suppose a prosecuting attorney learns that a friend has murdered a loner with no acquaintances. It is highly unlikely that anyone else will learn about the crime; and the friend states truthfully that he will henceforth be a law-abiding citizen. Nevertheless the attorney has no choice but to prosecute, if the community is going *to be* just, for if the murderer is not prosecuted, then the community compromises that identification. Thus it is not merely the fact that without punishments murders might increase; the identification of the political community as just requires punishment. By itself the liberal constitution that the Soviet Union adopted in 1936 tells little about the nature of that society, whereas an examination of which Soviets were actually punished, and for what acts, identifies the government as evil.

Retributive justice is sometimes claimed to be merely an outmoded doctrine endorsing unthinking retaliation. But that is not what is being depicted here. Rather it is what Joseph Butler described in 1726:

> The indignation raised by cruelty and injustice, and the desire of having it punished, which persons unconcerned would feel, is by no means malice. No, it is resentment against vice and wickedness: it is one of the common bonds, by which society is held together; a fellow-feeling, which each individual has in behalf of the whole species, as well as of himself. (1896 2:141)

"Deliberate resentment" is the term Butler uses for that "fellow-feeling," and if the term is understood here to mean that the resentment has been approved by the cool and deliberate sense of the community (a civicly controlled schadenfreude), we can say that deliberate resentment should be the foundation of retributive justice in America, a common bond that the people ought to cultivate in themselves, for example, by the kind of art they choose for Festival America, and for public schools. Further, students should get extensive practice as trial jurors by watching videos of trials, by deliberating on whether the defendant is guilty, and by comparing their deliberations with subsequent reflections by the jurors in actual cases. They could then discuss the quality of retributive justice in America, consider what changes they would make to improve it, and choose art to instill a common bond among themselves.

For political communities to be retributively just, punishments must be consistent with the deliberate resentment caused by a threat to the identity of the community. That identity will be determined by the kind of community the people wish to create and maintain. It will be up to an elite — political scientists, economists, lawyers, legislators, and so forth — to devise the simplest or most beautiful set of laws necessary to counter those threats, and then be up to administrators of justice — police, judges, lawyers, jailers, parole officers — to devise systems to carry out the laws effectively. This scheme is meant, in a contemporary setting, to embody the spirit of Jefferson's reflection: "Were I called upon to decide whether the people had best be omitted in the Legislative or Judiciary department, I would say it is better to leave them out of the Legislative. The execution of the laws is more important than the making [of] them"(1950 15:283). To some degree that spirit is already found in Vermont, where lay judges, who represent the values of the people, sit beside legally trained judges and participate in their decisions. There have been many attempts to eliminate lay judges, but they have so far all failed. One can certainly make legitimate criticisms of lay judges, but the legislature has not tried to replace them with a process that would ensure that the day-to-day operation of the court has the informed approval of the people. A Vermont Court of Common Reason could capture the spirit of Jefferson by embedding the common reason of the people into the exercise of the state's police and judicial power, so that the deliberate resentment that Vermonters feel toward wrongdoers is accurately reflected in the operation of their laws.

Let me emphasize once again the importance of having national and state Courts of Common Reason consider hypothetical case after hypothetical case of crimes and punishments for each. Their decisions would determine the common law (above, page 190). It would be the job of the trial jury or judge to determine which hypothetical case most closely fits the acts and circumstances of a guilty defendant. This determination would then assign the punishment, or a range of punishments, for the crime. Furthermore, the rules of trials could be changed to more nearly approach the following ideal: even a vigorous defense of a guilty person against a lukewarm prosecution would lead to a "guilty" verdict, whereas a lukewarm defense of an innocent person against a vigorous prosecution would still lead to a "not guilty" verdict. Here again hypothetical cases — and many experiments — would be indispensable in determining what changes, if any, to make in our present system. Finally, in specifying punishments, advisory juries must also be made aware that due to unavoidable randomness, to what evidence survives, to what witnesses are available, or to what they accurately remember, to mistakes by trial juries, and the like, the innocent will sometimes be convicted. They thus should weigh actual and hypothetical examples of wrongful punishments against those they propose for the guilty, and they should stipulate what would be appropriate for the state to do at the time of exoneration.

The identification of American communities as committed to the pursuit of happiness requires that punishments be retributive, but that very identification also requires, where possible, that they be reformative. For purposes of illustration let us imagine a group of inmates are just beginning a ten-year term for armed robbery. Let us suppose that any time after five years each will be eligible for parole provided they have spent, say, two thousand hours every year working successfully on liberal education and its practical application. "Men become builders by building, and lyre-players by playing the lyre," Aristotle said, "so too we become just by doing just acts, temperate by doing temperate acts . . . "(1984 2:1743). But such acts could be part of a game. Benjamin Franklin speculated that chess taught the moral dispositions of foresight, circumspection, and caution (1786 159). Today programmers, working with psychologists and others, should be able to devise specific interactive computer games so that play would require, in a virtual way, just acts, temperate acts and, in general, all the republican virtues, repeated and repeated and repeated until they become second nature for each prisoner. The aim would be to instill into the character of each prisoner the moral standards and manners that the American people expect of every free person. Further, by using their personal deliberators the robbers could learn about the possibility of flourishing and wonderful lives that are both greatly attractive to themselves — thus undermining a motive for crime — and acceptable to public Courts of Common Reason. Their emotional lives should be enriched as well, since their emotions — such as anger, fear, joy, shame — may appear at inappropriate times. For example, when Willie James Bosket, Jr., who was the most notorious criminal in the New York State prison system, got what he thought was proof that his father was a murderer, he was "thrilled"(Butterfield, Fox 1996 251). To help counter such destructive emotions we could have a competition for the best artistic productions that illustrate armed robbery from the victim's point of view. Inmates could be required to demonstrate knowledge of the winning artistic productions. Further, work might be required to compensate the victims of the robberies. The aim would be to give the criminals empathy for those injured by crime, an understanding of why justice requires that they be punished, and the habits, emotions, and experience necessary or desirable to live in a free society (such as feeling deliberate resentment at appropriate times). Perhaps, then, recidivism would be less likely. Great works of art have been produced when commissioned for many a purpose, so why not try to produce them to morally educate criminals? Maybe a work created under these circumstances might over time become as well-established as *Moby-Dick* or *Huckleberry Finn*. Teaching such art in schools might reduce crime in the next generation. In general, by requiring that inmates, to be eligible for parole, would have to satisfy the standards of civic and moral education laid down by the people, the freed convicts would each be in a better position than they were entering prison to successfully pursue happiness without violating any law. Again, my description is not meant to be complete or exact but to illustrate the kind of thing that ought to be done if punishment is to be in harmony with the informed values of the American people.

Distributive justice must likewise be procedurally determined by the standards of public deliberators. The identification of a society as distributively just requires that each individual be awarded according to the deliberate sense of distributive justice collectively held by the people. For example, a person might receive honors or money for contributions to the public happiness. "A perfect government," says an anonymous writer from Charleston in 1783, "should not only punish for crimes, but reward for a contrary conduct. Let humanity, public spirit and knowledge, be distinguished by particular honors"(RLGD 1783 25-6; cf. Pericles words in Thucydides 1928 1:341). The right to specify who deserves what with respect to such qualities as merit, need, wants, or aspirations is part of the political freedom of an independent people. For example, they might specify that all would deserve any wealth they could honestly get in an honest economy. In addition, advisory juries could decide a large number of hypothetical cases, on the basis of which public honors (such as the Presidential Medal of Freedom) or money (such as welfare) would be awarded. Administrators then could try, as closely as possible, to embody these values in practice.

To actually attain excellence justice would require much better measures than we now have. For instance, consider the principal indexes that are presently used to assess our nation's economic progress, say, the Gross Domestic Product, the unemployment rate, and the Consumer Price Index. These indexes could be moving in the "right" direction (the Gross Domestic Product rising, the unemployment index falling, and the Consumer Price Index remaining unchanged), but, in the considered judgment of the people, the state of the nation could be getting worse. For instance, if an increase in sickness or crime or pollution results in increased expenditure, the Gross Domestic Product goes up. Yet the people would not thereby be happier. *The people are the final authority and it is their considered judgments that must be measured if any index is to be regarded as an authoritative measure of their welfare.* Imagine applying this standard to the assessment to retributive justice. An advisory jury could by video review a trial, and then hear what, in retrospect, the police, judge, attorneys, defendant, trial jurors, and perhaps others have to say about it. The advisory jury could then discuss a series of questions such as: Were the selection procedures for the trial jury appropriate? Did the defendant have adequate representation? Was the punishment fair? Was the lawyer's fee appropriately determined? And so forth. On each of these questions the advisory jury would hear contrasting arguments (from people having no connection with the trial) that, for example, the jury selections procedures were or were not appropriate, or the defendant did or did not have adequate representation. Then, they will be asked: Overall, was the quality of justice in this case excellent, good, average, poor, or very poor? Using parallel deliberation (above, page 166), this procedure could simultaneously be applied to a random selection of trials and an index measuring the quality of retributive justice could be constructed. That index would, with a high degree of precision, give evidence to legislatures and judges of the quality of the judicial system and how it should be improved.

One could construct a similar index for distributive justice. The jury could answer such questions as: When a person purchases a house, or pays for hospital care, or takes a job, or receives welfare payments, is the transaction as honest and fair as it could be? Is the government doing an excellent, good, average, poor, or very poor job at devising laws to create a free and honest market, so that the healthy person with a good education gets what is deserved on the basis of merit? What kind of job is the government doing in administrating a backup welfare system so that, in case private charity fails, the person seriously retarded from birth gets what is deserved on the basis of need? From responses to such questions as these, an overall index of the quality of distributive justice could be devised and specific problem areas identified and remedied by legislatures.

Finally, we come to an index for social justice. Here advisory juries could interview randomly chosen citizens to determine, one by one, whether, the right to pursue happiness has been secured. For example, even if laws are equally applied, and there were equal opportunities in the economic and political spheres, it might be the habit of the majority to treat a minority with less dignity than others. Thus it might be common for someone to say "Thank you" if a Caucasian opens a door, but not otherwise. No law is violated, but many such habits in great variety can undermine the pursuit of happiness. By focusing on such issues, and by using an elaboration of techniques already suggested, it should be possible, though no doubt difficult, to devise an index of social justice.

The three kinds of justice are interrelated, so let us imagine that a single, unified *Justice* index is formed which combines retributive, distributive and social justice in relative amounts consistent with the informed values of the people. In America today a large number of ordinary polls are collected concerning the opinions and feelings of the public, but are any of them, or all of them together, as important as this one? The phrase "state-of-the-art" is applied to the most advanced devices and procedures to achieve a certain purpose. A state-of-the-art quest of justice would require the highest achievable standards in the measurement of the considered judgment of the people. One of the purposes of American perfectionist democracy is to create those standards so that individuals would have reliable feedback about the quality of their own society. That knowledge would create the conditions for relentlessly perfecting the pursuit of public happiness; it would enable us to make good on Benjamin Rush's claim that in America "the benefactor of mankind may realize all his schemes for promoting human happiness. Human nature here . . . yields to reason, justice, and common sense"(below, page 414). Again, efficiency would not be forgotten. Just as contemporary agriculture can produce more and higher quality food with far fewer farmers, compared with the eighteenth century, so we should aim, using a state-of the-art Justice index, to produce more and higher quality justice with far fewer lawyers and much less expense than we need today.

The possibility of a society with a continually rising quality of justice suggests another good measure of the caliber of government. One of the perennial criticisms of government by anarchists and libertarians is the coercive nature of taxation. But is it necessary to always exercise the coercive power? Even under the injustices experienced today, some people freely give money to the government out of their gratitude for what America has done for them. If each person's tax return contained a line, *"Additional voluntary tax,"* one could measure the percentage of these voluntary taxes compared to total tax revenues. We can guess that as American society becomes more just, this percent would increase. For instance, church giving suggests that those who believe they are tithing to a just God often do not resent those who pay little or nothing — even if they worship beside them. Some of these individuals want to *identify*, and not merely express, themselves as being grateful to God; the question whether anyone else knows about it, or what other people do, hardly enters their consciousness. The same holds true for those who want to *identify* themselves as patriots. Let us imagine that as justice increases so does voluntary taxation, because patriots are expressing gratitude to their country, until it is .01%, 1%, 5%, 10%, . . . , of total tax revenues. Then, one measure of the quality of government would be the increasing (or decreasing) percentage of voluntary taxation that members of the advisory juries freely contribute in their individual tax returns. For ease of exposition let us assume that the percentage of voluntary taxes given by the relatively informed (the advisory jury) is no different from that of the relatively uninformed (the people as a whole). We can then easily state a worthy long-term goal for America: to see if it is possible, by continually improving a state-of-the-art justice, to increase voluntary taxation to such an extent that coercive taxation becomes unnecessary. Coercive taxation would then become a fallback position to be used only when voluntary receipts are inadequate. No one knows if a completely voluntary system of taxation is possible where government precisely obeys the deliberate sense of the people. But let us suppose it is. We shall never bring about this desirable state of affairs unless we have a strong determination to improve the percentage of voluntary taxes to total tax receipts by making the economy more honest and the society more just. The attempt to make all taxation voluntary might not rest merely on selfless giving. Jefferson speaks approvingly of a case where "money is wanting for a useful undertaking, as a school, &c., for which a direct tax would be disapproved. It is raised therefore by a lottery, wherein the tax is laid on the willing only . . ."(1892 10 363; cf. Pufendorf 1934 2:769). Provided that the Court of Common Reason agrees that lotteries are appropriate way to raise taxes, there is no reason why they could not be used since all the reasons normally given — such as corrupting the people, or harming poor people disproportionally — would have, in the considered judgment of the people, been found to be unpersuasive.

A common criticism of American democracy is that the Declaration, the Constitution of 1787, and the Bill of Rights in fact produced only injustice for blacks, the poor, women, and Indians. White males, it is said, prosper at the expense of these groups, and this is no accident, as this was one of the intended effects of these documents. This charge has been discussed in Chapters 3 and 5 with respect to blacks. Here let us look at the other cases. First, the poor. The American economy is not only large; it is amazing and admirable in many ways. Yet when we look at it from the perspective of American political principles it has been a continuing disappointment. Since it is quite possible for a poor person to succeed in pursuing happiness and a rich person fail, the American political theory does not require equality of wealth. However, the kinds of poverty that make a life of excellence impossible should be defined by the Court of Common Reason and those kinds, as far as possible, be eliminated (recall Adams' comment above, page 280). Further, we should remember the distinction between voluntary and involuntary poverty (above, page 284). If poverty is valuable to some people, let them freely choose it. There is all the difference in the world between those who choose to be religious ascetics, on the one hand, and those children who suffer brain damage because their parents are too poor to get the right food, on the other. It does not take much exposure to such involuntary poverty to see that it is a great evil; voluntary poverty is something of a quite different order. There need be no attempt to eliminate it; indeed to attempt it would compromise individual liberty.

The Founders also wanted justice to include the rich. John Adams statement is perhaps typical: ". . . it must be remembered, that the rich are *people* as well as the poor; that they have rights as well as others; that they have as clear and as *sacred* a right to their large property as others have to theirs which is smaller; that oppression to them is as possible and as wicked as to the others; that stealing, robbing, cheating, are the same crimes and sins, whether committed against them or others"(1850 6:65; cf. 9). Adams surely means wealth acquired ethically, not wealth acquired through illegal or immoral means (cf. what I have called *democratic wealth,* above, page 282). Perhaps Adams was here influenced by *Leviticus* 19:15: "You shall do no injustice in judgment; you shall not be partial to the poor or defer to the great, . . ." In addition, the Bible has many injunctions to help the needy. This is well-known, but what is not so well known is that in ancient Greece there were also explicit statements favoring legal equality, and sympathy for the poor. Thus Demosthenes approvingly refers to a law which in part states: "And it shall not be lawful to propose a statute directed against an individual, unless the same apply to all Athenians"(1935 275; in eighteenth century language this would rule out bills of attainder). And Democritus expresses compassion for the poor: "When the powerful prevail upon themselves to lend to the indigent, and help them, and benefit them, herein at last is pity, and an end to isolation, and friendship, and mutual aid, and harmony among the citizens; and other blessings such as no man could enumerate"(Freeman 1966 114; cf. 103, 118; cf. also the words of Pericles in Thucydides 1928 1:323, 325). The Founders were in harmony with Biblical and pagan statements that were empathetic to the poor. Thus Madison remarks: "It is . . . certain, that there are various ways in which the rich may oppress the poor; in which property may oppress liberty; and that the world is filled with examples. It is necessary that the poor should have a defence against the danger"(Farrand 1937 3:451; cf. 1865 3:162, 1962 14:197-8). Behind the pseudonym of Publius, Hamilton could write: "Happy it is when the interest with which the government has in the preservation of its own power, coincides with a proper distribution of the public burthens, and tends to guard the least wealthy part of the community from oppression!"(1961 4:489). George Mason argued for "such a system of policy as would provide no less carefully for the rights . . . and happiness of the lowest than of the highest orders of Citizens" (Farrand 1937 1:49). John Adams also claimed that poor people have rights "undoubtedly, antecedent to all earthly government, — *Rights* that cannot be repealed or restrained by human laws — *Rights* derived from the great Legislator of the universe"(1977 1:112). The Founders did not want America to become a country where commercial values would always prevail over any other kind. In particular, they wanted property widely distributed so that a few rich, by controlling the subsistence of many, could not dominate the political process. In the words of Adams: "Harrington has Shewn that Power always follows Property. . . . The only possible Way then of preserving the Ballance of Power on the side of equal Liberty and public Virtue, is to make the Acquisition of Land easy to every Member of Society; to make a Division of the Land into Small Quantities, So that the Multitude may be possessed of landed Estates"(1977 4:210; cf. Harrington's definition of a *commonwealth* (2003 12)). Noah Webster agreed: "*A general and tolerably equal distribution of landed property is the whole basis of national freedom*"(1787 47). "[L]egislators cannot invent too many devices for subdividing property," Jefferson claimed, but he added that they should take "care to let their subdivisions go hand in hand with the natural affectations of the human mind"(1950 7:682).   He believed in progressive taxation: "Another means of silently lessening the inequality of property is to exempt all from taxation below a certain point, and to tax the higher portions of property in geometrical progression as they rise"(1950 8:682).   In addition, he argued that to "constrain the brute force of the people, [European governments] deem it necessary to keep them down by hard labor, poverty and ignorance, and to take from them, as from bees, so much of their earnings, as that unremitting labor shall deem necessary to obtain a sufficient surplus barely to sustain a scanty and miserable life"(1892 10:226). America offered a favorable contrast. He advocated educating the poor at public expense: "The object is to bring into action that mass of talents which lies buried in poverty . . . for want of the means of development . . ."(1903 15:156; cf. Thucydides 1928 1:323). Adams did likewise: "Laws for the liberal education of youth, especially of the lower class of people, are so extremely wise and useful, that, to a humane and generous mind, no expense for this purpose would be thought extravagant"(1850 4:199). Elsewhere he makes the point even more forcefully: ". . . the preservation of the means of knowledge, among the lowest ranks, is of more importance to the public, than all the property of all the rich men in the country"(1977 1:121). Paine suggested creating "a national fund, out of which there shall be paid to every person, when arrived at the age of twenty-one years, the sum of fifteen pounds sterling, as a compensation in part, for the loss of his or her [*nota bene*] natural inheritance, by the introduction of the system of landed property; And also, the sum of ten pounds per annum, during life, to every person now living, of the age of fifty years, and to all others as they shall arrive at that age"(1945 1:612-13). Perhaps this was the first proposal in America for Social Security. Franklin's statements on property are the most extreme: He states: "The Remissness of our People in Paying Taxes is highly blameable; the Unwillingness to pay them is still more so." He grants that "all the Property that is necessary to a Man, for the Conservation of the Individual and the Propagation of the Species, is his natural Right, which none can justly deprive him of" but he immediately adds that "all Property superfluous to such purposes is the Property of the Publick, who, by their Laws, have created it, and who may therefore by other Laws dispose of it, whenever the Welfare of the Publick shall demand such Disposition"(1907 9:138; cf. Locke's words above, page 39). In another place he makes unmistakably clear that the poor have a claim to property to protect their life and liberty in a manner equal to the rich:

> Private Property . . . is a Creature of Society, and is subject to the Calls of that Society, whenever its Necessities shall require it, even to the last Farthing; its Contributions therefore to the public Exigencies are not to be considered as conferring a Benefit on the Publick, entitling the Contributors to the Distinctions of Honor and Power, but as the Return of an Obligation previously received, or the Payment of a just Debt. . . . the important ends of Civil Society, and the personal Securities of Life and Liberty, . . . remain the same in every Member of the society; and the poorest continues to have an equal Claim to them with the most opulent, whatever Difference Time, Chance, and Industry may occasion in their Circumstances"(1907 10:59-60).

Of course, for Franklin as the other Founders, what constitutes "Necessities" or "public Exigencies" is something that must be decided in accordance with the cool and deliberate sense of the people.

For the United States to develop without both the rights of the poor and the rich being meticulously respected would violate the principles repeatedly expressed by those who founded it, in Madison's words, the United States "will equally respect the rights of property, and the property in rights"(above, page 43). Again, this issue was recognized by the ancient Greeks. Thus when speaking to a jury, Demosthenes says: ". . . if a poor man through stress of need commits a fault, is he to be liable to the severest penalties, while, if a rich man does the same thing through shameful love of gain, is he to win pardon? Where, then, is equality for all and popular government, if you decide matters in this way?"(1936 3:61; other expressions of equality can found in Isocrates 1928 3:345, Euripides 2002 265, 1998 55). Today we have the means both to measure, and maintain, legal equality. For example, each year public deliberators could examine, say, the ten richest and ten poorest persons accused of, or prosecuted for, the same type of crime. Any differences that violated the American people's sense of equal justice would have to be remedied by a change of law, administrative practice, and so forth. Were such tests and remedies regularly carried out, American society — using twenty-first-century standards — would finally live up to the words of the Magna Carta (1215): "To none will we sell, to none will we deny, to none will we delay right or justice"(Sandoz 1993 264). Again, consider two classes: first, those whose net worth is about a million dollars and, second, those whose net worth is about a thousand dollars. Comparing members of one class with members of the other, we can ask: Are they equally likely to lose, say, half their net worth through force or fraud, or through a inflation over time? If not, then there is no equal security of property, no equal protection of the laws, no economic justice.

Now let us consider justice for women. When Lucretia Mott, Martha C. Wright, Elizabeth Cady Stanton, and Mary Ann McClintock organized the Seneca Falls Convention in July of 1848, a meeting that marked the beginning of the woman's movement in this country, they chose an extended paraphrase of the Declaration of Independence in which to express the sense of the convention. It asserted that "we hold these truths to be self-evident: that all men and women are created equal"(Stanton, Anthony, and Gage 1899 1:70). The Declaration, and the natural rights tradition on which it is based, furnish no valid arguments that allow sex to be used to deny equality of rights. For instance, James Otis raised these questions in 1764: "Are not women born as free as men? . . . . Whether every man and woman were not [in a state of nature] equal? . . . . If upon the abdication [of the king] all were reduced to a state of nature, had not apple women and orange girls as good a right to give their respectable suffrages for a new king as the philosopher, courtier, petit maitre and politician? "(4, 6). A government founded on reason and justice must be founded on voluntary agreement and it would not be reasonable for women to freely agree to an inferior position in any compact that forms a state. However, unlike the application of the Declaration to blacks, which was clearly understood (although betrayed) in the eighteenth century, its application to women was not nearly so clear. *That women could not be denied the right to vote because their husbands or fathers have the right to vote* was, in the Founding era, an underived implication of the Declaration. The question of suffrage for women turned on the question of independence. As Alexander Hamilton pointed out in a different connection, "In the general course of human nature, *a power over a man's subsistence amounts to a power over his will*"(1961 4:663). Thus a person with land could participate in public affairs according to his best judgment of right and wrong, rather than being controlled by those who had a power over his livelihood. Hamilton elsewhere quoted Blackstone on this point with regard to voting: "The true reason . . . of requiring any qualification, with regard to property in voters, is to exclude such persons, as are *in so mean a situation*, that they are esteemed to have *no will* of their own. If these persons had votes, they would be tempted to dispose of them, under some undue influence, or other. This would give a great, an artful, or a wealthy man, a larger share in elections, than is consistent with general liberty"(Hamilton 1961 1:106; cf. Blackstone 1771 1:171, Montesquieu 1989 160 Adams 1977 4:210, Gouverneur Morris in Farrand 1937 202-3). This argument was more plausible in the eighteenth century than it is for us because voting was not then generally secret. Still, even at that time, some understood the weakness of such reasoning. Limiting voting privileges to freeholders, Madison points out "violates the vital principle of free Govt. that those who are to be bound by laws, ought to have a voice in making them"(Farrand 1937 3:453). The Founders did not seriously consider that the lack of independence for women might be due to unjust human laws rather than something built into women's nature.

The full implications of axioms of politics may be no more obvious than the full implications of axioms in mathematical thought. Thus just as Euclid did not see that it is impossible to trisect an arbitrary angle, given the axioms for his geometry, so Jefferson did not see that it is impossible to deny women the right to vote, given the axioms for his politics. In the eighteenth century, the term "men" included women in general contexts, and thus also in the axiom: "all men are created equal." For example, in 1752 David Hume wrote: "For as there is in all men, both male and female, . . . "(1985 381) and in 1792 Edmund Burke said: "Without this help such a deplorable Havock is made in the minds of men (in both sexes) . . . "(1958 7:390). A 1784 act of Rhode Island stated that "all men are entitled to life, liberty, and the pursuit of happiness . . . Be it therefore enacted . . . that no person or persons . . . shall be deemed or considered . . . slaves . . . in consequence of the condition of their mothers . . ."(RSRI 1865 7). I don't believe there is a single instance in any American eighteenth-century source whatsoever, where "men" in the Declaration, or in "all men are born free," or in a similar phrase, was understood as implying the freeing of male, but not female, slaves. In 1770 Jefferson himself gave the following argument in court: "Under the law of nature, all men are born free, every one comes into the world with a right to his own person, which includes the liberty of moving and using it at his own will. This is what is called personal liberty, and it is given him by the author of nature, because necessary for his own sustenance. The reducing the mother to servitude was a violation of the laws of nature . . . "(1892 1:376; cf. Locke 1988 394). To understand the word "men" in the Declaration as definitely or probably not applying to women is not to understand the term as it was commonly used in the eighteenth century.

Yet Jefferson did not draw the political implications. Thus in 1816 he wrote: "Were our State [Virginia] a pure democracy, in which all its inhabitants should meet together to transact all their business, there would yet be excluded from their deliberations, 1, infants, until arrived at years of discretion. 2, Women, who, to prevent depravation of morals and ambiguity of issue, could not mix promiscuously in the public meetings of men. 3, Slaves, from whom the unfortunate state of things with us takes away the rights of will and of property"(1892 10:45-6; cf. also 9:7 and Parsons 1778 28-9). The reasons given with respect to women are as fallacious as those with respect to slaves — the "unfortunate state of things" for slaves was not ordained by God or Nature, but by Virginians like Jefferson. Yet it by no means follows that the fallaciousness with respect to women was then as easily seen. The principal reason for this, I believe, is that it is easier to see a dark complexion or kinky hair as irrelevant to politics than it is to see sexual differences in this light. Nevertheless Jefferson in an abstract way had some inkling that the tradition in which he believed presupposed the full equality of women. Among barbarous people, he says, "force is law. The stronger sex imposes on the weaker. It is civilization alone which replaces women in the enjoyment of their natural equality"(1903 2:84). John Adams was also aware of the political equality of women in the abstract: "Whence arises the Right of the Men to govern Women, without their Consent?"(1977 4:208) but he never gave an answer.

Of course, some could see more clearly and concretely. In 1773, "Sally Tickle" complained:

> That the Men were always jealous of the intellectual Talents of Women, is very clear, from the Pains which they have always taken to exclude them from a Share in the Administration of publick Affairs, to debar them from a liberal Education, and on the contrary, to employ their Minds on Trifles. .... Let me press you then, — ye fair Ones, to know your own Importance, and to exert it. — — Confine your Attention no longer to the Concerns only of a Family. — — Consider yourselves

as intitled to a Suffrage, and possessed of Influence, in the Administration of the great Family of the Publick — — (836)

In 1790, Judith Sargent Murray also objected to the claim that women's "domestick employments are sufficient":

> I would calmly ask, is it reasonable, that a candidate for immortality, for the joys of heaven, an intelligent being, who is to spend an eternity in contemplating the works of Deity, should at present be so degraded, as to be allowed no other ideas, than those which are suggested by the mechanism of a pudding, or the sewing the seams of a garment? . . . Yes, ye lordly, ye haughty sex, our souls are by nature *equal* to yours; the same breath of God animates, enlivens, and invigorates us . . . [F]rom the commencement of time to the present day, there hath been females, as males, who, by the *mere force of natural powers*, have merited the crown of applause; who, *thus unassisted*, have seized the wreath of fame. (1995 7-8)

According to a common eighteenth-century view, the love of fame is a mark of nobility (Adair 1972 336). Hume states that in a person ruled by the love of fame, the "animal conveniences and pleasures sink gradually in their value, while every inward beauty and moral grace is studiously acquired and the mind is accomplished in every perfection which can adorn or embellish a rational creature"(1957 96, cf. 1985 86). Hamilton refers to pursuit of fame as "the ruling passion of the noblest minds"(1961 4:613). In the words of Gouverneur Morris, this passion is "the great spring to noble & illustrious actions"(Farrand 1937 2:53) and, in the words of Madison, it helps motivate "continual exertions of Genius"(1962 1:112). Consider some examples: the young (24) John Adams said: "I am not ashamed to own that a Prospect of an Immortality in the Memories of all the Worthy, to [the] End of Time would be a high Gratification of my Wishes"(1977 1:42). The young (23) Lincoln said he had no ambition "so great as that of being truly esteemed by my fellow men, by rendering myself worthy of their esteem"(1953 1: 8; cf. Wilson 2007 1:536)). The belief that the love of fame can be an overpowering motivation in great men goes back to the *Iliad*, and in later classical times it was even claimed that a successful drive for fame constitutes happiness: "Opinions differ, but my idea of the truly happy man is of one who enjoys the anticipation of a good and lasting reputation, and, confident in the verdict of posterity, lives in the knowledge of the fame that is to come"(Pliny [the Younger] 1969 2:85). Yet, the love of fame can also produce vices. In his *Discourses on Davila*, John Adams gives a detailed discussion of the "*passion for distinction*" that he claims is "a principal source of the virtues and vices, the happiness and misery of human life; and that the history of mankind is little more than a simple narration of its operation and effects"(1805 6:232, 234). Whether the love of fame produces virtues or vices depends on the character of the group that bestows fame. Hence those politicians who seek fame amongst mobs are despicable demagogues, whereas those who pursue eminence among the best are great-souled statesmen. The latter pursuit becomes a virtue since it is often an essential motivation in "noble and illustrious actions" and "continual exertions of Genius." Those that reject such fame sometimes reject the virtues that deserve it, often the very virtues that sustain public happiness. Nevertheless, whether the lust for fame is vile or honorable, self-love is at its root. Wanting attention and praise, women in the eighteenth century could honorably use their self-love to energize the making of a wonderful pudding, or an exquisite garment. In itself there is nothing wrong with this. Free societies have a large, overlapping, multitude of ways to satisfy the craving for approval by others. That is part of the appeal of a diverse society. What is wrong, however, is that women did not have the same liberal education and political freedom as men; they could thus not use their love of fame in politics, as men could, to invigorate their love of country. Yet it is in politics that the greatest fame can be sought. Machiavelli said that "no man is so much exalted by any act of his as are those men who have with laws and with institutions remodeled republics and kingdoms; these are, after those who have been gods, the first to be praised"(1965 1:114; cf. Adams 1850 5:189). According to Bacon, the first place of "*Soveraigne Honour*" is to the "*Founders of States, and Common-Wealths*"; "In the Second Place are *Legis-latores, Law-givers*"(2000a 164). Hume takes up the same theme: "Of all men, that distinguish themselves by memorable achievements, the first place of honour seems due to LEGISLATORS and founders of states, who transmit a system of laws and institutions to secure the peace, happiness, and liberty of future generations"(1985 54). Hamilton thought of himself in these terms. "The station of a member of C-----ss [= Continental Congress], is the most illustrious and important of any I am able to conceive. He is to be regarded not only as a legislator, but as the founder of an empire. A man of virtue and ability, dignified with so precious a trust, would rejoice that fortune had given him birth at a time, and placed him in circumstances so favourable for promoting human happiness(1961 1:380-1). Eighteenth-century American women of "virtue and ability" could not aspire to such eminence. Because they were excluded from politics, women were denied "the first place of honour" that many of the Founders achieved; they were capable of political virtues, but were forbidden to cultivate them. In 1775, two years before Hume's comment was published and three years before Hamilton's, anonymous article in the *Pennsylvania Magazine* (edited by Thomas Paine) argued that since reason demonstrates the equality of men and women, a woman could rightly complain: "Alas! while your ambitious vanity is unceasingly laboring to cover the earth with statues, with monuments, with inscriptions to eternalize, if possible, your names, and give yourselves an existence, when this body is no more, why must we be condemned to live and to die unknown?"(Paine 1945 2:35, 38). Men alone have the opportunity to infuse their patriotism with a powerful ambition for lasting fame that is rooted in self-love. That self-love helps some males become heroes, but it also produces the "haughty sex" that denies women their equal rights. In contrast, women's self-love cannot energize them to seek the greatest fame among the best, whether for mortal fame among the best of their contemporaries, or for immortal fame among the best of their posterity. Although women are thus not "haughty," their virtues appear petty compared to males, and their exclusion from politics leads to the paradoxical consequence that their love of country must be dispassionate. As Abigail Adams wrote to her husband:

> Patriotism in the female Sex is the most disinterested of all virtues. Excluded from honours and from offices, we cannot attach ourselves to the State or Goverment from having held a place of Eminence. Even in the freeest countrys our property is subject to the controul and disposal of our partners, to whom the Laws have given a soverign Authority. Deprived of a voice in Legislation, obliged to submit to those Laws which are imposed upon us, is it not sufficient to make us indifferent to the publick Welfare? Yet all History and every age exhibit Instances of patriotick virtue in the female Sex; which considering our situation equals the most Heroick of yours. (Butterfield, Lyman 1963 4:328).

By the philosophy of the American revolution, as rightly articulated by "Sally Tickle," Judith Sargent Murray, and Abigail Adams, women are morally equal to men; they ought to have the same opportunity as men to have their craving for fame animate their duty to create, preserve, and improve republican government. The love of political fame in women exhibited itself quite early in human history. More than three thousand years before the American revolution the Egyptian pharaoh Hatchepsut had an inscription put at the base of one of her obelisks: "Now my heart turns this way and that, as I think what the people will say. Those who shall see my monuments in years to come, and who shall speak of what I have done"(Tyldesley 1996 210). Some eighteenth-century women wanted the political fame that we know Hatchepsut gained, but they wanted it based on deserved "patriotick virtue." However, American laws made that fame impossible. Today these laws have changed, but we do not create the moral and political technology that might securely transform the powerful motivation of self-love into "patriotick virtue." "Bards . . . hold the keys of the gate by which Patriots, Sages and Heroes are admitted to immortality"(1992 6:297) says Washington. If we only had a Festival America, the people could authorize bards to bestow "immortality" on those women and men who best promote and perfect public happiness. History, too, could make a contribution. Herodotus says that the purpose of his history "is to prevent the traces of human events from being erased by time, and to preserve the fame of the important and remarkable achievements produced by both Greeks and non-Greeks"(1998 3). Tacitus says that "my conception of the first duty of history [is] to ensure that merit shall not lack its record and to hold before the vicious word and deed the terrors of posterity and infamy"(1969 3:625). By institutionalizing a rigorous democratic evolutionary paradigm (above, page 178) that would allow the public to approve a history of America, we would have the first "people's history" that deserves the name. What greater goad to political virtue, for talented women or men, than to there receive an unqualified place of honor, and to forever keep that place whenever the history is revised?

Since the legitimacy of the Constitution as the foundation of law presupposes the unalienable right of sexual equality — otherwise the agreement of women to the original contract is either not reasonable or not voluntary — what is presupposed by that Constitution cannot be legitimately contradicted within it. When describing the origin of a just political society, Madison said that "each individual being previously independent of the others, the compact which is to make them one society must result from the free consent of *every* individual"(1962 4:392). By this reasoning the Constitution, if it is legitimate, must presuppose sexual equality. George Clinton stated that the constitutions of free governments can be abused by legislators: "When laws are made, not contradictory to the letter of the constitution, but repugnant to the general good, the constitution is violated; because the general good is the foundation of the social compact(1998 10). The Ninth Amendment was intended to prevent such legislative abuse. In any case, sexual distinctions are not made anywhere in the Constitution of 1787, or in the Bill of Rights; the language is in terms of persons, and women are persons. Since the states set the requirements for voting, they were certainly free to give women the right to vote. In fact, beginning in 1776, women had and exercised their (constitutional) right to vote in New Jersey, and they kept that right until it was denied in 1807 (for details, see Klinghoffer and Elkis 1992). What was not clearly understood in the eighteenth century is that, since republican government presupposes political equality for women, and since the "United States shall guarantee to every state in this union a Republican form of government"(Article IV, Section 4), it was the duty of the federal government to secure their right to vote. After all, if, in articulating republican theory in opposition to the lack of American representation in Parliament, it was claimed that virtual representation is an "exploded Notion"(MTCP 1768 1), a "pernicious Doctrine"(JVP 1769 65), which "has been so often and so clearly refuted"(VPHR 1777 64), so that a state that gives only virtual representation deserves only virtual taxes and virtual obedience (cf. TJG 1794 153), then moral consistency does not allow women in general, much less single women with property, to be given only the virtual representation of their husbands or fathers (cf. Christian 1801 117). Of course, many leaders — either political or intellectual — might have denied such an implication; yet it is far from certain that the deliberate sense of the American people at that time would have proclaimed that patriotism in females (but not males) must be a disinterested virtue. But suppose it did. Such an issue transcends voting and the law. As Jefferson said: "This country, which has given to the world the example of physical liberty, owes to it that of moral emancipation also. . . . . The inquisition of public opinion overwhelms in practice the freedom asserted by the laws in theory"(Cappon 1959 2:569).

A purely procedural republic, then, with strict equality before the law, might be inadequate to achieve the ideals of the American revolution. It is possible for equality of males and females to exist in a technical, legal sense, but the actual operation of society to be socially unjust. For instance, many parents might give their sons numerous advantages that they deny to their daughters. If the American people as a whole aspire to republican virtue, experiments in Courts of Common Reason and Festival America could allow this sort of social injustice to be adequately defined, faced, and remedied, not by new laws, but by changes in public sentiment. To see how let us begin by considering a person who has lost a limb but, paradoxically, the limb *feels* both paralyzed and painful. The psychologist Vilayanur Ramachandran has shown that by using mirrors and other devices for creating carefully chosen illusions, the "paralysis" can be removed and the pain ceases, even though the patient knows they are illusions. Now remember James Sullivan whose reason told him to be a "pure republican" but that required blacks to be treated equally; "There is an objection to this, which embraces all my feelings; that is, that it will tend to a mixture of blood, which I now abhor"(above, page 122). In many, if not all, such cases where reason conflicts with moral feelings, might it not be prudent to test whether the paralysis and pain could be removed by having artists and psychologists cooperate to create carefully chosen illusions where again, all involved know they are illusions? Suppose that experiments in the Court of Common Reason show that the reason of the people is for strict moral, legal, and social equality between men and women, but nevertheless the people generally feel that women are inferior. In such a case, the people should be tested to see whether they would chose art in Festival America that might free them from their moral paralysis and the social pain that such paralysis entails. If illusions in the physical world have beneficial effects in minds suffering from irrational feelings, would it not be worth investigating whether illusions in the political world could also have beneficial effects? Ramachandran claimed that he had produced 'the first example in medical history of a successful 'amputation' of a phantom limb"(1998 49). It would be excellent evidence that the American revolution is awake and thriving, were the United States to become the first country in political history in which the people habitually modified their feelings to harmonize with their reason; in particular, the first country in which the people themselves selected art that produced successful amputations of what their common reason identified as their own phantom fears and moral delusions. Republican virtue will have reached an unprecedented level of excellence, and we could justly boast that America has paid what it owed to the world by giving to it a paradigm of moral emancipation.

    Finally, let us turn to the status of the American Indians. While it is true that the Declaration spoke of "merciless Indian Savages," they were referred to when speaking of warfare. There is no question that they were meant to be included in the equality proclaimed therein. "I believe the Indian . . . to be in body and mind equal to the white man", Jefferson declared (1892 3:138; cf. 1903 3: 78, 1950 8:185. See also Locke 1975 646 and 1989 206). Adams said that the "Indians had a right to life, liberty, and property in common with all men . . . "(1850

10:359). It is also clear that the Indian was often held in high esteem by whites (see Hallowell 1963 and Eid 1981). Here are some descriptions from eye-witnesses in the eighteenth century:

> One must have seen these people (the Indians I mean) to have any idea what a noble animal man is, while unsophisticated. I have been often amused with the descriptions that philosophers, in their closets, who never in their lives saw a man but in his improved or degraded state, give of uncivilized people; not recollecting that they are at the same time uncorrupted. . . . Of the class of social beings (for such they were) of whom I speak, let us judge from the traders who know their language and customs, and from the adopted prisoners who have spent years among them. How unequivocal, how consistent is the testimony they bear to their humanity, fortitude, fidelity, and generosity . . . (Grant 1846 50-1; cf. Atkin 1954 38)
>
> As moral men they [that is, the Indians] certainly stand in no need of European civilization. They are just, honest, liberal and hospitable to strangers; considerate, loving and affectionate to their wives and relations; fond of their children; industrious, frugal, temperate and persevering; charitable and forbearing. I have been weeks and months amongst them and in their towns, and never observed the least sign of contention or wrangling: never saw an instance of an Indian beating his wife, or even reproving her in anger. In this case they stand as examples of reproof to the most civilized nations, as not being defective in justice, gratitude, and a good understanding . . . (Bartram, William 1928 385)
>
> . . . the savages of North-America, are infinitely more virtuous than the inhabitants of the most polished nations of Europe. (Coram 1791 10)

The Indian way of life was often extremely attractive to whites. Again and again when whites lived with them and adopted their customs, they would refuse to return to "civilization," or returned only very reluctantly (see, for example, Franklin's account in 1959 4:481-83 or Crèvecoeur's in 1926 214-15). Patrick Henry thought so highly of the Indians that he supported a bill in the Virginia legislature that would give cash to encourage intermarriage among whites and Indians, and more cash for each child produced by such unions. By such means, he thought, we could produce both peace with the Indians and a superior race of human beings (Wirt 1847 170-74). John Marshall also supported the bill (Beveridge 1916 1:239-41). Even Jefferson approved of the mixing of whites and Indians (1903 10:363, 14:23, 16: 439, 452, 464).

The Indian way of life gave white Americans an example of what they believed was perfect freedom in a state of nature. Gouverneur Morris said that the "savage State was more favorable to liberty than the Civilized; and sufficiently so to life. It was preferred by all men who had not acquired a taste for property . . . "(Farrand 1937 1:533). Hence it is not surprising that the American revolutionists adopted an extraordinarily strict standard for a government to be good: No government is good unless people in an Indian-like state of freedom would voluntarily choose to live under it. Such a standard leaves open the possibility that no government whatsoever is good. Of course, the American revolutionists opted for some government since they saw many of the inconveniences of an Indian way of life, not to mention the cruelties that sometimes accompanied it, such as frequent warfare among the tribes, or despicable tortures and executions of captives. This illustrates the insecurity of Indian freedom. It is also limited. Had there never been governments it is hard to imagine that a Franklin, for example, could have had the freedom to become a printer, or even have known that printing was possible. Nor did Indian freedom include the enjoyment of representative art. Thus when Washington showed a John Trumbull portrait of himself to some Indian leaders "they were for a time mute with astonishment. At length one of the chiefs advanced towards the picture, and slowly stretched out his hand to touch it, and was still more astonished to feel, instead of a round object, a flat surface, cold to the touch. He started back with an exclamation of astonishment — "Ugh!" Another then approached, and placing one hand on the surface and the other hand behind, was still more astounded to perceive that his hands almost met"(Trumbull 1841 165). *Perfect freedom in a state of nature* was not as great as the freedom that could be introduced under republican government where, according to James Wilson, "each gains more by the limitation of freedom of every other member, than he loses by the limitation of his own. The result is, that civil government is necessary to the perfection and happiness of man"(DHRC 1976 2:356-57; cf. Locke 1988 305-6 and Cicero 1988 233). Yet whenever there was any doubt, less government was a better choice. In the words of Jefferson: ". . . were it made a question, whether no law, as among the savage Americans, or too much law, as among the civilized Europeans, submits man to the greatest evil, one who has seen both conditions of existence would pronounce it to be the last . . . "(1892 3:195; cf. Paine 1945 2:610). The Northwest Ordnance of 1787 specifically recognized the right of Indians to their way of life: "The utmost good faith shall always be observed towards the Indians; their lands and property shall never be taken from them without their consent; and in their property, right and liberty they never shall be invaded or disturbed, unless in just and lawful wars authorized by Congress; but laws founded in justice and humanity shall, from time to time, be made, for preventing wrongs being done to them, and for preserving peace and friendship with them"(Thorpe 1909 2:961; cf. Jefferson 1903 16:197). On June 15, 1789, Henry Knox sent a report to George Washington that said:

> The Indians being the prior occupants possess the right of the Soil—It cannot be taken from them unless by their free consent, or by the right of Conquest in case of a just War—To dispossess them on any other principle would be a gross violation of the fundamental Laws of Nature and of that distributive justice which is the glory of a nation. (Washington 1987 2:491; for details on what Knox and Washington were attempting to do, and the problems they faced, see Ellis 2007 127-64.)

Yet the treatment of Indians since then, whether by individuals or by state and federal governments, has often been a paradigm of morally repulsive acts. Apart from experiments in the Court of Common Reason, in Indian courts of common reason, and in hybrid courts, where the subjuries consist of six Indians and six from the general population, how are Indians ever to receive the "distributive justice" that has so long been denied them? We could not even know, with any degree of detail, what that "distributive justice" should be. So many politicians today revere the American revolution, but where are those advocating the painstaking moral and political experiments that are the secure basis for justifying actions in its name? Without courts of common reason or their equivalent, the professional lives of our politicians are fated to be profoundly inauthentic.

To conclude, justice cannot be ready-made but must instead be tailored to the informed values of the people (cf. Jefferson's words, above, page 187). Just governments are ergonomic. Adam Smith understood this idea years ago:

> The man of system seems to imagine that he can arrange the different members of a great society with as much ease as the hand arranges the different pieces upon a chess-board. He does not consider that the pieces upon the chess-board have no other principle of motion besides that which the hand impresses upon them; but that, in the great chess-board of human society, every single piece has a principle of motion of its own, altogether different from that which the legislature might choose to impress upon it. If these two principles coincide and act in the same direction, the game of human society will go easily and harmoniously, and is very likely to be happy and successful. If they are opposite or different, the game will go on miserably, and human society must be at all times in the highest degree of disorder. (1982 233-34)

Courts of common reason can be used to create a state-of-the-art justice, where the "principles of motion" of the people and their government coincide, and "the game of human society will go easily and harmoniously." But it should not go too easily and too harmoniously, for the philosophy of the American revolution aims at the strenuous principles of government that take the people into account, not only as they are, but as they wish to become. "The happy life," Aristotle declared, "is thought to be one of excellence; now an excellent life requires exertion, and does not consist in amusement"(1984 2:1860). The pursuit of happiness is an enterprise requiring enormous energy; an excellent government should never let its people rest in continual amusement, rather, it should relentlessly goad them to fulfill their greatest aspirations.

14

The Aesthetics of Aspiration

A study of the history of mathematics and science suggests that we should always try to understand both the abstract and physical universes as aesthetic phenomena, since the yearning for the beautiful has often been the most important motivation in the creation of revolutionary new proofs, experiments, or theories. Consider the words of some eminent twentieth-century mathematicians and scientists:

Francis Crick: ". . . [Gunther] Stent had argued that a scientific discovery is more akin to a work of art than is generally admitted. Style, he argues, is as important as content. . . . But what I think is overlooked in such arguments is the intrinsic beauty of the DNA double helix. It is the molecule which has style, quite as much as the scientists"(1974 768).

Paul A. M. Dirac: "It is more important to have beauty in one's equations than to have them fit experiment"(1963 47). ". . . it's most important to have a *beautiful* theory. And if the observations don't support it, don't be too distressed, but wait a bit and see if some error in the observations doesn't show up . . . you feel [beauty in a theory] . . . Just like beauty in a picture or beauty in music. You can't describe it, it's something — And if you don't feel it, you just have to accept that you're not susceptible to it. No one can explain it to you."(Judson 1980 198-9). "With all the violent changes to which physical theory is subjected in modern times, there is just one rock which weathers every storm, to which one can always hold fast — the assumption that the fundamental laws of nature correspond to a beautiful mathematical theory"(1954 143). When Dirac was asked about the origin of his discovery of the Dirac equation he answered: "I was not trying to solve directly some physical problem but to look for some pretty mathematics"(Thomsen 1981 397). He even wrote a paper called "Pretty Mathematics"(1982).

Albert Einstein: "Our experience hitherto justifies us in believing that nature is the realization of the simplest conceivable mathematical ideas. I am convinced that we can discover by means of purely mathematical constructions the concepts and the laws connecting them with each other, which furnish the key to understanding of natural phenomena"(1954 274). "After a certain high level of technical skill is achieved, science and art tend to coalesce in esthetics, plasticity, and form. The greatest scientists are always artists as well"(Calaprice 1996 171). In 1947 Hermann Bondi met Einstein and reports: "What I remember most clearly was that when I put down a suggestion that seemed to me cogent and reasonable, he did not in the least contest this, but he only said, 'Oh, how ugly.' As soon as an equation seemed to him to be ugly, he really rather lost interest in it . . . He was quite convinced that beauty was a guiding principle in the search for important results in theoretical physics"(Whitrow 1967 82).

Murray Gell-Mann: Gell-Mann was asked "how much did he find himself consciously applying the criterion of elegance?" His answer: "Constantly! Nothing but. Well, I mean, that together with trying to get the thing right! Trying to explain the data. But, you know, frequently a theorist will even *throw out* a lot of the data on the grounds that if they don't fit an elegant scheme, they're wrong. That's happened to me many times . . . There were nine experiments that contradicted [the theory of weak interaction] — all wrong. Every one. When you have something simple that agrees with all the rest of physics and really seems to explain what's going on, a few experimental data against it are no objection whatever. Almost certain to be wrong. Einstein was not very much perturbed when some early experiments showed the special theory of relativity to be wrong"(Judson 1980 22).

G. H. Hardy: "The mathematician's patterns, like the painter's or the poet's, must be *beautiful*; the ideas, like the colours or the words, must fit together in a harmonious way. Beauty is the first test: there is no permanent place in the world for ugly mathematics"(1969 85).

Werner Heisenberg: Heisenberg answered a question of Einstein as follows: "I believe, just like you, that the simplicity of natural laws has an objective character, that it is not just the result of thought economy. If nature leads us to mathematical forms of great simplicity and beauty . . . to forms that no one has previously encountered, we cannot help thinking that they are 'true,' that they reveal a genuine feature of nature"(1971 68). In a letter to a relative Heisenberg states that "the whole terrain of interrelationships in atomic theory is suddenly and clearly spread out before my eyes. That these interrelationships display, in all their mathematical abstraction, an incredible degree of simplicity, is a gift we can only accept humbly. Not even Plato could have believed them to be so beautiful"(Heisenberg, Elizabeth 1984 143-4). Elsewhere he says that Plato believes "the soul is awe-stricken and shudders at the sight of the beautiful, for it feels that something is evoked in it that was not imparted to it from without by the senses but has always been already laid down there in a deeply unconscious region"(1990 171).

Roger Penrose: "How . . . does one decide which things in mathematics are important and which are not? Ultimately, the criteria have to be aesthetic ones . . . that is, artistic values such as one has in music or painting or any other art form. . . . Even in experimental work, aesthetic criteria are very important. After all, you can talk about a beautiful experiment. I think this is certainly something that is strived for. It may not be the only thing, but to have an experiment which for some reason has an elegance about it is, I think, regarded as a great virtue. . . . There is also a more subtle rôle played by aesthetics, in connection with research, namely, as a means for obtaining results. This is an important aspect of the rôle of aesthetics which I do not think has been discussed very much"(1974 266-267).

Henri Poincaré: "The scientist does not study nature because it is useful; he studies it because he delights in it, and he delights in it because it is beautiful. If nature were not beautiful, it would not be worth knowing, and if nature were not worth knowing, life would not be worth living. . . . intellectual beauty is sufficient unto itself, and it is for its sake, more perhaps than for the future good of humanity, that the scientist devotes himself to long and difficult labors"(1921 366-7). "It may seem surprising to see emotional sensibility invoked apropos of mathematical demonstrations which, it would seem, can interest only the intellect. This would be to forget the feeling of mathematical beauty, of the harmony of numbers and forms, of geometric elegance. This is a true aesthetic feeling that all real mathematicians know, and it surely belongs to emotional sensibility. . . . The useful combinations are precisely the most beautiful, I mean those best able to charm this special sensibility that all mathematicians know, but of which the profane are so ignorant as often to be tempted to smile at it"(392-93).

Bertrand Russell: "Mathematics, rightly viewed, possesses not only truth, but supreme beauty — a beauty cold and austere, like that of sculpture, without appeal to any part of our weaker nature, without the gorgeous trappings of painting or music, yet sublimely pure, and capable of a stern perfection such as only the greatest art can show. The true spirit of delight, the exaltation, the sense of being more than man, which is the touchstone of the highest excellence, is to be found in mathematics as surely as in poetry"(1957 57).

The aesthetic delight that creative adults enjoy is common in children. Consider the areas in which child prodigies are possible: mathematics, physics, music, chess, and the like. Outside the area of their precocity the children are often quite "normal." How does it come about that they have such an extreme interest? Their dedication seems to derive from the aesthetic delight they take in their creations or discoveries, be it a mathematical theorem, a musical piece, or a strategy to checkmate. We have met this world, they say, and it is ours. Even this may be an understatement. They might better say, we know a beautiful world in which we have become more than conquerors, we are its lord and master. This sense of being lord over creation, of being like God, is also found in ordinary children in their creative play. This playful power, which we can keep as adults, is a mark of humanity. Friedrich Schiller expressed the point in a pair of epigrams: "With beauty man shall *only play*, and it is *with beauty only* that he shall play. . . . man only plays when he is in the fullest sense of the word a human being, and *he is only fully a human being when he plays*"(1982 107).

In Euclid and Galileo, in Archimedes and Newton, in Gauss and Kepler, in Gödel and Einstein, we see again and again the enormous importance of the aesthetic element in mathematics, physics, and astronomy. This element provides a link between poetry and mathematics, play and physics, music and biology, dance and technology. These considerations suggest that economists, political scientists, lawyers and politicians might seek beautiful laws and institutions not only for their own delight, but as a guide to economic and political truth. If beautiful laws work in astronomy or subatomic physics, might not we, as part of nature, require beautiful laws to reach public happiness? If so, then our public life should reflect energetic, imaginative, and powerful aspirations toward the simple, the elegant, and the beautiful.

But when we look at most of our laws we find little to excite our aesthetic sense. It hardly matters where one looks: our penal laws or our tax laws, our antitrust laws or our laws about children, our laws concerning interstate commerce, or our laws concerning retirement. Aesthetically they appear to be a vast wasteland. There is a kind of incongruity here: DNA is beautiful, the cell is beautiful, the organs of the body are beautiful, the brain is of transcendent economy and beauty, but the aesthetic element is generally treated as irrelevant for our laws and institutions. Imagine the human organism where the DNA, the cell, the organs, the brain, were all designed according to the "aesthetic" standards that were used in the twentieth century in creating our laws? What would your body be like if it were designed by a Congress that applied no more aesthetic criteria than it had typically used in income tax statutes? Humans could hardly have survived for so long without the remarkable beauty of their bodies; we need to infuse a comparable beauty into the body politic. And here we may lay to rest the rationalization that we cannot do so because the American polity is too complex. For the human body is more complex, but is nevertheless remarkably beautiful, as scientists and artists have shown for centuries. To create moral beauty in the body politic, we need the biomimicry of the democratic evolutionary paradigm in courts of common reason (above, page 178). Darwin ended *The Origin of Species* (1859) with these words: "There is grandeur in this view of life, with its several powers, having been originally breathed into a few forms or into one; and that, whilst this planet has gone cycling on according to the fixed law of gravity, from so simple a beginning endless forms most beautiful and most wonderful have been, and are being, evolved"(1985 459-60). We should try to duplicate that grandeur in our moral and political growth. To do so we will need the discipline of evolutionary developmental democracy to understand the body politic, just as we need the discipline of evolutionary developmental biology to understand the plants and animals. There are exceptional opportunities here for a new depth in national self-knowledge.

The particle theorist looks for beauty and the technologist creates it, the naturalist finds it and the artist embodies it, but what happens to our aesthetic sense when civic questions arise? Why is it not present? We can make some progress toward an answer, I believe, by considering the history of science, in particular, by considering Aristotle's theory of motion. According to Aristotle, motion in general can be understood the way we understand the motion of animals, including humans. If we examine this motion we immediately notice that it is easier to account for how the motion begins and for what end it proceeds, than it is to explain the details of the motion itself. For example, if one person serves to another's backhand at tennis, the latter's soul (and sole) initiates a movement of its body with the goal of hitting the ball over the net. Such a movement is so complicated that even today it is probable that a full analysis could not be given. Hence it is not surprising that Aristotle thought that motion on earth was *incapable* of exact definition. For a motion as simple as dropping a ball there were difficulties: Although the beginning of the motion could be described (releasing the ball from one's hand), and the end (the earth for which the ball has a natural affinity), the fact of acceleration was left mysterious. On the other hand, Aristotle thought he could give a complete account of celestial motion: it is exact, uniform, circular, eternal, and flawless. In his book *On the Heavens* he maintained that "there is something beyond the bodies that are about us on this earth, different and separate from them; and that the superior glory of its nature is proportionate to its distance from this world of ours" (1984 1:449). The Roman tradition continued such otherworldliness in the writings of Cicero (1951 177) and Seneca: ". . . it is a narrow mind that finds its pleasure in earthly things; it should turn from these to those above"(1970 2:443). Contrast this otherworldly attitude with that of Francis Bacon, who said vile and ugly "things must be taken into natural history no less than the finest and most precious. For natural history is not thereby defiled. For the Sun enters sewers as much as palaces, but still stays clean. . . . . what is worthy of existence is worthy of knowledge . . . "(2004 179-80). The Bible, like the Greek and Roman tradition, also has many expressions of otherworldliness. For instance, "Do not love the world or the things in the world. If any one loves the world, love of the Father is not in him. For all that is in the world, the lust of the flesh and the lust of the eyes and the pride of life, is not of the Father but is of the world" (1 *John* 2:15-16; cf. *Matthew* 6:19-21). It is hard to imagine that the rise of science and technology had this passage consistently been taken to heart. The low value often put on earthly concerns by the Greeks, Romans, and Christians made Aristotle's theory of motion difficult to correct; a hard problem (understanding the nature of terrestrial motion) was made impossible to solve because the realm in which a solution could be found was beneath careful observation and thought. Aristotle's assumptions, unlike Bacon's or Galileo's, prevented him from conducting experiments needed to formulate of an adequate theory of motion. His fateful mistake was dividing motion into two kinds: one kind was superior, precise, perfect, eternal, and celestial, the other was inferior, indefinite, imperfect, perishable, and terrestrial (cf. Cicero 1951 177). Today, as a result of science from the age of Bacon and Galileo onward, we know that the same laws, and the same elements, are involved in both celestial and terrestrial motion. Aristotle's error was due to his deprecation of earthly matter, an error that was perhaps related to his social class, since he thought contemplation vastly superior to using one's hands to work with matter (which Galileo's approach to science required). Had Aristotle believed both celestial and terrestrial motion was worthy of careful examination and measurement, it is possible he could have learned what Galileo eventually discovered.

If we now return to the problem of determining the reason for our failure to apply aesthetic categories to our economic and political life, we find that we bifurcate our activities (as Aristotle bifurcated the universe): Some activities are worthy of our aspirations for perfection and some are not. Thus the artist, the mathematician, the scientist, the poet, the athlete, the craftsman, are all expected to discipline themselves to an excellence the rest of us can only admire. In contrast, it is common for us to be completely cynical about government and business; politics is base, and money is the Biblical "filthy lucre"(1 *Timothy* 3:3, *Titus* 1:11); political science studies the lust for power, economics, the vicissitudes of greed. The activities these disciplines study are appropriate for burlesque and jokes, for sarcasm and cynicism, for conspiracy theories and moral loathing; they are not a place to look for simplicity, beauty, excellence, perfection, or sacred honor. For the eighteenth-century American revolutionists, however, the public arena was just such a place. They rejected otherworldliness in general. George Logan is typical; he declares that the "Holy Writings" and "Reason" tell us "the end which God had in view with regard to his Creatures, and particularly with respect to Man, was a state of perfection and happiness in this world"(1798 6). The widespread acceptance by the revolutionists of the view that it is our nature to aspire to "perfection and happiness" led them to invest the here and now of public affairs with enormous value. Some came to this conclusion for purely secular or purely religious reasons. Most, however, blended their civic and religious convictions, as in the claim by Benjamin Rush that "a Christian cannot fail of being a republican"(above, page 29). This is a radical alternative to the otherworldliness common in Christian tradition, perhaps best epitomized by Tertullian's declaration (*circa* 197): "But we who are insensible to all that burning for glory and greatness, have no need of banding together, nor is any thing more foreign to our taste than public affairs"(1842 80).

Today, we don't believe in our own worth as civic beings. We have enormous scientific daring; we put the Hubble telescope in the heavens, aim it at the stars and, in spite of troubles along the way, are dazzled by the execution, the precision, the results; but we have no comparable political daring, we do not put Jeffersonian wards on earth, aim them at ourselves, with the hope of being dazzled by the execution, the precision, the results. Imagine that we somehow made contact with a civilization belonging to another solar system. One can almost hear members of Congress saying: "Nothing — nothing whatsoever in all of human history — is of greater consequence than to find out who we have contacted, and to explore their life and thought." But if someone proposed a mechanism to find out who *we* are, and the nature of *our* informed values and considered judgments, how much chance would such a proposal have? Wards — the "most admirable of all human contrivances in government"(Jefferson, above, page 161) — are not objects of great curiosity, much less are politicians trying to create them satisfying twenty-first-century standards of epistemological excellence. If the Search for Extraterrestrial Intelligence (SETI) were successful, we would certainly be willing to spend billions, perhaps trillions, investigating that intelligence, yet, with the spirit of 1776 in a slumber, we spend virtually nothing to communicate with our own terrestrial intelligence through a politics of self-knowledge. The terrestrial *we* is inconsequential; the celestial *they* is of transcendental importance. Otherworldliness grips our souls.

How would we, as Americans, have to change in order to remedy this situation? To answer this question, let us again temporarily turn from political science to natural science, in this case from the American revolution to the Einsteinian revolution. Consider Einstein's greatest achievement: the General Theory of Relativity. Many years after its discovery the physicist Leopold Infeld said to Einstein, "I believe that special relativity theory would have been formulated with but little delay whether or not you had done it. The times were ripe for it." Einstein responded: "Yes, this is true, but not of the general relativity theory. I doubt if it would be known yet"(Infeld 1950 46). What, then, enabled Einstein to discover the General Theory? It was not his mathematical genius. If he is compared with the best contemporary mathematicians and physicists in that regard, Einstein does not stand out (cf. Ohanian 2008). Hermann Minkowski claimed that "Einstein's presentation of his deep theory is mathematically awkward — I can say that because he got his mathematical education in Zurich from me"(Reid, Constance 1970 112). David Hilbert put the point humorously by saying: "Every boy in the streets of Göttingen understands more about four-dimensional geometry than Einstein." But Hilbert added, "Yet, in spite of that, Einstein did the work and not the mathematicians"(142).

Einstein discovered a General Theory before anyone else, not because he had an absolutely superior mathematical talent, but because he was almost alone in searching for it. What, then, inspired him to look? Einstein's answer: a deep feeling for the rational beauty of the world. It was here that Einstein surpassed those who were, mathematically speaking, in his league or above it. This is what led him for years to aspire towards a theoretical beauty and simplicity for which others were not sufficiently motivated to look. In this respect he justly bears comparison with Kepler and Newton. Since it was his principal motivation, we ought to let Einstein himself describe the feeling:

> Although it is true that it is the goal of science to discover rules which permit the association and foretelling of facts, this is not its only aim. It also seeks to reduce the connections discovered to the smallest possible number of mutually independent conceptual elements. It is in this striving after the rational unification of the manifold that it encounters its greatest successes, even though [*nota bene*] it is precisely this attempt which causes it to run the greatest risk of falling a prey to illusions. But whoever has undergone the intense experience of successful advances made in this domain, is moved by profound reverence for the rationality made manifest in existence. (1941 213-14; cf. 1954 52).
>
> To know that what is impenetrable to us really exists, manifesting itself as the highest wisdom and the most radiant beauty which our dull faculties can comprehend only in their most primitive forms — this knowledge, this feeling, is the center of true religiousness. In this sense, and in this sense only, I belong in the ranks of the devoutly religious men. . . . It seems to me that the most important function of art and of science is to arouse and keep alive this feeling in those who are receptive. . . . I assert that the cosmic religious experience is the strongest and noblest driving force behind scientific research. No one who does not appreciate the terrific exertions, and above all, the devotion without which

pioneer creations in scientific thought cannot come into being, can judge the strength of the feeling out of which alone such work, turned away as it is from immediate practical life, can grow.   What a deep faith in the rationality of the structure of the world, and what a longing to understand even a small glimpse of the reason revealed in the world there must have been in Kepler and Newton to enable them to unravel the mechanism of the heavens in long years of lonely work!   Any one who only knows scientific research in its practical applications may easily come to a wrong interpretation of the state of mind of the men who, surrounded by skeptical contemporaries, have shown the way to kindred spirits scattered over all countries in all centuries.   Only those who have dedicated their lives to similar ends can have a living conception of the inspiration which gave these men the power to remain loyal to their purposes in spite of countless failures.   It is the cosmic religious sense which grants this power"(1931 96-7; 100; 100-2).

It is interesting to compare Einstein's words with Jefferson's: "I hold (without appeal to revelation) that when we take a view of the Universe, in it's parts general or particular, it is impossible for the human mind not to perceive and feel a conviction of design, consummate skill, and indefinite power in every atom of it's composition"(Cappon 1959 2:592; cf. Cicero 1951 177, 217).   Before Darwin it was virtually impossible to explain the order in the universe otherwise than by an intelligence (called "Nature's God" in the Declaration).   Even Hume reluctantly reverted to such an explanation at the end of his *Dialogues Concerning Natural Religion* (1998 129-30).   Darwin, however, explained how order is possible without intelligence, and thus Einstein's views have a curiously anachronistic flavor.

In any case Einstein's feelings about the universe drove him to formulate general relativity, about which an early commentator exclaimed: "Einstein's theory has the very highest degree of aesthetic merit: every lover of the beautiful must wish it to be true"(X [pseudonym] 1919 1189; cf. also Lorentz 1920 23).   "The theory of relativity," Dirac observed, "introduced mathematical beauty to an unprecedented extent into the description of Nature"(1939 123).   If a person possesses a feeling for something comparable to that which Einstein has for nature, let us say that the person has a *perfectionist respect* for it.   Some, like Einstein, may identify that feeling as religious; others may not.   In either case, the person is so committed to find awesome beauty and excellence that neither the enormous force of accumulated knowledge (which does not recognize that beauty and excellence), nor contrary experience (which might undermine that beauty or excellence), will shake his or her conviction.   The "accumulated knowledge" is understood by the person as so-called knowledge, and the "contrary experience" as deceptive appearance. Perfectionist respect has led to great revolutions, but let us as well keenly remember that here also there is "the greatest risk of falling prey to illusions."

Now let us ask: who first took an attitude of perfectionist respect toward mathematical objects? We do not know, but it may have been certain pre-Socratic thinkers of whom the best known is Pythagoras. The perfectionist respect exhibited by his school enabled the Pythagorean theorem (and many other results) to be discovered. Perhaps this was the first time in history when theoretical reason was united with religious and aesthetic emotions in a sustained and substantial way. The invention of pure geometry — one of the greatest intellectual achievements of all times — must have seemed rather foolish to many in the age of Pythagoras. What is a point? That which has no part. What is a line? That which has length, but no breath. These aesthetic ideals, however, eventually enabled more practical-minded persons — such as architects or navigators — to understand their craft. The very conception of a *kosmos*, which the Pythagorean school introduced, implies a universe that is structurally beautiful and perfect (cf. Guthrie 1967 7:38-9). The vision of a universal, heavenly harmony set the stage for ancient Greek astronomy and subsequently inspired both Copernicus and Kepler.

A perfectionist respect for mathematical objects that is explicitly based on religion did not die with the Pythagorean school. Thus the mathematician Charles Hermite (1822-1901) writes: "There exists, unless I am mistaken, an entire world consisting of the totality of mathematical truths, which is accessible to us only through our intelligence, just as there exists the world of physical realities; each one is independent of us, both of them divinely created"(quoted favorably by the logician Kurt Gödel (1906-1978), see 1995 3:323; Gödel himself, the greatest logician of the twentieth century, believed in God and an afterlife.) Hermann Weyl (1885-1955), who made fundamental contributions to mathematics and physics, begins a lecture with: "A mathematician steps before you, speaks about metaphysics, and does not hesitate to use the name of God"(1932 1). Later he says that "the mathematical lawfulness of nature is the revelation of divine reason"(11). Or consider, Georg Cantor (1845 -1918), who discovered a realm of transfinite (or infinite) numbers beyond the 1, 2, 3, ... that are so familiar to us. He states: "One must distinguish numbers as they are in and of themselves, in and of the Absolute Intelligence, and those same numbers as they appear in our limited discursive mental capacity and are defined (in different ways) by us for systematic or pedagogic purposes . . . The (cardinal numbers) are all independent from one another (taken absolutely), all are equally good and equally necessary metaphysically"(1979 231). ". . . the transfinites are just as much at the disposal of the intentions of the Creator and His absolutely infinite . . . Will as are the finite numbers"(229). Joseph Dauben, from whose excellent book I have just quoted, claims that there

> can be no mistake about Cantor's identification of his mathematics with some greater absolute unity in God. This also paralleled his identification of transfinite set theory with divine inspiration. (290) The theological side of Cantor's set theory, though perhaps irrelevant for understanding its mathematical content, is nevertheless essential for the full understanding of his theory and the development he gave it. Cantor believed that God endowed the transfinite numbers with a reality making them very special. (291) Later generations might forget the philosophy, smile at the abundant references to St. Thomas and the Church fathers, overlook his metaphysical pronouncements and miss entirely the deep religious roots of Cantor's later faith in the veracity of his work. But these all contributed to Cantor's resolve not to abandon his transfinite numbers for less controversial and more acceptable interests. Instead, his determination seems actually to have been strengthened in the face of opposition. His forbearance, as much as anything else he might have contributed, ensured that set theory would survive the early years of doubt and denunciation to flourish eventually as a vigorous, revolutionary force in scientific thought of the twentieth century. (299).

The depth of religious feeling of those who worship before an altar of mathematics is certainly as great as those who worship before altars of wood or stone.

Let us turn now from mathematics to astronomy. Kepler was the most important person in the transformation from ancient and medieval astronomy to its modern form. He searched for the beauty and excellence of the heavens using the five Platonic solids, he searched using musical harmonies, he searched using algebraic relationships. In spite of superstitions that were rife at the time — astrology and alchemy, numerology and witchcraft — superstitions from which Kepler himself was not immune, his search for rational beauty enabled him, like Einstein, to solve problems that no one else recognized as problems. Kepler's claim that the planets had elliptical orbits was so far ahead of his contemporaries that Galileo himself failed to appreciate it. Galileo's commitment to the beauty of circular motion blinded him to the significance of Kepler's laws (Panofsky 1954 20-31), a commitment that led to Galileo "to fall prey to illusions." Even Kepler himself did not see the full significance of his own laws, which were not understood until Newton formulated his universal law of gravitation.

Kepler's great discoveries began with something quite small. There was a discrepancy of a mere eight minutes of arc between theory and observation in the position of Mars. Kepler wrote: "If I had believed that we could ignore those minutes I would have patched up my hypothesis accordingly. But since it was not permissible to ignore them, those eight minutes point the road to a complete reformation of astronomy"(Koestler 1967 330; cf. Dijksterhuis 1961 307). Although no doubt every other astronomer of the time would have ignored the deviation, Kepler's perfectionist respect did not give him similar freedom: ". . . the all-wise Creator sought to make everything as good, beautiful and excellent as possible . . ."(Pauli 1955 168). ". . . it was absolutely necessary that the most perfect Creator should produce the most beautiful handiwork. For, 'it is not fitting (as Cicero says in his book *de Universitate* when quoting Plato's *Timaeus*), and has never been fitting, that he who is supreme should do anything except transcend in excellency' "(Koyre 1973 144; cf. Cicero 1975 184 and Plato 1957 33). The heavens are thus beautiful and excellent, but Kepler did not want to stop there: "There is nothing which I desired more to investigate thoroughly and to know than this: can I also find God within myself, God whom I readily grasp when contemplating the universe?"(Caspar 1993 221). Hence the same religious aspiration shaped Kepler's understanding of both the heavens and the soul:

> Those laws [which govern the material world] lie within the power of understanding of the human mind; God wanted us to perceive them when he created us in His image in order that we may take part in His own thoughts . . . Our knowledge [of numbers and quantities] is of the same kind as God's, at least insofar as we can understand something of it in this mortal life. (Holton 1956 350; Galileo also expressed this idea (1953 103)) Geometry is one and eternal, a reflection out of the mind of God. That mankind shares in it is one of the reasons to call man an image of God. (Caspar 1993 93) Geometry is the archetype of the beauty of the world. (Pauli 1955 156) Geometry, which before the origin of things was coeternal with the divine mind and is God himself (for what could there be in God which would not be God himself?), supplied God with patterns for the creation of the world, and passed over to Man along with the image of God; and was not in fact taken in through the eyes. (1997 304) The world is the corporeal image of God. The soul is the incorporeal image of God. (Caspar 1993 378)

It was Kepler's perfectionist respect for both the heavens *and* the inquiring human that gave him the powerful motive to overcome the old Aristotelian dichotomy of celestial/terrestrial on which even Copernicus had insisted. Hence he looked for rational beauty in both realms, and to continue to look in spite of difficulty after difficulty, failure after failure. In physics, Kepler's program culminated in Newton's universal law of gravitation, which showed that the exact same law was celestial and terrestrial. Hence it is not surprising that Newton expressed the same aesthetic passion as Kepler and Einstein: "Truth is ever to be found in simplicity, and not in the multiplicity and confusion of things . . . the world, which to the naked eye exhibits the greatest variety of objects, appears very simple in its internall constitution when surveyed by a philosophic understanding, and so much the simpler by how much better it is understood . . . It is the perfection of . . . God's works that they are all done with the greatest simplicity. He is the God of order and not of confusion . . . therefore . . . they that would understand the frame of the world must endeavour to reduce their knowledg to all possible simplicity . . ."(Manuel 1974 120).

If we now return to politics and ask who it was who first tried to found actual governments on the basis of a perfectionist respect for human beings the answer is clear: the American revolutionists. They too believed that God created the physical world and that its subtle beauty, reflecting God's perfection, is revealed in the theory and practice of natural science. "As far as we understand nature," Ethan Allen declared in 1784, "we are become acquainted with the character of God"(30; cf. Newton's belief that the transcendent subtlety of the solar system shows its "cause to be not blind and fortuitous, but very well skilled in mechanicks and geometry"(Newton 1779 4:432)). Writing a decade later, Thomas Paine agreed: "The creation is the Bible of the Deist. He there reads, in the handwriting of the Creator himself, the certainty of His existence and the immutability of His power . . ."(1945 1:599). But the American revolutionists typically believed that God created the moral world and that its subtle beauty, reflecting God's perfection, is revealed in the theory and practice of republican politics. Conceptions of human nature very similar to Kepler's can easily be found in the American revolutionary era. For example, in a sermon delivered in June 1748, Jonathan Mayhew said: "It is principally on account of our reason, that we are said to have been *created in the image of God*"(1749 39). Or consider again the 1787 words of Nathanael Emmons: "The dignity of man appears from his bearing the *image* of his Maker. . . . His soul is a transcript of the *natural* perfections of the Deity. God is spirit, and so is the soul of man; God is intelligence and activity, and so is the soul of man. In a word, man is the living image of the living God, . . . The truth is, rationality is the same in all intelligent beings. Reason is the same thing [*nota bene*] in God, in Angels, and in Men. As men therefore bear the *image* of God, in point of Rationality; so they possess all the *rational* powers and faculties, which bear any analogy to the divine intelligence . . ."(above, page 21). But if humans are fully worthy of perfectionist respect then, as John Adams exclaimed, we must create governments worthy of the same sentiment: "Objects of the most Stupendous Magnitude, Measures in which the Lives and Liberties of Millions, born and unborn, are most essentially interested, are now [June 9,1776] before Us. We are in the very midst of a Revolution, the most compleat, unexpected, and remarkable of any in the History of Nations. . . . Every Colony must be induced to institute a perfect Government"(1977 4:245). Not only is otherworldliness dead, the contemplation of perfection within ourselves requires the same kind of idealized thought experiments that occur in physics. "Whoever frames to himself an idea of a perfect republican government," says an anonymous author in the *Worcester Speculator* in October 1787, "must necessarily consider the inhabitants in the highest stages of refinement, possessing the moral and social virtues in the highest perfection"(WS 1787 56). Yet ideal contemplation was not enough, Galileo rolled balls down inclines, Adams wrote a constitution for Massachusetts. The Galilean and American revolutions were fueled by religious energy in the cause of human felicity, but they both were fully under the discipline of reason, observation, experiment, and procedures for self-correction.

As Kepler overcame the *celestial/terrestrial* distinction, so the Founding generation did the same for the *natural world/moral world* distinction. Adams maintained that we should study "government as you do astronomy, by facts, observations, and experiments; not by the dogmas of lying priests or knavish politicians"(1850 6:479). He complained: "Experiment, which is admitted in all other arts and Sciences, is totally unheeded in" the science of government (1954 Reel 123 64). Elsewhere he wrote: "The vegetable and animal kingdoms, and those heavenly bodies whose existence and movements we are as yet only permitted faintly to perceive, do not appear to be governed by laws more uniform or certain than those which regulate the moral and political world. Nations move by unalterable rules; and education, discipline, and laws, make the greatest difference in their accomplishments, happiness, and perfection"(1850 6:218). The laws that can be discovered by observation, experiment, and reason in the natural world can be discovered by the same means in the social world; the laws of morality and politics are just as "certain and uniform" as the laws of astronomy. And, according to Hamilton, they are just as mathematical. Hamilton asserts that postulates in geometry, such as "all right angles are equal to each other " are "of the same nature" as some fundamental principles of ethics and politics, such as "every power ought to be commensurate with its object." Upon such axioms "all subsequent reasonings must depend."(1961 4:456). In Euclidean geometry the Fourth Postulate claims that "all right angles are equal to one another"(1956 1:154); in American democracy the Declaration claims that "all men are created equal." Each is axiomatic and held to be self-evident, neither is given a proof, and both are perfect. In the beauty of aesthetic ideals, Euclidean geometry, Newtonian physics, and American politics were born. We need these ideals to understand the mathematical, physical, moral and political worlds. In America, Jefferson claims, there is a "lovely equality which the poor enjoys with the rich"(1950 8:636). What apparently made it "lovely" was the fact that in Jefferson's mind, the aesthetic ideals of equal rights of life, liberty, and the pursuit of happiness were closely approached by rich and poor. Even inequality for the revolutionists was understood aesthetically: "When we say, that all men are equal;" James Wilson tells us, "we mean not to apply this equality to their virtues, their talents, their dispositions, or their acquirements. In all these respects, there is, and it is fit for the great purposes of society that there should be, great inequality among men. In the moral and political as well as in the natural world, diversity forms an important part of beauty; and as of beauty, so of utility likewise"(2007 1:636-7; cf. Locke 1988 304 and Adams' words in Cappon 1959 2:355).

Wilson's observation that "diversity is an important part of beauty" is extraordinarily suggestive for revolutionary democracy. Consider the following quotation from a 1692 sermon by the English classical scholar, Richard Bentley. It is a passage that I find haunting:

> There is no universal reason . . . that a figure by us called regular, which hath equal sides and angles, is absolutely more beautiful than any irregular one. All pulchritude is relative; and all bodies are truly and physically beautiful under all possible shapes and proportions, that are good in their kind, that are fit for their proper uses and ends of their natures. We ought not then to believe that the banks of the ocean are really deformed, because they have not the form of a regular bulwark; that the mountains are out of shape, because they are not exact pyramids

or cones; nor that the stars are unskillfully placed, because they are not all situated at uniform distance. These are not natural irregularities, but with respect to our fancies only; nor are they incommodious to the true uses of life and the designs of man's being on the earth. (1836 3:194)

The examples here are remarkable because they loomed so large as instances of beauty in fractal geometry developed the twentieth century. Thus Mandelbrot begins *The Fractal Geometry of Nature* with the following words: "Why is geometry [that is, classical geometry] often described as 'cold' and 'dry'? One reason lies in its inability to describe the shape of a cloud, a mountain a coastline, or a tree"(1982 1). The new fractal geometry "reveals a totally new world of plastic beauty"(2). The elegant way fractal geometry articulates varieties of indefinitely great complexity in a sense confirms Bentley's aesthetic observations about nature. Perhaps the same sort of articulation might confirm Wilson's aesthetic sensibilities about our social nature; in particular, about the kinds of inequalities a free society should allow, or even promote (cf. Adams 1850 1:462), to reach a social justice in harmony with the deliberate sense of the people. Wilson's conception that beauty ought to be an essential part of republican freedom can be compared with Friedrich Schiller's (1795). After discussing the "most perfect of all the works to be achieved by the art of man: the construction of true political freedom," Schiller states, "if man is ever to solve that problem of politics in practice he will have to approach it through the problem of the aesthetic, because it is only through Beauty that man makes his way to Freedom"(1982 7, 9).

We can now see that a primary motive for the American revolution was not different from that behind the Keplerian or Newtonian revolutions: namely, a pursuit after the beautiful that results in an intense aspiration for perfection. A tax on tea seems rather trivial only if one ignores the aesthetics of aspiration. But that triviality — like the Keplerian eight minutes of arc — initiated a mighty revolution. "The people of the U. S.," Madison observed, "owe their Independence & their liberty, to the wisdom of descrying in the minute tax of 3 pence on tea, the magnitude of the evil comprized in the precedent"(1946 557). "So inscrutable is the arrangement of causes and consequences in this world," Jefferson marvels, "that a two-penny duty on tea, unjustly imposed in a sequestered part of it, changes the condition of all it's inhabitants"(1892 1:147). Eighteenth-century America certainly illustrated Aristotle's statement that "in revolutions the occasions may be trifling, but great interests are at stake"(1984 2:2070). But what did the revolutionary generation believe was at stake? They believed that the American revolution was the first, and perhaps the last, opportunity in human history to transform the political realm from one based on force and fraud, directed by ignorant authority, to one based on truth and freedom, directed by a self-governing people continually enlightened by an ongoing education in the liberal arts. The Bible told them God created light, but they believed it was only through natural science that one could learn of the beautiful and subtle details of God's design, such as Newton's using a prism to show white light is a mixture of a rainbow of colors. Similarly, the Bible told them God created liberty, but they believed it was only through moral science that they learned the beautiful and subtle details of God's design, such as Locke's discovery that God's liberty is worthy of revolution after "a long train of Abuses, Prevarications, and Artifices"(above, page 35).

The mathematics of Hermite, Cantor, and Gödel, the science of Galileo, Kepler, and Einstein, the politics of Washington, Adams, and Jefferson, were all driven by religious passion. But the resulting mathematics, science, and politics were not *based* on any religion. Although it originated with a Jew, and was motivated by religious emotion, relativity theory is not, in any sense, founded on Judaism. Likewise, although it originated with Christians, and religious emotion energized it, the "Government of the United States of America is not, in any sense, founded on the Christian religion"(ASP 1832 19). The quoted words are in the Tripoli Treaty that President Washington sent to the Senate in 1796. It was discussed there, ratified unanimously, and signed by President Adams, in 1797. In the liberal Protestant tradition that influenced the Founders, Christianity ought to be independent of politics. Jesus said: "Render to Caesar the things that are Caesar's, and to God the things that are God's"(*Mark* 12:17; cf. *Matthew* 22:21, *Luke* 20:25) and "My kingdom is not of this world . . . "(John 18:36, cf 6:15). Harrington points out (2003 26) that the Samuel story (above, page 10) shows that the people can even reject God himself as king. Locke said that "there is absolutely no such thing under the Gospel as a Christian commonwealth. . . . Christ . . . instituted no commonwealth"(1963 73, 75). Hence American governments should not, indeed could not, be founded on Christianity. In general, they must neither promote nor disparage the religious beliefs of its citizens, much less give a particular religion political sanction. Nor should they use religion to manipulate people, as the Romans did according to Polybius (1922 3:395-6), Strabo (1917 1:71), and Livy (1919 1:69) — a practice, unfortunately, that has not disappeared. As John Adams asked: "Was there ever a country, in which philosophers, politicians, and theologians believed what they taught to the vulgar?"(Haraszti 1952 290).

Hence, neither a genuine mathematician, nor a genuine scientist, nor a genuine American patriot is required to profess either a belief in, ar a disbelief in, any particular religion, or religion in general, in order, respectively, to be in good standing in the mathematical, scientific, or political communities. Washington believed in freedom for every religion so long as it members obeyed the law. Writing to the clergy of Philadelphia in 1797 he said: ". . . I view, with unspeakable pleasure, that harmony and brotherly love which characterizes the Clergy of different denominations, as well in this, as in other parts of the United States; exhibiting to the world a new and interesting spectacle, at once the pride of our Country and the surest basis of universal Harmony"(1931 35:416). Elsewhere he said he wanted Roman Catholics to "enjoy every temporal and spiritual felicity"(1931 31:22). Washington was the radical opposite of the vicious anti-Semitism of such Christians as St. Chrysostom (Maxwell 1966) and Luther (1955 47:123-306); he thought even toleration to be a insufficient criterion for religious freedom in America. As he eloquently put it in his August 17, 1790, reply to the Hebrew Congregation of Newport, Rhode Island: "It is now more that toleration is spoken of, as if it was by the indulgence of one class of people, that another enjoyed the exercise of their inherent natural rights. For happily the government of the United States, which gives to bigotry no sanction, to persecution no assistance, requires only that they who live under its protection should demean themselves as good citizens, in giving it on all occasions their effectual support"(1987 6:285, the phrases concerning bigotry and persecution come from the congregation's letter to Washington; cf. Paine's comments on toleration in 1945 1:291 and John Leland's in 1790 40). Nor was Washington alone in being friendly to Jews. For example, in Philadelphia on July 4, 1788, there was a parade that was larger than any spectacle hitherto attempted in the United States. Benjamin Rush reports that among the marchers were seventeen clergy: "The Rabbi of the Jews locked in the arms of two ministers of the gospel was a most delightful sight. There could not have been a more happy emblem contrived of that section of the new Constitution which opens all its power and offices alike not only to every sect of Christians but to worthy men of *every* religion"(1951 1:474). Adams' judgment of the Jewish people was perhaps the most favorable: ". . . for in spite of Bolingbroke and Voltaire, I will insist that the Hebrews have done more to civilize men than any other nation. If I were an atheist, and believed in blind eternal fate, I should still believe that fate had ordained the Jews to be the most essential instrument for civilizing the nations"(1850 9:609-10). Elsewhere he says: "The Hebrew unity of Jehovah, the prohibition of all similitudes, appears to me the greatest wonder of antiquity"(10:235). Adams was even a Zionist: "For I really wish the Jews again in Judea an independent nation"(1954 Reel 123 276). Madison likewise expresses a high opinion of Jews (see 1900 9:29-30). (For more examples of favorable comments, see Noah 1819 xxv-xvi, which reprints three letters about Jews from Madison, Jefferson and Adams, all written in 1818.)

I do not want to leave the impression that such judgments were uniformly high. Jefferson, for example, who could praise Jews and would personally treat them with respect, nevertheless refers to Jesus as "the great Reformer of the vicious ethics and deism of the Jews"(1903 14:386; cf. 15:260). Yet Jefferson, expressing the metaprotestantism (above, page 294) of the age, was also strongly critical of the Christians: "Millions of innocent men, women, and children, since the introduction of Christianity, have been burnt, tortured, fined, and imprisoned. . . . What has been the effect of this coercion? To make one half the world fools, and the other half hypocrites. To support roguery and error all over the earth"(1972 160). ". . . what blood, how many human lives have the words 'this do in remembrance of me' cost the Christian world!"(1983 344). "In every country and in every age, the priest has been hostile to liberty. He is always in alliance with the despot, abetting his abuses in return for protection to his own"(1903 14:119; cf. 2004 2:157 and Leland 1845 477). Franklin agrees: "the most dangerous Hypocrite in a Common-Wealth, is one who *leaves the Gospel for the sake of the Law*: A Man compounded of Law and Gospel, is able to cheat a whole Country with his Religion, and then destroy them under the *Colour of Law*"(1959 1:31; cf. 19:164). James Madison was equally disparaging: "Religious bondage shackles and debilitates the mind and unfits it for every noble enterprize every expanded prospect"(1962 1:112-3). "During almost fifteen centuries has the legal establishment of Christianity been on trial. What have been its fruits? More or less in all places, pride and indolence in the Clergy, ignorance and servility in the laity, in both superstition, bigotry and persecution"(1962 8:301). John Adams adds to the criticism: "As I understand the Christian religion, it was, and is, a revelation. But how has it happened that millions of fables, tales, legends, have been blended with both Jewish and Christian revelation that have made them the most bloody religion that ever existed?"(1850 10:235). For Adams the intellectual, the moral, and the religious must be merged: "Mystery! The mortal Poison to all freedom of Speech Writing and Printing. There can be no Mystery in Religion or Morality. The Head and the heart must be united; The Understanding the Will and the Affections must concur in every [*nota bene*] Act of Religion or Morality"(1954 Reel 188 35). "I almost shudder at the thought of alluding to the most fatal Example of the Abuses of Grief, which the History of Man kind has preserved. The Cross. Consider what Calamities that Engine of Grief has produced! With the rational Respect that is due to it, knavish Priests have added Prostitutions of it, that fill or might fill the blackest and bloodiest Pages of human History"(Cappon 1959 2:488; cf. Adams 1954 Reel 430 217a; One wishes that Adams had been reborn as a contemporary movie critic).

It would be easy for anyone trained in analytic philosophy to criticize the comments about God made by Hermite, Cantor, Gödel, Weyl, Kepler, Newton, Einstein, Washington, Adams, and Jefferson. By that analysis, there is a vagueness and ambiguity about the word "God" that undermines any truth or falsehood claim. If "God" is vague, then the situation is analogous to the vagueness of "rain," which enables us to say, with regard to a borderline case, "It is raining and it is not raining." "Rain" is somewhat vague, "God" is much more so. There can thus be no definite answer concerning God's existence because, with numerous borderline cases, we can often say "God exists and God does not exist." Even if we ignore vagueness, "God" is ambiguous, so "God exists" is always true in some senses of the term (*nature exists* or *love exists*), and always false in others (*Zeus exists* or *Marduk exists*). Finally, in "God exists" the word "exists" has it own ambiguity; one might be using it to refer, to a feeling (as in *headaches exist*), or to an ideal entity (as in *there exists a prime number between 25 and 30*), or to a material object (as in *there exists a natural satellite of the earth*). Hence the question — "Are you a theist, atheist, or agnostic?" — has no cognitive meaning because "Does God exist?" is a counterfeit question. The situation is comparable to, "Are you going to answer 'no' to this question?" where the answers ("yes," "no," "maybe") are all incorrect because the question is likewise counterfeit (although for a different reason). (See Kaufmann 1978 173-181 and Kurtz 1986 314-16 for more on philosophical, analytic criticism.) Yet even if this analysis be granted, it is irrelevant to the resulting mathematics or physics or political science. To repeat, what counts is evidence, proof, fruitfulness, extent of application, and aesthetic appeal, not motivation, whether based on true or delusionary beliefs. Furthermore, analytic critics are open to the charge that their capacity to feel has atrophied, that their emotional intelligence is low. As the secular humanist Paul Kurtz notes: "Perhaps it is the skeptic who is blind and ignorant. I have wondered at times: Is it I who lacks a religious sense, and is this due to a defect of character? The tone-deaf are unable to fully appreciate the intensity of music, and the colorblind live in a world denuded of brightness and hue"(1986 105). Some of the greatest creations of science and rationality have come from those whose intellectual powers are awesomely developed, but whose sense of wonder and religious feeling are childlike. They often appear clueless. Perhaps this is a desirable state that others should emulate. Or perhaps the religious emotion of these individuals clouds their philosophical reason so that while they pay the price of confused or false religious beliefs, they gain an extraordinarily intense and sustained drive for perfection which leads to intellectual achievements that their more judicious colleagues do not even try to attain, let alone actually match or exceed. Their religious emotion would then be like the affective disorder of manic depression, a condition that is not in itself desirable, but can nevertheless promote great creativity.

In any case, the American revolution was often animated by soul-stirring religious emotions that led to a perfectionist respect for human beings in their moral and political capacity. George Washington, speaking to the officers of the army in 1783, closed his address with these words: ". . . you will, by the dignity of your Conduct, afford occasion for Posterity to say, when speaking of the glorious example you have exhibited to Mankind, 'had this day been wanting, the World had never seen the last stage of perfection to which human nature is capable of attaining' "(1931 26:227). It is anachronistic to associate these sentiments with a contemporary cynicism, because Washington believed them with his whole heart and mind and soul. They are an expression of perfectionist emotion that, in Washington's case, was driven by religion. Biblical authority for the belief that *striving for the last stage of perfection is appropriate to the human condition* can be found in a number of places: for example, in the claim that we are made in the image of God (*Genesis* 1:26-7; 5:1; 9:6), or in God's words to Abram: "I *am* the Almighty God; walk before me, and be thou perfect"(*Genesis* 17:1), or in what the Lord said to Moses and his people, "You shall be holy; for I the Lord your God am holy"(*Leviticus* 19:2, cf. 11:44-5, 20:7, 26, *1Peter* 1:16), or in the command of Jesus: "Be ye therefore perfect, even as your Father which is in heaven is perfect"(*Matthew* 5:48). Washington's words ought to be compared with those of Lincoln in a speech delivered on July 10, 1858: "It is said in one of the admonitions of the Lord, 'As your Father in Heaven is perfect, be ye also perfect.' The Savior, I suppose, did not expect that any human creature could be perfect as the Father in Heaven; but He said, 'As your Father in Heaven is perfect, be ye also perfect.' He set that up as a standard, and he who did most towards reaching that standard, attained the highest degree of moral perfection. So I say in relation to the principle that all men are created equal, let it be as nearly reached as we can"(1953 2:501). Is it an accident that America's two greatest presidents were driven by perfectionist aspirations for the American people?

For Einstein "this universe of ours is something perfect and susceptible to the rational striving for knowledge," a view grounded in a cosmic religion that Einstein traced back to Spinoza. For Washington man is capable of a "last stage of perfection," and it is only through the striving for excellence in government that that stage can be achieved. His view was grounded in a civic religion whose historical roots are in Unitarianism. The Einsteinian revolution originated in a perfectionist naturalism; the Washingtonian revolution in a perfectionist humanism. In each case religious emotion fueled nonreligious reason. Ernst Mayr, the greatest evolutionary biologist of the twentieth century, once said, "People forget that it is possible to be intensely religious in the entire absence of theological belief"(Ruse 2003 335). Thus Einstein could say, "I am a deeply religious nonbeliever"(Calaprice 1996 158). In the same spirit we can say, "Washington was the leader of a deeply religious, but secular, revolution." The emotions that excited that revolution, like those of Einstein, led to new aesthetic standards, standards which can lure the noble and gifted to new levels of excellence. "If happiness is activity in accordance with excellence," Aristotle argued, "it is reasonable that it should be in accordance with the highest excellence"(1984 2:1860). American revolutionists were perhaps the first to apply Aristotle's judgment to *public* happiness. Let us listen to them: The 1776 constitution of Pennsylvania states that only "the great Governor of the universe . . . knows to what degree of earthly happiness mankind may attain, by perfecting the arts of government"(5:3082). "In our civil constitutions," Ezra Stiles declared, "those impediments are removed, which obstruct the progress of society towards perfection"(1783 35). Isaac Parker proclaimed that our "form of government . . . is acknowledged, by Europe as well as America, to be the most perfect republican system, which the ingenuity of man has yet devised," the "most prominent excellence" is that "it may be ameliorated without violence, and rendered more and more perfect, without disturbing the public tranquility"(1786 9). In 1792, Washington again asserted his perfectionism: "That the established government being the work of our own hands, with the seeds of amendment engrafted in the Constitution, may by wisdom, good dispositions, and mutual allowances; aided by experience, bring it as near to perfection as any human institution ever aproximated" (1931 32:47; cf. Madison 1962 14:324). Or we can listen to John Adams: "Poor weak Man, when will thy Perfection arrive? Perfectibility, I shall not deny: for a greater Character than [Joseph] Priestley or [William] Godwin has said, 'Be ye perfect' etc."(Cappon 1959 2:338). The aspirational rallying cry of the American revolution was and is: *Perfection is our passion, perfectibility, our practice.* We can never adequately appreciate the Declaration or the Constitution, as so many attempt to do so today, without understanding the perfectionist dreams of their creators. The pithy and awesome rhetoric of the Declaration was an essential part of its greatness. So was the language of the Constitution; in the words of Fisher Ames from 1788, "Considered merely as a literary performance, [the new Constitution] was an honour to our country"(DHRC 1976 6:1445).

Perfectionist ideals have often served as the inspiration and foundation of the most practical human creations. Thus Alan Turing, in the course of solving a highly theoretical problem in mathematical logic, gave the first definition (in 1936) of a perfect machine, a conception that captures the essence of any actual computer. But Turing's interests were not limited to ideal machines for he also directed the construction of one of the world's first computers. Jefferson's interests were likewise both ideal and practical. The ideal requirements for a political system described in the Declaration is an example of the former, whereas he was just as interested in the practical problems of constructing actual American governments. And for these governments he harbored perfectionist aspirations: "I dare say that in time all these [State governments] as well as their central government, like the planets revolving round their common sun, acting and acted upon according to their respective weights and distances, will produce that beautiful equilibrium on which our Constitution is founded, and which I believe it will exhibit to the world in a degree of perfection, unexampled but in the planetary system itself"(1892 7:210). (The belief that politics was scientific made solar-system comparisons common: see Webster, Noah 1785 35, Fobes 1795 26-7, and Farrand 1937 1:153, 165)). From a contemporary standpoint it is easy for us to dismiss Jefferson's claim as mere braggadocio. But if we wish to learn from Jefferson, instead of merely admiring or criticizing him, we might see this passage, coming from the past, as an implicit but powerful criticism of us. For although the Constitution had faults, it is nevertheless true that the Founders made stupendous efforts to create a political system that had a "degree of perfection" found in the Newtonian theory of planetary motion. James Wilson believed that through empirical investigation "the immortal Newton collected, arranged, and formed his just and beautiful system of experimental philosophy. By the same kind of process, our predecessors and ancestors have collected, arranged, and formed a system of experimental law, equally just, equally beautiful [*nota bene*], and, important as Newton's system is, far more important still"(2007 1:568). Suppose we ask: What political institutions, what economic programs, what set of laws, what voting procedures, were devised in the contemporary world where, using contemporary standards, the creators made equally stupendous efforts to create a "degree of perfection" that is found in Einstein's general theory of relativity? It is hard not to squirm with either embarrassment or shame at the answer. It is a commonplace today that an essential part of the revolutionary mathematics or revolutionary science of such thinkers as Euclid, Archimedes, Kepler, Newton, Euler, Gauss, Einstein, Gödel, or Mandelbrot was the introduction of new aesthetic standards and it was those standards, rather than just the content of what they produced, that most ensured their undying fame. Their perfectionism is rightly celebrated as a paradigm of knowledge because it is ultimately based on evidence, experiments, and proof. Today it is often wrongly assumed that a perfectionist in politics must either be an impractical dreamer, or a pernicious utopian, such as Plato, Marx, Hitler, or the Taliban. These men not only made no provisions that there could be free challenges to their theories for eminence in the political community, they also recommended, or carried out, political manipulation or lies or repression or torture or murder or terror to prevent such challenges. The fanatical aspect of the perfectionism of Osama ben Laden is revealed in *The Al-Qaeda Training Manual*: "The confrontation that we are calling for with the apostate regimes does not know Socratic debates . . . , Platonic ideals . . . , nor Aristotelian diplomacy. But it knows the dialogue of bullets, the ideals of assassination, bombing and destruction, and the diplomacy of the cannon and machine-gun"(MSJT 2005 11). The philosophy of the

American revolution promotes a radically different perfectionism that can be clarified by an analogy. In the Old Testament, there is a prohibition against graven images of God, presumably because any unchanging image of a living God is spurious, fraudulent, sacrilegious. Now recall Harrington's words from 1656: "As the form of a man is the image of God, so the form of a government is the image of man"(2003 273). Following these ideas, the Declaration patriot must continually say to herself: "I will not accept any graven ideology or graven utopia, no matter how tempting." The perfectionism of the Founders is living, not graven; it requires that the government and the economy be continually remade so as to be an exact, moving image of the changing, deliberate sense of living Americans. This new aesthetic standard is today generally ignored, or treated as an idle theory; it is not recognized that the mediocrity of our politics is not due to a deficiency in talent or opportunity, but to a deficiency in aesthetic aspiration. Graven, aesthetic ideals can be the source of great political evil: Hitler wanted a world without Jews and Islamists want a world without infidels, both in order to reach an aesthetic purity. For the same reason Jefferson wanted a country without blacks, a country unblemished by what he saw as the inferior beauty of their race. But he was also a leader of a revolution that declared an aesthetic ideal of universal moral equality, resulting in a society where perfect happiness is an asymptote that cannot be reached, but it can be progressively approached by following curves whose equations are derived from the common reason of a free, liberally-educated people.

This ideal generates an optimism that seems utterly baffling to our cynical age. Here is how James Wilson expresses it: "Where liberty prevails, the arts and sciences lift up their heads and flourish. Where the arts and sciences flourish, political and moral improvements will likewise be made. All will receive from each, and each will receive from all, mutual support and assistance: mutually supported and assisted, all may be carried to a degree of perfection hitherto unknown; perhaps hitherto not believed"(2007 1:524). Even Madison, who is rightly renowned for being keenly sensitive to the limitations and defects of human nature, and of the political consequences of those limitations and defects — even the sober, sober Madison expresses what appears to us to be an utterly naive confidence: "[T]he destined career of my country will exhibit a Government pursuing the public good as its sole object, . . . a Government . . . whose conduct within and without may bespeak the most noble of all ambitions — that of promoting peace on earth and good will to man"(1900 8:384-5).

Perhaps the greatest lesson that we can learn from the Founding era is that our political cynicism, far from being sophisticated or profound, is based on a philosophical mistake concerning our own humanity; we lack a perfectionist respect for ourselves as moral and political beings. Hence we get liberal programs and conservative platforms, we get new deals and new frontiers, we get WIN buttons and wars against drugs, we get tax cuts and government support for faith-based organizations, we get many, many things, but the one thing needful, a recognition of the great dignity and worth of human beings as political and economic persons, a recognition generating a powerful and sustained aspiration to express the musicality of a great people in beautiful laws and institutions meticulously devised to harmonize with their informed values — this is forgotten by our political leaders for whom aesthetic excellence is unachieved in fact, and undreamed of in principle. Weep, Declaration devotees, there are no longer any recitals of that musicality which is the joy of your desiring; you are awe-stricken by the founding aesthetic of America, its government is dead to it; weep in your alienation. Until members of Congress decide that it is supremely important to pass elegantly designed legislation which precisely expresses the common reason of society, until they decide that there is no permanent place in America for ugly or dishonest economic practices and institutions, until the President presents programs and reorganizes the government, so that we can exclaim: "the President's proposals have the very highest aesthetic merit: every lover of the beautiful must wish they will be passed," until, in other words, the aspiration for aesthetic excellence becomes an integral part of our nation's economic and political life — until then, the triumph of incompetence, corruption, and cynicism will be our justified worry. "It is so much easier to descry the little difficulties immediately incident to every great plan," James Madison observed, "than to comprehend its general & remote benefits, that further light must be added to the Councils of our Country before many truths which are seen through the medium of philosophy, become visible to the naked eye of the ordinary politician"(1962 13:25). The ultimate roots of our unyielding political difficulties are not the failures of politicians, however conspicuous they are, but the failure of inconspicuous philosophers to make "visible to the naked eye of the ordinary politician" the perfectionist aspirations necessary to redeem America's revolutionary heritage. The "Councils of our Country" include a Council of Economic Advisers to look after our economic prosperity, but no Council of Philosophic Advisors to look after our moral prosperity. If such a Council were formed, would it have any more important task than to recommend that the country create institutions through which the people could examine who they are, could articulate who they wish to become, could develop the reason, the passion, the liberal education necessary to forever perfect their pursuit of happiness? For what is America profited, if she shall gain the whole world, and lose her revolutionary soul?

Those who are contemptuous of "every great plan" inspired by aesthetic aspirations should consider their predecessors who scorned the aspiration for beauty in mathematics, science, and engineering; they should reflect that they might be just as wrong about law, economics, or politics. Otherwise, their mocking might continually deflect young people who are aesthetically inflamed from ever entering these professions, just as it commonly prevents the practitioners themselves from applying their aesthetic sensibility to their own activities. Is the justification of the cynic's laughter so strong that we should not even attempt to create the same respect for the moral and political world, as Euclid and Archimedes had for the abstract world, or as Kepler and Einstein had for the natural world? Would such cynics have said to the Pythagoreans and Euclid, prior to their great discoveries: "Pure mathematics is a chimera, why are you wasting your time?" Or would they have said early on to Kepler and Newton: "You don't *know* there is any simplicity or beauty there, so be realistic and give up?" If mathematical and scientific entrepreneurs can achieved eternal fame by taking great risks in the cause of simplicity, beauty, truth, and perfection, why should we tremble at the thought of taking such risks in morality, law, economics, and politics? One wishes it were possible to administer an aesthetic aphrodisiac to members of Congress that would arouse their desire for a climactic pleasure, which would only occur as they passed laws that were efficacious, exquisite, and consistent with the informed values of the people; and, in addition, as a fail-safe measure, in case the aphrodisiac ever failed, to award money, power, and fame to them in such a way as to become the functional equivalent of one. The reason we have not achieved the same magnificence in our moral sciences that we have achieved in mathematics, science, and engineering is not because the task is impossible to solve, or because human nature is depraved; rather, it is because our philosophy of aspiration is paltry, and our dreams are so petty that we do not even try. In our society "the relentless pursuit of excellence" is a slogan for a car, not a fact about our commitment to democracy. Our present government, even our civilization, is in many, many ways the best in the world, and for this, as an American, I am as grateful as I can possibly be. Yet these achievements are no longer adequate to solve our colossal political problems. Whether it be an individual or a people, the truly great do not attempt to be best by the standards of their time; rather, they introduce new standards of excellence that others do not have enough intelligence, imagination, determination, and passion to conceive and pursue. After more than two centuries, the transcendent importance of the aesthetic ideals introduced by the American revolution is still not understood, much less deeply felt and acted on; the spirit of 1776 continues to slumber and our politics is relentlessly small-souled.

In Kepler's time there was little perfectionist respect for the physical world. It was not recognized that there is a cosmos that manifests, in Einstein's words, "the highest wisdom and the most radiant beauty"(above, page 384); it was not recognized that, to understand this realm, massive efforts were required to discover the wisdom and beauty that exactly corresponds to the evidence we can get from nature by observation and experiment. Hence numerology, astrology, alchemy, and witchcraft flourished. In such areas it was impossible for practitioners to have consistently high standards of truth represented by scrupulous attention to evidence and proof. The emphasis instead was on verbal hocus-pocus and the manipulation of emotion. In our time there is little perfectionist respect for the political world. It is not recognized that, to understand this realm, massive efforts are required to discover the wisdom and beauty that exactly corresponds to the evidence we can get from the people's informed values by observation and experiment. Hence superstitions abound and it is almost impossible for politicians to have consistently high standards of truth. Instead the emphasis is on verbal hocus-pocus and the manipulation of emotion.

If we wish to achieve beauty and grace in our public life, then we must seek beauty and grace in our laws and public institutions. But this means not just seeking anticipated beauty, which in the end might not be there, but looking for unexpected beauty in the spirit of the American people. Pythagoras had a beautiful conception that everything could be understood in terms of whole numbers and their ratios. That conception was wrong, as the Pythagoreans themselves discovered when they showed that the diagonal of a square cannot be the ratio of two whole numbers. Rather the beauty of the geometric line concerns what today are called real numbers. Aristotle, Ptolemy, Copernicus, and Galileo had a beautiful conception that the orbits of the planets were perfect circles, which Kepler showed was wrong.

Einstein originally sought for his elegant general theory in a four-dimensional Euclidean geometry before he found it in a four-dimensional Riemannian geometry. "The most beautiful logical theory," Einstein tells us, "means nothing without comparison with the exactest experience"(Kepler 1951 13). The word "simple" in a scientific context does not mean simple in the sense of "simple as ABC." Simple means simplest, that is, that any complexity cannot be either eliminated or reduced. It is relatively easy to make "simple as ABC" theories that don't fit "the exactest experience," or unnecessarily complex ones that do (by using a series of *ad hoc* assumptions). It takes a great intellect, such as Kepler, Newton, Darwin, or Einstein, to formulate simple theories that both fit experience and greatly excite our aesthetic emotions. A scientific education is required before one can fully appreciate the simplicity associated with the work of these men, a liberal arts education (which includes science) is required before one can fully appreciate the simplicity associated with the work of Locke, Adams, Wilson, Jefferson, Madison and Hamilton. The basic laws that best support a free society are not simple as ABC, any more than are the laws that best describe nature. Even simplicity so qualified is not necessarily the same as beauty. In the words of Dirac: "The research worker, in his efforts to express the fundamental laws of Nature in mathematical form, should strive mainly for mathematical beauty. He should still take simplicity into consideration in a subordinate way to beauty. . . . It often happens that the requirements of simplicity and beauty are the same, but where they clash the latter must take precedence"(1939 124).

Yet whatever claims are made about simplicity or beauty, they must eventually be justified in terms of experience and proof — that is what keeps mathematics, physics, or political science from being mere aestheticism. Mere aestheticism gives us simplistic — not simple — solutions; it can arise where an inquirer becomes arrogant and believes that, because a theory appears simple and beautiful to the inquirer, it must be true. In politics, as in natural science, we must avoid this arrogance and adopt a *disciplined aestheticism*; hence, we should forever seek to demonstrate that there are aesthetically pleasing proposals that are also consistent with experiments that reveal the common reason of society. Of course, disciplined aestheticism considered as a methodological principle may not always be fruitful, but without it, simple and beautiful theories (if they exist) are unlikely to be found. Today we have no political Brahes who are generating highly accurate facts about the informed values of the people; hence, we can have no political Keplers or Newtons or Einsteins. If we had such individuals, they would have a perfectionist respect for humanity in general, and the American people in particular. They would be willing to spend long years, and untold hours of computer time until they finally discovered an elegant legal system that would embody the deliberate sense of the people. "The people," they might say, "would not pass up an opportunity to make the best laws for America that simple." There is hardly a more commonplace claim than: There are no simple answers to our problems. Anyone who reflects on the aesthetics of aspiration realizes the truth may be the exact opposite: There are no answers to our problems that are not simple. And even if there are no simple answers, there may be beautiful ones. Although it is a typical and justified complaint today that we lack moral leadership, it is seldom noticed that this failure cannot be remedied without a rebirth of aesthetic leadership.

The absence of a history of feudalism, or the incredible physical assets of the North American continent, are just two of many reasons that have been given for the tremendous political achievements of eighteenth-century Americans. In my judgment, however, by far the most important reason is their conviction that politics, properly understood, is a disciplined aestheticism, an arena where the most noble aspirations can be gratified, an arena where human excellence is rewarded with the greatest honor and the most lasting fame. The world of politics is not intrinsically ugly; it has become ugly because we understand it to be so. The question is one of esteem and of such importance that it may again be worthwhile to appreciate our mistake by reflecting on a similar error in the past. The ancient Greeks are often thought to have been deficient in engineering and technology, in the kind of talent that produces gadgets, mechanical inventions, and laborsaving devices. This is false. They devised such things as self-moving marionettes, sound effect machines in theaters, coin-operated vending machines (for holy water), water clocks, windmills, self-opening doors, steam engines, lottery machines, and catapults (for more details see Brumbaugh 1966 and 1989). The Greeks also constructed the Antikythera mechanism (circa 100 B.C.), which is an astronomical analog calculator, based on differential gearing, that has a sophistication not duplicated for over a millennium (for details, see Marchant 2006, Charette 2006, Freeth 2006, and Seabrook 2007). But why did the Greeks not use their proven technological capabilities to make substantial laborsaving devices, or to make energy? The usual answer is that with slavery there was no need to apply their inventions to ease work. Although there is some truth to this, the primary reason does not concern need. Slaves, after all, were sometimes expensive, and slavery did not prevent the rise of science and technology from the Middle Ages onward. The primary reason concerned prestige, and the association of slaves with manual labor. In the minds of many of the most talented Greeks there was a dogmatic, perhaps unconscious, cynicism about the material world, and about people who work with their hands for utilitarian purposes, such as mechanics or artisans. Hence, however obvious it is to us today, it would then have taken substantial imagination to counter social prejudice by thinking of using sophisticated technology to save labor. Even free artisans and mechanics were depreciated in the eyes of the intellectual and social elite because they often worked side by side with slaves. In general, the application of one's talents to the physical world was seen as demeaning. Thus if we look at the oldest Greek literary work — the *Iliad* — we find that Hephaestus, the divine craftsman, is the only god with physical defects. He is thrown out of heaven by his mother (Homer 1924 2:317) because he is lame. Although his works are marvelous (for example, see 2:315) he himself is subject to ridicule: "And laughter unquenchable arose among the blessed gods, as they saw Hephaestus puffing through the palace"(1:49). The Greeks extended this negative attitude to human craftsmen (Herodotus 1998 162). According to Xenophon, Socrates said that mechanical artisans were "quite rightly, held in very low esteem"(1995 121; cf. 131 ,235). According to Plato, Socrates argued that those who work with their hands were incapable of doing philosophy, it being unfortunate "when any poor creature who has proved his cleverness in some mechanical craft, sees here an opening for a pretentious display of high-sounding words and is glad to break out of the prison of his paltry trade and take sanctuary in philosophy. For as compared with other occupations, philosophy, even in the present case, still enjoys a higher prestige, enough to attract a multitude of stunted natures, whose souls a life of drudgery has warped and maimed . . . "(1955 203). Speaking of artisans Aristotle said that "the best form of state will not admit them to citizenship." He added that "no man can practise excellence who is living the life of a mechanic or labourer"(1984 2:2028). In the same spirit Plutarch depreciates the artisan and artist: "No generous youth, from seeing the Zeus at Pisa, or the Hera at Argos, longs to be Pheidias or Polycleitus; nor to be Anacreon or Philetas or Archilochus out of pleasure in their poems. For it does not of necessity follow that, if the work delights you with its grace, the one who wrought it is worthy of your esteem"(1914 3:5-7). Influenced by the Greeks, the Roman Cicero

deprecated mechanics: "Unbecoming to a gentleman . . . and vulgar
are the means of livelihood of all hired workmen whom we pay for
mere manual labour, not for artistic skill . . . And all mechanics are
engaged in vulgar trades; for no workshop can have anything liberal
about it"(2005 153).

Even Archimedes, the greatest mathematician of the ancient world,
belittled engineering. When the city of Syracuse was attacked in 214
B.C. by the Romans, they were repulsed by the catapults and other
machines devised by him. To these, Archimedes

> had by no means devoted himself as work worth of his serious effort, but most of
> them were mere accessories of a geometry practiced for amusement, since in
> bygone days Hiero the king had eagerly desired and at last persuaded him to turn
> his art somewhat from abstract notions to material things, and by applying his
> philosophy somehow to the needs which make themselves felt, to render it more
> evident to the common mind. . . . . And yet Archimedes possessed such a lofty
> spirit, so profound a soul, and such a wealth of scientific theory, that although his
> inventions had won him a name and fame for superhuman sagacity, he would not
> consent to leave behind him any treatise on this subject, but regarding the work of
> an engineer and every art that ministers to the needs of life as ignoble and vulgar,
> he devoted his earnest efforts only to those studies the subtlety and charm of which
> are not affected by the claims of necessity. (Plutarch 1914 5: 471, 479, 481).

In retrospect, this view is easily refuted. Archimedes would no doubt
be astounded to know, for example, that the cattle problem that he
made famous, and that confounded mathematicians for over two
thousand years, was solved in 1981 in under ten minutes by an
engineering device—a CRAY 1 computer (Nelson, Harry L. 1981 162,
164). For the first time, the 206,545 digits of the solution were written
out (using 47 computer pages). Today the solution could be
calculated in a fraction of a second.

The Greeks had all the ingredients needed to create a
technologically-based science that could improve the lot of ordinary
people, but many, perhaps all, of the best talents thought such an effort
was beneath their attention. Hence Greek societies would forever
require slaves and ignorant drudges; would forever be based on moral
inequality. This lack of esteem for common people, and the practical
problems of their work, hindered the creation of that dialectical
relationship between theory and technology which is the hallmark of
modern science. Both the Greeks and the Romans could on occasion
embody that relationship, but they failed to systematically employ it in
their science. That systematic application had to wait century upon

century until Christians, beginning in the Middle Ages, initiated a revolution by ignoring, or explaining away, otherworldly secular authorities and otherworldly Biblical passages. These Christians did not think either applied science or manual labor was "ignoble and vulgar," for God is the engineer of a world that is "very good"(*Genesis* 1:31; cf. 1 *Timothy* 4:4); and Jesus himself was a carpenter (*Mark* 6:3). As early as the twelfth century we have theologians, influenced by the Pythagoreans and Plato, saying that nature is rational, mathematical, and beautiful (cf. Stiefel 1977). The belief that these properties are exhibited in terrestrial matter, since they are the creation of a perfect God, meant that investigations that combined theoretical science with practical engineering were worthy of a life-long occupation of the most gifted and most devoted Christians. As heir and contributor to these ideas, Leonardo's words offer a sharp contrast to the disparagement of practical science common in Greek writings: "Instrumental or mechanical science is the noblest and above all others the most useful, seeing that by means of it all animated bodies which have movement perform all their actions"(1938 1:655); "Mechanics is the paradise of the mathematical sciences because by means of it one comes to the fruit of mathematics"(628). Francis Bacon also greatly respected the products of engineering. Speaking of printing, gunpowder, and the mariner's compass, he claimed that "no empire, no sect and no star seems to have exerted a greater effect and influence on human affairs than these mechanical innovations"(2004 195). There was nothing wrong with Archimedes choosing to spend his life on pure rather than applied science. Pure mathematics or theoretical science are surely among the greatest joys and achievements of the human mind. *Mathematics or science for the sake of mathematics or science* is a fine ideal, provided it is not an exclusive ideal. Unfortunately Archimedes not only made it a nearly exclusive ideal for himself, he also joined in the general deprecation of applied science that had long since became the prevailing view.

Nevertheless Plato and Aristotle have a point in asserting that, if one's life is entirely taken up in drudgery, a life of excellence is precluded. What they utterly failed to see was that drudgery could be relieved by engineering. Christians, however, eventually understood this, and had made sufficient progress by the seventeenth century so that Locke could argue: "No Man is so wholly taken up with the Attendance on the Means of Living, as to have no spare Time at all to think of his Soul, and inform himself in Matters of Religion. Were Men as intent upon this, as they are on Necessities of Life, who might not find many Vacancies, that might be husbanded to this Advantage of their Knowledge"(Locke 1975 708). Locke wanted to rearrange social practices so that life-long drudgery would be unnecessary for anyone. Hence he argued that the well-off should spend at least three hours a day in manual labor, and laborers, at least three hours improving their minds. This would enhance the health of the former and save the latter from "that horid ignorance and brutality to which the bulke of them is now every where given up." Were this done the "populace well instructed in their duty and removed from the implicit faith their ignorance submits them in to others would not be soe easie to be blown into tumults and popular commotions by the breath and artifice of designeing or discontented Grandees"(1991 2:494-5). To consider a mechanic, an artisan, a common laborer, to be a mere mechanic, a mere artisan, a mere common laborer, is dehumanizing, and paves the way for abuse.

As they did in so many other ways, the Founders generally followed Locke rather than the ancient custom of demeaning the common person. Thus Franklin says: "We are more thoroughly an enlightened people, with respect to our political interests, than perhaps any other under heaven. Every man among us reads, and is so easy in his circumstances as to have leisure for conversations of improvement, and for acquiring Information"(1907 9:88). When describing America, he says: "The Husbandman is in honor there, and even the Mechanic, because their Employments are useful. The People have a saying, that God Almighty is himself a Mechanic"(8:606). Washington could also praise the farmer: "I think . . . that the life of a Husbandman of all others is the most delectable.   It is honorable"(1931 29:414).   Madison adds to the chorus: "The life of the husbandman is pre-eminently suited to the comfort and happiness of the individual"(1962 14: 245; cf Cicero 2005 155).   And Jefferson famously said: "Those who labour in the earth are the chosen people of God, if ever he had a chosen people, whose breasts he has made his peculiar deposit for substantial and genuine virtue"(1972 164-5). Jefferson believed the farmer and mechanic should study "ethics, mathematics, chemistry and natural philosophy." He maintained the education of a merchant should include "ethics, mathematics, geography, political economy, history"(1903 15:211). Noah Webster exults: "In no country, is education so general — in no country, have the body of the people such a knowledge of the rights of men and the principles of government"(1787 49). John Adams boasts: "A native of America who cannot read and write is as rare . . . as a Comet or an Earthquake.   It has been observed, that we are all of us, lawyers, divines, politicians and philosophers. And I have good authorities to say that all candid foreigners who have passed thro' this country, and conversed freely with all sorts of people here, will allow, that they have never seen so much knowledge and civility among the common people in any part of the world"(1977 1:120; cf. 81 and Mayhew 1763 45). He believed that the "moral equality that nature has unalterably established among men, gives [husbandmen, merchants, and mechanics] an undoubted right to have every road opened to them for advancement in life and in power that is open to any others"(1850 5:457). In contrast to Plato, Aristotle, Archimedes, Plutarch, and Cicero, the American elite did not disrespect men merely because they worked with their hands, nor did those who worked with their hands believe themselves incapable of contributing to public deliberation. In 1776, mechanics in New York City asserted that though they were not competent to write constitutions, they were quite competent to judge them (Niles, Hezekiah 1822 442). Commoners can gain enough liberal arts education and self-knowledge to make them collectively capable of excellent self-government. The fact that some political leaders could be understood in terms of ordinary occupations was seen as a triumph by Benjamin Rush: "It would seem as if heaven stamped a peculiar virtue upon agriculture and mechanical arts in America by selecting WASHINGTON and FRANKLIN to be of the principal agents in the late Revolution. The titles of farmer and mechanic, therefore, can never fail of being peculiarly agreeable in the United States while gratitude and patriotism live in American breasts"(1951 1:472). Political thought in eighteenth-century America generally presupposed that the world of the common people — their rights, their common reason, their happiness —was worthy of intense and prolonged attention by the greatest intellects, the most powerful politicians, and the most noble human beings that America could produce.

In this context the following words of Einstein are chilling:

> Personally I am inclined to agree with Schopenhauer in thinking that one of the strongest motives that lead people to give their lives to art and science is the urge to flee from everyday life, with its drab and deadly dullness, and thus to unshackle the chains of one's own transient desires, which supplant one another in an interminable succession so long as the mind is fixed on the horizon of daily environment. (Planck 1932 8; cf. Schopenhauer 1948 1:405)

Einstein's otherworldliness is part of a long tradition, for example, Aristotle ("The scanty conceptions to which we can attain of celestial things give us, from their excellence, more pleasure than all our knowledge of the world in which we live . . . "(1984 1:1004), or Descartes ("It is our nature to have more admiration for the things above us than those that are on our level, or below"(1965 263).) (Further examples of the tradition are given above, page 381 and below, page 431). Clearly for Einstein the thought of spending his life as a politician would be distasteful and disgraceful. For then he would be chained to "everyday life" and his mind would be "fixed on the horizon of daily environment." When a friend gave him the six volumes of Gibbons's *The Decline and Fall of the Roman Empire,* he returned them a few days later and said: "Take them back. I can't read that stuff"(Woolf 1980 16). He thought "the distinction between a past, a present, and a future has the character of a tenaciously held illusion"(17; see also Feuer 1983 281). (One wonders how a timeless physics of the *cosmos* based on a beautiful reality can be appropriately justified by a changing *history* of physics based on a drab illusion.) After Hermann Broch gave him a copy of his novel *The Death of Virgil*, Einstein thanked him with these words: "I am fascinated by your *Virgil* — and am steadfastly resisting him. This book shows me clearly what I fled from when I sold myself body and soul to science — the flight from the I and WE to the IT"(Hoffman, Banesh 1972 254). The "I and WE" are incapable of moral freedom:

> *I do not believe in freedom of the will. Schopenhauer's words: 'Man can do what he wants, but he cannot will what he wills," accompany me in all situations throughout my life and reconcile me with the actions of others, even if they are rather painful to me. This awareness of the lack of freedom of will preserves me from taking too seriously myself and my fellow men as acting and deciding individuals . . .* (White and Gribbin 1994 262; cf. Feuer 1983 275 and Schopenhauer 1999 21, 38, 88.)

Einstein did not look for "the highest wisdom and the most radiant beauty" in history or politics. He was guided by a *cosmic* religious sense, but rejected a *terrestrial* religious sense. In sharp contrast, eighteenth-century American revolutionaries were guided by a religious sense that made no such distinction. They believed that man "may be preserved, improved, and perfected. The celestial as well as the terrestrial world knows its exalted but prescribed course"(Wilson 2007 1:464). They believed that "there can be no employment more agreeable to a benevolent mind, than a research after the best" in "the divine science of politicks"(Adams 4:1977 86). They believed that the "Citizens of America" were "Actors on a most conspicuous Theatre, which seems to be peculiarly designated by Providence for the display of human greatness and felicity"(Washington 1931 26:484-5; cf. Adams 1961 1:282). They believed the "wise and benevolent Author of nature has made the human race capable of continual advances towards a state of perfection and happiness." This progress "is to be carried further in America, than it has ever yet been in any place"(Williams, Samuel 1775 5, 22; cf 25). They believed that "Man is not merely so much lumpish Matter, or a *mechanical* Engine," but rather has "the Power of Self-determination, or Freedom of Choice (Gay 1759 12; cf. Rush 1786 15)). They thus took both themselves and others seriously "*as acting and deciding individuals*": "Has God made us *free agents*, in his own moral, intellectual image, and done honor to human nature in giving man dominion over the lower creation, then let us shew ourselves Men, behave with becoming *dignity*, and act the part of *reasonable*, as well as *accountable* beings"(Mellen 1795 33). For Einstein, humans are not free agents and hence are not "*accountable*," nor is the terrestrial world "exalted." Of course, Einstein did become involved in politics as Archimedes became involved in applied science. However, his involvement was only a duty deriving from his compassion for human beings, who nevertheless were not worthy of the perfectionist respect that he bestowed on the cosmos.

Bertrand Russell takes up the same ancient theme when he speaks of an "ordered cosmos, where pure thought can dwell as in its natural home, and where one, at least, of our nobler impulses can escape from the dreary exile of the actual world"(1957 57-58). For Russell and Einstein, the moral and political world, unlike the cosmos, has no enchanting majesty. And their views are widespread. What politician today would agree with James Wilson that "morals are undoubtedly capable of being carried to a much higher degree of excellence than the sciences, excellent as they are"(2007 1:525)? It is easy to find numerous Russellian mathematicians and Einsteinian physicists seeking simplicity, subtlety, and grandeur in a beautiful proof, theory, or experiment, but it is virtually impossible to find politicians who have similar aspirations. Indeed it is now common to understand *political* as a pejorative term, to think of politicians as mainly or completely corrupt, and even to understand the people as the masses, incapable of any thought or emotion that is not trivial or base. This was not true in the Founding era when most of the greatest talents (among white males) turned to political life. For them, the study of history was worthy of the most penetrating intellects; for them, politics could be the vocation of great-souled human beings; for them, a powerful aspiration for perfection did not require a "flight from the I and WE to the IT." Rather they sought to make the ideal actual in the historical here and now; they sought, in Washington's words "the last stage of perfection to which human nature is capable of attaining"(above, page 397), or in Madison's words, "a Government pursuing the public good as its sole object," a pursuit that embodies "the most noble of all ambitions —that of promoting peace on earth and good will to man"(above, page 401). Or let us listen to Benjamin Rush when he urges a correspondent to come to America: "Here everything is in a plastic state. Here the benefactor of mankind may realize all his schemes for promoting human happiness. Human nature here (unsubdued by the tyranny of European habits and customs) yields to reason, justice, and common sense. Come, sir, and spread the influence of science and religion among us. America seems destined by heaven to exhibit to the world the perfection which the mind of man is capable of receiving from the combined operation of liberty, learning, and the gospel upon it"(1951 1:316; remember that, for Rush, to receive the gospel is to become a republican, cf. above, page 29). For the Founding generation, human beings are political animals who flourish best in a self-governing community that aspires to an enduring perfectibility. To participate in the political process of such a community is part of the life of those who reach and maintain the pinnacle of excellence that it is possible for human beings to achieve; it is part of the life of those who are grandmasters in that great art they called the pursuit of happiness.

Speaking of an afterlife, Jefferson once closed a letter to John Adams with these words: "May we meet there again, in Congress, with our ancient Colleagues, and receive with them the seal of approbation 'Well done good and faithful servants' "(Cappon 1959 2:594). Hannah Arendt observes: "Here, behind the irony, we have the candid admission that life in Congress, the joys of discourse, of legislation, of transacting business, of persuading and being persuaded, were to Jefferson . . . a foretaste of an eternal bliss . . . "(1963 127). No doubt many today would assume that what goes on in Congress is closer to eternal misery than eternal happiness, but why must it be so? Let us look at some other societies. Charles Mann in *1491* tells us that the "Olmec, Maya, and other Mesoamerican societies were world pioneers in mathematics and astronomy — but they did not use the wheel. Amazingly, they had invented the wheel but did not employ it for any purpose other than children's toys"(2006 21-2). We think: how could they be so blind as not to see the usefulness of the wheel in transporting dirt, or stones, or anything else? The Greeks too were world pioneers in mathematics, astronomy, and in many, many other ways, including engineering capable of producing sophisticated differential gears and the steam engine. We think: how could they be so blind as not to use their technology to produce labor-saving devices? We Americans as well are world leaders in mathematics, science, and technology, but when we think about our ethical and political problems it never occurs to us to think in engineering terms. How can we be so blind? Engineering is not just applicable to hardware or wetware, it is applicable to software; through it computers or governments can be made ergonomic. Aristotle would never have invented chemistry because he lacked esteem for matter; Jefferson would never have believed that free blacks and free whites could live peacefully and happily in Virginia, because he lacked esteem for blacks; and we seldom think of basing public policy on the common reason of the people, because we think that such reason, if it exists at all, is a worthless lowest common denominator. Our respect for the American people *as citizens* is shattered into random bits. Hence we cannot imagine using our imagination to *fully* exploit *all* the liberal arts in order to produce a government that precisely reflects the informed values and considered judgments of the people. When referring to the laws of physics, Richard Feynman says "You can recognize truth by its beauty and simplicity"(1965 171). But our legislators apply no such aesthetic discipline to legal, economic, and political propositions. They do not have enough esteem for the people, and thus for their responsibilities as representatives, to seek a *democratic beauty* grounded in the deliberate sense of the community; Necessity may be the mother of invention, but she will be childless until she embraces Engineering. The Greeks did not think of energy, and the Mesoamericans did not think of transportation, in engineering terms; we make the same mistake with respect to ethics and politics. Our Necessity, like theirs, is barren. We employ thousands and thousands of software engineers devoted to amusement, as it were, devoted to toys with wheels, but virtually none devoted to a politics of self-knowledge that has the prospect of fostering our pursuit of happiness with hitherto undreamed of success. Weep again, 1776 patriots.

"Those who cannot remember the past are condemned to repeat it," said Santayana (1954 82); but remembering is not enough; one must habitually scrutinize the present for anything that might be comparable to past errors. It is clear that the Founders did so, and thus Hegel's famous words of 1822 are completely false when applied to America's birth: "Rulers, statesmen and nations are often advised to learn the lesson of historical experience. But what experience and history teach is this — that nations and governments have never learned anything from history or acted upon any lessons they might have drawn from it"(1975 21). Yet remembering the past might also create a nostalgia to repeat it — even where precedents are not appropriate. The revolutionary generation had no such nostalgia. "Is it not the glory of the people of America," Madison boasts, "that whilst they have paid a decent regard to the opinions of former times and other nations, they have not suffered a blind veneration for antiquity, for custom, or for names, to overrule the suggestions of their own good sense, the knowledge of their own situation, and the lessons of their own experience?"(1962 10:288; cf. Jefferson 1950 31:128). Madison's point has a larger significance that he was not in a position to see. Alfred Russel Wallace, who independently discovered evolution when Darwin did, remarked that humans do not need natural evolution to get a warm coat of fur if the climate turns cold (1864 clxiii). Animals do and will die out if the change is too rapid. In sharp contrast humans can survive, even as their natural bodies remained naked, because cultural change allows them to develop the hunting technology and needles to rapidly get tailored fur coats. Cultural change also allows them to rapidly create dogs and corn by human selection; they did not have to depend on natural selection. Today the rate of past cultural change can itself be too slow and thereby a threat to humanity, as when well-established but inappropriate ideas, manners, and habits, including many in religion or philosophy, are taught to children, who then maintain them as adults. Taking centuries to remove racism against blacks, or millennia to remove sexism against women, is highly dangerous. Speeding up cultural evolution may be as important to humanity now, as speeding up natural evolution by culture was important to humanity in the past. We have the power to control the nature and rate of both biological and cultural evolution to become, as it were, the first fully autonomous species. But this self-mastery can only be achieved by painstakingly exploring the rational powers of the people in courts of common reason. The moral geometry of the American revolution is democratic, not elitist, it is fractal, not classical, it is entrepreneurial, not immutable. There is grandeur in this view of ourselves, but it must be tested anew. The belief that the "rational powers of the mind are the glory of human nature"(Shute 1767 28) was widely held in the eighteenth century; Madison was merely applying that doctrine to the American people, whose reason, he believed, would indirectly control the new political institutions to create, abolish, or modify laws solely for the public good. Madison's belief could be retested by challenging the American people to display their "glory" in the new Courts of Common Reason. Then, our politicians could formulate, enact, and enforce laws to reflect that "glory." To the degree that that reflection is accurate and functional, to that degree America will become truly revolutionary. We must think in twenty-first century terms: *software engineering for machines, but no software engineering for humans* is a formula for political and cultural failure; instead of the world becoming all-American as the revolutionary generation hoped and foretold, it could easily become post-American as our unrevolutionary generation fears and predicts. Just as Euclid's perfectionist respect for mathematical objects requires elegant abstract proofs of the utmost rigor, and Kepler's belief that nature is the product of a perfect Creator requires that the laws of nature be both awesome and consistent with the maximum degree of observational exactitude, so Jefferson's perfectionist aspirations for America require that laws governing society exhibit both a rational beauty and the highest degree of fidelity to the informed consent of the citizens, a fidelity that must not only be ensured by careful observation and meticulous experiments but that, further, must be scrupulously respected in the execution of those laws. We must not let cynicism with regard to the civic capability of the people blind us to the possibilities of a politics of self-knowledge and an economics of honesty. When we treat the public with perfectionist respect, political science and economics will become genuine moral sciences, they will be driven by an aesthetic aspiration disciplined to the common reason of the people, they will be forms of play with the beautiful, with the consequence that America will become a restored and "most conspicuous Theatre," superbly designed and exquisitely engineered, "for the display of human greatness and felicity."

15

The Metaphysics of Aspiration

The term *metaphysics* is sometimes used as a synonym for the occult, or for superstition in general. Although some metaphysical writing justifies these meanings, it is a mistake to let charlatans characterize a discipline. We speak of science, science fiction, science fantasy, scientific nonsense. The same distinctions hold in metaphysics. *Metaphysics*, as the term ought to used, refers to a legitimate activity. The nature of this activity can be explicated by considering the situation in the several centuries before Euclid laid down his axioms for geometry. At that time an ideally beautiful and exciting realm of abstract objects had been discovered (points, lines, triangles, circles, etc.), but it was far from obvious how one would come to know these objects, or what the basis of such knowledge was. The several-hundred-year search that ended in success with Euclid's axioms is an example of what might be called the *metaphysics of geometry*. Here I am following Abraham Robinson, the discoverer of nonstandard analysis, who wrote an essay entitled "The Metaphysics of the Calculus"(1979), a title he took from the eighteenth-century mathematician d'Alembert (1821 1:288-93). In my judgment it is very important to teach students of mathematics its metaphysics: that is, an explanation of the methods and history that together explain how and why the axioms of the mathematical disciplines were chosen. Unfortunately, for example, Peano's axioms for arithmetic, or Zermelo's for set theory, seldom receive this kind of attention in textbooks. In addition to axioms, metaphysicians are also concerned with basic presuppositions. For example, there are some things geometers presuppose but do not make explicit in their axioms, such as the assumption that memory is to some extent reliable, or that symbols are relatively permanent and do not change when we are not looking. Naturally the metaphysician is not limited to one discipline but is concerned with the fundamental assumptions and presuppositions of knowledge in general. (My conception of metaphysis is indebted to Collingwood (1957), although it is not the same.)

Metaphysics, properly understood, is tied to experience. "I believe," Einstein once said, that every true theorist is a kind of tamed metaphysicist, no matter how pure a "positivist" he may fancy himself. . . . The tamed metaphysicist believes . . . that the totality of all sensory experience can be "comprehended" on the basis of a conceptual system built on premises of great simplicity. The skeptic will say that this is a "miracle creed." Admittedly so, but it is a miracle creed which has been borne out to an amazing extent by the development of science. (1950 13)

Any good metaphysics is "tamed," that is, it is the product of a disciplined aestheticism; but we need not limit ourselves to sensory experience of nature: mathematical experience and social experience are also relevant.

We now turn to the distinction between descriptive and prescriptive metaphysics. The aim of *descriptive* metaphysics is to ascertain the axioms and fundamental presuppositions of knowledge at a given time and place. Kant's claim in *The Critique of Pure Reason* that Euclidean geometry is a basic presupposition of (Newtonian) science is a metaphysical description. But it does not take an eighteenth-century metaphysician to make such an analysis: a twenty-first-century philosopher who carefully studied the history of eighteenth century Europe could do as well. He could even show where Kant made metaphysical mistakes by demonstrating, for example, that Newtonian science did not presuppose some of the things Kant maintained. Descriptive metaphysics is thus part of the history of ideas — including recent history. *Prescriptive* metaphysics concerns itself not with what our basic axioms and presuppositions are, but with what they *ought* to be. It consists of proposals that, if successful, would create a revolution in the area or areas in question. Or it can be universal. Thus Francis Bacon called for "a wholesale Instauration [= renewal] of the sciences, arts and of all human learning, raised on proper foundations"(2004 3). His articulation and defense of those new foundations provide an example of prescriptive metaphysics for a new civilization.

Prescriptive metaphysics begins not with a proof, but a declaration. For instance, Euclid said in effect that we hold these truths to be self-evident: that *a straight line can be drawn from any point to any point*, that *a circle can be drawn with any center and diameter*, that *all right angles are equal*, and so forth. With that declaration he initiated a revolution in geometry. Geometry had a series of further revolutions in the work of Lobachevsky, Riemann, Hilbert, and Mandelbrot. In each case fundamental assumptions and presuppositions were challenged. Geometry has not been a discipline that is essentially fixed for all time, and it may not be so in the future. But how can prescriptive metaphysical claims be tested? The answer: by the difficult process of reorganizing a discipline on the new foundation. To be successful the prescriptive metaphysician must show how this reorganization will solve certain fundamental problems in the existing scheme, or open up fresh and fruitful areas for investigation. It introduces a new way of understanding, a new way of speaking, a new paradigm. The community of scholars must then determine if the reorganization is not only better than the old scheme, but so much better that it is worth the effort and the intellectual risk involved in carrying out the reorganization in detail. This is why such revolutions may take a good deal of time. In the detailed reorganization, new fundamental objections may arise that were not apparent at the time of the proposal. A revolution is only completed when objections are answered and the community accepts the new axioms and presuppositions.

America began with a metaphysical Declaration. It proposed something new: namely, to reorganize an actual society so as to presuppose the equal dignity of every human being, whose perfection is to be a morally free and liberally educated person pursuing a flourishing life in the context of a politically free society. To accept a metaphysical presupposition ("we hold these truths") is to resolve always to place it beyond challenge in case of failure. For example, in physics, we rest all our physical experiments on the capacity of reality to be mathematized. In all cases where that cannot be achieved, the blame is put on faulty observation, or inadequate experimental procedures, or insufficient mathematical insight, or the like. That there is some way or other to mathematize reality is beyond challenge. Of course, that claim can be challenged, but the challenge is *about* physics, not physics itself. It is a metaphysical challenge and its investigation is part of the history and philosophy of science. That investigation might seek to demonstrate, for example, that all such challenges fail; that a physics which presupposes universal mathematization is superior as to any physics, such as Aristotle's, which does not ("The minute accuracy of mathematics is not to be demanded in all cases, but only in the case of things which have no matter. Therefore its method is not that of natural science; for presumably all nature has matter"(1984 2:1572)). Metaphysical claims about society should be treated similarly. When Madison said, we "rest all our political experiments on the capacity of mankind for self-government"(above, page 134) he was articulating a prescriptive metaphysical claim in harmony with the Declaration, a presupposition on which the revolutionized, future America must rest. A politician thus revolutionized cannot put blame for failure on the people. If, for instance, the trial jury system does not work well, then the blame must not be put on jurors, but on the design of trials, overzealous prosecutors, incompetent defense lawyers, judges who give misleading instructions, and so forth. For example, suppose a large number of hypothetical "whodunits" are presented to mock trial juries. Suppose the error rate in their assignments of guilt is at a certain level. However, an analysis shows that their errors are substantially due to three common fallacies of reasoning. It is found that an hour's instruction concerning these fallacies greatly reduces that rate. Henceforth, in the name of improving justice in America, all trial juries, before being impaneled, would get that hour of instruction. This example is meant to embody Jefferson's earlier quoted advice: "if we think [the people] not enlightened enough to exercise their control with a wholesome discretion, the remedy is not to take it from them, but to inform their discretion by education"(above, page 218). Jefferson is presupposing that there is always some way or other for the people to carry out their political tasks. After their initial failures Kepler or Einstein did not blame the universe for not having rational beauty, but blamed themselves for not being able to discover it. Similarly, investigators who accept the philosophy of the American revolution would not blame the people for irrational answers in Courts of Common Reason, but would put the blame on the structure of those courts, or on its procedures, or on badly framed questions, or on an incorrect understanding of the answers, or on bad education, and so forth. Again, if the metaphysical elements of the Declaration are challenged, it is up to historians and political philosophers who accept those elements to demonstrate, by persuasive argument, that a society based on those elements is superior to any that rejects them. Here we can mimic Einstein: "The skeptic will say that the Declaration is a 'miracle creed.' Admittedly so, but it is a miracle creed which has been borne out to an amazing extent by the history of America."

Yet the metaphysical foundation of a revolutionized America is not merely the presupposition that self-government is possible; rather, it is that utterly excellent self-government is a reasonable and desirable goal. To quote Madison's words again: "the destined career of my country will exhibit a Government pursuing the public good as its sole object"(above, page 401). Democrats today generally express a belief in self-government — *and* a disbelief in excellent self-government. They have no perfectionist respect for the people. Western science — now world science — is a kind of grand metaphysical experiment to test whether perfectionist respect for nature is justified. That it *is* justified is one of the great dreams of reason. In the same way, the American revolution is the grand metaphysical experiment that tests whether perfectionist respect for humans in their civic capacity is justified. George Washington, in his first inaugural address, declared this experiment to be crucial for all humanity: ". . . the preservation of the sacred fire of liberty, and the destiny of the Republican model of Government, are justly considered as deeply, perhaps as finally staked, on the experiment entrusted to the hands of the American people"(1931 30:294-5; cf. Farrand 1937 1:424 and DHRC 1976 2:359). Let us remember again that, for Washington, the revolution's ultimate goal was to reach "the last stage of perfection to which human nature is capable of attaining"(above, page 397). But just as the "miracle creed" of Einsteinian science assumes it is possible to find a set of basic laws that simultaneously fits all the evidence and gives transcendent aesthetic pleasure, so America's "miracle creed" assumes it is possible to find a set of constitutional laws that gives similar pleasure and, at the same time, creates ideal conditions to forever perfect both private and public happiness. There are no ultimate irreconcilable conflicts; in Washington's words, ". . . there is no truth more thoroughly established, than that there exists in the economy and course of nature, an indissoluble union between virtue and happiness, between duty and advantage, between the genuine maxims of an honest and magnanimous policy, and the solid rewards of public prosperity and felicity"(294, cf. Locke 1975 69 and Jefferson 1903 16: 282).

The experiments in the physical sciences occur in a political and economic environment that the scientist does not take into account in formulating theories. America, however, is an experiment in which the experimenters are also subjects of the experiment. It is a kind of experiment of experiments — a metaexperiment — to create the best political and economic conditions in which other experiments can be carried out — whether they belong to social life, the arts, the humanities, the sciences, the social sciences, business, technology, or whatever. America as an ideal is the greatest of the dreams of reason since it provides an environment in which reason's other dreams may be transformed into reality. Every lover of knowledge and the beautiful should hope she succeeds.

It is, I believe, much, much harder than most people think, to imagine the enormous benefits of true excellence in government. Consider, for example, a person who was best off at a point in the distant past — say, an Egyptian pharaoh. Average Americans are much better off in almost every way, from the freedom of fear from eclipses and comets, to the quality of dental and medical care available, to the variety of music that is at their fingertips, to . . . but who could not make this list indefinitely long? "Poverty under a democracy," said Democritus, "is as much to be preferred to so-called prosperity under an autocracy as freedom to slavery"(Freeman 1966 114). The American revolution is a revolution intended to appeal to everyone since it promises to protect each and every person's pursuit of happiness. But more than protection is achieved, for any person's pursuit of happiness is greatly enhanced if it occurs in a context where everyone else has an equal freedom for that pursuit. Were we to achieve true excellence in democratic government, perhaps the best-off people in contemporary America would prefer to be average or poor under that government, than to be kept in their present status.

It might seem the metaphysics of American democracy overlooks evil in human nature, that the gigantic debaucheries of Stalin, Hitler, Mao, and al-Qaeda make absurd any aspirations toward excellence in government. Yet a reading of the Founders shows that they were acutely aware of gross moral failures, an awareness that let to the complex system of checks and balances in the Constitution. It is a mistake to believe that the vast scale of evils that modern technology has produced necessitates a more pessimistic view of the prospects of humanity than earlier generations held on the basis of evils known to them. The same superior knowledge and technology that we possess, and that so greatly magnifies the abominations of earlier centuries, gives us superior opportunities for frustrating those evils. The possible size of those evils, however, makes the aspiration for political excellence more desperate.

Still, it might be wondered if a truly profound view of the human condition, a view that is articulated with an intimate acquaintance of human tragedies in all their depth, is at all consistent with American ideals. A long line of thinkers from Plato to Nietzsche has argued that democracy is incompatible with nobility. And it is with nobility that the great writers of tragedy — Aeschylus, Sophocles, Euripides, Shakespeare — have primarily been concerned. Whatever plausibility this view might have, it quickly evaporates under examination. For tragedy, as Aristotle maintained, is concerned with "actions and life" and not "persons"(1984 2:2320); there is thus no reason why a commoner is any less capable of noble acts than an aristocrat. Indeed if we look for an early American work that most nearly captures an ethos found in the great writers of tragedy, it is *Moby-Dick*. And

Melville makes quite clear his belief in the compatibility of democracy and tragedy:

> But this august dignity I treat of, is not the dignity of kings and nobles, but that abounding dignity which has no robed investiture. Thou shalt see it shining in the arm that wields a pick or drives a spike; that democratic dignity, which, on all hands, radiates without end from God; Himself! The great God absolute! The centre and circumstance of all democracy! His omnipresence, our divine equality! If, then, to meanest mariners, and renegades and castaways, I shall hereafter ascribe high qualities, though dark; weave round them tragic graces; if even the most mournful, perchance the most abased, among them all, shall at times, lift himself to the exalted mounts; if I shall touch that workman's arm with some ethereal light; if I shall spread a rainbow over his disastrous set of sun; then against all mortal critics bear me out in it, thou just Spirit of Equality, which hast spread one royal mantle of humanity over all my kind! Bear me out in it, thou great democratic God! (1952 114)

If we assume, apart from foreigners, that every inhabitant is a citizen, Melville's sentiment is implicit in Aristotle's belief that politicians should aim at making citizens "good and capable of noble acts"(1984 2:1738). On July 2, 1776, Washington tried to do just that when he sent general orders to his army: "Let us therefore rely upon the goodness of the Cause, and the aid of the supreme Being, in whose hands Victory is, to animate and encourage us to great and noble Actions"(1931 5:211; cf. Emmons 1787 892). Like Washington, contemporary politicians should inspire the common person individually, and the American people collectively, to noble action. If they achieve success, but nevertheless some final calamity overwhelms the country, would it not then be justifiable for some surviving Ishmael to wrap tragic graces around the American people, and to spread a rainbow over their disastrous set of sun? "I sincerely wish," John Jay observed in 1787, "that it may be clearly foreseen by every good citizen, that whenever the dissolution of the Union arrives, America will have reason to exclaim in the words of the poet, "Farewell! a long farewell, to all my greatness"(1890 3:267; cf. *King Henry VIII*, Act 3, Scene 2, line 352). Paine's vision of America coming to an end was described in similar heroic terms: "It will not then be said, here stood a temple of vast antiquity, here rose a babel of invisible height, or there a palace of sumptuous extravagance; but here, ah painful thought! the noblest work of human wisdom, the grandest scene of human glory, the fair cause of freedom rose and fell"(1796 9; cf. Dexter 1798 8).

For many citizens today the federal government is not perceived as heroic, but as distant, unresponsive, and small-souled. To these feelings of alienation are often added feelings of meaninglessness, the fear that in some profound sense their lives, their society, even the universe itself, has no moral foundation. Such feelings are sometimes given as an explanation, even a justification, for political apathy or despair or cynicism. Yet these experiences are hardly unique to our age. Alienation was the disturbing feeling that led Americans to rise up against the country they loved, against the country that had defined their identity. In 1767 Benjamin Franklin warned Lord Kames that "if Force is us'd, great Mischief will ensue, the affections of the People of America to this Country [Britain] will be alienated"(1959 14:67). In 1770 Edmund Burke, speaking in Parliament, said the colonies "grow every day into alienation from this country"(1981 2:285). The Americans then created a new nation that better fit their spirit. But that fit was not perfect. In a remarkable letter written to Gouverneur Morris on February 29, 1802, Hamilton writes:

> Mine is an odd destiny. Perhaps no man in the UStates has sacrificed or done more for the present Constitution than myself — and contrary to all my anticipations of its fate, as you know from the very beginning I am still labouring to prop the frail and worthless fabric. [During the Constitutional Convention Hamilton "acknowledged himself not to think favorably of Republican Government"(Farrand 1937 1:424).] Yet I have the murmurs of its friends no less than the curses of its foes for my rewards. What can I do better than withdraw from the Scene? Every day proves to me more and more that this American world was not made for me. (1961 25:544)

Had Hamilton's last sentence been unknown to me, and I was asked to guess its provenance, I would have said a student or faculty radical, in a moment of despair, at an American college or university in the 1960s. The experience of alienation could hardly be more poignantly expressed, yet Hamilton made outstanding contributions to republican government. Einstein felt alienated from most of the greatest physicists of the twentieth century because he stubbornly resisted quantum mechanics, a theory to which he nevertheless made outstanding contributions. It is a source of great wonderment that the whirlwinds of the American and quantum mechanical revolutions could be so powerful that the greatest opponent of each revolution was sucked into making brilliant contributions to what he strongly opposed. Anyone who claims that one must have faith in a revolution to be one of its leaders overlooks the subtleties of genius, honor, fame, and the human heart.

John Adams, with humor and irony, also expresses alienation: "From the year 1761, now more than fifty years, I have constantly lived in an enemy's country. And that without having one personal enemy in the world that I know of"(Schutz and Adair 1966 205). He also faces meaninglessness, yet without seeing it as a justification for political apathy or despair or cynicism. Adams thought that "without the Supposition of a future State, Mankind and this Globe appear to me the most sublime and beautifull Bubble and Bauble that Imagination can conceive"(Cappon 1959 2:486; cf. 399-400, 471, 530). Yet elsewhere he ruminates:

> A death bed, it is said, shews the emptiness of titles. That may be. But does it not equally shew the futility of riches, power, liberty, and all earthly things? The cloud-capt towers, the gorgeous palaces, the solemn temples, the great globe itself, appear the baseless fabric of a vision, and life itself a tale, told by an idiot, full of sound and fury, signifying nothing. Shall it be inferred from this, that fame, liberty, property, and life, shall be always despised and neglected? Shall laws and government, which regulate sublunary things be neglected, because they appear baubles at the hour of death? (1805 40; cf. John Witherspoon's similar reflections (1802 4:350) and Joseph Addison (from 1711): "The Death-Bed shews the Emptiness of Titles in a true Light"(Addison and Steele 1965 2:352).)

Adams means, I think, that even if the whole human world is destined to dissolve and leave not a rack behind, even if our earthly existence is in some ultimate sense futile, even then, it is worth bothering about "fame, liberty, property, and life," even then, the American revolution is worth pursuing. In that pursuit we might today see some hope of creating a humane existence, even if the universe is meaningless, and humanity itself is a bauble beginning as the accidental byproduct of a ghastly, evolutionary slaughterhouse, and destined to end, utterly devoid of any significance, in a cosmic nanosecond.

But is such a hope justified? It is certainly a widespread perception that Western science, starting with Copernicus, began something that undermines the belief that the universe has a moral meaning, and thereby, the belief that human action does. For example, in 1810 Goethe observed that perhaps no greater challenge than the teaching of Copernicus had confronted humankind, for with it, he said, so much went up in "dust and smoke: a second paradise, a world of innocence, poetry and piety, the testimony of the senses, the convictions of a poetic-religious faith . . ."(1949 395; cf. Emerson 1960 4:26). A similar nostalgia led William Butler Yeats in 1889 to become explicitly antiscientific (1989 8):

Seek, then,
No learning from the starry men,
Who follow with optic glass
The whirling ways of stars that pass —
Seek, then, for this is also sooth,
No word of theirs — the cold star-bane
Has cloven and rent their hearts in twain,
And dead is all their human truth.

In 1887 Nietzsche likewise saw humanity diminished by science:

> Has man perhaps become *less desirous* of a transcendent solution to the riddle of his existence, now that his existence appears more arbitrary, beggarly, and dispensable in the *visible* order of things? Has the self-belittlement of man, his *will* to self-belittlement, not progressed irresistibly since Copernicus? Alas, the faith in the dignity and uniqueness of man, in his irreplaceability in the great chain of being, is a thing of the past — he has become an *animal*, literally and without reservation or qualification . . . Since Copernicus, man seems to have got himself on an inclined plane — now he is slipping faster and faster away from the center into — what? into nothingness? into a "*penetrating* sense of his nothingness"? . . . *All* science . . . has at present the object of dissuading man from his former respect for himself, as if this had been nothing but a piece of bizarre conceit. (1969 155-6)

In 1917 Freud took up the same theme by arguing that science had given three mighty blows to human narcissism: the cosmological blow, due to Copernicus; the biological blow, due to Darwin; and finally the psychological blow, due to Schopenhauer and Freud himself. The latter is the realization that the human ego is not even master in the psychological world in which it is defined (1966 17:139-144; cf. 16:284-5 and Jones 1953 2:226).

Many contemporary scientists see little hope for a return to some kind of cosmic meaning. Steven Weinberg, in his book *The First Three Minutes*, presents a view (as of 1977) of the origin and destiny of the universe. He concludes: ". . . this present universe has evolved from an unspeakably unfamiliar early condition, and faces a future extinction of endless cold or intolerable heat. The more the universe seems comprehensible the more it also seems pointless"(144). Could our existence be any more "arbitrary, beggarly, and dispensable in the visible order of things" than this? If we move from the cosmological to the earthly level, "human truth" seems equally pointless. What was the purpose of the life and death of billions and billions of dinosaurs?

Or of their final extinction, which made possible the triumph of mammals, and ultimately, humans? We are the arbitrary creation of a brutal and grossly inefficient evolution. Here we have accident after accident and the fact that humanity exists in the precise way it does, from the birth of the universe until now, appears to require odds greater than any that have every been articulated, maybe than could be articulated. History seems just as arbitrary. In *Ecclesiastes* we read that "under the sun the race is not to the swift, nor the battle to the strong, nor bread to the wise, nor riches to the intelligent, nor favor to the men of skill; but time and chance happen to them all"(9:11). Solon said that "human life is entirely a matter of chance"(Herodotus 1998 15). Pascal pointed out with regard to Cleopatra's nose: "had it been shorter, the whole face of the earth would have been changed"(1950 51). The same might today be said of Darwin, who remarked that Fitz-Roy, the captain of the Beagle, almost rejected him "on account of the shape of my nose"(1887 1:50). The chaotic nature of history matches the chaotic nature of the weather, as exemplified in Edward Lorenz's question (1993 181): "*Does the Flap of a Butterfly's Wings in Brazil Set off a Tornado in Texas?*" Technically speaking chaos is a kind of mean between complete randomness and complete order. There is order, but the road to the present will always have elements of randomness. Jefferson and Madison (above, page 392) saw the mighty American revolution being provoked by a trivial tax on tea. Writing in 1812, John Adams recollects that "every measure of Congress, from 1774 to 1787 inclusively, was disputed with acrimony, and decided by as small majorities as any question is decided these days"(1850 10:23). How different our world would be if those "small majorities" had gone the other way. Adams believed that "this globe, and as far as we can see this Universe, is a theatre of vicissitudes"(1954 Reel 124 215). Consider the list of all the winners of all the state lotteries. What was the chance that it would now be just that list? Or consider the odds of success of the sperm from which any actual person has come, given millions of competitors in the womb. Rather than an untalented sibling, was a mother's hiccup what occasioned the conception of Aristotle or Leonardo or Shakespeare? And what is the chance that all the billions of humans that actually exist are here rather than unconceived brothers or sisters? And how many chance occurrences worldwide were required that allowed me to write these words and you to read them? It can be frightening to contemplate our chaotic world.

Nevertheless we should remember that the Ptolemaic system, which preceded the Copernican, had its own terrors. Consider Shakespeare's description in *Troilus and Cressida* (Act 1, Scene 3, lines 94 -103):

> But when the planets
> In evil mixture to disorder wander,
> What plagues and what portents, what mutiny?
> What raging of the sea, shaking of earth?
> Commotion in the winds, frights, changes, horrors
> Divert and crack, rend and deracinate
> The unity and married calm of states
> Quite from their fixture. O when degree is shaked,
> Which is the ladder to all high designs,
> The enterprise is sick.

Copernicus, Kepler, and Newton showed that the planets do not wander, states are not upset, and the awesome beauty and intelligence of the universal law of gravitation puts to shame all previous "high designs." Furthermore, the claim that science leaves room for no other conclusion except a complete nihilism hardly seems justified. Something might not matter in some larger or cosmic sense, but that doesn't mean it doesn't matter to the individual or, say, to the American people. Would the nihilist freely submit to harsh torture merely because she believed life has no ultimate meaning? Franklin said that he does "not perceive, that the Supreme takes it amiss, by distinguishing the Unbelievers in his Government of the World with any peculiar Marks of his Displeasure"(1907 10:34). Certainly those individuals or organizations that deny any divine meaning do not seem to have an existence any less moral, any less significant, or any less flourishing, than those that affirm it. Why should public happiness therefore fall apart if such "Unbelievers" become the majority? Private or public happiness can and should be meaningfully pursued whether or not there is a larger or cosmic meaning. Consider an existence dominated by gloom and depression, where lives are, to use Hobbes' phrase, "solitary, poore, nasty, brutish, and short"(1968 186). Compare that with an existence dominated by exuberance, a life of happiness, as described by Aristotle: "good birth, plenty of friends, good friends, wealth, good children, plenty of children, a happy old age, also such bodily excellences as health, beauty, strength, large stature, athletic powers, together with fame, honour, good luck, and excellence"(1984 2:2163). Whether individuals gain Hobbesian or

Aristotelian lives, as just described, certainly matters to each individual, even if there is no meaning at all to humanity itself, or to the universe. The same reasoning applies to public misery or happiness. Thus Lincoln was confronted by meaninglessness. On one occasion, just before reading aloud the "Tomorrow" speech of *Macbeth* (Act 5, Scene 5, lines 19-27), he said "it comes to me to-night like a consolation"(Forney 2:180-181). Nevertheless that "consolation" did not lead him to give up trying to preserve the Union; he didn't want America to become a failed state, even if life in some grand sense signifies nothing. Inferring that if a whole is devoid of meaning, the parts must also be devoid of meaning, is an instance of the fallacy of division, which can be illustrated by saying that because Noam Chomsky's well-known sentence — "Colorless green ideas sleep furiously"(1957 15). — is meaningless, it follows that the words that make it up are also meaningless. The American revolution does not require, but neither does it deny, extraterrestrial meaning; what it does is to create and sustain the conditions for (at least) a terrestrial meaning appropriate for flourishing lives. Hence even if in some larger or cosmic sense, meaninglessness has a victory, even if modernity has a sting, neither makes the pursuit of happiness through American revolution a vain or futile aspiration.

It is a curious fact that the oldest maps of the most southern parts of the globe, drawn at a time when cartographers used their imagination where they were ignorant, seem more accurate (because they largely guessed right about Antarctica) than somewhat later maps, when cartographers, with higher epistemological standards, left blank what they did not know. Suppose that from the vantage point of a millennium hence, a similar situation holds on the question of cosmic meaning: that is, because of higher epistemological standards in our era, the preponderance of educated opinion leaves the geography of cosmic meaning blank, but educated opinion will eventually, and substantially, re-establish past guesses of cosmic meaning with the same certainty we now have about Antarctica. Even if this be true, it would be foolish to base free societies today on cosmic meanings that are made doubtful by our present higher epistemological standards, because the societies themselves may then collapse due to the relentless criticisms of skeptics, and the ultimate truth may never be discovered. Believers thus have a motive to establish free societies in such a way as to be capable of weathering an age of skepticism, just as doubters have the same motive with regard to an age of belief. America should provide the field in which the controversy can peacefully, either continue indefinitely, or be decided, if that proves possible, once and for all.

Of those who deny that science leads to a complete nihilism, a majority perhaps believe it nevertheless results in the belittlement of human potentialities. These milder cases allow a perfectionist respect of nature by scientists, but they do not allow a perfectionist respect of human beings. There are no moral wonders of human nature to generate political wonder. Peter Medawar, winner of the 1960 Nobel Prize in Medicine, complains: "The real trouble is our acute sense of human failure and mismanagement, a new and specially oppressive sense of the inadequacy of men. So much was hoped of us, particularly in the eighteenth century. ... Once again our intellectuals have failed us; there is a general air of misanthropy and self-contempt, of protest, but not affirmation. ... To deride the hope of progress is the ultimate fatuity, the last word in poverty of spirit and meanness of mind"(1996 117-19). Yet self-belittlement of humanity did not begin in the twentieth century, or even with Copernicus. Plato, for example, had said that "a man whose thoughts are fixed on true reality has no leisure to look downward on the affairs of men"(1955 208). Since the "affairs of men" are not "true reality" it is not surprising to find Plato claiming that "nothing human is matter for great concern"(336). Again, the Greek playwright Philemon says: "D' you think there's any difference at all between a man and another animal? There's none except in shape; it's long, he's tall"(Edmonds 1961 3:7). Self-belittlement is also common in Judaism and Christianity. The "children of men," we are told by the Psalmist, "have all gone astray, they are all alike corrupt; there is none that does good, no, not one"(14:2-3; cf. 53:2-3 and *Romans* 3:10-12). Again, "I said in my heart with regard to the sons of men that God is testing them to show them that they are but beasts. For the fate of the sons of men and the fate of the beasts is the same, the one dies, so dies the other. They all have the same breath, and man has no advantage over the beasts; for all is vanity. All go to one place; all are from the dust, and all turn to dust again"(*Ecclesiastes* 3:18-20). In effect the Bible presents us with a belittling Darwinism, a doctrine that tells us we are great apes, mere beasts, with no advantage over bonobos, chimpanzees, gorillas, or orangutans; their breath is our breath, their fate our fate. Since contemporary thinkers can no more plausibly reject evolution than earlier thinkers could plausibly reject the Bible, psychologically, the problem of Darwinian nihilism for us, and Biblical nihilism for them, appear the same.

How did some former thinkers deal with the threat of nihilism? Let us look at John Donne. In his 1611 poem, *The First Anniversary,* he considers the depressing significance of science (1929 335):

> And new Philosophy cals all in doubt,
>
> The Element of fire is quite put out;
> The Sun is lost, and th'earth, and no mans wit
> Can well direct him, where to looke for it.
> And freely men confesse, that this world's spent,
> When in the Planets, and the Firmament
> They seeke so many new; they see that this
> Is crumbled out againe to his Atomis.
> "Tis all in peeces, all cohærence gone;

But Donne knew, as many today seem not to know, that the Bible also presents us with the challenge of nihilism. Thus his sermon of May 8, 1625, takes as its text Psalm 62:9: "Surely men of low degree are vanity, and men of high degree are a lie; to be laid in the balance, they are altogether lighter than vanity"(1953 6:292). Donne evades the hopelessness of this passage by showing that to read it unconditionally is to contradict other parts of the Bible:

> . . . we say, for the dignity of man, *Cui dixit,* of what creature did God ever say, *Faciamus,* Let us, us make it, All, all, the Persons together, and to imploy, and exercise, nor onely Power, but Counsaile in the making of that Creature? . . . David asks . . . with a holy wonder, *Quid est homo? What is man that God is so mindfull of him?* But I may have his leave, and the holy Ghosts, to say, since God is so mindfull of him, since God hath set his minde upon him, What is not man? Man is all. . . . He is not a piece of the world, but the world it selfe; and next to the glory of God, the reason why there is a world. . . . So that still, simply, absolutely, unconditionally, we cannot say, Surely men, men altogether, high or low, or meane, all are lesse than vanity. And surely they that pervert and distort such words as these, to such a use, and argue from thence, Man is nothing, no more than a worme, or a fly, and therefore what needs this solemne consideration of mans actions, it is all one what he does, for all his actions, and himselfe too are nothing; They doe this but to justifie or excuse their own lazinesse in this world . . . (1953 6:296, 297-8, 299; in 1609, Francis Bacon, using the Prometheus myth, had argued that "Man, if we look to final causes, may be regarded as the centre of the world" and that "the whole world works together in the service of man"(1860 8:147).)

Anyone who today wishes to awaken the American revolution must, like Donne, justify "solemne consideration of mans actions" and the perfectionist respect on which that consideration depends. And the method can be the same, for just as Donne shows that various parts and presuppositions of the Bible are inconsistent with interpreting it as affirming an absolute belittlement of human beings, so it can be shown that various parts and presuppositions of science are also inconsistent with affirming an absolute belittlement of human beings. For example, both a belittling *Ecclesiastes* and a belittling Darwinism proclaim that "man has no advantage over the beasts." But what advantages do the beasts have? The scientific study of artificial life suggests that natural life, like artificial life, is an embodiment of an indestructible abstract structure. Animals, including humans, have mortal bodies but, as it were, immortal "souls." Consider the game of ACE. In it two players take turns picking up cards from a set numbered one through nine. The object is to be the first player to get a set of three cards whose sum is fifteen. This game, although materially different, is actually the game of tick-tack-toe. This can be seen by studying the following grid:

$$6 \quad 1 \quad 8$$

$$7 \quad 5 \quad 3$$

$$2 \quad 9 \quad 4$$

Analysis of the grid shows that to every game of Ace there is exactly one of tick-tack-toe, and vice versa. These games are related by what mathematicians call an *isomorphism*, that is, they have the same number of elements, and the structures of the games are identical. The essence or, using our analogy, the soul of tick-tack-toe does not consist of X's and O's, or of cards marked 1 through 9; rather, it is the abstract structure common to its many different material versions. Notice that the structure is eternal; it is no more possible to destroy that structure than it is possible to destroy the number 17, or the square root of 2. To each living thing at a given time, there evidently also corresponds an abstract artificial life structure. (One wonders: Is there something in the universe that is isomorphic to me, but is materially very unlike myself, like the material difference between ACE and tick-tack-toe, only more so?) It follows that the game of life for an individual person is just as eternal as the game of tick-tack-toe. Of course, it might have happened that no one thought up 17, the square root of 2, or tick-tack-toe. But once contemplated, we can say, of an actual tick-tack-toe game played on a blackboard, "chalk dust thou *art*, and, when erased, unto chalk dust shalt thou return." The abstract structure, of which the blackboard game is an instantiation, is not destroyed: instances of it were played countless times before and will be replayed countless times again. The game of life could likewise be replayed countless times, as Hinduism suggests, perhaps in parallel universes, as contemporary scientific speculations sometimes maintain. Thus Ecclesiastical Darwinism, which proclaims "all are of the dust and all return to dust again"(3:20; cf. *Job* 34:15) may be true but misleading. (If there were only two choices, one wonders how many persons would prefer an omnipotent god who creates and insures a happy but once-and-done finite life, to a happy eternal life, but no god.)

Further, self-belittlement by humans, if carried to extremes, belittles the claim of self-belittlement. If we were completely worthless, we would not be able to comprehend, much less prove, that fact. Donne's solution to Biblical self-belittlement and nihilism is an early indication of a change in understanding the Bible, a change that ultimately led to its republican interpretation in America (above, page 28). Americans applied that interpretation to science as well as the Bible. Consider an analogy. If, in the traditional game of tick-tack-toe, someone proposed a *strategy* of trying to achieve two ways of getting four-in-a-row, this would be incompatible with the *rules* of the game (since there would be no possibility of getting four-in-a-row). Moral science (the strategies for successful pursuits of happiness) must be in harmony with natural science (the rules of the universe, so to say). But the practice of science should also be in harmony with moral science; there should no experimental torture, however scientifically planned, on unwilling subjects. For republicans, science is made for humans, not humans for science. Here we can state the Principle of Integrity for scientific disciplines: No interpretation of experimental or theoretical results is acceptable if that interpretation would make the pursuit of science pointless, or wrong. For example, Einstein's view of humans (above, page 412) violates this principle. It makes the discipline of science senseless, since there can be no ethical preference for truth over falsehood. His friend Max Born called Einstein's claim "quite abhorrent"(1971 155). Unfortunately Einstein's view is not passé. We are often told that science has proven the self is a mere apparition, that the belief that we can control our thoughts or actions is an illusion, that we are no more than biological robots in a world devoid of value or meaning. Were this true without qualification, the practice of science, and the ethics and politics that nurtures it, would be nugatory. Scientific nihilism cannibalizes science itself.

Just as Galileo, Kepler, and Newton presupposed that one theory applies to the celestial and terrestrial worlds, so Locke and the Founding generation presupposed one theory applies to the natural and moral worlds. The content of science is forced upon us, but we have freedom in the choice of problems to be investigated and experiments to be conducted, including some freedom in the interpretation of results. There is today no more important metaphysical pursuit than to find an adequate set of metaphysical presuppositions for contemporary science that can be consistently combined with an adequate set for a free society. Those dedicating themselves to that pursuit would, like the Founding generation, be entrepreneurs in the cause of humanity.

Suppose we ask: Could there be any objective scientific evidence that the world has a moral meaning? Scientists have generally agreed that the question is not scientific. Yet how well-grounded is this answer? For example, for a long time scientific evidence supported an eternal universe; to talk about it as having a beginning was thought to be unscientific, even meaningless. Then in 1964 Arno Penzias and Robert Wilson tried to measure radio noise coming from gas surrounding our galaxy. Their serendipitous discovery, for which they received a Nobel Prize, was a cosmic microwave background radiation that provided evidence for the universe having a beginning. But where would we look for evidence of moral meaning? Since the only certain source of meaning that we know is ourselves, we might try looking at what is known about human origins. How did the thinking and emotions by which humans found meaning come into existence? Science answers: by an evolutionary process that is universally exhibited in the history of all life. But when we inquire in response to what did such things as our resourceful intelligence, our refined emotions, our aesthetic sensibility, prove their survival value, the answer remains speculative. In my judgment, the most plausible answer is: in response to rapidly changing social competition within prehuman or early human colonies. The intelligence capable of creating the calculus, the emotion capable of romantic love, the aesthetic sensibility that delights in a Beethoven symphony did not, it would seem, come into existence because they were needed to protect us against lions, or because it was necessary to put food in prehuman bellies. The other great apes, the monkeys, and the baboons survived without such capabilities. Although Darwinian evolution had been, and remains, one of the most fruitful ideas in the history of science, it has rendered mysterious something that had formerly been clear from Biblical tradition. According to that tradition, we were made by God in his image. Our mental life, although imperfect, was of the same kind as his, so there was always the possibility of understanding the universe, at least to some degree. Kepler, Newton, and Einstein believed they were, to some extent, rethinking the thoughts of Nature's God. If true, then God is a mathematician, and their theories, in a significant measure, really do apply to the universe. But what if Biblical tradition is rejected? "With me," said an anxious Darwin, "the horrid doubt always arises whether the convictions of man's mind, which has been developed from the mind of the lower animals, are of any value or at all trustworthy. Would any one trust in the convictions of a monkey's mind, if there are any convictions in such a mind?"(1887 1:285). But if human convictions are all untrustworthy, how can the theory of evolution, or science itself, be justified? It is a "horrid doubt" that they cannot. We could try to limit the universality of this doubt by applying the thought to itself (if we can't trust our minds at all, then our doubt is untrustworthy). Even if we are successful, we ought to ask: Why should our resourceful intelligence, refined emotions, and aesthetic sensibilities, that come into existence by being highly social animals, be just what is needed to understand the universe? The religious answer of *God* or the secular answer of *happy accident* result in an unjustifiable end to inquiry. Yet this is what the best physicists have typically given us. Thus Einstein says: "Even if the axioms of [Newton's theory of gravitation] are proposed by man, the success of such a project presupposes a high degree of ordering of the objective world, and this could not be expected *a priori*. That is the "miracle" that is being constantly reinforced as our knowledge expands. . . . . Oddly, enough, we must be satisfied to acknowledge the "miracle" without there being any legitimate way for us to approach it"(1987 131, 133). Weyl says: "But this ultimate foundation for the ratio governing the world, we can find only in God; it is one side of the Divine Being. Thus the ultimate answer lies beyond all knowledge"(28). Wigner says: "The miracle of the appropriateness of the language of mathematics for the formulation of the laws of physics is a wonderful gift which we neither understand nor deserve"(1960 14). Dirac says: "It seems to be one of the fundamental features of nature that fundamental physical laws are described in terms of a mathematical theory of great beauty and power, needing quite a high standard of mathematics to understand it. You may wonder: Why is nature constructed along these lines? One can only answer that our present knowledge seems to show that nature is so constructed. We simply have to accept it"(1963 53). In contrast, the history of mathematics and science suggests that continuing acceptance of a fact is neither reasonable or fruitful, we should always wonder why, we should always look for a "legitimate way for us to approach it." For example, Cantor rejected the idea that infinity is an inquiry stopper; instead he developed a mathematics of the infinite in order to gain a more profound conception of God. Again, since Galileo it was known that all objects of whatever weight fall at the same rate in a vacuum. From a Newtonian point of view this equality was entirely coincidental — the stronger gravitational attraction of heavier objects (which initiated motion) just happened to be exactly matched by their stronger inertial force (which retarded motion). Einstein showed that this equality was not accidental, that gravitation and inertia were really the same force seen from different points of view. The history of mathematics and science suggest that, regardless of whether we are want to know more about God, or want to eliminate all appeals to God, there should be no elimination of wonder, no inquiry stoppers.

So could there then be some connection between the evolutionary process by which we gained the ability to think mathematically, and the structure of the universe? Penzias and Wilson used a highly sophisticated antenna — created for the purpose of communication — to discover evidence for the universe having a beginning. Could some future political scientists use highly sophisticated courts of common reason — created for the purposes of regulating the economic and political activities of Americans — to discover evidence connecting the deliberate sense of human communities, and the universe, or its meaning? Of course, *prima facie* there seems to be no possible relation. Yet *prima facie* there seems to be no connection between the tides and the moon; but Kepler claimed there was. Initially that idea seemed fanciful. Galileo himself used it as a sign that Kepler lacked the scientific spirit (1953 462). Yet if there is no connection, why is there a consistent correlation between the rhythm of the moon and the rhythm of the tides? If there is no connection between the social problems in prehuman communities and the structure of the world, why is there a correlation between our intelligence, emotions, and sensibilities created in response to those problems, on the one hand, and our ability to understand the universe, on the other? Is our universe a fractal in some relevant sense, so that the talents needed to *survive* locally include those that are needed to *understand* cosmologically? We should investigate how we might ultimately explain — rationally, scientifically, and metaphysically —what Einstein, Weyl, Wigner, and Dirac find baffling; we should try to lay Darwin's "horrid doubt" to rest. As part of this investigation, would it not be reasonable to investigate the common reason of the people of the earth?

Likewise we should continue to wonder about the apparent randomness of human existence. Consider the following sequence of digits:

785398163399744830961566084581987757 . . .

What does it signify? Could you name the next digit? Initially it seems to be inscrutable, an incompressible, brute, mathematical fact, with no "legitimate way for us to approach it." Some will no doubt pronounce it to be so after a few minutes, yet a rational and industrious person might keep at the problem for quite a long time. She might eventually try multiplying the first four digits by 2, then 3, then 4, to see if anything familiar shows up. The latter yields 31412. Since this number looks like the beginning of the decimal expansion of π, she confirms this hunch by checking the other digits. Hence the sequence is not random but represents the decimal expansion of $\pi/4$. She might then recall that there is a simple and elegant way, discovered by Leibniz, to represent $\pi/4$ by series of fractions. That is,

$$\pi/4 = 1 - 1/3 + 1/5 - 1/7 + 1/9 - 1/11 + 1/13 - 1/15 + . . .$$

Thus what was initially seen as a meaningless sequence of digits, where naming the next one seems impossible, can be transformed into a highly ordered sequence of fractions, where naming the next one is easy (cf. Jauch 1973 63 and Hofstadter 1979 408-9.). Again, imagine a flat surface marked with parallel lines an inch apart. An inch long needle is repeatedly and randomly dropped on the surface n times. Let P_n be a fraction where the numerator is the number of times the needle crossed a line, and the denominator is, n,. Amazingly, as n grows larger, $2/ P_n$ gets arbitrarily close to π (cf. Beckmann 1971 159-65). π is, as it were, the telos of the random process. These examples show that apparent randomness is no guarantee that the reality represented cannot be understood as orderly and meaningful; nor does a random process mean that it will not move toward a specific outcome. So is there, with regard to the apparently random, evolutionary process that created humans, an equivalent either of multiplying the first four digits by four, or of discovering a telos toward which that randomness is progressing? We do not know, but the very old general question of the relationship of order and chance was certainly asked in eighteenth-century America.

"Quest[ion] 1. Is this stupendous & immeasurable universe governed by eternal fate? 2. Is it governed by chance[?] 3. Is governed by caprice anger or resentment & vengeance[?] 4 Is it governed by intelligence wisdom and benevolence[?]"(1954 Reel 124 188). John Adams picked the fourth alternative after asking these questions, which today continue to haunt us. Thus there are nihilists who proclaim that a flourishing life is meaningless in a meaningless world, and some of them even say that it is meaningless to even affirm or deny such things. But perhaps they also "doe this but to justifie or excuse their own laziness in the world." Could a rational and industrious person, or a rational and industrious people, show them to be wrong? Of course this is speculation, but in the intellectual world, as in the financial, one cannot accumulate unless one speculates, even though speculations often fail. The possibility that there is a world of beauty in the deliberate sense of the people might be enough to attract individuals today whose childlike wonder make them kindred spirits to Aristotle, Kepler, Newton, Darwin, or Einstein. Moral, scientific, or political entrepreneurs would not, any more than their commercial counterparts, need assurance ahead of time that they will succeed. "What really interests me," Einstein once proclaimed, "is whether God had any choice in the creation of the world"(Holton 1971 20). We can say: What really interested the American revolutionists were the choices that Nature's God made in creating the moral and political world. It seems possible that in trying to fulfill that dream of political knowledge we will make progress in answering some of the most puzzling philosophical questions of all time: Who are we? Why are we here? How can we understand the universe? Do we — and our universe — contain a kind of code which, if broken, will reveal meaning? Or is Adams' option 2 the final word, the order in the universe being merely a statistical fluke? Even if these questions remain unanswered, might we not discover new things, such as showing, through a study of the brain and the deliberate sense of the people, that Plato's brilliant analogy between the just man and the just society is more than a metaphor, that private and public happiness are structurally identical? (1955 55; cf. the comments of Hobbes and Wilson above, page 194). In that case, the Constitutional phrase — "to form a more perfect Union" — should gain an additional ethical meaning: to create within oneself a *tripartite integrity*, consisting of all the intellectual, emotional, and volitional elements that make up one's person (cf. Adams' words above, page 396). Again, might not the science of common reason help us prove empirically that Americans, in a calm, reflective, and deliberate mood, actually hold some moral and political propositions to be self-evident? But what are they? It wonders me, to use a Pennsylvania Dutch expression.

Copernicus began a revolution in our knowledge of the universe by asking a new question about the solar system: How would the mathematics of celestial prediction be transformed if the earth and other planets revolve around the sun? Locke and the Founders began a revolution in our knowledge of ourselves by asking a new question about political systems: How would the structure of government be transformed if the just powers of government depended only on the informed consent of the people? For so many people today politics has lost its savor; they believe it has become a mere vehicle to further the interests of the politician, or th class to which she belongs. It would certainly help minimize this attitude if we had politicians who would energetically strive to find simple and beautiful laws that are not merely pleasing to them but, using the highest achievable standards of accuracy, could be proven to be in harmony with the informed values of the American people. Today our political science, economics and philosophy contain some work of very high quality, but there are few things in them to inspire our politicians to act anew in the spirit of 1776. If our capacity for intelligent thought, emotional refinement, and aesthetic sensibility evolved to make us better fit to deal with social problems, it is a great irony that the magnificent success of the natural sciences, which depended on these capacities, is not duplicated by contemporary social science. In the eighteenth century the American revolution was a self-conscious attempt to repeat the success of natural science in the political life of America. To be true to that revolution politicians can hardly ignore that aspiration.

Yet we ought never to forget our limitations in our aspirations as inquirers. The significance of the answers that the American people give to questions will not necessarily be immediately clear to us. Those who try to complete the American revolution must be ready for an intellectual Valley Forge, where a very long winter might pass before even the smallest victory is won. Walt Whitman thought "that a new Literature, perhaps a new Metaphysics, certainly a new Poetry, are to be, in my opinion, the only sure and worthy supports and expressions of the American Democracy"(1964 2:416). The politics of self-knowledge — including Festival America — is meant to provide that new poetry, literature, and metaphysics. Perhaps the people themselves will at some point become discouraged at the magnitude of their task, or devastated because a major decision, which they authorized after wrenching soul-searching, proved disastrous. In such dark moments Festival America could invigorate their morale to try again, to reaffirm their commitment to revolutionary democracy as described by John Jay in 1788: "While reason retains her rule, while men are as ready to receive as to give advice, and as willing to be convinced themselves, as to convince others, there are few political evils from which a free and enlightened people cannot deliver themselves"(above, page 7).

We are surely still in ignorance about the ultimate nature of ourselves and our world. This is one of the reasons American democracy allows the freedom to act according to a wide variety of religious and metaphysical positions. Yet there are limits to the freedom of action. For example, in his notes on Locke, Jefferson wrote:

> whatsoever is lawful in the Commonwealth, or permitted to the subject in the ordinary way, cannot be forbidden to him for religious uses; & whatsoever is prejudicial to the commonwealth in their ordinary uses & therefore prohibited by the laws, ought not to be permitted to churches in their sacred rites. for instance, it is unlawful in the ordinary course of things or in a private house to murder a child. it should not be permitted any sect then to sacrifice children: it is ordinarily lawful (or temporally lawful) to kill calves or lambs. they may therefore be religiously sacrificed. but if the good of the state required a temporary suspension of killing lambs (as during a siege); sacrifices of them may then be rightfully suspended also, this is the true extent of *toleration*." (1950 1:547; cf. Locke 1963 65-7)

Jefferson's position is still upheld. On June 11, 1993, the Supreme Court ruled, without mentioning Locke or Jefferson, that the Santeria church could practice animal sacrifice (such as killing goats, chickens, guinea hens, and doves), which the city of Hialeah in Florida had forbidden. The law in this case failed to satisfy the requirements of neutrality and general applicability (508 U.S. 520).

Republican government requires that religious persons obey secular laws based on common reason but, apart from that, their religious freedom is guaranteed. The separation of church and state brought about by Mason, Jefferson, and Madison is similar to other separations in the history of mathematics and science. By the time of

Euclid, mathematics was separated from the "church of Pythagoras," according to which the ground for at least some mathematical propositions was religious. Mathematics became, so to say, "republican mathematics," a discipline based solely on the common reason of mathematicians; a reason that required that mathematical assertions to be self-evident propositions, or validly drawn propositions from them. Beyond that, "republican mathematics" allowed freedom of choice among a wide range of religious or metaphysical beliefs. Arithmetic, for example, is neutral on the question of whether numbers are eternal objects fixed in the nature of things (as the Platonists would say), or abstractions from everyday experience (as the Aristotelians would say), or objects created by God (as some Christians would say). However, arithmetic is not neutral on every conceivable religious or metaphysical claim. For example, it cannot operate on the presupposition, apparently held by the early Pythagoreans on religious grounds, that natural numbers are the essence of all things, because this presupposition is inconsistent with the mathematical proof that, *if the side of a square is represented by a natural number, the diagonal cannot be either represented by a natural number or by the ratio of two natural numbers. Mutatis mutandis*, similar things could be said about the separation of church and science effected by the science of Galileo, Kepler, Newton and their successors. The result of that separation was, as it were, "republican science," defined by the common reason of all scientists. It is neutral on a large variety of religious or metaphysical beliefs, but not all of them. Thus it is neutral on the question of whether the universe was created by God (as the Christians would say), or whether it had no such creator (as atheists would say); but it cannot operate on the presupposition (made by Aristotle, Ptolemy, Copernicus, and Galileo) that *celestial motion is perfect and therefore must be circular* because this presupposition is inconsistent with repeatable, scientific observations. Republican government likewise operates with great neutrality. When Washington expressed his desperation for "good workmen," he said: "they may be of Assia, Africa, or Europe. They may be Mahometans, Jews, or Christian of any Sect — or they may be Athiests"(1992 1:232). An enlarged but similar neutrality applies when a republican government is looking for a good employee, or judging whether a person is a good citizen. Nevertheless, Republican government cannot be absolutely neutral; for example, it cannot be neutral on the claim that some people are chosen by God to be superior in their rights. Republican government, like the mathematical or scientific establishment, is a reason-based organization.

To conclude, we can ask the moral skeptic a number of things: First, how do you deal with the issue of self-reference? Does not meaningful conversation about nihilism presuppose the moral imperative to seek truth rather than falsehood? Second, why be skeptical ethically, but not metaethically? Should you not, standing back and looking at ethical skepticism, see in it, as in other points of view, grounds for some doubt? "A true sceptic," said David Hume, "will be diffident of his philosophical doubts, as well as of his philosophical conviction"(above, page 292). Third, moral skepticism is controversial and must be investigated carefully; to do so, won't you need some space and time that would require the protection of a free government like the United States? Finally, just as the skeptic with regard to the material world (such as a follower of the philosopher George Berkeley) must convince the community of scientists in order to establish that view, don't you, as a moral skeptic, need to convince the political community? Being "right" is not enough, for if you are truly right, then the argument for moral skepticism should be convincing in an rational environment where there is a fair competition with other views. Creating that environment is what a court of common reason is intended to do. It is for the people to determine the extent to which skeptical arguments are to be effective in public policy. For example, an extreme skeptic might claim that one can never have enough evidence to prove a person guilty of a crime and that, even if we could, the attribution is meaningless since there are no crimes. The most credulous would allow any charge of guilt by the state to be sufficient evidence of it, and would accept virtually anything as being a crime, such as witchcraft. The people must decide where the administration of justice should lie between the extremes. Similarly for other cases. In general, a free people are, as Jefferson said, "independent of all but moral law"(above, page 181); they must use their common reason to choose what axioms and presuppositions will serve as the philosophical foundation of their own society. If, under favorable conditions for careful and thorough deliberation, they in fact consciously choose to violate moral law, or end their own free society, then the American experiment is a failure. On the other hand, if within the bounds of that law they choose the axioms and presuppositions of their government so as to secure and enlarge their freedoms, we would have an utterly new phenomenon in the history of the world, a metaphysics of, by, and for the people, a metaphysics of American democracy. But by what logic could a people achieve such a goal?

16

The Logic of Aspiration

The technique used for axiom discovery in metaphysics is the same as that in mathematics. Betrand Russell calls the latter "the regressive method of discovering premises." It illustrates "the close analogy between the methods of pure mathematics and the methods of the sciences of observation"(1973 272)). I will try to explain this "regressive method" by showing that it is also the same procedure used in the game of Eleusis. The game was invented by Robert Abbot in the Fall of 1956. Over a period of time the rules were refined in order to make it a good simulation of the scientific method. Today, using computer technology, it is possible to create games that even more closely reflect that method. However, for our purposes, Eleusis is adequate. (See Abbot, Robert 1963 73-92, and 1977 as well as Gardner 1959, 1961 165-173, for the complete rules and history of the game.) Eleusis uses ordinary playing cards. Before play begins, the dealer secretly invents a rule that the players attempt to discover as the game proceeds. The play is designed to provide more and more clues as to what that rule is. The dealer creates the rule and provides the clues, and is thus commonly called either "God" or "Nature."

After the players receive their cards (14 each), the game begins when the dealer places a card face up. This is the starter card. Players take turns showing a card from their hand to the dealer. The dealer, who receives no cards, will tell each player whether the card the player chooses conforms to the secret rule. If the card is correct, it will be placed next to the last correctly-played card (and be called a "mainline" card); if it is incorrect, it will be placed below the previously played card (and be called a "sideline" card). Each player tries to get rid of all cards in his hand. A correct play will decrease a hand by one card. An incorrect play requires the player to pick up two cards from a deck of previously unused cards and thus increases a hand by one card. Each player, on his or her turn, must play one card but may play up to four. Here are some examples of rules:

1. Play a card so as to alternate colors.
2. Play a card so as to alternate odd and even cards.
3. Play a card of the same suit or same value as the last correctly-played card.
4. If the last correctly-played card is even, play a club or a diamond; otherwise, play a heart or a spade.

The reader might enjoy trying to figure out the secret rule for the following sequence of cards. The answer will be given below.

Starter
card

K	10	5	8	9	2	5	4	4	J	K	8	9	Mainline
H	C	H	S	H	C	D	H	C	C	D	C	S	cards

	Q	3		J			5			6	Sideline
	S	H		D			C			C	

	2					7		4	
	S					D		S	

								2	cards
								D	

Eleusis is designed so that a dealer is penalized for choosing a rule that is either too easy or too hard. Without this feature the dealer could easily choose rules so difficult that no player could discover them. Furthermore, after a certain point in each round, players may be expelled if they make incorrect moves. Another interesting aspect of the game is the role of Prophet. If a player believes he knows the rule, he can declare himself a Prophet. The Prophet then answers for the dealer (God or Nature). He continues as a Prophet as long as he answers correctly. If he answers incorrectly, he is a False Prophet and receives an appropriate penalty. By the scientific analogy: "The Prophet would be a Scientist Who Published. A False Prophet would be a Scientist Who Published Too Early"(Abbot, Robert 1977 16). The identification of False Prophets through reason illustrates the sharp difference between mathematical or scientific "prophets" on the one hand, and those of "faith-based" religion, on the other. Eleusis, mathematics, science, and engineering do not tolerate any "prophets" immune to rational criticism and revision, nor is it necessary that religion tolerate them (cf. above, page 299).

Martin Gardner considers the fantasy that

God or Nature may be playing thousands, perhaps a countless number, of simultaneous Eleusis games with intelligences on planets in the universe, always maximizing his or her pleasure by a choice of rules that the lesser minds will find not too easy and not too hard to discover if given enough time. The supply of cards is infinite, and when a player is expelled, there are always others to take his place. Prophets and False Prophets come and go, and who knows when one round will end and another begin? Searching for any kind of truth is an exhilarating game. It is worth remembering that there would be no game at all unless the rules were hidden. (1977 25)

In Eleusis the use of any secret rule not depending solely on the correctly-played cards is prohibited. Thus one could not make the rule depend on the time of day, or whether anyone is eating during a given play. However, we have no assurance that God or Nature abides by such a prohibition in the design of the physical or moral world. For example, we could imagine that the successful pursuit of happiness could become more subtle and difficult depending on the success of the pursuer so far. Or consider a game of Eleusis in which the rule is to play a red card if there are zero or an even number of sideline cards; otherwise, play black. Then two games of Eleusis, which have different players but seek this same rule, might produce two sets of mainline cards that have no discoverable common order. If the universe were like this, its nature would in part depend us. There are physicists who believe quantum mechanics exhibits this sort of feature (see, for example, Woolf 1980 354-6, and Wigner 1967 172).

Let us now solve the above Eleusis problem. The hypothesis "Play a card so as to alternate colors" is simplistic since this hypothesis, although consistent with the cards as played for a while (through the five of diamonds), eventually is refuted by experience (when the dealer says "Right" to the play of the four of hearts). On the other hand, the following rule is consistent with the cards played but is too complex: "If the last correctly-played card is red, but not the five of hearts, play a card of equal or lesser value; if it is the five of hearts, play black. If the last correctly-played card is black, but not the ten of clubs, play a card of higher value; if it is the ten of clubs, play red." This hypothesis has undesirable *ad hoc* features and is needlessly complex. Unacceptable hypotheses are those that are inconsistent with the evidence, or possess *ad hoc* features, or are needlessly complex. Much of what counts as "bad science," whether natural or social, is of this sort. A simple hypothesis consistent with the evidence is: "If the last correctly-played card is red, play an even card; otherwise, play an odd card." The scientist, whether natural or social, should strive for the simplest or most beautiful hypothesis consistent with the evidence. Likewise, the legislator should seek the simplest or most beautiful laws consistent with the informed values of the people. Endorsing unnecessarily complex laws is a fault in both the scientist and legislator, it represents a failure of the aesthetic sense, and is a potential hinderance to both scientific and social progress.

We can use Eleusis to give a more exact characterization of the scientific understanding of "simple." Imagine that the game of Eleusis is translated into the language of computers (that is, a sequence of zeros and ones) and you are playing Eleusis with the computer. For a given game at a given time, let the simplest hypothesis for the secret rule be defined as the shortest computer program (represented by zeros and ones) that will produce the given ordering of cards (also represented by zeros and ones). (The alphabetic order 01 will decide among programs of equal length.) If we assume that the computer has found that program by testing all possibilities, then simplicity can be precisely measured. Imagine you give your proposal for the simplest hypothesis. The computer will translate your answer into a series of zeros and ones, and compare the length of your answer with the simplest program. If the latter is the same length, you get a score of 100%, if it is half as long, you will get a rating of 50%, and so on. Note that a random sequence, which by definition has no secret rule, is incompressible, the shortest program could not be much shorter than the sequence itself. (For details on this conception of simplicity, see Solomonoff 1964.) Perhaps the most profound results in mathematics or science are those showing that a sequence of digits which seems random is in fact governed by a simple rule. Thus the sequence of the billion initial digits in the decimal expansion of π may appear to be random, but it is not, since a brief program for creating the decimal expansion of the ratio of the circumference of a circle to its diameter will enable the machine to produce the digits. Newton's rule of universal gravitation showed that the wandering motions of the planets (and much else) could be exactly described by a brief rule. In the actual practice of mathematics or science or politics we would want, not necessarily the simplest hypothesis or law absolutely, because that hypothesis may be too subtle for any human to understand, or be utterly alien to our way of thinking. Instead, we would want the simplest one, assuming it exists, which, respectively, the community of mathematicians, scientists, or citizens would deem understandable and beautiful.

The guesses, the experiences, and the reasoning, that Eleusis players use to discover the secret rule mirrors the scientific method, but the phrase "scientific method" may suggest something too narrow, for the game clarifies the use of reason in the wide sense of the term, the sense that the ancients meant when they said reason is what distinguishes humans from animals. Thus we may say a human baby is a natural Eleusis player who learns language by formulating the simplest semantical and grammatical rules from initially meaningless sequences of sounds coming from speakers in her environment. Later the child learns to hypothesize motives of others by finding the simplest possibility consistent with the evidence. Since the historian does the same thing, he also is, as it were, playing a game of Eleusis.

Eleusis can help us understand why Jefferson considered Bacon, Locke and Newton "as the three greatest men that ever lived, without any exception, and as having laid the foundation of those superstructures which have been raised in the Physical and Moral sciences . . ."(1950 14:561; cf. Voltaire 1733 84, Adams 1977 1:42-3, and Wilson 2007 604-5, 619). Jefferson thought that Bacon invented the scientific method (the game of Eleusis, so to say), and thus believed Bacon could ground his thinking, as his predecessors could not, in the natural world. It is thus not surprising that Jefferson's most famous words reflect Bacon's ethos and language: "Is it not a common principle, that the law favoureth three things: life, liberty, and dower? And what is the reason of this favour? This, because our law is grounded upon the law of nature, and these three things do flow from the law of nature; preservation of life, natural; liberty, which every beast or bird seeketh and affecteth, natural; the society of man and wife, whereof dower is the reward, natural"(Bacon 1860 15:225; cf. Coke 1670 125a). ("Dower" is used in the figurative sense of *endowment*; it means "marital bliss," which is the natural reward of "the society of man and wife.").

Turning to Newton and Locke, Jefferson would have agreed with Madison that they "established immortal systems, the one in matter, the other in mind"(1900 6:93; cf. Emmons 1787 18). Newton, as it were, was the best Eleusis player when the secrets were physical, Locke when they were moral. Put in these terms, the trouble with our society is that we honor Newton and forget Locke. It is often claimed that the moral, economic, and political catastrophes of the twentieth century show the limitations of reason. But these catastrophes were due to the combination of using deliberative reason in the physical sciences (and thus our power was very great) and the failure to adequately use it in the moral sciences (and thus our ability to use that power wisely was unnecessarily compromised). Members of Congress seem utterly ignorant of the fact that our revolutionary heritage requires that they respond to these cataclysmic failures by better knowing and following the outcome of the people's deliberative reason, and that to do this they must create a contemporary equivalent of Jefferson's system of wards. Some of Galileo's opponents refused to look through his telescope (Drake 1978 162, 165); likewise, our politicians refuse, as it were, to look through Jefferson's telescope to see, in detail, the moral and political landscape created by the common reason of society. That great landmass remains *terra incognita*; but no president has sent a Lewis and Clark to explore it. When it comes to moral and political technology, America is an undeveloped country.

Abolitionists in the eighteenth century recognized that it was not enough to free the slaves; care must also be exercised in preparing them for their freedom (for example, PHNOD 1998 329). A similar care is necessary to prepare the people for the enlargement of freedom required by American perfectionist democracy. Eleusis, although it serves the purpose of illustrating some aspects of the use of reason, is not subtle enough to provide exercise in all the reasoning necessary for the pursuit of private and public happiness. For instance, in practice, nature in science, or the people in politics, often speak with less clarity than the Eleusis dealer. More subtle games could be invented by a competition. For example, imagine a contest whose prize is a substantial honor or fortune. It would go to the person who produces the best game, computerized or not, which satisfies the following conditions: First, the game must mirror, as does Eleusis, the use of reason in the search for discovering or achieving some goal, such as truth, or a happy life. Second, anyone who is not considered mentally deficient (by the standards of the people) must be able to play the game. Third, the game must be fun to play, the kind of game that might become a national pastime. A series of such contests — each chosen by a democratic evolutionary paradigm (above, page 178)— could help produce the games necessary to prepare citizens for service on an advisory jury. These games could be of great variety; one might even imagine that a casino might adapt one of them to produce a kind of "republican bingo"! (For actual examples of games that people voluntarily play for pleasure, but whose outcomes have a useful social purpose, see von Ahn 2006.) To provide for their metaphysical tasks, a fun-to-play axiom game for school children might also be devised. In the game they might be given ten statements and told that seven follow logically from just three of them. They would then take turns trying to find the three and carry out the deductions. In time they could study the history behind the various formulations of the political axioms presupposed by free societies, eventually analyzing and debating what are the best axioms to adopt. By giving such practice year after year with regard to many different kinds of such subject matter, schools could prepare their graduates for their duties as autonomous citizens and, by the bye, impart a life-long love of recreational politics.

Consider Euclid. Euclid had to guess that *all right angles are equal* is a suitable axiom (= secret rule). Once Euclid made all his guesses, he had to show that it was plausible that they were the simplest axioms from which all the propositions could be derived that he, and other members of the community of geometers, already believed to be true on the basis of their mathematical experience, both old (= mainline and sideline cards already played) and new (= cards played after the formulation of the rule). He was a great simplifier, organizer, and explainer; In eighteenth-century terms, he was a Mathematical Prophet articulating the Laws of Geometry and of Geometry's God. But no faith is implied, only hope that he is a true prophet. Turning now to politics we can follow Lincoln in saying that the "principles of Jefferson are the definitions and axioms of free society"(1953 3:375). One must use historical experience to show that this set of definitions and axioms are the simplest or most beautiful to derive the propositions of a free society that the people, represented by the Court of Common Reason, believe to be true. Naturally the search for the axioms of a free society is an activity in which we would use the most rigorous democratic evolutionary paradigm and the highest quality sandwich (above, page 199) that is practically achievable at a given time. This activity would be a contemporary embodiment of Jefferson's doctrine: "Questions of natural right are triable by their conformity with the moral sense and reason of man."(1903 3:235; cf. Jefferson words below, page 463). Of course, one must continually look for new axioms, and periodically check if those already accepted appear justified in light of new experiences or further reflections. John Adams argued that the basis of our political liberties must be found in "the constitution of the intellectual and moral world"(1850 3:463). Yet the nature of that constitution may be perpetually controversial. In a society organized by a politics of self-knowledge, the people must decide, amid all the controversy, by soul-searching under uncertainty, what constitution to accept, what part of it to declare as the metaphysical foundation of their society, and what goals they, as a people, should aspire to. *Be careful what you wish for* is an admonition as appropriate for societies as it is for individuals. In a fully democratic and independent country it is the people who will examine their own dreams for happiness; they will become, and continually remain, the metaphysicians of their own democracy, collectively their own philosopher-king. This does not mean that a scholar, or an ordinary citizen, should not try to uncover presuppositions that are simultaneously metaphysical and political. It only means that if they do, they must have their results confirmed in the Court of Common Reason just as the scientists must have their results confirmed by the community of scientists. The axioms we *hold* to be true ought to be determined by the deliberate majority of the people; those axioms that *are* true are those that forever keep that majority. Harrington's words from 1656 are here quite relevant: "And if reason be nothing else but interest, and the interest of mankind be the right interest, then the reason of mankind must be right reason. Now compute well, for if the interest of popular government come the nearest unto the interest of mankind, then the reason of popular government must come nearest unto right reason"(2003 22). The Founding era in America was an attempt to test whether "the reason of popular government must come nearest unto right reason." If we aspire to "compute well," should we not carry out this test anew, with the highest degree of honesty, thoroughness, and excellence that could be achieved in the twenty-first century?

Now let us consider another aspect of playing Eleusis. When playing, it is useful to consider the character of the dealer (= (God or Nature)) in trying to discover the secret rule. For example, a mathematically inclined dealer might prefer to let the secret rule depend on even or odd numbers, while a person who had artistic temperament might choose a rule that depends on color and one-eyed jacks. Hence information about the dealer obtained in one game of Eleusis might be useful in the next. In guessing the character of the dealer one is really having a side game of Eleusis whose purpose is to confirm, or refute, those guesses. In the eighteenth century certain presuppositions in the game of life were made about the "dealer." These assumptions they believed were necessary to make meaningful the politics of a free society. I will now list some of these eighteenth-century assumptions although I will sometimes illustrate them by examples from later centuries. I do not mean to suggest that they were universally made — meaninglessness could be expressed even in that age (above, page 426). My only claim is that they were typical, both for the intellectual elite and the ordinary person.

God created laws of morality. God could have created a morally arbitrary world, that is, a world with no moral order. This would be like an Eleusis dealer answering "Right" or "Wrong" at random. Nihilism would then be the true philosophy. God, however, did not do this (cf. Adams' words above, page 438). God is rational — reason is the voice of God within us (see Locke 1988 205, 1975 598, 698;

Jefferson 1892 4:432) — and his sublime rationality can by found both in the physical and moral world. This "miracle creed" had been proclaimed by Kepler and Newton for the physical world, and by Locke and Jefferson for the moral world.

Humans are made in the image of God. Humans thus have dignity. The metaphysical presupposition that we are to some degree like God was required by science (were we wholly unlike God we could not discover his "secret rules"), and it was sometimes explicitly made by scientists. Examples are Kepler ("Those laws [which govern the material world] lie within the power of understanding of the human mind; God wanted us to perceive them when he created us in His image in order that we may take part in His own thoughts"(above, page 388)) and Descartes (". . . I am made in the image and likeness of God"(1951 51)). American revolutionary philosophy in the eighteenth century made the same presupposition (above, page 389), the Darwinian "horrid doubt" had not yet arisen. If the dealer in Eleusis thinks in a way entirely different from the other players, the game is meaningless since the players have no chance of success. However, Eleusis can fail to be meaningful even if the dealer thinks in a similar way to the dealer. This brings us to the next assumption.

God is not a deceiver. This is the formulation of Descartes (1951 71). If God wanted to deceive us there is no power that we have that could prevent him. For example, imagine a dealer at Eleusis answering "Right" or "Wrong" according to whether the decimals in the expansion of π, beginning with the 10^a digit, where a is a centillion, are even or odd. That is, if the 10^a digit is even, the dealer would say "Right" after the first card is played; if the next digit is odd, he would say "Wrong" after the second card, and so on. Thus, although there is a rule governing the dealer's answers, the game is an artful deception because the rule is undiscoverable by the players. When we play Eleusis we assume the dealer gives us a chance to win; when we play American politics we assume God does likewise. To use Jefferson's words: "I have no fear that the result of our experiment will be that men may be trusted to govern themselves without a master. Could the contrary be proved, I should conclude either that there is no god, or that he is a malevolent being"(1950 11:526).

God is subtle but he is not malicious. This famous aphorism of Einstein (Clark 1971 422) must be added to that of Descartes because the pursuit of knowledge is not easy. That is, God as the "Eleusis dealer" has not made the rules impossible to discover (God is not malicious), nor has he made it too easy (God is subtle). The work of

Pythagoreans (magnitudes may be of irrational length), of Copernicus (the earth moves around the sun), of Galileo (heavy objects fall at the same rate as lighter objects), of Kepler (planets move in elliptical, not circular, orbits), of Einstein (the geometry of the world is Riemannian, not Euclidean), all show that God is subtle. And the same subtlety one finds in the mathematical and physical worlds is exhibited in the moral world. Thus the Constitution does not establish a monarchy, an aristocracy, or a pure democracy, but rather a mixture that includes representatives, checks and balances of power, bills of rights, presidential vetoes, judicial review, and so forth. Reality — whether mathematical, physical, or moral — has presented us with subtlety, subtlety, subtlety, and yet again more subtlety. Nevertheless we are not maliciously excluded from its discovery. Einstein said that by his aphorism he had meant: "Nature conceals her mystery by means of her essential grandeur, not by her cunning"(Clark 1971 422). This aesthetic element is introduced by the next presupposition.

God has an aesthetic sense. The same God that made the physical universe also made our moral nature. This suggests that the "essential grandeur" that exists in nature may also be found in the moral world. Since part of the "essential grandeur" of the natural world is mathematical, could the same be true of the moral world? Locke, Wilson, and Hamilton thought so (1975 549-50, 566, cf. 516, 565; 2007 1:508, 512-13; 1961 4:456-60). Franklin even worked out a *"Moral Algebra"*(above, page 20). Writing software for American perfectionist democracy will allow explicit tests of the extent to which mathematics is relevant to that morality and politics, for example, by assessing its role in collective deliberative decision. Consider this possibility. We know that various laws are related to one another logically. The study of these relations is part of "legal logic." We also know that logical relations can be represented mathematically. Could we arrange our laws so that the various logical nets are mathematically elegant? For example, Newton devised a single law for phenomena as different as the fall of an apple and the orbit of the moon. Could a single legal structure be applied to two areas of human activity that initially seem quite different? Again, the rippling movement of a swimming fish takes the form of a sine wave. Could we so devise our laws that changes in the informed values of the people would lead to changes in the laws that can, Eleusis-like, be described in a simple way? "The mathematician plays a game," Dirac observes, "in which he himself invents the rules while the physicist plays a game in which the rules are provided by Nature, but as time goes on it becomes increasingly evident that the rules which the mathematician finds interesting are the same as those which Nature has chosen"(1939 124). (Is Dirac saying that the minds of mathematicians, at least, are made in the image of Nature?) It might also be possible that some of the games which the mathematician finds interesting will be the same as those which a cool and deliberate human nature has chosen. Perhaps a mathematics of happiness already exists but the possibility of its application to society is unknown. We should not presuppose that God was a mathematical genius when he devised the laws relevant to nature, but was a mathematical nincompoop when he devised the laws relevant to politics. If the fundamental laws of nature satisfy the triad of beauty, subtlety, and grandeur, we should not be satisfied with anything less from ethics, politics, economics, or jurisprudence.

The above listing of presuppositions about the "dealer" is a beginning sketch. They are expressed in theological language because it seems likely that, for most eighteenth-century Americans, including the Founders, this formulation is the most appropriate. In a contemporary articulation of the metaphysical presuppositions of a free society, there would be good reason not to express them in that language. Let me explain why by considering the analogous situation in mathematics. Suppose someone says: "There exists a prime number between 85 and 90, but there does not exist a prime number between 185 and 190." What is the nature of these entities? Christian platonists claim that prime numbers are conceptual objects created by God, realists that they are patterns fixed in the abstract nature of things, formalists that they are artifacts of a symbol game, intuitionists that they are psychological constructions. Most mathematicians are realists, but it does not follow that nonrealists are inferior mathematicians, or less devoted to mathematics. Embracing a position on the nature of mathematical entities may influence the choice of problems, and the style of proof, but mathematics as a discipline can go forward without a deciding whether the position is true. Such understandings are parts of mathematical "rights of conscience." The same considerations hold for political science. The nature of rights or values, for example, can be given a variety of interpretations — with or without God, for instance — but these interpretations are part of the political "rights of conscience." It is no more necessary to decide whether or not God created rights to have a flourishing political society, than it is to decide whether or not God created numbers to have a flourishing mathematical community.

Absent a decision about these controversial matters, mathematics and politics, both as disciplines and practice, can progress.

Politically, this attitude can be found quite early in American history. For example, a town-meeting of Flushing, New York (then New Netherlands) approved a letter that was sent to Governor Stuyvesant. In it we find the following phrase: "The law of love, peace and liberty in the states extending to Jews, Turks and Egyptians, as they are considered sons of Adam . . . "(Harrington, R. Ward 1993 107). America was here headed in a Lockean direction without Lockean influence, for this occurred in 1657, when Locke was just twenty-five and had yet to formulate his political philosophy. Thirty-two years later Locke writes: ". . . neither *Pagan* nor *Mahometan*, nor *Jew*, ought to be excluded from the civil rights of the commonwealth because of his religion"(1963 103). When the bill on freedom of religion was before the Virginia legislature, an amendment was proposed that would make it specific to Christianity. Its defeat, Jefferson reports, was "proof that [the legislators] meant to comprehend, within the mantle of it's protection, the Jew and the Gentile, the Christian and Mahometan, the Hindoo, and infidel of every denomination"(1892 1:62). A belief in Christianity was no more required to be a citizen in good standing in Virginia than being a realist is required to be a mathematician in good standing in the American Mathematical Association. Protestants were a large majority in Virginia, but by exercising self-restraint — one might even say by exhibiting a magnanimous character — the state legislature showed that it wished Virginia to be a cosmopolitan community with regard to religion. Speaking of the federal government, John Leland declared: "Let a man be Pagan, Turk, Jew or Christian, he is eligible to any post in that government"(1791 28). The adoption of the axioms of a society that intends to be cosmopolitan in its laws and behavior — and this is what Americans claimed — can only include those axioms necessary for a free society, not all the axioms to which a majority (even of atheists) might happen to agree at a given time. If the Court of Common Reason restricts itself in this way, America would have a good chance to redeem its birth by building a highly successful pursuit-of-happiness civilization that is universally ergonomic, a civilization where citizens, however different from one another, would each be able to declare: "This American world was made for me." Using theological language today in articulating the axioms of democracy would contradict the cosmopolitan spirit of the American revolution, for such language would leave out not only secularists (agnostic or atheistic) but, in addition, members of godless religions, such Buddhism, Jainism, Confucianism, Taoism, and some forms of Hinduism. Similar remarks apply to the phrase "under God" in the Pledge of Allegiance. On the other hand, antitheistic language ("there is no god") would likewise be inappropriate. A nontheistic mathematics, science, or politics, does not prevent believers from giving the foundations of these disciplines their own religious interpretation; nor does it prevent nonbelievers from thinking there is no such further foundation.

Hence the structure of the courts of common reason ought to encourage moral self-restraint by majorities. This notion can be clarified by considering an explicit example of logical self-restraint. It by no means follows that because something is true, one always has the logical right to assert that truth. For example, consider: "Ralph has never verbally asserted this statement." At a definite time we might consistently, truthfully, and verbally assert that statement, but Ralph could not. That is, he would have to forbear verbally asserting the proposition if he wished to preserve its truth, although he might assert it in other ways (say, by writing it). Now morality can introduce similar limits. For example, the most meek person in the world would have to forbear explicitly asserting the truth about her maximal meekness (for otherwise it would very probably be false). Similarly many Christians in eighteenth-century America believed that Christianity was constrained in the means that could be used to assert the truth of Christianity. Let me quote from the Virginia Declaration of Rights of June 12, 1776:

> That Religion, or the duty we owe to our *Creator*, and the manner of discharging it, can be directed only by reason and conviction, not by force or violence; and, therefore, all men are equally entitled to the free exercise of religion, according to the dictates of conscience; and that it is the mutual duty of all to practise Christian forbearance, love, and charity, towards each other. (Mason 1970 1:289)

The separation of the church and state in America had the support, then and now, of many minorities, whether religious or not. However, historically speaking, its main support came from Protestants who believed that Christian love and charity, based directly on the teaching of Jesus, was inconsistent with Christianity's being declared or used in governmental contexts. In the words of the Baptist minister, John Leland: "no body politic can form a christian government and administer the same; without breaking the rules of pure christianity"(1801 33; cf. TAP 1791 97). In sum, the assertion of Christianity through state power nullifies Christianity itself; if the meek were going to inherit the earth, as Jesus foretold, it can only be done by persuasion and example alone, not by means incommensurate with meekness.

By reflecting on such examples we come to the following principle of scientific or moral self-restraint: *Statements, or imperatives, should not be asserted when that assertion is incompatible with their being true or right.* If an assertion is inconsistent with the presuppositions of science itself, for example, then self-restraint ought be exercised, since science is *par excellence* an activity of reason. This restraint, however, is not always recognized. Consider Freud. In order to propagate his own theories of human nature, he had to except himself from those theories. For example, Freud claimed that Adler's "theory does what . . . our conscious thought in general does — namely, makes use of a *rationalization* . . . in order to conceal the unconscious motive"(1966 14:52). Freud does not, however, understand his own theory of psychoanalysis as a rationalization. He, *qua* psychoanalyst, did not do "what . . . our conscious thought in general does." Another example: "The psychical apparatus is intolerant of unpleasure; it has to fend it off at all costs, and if the perception of reality entails unpleasure, that perception — that is, the truth — must be sacrificed"(1966 23:237). But, as Freud often pointed out (for example, 1966 17:141-44), psychoanalysis itself causes a psychological wound, and so we emphatically do not wish it to be true. Yet the "psychical apparatus" of Freud did not "fend it off at all costs," he did not sacrifice the "truth." Again, Freud says that "thought is after all nothing but a substitute for a hallucinatory wish . . . "(1966 5:567; cf. Jones 1966 1:401) but, as before, Freud did not understand psychoanalytic theory to be a "substitute for a hallucinatory wish." We can only conclude that, if Freud's theory happens to be true, neither he nor any other human has a right to assert it.

The case is similar for Marx. These are his words:

> In the social production which men carry on they enter into definite relations that are indispensable and independent of their will; these relations of production correspond to a definite stage of development in their material powers of production. The sum total of these relations of production constitutes the economic structure of society — the real foundation, on which rise legal and political superstructures and to which correspond definite forms of social consciousness. The mode of production in material life determines the general character of the social, political and spiritual processes of life. It is not the

consciousness of men that determines their existence, but, on the contrary, their social existence determines their consciousness. (1913 11-12)

According to Marx, a person's political theories, for example, cannot be the result of free choice after careful investigation of the evidence. Rather, whether the person is aware of it or not, the content of the theory is determined by the social class of the theorist, and the underlying economic forces of the time and place. Yet Marx did not claim that he was expressing his class prejudices, or being a puppet to some mode of production. Rather he believed that he was discovering profound truths about man, economics, and society. The rest of us are the puppets. Marx had no intellectual claim to ownership of some of the ideas he was trying to sell. Indeed a person who attempts to understand Marx can be put into the position of reading a sign that says: "Ignore this sign." For example, when Engels agrees with Marx's theory, his doing so contradicts that agreement, because given Engels' class, he should be unable or unwilling to do so.

The difficulties for behaviorism (to take a third example) are just as large and may be illustrated by the parable of

The Stultifying Behaviorist

A lesbian, who wished to become a heterosexual, had come to Renniks, a behavioral psychologist, who assured her that she would become heterosexual if she would submit to certain behaviorist procedures. The patient submitted and Renniks' claim proved true. Next a Freudian came saying that he was despondent because he thought of himself and others in terms of the Oedipus complex, the death instinct, narcissism, repression and all the other conceptual animals in the depressing Freudian zoo. Again, Renniks promised change using behaviorist techniques, and the person left therapy as a happy ex-Freudian. Finally, another behaviorist arrived and wanted Renniks to use behaviorist techniques to make him a nonbehaviorist. Renniks used them and was completely successful. Moral: Those who go beyond freedom and dignity go beyond logic and science.

It will not do for a Freud or a Marx or a behaviorist to claim that "someday" an explanation of their own activity will be forthcoming in their own terms. This would be like Carol claiming that "someday" she will prove: *Carol cannot prove this statement.* Success would contradict the claim. She, unlike ourselves, has no assertion rights with respect to that statement. As the want of a nail can cost a king his kingdom, so the failure to pay attention to something as "small" as the doctrine of assertion rights, can cost a theorist a adequate view of human nature. The study of mathematical logic can help one see in precise detail what has been known in a general way for thousands of years: namely, that problems of self-reference are important, subtle, and very hard to solve (see DeLong 2004, Hofstadter 1979, 1985 and Suber 1990). There is no Freudian or Marxist or behaviorist explanation of, respectively, Freud or Marx or, say, B. F. Skinner. Each of their doctrines becomes self-stultifying when applied to its author. It seems then that dignity is presupposed in the practice of science itself. It is as much a metaphysical presupposition of science as the claim that physical reality is everywhere subject to mathematization. As such, it has a different logical status than the detailed claims of the science. It is the difference between an empirical generalization and a principle of interpretation of experience. *All human blood is red* is an empirical generalization. One example, say, of a human with natural green blood could prove the generalization false. *Every disease has a cause* is a principle of interpretation in pathology (see Collingwood 1957 285-343). Any claim that there is a disease, say cancer, that has no cause would be countered by the pathologist with: "Cancer has a cause (or set of causes), but we have not yet discovered it." It is the mistake of the dogmatist to treat an empirical generalization as a principle of interpretation. Thus a dogmatist on the issue of red blood would deny that green blood is really blood — even if the dogmatist drew it out of the green-blooded person himself. But it is likewise a mistake to understand a principle of interpretation as an empirical generalization. A pathologist who tried to prove that *every disease has a cause* by looking at pneumonia, hepatitis, and polio would be logically confused. For this claim is presupposed by pathology itself and is not subject to proof (or refutation) from within the discipline. *Every human has dignity* is a principle of interpretation in the moral science of politics, as *every disease has a cause* is one in the natural science of pathology. Both are metaphysical presuppositions. And it was the interpretation of politics as a moral *science*, a science that needed political technology to progress, a science fully comparable with natural science, it was this interpretation that made the American revolution truly revolutionary.

Hence it is a mistake when Marx, Freud, and Skinner, try to disprove dignity within what they believe is a scientific discipline. The denial of dignity in human nature not only makes Marxism, Freudianism, and behaviorism incoherent with regard to assertion rights, it protects the doctrines from falsification by critics. For each can always appeal to the disability of the critic instead of having to prove the incorrectness of the criticism. Freud is typical. Consider his characterization of a patient's objections or doubts about psychoanalysis: "To the skeptic we say that the analysis requires no faith, that he may be as critical and suspicious as he pleases and that we do not regard his attitude as the effect of his judgment at all, for he is not in a position to form a reliable judgment on these matters; his distrust is only a symptom like other symptoms and it will not be an interference, provided he conscientiously carries out what the rule of the treatment requires of him"(1966 12:126). If one takes this attitude toward a patient, the psychoanalyst can easily dismiss unwanted criticisms as "symptoms." Freud treated his scientific critics in the same way if they criticized a fundamental tenet of psychoanalysis. For example, Havelock Ellis wrote an article in which he maintained that Freud was an artist rather than a scientist. As Ernest Jones informs us, "Freud called that 'a highly sublimated form of resistance.' Writing to me, he described Ellis's essay as 'the most refined and amiable form of resistance, calling me a great artist in order to injure the validity of our scientific claims"(1966 3:21). Freud also made this charge in print (1966 18:263). Jones goes on to say that "Havelock Ellis, at one time the leading pioneer in the world on the subject of sexuality, had at first been enthusiastic about Freud's contributions, but, then finding himself quite displaced by Freud, his jealous nature led him to write about Freud's work in an increasing carping spirit which ended in a completely negative attitude"(1953 3:21). However, the jealous nature of Ellis might have led him to think up valid objections to psychoanalysis that demolish it completely. Neither Ellis's alleged jealous motives, nor his alleged resistance, entail the falsehood of his claims, as Freud and Jones seem to believe.

It does not matter whether a critic is disqualified because of her psychosexual development, or her economic class, or the accidental reinforcement she received up to the present. It is a flight from criticism to assert that the environment alone controls her thoughts and actions. Ideologues are protected from criticism by taking as a principle of interpretation the incompetence of their critics. An ideologue who is a Marxist, for example, may not immediately know the economic roots of a criticism of Marxism, yet his principles are enough to ensure not only that they are there, but that understanding the roots will vitiate the critique. By committing the fallacy of *argumentum ad hominem*, ideologues are protected from any necessity of revising their views in light of criticism; they reject criticism merely because of its source, without carefully considering its content. Honesty and self-knowledge requires a vigilance in looking for errors in one's own thought and action, for there is always the possibility that a critic, however motivated, has discovered errors. There is no suggestion here that all Freudians, Marxists, or behaviorists are ideologues. Many are not. Ideologues are found in most, perhaps all, schools of thought. Nor is there any suggestion that the response to critics cannot be strong and vigorous. A willingness to listen to critics is part of recognizing their dignity, it does not mean one must agree with them.

Dignity is a basic undefined term in ethical axioms, as *natural number* is in the axioms for number theory. Disciplines must use some undefined terms for otherwise there is an infinite regress of definitions. Nevertheless undefined terms get their meaning contextually, that is, they mean whatever makes the axioms true. *Is a natural number* applies to members of any set (such as 0, 1, 2, . . .) that makes all the axioms for number theory true; *has dignity* applies to the members of any set (such as the set of humans) that make all the axioms of morality true. One can give examples exhibiting the property of being a natural number, or exhibiting the property of dignity, but examples are not definitions. Logicians have discovered some amazing things about natural numbers. For example, they have shown that there is no finite set of axioms that is adequate to derive all the statements of arithmetic that we know are true (see Tarski 1949 75 and Kleene 1967 278-80). Even with an infinite set of axioms, there will be still be an infinite number of true statements about natural numbers that we will not be able to prove from the axioms. When such truths are discovered, new axioms can be added to prove them. Hence the arithmetic of natural numbers seems to have an essential historical and progressive aspect that is lacking in some other areas of mathematics, such as elementary geometry, where all truths, and only truths, can be proven (see DeLong 2004 60). Just as the properties of natural numbers admit no complete axiomatization — that is, they are inexhaustible (Gödel 1995 3:305) — so the properties of humans may likewise be inexhaustible and admit no complete description. Of course, the analogy should not be pushed too far. Nevertheless, it suggests the logical difficulties that may exist in trying to describe and understand ourselves; perhaps natural languages are as inadequate to give a complete description of human nature as formal languages are to give a complete description of the natural numbers. Whether or not such a conception is true is, of course, a debatable point, but we must make allowance for that possibility in our political theory. For example, as we have seen (above, page 151), Madison's justification of the Ninth Amendment included the argument that a complete characterization of human rights is impossible. Some of the rights that were then recognized had their roots in history ("the rights of Englishmen") and some of the rights we recognize today are likewise founded in our revolutionary history. These rights can be stated, but it is likely that the task of articulating a complete characterization of all human rights, like articulating a complete characterization of all the properties of natural numbers, is impossible.

In any case, all the rights we have asserted, or intend to assert, should be consistent with what we know about human nature. Classic statements of this naturalism can be found in Aristotle and Cicero. Thus Aristotle says: "the things which are just not by nature but by human enactment are not everywhere the same, since constitutions also are not the same, though there is but one which is everywhere by nature the best"(1984 2:1791). And Cicero claims there is

> a law which is a law not of the statute-book, but of nature; a law which we possess not by instruction, tradition, or reading, but which we have caught, imbibed, and sucked in at Nature's own breast; a law which comes to us not by education but by constitution, not by training but by intuition. (1931 17; cf. Rush 1786 2). True law is right reason in agreement with nature; it is of universal application, unchanging and everlasting; it summons to duty by its commands, and averts from wrongdoing by it prohibitions . . . . And there will not be different laws at Rome and at Athens, or different laws now and in the future, but one eternal and unchangeable law will be valid for all nations and all times, and there will be one master and ruler, that is, God, over us all, for he is the author of this law, it promulgator, and its enforcing judge. (1988 211; cf. 333, 329)

An Aristotelian and Ciceronian cosmopolitanism became part of the American revolution; in Jefferson's words: "The principles on which we engaged, of which the charter of our independence is the record, were sanctioned by the laws of our being, . . . "(1903 16:349). Hence it is that James Wilson claims that the "knowledge of human nature is of all human knowledge the most curious and the most important"(2007 1:585) and John Adams commands "Know thyself, human Nature!"(Cappon 1959 2:334) The evidence that there is a universal human nature has now been explosively enlarged, most spectacularly in the articulation of the human genome. The knowledge we get from biology and the other sciences must be part of the considerations in any new formulation of the metaphysics of democracy. The ultimate aim is, as it were, to articulate and interpret the moral and political genome of human beings so that, as far as possible, civilizational discontents could be progressively reduced. Such a genome, like its biological counterpart, is grounded in history, and is not fixed. It does not presuppose that we are all alike morally or politically, any more than a biological genome presupposes that we are all clones with no biochemical individuality. Yet its articulation would allow us to better determine the customs and laws that fit human nature (at a given time) and are most likely to produce flourishing lives for all. America is Delphic-based civilization; without that base the American revolution dissolves into thin air.

As a thought experiment, imagine a statistically valid advisory jury for the world population. We could use the distributed intelligence of such a jury to create a common reason of humanity, or a world deliberate sense, which could give authoritative advice about what constitutes, say, crimes against humanity. We cannot know the exact nature and extent of those crimes without a careful and empirical investigation of human nature. Similar things could be said about virtues for humanity, or laws governing relations between nations. By studying the way different subjuries reason, we could investigate, as part of cognitive science, the extent to which there is a universal reason, or a universal morality, imbedded in the human psyche. We would be investigating deep reason or deep morality, corresponding to the inquiry of linguists who look for the deep structures that serve as the basis of all human languages. Of course, we would simultaneously be learning about deep superstition or deep immorality. (An example of deep superstition would be the fallacies of probability to which all humans seem naturally prone.) This psychological archaeology might reveal such things as deep religion, deep consciousness, deep play, deep aspiration, deep virtue, deep happiness (= secular equivalent of blessedness?), or deep vice (= secular equivalent of original sin?). Darwin may have been talking about deep vice when, in one of his notebooks, he said: "Our descent . . . is the origin of our evil passions!!— The Devil under form of Baboon is our grandfather!"(1987 550). The idea that education should protect us from built-in moral imperfections is old; in the words of Milton: "The end then of Learning is to repair the ruines of our first Parents by regaining to know God aright"(1673 97). James Wilson, typical for his time, believed that that repair should be made by reason since it enables us "to discover and correct the mistakes, of the moral sense"(2007 1:515; cf. 452). As we empirically investigate the nature of our common humanity using reason to articulate the moral and political genome of the human race, we would be getting to know ourselves aright, and thus better able to repair the ruins of our common evolution. Are the social games we play merely sophisticated versions of baboon morality? Perhaps a global politics of self-knowledge will reveal a dark humanity as puzzling as the dark matter currently challenging physicists. Linguists, when they study universal characteristics of contemporary languages, also learn something about prehistoric languages. Likewise if we investigate deep humanity, we can learn something about the prehistory of morals and reason. In the same notebook, Darwin writes that Plato "says in Phædo that our 'necessary ideas' arise from the preexistence of the soul, are not derivable from experience.— read monkeys for preexistence"(1987 551; cf. Plato 1937 1:456-62). Preexistence had no empirical basis in ancient Greece; now it does, and with a breath and depth that would perhaps astonish even Darwin. We know that human preexistence began in an apelike way and continued in a variety of hominids until *Homo sapiens* appeared. (One wonders: if humans had a preexistence as animals, could they have a post-existence as gods?) Darwin also said: "Origin of man now proved.— Metaphysics must flourish.— He who understands baboon . . . would do more towards metaphysics than Locke"(1987 539). Although contemporary metaphysics must be based on history and empirical science, both emphasized by Locke, it can nevertheless greatly transcend Locke, because our knowledge of history, biology, and the logic of metaphysics greatly transcends his age.

If an empirically-based metaphysics were created under the impetus of an aroused American revolution in the twenty-first century, it by no means follows that religious fervor would not again be part of the driving force. Science, which undermines religious faith for some, deepens and augments it for others. For example, a Christian of the latter sort might argue as follows:

Scientists ought to think of their quest in religious terms. Galileo did. He rejected the idea that God is "any less excellently revealed in Nature's actions than in the sacred statements of the Bible," and he quotes Tertullian (c. 160 - c. 220) approvingly: "We conclude that God is known first through Nature, and then again, more particularly, by doctrine; by Nature in His works, and by doctrine in His revealed word"(Galileo 1957 183; cf. Tertullian 1972 1:47).

Kepler also thought of science in religious terms: "I wanted to become a theologian; for a long time I was restless: Now, however, observe how through my effort God is being celebrated in astronomy"(Holton 1956 351). Again, Newton writes: "When I wrote my Treatise about our System, I had an eye on such principles as might work with considering men, for a belief of a Deity: and nothing can rejoice me more than to find it useful for that purpose"(1779 4:429). Nor is this attitude passé. On June 27, 2000, when the breaking of the human genetic code was announced, Francis Collins, the head of the NIH Human Genome Project, stated: "We have caught the first glimpses of our instruction book, previously known only to God"(Wade 2000 A21, Collins 2006 3). That was no mere manner of speaking, for Collins is a dedicated Christian (Liles 1992, Collins 2006). There are also many organizations — for example, the American Scientific Affiliation — made up of scientists who believe both in the authority of religion and the integrity of science. Embracing this ethos, we can say that if "in the beginning, God created the heavens and the earth"(*Genesis* 1:1), and if "in the beginning God existed, and reason (or mind) was with God, and that mind was God"(Jefferson's translation of *John* 1:1, Cappon 1959 2:593), then the physics of the big bang discloses the details of God's reason. If the "heavens are telling the glory of God"(*Psalms* 19:1), then the theories of Galileo, Kepler, Newton, and Einstein reveal some of the transcendent, but hidden, grandeur of God. If God said "Let there be light"(*Genesis* 1:3), then Maxwell's differential equations for electromagnetic radiation reveal the subtle reality of what God spoke into existence. If "ever since the creation of the world [God's] invisible nature . . . has been clearly perceived in the things that have been made"(*Romans* 1:20), then the natural world as portrayed by science discloses the character of "Nature's God," a God who, in Kepler's words, "wishes to be recognized from the book of nature"(1951 31). The physician Thomas Browne agrees: "There are two bookes from whence I collect my Divinity; besides that written one of God, another of his servant Nature, that universall and publique Manuscript, that lies exposed to the eyes of all"(1642 26). Today we know this Manuscript tells us that the atoms of our bodies were formed in the stars; hence our womb is cosmological, Nature's God is our God, and we are his stardust children. The opportunities to know him are thus not limited to the Book of Scripture and the Book of

Nature; his third book, the Book of Humanity, likewise proclaims his majesty and glory. Consequently, if "in the day that God created man, in the likeness of God made he him"(*Genesis* 5:1) then understanding the human genome helps us understand something about God. If "God is spirit"(*John* 4:24), and if the "spirit of man is the lamp of the Lord, searching all his innermost parts"(*Proverbs* 20:27), if Nature's God made man "a little lower than the angels, and hast crowned him with glory and honour"(*Psalms* 8:3-5), and if the "kingdom of God is within you"(*Luke* 17:21), then the deliberate voice representing the soul-searching reason of the people might tell us something, previously unknown, about God's *will*, about God's *reason*, about God's *politics*. Jesus says "where two or three are gathered in my name, there am I in the midst of them"(*Matthew* 18:20). St. Paul says: "Examine yourselves, to see whether you are holding to your faith. Test yourselves. Do you not realize that Jesus Christ is in you?"(2 Corinthians 13:5). If these statements are true, would not religious experiments in the Book of Humanity, conducted with the utmost honesty, be appropriate? Imagine a private deliberator consisting of 100,000 subjuries of three sincere Christians each. Might not a deliberate majority of these subjuries, ready to "examine" and "test" themselves, more accurately reflect the character of Jesus than any individual, even a church leader? Jefferson wanted to see the spread of "rational Christianity," and illustrated it by abridging the Gospels of everything he considered superstitions (1983). He said, "I trust that there is not a *young man* now living in the United States who will not die a Unitarian ." (Adams was also a Unitarian (1954 Reel 430 216).) Jefferson disclosed, "I am a real Christian, that is to say, a disciple of the doctrines of Jesus"(1903 15:323, 385, 14:385; cf. 10:380). As Jefferson originally wrote the Declaration, the American revolution was based on the "laws of nature and of nature's god," on truths held to be "sacred," on "sacred rights of life & liberty," which were pledged with "sacred honor." He believed that America, rightly understood, is a grand scientific experiment, founded in human nature, but driven by religious aspiration. Adams asserted that the "*general Principles*" of the American revolution were the "general Principles of Christianity, in which all . . . Sects were United: And the *general Principles* of English and American Liberty, . . . which had United all Parties in America"(Cappon

1959 2:340-1). As a universal world view, Darwinian evolution has not been demonstrated. Einstein once remarkably remarked: "No one must think that Newton's great creation can be overthrown in any real sense by [relativity] or by any other theory. His clear and wide ideas will for ever retain their significance as the foundation on which our modern conceptions of physics have been built"(1919 14). By the late nineteenth century many scientists rightly believed that Newtonian science triumphed and would live on, but then, through a hasty generalization, concluded that Newtonian scientism, that is, Newtonianism considered as a world view, also triumphed. This fallacious reasoning was exposed when quantum mechanics, relativity, and the theory of chaos demonstrated that the truths of Newton are not universal. In the spirit of Galileo, Kepler, Newton, Einstein, Jefferson, and Adams, Christian denominations — and not only Christian — could use private deliberators to conduct an indefinitely large number of experiments searching for the deep religion buried in their own humanity. Such experiments, provided they are conducted with painstaking care and are repeatable by nonbelievers, might similarly undermine Darwinian scientism *without undermining Darwinian science*, a science that could, like Newtonian science, live on; indeed such experiments might undermine secularism itself, *considered as a universal world view.*

A philosopher, skeptical of religion, might react with a smile, even contempt. Let us imagine her analysis of the Christian's argument:

Xenophanes' (*circa* 530 B.C.) observation is still relevant: "Aethiopians have gods with snub noses and black hair, Thracians have gods with grey eyes and red hair"(Freeman 1966 22). The Christian's sophistical reasoning merely expresses an unconscious, megalomaniacal ambition that says: "I was born in the right religion, others have to change theirs to mine if they want truth." The references to Jesus are bizarre pseudoscience, a product of the same megalomania: "Let us make God in our image, after our likeness." Christians fail to make the simple observation that religion is like language, that is, it is not universal like mathematics and science, whose truths can be discovered independently. It is merely cultural superstition, like believing that, if a black cat walks in front of you, it will bring bad luck. "God's son" did not appear to the ancient Chinese or the American Indians. Appeals to the Bible are appeals to what deserves no authority. Consider, for example, that it gives approval to immoral behavior and reprehensible punishments: These include One, the stoning of witches (*Leviticus* 20:27), blasphemers (24:10-16), worshipers of foreign gods (*Deuteronomy* 17:2-7), insolent sons (21:18-21), those who pick up sticks on the sabbath (*Numbers* 15 32-6), and brides who are not virgins (*Deuteronomy* 22:20-21); Two, the killing of female fornicators (*Genesis* 38:24, *Leviticus* 21:9), male homosexuals (*Leviticus* 20:13), heretics (*Deuteronomy* 18:20), worshipers of other gods (*Deuteronomy* 13:12-16), those who work on the Sabbath (*Exodus* 35:2), those who curse their father or mother (*Leviticus* 20:9), and those who lend money at interest (*Ezekiel 18:5-17*); Three, destroying of places of worship of subordinate peoples (*Exodus* 34:13, *Deuteronomy* 7:5, 25; 12:1-3); Four, human sacrifices (*Exodus* 22:29, *Joshua* 6:26, *Judges* 11:29-39, *1Kings* 16:34, Ezekiel 20:26); Five, slavery (*Genesis* 9:20-27; *Exodus* 21:7; *Leviticus* 25:44-46; *Deuteronomy* 15:15-17; *Joel 3:8, Ephesians 6:5; Colossians 3:22; 1 Timothy 6:1-2; Titus 2:9; 1 Peter 2:18-25*); Six, cannibalism (*Leviticus* 26:29; *Deuteronomy* 28:53; 2 Kings 28:29; Isaiah: 9:20, 49:26; Jeremiah 19:9; Lamentations 4:10; Ezekiel 5:10*); Seven, genocide or the slaughter of innocents (*Genesis* 7:19-23; *Numbers* 31:17-8; *Deuteronomy* 3:1-7, 7:1-2, 16, 20:16-17; *Joshua* 6:21, 8:1-29, 10:1-42, 11:16-20; 1 *Samuel* 15:1-31; *Psalms* 137:9; *Ezekiel* 9:5-6; *Hosea* 13:16). Yet Jews and Christians consider their respective Bibles "sacred" and the "word of God." It is impossible to detest this mythology with the vigor that it deserves. Sacred religion based on superstition and faith must be replaced by secular philosophy based on evidence and reason.

What this skeptical philosopher should understand is that religious inspiration has not always led to superstition, moral abominations, terrorism, and war; that it has on occasion been, and may yet again be, the engine of great and wonderful revolutions in mathematics, art, music, science, and politics; that all living scientists (whether they like it or not) stand on the shoulders of Christians who created modern science (and who themselves had debts to Islam and Judaism); that, just as the atheist does not reject science produced under the influence of a bipolar affective disorder, so, even if she believes religion is caused by a mental virus, or temporal lobe epilepsy, or religious child abuse, she should not reject scientific claims merely because they were inspired by a faith that she believes to be both immoral and absurd.

The twentieth century's greatest scientist (Einstein), and its greatest logician (Gödel), were intimately familiar with skeptical philosophical arguments, yet both rejected them, and remained believers (albeit each in his own way). On the other hand, since Darwin, at least, methodological parsimony rules out scientific references to God, since there is an evidenced-based, coherent explanation of the natural order without a designer. Even if true or held to be self-evident, the axiom *God created points and lines* added to Euclid's would never be needed in geometric proofs, nor would *God created the universe and humanity* ever be needed for demonstrations in physics or biology. Nevertheless, w *ith regard to its motivation,* mathematics, science, and engineering rightly tolerate religious, non-religious, or antireligious, diversity, just as they tolerate neurodiversity. Are there any atheists who reject set theory because Cantor was religiously motivated to discover it? Or any theists who reject the concept of a Turing machine because its originator was an atheist? Mathematical, scientific, or engineering claims are judged by the excellence of their proofs, experiments, theory, practice, aesthetics, and fruitfulness, not by the worthiness of the sources of their inspiration, or by the personality of the first professors. Likewise for political science and politics (cf. Adams' words above, page 301). Whether the mathematical discipline called *set theory*, or the political experiment called *America*, is given a religious or secular interpretation, therefore, depends on the character of the mathematician or citizen, not the nature of the discipline or the experiment. Science greatly enlarges what we know we do not know; and we *know* we have insufficient evidence for any universal world view, at least for now, and maybe forever. The history of cosmology, for example, is a history of many hasty generalizations, whose lesson is that we need to discipline ourselves into a strong epistemological modesty. At present, then, all world views are realms of fears and hopes, of faith and speculations, of political manipulation and moral yearning, not knowledge.

It is commonplace today for religions such as Judaism, Christianity, and Islam to receive strong, and often justified, ethical and epistemological criticism. It is rare for philosophy to receive comparable treatment, although it is likewise vulnerable. So let us see how the skeptical philosopher's attack on Christianity could be mimicked with a comparable critical assault directed at philosophy:

> The writings of the great philosophers are jam-packed with moral and political horrors. Consider Kant. In 1793 he said that if "a people now subject to a certain actual legislation were to judge that

in all probability this is detrimental to its happiness, what is to be done about it? Should the people not resist it? The answer can only be that, on the part of the people, there is nothing to be done about it but to obey"(1996 297). The significance of the mind-set that Kant is here advocating can be appreciated by turning to the words of Rudolf Höss, the commandant of Auschwitz: "Since the Führer himself had ordered 'The Final Solution to the Jewish Question,' there was no second guessing for an old National Socialist, much less an SS officer. 'Führer, you order. We obey' was not just a phrase or a slogan. It was meant to be taken seriously"(1992 153). Again, " 'Führer, give the order — we obey!' was not just an empty phrase for all of the SS. Himmler educated the SS, particularly the officers, to carry out this concept no matter what"(271). For Kant, rebellion is never a legitimate way for a people to get rid of a despot: "And this prohibition is *unconditional*, so that even if that [supreme legislative] power or its agent, the head of state, has gone so far as to violate the original contract and has thereby, according to the subjects' concept, forfeited the right to be legislator inasmuch as he has empowered the government to proceed quite violently (tyrannically), a subject is still not permitted any resistance by way of counteracting force"(298). This, of course, contradicts the Lockean doctrine of justified revolution written into the Declaration of Independence seventeen years earlier. In 1795 Kant argued for the "principle of the publicity of public right" according to which "a people asks itself, before the establishment of the civil contract, whether it dares to make publicly known, the maxim of its intention to rebel upon occasion. It is easily seen that if one wanted to make it a condition, in establishing a constitution for a state, that in certain cases force would be exercised against its head, the people would have to arrogate to itself a legitimate power over him. But in that case he would not be head, or, if both were made a condition of establishing a state, no state at all would be possible, though the people's aim was to establish one"(348; see also 301 and 463). This claim is preposterous; eleven years before Kant published these words, the New Hampshire Constitution's purpose was not made impossible because it contained the following declaration: "The doctrine of non-resistance against arbitrary power, and oppression, is absurd, slavish, and destructive of the good and happiness of mankind (above, page 152; cf. the Virginia

Constitution of 1776, Mason 1970 1:287 and Madison's words below, page 493). "There is," according to Kant, "no right of *sedition (seditio)*, still less to *rebellion (rebellio)*"(1996 463). By comparison, six years earlier James Wilson said that a "revolution principle certainly is, and certainly should be taught as a principle of the constitution of the United States, and of every State in the Union"(above, page 226). Given Kant's "*unconditional*" principle against revolution, it is easy to imagine what he would have said, had he been present at the meetings that produced the American revolution, or the successful slave insurrection in Saint Domingue. His doctrine is so radically contrary to the spirit of 1776 that he enunciates what ought to be called the *Totalitarian Imperative*: "[A] people has a duty to put up with even what is held to be an unbearable abuse of supreme authority"(1996 463). Could there be any more ugly consequence of secular philosophy than this? Rather than "Work Makes You Free," Rudolf Höss, with more justification, could have used Kant's Totalitarian Imperative for the motto at Auschwitz. Thus those victims who, without violent resistance, obeyed the Nazi soldiers who came to take them to the death camps, were acting consistently with what Kant prescribes; they were submitting to an "unbearable abuse of supreme authority." He even argues that it is wrong to lie to a murderer about the location of his intended victim (611-15). Thus those courageous individuals who lied to the Nazi's murderers concerning the whereabouts of Jews should be condemned by his standards, whereas those who told the truth should be commended. In 1797 he stated that it "is the formal *execution* of a monarch that strikes horror in a soul filled with the idea of human rights"(464). A decade earlier the soul of John Adams was certainly "filled with the idea of human rights." but he felt no such horror: "The right of a nation to kill a tyrant, in cases of necessity, can no more be doubted, than that to hang a robber, or kill a flea"(1850 6:130; cf. the words of Isocrates and Locke above, page 227). Or consider the title of one of John Milton's books (1649): *The Tenure of Kings and Magistrates: Proving, That It is Lawfull, and Hath Been Held So Through All Ages, For Any, Who Have the Power, to Call to Account a Tyrant, or Wicked King, and After Due Conviction, to Depose, and Put Him to Death; If the Ordinary Magistrate Have Neglected, or Deny'd to Doe It.* (cf. Mayhew 1750 37-9.) In sharp contrast, Kant rejects the rule of law for the rule of persons; he claims that the people "never has the least right to punish [a monarch], the head of state, because of his previous administration, since everything he did, in his capacity as head of state, must be regarded as having been done in external conformity with rights, and he himself, as the source of the law, can do no wrong"(1996 464). Compare Paine's words written six years before Kant's: "When it is laid down as a maxim, that *a king can do no wrong*, it places him in a state of similar security with that of idiots and persons insane, and responsibility is out of the question with respect to himself"(1945 1:339). By giving the monarch the power to act tyrannically, Kant gives him the right: "Power and right are convertible terms, when the law authorizes the doing of an act which shall be final, and for the doing of which the agent is not responsible"(Alexander Hamilton, above, page 193). Every twentieth-century totalitarian could correctly claim he always acted within his Kantian right. Kant thought that the "formal execution of a monarch . . . must be regarded as a complete *overturning* of the principles of the relation between a sovereign and his people (in which the people, which owes its existence only [*nota bene*] to the sovereign's legislation, makes itself his master)"(1996 464). Had the German people formally tried Hitler after a successful revolution, it would have been contrary to Kantian doctrine, as were the Nuremberg trials, the prosecution of Augusto Pinochet, and the trial of Slobodan Milošević. Since "the people never has a coercive right against the head of state"(301), it is hard to believe that Kant would not judge the impeachment clause in the Constitution (Article II, Section 4) to be a reprehensible mistake. Kant was also a racist: "This fellow was quite black from head to foot, a clear proof that what he said was stupid"(2003 113). Here Kant is himself stupid, since he cannot avoid even a flagrant example of the fallacy of *argumentum ad hominem*. He said the Negro was "strong, fleshly, supple, but in the midst of the bountiful provision of his motherland lazy, soft and dawdling"(Count 1950 22). For Kant, blacks had a slave mentality that made them incapable of self-government or civilization (Louden 2000 100, 105). In sharp contrast to Kant, there .was a large literature defending the intelligence, character, and rights of blacks in eighteenth-century America (above, pages 51-57, 70). There were also a substantial number of writers in Kant's time who defended the rights of women, such as Paine, Condorcet, Olympe de Gouges, and Wollstonecraft. Another was

Theodor Gottlieb von Hippel (1979, 1994; see also Schröder 1997). He was mayor of Königberg and was often invited to Kant's home. Kant, however, was a gross sexist: "As concerns scholarly women: they use their *books* somewhat like their *watch*, that is, they carry one so that it will be seen that they have one; though it is usually not running or not set by the sun"(2006 209); "Thus for the most part we have the greatest love for those we revere less, for example, the female sex"(1997 14); "Womenfolk have little wisdom, but much prudence"(16); "Womenfolk are able to select good means, but not good ends"(21); "In regard to sex, we notice that women are more exposed to avarice than men, which is doubtless also in keeping with their nature"(171); "In marriage the man woos only his *own* wife, but the woman has an inclination for *all* men"(1006 208). When the racist Jefferson wanted to disparage blacks he said they couldn't do geometry (above, page 78); the sexist Kant comes to the same conclusion about women. Women have a beautiful understanding (in contrast to the deep understanding of men) that means a "woman therefore will learn no geometry. . . . . Her philosophy is not to reason, but to sense"(2003 79). By way of contrast, Benjamin Rush believed "that the female temper can only be governed by reason, and that the cultivation of reason in women, is alike friendly to the order of nature, and to private as well as public happiness"(1787 25). "I hardly believe that the fair sex is capable of principles"(2003 81) says Kant; women are only capable of "beautiful" or "adoptive" virtues, not the "genuine" or "noble" virtue "which rest upon principles"(81, 61), and is therefore appropriate to men. Morally speaking women can never achieve what the best men achieve. They also need marriage to be completed, whereas superior men do not marry or become intimately involved with them, sexual intercourse being akin to cannibalism (1996 495, 1999 521). When Kant says, "All human beings are equal to one another"(1996 xviii), or "Woman becomes free by marriage"(2006 211), these must not be thought of as ordinary claims; rather, they are Orwellian expressions, using language characteristic of totalitarian governments ("Work Makes You Free"). If powerful monarchs committed rapes, murders, and other crimes, Kant wanted them to get away with it; whereas he granted vulnerable people no effective defense against the numerous oppressions that they might suffer. Thus he maintains that the "only qualification for being a citizen is being fit to vote" and that such people as apprentices to merchants or artisans, domestic servants, woodcutters, private tutors, and women are not fit to vote (1996 458). When Kant wrote these words, women and all the others he mentioned, had been voting for many years in New Jersey (above, page 371). Kant argues that if a person leaves a marriage "the other partner is justified, always and without question, in bringing its partner back under its control, just as it is justified in retrieving a thing"(427). In a Kantian country runaway wives are fugitive slaves where, unlike husbands, they are not citizens, and therefore they cannot use their voting power to get legal protection against abusive spouses. For Kant even an innocent child is a thing unless blessed by the state: A "child that comes into the world apart from marriage is born outside the law (for the law is marriage) and therefore outside the protection of the law. It has, as it were, stolen into the commonwealth (like contraband merchandise), so that the commonwealth can ignore its existence (since it was not right that it should have come to exist in this way), and can therefore also ignore its annihilation"(1996 477). Evidently he would have had no objection if Alexander Hamilton had been murdered as a child. For Kant, the people owe their existence to the state, and it is the state that rightly determines whether they are to be treated as persons or contraband things. Kant would not have wanted parents to resist the soldier who grabs their child out of their hands to carry out Herod's decree. Instead they should be apathetic (like a Stoic), recognizing that their public duty to the tyrant overrules their private duty to protect their child. If children can be placed outside the law, why cannot a dictator decree that the same should apply to adults whose parents were not married when they were born? Or why can't Hitler destroy all Jews, homosexuals, and gypsies since, under his government, they should not even exist? In a Kantian world, the prosperity of governmental injustice would not be disturbed; victims would have no *right* to resist violently, or even passively, if the ruler would issue a decree against passive resistance. For Jefferson, "Rebellion to Tyrants is Obedience to God"(above, page 227). For Kant, Extremism in Servility toward Tyrants is No Vice; whereas Moderation in Callousness toward Vulnerable Humans is No Virtue. Thus Kant has no sympathy for a person who attempts suicide; rather, such a person "disposes over his life, he sets upon himself the value of a beast. But he who takes himself for such, who fails to respect humanity, who turns himself into a thing, becomes an object of free choice for everyone; anyone, thereafter, may do as he pleases with him; he can be treated by others as an animal or a thing; he can be dealt like a horse or dog, for he is no longer a man; he has turned himself into a thing, and so cannot demand that others should respect the humanity in him, since he has already thrown it away himself"(1997 147). Well, we can make an beast, such as an ox, into our slave, and we can split a thing, such as firewood, into two pieces. But Kant does not stop at suicide: "A man is not entitled to sell his limbs for money, not even if he were to get 10,000 thalers for one finger; for otherwise all the man's limbs might be sold off. One may dispose of things that have no freedom, but not a being that itself has free choice. If a man does that, he turns himself into a thing, and then anyone may treat him as they please, because he has thrown his person away; as with sexual inclinations, where people make themselves an object of enjoyment, and hence into a thing"(127). So, for Kant, it is often quite justifiable to treat others *merely* as a means to our end, even if that end be grossly immoral. This claim is thoroughly irrational: even if we agree that some persons make a grave error and treat themselves as mere animals or things, we gain no right to treat them in same way. Every friend of humanity would agree with Samuel Hopkins: "Tho' the *Indians*, are sunk below the Dignity of human Nature, and their Lust after Drink exposes them to be cheated out of what little they have; yet this gives us no Right to deal unjustly by them. They have a natural Right to Justice . . ."((1693-1755) 1757 10). Again, Kant says that sexual desire "is nothing more than appetite. But, so considered, there lies in this inclination a degradation of man; for as soon as anyone becomes an object of another's appetite, all motives of moral relationship fall away; as object of the other's appetite, that person is in fact a thing, whereby the other's appetite is sated, and can be misused as such a thing by anybody"(156). The masturbator, the homosexual, the person who has sex with animals, "no longer deserves to be a person"(161). Ethically, for Kant, the vast majority of adult human beings may be treated as animals or things (and the monarch has the power and right to treat everyone, including himself, in such a way). Kant is willing to glaringly violate the ethics of expression (above, page 76) by, for example, advocating tenets that could substantially increase the mistreatment of women, blacks, and the poor, delay their emancipation from unequal laws and demeaning social practices, embolden the licentiousness of dictators, and increase the passivity of the population. Kant had a depraved indifference to the possible consequences of his words; in a moral but not legal sense, he was certainly guilty of *reckless endangerment.* Suppose a senior engineer, with malice aforethought, and on a number of occasions, designs artful errors into specifications for airplanes and these errors directly result in the deaths of hundreds, and indirectly thousands when other engineers follow his lead. Would he not deserve our strong moral condemnation (even if he otherwise made important contributions to technology)? A similar judgment applies to Kant. He was the most important figure in the many contributions that philosophy made to totalitarianism, and thus to the Gulag and Holocaust. Kant should be known as *the* philosopher of totalitarianism, which is a paradigm of the transcendent evil that humans can create. Yet how is this fanatical, bigoted crackpot, this trash-talking enemy of humanity, described in histories of philosophy? One of the greatest moral philosophers of all time! (One shudders to think what a great immoral philosopher would be like.) Philosophy is a fraudulent discipline of bait and switch; students learn about its wonders, but then are presented with counterfeits who embody no such wonders. Philosophy supposedly teaches love of wisdom, but Kant is a political and sexist hack; philosophy is supposed to teach epistemological modesty, but Kant is an ignorant and arrogant know-it-all; philosophy is supposed to teach good judgment but Kant's works are filled with paradigms of bad judgment (for example, that masturbation is greatly immoral and worse than suicide (1996 549; 1997 127, 161); philosophy is supposed to improve character, but Kant is a malevolent human being (otherwise, why would he write such terrible things?); philosophy is supposed to give you self-knowledge, but Kant is so grossly *self-deceived* that he cannot even see the obvious contradiction between his beliefs about, say, sex or women, and the teachings that made him famous. If, contrary to overwhelming evidence, Kant really believed that humans have innate dignity, are morally equal, and are ends in themselves, he should find the above quoted doctrines of his to be morally repulsive. He also maintained that the "human being is by nature evil"(1996a 79). So did he ever have enough integrity, wonder, and self-insight to consider the possibility that promoting the quoted doctrines might be an expression of that natural evil in himself? LOL. And Kant is no exception. From the beginning many of the greatest philosophers present one horror story after another. The conception of Tacitus that history should "hold before the vicious word and deed the terrors of posterity and infamy"(above, page 370) has no place in the subhonest "histories" of philosophy that professors generally give students to read. These books are literary sycophancy, mere spin-doctoring accounts of what each great philosopher should have believed and said according to "historians" who live in states of denial where "vicious words or deeds" disappear; students are not told what the historical, flesh-and-blood philosopher actually believed and said unless it does not reflect badly either on his character or on philosophy itself. They get silence, evasions, euphemisms, and bizarre interpretations, one vast cover up of moral stupidities and abominations; it is as if great philosophers, qua philosophers, are capable of innocent mistakes (like those in arithmetic), but never any errors that might be worthy of moral condemnation; they are placed "in a state of similar security with that of idiots and persons insane, and responsibility is out of the question." Teaching from these texts is truly a kind of philosophical teenage abuse.

When we survey history it is hard to judge which moral abominations are worse: those committed by those with religious motives, or by those with secular ones. It is made even harder because sometimes those with secular motives pretend they are religious, and vice versa. But the source of the problem is not religious or secular motives, but arrogant or fanatical belief where reason has been rendered impotent, a failure to achieve, whether in the habits of individuals and in the institutions of society, a bend-over-backwards honesty (see Feynman's description above, page 344). If it is asserted that the Bible is sacred or authoritative, or that some great philosopher is a worthy guide to standards of belief or action, a bend-over-backwards honesty would require that *those making the assertions* should conscientiously scrutinize, and present, the best possible argument against their own claims (the radical opposite of a straw man), especially with regard to any moral culpability of the person or tradition they are trying to champion. The purpose of the preceding two dialogues is to illustrate the kind of *one-sided* argument that ought to be considered according to the standards of a bend-over-backwards honesty. Of course, the champions should then give the other side, and conclude with the most judicious interpretation they could muster. Many of our greatest ethical and political failures were, and are, due to a refusal to adopt a bend-over-backwards honesty in the teaching of the humanities. (One wonders how many millions of lives might have been saved if, from the beginning, that honesty had always been achieved when Marx was discussed.) The acts of torture or murder that Stalin or Hitler may personally have carried out would not raise them above the ranks of common criminals. It is only their words that took them into the greatest depths of moral depravity, it is only their words that led others to commit atrocities in their name; it is only their words that led to catastrophic effects on tens of millions of people. Crimes of the tongue or pen are the origin of the extreme crimes of the sword; they can be weapons of mass destruction. And if we hold Stalin or Hitler responsible for their words in presenting them as paradigms of evil, should we not hold religious figures and philosophers for theirs? It is true that generally a writer's words are not as certainly consequential as those of heads of government, and their influence is often a longer time in coming. Nevertheless they can be just as deadly. Of course, authors have less control over how their words will be used than political leaders do, but that does not mean they have no control. (If you were a totalitarian leader, would you choose Marx or John Stuart Mill as your patron philosopher?) It is an abomination for authors to express themselves in such a way that their words can afterwards be easily exploited by those with evil purposes. Even if the "private" or "real" or "deep" meaning is entirely reasonable and moral, it is nevertheless grossly unethical to let the "public" or "apparent" or "surface" meaning be immoral, since that meaning might be the effectual one. Words in religious or philosophical contexts can be as powerful as those in political contexts; both their content, and the way they are expressed, can be important influences in the commission of unspeakable crimes and devastating wars. *Reckless endangerment* is an important category of ethical criticism that should be applied to spoken and written language. We think it prudent to deny weapons to mentally unstable persons; should we not also think it prudent to obstruct, by withering criticism, any pernicious influence that morally unstable speakers and writers might have? American culture at large, but especially students, ought to be direct beneficiaries of the best investigative scholarship that requires a fearless examination into the integrity and moral decency of both religious and secular figures so as to nullify every harmful effect they might have, an examination that should be conducted with a bend-over-backwards honesty that even the most fastidiously upright scientist might admire.

Today we have the resources in logic and science, in engineering and the social sciences, in the liberal arts in general, to conduct political experiments with that bend-over-backwards honesty. Through an extraordinarily careful design of courts of common reason, there is the prospect of a free people producing a moral stability appropriate to their ongoing pursuit of public happiness. The demanding soul-searching necessary for such an endeavor would help America, as a nation, to stay mentally sharp and spiritually vigorous. Nations, no less than individuals, often become cautious and less creative as they becomes older, but not always. Creative people, such as a Picasso or an Einstein, seem childlike even as adults. It is possible that our superiority to other animals rests on the neotenous fact that humans remain childlike longer than other animals. (One wonders if the maturing of a chimpanzee, bonobo, orangutan, or gorilla, could be substantially delayed, whether the animal would gain more humanlike powers?) Perhaps those nations that will best meet the challenges of a rapidly changing world are those that civically keep their youthful features, such as playfulness, openness to new ideas, curiosity, honesty, and enthusiasm. Of course we would not want all the youthful features of children — for example, their ignorance and amorality. Yet among the youthful features of America is there any more exhilarating than the aspiration for political excellence that marked its birth? On July 4, 1778, David Ramsay described the expected consequences:

> None can tell to what perfection the arts of government may be brought. May we not therefore expect great things from the patriots of this generation, jointly co-operating to make the new-born republic of America as compleat as possible? Is it not to be hoped, that human nature will here receive her most finished touches? That the arts and sciences will be extended and improved? That religion, learning, and liberty, will be diffused over the continent? And in short, that the American editions of the human mind will be more perfect than any that have yet appeared? Great things have been achieved in the infancy of states; and the ardour of a new people, rising to empire and renown, with prospects that tend to elevate the human soul, encourages these flattering expectations. (1779 3; cf. Barlow 1787 20 and Wilson's comments at DHRC 1976 2:582)

America was built on a philosophy of moral aspiration. The third dimension of American perfectionist democracy is meant to capture the spirit of that philosophy by providing a setting, through which a free people can stir themselves to achieve the aspirations that their politics of self-knowledge reveals. It is not certain that this, any more than the other two dimensions, can be carried out. American perfectionist democracy is an experiment, but if this experiment is pursued with great energy, daring, imagination, and excellence in execution, we might recapture the spirit of 1776, we might recapture our lost and glorious youth.

17

A New Order of the Ages

"Democracy" in eighteenth-century America meant what it means today: self-rule by the people. Since that was the proclaimed object of the revolution and the Constitution of 1787 it is certainly ironic that we find some very strong denunciations of democracy by revolutionary leaders. Thus, in June of 1788, Hamilton says: "Experience has proved, that no position in politics is more false than this [that is, that a pure democracy would be the most perfect form of government]. The ancient democracies, in which the people themselves deliberated, never possessed one feature of good government. Their very character was tyranny; their figure deformity; When they assembled, the field of debate presented an ungovernable mob, not only incapable of deliberation, but prepared for every enormity"(1961 5:38-9; cf. Madison 1962 10:267 and Elbridge Gerry at Farrand 1937 1:48). Modern scholarship has not ratified Hamilton's sweeping and harsh judgment. Athenian democracy was very much concerned with liberty and equality (Hansen 1989 25-28). Compare Greeks to Americans: On the one hand, when speaking of jurors in Athens, the orator Hyperides (390-322 B.C.) says that "there is not in the whole world a single democracy or monarch or race more magnanimous than the Athenian people, and that it does not forsake those citizens who are maligned by others, whether singly or in numbers [*nota bene*], but supports them"(Maidment and Burtt 1951 2:487); on the other hand, John Adams remarks: "I never knew a jury, by a verdict, to determine a negro to be a slave. They always found them free"(above, page 156). Again, Demosthenes claims that ". . . Greeks in every city are divided into . . . two parties — the one desiring neither to rule others by force nor to be slaves to any man, but to enjoy liberty and equality under a free constitution; the other eager to rule their fellow-countrymen . . . "(1998 273); whereas Lincoln declares: "As I would not be a *slave* so I would not be a *master*. This expresses my idea of democracy. Whatever differs from this, to the extent of the difference, is no democracy"(1953 2:532). It is quite unlikely there is any influence here, just similar observations generated by somewhat similar circumstances.

In any case, there is substantial evidence that the Founders thought of their revolution as democratic. Even the young Hamilton defended democracy with built-in safeguards (which is, of course, what we mean by democracy today). As he put it in 1777: "A representative democracy, where the right of election is well secured and regulated & the exercise of the legislative, executive and judiciary authorities, is vested in select persons, chosen *really* and not *nominally* by the people, will in my opinion be most likely to be happy, regular and durable"(1961 1:255; cf. 5:150). Noah Webster said: ""A representative democracy seems . . . to be the most perfect system of government that is practicable on earth"(1785 11). James Winthrop declared: "This glorious [American] revolution exhibited to the world, A R e p r e s e n t a t i v e D e m o c r a c y"(1795 32; cf. Clinton 1798 7). Representation was also stressed by Jefferson. The ancient Greeks, he said, "knew no medium between a democracy (the only pure republic, but impracticable beyond the limits of a town) and an abandonment of themselves to an aristocracy, or a tyranny independent of the people. . . . The full experiment of a government democratical, but representative, was and is still reserved for us. . . . The introduction of this new principle of representative democracy has rendered useless almost everything written before on the structure of government . . ."(1903 15:65-66; cf. Phocion 1795 11, Tench 1788 18, and Wilson's comments at DHRC 1976 2:343-4 and 354). Elsewhere Jefferson states that "we of the United States . . . are constitutionally and conscientiously democrats"(1892 10:22). James Wilson expressed a similar view in the Constitution's ratifying debate in Pennsylvania: "What is the nature and kind of that government which has been proposed for the United States by the late Convention? In its principle, it is purely democratical. But that principle is applied in different forms, in order to obtain the advantages and exclude the inconveniences of the simple modes of government"(DHRC 1976 2:363, cf. 349 and18:10). Later he claims, that the Constitution is democratic "is evident from the manner in which it is announced: 'WE, THE PEOPLE OF THE UNITED STATES' . . . all authority of every kind is *derived by* REPRESENTATION *from the* PEOPLE, *and the* DEMOCRATIC *principle is carried into every part of government.*"(2:494, 497). Referring to the federal Constitution, the Chief Justice of the Massachusetts Supreme Judicial Court asserted that "the whole building is democratic"(6:1433), whereas a Virginia commentator said "it secures us inviolably our rights and prerogatives as a republican nation, preciously preserving the nature of a government purely democratical"(8:164). John Adams said that "democracy must be an essential , an integral part of the sovereignty, and have a control over the whole government, or moral liberty cannot exist, or any other liberty"(Adams 1850 6:477-8; cf. 4:289; but note Adams' strictures at 6:477, 484-5 as well as in Schutz and Adair 1966 52)). In America, by the beginning of 1787, Adams thought "there is reason to hope for all the equality, all the liberty, and every other good fruit of an Athenian democracy, without any of its ingratitude, levity, convulsions, or fractions"(1850 4:492). To achieve this hope the Founders created a democracy with protections for minorities, multiple modes of representation, checks and balances of powers among the legislative, executive, and judicial branches, and so forth. These principles are the core of American revolutionary government and are expressed in the Declaration, the Constitution of 1787, and the Bill of Rights.

Yet the spirit of this kind of government is commonly violated by the representatives of the people. In the *Federalist* Madison makes an observation that should have been taken to heart by all future members of Congress:

> What indeed are all the repeating, explaining and amending laws, which fill and disgrace our voluminous codes, but so many monuments of deficient wisdom . . . It will be of little avail to the people that the laws are made by men of their own choice, if the laws be so voluminous that they cannot be read, or so incoherent that they cannot be understood; if they be repealed or revised before they are promulgated, or undergo such incessant changes that no man who knows what the law is to-day can guess what it will be tomorrow. Law is defined to be a rule of action; but how can that be a rule, which is little known, and less fixed? (1962 10:538-9; cf. 9:353-54, Hamilton 1961 4:651, Jefferson 1950 442, Wilson 2007 2:869-70, Cooke 1770 15, Hitchcock, Gad 1774 32, Montesquieu 1989 602-16, Sidney 1990 466, Harrington, James 2003 288-9; Tacitus 1969 3:567.)

It would be hard to top Madison's words for a succinct criticism of Congress as it has actually developed. The vices of which he speaks have grown exponentially. Given the disregard, not to say contempt, that Congress has for so long, and so consistently, shown for Madison's warning, it is hard to imagine anything short of a Court of Common Reason bringing about a reformation. With it, the people, after due consideration, will be able to advise nullification of laws that do not satisfy *their* standards of reasonableness, simplicity, elegance, stability, and, on occasion, grandeur. The republican legislator must constantly remember Madison's criterion: "the cool and deliberate sense of the community . . . actually will in all free governments ultimately prevail over the views of its rulers"(above, page 158). Just as Kepler and Newton reduced the bewildering evidence about the motion of the planets to simple laws that experience would not falsify, so legislators should reduce the bewildering evidence about the people's views to simple laws that the people will not wish to nullify. In physics, laws become meaningless if arbitrarily complex; in politics, laws become "monuments of deficient wisdom" for the same reason. Many of our laws are so incoherent, ambiguous, and burdensome that they encourage their own violation. They seem to contain little trace of lightness, of simplicity, of elegance, of gracefulness, of musicality, and never, never, never, are they tested against the cool and deliberate sense of the community determined in as precise a way as possible. Instead, *ad hoc-itis* has swollen them beyond belief, and unnecessary complexity is as pervasive as it is pernicious.

So let us imagine an amendment to the Constitution that would require that legislators meet Madisonian standards. It could be called the Aesthetic Amendment: "Acts of Congress shall contain neither arbitrary distinctions nor meaningless imperatives; nor shall laws be unreasonably complicated or mutable." Let me give illustrations of acts that would plausibly become unconstitutional by this Amendment.

First, an example of arbitrary distinctions are those laws written for the convenience of one person. Consider the case of Louis B. Mayer, the movie magnate: "Mr. Mayer," the attorney Louis Eisenstein tells us,

> was about to retire from his eminent position as a contributor to American culture. He had faithfully served his employer for about 20 years; on retirement he was entitled to share in the future profits of his employer for about 5 years or until his death; and his contract of employment had so provided for about 12 years. Instead of assuming the risk of future operations, Mr. Mayer desired to depart with one large lump-sum payment. However, if he took the payment, relatively little would remain after taxes. The Finance Committee was informed of his acute problem, and proved to be a friend in need. (1961 156).

So, without mentioning Mayer, the Committee wrote a law that applied only to him. Thus, to benefit by the law, you have to work for a company for twenty years, have rights to future profits for five or more years, have such rights at least twelve years before you stopped work, have such rights before August 16, 1954, and so forth (see Stern, Philip M. 1973 41). The decision not to use the word "Mayer" in this tax law facilitated hypocrisy and self-deception, not unlike the decision not to use the word "slave" in the Constitution. Loudly we proclaimed that our Constitution is the legal foundation for the land of the free, but then softly we interpreted it to uphold slavery; loudly we declared our laws apply equally to all, but then softly we write a law that in fact applies only to Mayer. To have been candid in these cases would have bothered one's conscience, or one's constituency, too much. The Committee in its defense could argue that the law sometimes creates unintended hardships on a specific individual which laws applying only to that individual can relieve. This may be true enough but is it creditable that, had Mayer been poor and the tax law was about to reduce him to that utter destitution, he could equally well have persuaded Congress to pass a special law covering only his case? Deceit has become routine: In tax bills, arcane language is used to hide the purpose of helping one individual or one corporation; in appropriation bills, anonymous earmarks often have the same purpose. The Biblical warning — "That the hypocrite reign not, lest the people become ensnared"(Job 34:30) — is forgotten; the revolutionary ideal — "no shadow of deception should ever be offered to the people"(Joel Barlow above, page 235) — is inoperative.

Second, consider an example of a meaningless imperative. Section 7 of Public Law 95-435 (October 10, 1978) reads as follows: "Beginning with Fiscal Year 1981, the total budget outlays of the Federal Government shall not exceed its receipts." This commitment was reaffirmed in Public Law 96-5 (April 2, 1979). Congress made no attempt to obey its own law; fiscal 1981 ended with a deficit of nearly 58 billion dollars. Yet things are not what they seem. Let me quote Section 3 of Public Law 96-389 in full:

> Strike section 7 of Public Law 95-435, the Bretton Woods Agreements Act Amendments of 1978, which reads: "Beginning with Fiscal Year 1981, the total budget outlays of the Federal government shall not exceed its receipts.", and insert in lieu thereof: "The congress reaffirms its commitment that beginning with Fiscal Year 1981, the total budget outlays of the Federal Government shall not exceed its receipts.".

Far from reaffirming its commitment the new act was completely hortatory and was meant to replace a law with force by a deceptive imperative.

Third, let us look at an unreasonably complicated or mutable law. Here many major pieces of legislation would qualify, but the income tax laws as they existed, say, in 1960 or 1970 or 1980 or 1990 or 2000 will suffice. Jefferson once said that "ignorance of the law is no excuse, in any country. If it were, the laws would lose their effect, because it can always be pretended"(1903 6:401). But there is a contrary danger. Laws can be made so numerous, complicated, enigmatic, and mutable as to make it possible for rulers, at their discretion, to fine, arrest, or imprison citizens while making the colorable claim that they are merely following the law. The rule of law here becomes a masquerade. Using Madisonian standards, ignorance of the income tax laws *should* be an excuse whenever the specific violation is unreasonable for citizens to know because the laws are too voluminous, incoherent, or changeable. Judging ourselves by the Madisonian standard that "the cool and deliberate sense of the community . . . actually will in all free governments ultimately prevail over the views of its rulers" we can only conclude that we do not yet have a free government with respect to taxes, unless we are going to maintain the highly dubious proposition that, after more than two centuries, our present tax laws finally represent the triumph of the considered views of the people over the opinions, considered or not, of political leaders. Eighteenth-century legislators in the South worried about blacks, not in terms of American freedoms, but in terms of slave revolts; our legislators worry about income taxes, not in terms of American freedoms, but in terms of tax revolts. To create an ergonomic tax system appropriate to the American people, we must find out how, after serious deliberation, *their* sense of economic justice and *their* aesthetic sense interact. Our tax policies generate arguments galore, but no one is exhibiting the spirit of the American revolution by collecting the evidence, and doing the hard work, needed satisfy Madisonian standards.

The intended effect of the Aesthetic Amendment is to reduce dishonest or careless law-making, and to goad legislatures to pursue the disciplined aesthetic standards intrinsic to the American revolution. Those who resist those standards because they seem coldly inhuman are, I believe, numb to the enormous passion that drives the aspiration for perfection. Their range of feeling is too narrow. The physicist Richard Feynman once asked a haunting question: "What men are poets who can speak of Jupiter if he were like a man, but if he is an immense spinning sphere of methane and ammonia must be silent?"(Feynman, Leighton, and Sands 1963 1:3-6). Could we not ask: What persons are friends of humanity who can warmly aspire to perfection if the activity is mathematics or music or gymnastics or architecture, but can only feel a paralyzing chill — thinking "Utopian! Utopian!" — if the activity is politics? When a scheme is called utopian it may merely mean a lack of desire, imagination, and determination, not the impossibility of actuality. We ought to be disgusted with the crudities of much in American law and dream of simple, beautiful, subtle, and grand laws that never were, and ask the people "Why not?"

There is a single proof in mathematics that originally was nearly 15,000 pages long but scattered in many places. In the nineteen-eighties mathematicians began trying to drastically cut its length while greatly increasing its perspicuity (see Gorenstein 1985 for details). The effort is continuing. Progress in mathematics is facilitated by a relentless striving for simplicity and lucidity. The same is true in democracy. But how many legislators are taking 15,000 pages of statute laws and attempting to drastically cut their length, while greatly increasing their perspicuity? "Laws are made for men of ordinary understanding," Jefferson said, echoing the Madisonian theme, "and should, therefore, be construed by the ordinary rules of common sense"(1892 10:231). Our laws can often not be understood by persons of "ordinary understanding," nor "construed by the ordinary rules of common sense." Early on in the computer revolution it was widely argued that we should all become computer literate, but it was later seen that a truly sophisticated computer would adapt to people of ordinary understanding — there would be no need for special literacy. Similarly, there should be no special literacy necessary for understanding the law as it applies to oneself; in a democracy, laws are made for the people, not the people for the laws. Of course, an ordinary person need not understand highly technical laws, such as those applying to regulated businesses (drugs, airlines, insurance, and so forth). However, the people who are directly involved should be able to understand them, and the goals of the legislation should be approved by the people.

Creating courts of common reason would awaken the spirit of 1776, but they would not be sufficient to keep it awake. That spirit burst forth in the revolutionary era with a speed and vigor that from our vantage point is astonishing. Yet the strength of the spirit became unsteady and, after a generation, it was often "slumbering." Even in the eighteenth century those who were most consistent in opposing slavery generally acted with religious, not political, motivation. The Founders failed to develop institutions that would sustain their own revolution. I do not believe that they can justly be blamed for that failure. They were engaged in an unprecedented enterprise, and were not in a good position to anticipate the coming slumber, which itself was hard to recognize because it came intermittently and by degrees. We do not have that excuse. To keep a revolutionary spirit energetic and robust it must be subjected to revolutionary exercises on a regular basis. Such exercises can only be obtained by returning to first principles, by reexamining, and perhaps revising, the fundamental documents of American democracy. In 1775 Silas Deane hoped for a "complete & perfect American Constitution, the only proper one for Us"(CNYHS1886 38-39). So let us revise our present Constitution until it becomes the only proper one for us, that is, one in perfect harmony with the common reason of society using the highest achievable, twenty-first-century standards for the determination of that harmony.

Any proposal to revise the Constitution will be meant with at least three objections. First, it will be claimed that it is dangerous. Yes, we might answer, attempting to rewrite the Constitution involves substantial risks, but certainly these risks are no greater than those taken in 1787. Should we be less daring and less imaginative in the cause of freedom than our forefathers? Must we live off the product of their revolution *ad infinitum* without ever creating a constitution that is the product of *our* revolution? Given time, is the Constitution to eventually include scores, or hundreds, or thousands of amendments with never a thought to starting afresh, with never a thought that a spirit of *ad hoc-itis* might be completely inappropriate for the American people? The American revolutionists preached a sermon on virtue, reason and excellence, a sermon I have tried to articulate in this book. We cannot practice what they preached without returning to first principles, without being willing to rewrite foundational documents, without being guided by the ideals of dignity and equality before the law. Why should we allow ourselves to be reduced to a footnote of a glorious revolutionary past when the resources of contemporary America give us an even more glorious, revolutionary opportunity?

Second, it will be said that these documents are too sacred to be changed. But the documents are not religious scriptures, nor are the Founders gods. Imagine that a young initiate into Judaism or Christianity studies the Torah or the Bible, and then decides to emulate the *creativity* of Moses or Jesus. Since both Moses and Jesus borrowed from existing religions in founding their own, the initiate likewise borrows from Judaism and Christianity. She wants to create *new* sacredness, not merely honor past sacredness. She becomes a prophet and composes a scripture with the aim of establishing a religion that has higher ethical standards, more truth, and greater spiritual beauty than either Judaism or Christianity. May we say that the initiate missed the point of much orthodox religion, for whatever else it means, it includes taking an attitude toward sacred scriptures and personages that puts them beyond substantial revision, criticism, or replacement? Adopting this kind of religious attitude toward the Declaration or the Constitution is completely inappropriate. These documents are human creations and, as such, there is always the possibility they can be improved. Wilson said that the right of the people to change constitutions is "a right, of which no positive institution can ever deprive them"(DHRC 1976 2:362). Our aim is to allow the people to exercise their right by developing a set of procedures and institutions for rewriting foundational documents, procedures which are so good that we would be quite confident that they would yield the best constitutions which it is humanly possible to produce at this time and place. Madison believed that since the Federal government contained "within itself a provision for its own amendment, as experience may point out its errors," it would, under wise and virtuous leaders, "approach as near to perfection as any human work can aspire . . ."(1962 14:324). The aspiration for a theoretical perfection, which is unachievable in practice, should serve as an eternal enticement to higher and higher levels of Constitutional excellence. The impossibility of perfection should certainly not excuse getting any new constitution at all; in Madison's words: ". . . if any constitution is to be established by deliberation & choice it must be examined with many allowances, and must be compared not with the theory, which each individual may frame in his own mind, but with the system which it is meant to take the place of; and with any other which there might be a possibility of obtaining"(1900 5:49; cf. Aristotle 1984 2:2045). In his *Autobiography* Franklin said that "tho' I never arrived at the Perfection I had been so ambitious of obtaining, but fell far short of it, yet I was by the Endeavour made a better and happier Man than I otherwise should have been, if I had not attempted it"(1986 73). This sentiment applies, *mutatis mutandis,* to public aspiration for perfection: for without it, we will not be able to attain the great goal of the American revolution which is, in the words of David Ramsay, to create a government that will "extend human happiness to its utmost possible limits"(1779 3).

Third, it will be claimed that we lack the talent to carry out constitutional revision wisely. Is this believable with three hundred million people from which to draw? Consider Paine's observation from 1792:

> There is existing in man, a mass of sense lying in a dormant state, and which, unless something excites it to action, will descend with him, in that condition, to the grave. As it is to the advantage of society that the whole of its faculties should

be employed, the construction of government ought to be such as to bring forward, by a quiet and regular operation, all that extent of capacity which never fails to appear in revolutions. (1945 1:368)

Paine's objective could be achieved by creating a government that, in its "quiet and regular operation," is permanently revolutionary. We are willing to spend more than fifty years and very large sums trying to create a controlled thermonuclear fusion to fully unlock the enormous energy in dormant matter; should we not be willing to spend even more time and money to create a controlled ethico-political revolution to fully unlock the enormous human energy available for public happiness?

Let us imagine, then, that the President launches a project to rewrite the foundational documents of the United States. Since attempting to revise fundamental documents involves great risks, it would not begin until it is shown that public deliberators have worked well for years, and until such rewriting has been successfully tried on actual villages, towns, cities, regional governments, and states. (Note that the Constitution of 1787 was preceded by constitutional writing for the states.) Further, there would be many fail-safe procedures along the way, such as allowing the President, or a majority of Congress, or the Supreme Court, or the Court of Common Reason, to delay or even terminate, the process. However, although prudence will rightfully dictate extraordinary fail-safe measures, the aspiration for excellence will not allow prudence to forever frustrate revolutionary change. The description which follows is a rough characterization of the sort of process that would be needed.

A special, and quite large, Constitutional Court of Common Reason is set up that spends ten years dealing exclusively with constitutional issues. It would operate according to procedures set by the regular Court of Common Reason. At the end of this period the Constitutional Court would pick — from its own membership — the delegates to a federal constitutional convention. The delegates could be chosen by successive rounds of election, either directly, by using a democratic evolutionary paradigm (above, page 178), or indirectly, by using a filtration scheme. In the Constitutional Convention Madison was critical of the proposal that the House of Representatives would be elected by the state legislatures (some of which are "composed of men already removed from the people by an intervening body of electors"). He objected because the House members would then elect the Senators, the House and the Senate would then elect the President, and the President would then appoint others to lesser governmental positions. Madison "was an advocate for the policy of refining popular appointments by successive filtrations, but thought it might be pushed too far"(Farrand 1937 1:50). Hence whatever scheme of choice is used, it must, via a metajury, have the prior approval of the people.

Aristotle claimed that "it is improper that the person to be elected should canvass for the office; the worthiest should be appointed, whether he chooses or not"(1984 2:2017). The Court of Common Reason must establish the set of qualities that it would want in their ideal delegates, and in their ideal mix of delegates. Then, using these standards, the Constitutional Court could choose the "worthiest" from its membership, regardless of the wishes of the persons chosen. Presumably most would be willing to serve, since they have participated so far, and the best do not attempt to evade their duties. Creating such a system is part of the Jeffersonian ideal: "The natural aristocracy I consider as the most precious gift of nature for the instruction, the trusts, and government of society. . . . May we not even say that that form of government is the best which provides the most effectually for a pure selection of these natural aristoi into the offices of government?"(Cappon 1959 2:388). Jefferson's ideal is old. Thus Isocrates (435 - 388 B.C.) says: "And how, pray, could one find a democracy more stable or more just than this, which appointed the most capable men to have charge of its affairs but gave to the people authority over their rulers?"(1928 2:121). Again, in 1656 James Harrington argued that "a natural aristocracy diffused by God throughout the whole body of mankind," is "such as the people have not only a natural but a positive obligation to make use of as their guides; as where the people of Israel are commanded to *take wise men and understanding and known among their tribes, to be made rulers over them*"(2003 23; cf. *Deuteronomy* 1:13, *Exodus* 18:19-26). Harrington thought that "a true and natural aristocracy" is "the deepest root of a democracy that hath been planted,"(170) that "where men excel in virtue, the commonwealth is stupid and unjust if accordingly they do not excel in authority"(35; cf. Wilson 2007 1:537). But Harrington was well aware that the "wisdom of the few may be the light of mankind, but the interest of the few is not the profit of mankind, nor of a commonwealth"(24). John Adams, perhaps influenced by Harrington, argued that the aristoi "are the most difficult Animals to manage, of anything in the whole Theory and practice of Government"(Cappon 1959 2:352). One of the purposes of courts of common reason is to bridle these "most difficult Animals," so that, no matter how extreme their passion for fame and power, their *actions* will be constrained to be meticulously faithful to both the commonwealth and humanity. Nietzsche said that "perfecting consists in the production of the most powerful individuals, who will use the great mass of the people as their tools"(1968 349). The radical opposite of this claim is the ideal of American democracy, where talented and forceful aristoi, however difficult, will be compelled to act in the interest of the people who, being tools of no one, will continually exercise their moral freedom to perfect the pursuit of public happiness and, thereby, to perfect civilization itself.

We will assume that the charge to the aristoi chosen for the constitutional convention would be, first, to achieve the highest standards of fidelity to the informed values and considered judgments of the American people and, second, to embody those values and judgments in a document of great structural elegance and literary grace. The members of the constitutional convention could spend a few years revising the federal Constitution. For example, they might start by rewriting it in language appropriate to the twentieth-first century; there would be no archaic terms such as "bill of attainder," nor any reference merely to the press when communication media is now meant. They could periodically test their preliminary ideas by experimenting with them in the Constitutional Court, using a democratic evolutionary paradigm that would have the advantage of being able to begin anew in a sense that is impossible in biological evolution. The standards for the final adoption process would be very rigorous. Among other requirements, at least three-quarters of the subjuries of the regular Court of Common Reason would have to approve it. Madison said that the Constitution, as it came from the Convention that produced it, "was nothing more than the draft of a plan, nothing but a dead letter, until life and validity were breathed into it by the voice of the people, speaking through the several State conventions. If we were to look, therefore, for the meaning of the instrument beyond the face of the instrument, we must look for it, not in the General Convention, which proposed, but in the State Conventions, which accepted and ratified the Constitution"(1900 6:272; cf. 1946 544, and Wilson in DHRC 1976 2:483-4). The new Constitution, then, will have life breathed into it by the spirit of the people, speaking through federal and state Courts of Common Reason, and it will mean whatever the people understood it to mean when they approved it. The words of the Constitution can hardly be the voice of the people if there is no way to know their sentiment whenever it is contrary to interpretations given by legislators,

presidents, or judges. The opportunities to make constitutional legal
science more scientific are great indeed, and traditional arguments
about "judicial supremacy" or "original intent" or"contemporary
interpretation" would be completely transformed, if not rendered
altogether obsolete.

Finally, we will suppose that the Court of Common Reason would
decide if any social classes are in need of special treatment when it
comes to constitutional approval. If there are, the Court would identify
these classes, which might include age, race, sex, economic condition,
area of the country, and so forth. Then special courts of common
reason would be set up consisting of a representative sample of each
of these classes. One of these courts, for instance, might consist only
of poor people, and it would have to be shown that the new
Constitution had the informed approval of two-thirds of them. To
achieve such a result, hybrid courts might be needed to make
compromises. The aim is to be able to say that the new Constitution
represents the common reason not just of the American people as a
whole, but of each of its politically relevant classes. Thus there should
be no good grounds for saying of the new constitution, as it was
sometimes said of the old, that it favored the pursuit of happiness of a
chosen few, and thereby betrayed the ideal of equality declared at
America's conception. If the new constitution attains the highest
degree of achievable excellence, perhaps we will someday be able to
satisfy Paine's criterion when we brag about America: "When it shall
be said in any country in the world, 'My poor are happy; neither
ignorance nor distress is to be found among them; my jails are empty
of prisoners, my streets of beggars; the aged are not in want, the taxes
are not oppressive; the rational world is my friend, because I am a
friend of its happiness':— when these things can be said, then may
that country boast of its constitution and its government"(1945 1:446).

After all these experiments both the state Courts of Common
Reason and the state constitutional conventions would be asked to
approve the new federal Constitution. By that time, perhaps, approval
would be a formality. What might such a document look like? We
cannot know but again, for purposes of illustration, let me speculate.
In the speech in which Madison introduced what became the Bill of
Rights he argued, "That there be prefixed to the constitution a
declaration — That all power is originally vested in, and consequently
derived from the people. That government is instituted, and ought to
be exercised for the benefit of the people; which consists in the
enjoyment of life and liberty, with the right of acquiring and using
property, and generally of pursuing and obtaining happiness and

safety. That the people have an indubitable, unalienable, and indefeasible right to reform or change their government, whenever it be found adverse or inadequate to the purposes of its institution"(1962 12:200; my emphasis). This seems to me to be an excellent idea. The "Declaration" section of the new Constitution could draw on the Declaration of Independence but, being cosmopolitan, there would be no reference to "Nature's God," or any ambiguity that all humans begin with equal moral worth. It would include the metaphysical axioms by which American society and government must operate.

The Declaration section could also draw on the Preamble of the 1787 Constitution, which without change is cosmopolitan. Evidence that it is cosmopolitan can be had by considering a remarkable set of parallel expressions. One of the oldest law codes, that of Lipit-Ishtar, which was unknown in the eighteenth century, contains a Prologue uncannily similar to the Preamble. (The following quotation from Lipit-Ishtar is taken from Pritchard 1969 159. The parallels were first pointed out by James T. McGuire (1994). Anu is the god of the sky, while Enlil is the god of kingship and the king of the gods.)

Sumeria, circa 1900 B.C.	*United States, September 17, 1787.*
The Law Code of Lipit-Ishtar	*The Federal Constitution*
Prologue	*Preamble*
. . . when Anu (and) Enlil had called Lipit-Ishtar . . . to the princeship of the land	WE, THE PEOPLE OF THE UNITED STATES
in order to	in Order to form a more perfect Union,
establish justice in the land,	establish Justice,
to banish complaints,	insure domestic Tranquility,
to turn back enmity and rebellion by the force of arms,	provide for the common defence,
(and) to bring well-being to the Sumerians and Akkadians,	promote the general Welfare,
then I, Lipit-Ishtar . . . [estab]lished [jus]tice in [Su]mer and Akkad in accordance with the word of Enlil. Verily, in those [days] I *procured . . .* the [fre]edom of the [so]ns and	and secure the Blessings of Liberty to ourselves and our Posterity, do ordain and establish this Constitution for the United States of America.

daughters of [Nippur], the [so]ns and
daughters of Ur, the sons and daughters
of [I]sin, the [so]ns and daughters of
[Sum]er (and) Akkad *upon whom . . .*
slaveship *. . . had been imposed. . . . .*

The Laws   ARTICLE I.

John Jay said the Preamble's purposes "collectively comprise every thing requisite, with the blessings of Divine Providence, to render a people prosperous and happy"(Dallas 1790 2:475). It certainly seems likely that Lipit-Ishtar would have said something comparable about his Prologue. In any case, just before the Iraqis began to write their constitution during the Iraq war, would it not have been politic for President Bush to have publicly recognized that ancestors of the Iraqis articulated their intent, more than 3600 years before the Founders, to achieve universal civic goals toward which Americans were, and still are, striving?

The Declaration section could also contain a revision of the old Bill of Rights. (John Adams organized the Massachusetts Constitution: Preamble, Bill of Rights, Frame of Government.) New rights could be added, such as the right to create private and personal deliberators. The status of rights — whether they are created by gods or God, or nature, or aliens, or are artifacts of a political game preceding the Constitution — would be left deliberately ambiguous. Such judgments would be part of the individual's freedom of conscience. Lastly, it would assert that it is the government's function to protect these rights as well as any others that might be shown, from time to time, to be desired by the common reason of the people. This statement could be so framed as to perform the function of the old Ninth Amendment. Throughout there would be a attempt to have all statements consistent with our deep humanity as revealed by the liberal arts.

Following the Declaration section would come the "Structural" section describing the design of the government and delineating the function of its various branches. These would include the traditional executive, legislative, judicial as well as a fourth deliberative branch to administer public courts of common reason. The Constitution would end with a "Renewal" section describing the amending process, including a requirement that the Constitution be ratified again, or replaced, in fifty years. The renewal requirement is meant to fulfill

Jefferson's revolutionary idea that constitutions be rewritten by each generation (1950 15:396).

John Adams rightly called himself the "principal Engineer"(1977 9:388) of the Massachusetts constitution. *Civic* engineers responsible for the creation of constitutions, like *civil* engineers responsible for the creation of public works, should be masters at expressing the spirit of the people, a task that requires such things as meticulous preparation, careful observation, controlled experiment, technological prowess and monumental, even awesome, beauty. (The pejorative "social engineer" is applied to those who don't exhibit this combination of qualities.) Civic engineering in this sense must be an ongoing, disciplined activity if America is to have the best government. It could be divided into several divisions, such as ethical, political, legal, educational, and philosophical. "There is not in the whole science of politicks a more solid or a more important maxim than this," James Wilson observed, "that of all governments, those are the best, which, by the natural effect of their constitutions, are frequently renewed or drawn back to their first principles"(2007 1:698). Similar statements can be found in Machiavelli (1965 1:419), Sidney (1990 150), Trenchard and Gordon (1995 1:121) and Montesquieu (1989 121), although Wilson's observation is almost a direct quotation from Bolingbroke's *Remarks on the History of England* (1972 165), in a passage that attributes the idea to Machiavelli. George Mason's Virginia Declaration of Rights (June 12, 1776) also asserts the maxim: "That no free Government, or the blessings of liberty, can be preserved to any people but by . . . frequent recurrence to fundamental principles"(1970 1:289; cf. also the constitutions of Massachusetts (Thorpe 3:1892), New Hampshire (4:2457), Pennsylvania (5:3083), Vermont (6:3471)). By making that recurrence regular, and by using procedures favorable to deliberation, the Renewal section would continually force the American people, as our present Constitution does not, into a soul-searching Delphic exercise to determine who they are and who they want to become; it would arouse and invigorate the spirit of 1776; it would make the American revolution permanent. We could then outdo the eighteenth century in revolutionary politics by as much as we have outdone it in revolutionary natural science and technology; we could become the world's first thoroughly revolutionary people.

It is easy to imagine an opponent objecting: "This is all very well, but suppose the people make catastrophic choices, say, by including references to Moses, Jesus, or Mohammed in the Constitution, what then?" The answer is: "If your belief that this is a catastrophic choice is rational, then you should be able to produce a convincing argument to that effect. This or a similar argument would be used in the Constitutional Court of Common Reason. Remember that the advisory jury, both before and after its decisions, would be shown to have a very high level of collective intelligence. In addition, the members of that Court would hear the testimony of historians, political scientists, and philosophers on the consequences of such a choice, would see plays illustrating its effects, and so forth. The opponent, unconvinced, might say: "Well, I am going to set the conditions for accepting a new constitution extraordinarily high." To which the answer is: "Excellent! Excellent! However, you cannot set them so high that they can never be met. Otherwise, you, as a professed democrat, will be considered a hypocrite or self-deceiver, just as some so-called abolitionists were so considered when they continually set unachievable conditions for liberating the slaves. Or are you saying that you are smart enough to discern political truths, but not smart enough to convince ordinary people that they are true?" "The point is, I do not want to trust my liberty to ordinary people." "And who do you want to entrust your liberties to? Why should we not call you an aristocrat or monarchist?"

Jefferson's comments on Hume are relevant here. He quotes Hume's statement that "the commons established a principle, which is noble in itself, and seems specious [plausible], but is belied by all history and experience, *that the people are the origin of all just power*"(Hume 1879 5:284). Exasperated, Jefferson exclaims, "And where else will this degenerate son of science, this traitor to his fellow men, find the origin of *just* powers, if not in the majority of society? Will it be in the minority? Or in an individual of that minority?"(1903 16:44). In sharp contrast Jefferson said his "most earnest wish is to see the republican element of popular control pushed to the maximum of its practicable exercise. I shall then believe that our Government may be pure and perpetual"(1903 15:65). We still do not know what that maximum is. Yet we do know one thing: Popular control can be improved. For Jefferson, the term *republic* means "a government by its citizens in mass, acting directly and personally, according to rules established by the majority; and that every other government is more or less republican, in proportion as it has in its composition more or less of this ingredient of the direct action of its citizens"(1903 15:19). It is an embarrassing fact that today popular control hardly means more than the minimum of periodic elections and a few referenda. A large element of Hume lives on in our consciousness. To end our apathy and cynicism with regard to the people, we need a large-scale test of American perfectionist democracy such as, for example, creating a Court of Common Reason for one of the smaller states. Large experiments can introduce revolutionary change. Thus even though ENIAC was only a programmed calculator and not a computer, its success in 1945 demonstrated that electronic computers were possible and useful. The tremendous demand for them then led to an intense competition for computing excellence. And there is no end in sight. Everyone believes the next generation of computers will be more useful than the present generation. The world of computers — indeed the worlds of science and technology as a whole — are in a state of perpetual innovation. Like the ENIAC, an experimental Court of Common Reason for a state might not work particularly well, but it might work better than any alternative, and would allow unsolved problems to be successfully attacked. If so, the enormous demand for better democratic government could create an intense competition for democratic excellence, and courts of common reason could be improved beyond all reasonable expectation. Our present political cynicism would disappear, and we would wipe the condescending smile off our face when contemplating Madison's belief that "the destined career of my country will exhibit a Government pursuing the public good as its sole object"(above, page 401).

Yet how could government officials be persuaded to construct such a test? In my judgment the American people must be made aware of their ability and responsibility to directly govern themselves. This could be done through individual initiative. Theoreticians could turn their attention to the problems of American perfectionist democracy. There are many relevant disciplines: from the well-known, such as probability theory, group psychology, voting theory, nonlinear systems, or game theory; to the more arcane or speculative, such as the Delphi method, fractal statistics, fuzzy logic, the logic of question and answer, prediction markets, or algorithmic information theory. Some democratic organizations, such as unions or churches, might be willing to risk tests of the theoreticians' work. A large number of experiments would be necessary to determine the best deliberator software for a given purpose, but some foundations or universities might underwrite this research, or a company such as IBM or Microsoft or Google might see profit opportunities there. There is no need to await government action. Rather, government action could follow successful private initiatives. Of course, the government could lead; the Supreme Court might require the executive branch to prove its claim in a Ninth Amendment case, a single well-place legislator might require the necessary research funds in exchange for his or her vote on another issue, or the President might propose experimenting with courts when the country is united, as it was under Bush immediately after 9/11. In a speech given on September 12, 1962, President Kennedy said that the "goal [of going to the moon] will serve to organize and measure the best of our energies and skills; because that challenge is one that we're willing to accept; one we are unwilling to postpone, and one which we intend to win"(1962 16). That daring scientific and technological spirit must now be applied to ourselves. On October 22, 1788, Franklin wrote to a foreign correspondent: "We are making Experiments in Politicks; What Knowledge we shall gain by them will be more certain, tho' perhaps we may hazard too much in that Mode of acquiring it"(1907 9:666). When will we again be daring enough to "perhaps . . . hazard too much" by "making Experiments in Politicks," because the new goal of creating superbly functional personal, private, and public deliberators "is one that we are willing to accept, one we are unwilling to postpone, and one which we intend to win"? Such a win would demonstrate to the people of the earth that America is embarked on a great-souled endeavor that their own candid reason would instruct them to join and perfect.

From the 1950s through the 1970s it was commonly claimed that nuclear war was "unthinkable" but, in fact, it was often thought about, and sometimes even considered. What was probably never thought about, and certainly never seriously considered, was the possibility of creating a permanent democratic revolution in which the first principles of our government would be continually challenged and checked against the common reason of society. Is it possible that beneath the rhetoric and braggadocio of our politicians lies a spirit for which the unthinkable is America's own revolutionary history? I share the great anxiety of those who shudder at the thought of a constitutional convention under the political conditions that exist today. But we can change those conditions. And we must. In 1765 John Adams made a judgment that applies to contemporary politics to a painful degree: "The true source of our sufferings has been our timidity. We have been afraid to think. We have felt a reluctance to examining into the grounds of our privileges . . ."(1850 3:458-59). Independence for the nation, no less than autonomy for the individual, requires the risks of deliberative soul-searching, the risks of self-knowledge, the risks of fundamental change. We have not pondered long and hard about the awesome intelligence, the moral power, the revolutionary aspirations that a deliberating people might demonstrate under the right conditions, much less have we have tried to create the political technologies necessary for actual experiments. If the latter are successful, perhaps some or all of the initial structural restrictions on direct action by the people will be seen as mere training wheels of freedom, that a liberally-educated and independent people will eventually throw off. In time, it might even be possible to revive the Athenian ideal of citizens as the sole *legislators,* and not restrict them to an advisory role (cf. Locke's words: "the people have a Right to act as Supreme, and continue the legislative in themselves"(above, page 34)). As a client might decide to take over more and more functions that had hitherto been carried out by the client's lawyer, so advisory juries might begin by giving advice, but gradually act directly, until control by juries reaches "the maximum of its practicable exercise," whatever that maximum be at a given time. But this dream of Jefferson will never come true unless we, as a people, act on James Wilson's dictate: "A nation should aim at its perfection"(2007 1:539). To aim at it, we must think about it, we must start the process by which *our* first principles, and *our* political ideals, authenticated by experiments revealing the common reason of the people, could be stated in declarations and embodied in constitutions and laws with an ever-increasing degree of excellence. We must again become American revolutionaries.

In March of 1776 John Adams rejoiced that he had "been sent into life, at a time when the greatest law-givers of antiquity would have wished to have lived. How few of the human race have ever enjoyed an opportunity of making an election of government more than of air, soil, climate, for themselves or their children. When! Before the present epoch, had three millions of people full power and a fair opportunity to form and establish the wisest and happiest government that human wisdom can contrive?"(1977 4:92). Today we have an even greater opportunity, but to seize it we must think anew and act anew. American perfectionist democracy is both a renaissance of the spirit of 1776, and a reformation of our present practice. Undertaking to new-model our civilization in that spirit is not without its dangers, as I have emphasized again and again. Yet the substantial risk of complete failure did not prevent the creation and adoption of the Constitution of 1787. Its creators were moral and political entrepreneurs willing to take great risks for the sake of great achievement. They bring John Milton's words to mind: "I cannot praise a fugitive and cloister'd vertue, unexercis'd & unbreath'd, that never sallies out and sees her adversary, but slinks out of the race, where that immortall garland is to be run for, not without dust and heat. Assuredly we bring not innocence into the world, we bring impurity much rather: that which purifies us is triall, and triall is by what is contrary"(1644 12). The "vertue" of the American people ought not to be "fugitive and cloister'd"; the people ought to be purified by the "triall" of contraries in courts of common reason, purified by being confronted, again and again, with America's most excruciatingly difficult moral and political problems. For then the people might achieve "that purity of Heart, and Greatness of soul which," John Adams believed "is necessary for an happy Republic"(1977 4:125). The people are the core of the democratic process; no government is truly democratic if it allows them to evade their responsibility, their freedom, their autonomy, by making hard and fateful decisions for them. Or do we slink out of the race for the immortal garland of unprecedented excellence in the pursuit of democratic perfection because of fear of what the people, after agonistic deliberation and soul-searching reflection, might decide? Is a cloistered virtue in the cause of democracy the best the twenty-first century can achieve?

The aspiration for perfection requires attention to details and a willingness to change the smallest item, a contemporary political equivalent of recognizing as a problem the Keplerian eight minutes of arc, or of rightly fearing a two or three pence tax on tea. Let us listen to James Wilson, speaking in Philadelphia on July 4, 1788: "A progressive state is necessary to the happiness and perfection of man. Whatever attainments are already reached, attainments still higher should be pursued. Let us, therefore, strive with noble emulation. Let us suppose we have done nothing, while any thing yet remains to be done. Let us, with fervent zeal, press forward, and make unceasing advances in every thing that can support, improve, refine, or embellish society"(2007 1:292). But can we claim a "progressive state" if we accept an amending process for our Constitution that in effect is limited to major changes? To attain the best government it is humanly possible to achieve at this particular time and place, we must "suppose we have done *nothing*, while *any thing* yet remains to be done." The revolutionary ideal embodied in the invention of America is a passionate and relentless activity of perfecting the pursuit of happiness. It is a inexhaustible process of transcendence: "Whatever attainments are already reached, attainments still higher should be pursued." If we truly respect and care about the American people, this conception must be applied to the Constitution, the foundation of our public happiness. A rewritten Constitution might be an elegant refinement of the present one, but that does not mean it would not be revolutionary. After all, Einsteinian physics was a elegant refinement of Newtonian physics.

Unfortunately, the concept of *democratic excellence* is now often thought to be an oxymoron: "it has been said that democracy is the worst form of Government except all those other forms that have been tried from time to time .   .   . "(1974 7:7566). These words of Winston Churchill convey a belief that is expressed again and again. Yet the belief is only partly true. Democracy is better than its rivals. It is also true that the serious faults which democracies exhibit worldwide provide evidence that democracy may at present be a bad form of government. In certain respects, a rival, such as the government of Singapore, might be better. But that it *must* be a bad form, or that it *must* be inferior in any respect whatsoever to its rivals, is doubtful. We do not have to embrace the soft bigotry of low expectations by assuming that the people can never become exceptionally skillful in the art of social decision, that they can never achieve self-mastery in the pursuit of their own public happiness. Here are Madison's words from the Constitutional Convention: "The people were in fact, the fountain of all power, and by resorting to them, all difficulties were got over. They could alter constitutions as they pleased. It was a principle in the Bills of rights, that first principles might be resorted to"(Farrand 1937 2:476). Few today argue that the people can alter constitutions as they please, or that by resorting to them all difficulties can be gotten over, or that they are capable of dealing with first principles. We say that the people have ultimate authority, but we refuse to create the institutions which could make that a living reality; we have become timid and pessimistic democrats. Yet we need only look at the phenomenology of the spirit of 1776 to realize that using those institutions to resort to first principles and to rewrite constitutions might enable us to justly boast that we had been sent into life at a time when the greatest law-givers of eighteenth-century America would wished to have lived.

Nevertheless, Madison's worries about revising constitutions must be considered:

> every appeal to the people would carry an implication of some defect in government, frequent appeals would in great measure deprive the government of that veneration which time bestows on every thing, and without which perhaps the wisest and freest governments would not possess the requisite stability. .   .   . In a nation of philosophers .   .   . [a] reverence of the laws, would be sufficiently inculcated by the voice of an enlightened reason. But a nation of philosophers is as little to be expected as the philosophical race of kings wished for by Plato. And

in every other nation, the most rational government will not find it a superfluous advantage to have the prejudices of the community on its side. (1962 10:461-62; cf. also 13:22-25)

These worries, it seems to me, can be put to rest. In the first place, fifty-year intervals are not "frequent appeals," but the process described above would, I believe, satisfy Jefferson's, Mason's, and Wilson's "frequency" requirements, since the people would be involved in the revision of their constitutions as an ongoing political activity. This process would also exhibit, to ourselves and the world, the revolutionary nature of American civilization. Of course, it would eventually be up to the people to decide how often they wished to rewrite constitutions — my choice of fifty years is a guess. Second, if a revision actually occurred in a manner comparable to that described above, the nation could rightly boast that it was a "rational" government — perhaps even the "most rational government." It could create a constitutional version of Festival America to help get the "prejudices of the community on its side." Art and ritual could instill with patriotic emotion what the reason of the people had first, in a cool and deliberate mood, concluded is right. *Passion disciplined by reason* — the definition of emotional integrity — is not inferior to untutored feeling or prejudices in either intensity or effect; it produced the most sublime creations in mathematics, science, and engineering; and it is the only force capable of significantly perfecting the pursuit of happiness in the twenty-first, or any other, century. Further, this conception can be understood in either secular or religious terms (for the latter, cf. Reese's words above, top of page 27). The Festival might last a week and would celebrate the launching of the new Constitution, in song, dance, theater, music, ritual, and spectacle. The Declaration and Renewal sections could be composed with the aim of inspiring awe. (Both the Law Codes of Lipit-Ishtar and Hammurabi contain Prologues and Epilogues that are highly poetic and impassioned.) These sections might be set to music, incorporated in a new national anthem, provide the basis for any pledge of allegiance, and inspire themes for a dozen plays. (Putting such things to music is hardly an innovation: "Ballad for Americans" (Earl Robinson, John Latouche) contains words from the Declaration; "We the People" (Ruth Schram) is a musical version of the Preamble; and Neely Bruce has composed the "Bill of Rights: Ten Amendments in Eight Motets.") The sections could be written knowing they would be put to these uses; they could be eloquent when read, stirring when sung, and organized to ease memorization by students in secondary schools.

What is learned by heart is taken to heart; children would be identifying themselves with the ethical and political basis of American civilization. Aristotle's comment is relevant: "The best laws, though sanctioned by every citizen of the state, will be of no avail unless the young are trained by habit and education in the spirit of the constitution . . . "(1984 2:2080). This conception was adopted by the American revolutionists. Charles Cotesworth Pinckney thought the Declaration of Independence was a "charter which our babes should be taught to lisp in their cradles; which our youth should learn as a *carmen necessarium*, or indispensable lesson; which our young men should regard as their compact of freedom"(Elliot 1836 4:301). "As soon as [any child in America] opens his lips," Noah Webster declares, "he should rehearse the history of his own country; he should lisp the praise of liberty . . ."(1790 23). Nor should such rehearsals be only for youth. John Adams's diary for August 14, 1769 states: "Dined with 350 Sons of Liberty . . . We had also the Liberty Song . . . and the whole Company joined in the Chorus. This is cultivating the Sensations of Freedom. There was a large Collection of good Company. Otis and [Samuel] Adams are politick, in promoting these Festivals, for they tinge the Minds of the People, they impregnate them with the sentiments of Liberty . . . "(1961 1:341; the song was written by John Dickinson. Paine, by he way, was the probable author of the popular song "Liberty Tree."). If democratic festivals fostered revolution in the eighteenth century, might it not be politic to establish, with great emotional integrity, festivals to advance that revolution in the twenty-first?

The American people do not have a special place within the American revolution, they are the American revolution; their pursuit of happiness and the flourishing of all humanity is its quintessence. To emphasize their ultimate supremacy, there should be no *official* written copy of the new Constitution. Rather, we should reintroduce the oral tradition of our preliterate ancestors and have the only official version be preserved, not in argon gas, but in the collective memory of what the American people spoke into existence. It would then be clear, as it now is unfortunately not, that the people give the Constitution the only life it has, and that any authoritative understanding of its text must finally rest in their minds and hearts. In James Wilson's sense, our toasts would all become "politically correct" (above, page 235), because the awe that patriots feel toward the new Constitution would not be to parchment under glass, but to the sublime spirit of the American people in its finest political expression, a spirit that protects our individuality, our freedoms, our pursuits of happiness. Given the way the new Constitution was created and preserved, given its frequent expression in song, in art, in pledges of allegiance, given the extraordinary capacity for spectacle that contemporary technology has made possible, the new government will inevitably have more than the "prejudices of the community on its side"; it will have the fervent and rational support of the citizens of the United States, because they authorized it to be the supreme embodiment of their common humanity. Jefferson hoped the impact of the European Age of Reason, which was created through the influence of science and technology, would in America produce the Age of Common Reason, through the influence of ethics and politics. "Life is of no value but as it brings us gratifications," he says. "Among the most valuable of these is rational society. It informs the mind, sweetens the temper, chears our spirits, and promotes health"(1950 6:550). The aim of the revolution is to create, maintain, and continually perfect American civilization based on that society.

From the beginning the revolutionists often asserted that their pursuit was in the name of humanity. "The cause of America, " Paine declared in January 1776, "is in a great measure the cause of all mankind"(1945 1:3). Writing from Paris in 1777, Franklin observed: ". . . 'tis a Common Observation here, that our Cause is *the Cause of all Mankind*, and that we are fighting for their Liberty in defending our own. 'Tis a glorious task assign'd us by Providence; which has, I trust, given us Spirit and Virtue equal to it, and will at last crown it with Success"(1907 7:56; see also 1959 23:473, Jefferson 1903 10:324-5, and Adams 1850 7:393). David Ramsay continued the same theme in his Independence Day speech in 1778: ". . . I am confident that the cause of America is the cause of human nature, and that it will extend its influence to thousands who will never see it, and procure them a mitigation of the cruelties and oppressions imposed by their arbitrary taskmasters"(1779 3). In 1779 Washington declared that "Our cause is noble, it is the cause of Mankind!"(1931 14:313). In a booklet published in the same year, Gouverneur Morris wrote: "The portals of the temple we have raised to freedom, shall . . . be thrown wide, as an asylum to mankind. America shall receive to her bosom and comfort and cheer the oppressed, the miserable and the poor of every nation and of every clime. . . . In becoming acquainted with the religions, the customs and the laws, the wisdom, virtues and follies and prejudices of different countries, we shall be taught to cherish the principles of general benevolence. We shall learn to consider all men as our brethren, being equally children of the Universal Parent - - - that God of the heavens and the earth . . ."(1779 122). This booklet was "published according to a resolution of Congress." Thus eight years before the Constitution, it was the understanding, authorized by Congress, that America, if it lived according to its ideals, was to have a cosmopolitan attraction, and thus destined to be made up of individuals coming from all cultures ("every nation") and all races ("every clime"). A year later, in a Pennsylvania law for the gradual elimination of slavery, we find this phrase: "We esteem it a peculiar blessing granted to us, that we are enabled this day, to add one more step to universal civilization, . . ."(LESS 1780 296). In 1781 Adams said that America's "cause is that of all nations and all men; and it needs nothing but to be explained, to be approved"(1850 7:393). At the Constitutional Convention, Morris said that he "came here as a Representative of America; he flattered himself he came here in some degree as a Representative of the whole human race"(Farrand 1937 1:529). By adopting the Constitution, James Wilson declared, "we shall probably lay a foundation for erecting temples of liberty in every part of the earth"(2007 1:284). The cosmopolitan appeal of America does not entail the Stoic ideal of equalizing feelings for the joys and afflictions of an arbitrarily chosen person with those for one's own family. It seems highly likely that eighteenth-century Americans would agree with Adam Smith: "The man who should feel no more for the death or distress of his own father, or son, than for those of any other man's father or son, would appear neither a good son nor a good father"(1976 142). Nor does American cosmopolitanism entail the civic indifference that can be found in Greek philosophy as early as Democritus (circa 460 - 370 B.C.): "To a wise man, the whole earth is open; for the native land of a good soul is the whole earth"(Freeman 1966 113; cf. Cicero 1960 533-34, Seneca 1970 2:447, 1989 1:201, Epictetus 1928 1:63, Diogenes Laertius 1925 2:65). Rather, the cosmopolitan ideal of America requires that neither its laws or its behavior contradicts the normative standards built into humanity. Those standards would not require a woman, who can rescue only one child out of a number in mortal danger, to save a randomly chosen child, as Stoicism dictates, rather than her own child, as love dictates. "The essence of being human," George Orwell said, "is that one does not seek perfection, that one is sometimes willing to commit sins for the sake of loyalty, that one does not push asceticism to the point where it makes friendly intercourse impossible, and that one is prepared in the end to be defeated and broken up by life, which is the inevitable price of fastening one's love upon other individuals"(1949

89). The same holds true for love of country. In 1797 John Jay said, "I wish to see our people more Americanized," by which he meant that Americans should "feel and act as an independent nation"(1890 4:232). But then its citizens might be willing to do many things — for example, to fight and die for America — that they would not do for any other country. American perfectionist democracy is not founded on the cosmopolitan ideals of a "universal civilization" in the abstract, since that might jeopardize legitimate personal, cultural, or regional identities of a diverse citizenry; or it might even suggest the falsehood that we can completely escape biography and history. Rather, American perfectionist democracy is based on universal ideals as humanized by the common reason, decency, and loves of the American people, qualities that would be disclosed in their soul-searching deliberations to secure the blessings of liberty to themselves and their posterity.

The Founders wanted America not only to have ubiquitous appeal to its citizens, they wanted it to be a source of inspiration for all humanity. Writing to John Dickinson, Jefferson maintained that a

> just and solid republican government maintained here, will be a standing monument and example for the aim and imitation of the people of other countries; and I join with you in the hope and belief that they will see, from our example, that a free government is of all the others the most energetic; that the inquiry which has been excited among the mass of mankind by our revolution and it's consequences, will ameliorate the condition of man over a great portion of the globe. (1892 8:8; cf. 5:147 and 8:159; see also Ramsay's comments in 1779 2, Hamilton 's in 1961 3:557; Morris's in Farrand 1937 1:529, James Wilson's and Madison's in DHRC 1976 2:584, 10:1498-99, and 1900 9:157.)

Nor were Americans the only ones who believed that America could serve as a model. Europeans did as well. From Germany, in 1782, Johann Christian Schmohl maintained that "Europe on its own does not have enough strength to reform itself. But examples and help from others may yet effect something. It is America that will be Europe's savior. America will nobly repay the tyranny and devastation it suffered at Europe's hands with liberty and affluence instead"(Dipple 1977 311). (Reading this comment it is hard not to think of the World Wars I and II.) A dozen years later, Bernhard Christoph Faust wrote to George Washington : "The United States of America first broke the yoke of serfdom, proclaiming liberty and human rights to men and nations. It will be the free states of the New World that will engender the present and future happiness of the peoples of the Old World"(311). In England, Joseph Priestley wrote that the "noble example of America" would lead every country to become "flourishing and happy"(1791 146). In France, the Abbé Raynal, writing about Americans, said: "Their cause is that of the whole human race; it becomes our own . . . . And may your duration, if it be possible, equal the duration of the whole world"(1781 173, 181). In 1778 Turgot wrote that "the Americans are bound to become great, not by war but by culture. . . . All right-thinking men must pray that this people may arrive at all the prosperity of which they are capable. They are the hope of the human race. They should be the model"(1884 302-3; cf. Morgan 1815 73-4). Condorcet claimed that "the declaration by which [America] declared her independence is a simple and sublime statement" of the rights of man. He expounded on the "advantages of the American revolution relative to the preservation of peace in Europe" and "relative to the perfectibility of the human race"(Echeverria 1968 91, 96, 100). In the same vein, Diderot wrote: "After some centuries of general oppression, may the revolution that has just taken place overseas, by offering to all the inhabitants of Europe an asylum from fanaticism and tyranny, instruct those who govern men on the legitimate use of their authority"(Wilson, Arthur 1972 707). In my judgment, the best way we can help foreign countries is not by giving economic or military aid, though these on occasion may be necessary, but by returning to first principles and rewriting our Constitution in such a way as to be a paradigm of twenty-first-century excellence in revolutionary democracy. Such an exercise would be a peaceful equivalent of war against everything that stands in the way of the flourishing of humankind.

But that peaceful equivalent of war has many fronts; rewriting our Constitution is just one. Here is another: We could invite foreigners, on regular occasions, to take part in our courts of common reason. Consider the relations between the United States and some foreign country. What should the foreign policy of each country be to the other? Imagine that, say, fifty subjuries from the American Court of Common Reason study the culture of the foreign country for six months. They learn something about its history, language, art, science, government, economy, geography. They travel to the country, staying three months. They live in homes, visit factories, go to the theater, talk to government leaders, artists, teachers, farmers, and factory workers. The foreign country, we will suppose, also has fifty subjuries that study America in a like manner. In this way the jurors from each country could learn from the other and attempt to change those aspects of their society where the other does a better job. For example, the people of the American advisory jury might judge that the other country protects orphans better than the United States generally does. They might then recommend that the Court of Common Reason place this issue on its agenda. And so forth.

Now suppose a hybrid court is set up consisting of a hundred subjuries, each containing six Americans and six foreigners. Its purpose is to resolve any international disputes that the two countries might have. After doing so, it would be up to the legislators and diplomats to formulate and carry out the proposed resolutions. Of course, for various reasons the establishment of a hybrid court might be impossible — the cultural differences might be too great or the foreign government might forbid its citizens from taking part. Then the next best thing ought to be done, such as using recent emigres, citizens from countries that have some substantial similarity to it, and the like. This is hardly as good as using actual citizens but in political science, as in the physical sciences, indirect methods are often the only ones available. Even in America itself indirect methods will have to be used for groups such as the Amish who might refuse to participate in courts of common reason. Nevertheless, if hybrid courts could help regulate the relations between countries, they might become one of the most effective institutions for peace the world has ever known.

In 2000 Kasparov played a single game of chess, using the Internet, against 58,000 players whose moves were decided by majority vote. Kasparov won but, such was the power of distributed intelligence, that it produced, in the words of Kasparov, "one of the greatest games of chess ever played"(2000 202). Would it not be prudent to see if the same power of distributed intelligence, with tighter controls and suitably adapted to politics, could produce magnificent achievements in the cause of humanity? Thus we could ask the members of foreign courts of common reason to give us their considered judgment of early drafts of the new American Constitution in order that, on the one hand, Americans could consider these comments in their quest for excellence and, on the other hand, foreigners could directly experience American freedom, a firsthand chance to see a people at once democratic and revolutionary. They could experience the winning art in Festival America. Parts of the Festival could be opened to the world so that, among other things, peoples who have been grievously wronged by American power could express their complaint directly to the American people. The wretched of the earth could find an artistic voice that would be heard by the fortunate of the earth. We might expect that foreigners could teach

Americans a good deal and we should be eager to learn. Perhaps others, seeing what America is trying, will start their own revolution and, being more desperate, or more virtuous, actually carry it out with more speed and more excellence. So be it. As John Adams has stated: "There is no special providence for Americans, and their nature is the same with that of others"(1850 4:401). If American civilization saw a little further, at least in some ways, it was by standing on the shoulders of giant civilizations, but it has no monopoly on democratic revolution any more than it has on technological or scientific revolution. Technology and science are universal because its laws are built into nature, economics and politics are likewise universal because their laws are built into human nature. As I have emphasized again and again, this conception is classical. Thus Marcus Aurelius (121-180 A. D.) says: "If mind is common to us all, then we have reason also in common — that which makes us rational beings. If so, then common too is the reason which dictates what we should or should not do. If so, then law too is common to us all. If so, then we are citizens. If so, we share in a constitution. If so, the universe is a kind of community"(2006 24). What the classical world lacked was an understanding that any claimed universality must be justified by careful, detailed observation and experiment, and it lacked an appreciation that it must not neglect the importance of biography and history in human nature. We can not only repair these deficiencies, we possess the means to make such a conception functional.

Let's see how. Suppose that the relations between the United States and some other country are exceedingly good — travel and trade restrictions have been eliminated, all disputes are minor and there is an established procedure for settling them. The harmony is so great that the other country wants to join the United States. The possibility that such an event might occur would be greatly increased, I believe, by using the Court of Common Reason to give new life to the Tenth Amendment (above, page 150), or its future version in any revised Constitution. Its purpose was to restrict the powers of the Federal government to the powers explicitly named. By the Declaration, it is the people's right to delegate powers to governments; some of those not delegated to the Federal government are delegated to the states, and those not delegated to either are retained by the people. For example, the power to set the value of coins is delegated to the Federal government, the power to regulate various aspects of education is delegated to the state governments, and the power to determine the content of speech is reserved to the people. Now the people of the foreign country would want to ask: Do the people of the United States delegate enough powers to the states so that our culture, our rights, our individuality, will be enhanced when our country becomes one or more states in the United States? And the people of the United States will want to ask: Have the political skills of the people of the foreign country become sufficiently proficient as to enhance the prosperity of American democracy? Let us suppose that, in the considered judgment of the people of both countries, the answers to each question is "yes." Imagine that the foreign country joins our union and that the arrangement works superbly well. Then others, seeing the enlargement of freedom and public happiness achieved by both countries, might want to join. The communications system that gives us a global village could also give us a global revolutionary democracy. Perhaps, at some point, a revised American constitution would cover the entire earth, becoming an expression of the common reason of all humanity. We would then have an all-American world, in which global federalism would be achieved, and a new Festival Earth would celebrate our common humanity.

To reach this end, hybrid juries could routinely be used for mediation. Thus the conflict between the Israelis and Palestinians might be reduced or resolved by using mediation advisory juries, where each subjury would consist of four Israelis, four Palestinians, and, say, four Americans. In addition, global environmental disputes could be resolved. On the environment Jefferson claimed that it was a self-evident truth " '*that the earth belongs in usufruct to the living*' : that the dead have neither powers nor rights over it"(1950 15:392; usufruct = right of use without harm to what is used). From this he reasoned that debts ought not be passed on to succeeding generations Madison rightly objected to Jefferson's inference, saying that "if the earth be the gift of *nature* to the living, their title can extend to the earth in its *natural* State only. The *improvements* made by the dead form a debt against the living who take the benefit of them. This debt cannot be otherwise discharged than by a proportionate obedience to the will of the Authors of the improvements"(1962 13:19). Hence it would be right to pass on some of the costs of the revolutionary war to future generations since they benefitted by that war. We could likewise say that it would be right for the people of the earth to periodically decide how much of the cost of environmentalism should be passed onto posterity. This would apply both to conserving and improving the natural ecology of the earth, or to creating and enhancing the civic ecology of a global revolutionary democracy.

In many ways the concept of a deliberator provides extraordinary opportunities for peaceful conflict resolution. The technology is new but the two principles on which it is based are old. The first was expressed by Leibniz around 1666: "If controversies were to arise, there would be no more need of disputation between two philosophers than between two accountants. For it would suffice to take their pencils in their hands, to sit down to their slates, and to say to each other (with a friend as witness, if they like): Let us calculate"(Russell, Bertrand 1937 170; cf. Leibniz 1960 7:200). The second, expressed by John Jay (above, page 7), says, in effect, that those who are free and autonomous can settle disputes by saying to each other: Let us deliberate. Understanding the relationship between the principles of calculation and deliberation would involve such topics as Turing machines, deliberating brains, group dynamics, perhaps quantum computers, and much more. Fortunately, thorough knowledge here is no more necessary than understanding the nature of electricity was necessary to construct generators. Calculation and deliberation have been central to peaceful conflict resolution throughout history, whether we consider simple counting or complex economic models, whether we look at ordinary dialogue, or sophisticated discussions of major agreements between powerful state adversaries. An immersion of the technology of computers *and* deliberators into American civilization is meant to be a continuation of that trend.

By applying their deliberative skills of political freedom, ordinary people all over the world could promote harmony and reconciliation; they might succeed whenever and wherever the experts, politicians, and diplomats are failing. This may seem to be an unrealizable fantasy, but such a judgment may not be well-founded. If anyone had predicted in 1945 that, fifty years hence, computers much more powerful than the ENIAC would be microscopic and be made in the millions, that too would have seemed to be a crazy, unrealizable fantasy. Yet it came to pass. With respect to an innovative technology the future cannot be known. If somehow a global revolutionary democracy actually came to pass, we could then claim, in a geographical sense, to have pushed "the republican element of popular control . . . to the maximum of its practicable exercise," we could claim to have achieved *Novus Ordo Seclorum* — a new order of the ages — which was the motto that the generation of 1776 put on the Great Seal of the United States. When the Great Seal was instituted on June 20, 1782, that order was described as "the beginning of the New America Æra, which commences from" July 4, 1776 (Patterson and Dougall

1976 85). The transformation of human history that began with the birth of the American revolution was thought of in redemptive terms, both here and abroad. Abroad, in 1785, Richard Price could write: "Perhaps I do not go too far when I say that, next to the introduction of Christianity among mankind, the American revolution may prove the most important step in the progressive course of improvement"(1991 119; cf. 1815 73-4). The American revolutionists had already adopted this point of view; they recognized July 4, 1776, in the same way and place that they recognized the divine transformation of the human condition that began with the birth of Christ. Thus the Articles of Confederation ends with the statement: "Done at Philadelphia in the state of Pennsylvania the ninth Day of July in the Year of our Lord one Thousand seven Hundred and Seventy-eight, and in the third year of the independence of America"(DHRC 1976 1:93). The journal of the Constitutional Convention begins: "On Monday the 14th of May. A. D. 1787. and in the eleventh year of the independence of the United States of America . . . "(Farrand 1937 1:1) and the Constitution itself ends with: "done in Convention by the Unanimous Consent of the States present the Seventeenth Day of September in the Year of our Lord one thousand seven hundred and Eighty seven and of the Independence of America the Twelfth." The first use of the Great Seal of the United States was in a treaty with France. The end of the proclamation announcing that agreement reads as follows: "Given at the City of New-York, the ninth day of April in the year of our Lord 1790, and of the sovereignty and independence of the United States the fourteenth"(Patterson and Dougall 1976 156). The conclusion of the document creating the capital of the United States reads: "Done at the city of Philadelphia, this twenty-fourth day of January, in the year of our Lord one thousand seven hundred and ninety-one, and of the independence of the United States, the fifteenth"(Washington 1791 1). The Founders believed that the decision to initiate the revolution was, in the words of John Adams, ". . . the greatest Question . . . which ever was debated in America, and a greater perhaps, never was or will be decided among Men"(above, page 1; cf. Palmer 1797 8). They believed that the transformation of the human spirit that began on July 4, 1776, would eventually produce a revolution in humanity's understanding of itself, whose consequence would be a cool and deliberate politics of self-knowledge, capable of creating peace on earth and good will toward men.

"Our city has so far surpassed other men in thought and speech," Isocrates boasted, "that students of Athens have become the teachers of others, and the city has made the name 'Greek' seem to be not that of a people but of a way of thinking; and people are called Greeks because they share in our education rather than in our birth"(2004 40). Americans likewise claimed a radical conceptual change: "Our style and manner of thinking," Paine declared "have undergone a revolution more extraordinary than the political revolution of the country"(above, page 225). By this "style and manner of thinking" Americans hoped to create a new paradigm of human society that would, in the words of James Wilson, "outshine the glory of Greece"(2007 1:432; cf. 1788 1; Paine 1945 1:123-4. 371-72). America would become the first ergonomic civilization, precisely tailored to human nature so as best to promote universal human flourishing. Whereas Pericles, speaking for the Athenians, boasted that "our city as a whole is the school of Hellas"(Thucydides 1928 1:331), Americans believed their civilization could be a school for all humanity. It would be a society so excellent that America, which had learned so much from the rest of the world, would become its teacher and that, in time, the word *American* would signify not only the people of the United States but an innovative, universal civilization, created by the spirit of 1776, and characterized by a continuing democratic revolution, constantly devoted to perfecting public happiness and private flourishing. A century earlier the word *America* had a different meaning which Locke expressed when he stated that "in the beginning all the World was *America*"(1988 301). Locke meant that the condition of being without government, which then largely prevailed in America, was, in the distant past, the common lot of humanity. Americans aspired to change that meaning by creating a new American era in which the ideals of their revolution and the principles of their government would spread to all parts of the globe: "God grant," Benjamin Franklin declared in 1789, "that not only the Love of Liberty, but a thorough Knowledge of the Rights of Man, may pervade all the Nations of the Earth, so that a Philosopher may set his Foot anywhere on its Surface, and say, 'This is my Country'"(1907 10:72). It was thus the hope of the American revolutionists, a hope which is as attractive today as it was in 1776, that it will become the common lot of all people to share in an enduring democratic revolution and that thereby, in this revised sense, all the world will again become America.

Epilogue

Posterity and American Revolutionary Ideals

"O! Ye unborn Inhabitants of America! Should this Page escape it's destin'd Conflagration at the Year's End, and these Alphabetical Letters remain legible, — when your Eyes behold the Sun after he has rolled the Seasons round for two or three Centuries more, you will know that in Anno Domini 1758, *we dream'd of your Times"*(1757 16).

Nathaniel Ames in his almanac for 1758.

"Reason, humanity and religion, all conspire to teach us, that we ought in the best manner we can, to provide for the happiness of posterity. We are allied to them by the common tie of nature: They are not here to act their part; A concern for them is a debt which we owe for the care which our progenitors took for us"(33).

Simeon Howard in a sermon preached on June 7, 1773.

"Posterity! You will never know, how much it cost the present Generation, to preserve your Freedom! I hope you will make a good Use of it. If you do not I shall repent in Heaven, that I ever took half the Pains to preserve it"(Butterfield, Lyman 1963 2:224).

John Adams to Abigail Adams, April 26, 1777.

We were part of the dreams of eighteenth-century Americans. Posterity was continually on their minds. On October 23, 1769, an anonymous author writes: ". . . posterity must know, that the present generation had a just sense of, and religious regard to, their rights both civil & sacred, and exerted themselves with all possible ardor to defend and preserve them"(MF 1769 1). On December 23, 1776, John Jay declared that "we do not fight for a few acres of land, but for freedom — for the freedom and happiness of millions yet unborn"(1890 1:113). On July 4, 1778, David Ramsay explained the reality of the revolution: "We are laying the foundation of happiness for countless millions. Generations yet unborn will bless us, for the blood-bought inheritance we are about to bequeath them"(1779a 4). On May 8, 1785, John Adams declared the United States was "destined beyond a doubt to be the greatest power on earth"(1850 8:246; cf Morse 1789 469). On December 20, 1800, Gouverneur Morris said that the "proudest empire in Europe is but a bauble compared to what America *will* be, *must* be, in the course of two centuries, perhaps of one"(Hosack 1829 257) The Constitution (written by Morris) was intended to "secure the Blessings of Liberty to ourselves and our Posterity." One wonders what the Founders would think of us. I suspect they would in many ways be immensely proud of what their political baby has become. If by some miracle they were suddenly recreated, would it not be a pleasure to be their guide as they explored contemporary America? What a delight it would be to take Washington for a ride in a military jet, or to teach Jefferson how to use a word processor. "It has ever been my hobby-horse," John Adams wrote to Count Sarsfield in 1786, "to see rising in America an empire of liberty, and a prospect of two or three hundred millions of freemen, without one noble or one king among them. You say it is impossible. If I should agree with you in this, I would still say, let us try the experiment, and preserve our equality as long as we can"(1850 9:546). If Adams is looking at us from an afterlife he must be delighted to see that the American experiment produced "two or three hundred millions of freemen, without one noble or one king among them," he would be delighted to know that America became "the greatest power on earth." Nevertheless I believe Adams' pleasure would be bittersweet. For although he would be astounded by how much we know and have, compared to his generation, he would be appalled at our ignorance of the philosophy of the American revolution. That philosophy, which Adams correctly claimed was "hackneyed in Congress for two years before" the Declaration (1850 2:514), is today seldom embodied in decisive action by *our* Congress. With few exceptions, it has become part of the historical veneer of our current political life, with no influence on substance, even after September 11, 2001.

Why? One answer is that ideals are thought to be impractical, or pernicious. Yet this has hardly been shown to be true for ideals in general, or democratic ideals in particular. In any case, it is rejected by many. As I tried to discover a better answer I thought back to Washington, Jefferson, and Madison. The environment in which they lived made it difficult, though hardly impossible, to think clearly and speak forthrightly about blacks and slavery. Could it be that something similar is interfering with our ability to think clearly and speak forthrightly about revolutionary democracy? For myself, at least, there was. I had accepted that usual presupposition that common people are necessarily deficient in deliberation, reason, and motivation, and thus capable at best of a crude form of self-government, in which they are only needed to get rid of bad rulers, decide a few referenda, serve on trial juries; everything else should be the responsibility of some elite or other. As a result of reading eighteenth-century American literature, I came to doubt, and finally reject, this presupposition. Jefferson kept a *Literary Commonplace Book* containing the passages of literature he most admired, and which he would reread for pure pleasure. I found that keeping and rereading the *American Revolution Commonplace Book* that is spread throughout this volume, to also be pleasurable, and it awakened in me the spirit of democratic revolution. What would be the consequences, I asked, if that spirit animated American government and society?

This book is my answer to that question. It is an expression of my hobbyhorse that America should again become a revolutionary society in the spirit of 1776. And if that is impossible, I would still say let us energetically pursue the experiment as far as we can. However, writing the book led to difficulties which incredibly I did not anticipate, and which, in any case, I could not overcome. The American revolution is a total revolution that has a multifaceted character with implications for virtually all aspects of civilization. Any book which argues for awakening its spirit must deal with that totality, and it must portray that awakening as requiring an awesome effort. I thus found myself engaged in a project for which my abilities were far from adequate. Talent is not always created by desire, however strong. I was completely incapable of practicing the brevity I sought; instead I felt forced again and again into a wordy description and defense. Further, I felt intimidated by trying to comprehend a sizable group of Founders, many of whom were polymathic geniuses and all of whom had the additional tremendous advantage of living at a time and place that had the ambience of revolution. Every day brought laments from me, that I lacked the energy, range, and depth of their intellects; that I sorely needed their capacity for felicity of expression; that I did not have the support of a politically revolutionary environment. In trying to appropriate their words and wisdom, and those of the eighteenth-century revolutionary generation as a whole, to our present situation; in trying to emulate their use of mathematics, science, classics, history, politics, economics, and philosophy in my exposition; I had to dance continually at the limits of, and no doubt sometimes beyond, my knowledge and abilities. I well knew that I would be charged, even rightly, with pedantry, with pretension, with trying to appear to know much more than I do. Nevertheless I accepted these consequences because I also well knew that it was only by articulating the ramifications of *their* words and wisdom for our times, words which often drew on their European predecessors, that I could even hope to create a new, or renewed, dissatisfaction in the reader with our political life, with our culture, and, above all, with our unrevolutionary aspirations. As we were part of the dreams of the generation that initiated the American revolution, so I wanted to make their times part of our dreams — in order to recapture the élan for noble ideals, ideals which today are so easily forgotten, or disparaged, or expressed as a mere abstract principles unconnected with vigorous thought or action.

In composing my case for the advantages of the American revolution in the twenty-first century, I found myself remembering something Francis Bacon wrote a century and a half before it started. I could not help thinking that he explained why we should strive to awaken the spirit of 1776. Bacon takes the claim of Columbus, that the winds off the coast of Portugal are evidence of land to the west, and uses it in a metaphor when arguing that we should form our beliefs not from authority, but from experience and reason:

> . . . even if the breath of hope blowing from *that new continent* were much weaker and less perceptible, yet I have decided that (unless we evidently wish to be mean of soul) we must make the attempt. For not to try and not to succeed are quite different risks, for by not trying we cast aside an immense good but by not succeeding we lose a little human labour. But from what I have said, and also from what I have not, it seems to me that we have a great deal of hope, not only to persuade a keen man to have a go, but also to make a wise and moderate man believe in it. (2004 173)

Even if the breeze of hope that blows from the American revolution were fainter than I have depicted it, the attempt to create American perfectionist democracy has to be made "for not to try and not to succeed are quite different risks." Universal human flourishing is such a great good, possibly even the greatest good, that the opportunity must be taken, since the faintest of reasonable hopes is sufficient when the prize to be reached is so august. In that effort both the nondogmatic believer (expecting success) and the nondogmatic skeptic (expecting failure) must say; "Let the experiments begin!" The conception of a deliberate sense of the community, or a common reason of society, is an especially rich source for scholarly inquiry, for commercial development, for economic and political deeds. Is it credible, if Jefferson somehow had lived three hundred years and remained vigorous, that he would abandon his idea that wards are the "wisest invention ever devised by the wit of man for the perfect exercise of self-government, and for its preservation"(1892 10:41); that he would believe that because wards couldn't scale up beyond a village in the eighteenth century, they couldn't scale up any further in the twenty-first; that he would now be as passive or as unimaginative as our politicians have generally been in trying to fully instill the American revolutionary spirit into our civilization?

Jefferson also observed that the "generation which commences a revolution can rarely compleat it"(Cappon 1959 2:596; cf. Noah Webster's words in 1790 83-4). Can our generation complete it? The word "complete" is ambiguous and I can think of no better way to finish this book than to make clear the senses in which one can talk about completing the American revolution. The first sense is *conceptual* completeness. It is illustrated by Adams when, on June 9, 1776, he wrote, "We are in the very midst of a Revolution, the most compleat, unexpected, and remarkable of any in the History of Nations"(1977 4:245; cf. Butterfield, Lyman 1963 2:34). By "compleat" he meant perfect, that is, nothing needed to be added to the conception held in the hearts and minds of Americans. In this sense we might say the scientific method is complete because nothing needs to be added to it from any other source. Our understanding of the method might improve as when, for example, the idea of a double-blind experiment was developed. However, this improvement was due to the development of the scientific method itself, rather than to some extrinsic factor. Just as the scientific method is a self-correcting and self-perfecting procedure for solving epistemological problems in the natural world, so the philosophy of the American revolution is a self-correcting and self-perfecting procedure for solving social and political problems in the moral world. Each is a complete application of reason and experiment to a specific realm. Thomas Paine also meant the first sense of "complete" when he used its superlative form: "These are the times that try men's souls," he declared in December of 1776, but in April of 1783 he added that such times "are over — and the greatest and completest revolution the world ever knew, gloriously and happily accomplished"(1945 1:50, 230). He was certainly as wrong as he could be in saying "accomplished." For how could it be accomplished if, as Paine himself had elsewhere complained (1945 2:16-19; cf. above, page 52), there were hundreds of thousands of negroes in slavery? Unfortunately, the same holds true today with regard to the scientific revolution: it is conceptually complete but not yet accomplished, because so many turn to scientifically worthless explanations, such as numerology, astrology, and creationism.

Now consider a second sense that might be called *institutional* completeness. To say that the scientific revolution is complete in this sense is to say there exists a substantial community of scholars and technologists, and well-established institutions, all devoted to the pursuit of knowledge through observation, experiment, and logical proof. The same sense can be applied to politics. In February 1788, David Ramsay wrote to Benjamin Rush: ". . . I shall wait the event of the new constitution. The revolution cannot be said to be completed till that or something equivalent is established"(1943 553; cf. Hall, Aaron 1788 6-7). Completing the American revolution in this sense means the creation of a institution for the indefinite preservation of the revolutionary spirit. In November of 1787 James Wilson could say: "Oft have I viewed with silent pleasure and admiration the force and prevalence, through the United States, of this principle — that the supreme power resides in the people; and that they never part with it. It may be called the *panacea* in politicks. There can be no disorder in the community but may here receive a radical cure"(2007 1:191-2). We have fewer opportunities for such pleasure and admiration today. The creation of a set of wards was Jefferson's proposal to embody the spirit of 1776 into permanent institutional practice and "compleat" the revolution institutionally. The Court of Common Reason is merely a new-modeling of Jefferson's idea to make it appropriate for the twentieth-first century, and we might say that the American revolution cannot be completed in an institutional sense until it, or something equivalent, is established. Franklin once made a prediction about the exciting future of physical science:

> The rapid Progress *true* Science now makes, occasions my regretting sometimes that I was born too soon [cf. also 1907 6:44]. It is impossible to imagine the Height to which may be carried, in a thousand years, the Power of Man over Matter. We may perhaps learn to deprive large Masses of their Gravity, and give them absolute Levity, for the sake of easy Transport. Agriculture may diminish its Labour and double its Produce; all Diseases may by sure means be prevented or cured, not excepting even that of Old Age, and our Lives lengthened at pleasure even beyond the antediluvian Standard. O that moral Science were in as fair a way of Improvement, that Men would cease to be Wolves to one another, and that human Beings would at length learn what they now improperly call Humanity! (8:10)

Again, should Franklin somehow be rejuvenated what a joy it would be to show him a laser printer, to take him on an airplane, to describe the Green Revolution, to show him what we are now doing with electricity, to tell him about modern medicine, DNA technology, and anti-aging research. We could explain that these things have been brought about — with much more to come — because the scientific revolution has been institutionally completed. And then we would, with great mortification, have to admit that we do not even know whether the American revolution could bring about a similar improvement in "moral Science" since, although we are constantly invoking that revolution, we have made little attempt to institutionally complete it. But, if and when we do, the spirit of 1776 will permeate our governments, our education, our very souls, and the word *American* will again connote a persistent perfecting of the pursuit of happiness, something, if successful, we could properly call Humanity.

Finally, let us call the third sense *temporal* completeness, which means to bring to an end. The American revolution is already conceptually complete. It is institutionally incomplete although, with a great effort, we might, in that sense, be able to complete it. But it is incapable of ever being temporally completed. We could rightfully claim today what Benjamin Rush claimed on Independence Day in 1787: "There is nothing more common, than to confound the terms of *American revolution* with those of *the late American war*. The American war is over: but this is far from being the case with the American revolution. On the contrary, nothing but the first act of the great drama is closed. It remains yet to establish and perfect our new forms of government; and to prepare the principles, morals, and manners of our citizens, for these forms of government; after they are established and brought to perfection"(Niles, Hezekiah 1822 402; see also Rush 1951 1:388, Hitchcock, Enos 1788 9, Crèvecoeur in DHRC 1976 18:17, and Webster 1790 84). Once the scientific and American revolutions are embodied in well-established institutions, each will continue indefinitely (cf. the words about perfection by Locke and Wilson, above, pages 287 and 501, respectively). An unceasing dedication to perfecting science and politics institutionally is a necessary foundation for periodically achieving a new excellence in "the principles, morals, and manners of our citizens," a new excellence in the art of living well. We ought to speak of these revolutions as permanent or continuing, and the cause of science and America as intrinsic to the cause of humanity.

The principles that were explicated in the Declaration of Independence remain a potent source of inspiration to political greatness. They presuppose a modification of Aristotle's maxim (1984 2:1987), so that it now becomes: Humans by nature are *revolutionary* political animals. We are, and must understand ourselves as, progressive beings. Hence after more than two centuries the issue facing the United States is not Lincoln's question that asks "whether that nation, or any nation so conceived, and so dedicated, can long endure," but rather "whether that nation, or any nation so conceived, and so dedicated, can live up to the revolutionary principles on which it was founded." If the Declaration is ever truly embodied in our public life we can be certain that, should some tragedy overtake us, there will be a rainbow over our disastrous set of sun. Yet if America prevails, we need not have any doubts about posterity's view of that embodiment. Lincoln made this point with regard to his generation:

> Let us re-adopt the Declaration of Independence, and with it, the practices, and policy, which harmonize with it. Let north and south — let all Americans — let all lovers of liberty everywhere — join in the great and good works. If we do this, we shall not only have saved the Union; but we shall have saved it, as to make, and to keep it, forever worthy of the saving. We shall have so saved it, that the succeeding millions of free happy people, the world over, shall rise up, and call us blessed, to the latest generations. (1953 2:276, cf. 546-7)

If *we* attempt to readopt the Declaration, using the most rigorous standards for high fidelity to the deliberate sense of the people that it is now possible to achieve, then, paradoxically, we must rewrite it, and the Constitution that was composed in its spirit. A President who could inspire the people to rededicate themselves to this task would be revolutionary in a sense that only Washington and Lincoln were; such a President could, like Pericles or Elizabeth, rightly give a name to the age, an age establishing unprecedented moral prosperity.

Are we ready to take that revolutionary risk? John Adams, writing from London, said that the Convention that produced the Constitution was "the greatest effort of national deliberation that the world has ever seen"(1850 6:220). But if we took the risk and succeeded in completing the American revolution by creating new institutions adequate for its ideals, we could then reply: "Forgive us, Mr. Adams. Your generation, with its Declaration, Constitution, and Bill of Rights, showed that you aspired to the highest degree of political excellence that was then possible. You did not have to create an American revolution; you could have been satisfied with an American rebellion. You did not have to create the Constitution of 1787 or the Bill of Rights; you could have been satisfied to tinker with the Articles of Confederation. We too could have been satisfied with the fundamental political documents and institutions that we inherited from you and subsequent generations. Yet it was the striving for political excellence exemplified by your generation that inspired us to create, in contemporary America, a new perfection in government of, by, and for the people. As a result we have continued your revolution by revising the magnificent documents you have bequeathed to us. We have used standards of excellence that were impossible to achieve, or even imagine, in your age and have thus far exceeded the effort of national deliberation represented by the creation and adoption of the Constitution of 1787. But you need not repent in heaven, for our success demonstrates that we have made the good use of the freedom your generation created, and it was possible only because we dreamed of your times."

References

All references, except a few fully cited in the text, are listed below. No others are included and hence this section is not a bibliography of works consulted. That would have been so long as to be meaningless. A reference in the text is indicated by a parenthesis that gives the author or editor, the date of publication, the volume number, and the page number. From this abbreviation, and the list that follows, the full citation can easily be found. For example, "(Jefferson 1903 7:23)" means page 23 of volume seven of *The Writings of /Thomas Jefferson* (Washington: Thomas Jefferson Memorial Association, 1903), edited by Andrew A. Lipscomb. If, in a particular context, the item referred to is clear, the name, or the name and date, are omitted. In this context, for example, "(48)" refers to page 48 of volume seven of *The Writings of Thomas Jefferson.* If an author has published two or more works in a single year, they are distinguished by adding a lower case letter following the date. If the citation is to a multivolumed work published over a number of years only the date of the first volume is given. Thus "Jefferson 1950 10:44" refers to page 44 of the tenth volume of *The Papers of Thomas Jefferson* even though that particular volume was published in 1954. In the listing below, however, both the date of the earliest, and the latest, published volume is given. If a passage is quoted two or more times, only in the first or longest quotation is cited; for the others a page number of the present work is given to where the first or longest quotation appears. Throughout the book "Adams" or "Bacon" or "Wilson," used without qualification, whether in the text or references, refers to John Adams or Francis Bacon or James Wilson. Finally, if a particular work either has no listed author or editor, or too many to be conveniently listed, then it is referred to by the first word in the title; otherwise, by an abbreviation taken from the first letters of words in the title or periodical. It is alphabetically placed below (in capitals) as if that title or abbreviation were the name of the author. Thus "MA" is the "author" of items in the *Massachusetts Archives.* This system of reference eliminates footnotes and endnotes, while enabling a reader to quickly find the full citation. It is, in particular, much better than the commonly used scheme that makes so much use of "*op. cit.*", an expression that is quite indefinite as to where the full citation can be found. Finally, to more fully convey the flavor of the original, I have sometimes given the full title of eighteenth-century works, even though some are very long.

AA
  1837   *American Archives.* Fourth Series, Volume 1. Washington: Clair Clarke
            and Peter Force.
Abbot, Abiel
  1799   *Traits of Resemblence in the People of the United States of America to
            Ancient Israel.* Haverhill, Massachusetts: Moore & Stebbins.
Abbot, Robert
  1963   *Abbot's New Card Games.* New York: Funk & Wagnalls.
  1977   *The New Eleusis.* Box 1175, General Post Office, New York, N.Y.,
            10001.
Adair, Douglas
  1974   *Fame and the Founding Fathers.* Edited by Trevor Colbourn.
            Indianapolis, Indiana: Liberty Fund.
Adams, John
  1785   "John Adams to Elbridge Gerry, Auteuil, France, 28 April 1785." *The
            Gilder Lehrman Institute of American History*, Document GLC00024.

1805   *Discourses on Davila*. Boston: Russell and Cutler.
1850-56   *The Works of John Adams*. Edited by Charles Francis Adams. 10
            volumes. Boston: Charles C. Little and James Brown.
1954-59   *The Microfilm Edition of the Adams Papers*. Boston: Massachusetts
            Historical Society.
1961   *Diary and Autobiography of John Adams*. Edited by L. H. Butterfield et al.
            4 volumes. Cambridge: Harvard University Press.
1977-2006 *The Papers of John Adams*. Edited by Robert Joseph Taylor et al. 13
            volumes. Cambridge: Harvard University Press.
Adams, Samuel
1904-08   *The Writings of Samuel Adams*. Edited by Harry Alonzo Cushing. 4
            Volumes. New York: G .P. Putnam's Sons.
Addison, Joseph and Richard Steele
1965   *The Spectator*. Edited by Donald F. Bond. 5 volumes. Oxford: Clarendon
            Press.
Aeschines
1919   *The Speeches of Aeschines*. Edited by Charles Darwin Adams. London:
            William Heinemann.
Aeschylus
1996   *Suppliant Maidens, Persians, Prometheus, Seven Against Thebes*.
            Volume 1. Translated by Herbert Weir Smyth. Cambridge: Harvard
            University Press.
1991   *The Suppliants*. Translated by Peter Burian. Princeton: Princeton
            University Press.
Agrippa (pseudonym)
1788   "To the Massachusetts Convention." *Massachusetts Gazette* (January 29):
            2
Aldridge, A. Owens
1953   "Thomas Paine and the N. Y. *Public Advertiser.*" *The New-York Historical
            Society Quarterly* 37 (October): 361-382.
ADLSSK
1971   "Attempted Defection by Lithuanian Seaman Simas Kudirka." *Hearings
            Before the Subcommittee on State Department Organization and Foreign
            Operations of the Committee on Foreign Affairs, House of
            Representatives, Ninety-First Congress, Second Session, December 3, 7,
            8, 9, 14, 17, 18, and 29, 1970*. Washington: U.S. Government Printing
            Office.
Alcidamas
2002   *Alcidamas: The Works & Fragments*. Edited by J. V. Muir. London:
            Bristol Classical Press.
Alembert, Jean Le Ron d'
1821-22   *Oeuvres de d'Alembert*. 5 volumes. Paris: A. Belin.
Alison, Hugh
1769   *Spiritual Liberty, A Sermon Delivered at James-Island, in South-Carolina,
            October, the 9th, 1769*. Charleston: [David Bruce].
Allen, Carlos R., Jr.
1963   "David Barrow's *Circular Letter* of 1798." *William and Mary Quarterly*,
            Third Series 20 (July): 440-51.
Allen, Ethan
1784   *Reason the Only Oracle of Man, or A Compenduous System of Natural
            Religion*. Bennington, Vermont: Haswell & Russell.
Allen, John
1774   *Watchman's Alarm to Lord N—h*. Salem: E. Russell.
AM
1788   "To the Editor of the European Magazine." *The American Magazine*
            (May): 391-94.
Ames, Nathaniel
1757   *An Astronomical Diary: or, an Almanac for the Year of our Lord Christ
            1758*. New Haven: J. Parker.
ARDM
1787   *The Address and Reasons of Dissent of the Minority of the Convention of*

the State of Pennsylvania, to their Constituents. [No place or publisher given.].

Arendt, Hannah
1963   On Revolution. New York: Viking Press.
Aristotle
1984   The Complete Works of Aristotle. Edited by Jonathan Barnes. 2 volumes. Princeton: Princeton University Press.
Arrow, Kenneth
1967   "Values and Collective Decision-Making." In Philosophy, Politics, and Society. Third Series, edited by Peter Laslett and W. G. Runciman, 215-32. Oxford: Basil Blackwell.
1987   "Arrow's Theorem." In The New Palgrave: a Dictionary of Economics, 4 volumes, edited by John Eatwell, Murry Milgate, and Peter Newman, 1:124-6. London: Macmillan.
Ash, John
1775   The New and Complete Dictionary of the English Language. 2 volumes. London: E. C. Dilly.
ASP
1832   American State Papers: Class I, Foreign Relations, Volume II. Edited by Walter Lowrie and Matthew St. Clair Clarke. Washington: Gales and Seaton.
Atkin, Edmond
1954   Indians of the Southern Colonial Frontier: the Edmond Atkin Report and Plan of 1755. Edited by Wilbur R. Jacobs. Columbia: University of South Carolina Press.
Aubrey, John
2000   Brief Lives together with An Apparatus for the Lives of our English Mathematical Writers and The Life of Thomas Hobbes of Malmesburry. Edited by John Buchanan-Brown. London: Penguin Books.
Backus, Isaac
1771   The Doctrine of Sovereign Grace Opened and Vindicated. Providence: John Carter.
Bacon, Francis
1860-65   The Works of Francis Bacon. Edited by James Spedding et al. 15 volumes. Boston: Brown and Taggard (volumes 1, 12, 14), Taggard and Thompson (volumes 2-11, 13, 15).
2000   The Advancement of Learning. Edited by Michael Kiernan. Oxford: Clarendon Press.
2000a   The Essayes or Counsels, Civill and Morall. Edited by Michael Kiernan. Oxford: Clarendon Press.
2004   The Instauratio magna Part II: Novum organum and Associated Texts. Edited by Graham Rees with Maria Wakely. Oxford: Clarendon Press.
Bacon, Roger
1928   The Opus Majus of Roger Bacon. Translated by Robert Belle Burke. 2 volumes. Philadelphia: University of Pennsylvania Press.
Bailey, Nathan
1773   A Universal Etymological English Dictionary. London: J. Burkland.
Baldwin, Simeon
1788   An Oration Pronounced Before the Citizens of New-Haven, July 4th, 1788; in Commemoration of the Declaration of Independence and Establishment of the Constitution of the United States of America. New Haven: J. Meigs.
Barlow, Joel
1787   An Oration, Delivered at the North Church in Hartford, at the Meeting of the Connecticut Society of the Cincinnati, July 4th, 1787. Hartford: Hudson and Goodwin.
1793   A Letter to the National Convention of France, on the Defects in the Constitution of 1791, and the Extent of the Amendments Which Ought to be Applied. New York: Thomas Greenleaf.
Barnett, Randy E.
1989-93   The Rights Retained by the People: the History and Meaning of the Ninth

Amendment. 2 volumes. Fairfax, Virginia: George Mason University Press.

Bartram, John
1992 *The Correspondence of John Bartram: 1734-1777*. Edited by Edmund Berkeley and Dorothy Smith Berkeley. Gainesville: University Press of Florida.

Bartram, William
1928 *The Travels of William Bartram*. Edited by Mark van Doren. New York: Dover Publications.

Beckmann, Petr
1971 *A History of π*. New York: St. Martin's Press.

Benezet, Anthony
1767 *A Caution and Warning to Great-Britain, and Her Colonies, in a Short Representation of the Calamitous State of the Enslaved Negroes in British Dominions*. Philadelphia: D. Hall and W. Sellers.

Bentham, Jeremy
1859 *The Works of Jeremy Bentham*. Edited by John Bowring. 10 volumes. London: Simpkin, Marshall.
1968-88 *The Correspondence of Jeremy Bentham*. Edited by Timothy L. S. Sprigge. 10 volumes. London: Athlone Press.

Bentley, Richard
1836-38 *The Works of Richard Bentley*. Edited by Alexander Dyce. 3 volumes. London: F. Macpherson.

Bentley, William
1790 *A Sermon Preached at the Stone Chapel in Boston, September 12, 1790*. Boston: Samuel Hall.

Berend, Daniel and Jacob Paroush
1998 "When is Condorcet's Jury Theorem valid?" *Social Choice and Welfare* 15 (August): 481-488.

Berenson, Bernard
1948 *Aesthetics and History in the Visual Arts*. New York: Pantheon.

Bethell, Nicholas
1974 *The Last Secret: the Delivery to Stalin of Over Two Million Russians by Britain and the United States*. New York: Basic Books.

Beveridge, Albert J.
1916-19 *The Life of John Marshall*. 4 volumes. Boston: Houghton Mifflin.

BGCJ
1787 *The Boston Gazette and the Country Journal*. December 3, 1787, 1.

Blackmon, Douglas
2008 *Slavery by Another Name; the Re-Enslavement of Black People in America from the Civil War to World War II*. New York: Doubleday.

Blackstone, William
1771-72 *Commentaries on the Laws of England in Four Books*. 4 volumes. Philadelphia: Robert Bell.

Bland, Richard
1766 *An Inquiry Into the Rights of the British Colonies*. Williamsburg: Alexander Purdie.

Blumenbach, Johann Friedrich
1865 *The Anthropological Treatises of Johann Friedrich Blumenbach*. London: Longman, Green, Longman, Roberts & Green.

Bolingbroke, Henry St. John, Viscount
1972 *Historical Writings*. Edited by Isaac Kramnick. Chicago: University of Chicago Press.

Born, Max
1971 *The Born-Einstein Letters*. Translated by Irene Born. New York: Walker.

Bostonian (pseudonym]
1792 *Effects of the Stage on the Manners of a People: and the Propriety of Encouraging and Establishing a Virtuous Theatre*. Boston: Young and Etheridge.

Boswell, James
  1953   *Boswell on the Grand Tour: Germany and Switzerland, 1764.* Edited by
            Frederick A. Pottle. New York: McGraw-Hill.

Bourne, H. R. Fox
  1876   *The Life of John Locke.* 2 volumes. New York: Harper and Brothers.
Brams, Steven J. and Peter C. Fishburn
  1983   *Approval Voting.* Boston: Birkhäuser.
Brams, Steven J., Peter C. Fishburn, and Samuel Merrill, III
  1988   "The Responsiveness of Approval Voting: Comments on Saari and Van
            Newenhizen." *Public Choice* 59: 121-131.
  1988a   "Rejoinder to Saari and Van Newenhizen." *Public Choice* 59: 149.
Branagan, Thomas
  1804   *A Preliminary Essay, on the Oppression of the Exiled Sons of Africa.*
            Philadelphia: John W. Scott.
Brissot de Warville, Jacques-Pierre
  1788   *A Critical Examination of the Marquis de Chatellux's Travels in North
            America.* Philadelphia: Joseph James.
  1964   *New Travels in the United States of America, 1788.* Edited by Durand
            Echeverria. Cambridge: Harvard University Press.
Browne, Thomas
  1642   *Religio Medici.* [London]: Andrew Cooke.
Bruce, William Cabell
  1922   *John Randolph of Roanoke, 1773-1833.* Second edition. New York: G.
            P. Putnam's Sons.
Brumbaugh, Robert S.
  1966   *Ancient Greek Gadgets and Machines.* New York: Thomas Y. Crowell.
  1989   *Platonic Studies of Greek Philosophy: Form, Arts, Gadgets, and
            Hemlock.* Albany: State University of New York Press.
Bruns, Roger
  1977   *Am I Not a Man and a Brother: The Antislavery Crusade of Revolutionary
            America: 1688-1788.* [New York]: Chelsea House Publishers.
Brutus (pseudonym)
  1787   "To the Citizens of the State of New-York." *The New-York Journal, and
            Weekly Register* (November 1): 2.
BTDM
  1790   "By This Day's Mail." *The Federal Gazette and Philadelphia Evening Post*
            (July 14): 3.
BTEM
  1790   "By Thursday Evening's Mail." *Columbia Centinel* (October 9): 30.
Buchanan, George
  1793   *An Oration Upon the Moral and Political Evil of Slavery, for Promoting
            the Abolition of Slavery, and the Relief of Free Negroes, and others
            unlawfully held in Bondage, Baltimore, July 4, 1791.* Baltimore: Philip
            Edwards.
Burke, Edmund
  1958-78   *The Correspondence of Edmund Burke.* 10 volumes. Edited by Thomas W.
            Copeland. Chicago: University of Chicago Press.
  1981-2000 *The Writings and Speeches of Edmund Burke.* 7 volumes. Edited by Paul
            Langford, et al. Oxford: Clarendon Press.
Butler, Joseph
  1896   *The Works of Joseph Butler, D.C.L., Sometime Lord Bishop of Durham.*
            Edited by W. E. Gladstone. 2 volumes. Oxford: Clarendon Press.
Butterfield, Fox
  1996   *All God's Children: The Bosket Family and the American Tradition of
            Violence.* New York: Avon Books
Butterfield, Lyman Henry, et al.
  1963-73   (editor) *Adams Family Correspondence.* 4 volumes. Cambridge: Harvard
            University Press.
Byrnes, Daniel
  1775   *A Short Address to the English Colonies in North-America.* Wilmington:

James Adams.

Byrnes, James F.
1947   *Speaking Frankly.* New York: Harper and Brothers.
1958   *All In One Lifetime.* New York: Harper and Brothers.

C
1801   "Communication." The Mercury and New-England Palladium 18
        (November 6): 2

CFGSM
1778   *A Constitution and Form of Government for the State of Massachusetts-Bay.* Boston: J. Gill.

Calaprice, Alice
1996   (editor) *The Quotable Einstein.* Princeton: Princeton University Press.

Calhoun, John C.
1999   *The Papers of John C. Calhoun.* Volume 25. Edited by Clyde N. Wilson
        and Shirley Bright Cook. Columbia: University of South Carolina Press.

Calvin, John
1948   *Commentaries on the Epistle of Paul the Apostle to the Romans.* Edited
        by John Owen. Grand Rapids, Michigan: Wm. B. Eerdmans.
1960   *Institutes of the Christian Religion.* Edited by John T. McNeill. 2
        volumes. Philadelphia: Westminster Press.

Cappon, Lester J.
1959   (editor) *The Adams-Jefferson Letters.* 2 volumes. Chapel Hill: University
        of North Carolina Press.

Caspar, Max.
1993   *Kepler.* Translated and Edited by C. Doris Hellman, with a new
        introduction and references by Owen Gingerich. New York: Dover
        Publications.

CDVALE
1787   "Curious Dissertation on the Valuable Advantages of a Liberal Education."
        New-Jersey Magazine and Monthly Advertiser." 1 (January): 49-55.

Chaitin, Gregory J.
1987   *Information, Randomness & Incompleteness: Papers on Algorithmic
        Information Theory.* Singapore: World Scientific.
1990   "A Random Walk in Arithmetic." *New Scientist* 125 (March 24): 44-46.

Charette, François
2006   "High Tech from Ancient Greece." *Nature* 444 (November 30): 551-2

Chase, Frederick
1928   *A History of Dartmouth College.* Second Edition. Volume 1. Edited by
        John K. Lord. Brattleboro: Vermont Publishing Co.

Chauncy, Charles
1784   *The Benevolence of the Deity, Fairly and Impartially Considered.*
        Boston: Powars & Willis.

Chomsky, Noam
1957   *Syntactic Structures.* The Hague: Morton & Co.

Christian, Edward
1801   *Notes on Blackstone's Commentaries, Which are Calculated to Answer all
        the Editions.* Volume 5. Boston: I. Thomas and E.T. Andrews.

Churchill, Winston S.
1974   *Winston S. Churchill, His Complete Speeches: 1897-1963.* Edited by
        Robert R. James. 8 volumes. New York: Chelsea House.

Cicero
1931   *The Speeches.* Edited by N. H. Watts. London: William Heinemann.
1937   *The Speeches.* Edited by Louis E. Lord. London: William Heinemann.
1951   *De Natura Deorum, Academica.* Translated by H. Rackham. London:
        William Heinemann.
1958   *The Speeches.* Edited by R. Gardner. 2 volumes. London: William
        Heinemann.
1960   *Tusculan Disputations.* Translated by J. E. King. Cambridge: Harvard
        University Press.
1975   *De Divinatione, De Fato, Timaeus.* Edited by Remo Giomini. Leipzig: B.
        G. Teubner.

1988   *De Re Publica, De Legibus.* Edited by Clinton Walker Keyes. London: William Heinemann.

2005   *De Officiis.* Translated by Walter Miller. Cambridge: Harvard University Press.

Clark, Ronald W.

1971   *Einstein: the Life and Times.* New York: World Publishing Company.

Clavelin, Maurice

1974   *The Natural Philosophy of Galileo: Essays on the Origins and Formation of Classical Mechanics.* Cambridge: MIT Press.

Clinton, George

1798   *An Oration, Delivered on the Fourth of July, 1798, Before the General Society of Mechanics and Tradesmen, the Democratic Society, the Tammany Society or Columbian Order, the New York Cooper Society, and a Numerous Concourse of Other Citizens.* New York: M.L. & W. A. Davis.

CNYHS

1887   *Collections of the New-York Historical Society for the Year 1886.* New York: [No publisher given.].

Coffin, Joshua

1845   *A Sketch of the History of Newbury, Newburyport, and West Newbury, From 1635 to 1845.* Boston: Samuel G. Drake.

Coffin, William Sloane, Jr.

1977   *Once to Every Man: a Memoir.* New York: Atheneum.

Cohen, William

1969   "Thomas Jefferson and the Problem of Slavery." *Journal of American History* 56 (December): 503-526.

Coke, Edward

1670   *The First Part of the Institutes of the Laws of England. Or, A Commentarie Upon Littleton, Not the Name of the Lawyer only, but of the Law It Self.* London: Society of Stationers.

2003   *The Selected Writings and Speeches of Sir Edward Coke.* 3 volumes. Edited by Steve Sheppard. Indianapolis, Indiana: Liberty Fund.

Coleman, Thomas

1643   *The Christians Covrse and Complaint, Both in the Pursuit of Happinesse Desired, and for Advantages Slipped in that Pursuit: a Sermon Preached to the Honorable House of Commons on the Monethly Fast Day, August 30, 1643.* London: Christopher Meredith.

Coles, Edward

1927   "Letters of Edward Coles." *William and Mary Quarterly*, Second Series 7 (January): 32-41.

Collingwood, R. G.

1957   *An Essay on Metaphysics.* Oxford: Clarendon Press.

1958   *The Principles of Art.* New York: Oxford University Press.

1960   *The Idea of Nature.* New York: Oxford University Press.

Collins, Francis S.

2006   *The Language of God: A Scientist Presents Evidence for Belief.* New York: Free Press.

Colman, Benjamin

1774   "For the Essex Journal." *The Essex Journal and Merimack Packet: or The Massachusetts and New-Hampshire General Advertiser* 1 (July 20): 4.

Condorcet, Jean-Antoine-Nicolas de Caritat, marquis de

1994   *Condorcet: Foundations of Social Choice and Political Theory.* Edited by Iain McLean and Fiona Hewitt. Brookfield, Vermont: Edward Elgar.

Conrad, Clay S.

1998   *Jury Nullification: The Evolution of a Doctrine.* Durham: North Carolina Carolina Academic Press.

Cooke, Samuel

1770   *A Sermon Preached at Cambridge in the Audience of His Honor Thomas Hutchinson, Esq; Lieutenant-Governor and Commander in Chief; The Honorable His Majesty's Council, and the Honorable House of Representatives, of the Providence of the Massachusetts-Bay in New-England, May 30th, 1770.* Boston: Edes and Gill.

Cooper, David
1783   *A Serious Address to the Rulers of America, On the Inconsistency of their Conduct respecting Slavery: forming a Contrast between the Encroachments of England on American Liberty, and, American Injustice in tolerating Slavery.* Trenton: Isaac Collins.
Cooper, John
1780   "To the Publick." *New-Jersey Gazette* 3 (September 20): 2.
Cooper, Samuel
1780   *A Sermon Preached Before His Excellency John Hancock, Esq; Governour, the Honourable the Senate, and House of Representatives of the Commonwealth of Massachusetts, October 28, 1780.* [Boston]: T. and J. Fleet, and J Gill.
Coram, Robert
1791   *Political Inquiries: To Which is Added, a Plan for the General Establishment of Schools Throughout the United States.* Wilmington: Andrews and Byrnberg.
Count, Earl W.
1950   (editor) *This is Race: An Anthology Selected from the International Literature on the Races of Man.* New York: Henry Schuman.
Countryman, A [pseudonym]
1787   "Letter II." *The New-York Journal, and Weekly Register* (December 13): 2.
1787a   "Letter III." The New-York Journal, and Weekly Register (December 20): 2.
Coxe, Tench
1788   *An Examination of the Constitution for the United States of America, Submitted to the People by the General Convention, at Philadelphia, the 17th. day of September, 1787.* Philadelphia: Zachariah Poulson.
CPS
1788   *The Constitution of the Pennsylvania Society, for Promoting the Abolition of Slavery, and the Relief of Free Negroes, Unlawfully Held in Bondage.* Philadelphia: Francis Bailey.
Craig, Edward
1998   (editor) *Routledge Encyclopedia of Philosophy.* 10 volumes. London: Routledge.
Crawford, Charles
1783   *Liberty: a Pindaric Ode.* Philadelphia: Robert Aitken.
Crèvecoeur, Hector Saint John de
1926   *Letters from an American Farmer.* London: J. M. Dent.
Crick, Francis
1974   "The Double Helix: a Personal View." *Nature* 248 (April 26): 766-69.
Culbert, David
1980   (editor) *Mission to Moscow.* Madison: University of Wisconsin Press.
Cumings, Henry
1784   *A Sermon Preched In Billerica, December 11, 1783.* Boston: T, and J. Fleet.
D***, F***, H*** [pseudonyms]
1776   "DIALOGUE on CIVIL LIBERTY." *The Pennsylvania Magazine: or American Monthly Museum* 2 (April): 157-67.
Dallas, A. J.
1790-1807 *Reports of Cases Ruled and Adjudged in the Several Courts of the United States and of Pennsylvania Held at the Seat of the Federal Government.* 4 volumes. Philadelphia: J. Ormrod.
Dallin, David J., and Boris I. Nicolaevsky
1947   *Forced Labor in Soviet Russia.* New Haven: Yale University Press.
Dana, James
1790   "The African Slave Trade. A Discourse Delivered in the City of New-Haven, September 9, 1790, Before the Connecticut' Society for the Promotion of Freedom." New-Haven: Thomas and Samuel Green.
Daniel, Pete
1972   *The Shadow of Slavery: Peonage in the South: 1901-1969.* Urbana:

University of Illinois Press.

1989   (editor) *The Peonage Files of the U.S. Department of Justice, 1901-1945.* 26 microfilm reels. Frederick, Maryland: University Publications of America.

Darwin, Charles

1887-88   *The Life and Letters of Charles Darwin.* 2 volumes. New York: D. Appleton.

1987   *Charles Darwin's Notebooks, 1836-1844.* Edited by Paul H. Barrett et al. Ithaca: Cornell University Press.

1987a   *The Correspondence of Charles Darwin.* Volume 3. Cambridge: Cambridge University Press.

1985   *The Origin of Species by Means of Natural Selection or The Preservation of Favoured Races in the Struggle for Life.* London: Penguin Books.

Dauben, Joseph Warren.

1979   *Georg Cantor: His Mathematics and Philosophy of the Infinite.* Cambridge: Harvard University Press.

Davies, Samuel

1751   *Miscellaneous Poems.* Williamsburg, Virginia: William Hunter.

Davis, David Brion

1975   *The Problem of Slavery in the Age of Revolution: 1770-1823.* Ithaca: Cornell University Press.

Davison, R. R.

1983   "I Thought Americans Were Good." *The Wall Street Journal* (September 23): 31.

Day, Thomas

1784   *Fragment of an Original Letter on the Slavery of the Negroes, Written in the Year 1776.* Philadelphia: Francis Bailey.

1798   *An Oration on Party Spirit, Pronounced Before the Connecticut Society of Cincinnati, Convened at Hartford, for the Celebration of American Independence, on the 4th of July, 1798.* Litchfield: T. Collier.

DeLong, Howard

1971   "Unsolved Problems in Arithmetic." *Scientific American* 224 (March): 50-60.

1991   *A Refutation of Arrow's Theorem.* Lanham, Maryland: University Press of America.

2004   *A Profile of Mathematical Logic.* Mineola, New York: Dover Publications. [First published in 1970 by Addison-Wesley, Reading, Massachusetts. The Dover edition reproduces the second printing (1971).]

Demosthenes

1926   *De Corona* and *De Falso Legatione.* Edited by C. A. Vince and J. H. Vince. London: William Heinemann.

1935   *Demosthenes Against Meidias, Androtion, Aristocrates, Timocrates, Aristogeiton.* Edited by J. H. Vince. Cambridge: Harvard University Press.

1936-39   *Private Orations.* Edited by A. T. Murray. 3 volumes. Cambridge: Harvard University Press.

1998   *Olynthiacs; Philippics: Minor Public Speeches: Speech Against Leptines.* Edited by J. H. Vince. Cambridge: Harvard University Press.

Descartes, René

1951   *Meditations.* Edited by Laurence J. Lafleur. New York: Liberal Arts Press.

1965   *Discourse on Method, Optics, Geometry, and Meteorology.* Edited by Paul J. Olscamp. Indianapolis: Bobbs-Merrill.

Dexter, Andrew

1798   *An Oration, on the Importance of Science and Religion, Particularly to American Youth.* Providence: Carter and Wilkins.

De Witt, John

1787   "To the Free Citizens of the Commonwealth of Massachusetts." *American Herald* (October 29): 2.

DHCUSA

1894-1905 *Documentary History of the Constitution of the United States of America:*

1786-1870. 5 volumes. Washington: Department of State.

DHNPUS
1969　　　　*A Documentary History of The Negro People in the United States.* Edited by Herbert Aptheker. New York: Citadel Press.

DHRC
1976-2008 *The Documentary History of the Ratification of the Constitution.* Edited by Merrill Jensen et al. Volumes 1-10 and 13-22. Madison: State Historical Society of Wisconsin.

Dickinson, John
1766　　　　*An Address to the Committee of Correspondence in Barbados. Occasioned by a Late Letter from Them to their Agent in London. By a North-American.* Philadelphia: William Bradford.

1768　　　　*Letters from a Farmer in Pennsylvania to the Inhabitants of the British Colonies.* Boston: Edes Gill.

1774　　　　*An Essay on the Constitutional Power of Great-Britain Over the Colonies in America.* Philadelphia: William and Thomas Bradford.

Dijksterhuis, E. J.
1961　　　　*The Mechanization of the World Picture.* Oxford: Clarendon Press.

Diogenes Laertius
1925　　　　*Lives of Eminent Philosophers.* Translated by H. D. Hicks. 2 volumes. London: William Heinemann.

Dipple, Horst
1977　　　　*Germany and the American Revolution: 1770-1800.* Chapel Hill: University of North Carolina Press.

Dirac, P. A. M.
1939　　　　"The Relation between Mathematics and Physics." *Proceedings of the Royal Society of Edinburgh* 59: 122-129.

1954　　　　"Quantum Mechanics and Aether." *The Scientific Monthly* 78 (March): 142-146.

1963　　　　"The Evolution of the Physicist's Picture of Nature." *Scientific American* 208 (May): 45-53.

1982　　　　"Pretty Mathematics." *International Journal of Theoretical Physics* 21: 603-605.

Donne, John
1953-62　　*The Sermons of John Donne.* Edited by George R. Potter and Evelyn M. Simpson. 10 volumes. Berkeley: University of California Press.

1929　　　　*The Poems of John Donne.* Edited by H. J. C. Grierson. London: Oxford University Press.

Douglass, Frederick
1950-55　　*The Life and Writings of Frederick Douglass.* Edited by Philip S. Foner. 4 volumes. New York: International Publishers.

1962　　　　*Life and Times of Frederick Douglass, Written by Himself.* New York: Collier Books.

1979-1985 *The Frederick Douglass Papers; Series One: Speeches, Debates, and Interviews.* Edited by John W. Blassingame. 3 volumes. New Haven: Yale University Press.

DPCUS
1854　　　　*The Debates and Proceedings in the Congress of the United States.* Fourteenth Congress, First Session. Washington: Gales and Seaton.

Drake, Stillman
1978　　　　*Galileo at Work, His Scientific Biography.* Chicago: University of Chicago Press.

DRUC
1775　　　　*A Declaration by the Representatives of the United Colonies of North-America, Now Met in General Congress at Philadelphia, Setting Forth the Causes and Necessity of Their Taking up Arms.* Philadelphia: E. Russell.

DSB
1945　　　　*The Department of State Bulletin* 13 (August 12). Washington: Office of Public Communication.

1952　　　　*The Department of State Bulletin* 27 (September 1). Washington: Office of Public Communication.

DTPI
1989   "Democratic Theory and the Public Interest: Condorcet and Rousseau Revisited." *American Political Science Review* 83 (December): 1317-1340.
Dunn, Susan
1999   *Sister Revolutions: French Lightning, American Light.* New York: Farber and Farber.
Dwight, Jasper [pseudonym for William Duane]
1796   *A Letter to George Washington, President of the United States: Containing Strictures on His Address of the Seventeenth of September 1796, Noting His Relinquishment of the Presidential Office.* Philadelphia: [No publisher given.].
Dwight, Theodore
1794   *An Oration, Spoken Before "The Connecticut Society, For the Promotion of Freedom and the Relief of Persons Unlawfully Holden in Bondage."* Hartford: Hudson and Goodwin.
Dyke, Daniell
1642   *The Mystery of Selfe-Deceiving; or, A Discovrse and Discovery of the Deceitfulnesse of Mans Heart.* London: Richard Bishop.
Echeverria, Durand
1968   "Condorcet's *The Influence of the American Revolution on Europe.*" *William and Mary Quarterly*, Third Series 25 (January): 85-108.
Edmonds, John Maxwell
1961   *The Fragments of Attic Comedy.* 3 volumes. Leiden: E. J. Brill.
Edwards, Jonathan
1791   *The Injustice and Impolicy of the Slave Trade, and of the Slavery of the Africans: Illustrated in a Sermon Preached Before the Connecticut Society for the Promotion of Freedom, and for the Relief of Persons Unlawfully Holden in Bondage, at Their Annual Meeting in New-Haven, September 15, 1791.* New-Haven: Thomas and Samuel Green.
Eid, Leroy V.
1981   "Liberty: The Indian Contribution to the American Revolution." *The Midwest Quarterly* 23 (Spring): 279-98.
Einstein, Albert
1919   "Time, Space and Gravitation: The Newtonian System." *The Times (November* 28): 13-14.
1931   "The Meeting Place of Science and Religion." In *Has Science Discovered God?.* Edited by Edward H. Cotton. New York: Thomas Y. Crowell.
1941   "Science and Religion." In *Science, Philosophy, and Religion*, 209-214. New York: Conference on Science, Philosophy and Religion in their Relation to the Democratic Way of Life, Inc
1950   "On the Generalized Theory of Gravitation." *Scientific American* 182 (April): 13-17.
1954   *Ideas and Opinions.* Edited by Carl Seelig. New York: Crown Publishers.
1987   *Letters to Solovine.* New York: Philosophical Library.
Einzig, Paul
1966   *Primitive Money in its Ethnological, Historical and Economic Aspects.* Second edition. Oxford: Pergamon.
Eisenhower, Dwight D.
1948   *Crusade in Europe.* Garden City: Doubleday.
1953   "Text of President Eisenhower's Speech to Dinner at the Waldorf." *New York Times* (May 3): 21.
Eisenstein, Louis.
1961   *The Ideologies of Taxation.* New York: Ronald Press.
Elihu (pseudonym)
1788   "For the American Mercury." *The American Mercury* (February 19): 3.
Eliot, Andrew.
1771   *A Discourse on Natural Religion Delivered in the Chapel of Harvard College in Cambridge, New-England, May 8, 1771. at the Lecture Founded by the Hon. Paul Dudley, Esq:.* Boston: Nicholas Bowes.
1774   *Twenty Sermons.* Boston: John Boyle.

Eliot, Jared
1749   A Continuation of the Essay upon Field-Husbandry, As it is or may be Ordered in New England. New London, Connecticut: T. Green.

Elliot, Jonathan
1836   *The Debates in the Several State Conventions on the Adoption of the Federal Constitution, as Recommended by the General Convention at Philadelphia, in 1787.* 4 volumes. Washington: Printed for the Editor.

Elliott, Mark R.
1973   "The United States and Forced Repatriation of Soviet Citizens, 1944-47." *Political Science Quarterly* 88 (June): 253-75.
1982   *Pawns of Yalta: Soviet Refugees and America's Role in Their Repatriation.* Urbana: University of Illinois Press.

Ellis, Joseph
2000   *Founding Brothers: The Revolutionary Generation.* New York: Alfred A. Knopf.
2007   *American Creation: Triumphs and Tragedies at the Founding of the Republic.* New York: Alfred A. Knopf.

Emerson, Ralph Waldo
1960-82   *The Journals and Miscellaneous Notebooks of Ralph Waldo Emerson.* Edited by Alfred R. Ferguson. 16 volume. Cambridge: Harvard University Press.

Emmons, Nathanael
1787   *The Dignity of Man. A Discourse Addressed to the Congregation in Franklin, Upon the Occasion of Their Receiving from Dr. Franklin, the Mark of his Respect, in a Rich Donation of Books, Appropriated to the Use of a Parish-Library.* Providence: Bennett Wheeler.

Epictetus
1928-2000 *The Discourses as Reported by Arrian, The Manual, and Fragments.* Edited by W. A. Oldfather. 2 volumes. London: William Heinemann and Cambridge: Harvard University Press.

Epstein, Julius
1970   "Forced Repatriation: Some Unanswered Questions." *The Russian Review* 29 (April): 209-10.
1973   *Operation Keelhaul: the Story of Forced Repatriation from 1944 to the Present.* Old Greenwich: Devin-Adair.

Ernst, Robert
1968   *Rufus King: American Federalist.* Chapel Hill: University of North Carolina Press.

Euclid
1956   *The Thirteen Books of Euclid's Elements.* Second edition. Edited by Thomas Little Heath. 3 volumes. New York: Dover Publications.

Euripides
1998   *Suppliant Women, Electra, Heracles.* Edited by David Kovacs. Cambridge: Harvard University Press.
1999   *Trojan Women, Iphigenia Among the Taurians, Ion.* Edited by David Kovacs. Cambridge: Harvard University Press.
2002   *Helen, Phoenician Women, Orestes.* Edited by David Kovacs. Cambridge: Harvard University Press.

Evans, Emory G.
1963   (editor) "A Question of Complexion: Documents Concerning the Negro and the Franchise in Eighteenth-Century Virginia." *The Virginia Magazine of History and Biography* 71 (October): 411-15.

Farr, James
1986   " 'So Vile and Miserable an Estate' : the Problem of Slavery in Locke's Political Thought." *Political Theory* 14 (May): 263-289.

Farrand, Max
1937   (editor) *The Records of the Federal Convention of 1787.* Revised edition. 4 volumes. New Haven: Yale University Press.

Farrar, Cynthia
1988   *The Origins of Democratic Thinking: the Invention of Politics in*

Classical Athens. Cambridge: Cambridge University Press.

Farrington, Benjamin
1964   *The Philosophy of Francis Bacon.* Liverpool: Liverpool University Press.

Federal Farmer (pseudonym)
1787   *Observations leading to a fair examination of the system of government, proposed by the late Convention; and to several essential and necessary alterations in it. In a number of letters from the Federal Farmer to the Republican.* [No place or publisher given.].
1788   *An Additional Number of Letters prom the Federal Farmer to the Republican.* [No place or publisher given.].

Feuer, Lewis S.
1983   "Noumenalism and Einstein's Argument for the Existence of God." *Inquiry* 26 (September): 251-85.

Feynman, Richard P.
1965   *The Character of Physical Law.* Cambridge: M. I. T. Press.
1989   *"What Do You Care What Other People Think? ": Further Adventures of a Curious Character.* Edited by Ralph Leighton. New York: Bantam Books.
1997   *Surely You're Joking, Mr. Feynman!* New York: W. W. Norton.
1999   *The Pleasure of Finding Things Out: The Best Short Works of Richard B. Feynman.* Edited by Jeffrey Robbins. Cambridge, Massachusetts: Helix Books.

Feynman, Richard P., Robert G. Leighton, and Matthew Sands
1963-65 *The Feynman Lectures on Physics.* 3 volumes. Reading, Massachusetts: Addison-Wesley.

Finkelman, Paul
1990   "The Kidnapping of John Davis and the Adoption of the Fugitive Slave Law of 1793." *The Journal of Southern History* 56 (August): 397-422.
1994   "Thomas Jefferson and Antislavery." *Virginia Magazine of History and Biography* 102 (April): 193-228.
1998   "The Problem of Slavery in the Age of Federalism." In *Federalists Reconsidered*, edited by Doron Ben-Atar and Barbara G. Oberg, 135-56. Charlottesville: University Press of Virginia.

Fitzgerald, C. P.
1935   *China: a Short Cultural History.* London: Cresset Press.

FL
1776   *Four Letters on Interesting Subjects.* Philadelphia: Styner and Cist.

Flavell, John
1709   *Husbandry Spiritualized.* Boston: John Allen. [Originally published in London by John Boulter in 1669.]

Flournoy, H. W.
1890   (editor) *Calendar of Virginia State Papers and Other Manuscripts from January 1, 1799 to December 31, 1807; Preserved in the Capitol, at Richmond.* Volume 9. Richmond: James E. Goode.

Floyd, Marcus W.
1947   *Displaced Persons.* Frankfurt-AM-Main: United States Army, Office of the Chief Historian, European Command.

Fobes, Peres
1795   *A Sermon, Preached Before His Excellency Samuel Adams, Esq, Governour, His Honour Moses Gill, Esq. Lt. Governour, the Honourable the Council, Senate, and House of Representatives of the Commonwealth of Massachusetts, May 27th, 1795.* Boston: Mercury Press.

Forney, John W.
1881   *Anecdotes of Public Men.* Volume 2. New York: Harper & Brothers.

Foster, Sir Augustus John
1954   *Jeffersonian America: Notes on the United States of America Collected in the Years 1805-6-7 and 11-12.* Edited by Richard Beale Davis. San Marino, California: The Huntington Library.

Franklin, Benjamin
1786   "The Morals of Chess." *The Columbian Magazine, or, Monthly Miscellany.* 1 (December): 159-61.

1907   *The Writings of Benjamin Franklin.* Edited by Albert Henry Smyth. 10 volumes. New York: Macmillan.

1959-2006 *The Papers of Benjamin Franklin.* Edited by Leonard W. Labaree and William B. Willcox. 38 volumes. New Haven: Yale University Press.

1986   *Benjamin Franklin's Autobiography.* Edited by J. A. Leo LeMay and P. M. Zall. New York: W. W. Norton.

Freeman, Kathleen
1966   *Ancilla to the Pre-Socratic Philosophers.* Cambridge: Harvard University Press.

Freeth, Tony, et al.
2006   "Decoding the Ancient Greek Astronomical Calculator Known as the Antikythera Mechanism." *Nature* 444 (November 30): 587-91.

Freud, Sigmund
1966-74   *The Standard Edition of the Complete Psychological Works of Sigmund Freud.* Edited by James Strachey. 24 volumes. London: Hogarth Press.

FRUS
1955   *Foreign Relations of the United States, Diplomatic Papers, The Conference at Malta and Yalta, 1945.* Washington: United States Government Printing Office.

1966   *Foreign Relations of the United States, Diplomatic Papers 1944, Europe.* Volume 4. Washington: United States Government Printing Office.

1967   *Foreign Relations of the United States, Diplomatic Papers 1945, Europe.* Volume 5. Washington: United States Government Printing Office.

1969   *Foreign Relations of the United States, 1946, The British Commonwealth; Western and Central Europe.* Volume 5. Washington: United States Government Printing Office.

Gales, Joseph
1834-56   (editor) *The Debates and Proceedings in the Congress of the United States.* 42 volumes. Washington: Gales and Seaton.

Galilei, Galileo
1953   *Dialogue Concerning the Two Chief World Systems — Ptolemaic & Copernican.* Translated by Stillman Drake. Berkeley: University of California Press.

1957   *Discoveries and Opinions of Galileo.* Edited by Stillman Drake. New York: Anchor Books.

1960   *The Assayer.* In *The Controversy on the Comets of 1618*, translated by Stellman Drake and C. D. O'Malley. Philadelphia: University of Pennsylvania Press.

Gardner, Martin
1959   "An Inductive Card Game." *Scientific American* 200 (June): 160-68.

1961   *The Second Scientific American Book of Mathematical Puzzles & Diversions.* New York: Simon and Schuster.

1974   "On the Paradoxical Situations that Arise from Nontransitive Relations." *Scientific American* 231 (October): 120-25.

1977   "On Playing New Eleusis, the Game that Simulates the Search for Truth." *Scientific American* 237 (October): 18-25.

Gay, Ebenezer
1759   *Natural Religion, as Distinguish'd from Revealed: a Sermon Preached at the Annual Dudleian-Lecture, at Harvard-College in Cambridge, May 9, 1759.* Boston: John Draper.

Gillard, John T.
1934   "Lafayette, Friend of the Negro." *Journal of Negro History* 19 (October): 355-71.

Glanz, James
2000   "New Tactic in Physics: Hiding the Answer." *New York Times* (August 8): F1, F4.

Gödel. Kurt
1995   *Collected Works.* Edited by Solomon Feferman. Volume 3. New York: Oxford University Press.

Goethe, Johann Wolfgang
1949   *Naturwissenschaftliche Schriften, Erster Teil.* Zurich: Artemis-Verlag.

Goodell, William
  1845   American Constitutional Law, in its Bearing Upon American Slavery.
            Second edition. Utica, New York: Lawson & Chaplin.

Gordon-Reed, Annette
  1999   Thomas Jefferson and Sally Hemings: An American Controversy.
            Charlottesville: University Press of Virginia.
Gorenstein, Daniel
  1985   "The Enormous Theorem." Scientific American 253 (December):
            104-115.
Graham, Ronald L. and Joel H. Spencer
  1990   "Ramsey Theory." Scientific American 263 (July): 112-117.
Grant, Anne
  1846   Memoirs of an American Lady, with Sketches of Manners and Scenery in
            America, as They Existed Before the Revolution. New York: D. Appleton.
Grigsby, Hugh Blair
  1890   The History of the Virginia Federal Convention of 1788. Volume 1.
            Richmond, Virginia: Virginia Historical Society.
Griswold, Charles L. , Jr.
  1991   "Rights and Wrongs: Jefferson, Slavery and Philosophical Quandaries."
            In A Culture of Rights: The Bill of Rights in Philosophy, Politics and
            Law — 1791 and 1991, edited by Michael J. Lacey and Knud Haakonssen,
            144-214. Washington: Woodrow Wilson International Center For
            Scholars and Cambridge University Press.
Grofman, Bernard and Guillermo Owen
  1986   (editors) Information Pooling and Group Decision Making: Proceedings
            of the Second University of California, Irvine, Conference on Political
            Economy. Greenwich, Connecticut: Jai Press.
Grotius, Hugo
  1738   The Rights of War and Peace, in Three Books. Wherein are Explained, the
            Law of Nature and Nations, and the Principle Points Relating to
            Government. Edited by J. Barbeyrac. London: W. Innys [and others].
  1913   De Jure Belli ac Pacis Libri Tres, In quibus Jus Naturæ & Gentium, item
            Juris Publici præcipua explicantur. 2 volumes. Translated by Francis W.
            Kelsey. Washington: Carnegie Institute of Washington (volume 1) and
            Oxford: Clarendon Press (volume 2).
  1926-36   The Jurisprudence of Holland. Translated by R. W. Lee. 2 volumes.
            Oxford: Clarendon Press.
Guthrie, W. K. C.
  1967   "Pythagoras and Pythagoreanism." In The Encyclopedia of Philosophy,
            edited by Paul Edwards, 8 volumes, 7: 37-9. New York: Macmillan & Free
            Press.
Hall, Aaron
  1788   An Oration, Delivered at the Request of the Inhabitants of Keene, June 30,
            1788; to Celebrate the Ratification of the Federal Constitution by the
            State of New Hampshire. Keene, New Hampshire: James D. Griffith.
Hall, Francis
  1819   Travels in Canada, and the United States, in 1816 and 1817. Second
            edition. London: Strahan and Spottswoode.
Hallowell, A. Irving
  1963   "American Indians, White and Black: The Phenomenon of
            Transculturalization." Current Anthropology 4 (December): 519-31.
Hamilton, Alexander
  1961-87   The Papers of Alexander Hamilton. Edited by Harold C. Syrett. 27
            volumes. New York: Columbia University Press.
Hammond, Isaac W.
  1889   "Slavery in New Hampshire." Magazine of American History 21
            (January): 62-65.
Hancock, John
  1774   An Oration Delivered March 5, 1774, at the Request of the Inhabitants of
            the Town of Boston: to Commemorate the Bloody Tragedy of the Fifth of

March 1770. Boston: Edes and Gill.

Hansen, Mogens Herman
1989   *Was Athens a Democracy?* Copenhagen: The Royal Danish Academy of Sciences and Letters.

Haraszti, Zoltán
1952   *John Adams & The Prophets of Progress.* Cambridge: Harvard University Press.

Hardy, Godfrey Harold
1969   *A Mathematician's Apology.* Cambridge: Cambridge University Press.

Harrington, James
2003   *The Commonwealth of Oceana* and *A System of Politics.* Edited by J. G. A. Pocock. Cambridge: Cambridge University Press.

Harrington, R. Ward
1993   "Speaking Scripture: The Flushing Remonstrance of 1657." *Quaker History* 82 (Fall): 104-109.

Hart, Levi
1775   *Liberty Described and Recommended; in a Sermon, Preached to the Corporation of Freemen in Farmington, at Their Meeting on Tuesday, September 20, 1774, And Published at Their Desire.* Hartford: Eben. Watson.

Hegel, Georg Wilhelm Friedrich
1975   *Lectures on the Philosophy of World History.* Edited by H. B. Nisbet and Duncan Forbes. Cambridge: Cambridge University Press.

Heisenberg, Elizabeth
1984   *Inner Exile: Recollections of a Life with Werner Heisenberg.* Boston: Birkhäuser.

Heisenberg, Werner
1971   *Physics and Beyond: Encounters and Conversations.* New York: Harper & Row.

1990   *Across the Frontiers.* Woodbridge, Connecticut: Oxbow Press.

Hempel, Carl G.
1952   *Fundamentals of Concept Formation in Empirical Science.* Volume 2, number 7 of the *International Encyclopedia of Unified Science.* Chicago: Chicago University Press.

Henig, William Walter
1819-23   (editor) *The Statutes at Large; Being a Collection of all the Laws of Virginia, from the First Session of the Legislature, in the year 1619.* 13 volumes. New York: R. & W. & G. Bartow, et al.

Herodotus
1998   *The Histories.* Edited by Robin Waterfield and Carolyn Dewald. New York: Oxford University Press.

Hewatt, Alexander
1779   *An Historical Account of the Rise and Progress of the Colonies of South Carolina and Georgia.* London: Alexander Donaldson.

Hichborn, Benjamin
1784   *An Oration, Delivered July 5th, 1784 at the Request of the Inhabitants of the Town of Boston; in Celebration of the Anniversary of American Independence.* Boston: John Gill.

Hippel, Theodor Gottlieb von
1979   *On Improving the Status of Women.* Edited by Timothy F. Sellner. Detroit: Wayne State University Press.

1994   *On Marriage.* Edited by Timothy F. Sellner. Detroit: Wayne State University Press.

Hippocrates
1923-95   *Hippocrates.* Edited and translated by W. H. S. Jones and Paul Potter. London: William Heinemann.

Hitchcock, Enos
1788   *An Oration: Delivered July 4, 1788, at the Request of the Inhabitants of the Town of Providence, in Celebration of the Anniversary of American Independence, and of the Accession of Nine States to the Federal Constitution.* Providence: Bennett Wheeler.

Hitchcock, Gad
1774   A Sermon Preached Before His Excellency Thomas Gage, Esq; Governor:
        The Honorable His Majesty's Council, and the Honorable House of
        Representatives, of the Province of the Massachusetts-Bay in New-
        England, May 25th, 1774. Being the Anniversary of the Election of His
        Majesty's Council for said Province. Boston: Edes & Gill.
1775   A Sermon preached at Plymouth December 22d, 1774. Being the
        Anniversary Thanksgiving, in Commemoration of the First Landing of
        our New-England Ancestors in that Place, Anno Dom. 1620. Boston:
        Edes & Gill.
Hitler, Adolf
1976   Hitler's Secret Conversations: 1941-1944. New York: Octagon Books.
Hoare, Prince
1820   Memoirs of Granville Sharp, Esq. London: Henry Colburn.
Hobson, John
1799   Prospectus of a Plan of Instruction for the Young of Both Sexes, Including
        a Course of Liberal Education for Each. Philadelphia: D. Hogan.
Hobbes, Thomas
1968   Leviathan. Edited by C.B. Macpherson. Middlesex: Penguin Books.
1998   On the Citizen." Edited by Richard Tuck and Michael Silverthorne.
        Cambridge: Cambridge University Press.
Hoffman, Benesh
1972   Albert Einstein: Creator and Rebel. New York: New American Library.
Hoffman, Paul
1998   The Man Who Loved Only Numbers: The Story of Paul Erdös and the
        Search for Mathematical Truth. New York: Hyperion.
Hofstadter, Douglas R.
1979   Gödel, Escher, Bach: an Eternal Golden Braid. New York: Basic Books.
1985   Metamagical Themas: Questing for the Essence of Mind and Pattern. New
        York: Basic Books.
Holton, Gerald
1956   "Johannes Kepler's Universe: Its Physics and Metaphysics." American
        Journal of Physics 24 (May): 340-51.
1971   Review of Ronald W. Clark, Einstein: the Life and Times. New York
        Times Book Review (September 5): 1, 18-20.
Homer
1924-29 The Iliad. Translated by A. T. Murray. 2 volumes. New York: G. P.
        Putnam's Sons.
Hopkins, Samuel (1693-1755)
1757   An Address to the People of New-England. Representing the Very Great
        Importance of Attaching the Indians to their Interest; not Only by
        Treating Them Justly and Kindly; But by Using Proper Endeavors to Settle
        Christianity Among Them. Philadelphia: B. Franklin and D. Hall.
Hopkins, Samuel (1721-1803)
1770   Rare Observations. Providence: John Carter.
1787   [No title.] Providence Gazette and Country Journal 24 (October 6): 1-2.
Horne, Alistair
1988   "Blame for a Tragic Blunder." The Sunday Times (October 2): C2
Hosack, David
1829   Memoir of De Witt Clinton. New York: J. Seymour.
Höss, Rudolf
1992   Death Dealer: The Memoirs of the SS Kommandant at Auschwitz. Edited
        by Steven Paskuly. Buffalo, New York: Prometheus Books.
Howard, Simeon
1773   A Sermon Preached to the Ancient and Honorable Artillery-Company, in
        Boston, New-England, June 7th, 1773. Being the Anniversary of Their
        Election of Officers. Boston: John Boyles.
1780   A Sermon Preached Before the Honorable Council, and the Honorable
        House of Representatives of the State of Massachusetts-Bay, in New-
        England, May 31, 1780. Boston: John Gill.

Hume, David
1879   *The History of England.* 6 volumes. New York: Harper & Brothers.
1957   *A Inquiry Concerning the Principles of Morals.* Edited by Charles W. Hendel. New York: Liberal Arts Press.
1968   *A Treatise of Human Nature.* Edited by L. A. Selby-Bigge. Oxford: Clarendon Press.
1985   *Essays: Moral, Political, and Literary.* Edited by Eugene F. Miller. Indianapolis: Liberty Classics.
1998   *Principal Writings on Religion* including *Dialogues Concerning Natural Religion* and *The Natural History of Religion.* Edited by J. C. A. Gaskin. Oxford: Oxford University Press.
Humphrey, Edward Frank
1924   *Nationalism and Religion in America: 1774-1789.* Boston: Chapman Law Publishing Company.
Hutcheson, Francis
1969-71 *Collected Works of Francis Hutcheson.* 7 volumes. Edited by Bernard Fabian. Hildesheim: Georg Olms Verlagsbuchhandlung.
Hutchinson, Thomas
1776   *Strictures upon the Declaration of the Congress at Philadelphia; In a Letter to a Noble Lord, &c.* London: [No publisher given.].
Imlay, Gilbert
1797   *A Topographical Description of the Western Territory of North America.* Third edition. London: F. Debrett.
Infeld, Leopold
1950   *Albert Einstein: His Work and Its Influence on Our World.* Revised edition. New York: Charles Scribner's Sons.
Inge, Francis
1941   "Report of Disposition of Criminal Case." File 50-745 (October 27), Record Group 60, Department of Justice, National Archives and Records Administration.
Isocrates
1928-1945 *Isocrates.* Edited by George Norlin and La Rue Van Hook. 3 volumes. Cambridge: Harvard University Press.
2004   *Isocrates II.* Translated by Terry L. Papillon. Austin: University of Texas Press.
Jackson, Luther P.
1930   "Manumission in Certain Virginia Cities." *Journal of Negro History* 15 (July): 278-314.
Jackson, Robert H.
1955   *The Supreme Court in the American System of Government.* Cambridge: Harvard University Press.
James I
1918   *The Political works of James I.* Edited by Charles Howard McIlwain. Cambridge: Harvard University Press.
Jauch, J. M.
1973   *Are Quanta Real?: a Galilean Dialogue.* Bloomington: Indiana University Press.
Jay, John
1788   *An Address to the People of the State of New-York, on the Subject of the Constitution* Agreed upon at Philadelphia. New-York: Samuel and John Loudon.
1890-93 *The Correspondence and Public Papers of John Jay.* Edited by Henry P. Johnston. 4 volumes. New York: G. P. Putnam's Sons.
1975   *John Jay.* Edited by Richard B. Morris. New York: Harper & Row.
Jefferson, Thomas
1792   General Records of the Department of State, Record Group 59, Inventory 15, 100. Domestic Letters (Letters Sent), 1784-1906, Microfilm (M-40, Roll 4, 355-56). National Archives and Records Administration.
1892-99 *The Writings of Thomas Jefferson.* Letter-press edition. Edited by Paul Leicester Ford. 10 volumes. New York: G. P. Putnam's Sons.
1903   *The Writings of Thomas Jefferson.* Library edition. Edited by Andrew A.

Lipscomb. 20 volumes. Washington: Thomas Jefferson Memorial Association.

1950-90   *The Papers of Thomas Jefferson.* Edited by Julian Parks Boyd et al. 23 volumes. Princeton: Princeton University Press.

1972   *Notes on the State of Virginia.* Edited by William Peden. New York: W. W. Norton.

1976   *Thomas Jefferson's Farm Book, with Commentary and Relevant Extracts from Other Writings.* Edited by Edwin Morris Betts. [Charlottesville]: University Press of Virginia.

1983   Jefferson's Extracts from the Gospels: "The Philosophy of Jesus" and "The Life and Morals of Jesus." Edited by Dickinson W. Adams. Princeton: Princeton University Press.

1997   *Jefferson's Memorandum Books.* Edited by James A. Bear, Jr. and Lucia C. Stanton. 2 volumes. Princeton: Princeton University Press.

2004-08   *The Papers of Thomas Jefferson. Retirement Series.* 4 volumes. Edited by J. Jefferson Looney. Princeton: Princeton University Press.

JEPCM

1838   *The Journals of Each Congress of Massachusetts in 1774 and 1775, and of the Committee of Safety.* Edited by William Lincoln. Boston: Dutton and Wentworth.

Jespersen, Otto

1968   *Growth and Structure of the English Language.* New York: Free Press.

Johnson, Samuel

1969   *The Rambler.* Edited by W. J. Bate and Albrecht B. Strauss. 3 volumes. New Haven: Yale University Press.

1977   *Political Writings.* Edited by Donald J. Greene. New Haven: Yale University Press.

1978   *Sermons.* Edited by Jean Hagstrum and James Gray. New Haven: Yale University Press.

1990   *Rasselas and Other Tales.* Volumes 16 of *The Yale Edition of the Works of Samuel Johnson.* Edited by Gwin J. Kolb. New Haven: Yale University Press.

Johnson, William

1812   *Reports of Cases Adjudged in the Supreme Court of Judicature of the State of New-York.* Volume 3. New York: C. Wiley.

Johnston, James Hugo

1970   *Race Relations in Virginia & Miscegenation in the South: 1776-1860.* Amherst, Massachusetts: University of Massachusetts Press.

Johnstone, Abraham

1797   *The Address of Abraham Johnstone, a Black Man, Who was Hanged at Woodbury, in the County of Glocester, and State of New Jersey, on Saturday the 8th Day of July Last.* Philadelphia: [No publisher given.]

Jones, Ernest

1953   *The Life and Work of Sigmund Freud.* 3 volumes. New York: Basic Books.

Judson, Horace Freeland

1980   *The Search for Solutions.* New York: Holt, Rinehart and Winston.

JVP

1769   *Journal of the Votes and Proceedings of the General Assembly of the Colony of New-York.* New York: Hugh Gaine.

Kant, Immanuel

1996   *Practical Philosophy.* Edited by Mary J. Gregor. Cambridge: Cambridge University Press.

1996a   *Religion and Rational Theology.* Edited by Allen W. Wood and George Di Giovanni. Cambridge: Cambridge University Press.

1997   *Lectures on Ethics.* Edited by Peter Heath and J. B. Schneewind. Cambridge: Cambridge University Press.

1999   *Correspondence.* Edited by Arnulf Zweig. Cambridge: Cambridge University Press.

2003   *Observations on the Feeling of the Beautiful and Sublime.* Translated by John T. Goldthwait. Berkeley: University of California Press.

2006   *Anthropology from a Pragmatic Point of View.* Edited by Robert B. Louden. Cambridge: Cambridge University Press.

Kaplan, Sidney
1973   *The Black Present in the Era of the American Revolution: 1770-1800.* Washington: Smithsonian Institution Press.

Kasparov, Garry
2000   *Kasparov Against the World: The Story of the Greatest Online Challenge.* New York: KasparovChess Online.

Kaufmann, Walter
1978   *Critique of Religion and Philosophy.* Princeton: Princeton University Press.

Kelso, William M.
1986   "Mulberry Row: Slave Life at Thomas Jefferson's Monticello." *Archaeology* 39 (September/October): 28-35.

Kemeys, John Gardner
1785   *Free and Candid Reflections Occasioned by the Late Additional Duties on Sugars and on Rum; Submitted to the Consideration of the British Ministry, the Members of Both Houses of Parliament, and the Proprietors of Sugar Estates in the West-India Colonies.* Dublin: P. Byrne.

Kennedy, John F.
1962   "Transcript of Kennedy Remarks on Space Challenge." *New York Times* (September 13): 16.

Kenrick, William
1773   *A New Dictionary of the English Language.* London: J. & F. Rivington.

Kepler. Johannes
1951   *Life and Letters.* Edited by Carola Baumgardt. Introduction by Albert Einstein. New York: Philosophical Library.
1997   *The Harmony of the World.* Edited by E. J. Aiton, A. M. Duncan, and J. V. Field. Philadelphia: American Philosophical Society.

Ketcham, Ralph L.
1960   "The Dictates of Conscience: Edward Coles and Slavery." *The Virginia Quarterly Review* 36 (Winter): 46-62.

Keynes, John Maynard
1973   *The Collected Writings of John Maynard Keynes.* Volume 7. London: Macmillan.

King, Martin Luther, Jr.
1986   *A Testament of Hope: the Essential Writings of Martin Luther King, Jr.* Edited by James Melvin Washington. San Francisco: Harper & Row.

Kleene, Stephen Cole
1967   *Mathematical Logic.* New York: John Wiley & Sons.

Klinghoffer, Judith Apter and Lois Elkis
1992   " 'The Petticoat Electors': Women's Suffrage in New Jersey, 1776-1807." *Journal of the Early Republic* 12 (Summer): 159-193.

Koestler, Arthur
1967   "Johannes Kepler." In *The Encyclopedia of Philosophy*, edited by Paul Edwards, 8 volumes, 4: 329-33. New York: Macmillan and Free Press.

Koppes, Clayton R. and Gregory D.
1987   *Hollywood Goes to War: How Politics, Profits, and Propaganda Shaped World War II Movies.* New York: Free Press.

Koyre, Alexandre
1973   *The Astronomical Revolution.* Ithaca: Cornell University Press.

Kudirka, Simas
1978   *For Those Still At Sea.* New York: The Dial Press.

Kuran, Timur
1995   *Private Truths, Public Lies : the Social Consequences of Preference Falsification.* Cambridge: Harvard University Press.

Kurtz, Paul
1986   *The Transcendental Temptation: a Critique of Religion and the Paranormal.* Buffalo: Prometheus Books.

La Boétie, Estienne de
1988   *Slaves By Choice.* Edited by Malcolm Smith. Egham, Surrey:

Runnymede Books.

Lafayette, Marquis de

1976   *The Letters of Lafayette to Washington: 1777-1799.* Edited by Louis Gottschalk. Philadelphia: The American Philosophical Society.

1977-83   *Lafayette in the Age of the American Revolution: Selected Letters and Papers, 1776-1790.* Edited by Stanley J. Idzerda, et al. 5 volumes. Ithaca: Cornell University Press.

Langdon, Samuel

1775   *Government corrupted by Vice, and recovered by Righteousness. A Sermon Preached Before the Honorable Congress of the Colony of the Massachusetts-Bay in New England, Assembled in Watertown, on Wednesday the 31st Day of May, 1775.* Watertown: Benjamin Edes.

1788   *The Republic of the Israelites an Example to the American States.* Exeter: Lamson and Ranlet.

La Rochefoucauld, Francois, duc de

1778   *Maxims and Moral Reflections.* Philadelphia: Robert Bell.

Leibniz, Gottfried Wilhelm

1710   "Annotatio de quibusdam Ludis." *Miscellanea Berolinensia.* Volume 1. Berolini: Johan. Christ. Papenii.

1951   *Leibniz Selections.* Edited by Philip P Wiener. New York: Charles Scribner's Sons.

1960-1   *Die philosophischen Schriften von Gottfried Wilhelm Leibniz.* Edited by C. I. Gerhardt. 7 volumes. Hildesheim: Olms Verlagsbuchhandlung.

Leland, John

1790   *The Virginia Chronicle.* Fredericksburg [Virginia]: T. Green.

1791   *The Rights of Conscience Inalienable, and Therefore Religious Opinions not Cognizable by Law.* New London [Connecticut]: T. Green & Son.

1791a   *A Circular Letter of Valediction, on Leaving Virginia, in 1791.* [Bound in Nips 1994.]

1801   *A Blow at the Root, Being a Fashionable Fast Day Sermon, Delivered at Cheshire, April 9th, 1801.* Suffield [Connecticut]: Edward Gray.

1845   *The Writings of the Late Elder John Leland.* Edited by L. F. Greene. New York: W. Wood.

Leonardo, da Vinci

1964   *Leonardo da Vinci on Painting: a Lost Book (Libro A).* Edited by Carlo Pedretti. Berkeley: University of California Press.

Lessing, Gotthold Ephraim

1956   *Lessing's Theological Writings.* Edited by Henry Chadwick. London: Adams & Charles Black.

LESS

1780   *Laws Enacted in the Second Sitting of the Fourth General Assembly, of the Commonwealth of Pennsylvania. Which Commenced at Philadelphia, on Wednesday the 19th day of January, in the Year of our Lord One Thousand Seven Hundred and Eighty.* [Philadelphia: John Dunlap]

Levy, Steven

1992   *Artificial Life: A Report from the Frontier Where Computers Meet Biology.* New York: Vintage Books.

LFV

1816   *Letters from Virginia, Translated from the French.* Baltimore: Fielding Lucas, Jr.

Liles, George

1992   "God's Work in the Lab: Geneticist Francis Collins Makes the Case for Faith." *MD* (March 1992): 43-50.

Lincoln, Abraham

1953-55   *The Collected Works of Abraham Lincoln.* Edited by Roy P. Basher. 9 volumes. New Brunswick, New Jersey: Rutgers University Press.

Linn, William

1800   *Serious Considerations on the Election of a President: Addressed to the Citizens of the United States.* New-York: John Furman.

Livy

1919-1959 *Livy.* Edited by B. O. Foster. 14 volumes. London: William Heinemann.

Locke, John
1824 *The Works of John Locke*. Twelfth edition. 9 volumes. London: C. and J. Riverton.
1963 *A Letter Concerning Toleration*. Edited by Mario Montuori. The Hague: Martinus Nijhoff.
1975 *An Essay Concerning Human Understanding*. Edited by Peter H. Nidditch. Oxford: Clarendon Press.
1988 *Two Treatises of Government*. Edited by Peter Laslett. Cambridge: Cambridge University Press.
1989 *Some Thoughts Concerning Education*. Edited by John W. Yolton and Jean S. Yolton. Oxford: Clarendon Press.
1991 *Locke on Money*. Edited by Patrick Hyde Kelly. 2 volumes. Oxford: Clarendon Press.
1999 *The Reasonableness of Christianity as delivered in the Scriptures*. Edited by John C. Higgins-Biddle. Oxford: Clarendon Press.
2006 *An Essay Concerning Toleration*. Edited by J. R. Milton and Philip Milton. Oxford: Clarendon Press.

Loewen, James W.
1996 *Lies My Teacher Told Me: Everything Your American History Textbook Got Wrong*. New York: Touchstone.

Logan, George
[1798] *An Address on the Natural and Social Order of the World, As Intended to Produce Universal Good; Delivered Before the Tammany Society, at Their Anniversary, on the 12th of May, 1798*. Philadelphia: Benjamin Franklin Bache.

Long, Edward
1774 *The History of Jamaica*. 3 volumes. London: T. Lowndes.

Lorentz, H. A.
1920 *The Einstein Theory of Relativity*. New York: Brentano's.

Lorenz, Edward N.
1993 *The Essence of Chaos*. Seattle: University of Washington Press.

Louden, Robert B.
2000 *Kant's Impure Ethics: From Rational Beings to Human Beings*. New York: Oxford University Press.

Lublin, Joanne S.
1974 "On King! On Huskies! You've Got to Trace Yukon Land for Fans." *The Wall Street Journal* (November 26): 1, 42.

Luther, Martin
1955-86 *Luther's Works*. Edited by Jaroslav Pelikan and Helmut T. Lehmann. 55 volumes. Saint Louis: Concordia Publishing House (volumes 1-30) and Philadelphia: Fortress Press (volumes 31-55).

Lysias
2000 *Lysias*. Translated by S. C. Todd. Austin: University of Texas Press.

MA
n. d. *Massachusetts Archives*. 328 volumes. Located in Boston at the State House.

MacDonogh, Giles
2007 *After the Reich: The Brutal History of the Allied Occupation*. New York: Basic Books.

Machiavelli, Niccolò
1965 *Machiavelli: The Chief Works and Others*. Edited by Allan Gilbert. 3 volumes. Durham, North Carolina: Duke University Press.
1998 *Discourses on Livy*. Translated by Harvey C. Mansfield and Nahan Tarcov. Chicago: University of Chicago Press.

MacMaster, Richard K.
1972 "Arthur Lee's 'Address on Slavery': An Aspect of Virginia's Struggle to End the Slave Trade, 1765-1774." *The Virginia Magazine of History and Biography* 80 (April): 41-157.

Macmillan, Harold
1984 *War Diaries: Politics and War in the Mediterranean, January 1943-May 1945*. New York: St. Martin's Press.

Madison, James
1865   *Letters and Other Writings of James Madison*. 4 volumes. Philadelphia: J. B. Lippencott.
1900-10   *The Writings of James Madison*. Edited by Gaillard Hunt. 9 volumes. New York: G. P. Putnam's Sons.
1946   "Madison's 'Detached Memoranda'." Edited by Elizabeth Fleet. *William and Mary Quarterly*, Third Series 3 (October): 534-68.
1962-91   *The Papers of James Madison*. Edited by William Thomas Hutchinson et al. 17 volumes. Chicago: University of Chicago Press (volumes 1-10) and Charlottesville: University Press of Virginia (volumes 11-16).

Maidment, K. J. and J. O. Burtt
1941-54   (editors) *Minor Attic Orators*. 2 volumes. Cambridge: Harvard University Press.

Mandelbrot, Benoit B.
1977   *Fractals: Form, Chance, and Dimension*. San Francisco: W. H. Freeman.
1982   *The Fractal Geometry of Nature*. San Francisco: W. H. Freeman.

Mandeville, Bernard
1710   "Lucinda's Day." *The Female Tatler* 107 (From Friday March 17, to Monday March 20, 1710): 1.
1924   *The Fable of the Bees: or, Private Vices, Publick Benefits*. Edited by F. B. Kaye. 2 volumes. Oxford: Clarendon Press.

Mann, Charles C.
2006   *1491*. New York: Vintage Books.

Manuel, Frank Edward
1974   *The Religion of Isaac Newton*. Oxford: Clarendon Press.

Marchant, Jo
2006   "In Search of Lost Time." *Nature* 444 (November 30): 534-38.

Marcus Aurelius
2006   *Meditations*. Translated by Martin Hammond. London: Penguin Books.

Martin, Luther
1788   *The Genuine Information, Delivered to the Legislature of the State of Maryland, Relative to the Proceedings of the General Convention, Lately Held at Philadelphia; by Luther Martin, Esquire, Attorney-General of Maryland, and One of the Delegates in the Said Convention*. Philadelphia: Eleazer Oswald.

Martin, Mike W.
1985   (editor) *Self-Deception and Self-Understanding: New Essays in Philosophy and Psychology*. Lawrence: University Press of Kansas.
1986   *Self-Deception and Morality*. Lawrence: University Press of Kansas.

Marshall, George C.
1947   "Concern Expressed on Resettlement of Displaced Persons." *The Department of State Bulletin* 17 (July 27).
1947a   "Policy on Repatriation of Displaced Persons." *The Department of State Bulletin* 16 (June 1).

Marshall, John
2000   *The Papers of John Marshall*. Edited by Charles F. Hobson. Volume 10. Chapel Hill: University of North Carolina Press.

Marx, Karl
1913   *A Contribution to the Critique of Political Economy*. Chicago: Charles H. Kerr.

Mason, George
1970   *The Papers of George Mason: 1725-1792*. Edited by Robert A. Rutland. 3 volumes. Chapel Hill: University of North Carolina Press.

Mason, John
1789   *Self-Knowledge: A Treatise, Shewing the Nature and Benefit of that Importance Science, and the Way to Attain It*. Worcester, Massachusetts: Isaiah Thomas.

Matthewson, Tim.
1982   "Abraham Bishop, 'The Rights of Black Men,' and the American Reaction to the Haitian Revolution." *Journal of Negro History* 67 (Summer): 148-154.

Maxwell, C. Mervyn
    1966   "Chrysostom's Homilies Against the Jews: An English Translation." Ph. D dissertation. University of Chicago.

Mayhew, Jonathan
    1749   *Seven Sermons.* Boston: Rogers and Fowle.
    1750   *A Discourse Concerning Unlimited Submission and Non-Resistance to the Higher Powers.* Boston: D. Fowle.
    1763   *Observations on the Charter and Conduct of the Society for the Propagation of the Gospel in Foreign Parts.* Boston: Richard and Samuel Draper.

McGuire, James T.
    1994   *The Sumerian Roots of the American Preamble.* Larkspur, California: Lough Erne Press.

McLaughlin, Brian P. and Amélie Oksenberg Rorty
    1988   (editors) *Perspectives on Self-Deception.* Berkeley: University of California Press.

McLaughlin, Kathleen
    1946   "Soviet Deserters Suicides in Dachau." *New York Times* (January 20): 25.

Meade, Robert Douthat
    1957   *Patrick Henry: Patriot in the Making.* Philadelphia: J. B. Lippincott.

Medawar, Peter
    1996   *The Strange Case of the Spotted Mice.* Oxford: Oxford University Press.

MEG
    1768   "*Messieurs* Edes & Gill." *Boston Gazette and Country Journal* 367 (February 22): 1.

Mellen, John
    1765   *Fifteen Discourses upon Doctrinal Connected Subjects.* Boston: Edes and Gill.
    1795   *The Great and Happy Doctrine of Liberty.* Boston: Samuel Hall.

Melville, Herman
    1952   *Moby Dick Or, The Whale.* New York: Hendricks House.

MF
    1769   "*Messi'rs* FLEETS." *Boston Evening-Post* (October 23): 1.

MFC
    1787   "For the Centinel." *Massachusetts Centinel* (October 13).

M'Henry, James
    1792   "A Letter from mr. James M'Henry." *American Museum* 12 (July to December): 185-187.

MHS
    1917-25   *Warren-Adams Letters: Being Chiefly a Correspondence Among John Adams, Samuel Adams, and James Warren.* Boston: Massachusetts Historical Society.

MHSC
    1835   *Massachusetts Historical Society, Collections, for the Year 1795.* First Series. Volume 4. Boston: John H Eastburn.
    1877   *Massachusetts Historical Society, Collections.* Fifth series. Volume 3. Boston: Massachusetts Historical Society.
    1900   *Massachusetts Historical Society, Collections.* Seventh series. Volume 1. Boston: Massachusetts Historical Society.

Mill, John Stuart
    1965   *Mill's Essays on Literature and Society.* Edited by J. B. Schneewind. New York: Collier Books.
    1978   *On Liberty.* Edited by Elizabeth Rapaport. Indianapolis: Hackett.

Miller, Helen
    1975   *George Mason: Gentleman Revolutionary.* Chapel Hill: University of North Carolina Press.

Miller, John Chester
    1977   *The Wolf by the Ears: Thomas Jefferson and Slavery.* New York: Free Press.

Milton, John
    1644   *Areopagitica; a Speech of Mr. John Milton For the Liberty of Unlicenc'd*

Printing, To the Parliament of England. London: [No publisher given.]

1673   *Poems, &c. Upon Several Occasions. Both English and Latin, &c. Composed at Several Times. With a Small Tractate of Education to Mr. Hartlib.* London: [No publisher given.]

1692   *A Defence of the People of England, in Answer to Salmasius's Defence of the King.* [Amsterdam]: [No publisher given.].

Minsky, Marvin

1980   "Interview with Marvin Minsky." An interview by C. Roads. *Computer Music Journal* 4 (Fall): 25-39.

Montesquieu, Charles de Secondat, baron de,

1989   *The Spirit of the Laws.* Edited by Anne M. Cohler, Basia Carolyn Miller, and Harold Samuel Stone. Cambridge: Cambridge University Press.

Moore, Clement Clarke

1804   *Observations Upon Certain Passages in Mr. Jefferson's Notes on Virginia.* New York: [No publisher given.].

Moore, George H.

1866   *Notes on the History of Slavery in Massachusetts.* New-York: D. Appleton.

Moore, Jason Kendall

2000   "Between Expediency and Principle." *Diplomatic History* 24 (Summer): 381-404.

Moore, Wayne, R

1970   *Foundations of Mechanical Accuracy.* Bridgeport: Moore Special Tool Company.

Morgan, Richard

1815   *Memoirs of the Life of the Rev. Richard Price.* London: R. Hunter and R. Rees.

Morgenstern, Oskar

1963   *On the Accuracy of Economic Observations.* Second edition. Princeton: Princeton University Press.

1973   "Game Theory." In *Dictionary of the History of Ideas*, edited by Philip P. Wiener, 5 volumes. New York: Charles Scribner's Sons.

Morison, Samuel and Henry Steele Commager

1956   *The Growth of the American Republic.* 2 volumes. Fourth edition, seventh printing. New York: Oxford University Press.

Morris, Gouverneur

1779   *Observations on the American Revolution.* Published According to a Resolution of Congress, by Their Committee. Philadelphia: Styner and Cist.

1888   *The Diary and Letters of Gouverneur Morris.* Edited by Anne Cary Morris. 2 volumes. New York: Charles Scribner's Sons.

Morse, Jedidiah

1789   *The American Geography; or A View of the Present Situation of the United States of America.* Elizabethtown, [New Jersey]: Shepard Kollock.

Morton, Louis

1941   *Robert Carter of Nomini Hall: A Virginia Tobacco Planter of the Eighteenth Century.* Williamsburg, Virginia: Colonial Williamsburg.

MPCUS

1792   *Memorials Presented to the Congress of the United States of America by the Different Societies Instituted for the Promotion of the Abolition of Slavery.* Philadelphia: Francis Bailey.

MSJT

2005   *Military Studies in the Jihad against the Tyrants: THE AL-QAEDA TRAINING MANUAL.* Edited by Jerrold M. Post. Maxwell Air Force Base, Alabama: USAF Counterproliferation Center.

MTCP

1768   *To the Merchants, and Traders, of the City of Philadelphia.* Philadelphia: [No publisher given].

Murray, Judith Sargent

1995   *Selected Writings of Judith Sargent Murray.* Edited by Sharon M. Harris.

New York: Oxford University Press.

Musonius Rufus, Caius
1947 *Musonius Rufus: "The Roman Socrates."* Edited by Cora E. Lutz. New Haven: Yale University Press.

NAS
1841 *National Anti-Slavery Standard.* (December 2): 102.

Nash, Gary B.
1990 *Race and Revolution.* Madison: Madison House.

Nelson, Harry L.
1981 "A Solution to Archimedes' Cattle Problem." *Journal of Recreational Mathematics* 13 (July): 162-76.

Nelson, William
1916 *New Jersey Biographical and Genealogical Notes.* Volume 9 of the *Collections of the New Jersey Historical Society.* Newark: New Jersey Historical Society.

Nelson, William Edward
1975 *Americanization of the Common Law: The Impact of Legal Change on Massachusetts Society, 1760-1830.* Cambridge: Harvard University Press.

Newbeck, Phyl
2004 *Virginia Hasn't Always Been for Lovers: Interracial Marriage Bans and the Case of Richard Loving and Mildred Loving.* Carbondale: Southern University Press.

Newton, Isaac
1779-85 *Isaaci Newtoni Opera quæ exstant omnia.* Edited by Samuel Horsley. 5 volumes. London: J. Nichols.

NGSQ
2001 *National Genealogical Society Quarterly.* Volume 89 (September).

Nietzsche, Friedrich
1966 *Beyond Good and Evil.* Edited by Walter Kaufmann. New York: Vintage Books.
1967 *The Birth of Tragedy and The Case of Wagner.* Edited by Walter Kaufmann. New York: Vintage Books.
1968 *The Will to Power.* Edited by Walter Kaufmann. New York: Vintage Books.
1969 *On the Genealogy of Morals and Ecce Homo.* Edited by Walter Kaufmann. New York: Vintage Books.

Niles, Hezekiah
1822 (editor) *Principles and Acts of the Revolution in America.* Baltimore: William Ogden Niles.

Niles, Nathaniel
1774 *Two Discourses on Liberty; delivered at the North Church, in Newbury-Port, on Lord's Day, June 5, 1774, and Published at the General Desire of the Hearers.* Newbury-Port: I. Thomas and H. W. Tinges.

Nips, Jack [pseudonym for John Leland]
1794 *The Yankee Spy.* Boston: John Asplund.

Noah, Mordecai Manuel
1819 *Travels in England, France, Spain, and the Barbary States, in the Years 1813-14 and 15.* New York: Kirk and Mercein.

Noble, Oliver
1775 *Some Strictures Upon the Sacred Story Recorded in the Book of Esther.* Newbury-port, New-England: E. Lunt and H. W. Tinges.

Noonan, John T, Jr.
1977 *The Antelope: the Ordeal of the Recaptured Africans in the Administrations of James Monroe and John Quincy Adams.* Berkeley: University of California Press.

OED
1989 *The Oxford English Dictionary.* Second edition. Prepared by J. A. Simpson and E. S. C. Weiner. Oxford: Clarendon Press.

Ohanian, Hans C.
2008   *Einstein's Mistakes: the Human Failings of Genius*. New York: W. W. Norton.
Oldschool, Oliver
1804   "Observations upon certain passages in Mr. Jefferson's Notes on Virginia." *The Portfolio* 4 (#31, #32, #33): 244-45, 250-52, 268-69.
Onishi, Norimitsu
2003   "Japanese Workers Get Word From on High: Drop Formality." *New York Times* (October 30): A1.
Othello
1788   "Essay on Negro Slavery." *American Museum* 4 (November): 414-17.

Otis, James
1764   *The Rights of the British Colonies Asserted and Proved*. Boston: Edes and Gill.
PAH
1773   "*The Pursuit after* HAPPINESS." *The Virginia Gazette* (November 18): 1.
Paige, Lucius R.
1883   *History of Hardwick, Massachusetts*. Boston: Houghton, Mifflin.
Paine, Thomas
1796   *Letter to George Washington*. Philadelphia: Benj. Franklin Bache.
1945   *The Complete Writings of Thomas Paine*. Edited by Philip S. Foner. 2 volumes. New York: Citadel Press.
Palmer, Elihu
1797   *An Inquiry Relative to the Moral & Political Improvement of the Human Species*. New York: John Crookes
Panofsky, Erwin
1954   *Galileo as a Critic of the Arts*. The Hague: Martinus Nijhoff.
Parker, Isaac
1796   *An Oration, Delivered at Castine, July 4, 1796, at the Celebration of the Twentieth Anniversary of American Independence*. Boston: Samuel Hall.
Parrish, John
1806   *Remarks on the Slavery of the Black People*. Philadelphia: Kimber, Conrad & Co. .
Parsons, Theophilus
1778   *Result of the Convention of Delegates Holden at Ipswich in the County of Essex, Who Were Deputed to Take into Consideration the Constitution and Form of Government, Proposed by the Convention of the State of Massachusetts-Bay*. Newbury-Port: John Mycall.
PAS
1789-1794 *Pennsylvania Abolition Society, Committee of Correspondence Letterbook*. Volume 1. In Historical Society of Pennsylvania Collections, Philadephia, Microfilm Reel 11.
Pascal, Blaise
1950   *Pascal's Pensées*. Edited by H. F. Stewart. New York: Pantheon Books.
Patterson, Bennett B.
1955   *The Forgotten Ninth Amendment*. Indianapolis, Indiana: Bobbs-Merrill.
Patterson, Richard S. and Richardson Dougall
1976   *The Eagle and the Shield: a History of the Great Seal of the United States*. Washington: U. S. Government Printing Office.
Patterson, Samuel White
1941   *Horatio Gates: Defender of American Liberties*. New York: Columbia University Press.
Pauli, Wolfgang
1955   "The Influence of Archetypal Ideas on the Scientific Theories of Kepler." In *The Interpretation of Nature and the Psyche*, 151-240. New York: Pantheon Books.
Payson, Phillips
1778   *A Sermon Preached Before the Honorable Council, and the Honorable House of Representatives, of the State of Massachusetts-Bay, in New-England, at Boston, May 27, 1778*. Boston: John Gill.

PCSMC
1982   *Publications of the Colonial Society of Massachusetts. Collections.* Volume 59. Boston: Colonial Society of Massachusetts.

PCSMT
1904   *Publications of The Colonial Society of Massachusetts. Transactions 1899, 1900.* Volume 6. Boston: Colonial Society of Massachusetts.

Pennington, James W. C.
1849   *The Fugitive Blacksmith.* Second edition. London: Charles Gilpin.

Penrose, Roger
1974   "The Rôle of Aesthetics in Pure and Applied Research." *The Institute of Mathematics and Its Applications*10 (July/August): 266-271.

Perry, William
1777   *The Royal Standard English Dictionary.* Boston: Thomas & Andrews, West & Richardson, and E. Cotton.

Peterson, Christopher and Martin E. P. Seligman
2004   *Character Strengths and Virtues: A Handbook and Classification.* New York: Oxford University Press.

PGGC
1776   "A Proclamation By the GREAT and GENERAL COURT of the Colony of MASSACHUSETTS-BAY." *Journal of the Honourable House of Representatives, At a Great General Court or Assembly for the Colony of Massachusetts-Bay in New-England."* [Watertown, Massachusetts: Benjamin Edes.]

PHNOD
1998   *Petition Histories and Nonlegislative Official Documents.* Edited by Kenneth R. Bowling et al. Volume 8. Baltimore: Johns Hopkins University Press.

Phocion [pseudonym for Henry William De Saussure]
1795   *Letters on the Questions of the Justice and Expediency of Going into Alterations of the Representation in the Legislature of South-Carolina, as Fixed by the Constitution.* Charleston: Markland & M'Iver.

Piattelli-Palmarini, Massimo
1994   *Inevitable Illusions: How Mistakes of Reason Rule our Minds.* New York: John Wiley.

Pico della Mirandola, Giovanni
1948   "Oration on the Dignity of Man." In *The Renaissance Philosophy of Man*, edited by Ernest Cassirer, Paul Oskar Kristeller and John Herman Randall, Jr., 223-254. Chicago: University of Chicago Press.

Pinkney, William
1790   *Speech of William Pinkney, Esq. In the House of Delegates of Maryland, At their Session in November, 1789.* Philadelphia: Joseph Crukshank.

Planck, Max
1932   *Where is Science Going?* New York: W.W. Norton.

Plato
1937   *The Dialogues of Plato.* Edited by Benjamin Jowett. 2 volumes. New York: Random House.
1955   *The Republic of Plato.* Edited by Francis Macdonald Cornford. New York: Oxford University Press.
1957   *Plato's Cosmology.* Edited by Francis Macdonald Cornford. New York: Liberal Arts Press.
1957a   *Plato's Theory of Knowledge.* Edited by Francis MacDonald Cornford. New York:Liberal Arts Press.

Pliny [the Younger]
1969   *Letters and Panegyricus.* Translated by Betty Radice. 2 volumes. Cambridge: Harvard University Press.

Plutarch
1914-26   *Plutarch's Lives.* Translated by Bernadotte Perrin. 11 volumes. London: William Heinemann.
1927-2000   *Moralia.* Translated by Frank Cole Babbitt. 15 volumes. London:William Heinemann.

PMHS
1875   *Proceedings of the Massachusetts Historical Society: 1873-1875.*
            Boston: John Wilson & Son.
Poincaré, Henri
1921   *The Foundations of Science.* Translated by George Bruce Halsted. New
            York: Science Press.
Polyænus
1974   *Polyænus's Stratagems of War.* Translated by R. Shepherd. Chicago: Ares
            Publishers.
Polybius
1922-27   *The Histories.* Translated by W. R. Paton. London: William Heinemann.

Pope, Alexander
1970   *An Essay on Man.* Edited by Maynard Mack, New Haven: Yale University
            Press.
Porter, David D.
1886   *The Naval History of the Civil War.* New York: Sherman Publishing
            Company.
PPAJ
1987   "Practice and Potential of the Advisory Jury." *Harvard Law Review* 100
            (April): 1363-81.
Price, Richard
1948   *A Review of the Principal Questions in Morals.* Edited by D. Daiches
            Raphael. Oxford: Clarendon Press.
1991   *Political Writings.* Edited by D. O. Thomas. Cambridge: Cambridge
            University Press.
Priestley, Joseph
1791   *Letters to the Right Honourable Edmund Burke, occasioned by his
            Reflections on the Revolution in France, &c.* Birmingham: Thomas
            Pearson.
Pritchard, James B.
1969   *Ancient Near Eastern Texts Relating to the Old Testament.* Third Edition.
            Princeton: Princeton University Press.
PSLUSA
1845   *The Public Statues at Large of the United States of America.* Boston:
            Charles C. Little and James Brown.
Pufendorf, Samuel
1934   *De jure naturae et gentium.* Translated by C. H. Oldfather and W. A.
            Oldfather. 2 volumes. Oxford: Clarendon Press.
Ramachandran, V. S. and Sandra Blakeslee
1998   *Phantoms in the Brain: Probing the Mysteries of the Human Mind.* New
            York: William Morrow.
Ramsay, David
1779   "An Oration on the Advantages of American Independence." *The
            Pennsylvania Gazette, and Weekly Advertiser.* Number 2536 (January
            20).
1779a   "An Oration on the Advantages of American Independence [continued]."
            The Pennsylvania Gazette, and Weekly Advertiser. Number 2537 (January
            27).
1789   *The History of the American Revolution.* 2 volumes. Philadelphia:
            Aitken & Son.
1943   "David Ramsay on the Ratification of the Constitution in South Carolina,
            1787-1788." Edited by Robert L. Brunhouse. *Journal of Southern
            History* 9 (November 1943): 549-555.
Rauschning, Hermann
1940   *Hitler Speaks: A Series of Political Conversations with Adolph Hitler on
            his Real Aims.* London: Thornton Butterworth.
Ravitch, Diane
2003   *The Language Police: How Pressure Groups Restrict What Students Learn.*
            New York: Alfred A. Knopf.

Raynal, Abbé (Guillaume-Thomas-François)
  1781   *The Revolution of America, by the Abbé Raynal.* London: L. Davis.
Reese, Thomas
  1788   *An Essay on the Influence of Religion, In Civil Society.* Charleston, South Carolina: Markland & M'Iver.
Reid, Constance
  1970   *Hilbert.* New York: Springer-Verlag.
Reid, Thomas
  2002   *Essays on the Intellectual Powers of Man.* Edited by Derek R Brookes. University Park, Pennsylvania: Pennsylvania State University Press.
Rice, David
  1792   *Slavery Inconsistent with Justice and Good Policy.* Philadelphia: Parry Hall.
RLGD
  1783   *Rudiments of Law and Government, Deduced From The Law of Nature; Particularly Addressed to the People of South-Carolina, But Composed on Principles Applicable to All Mankind.* Charlestown: John M'Iver.
RNSV
  1787   Review of *Notes on the State of Virginia. The European Magazine, and London Review.* Volume 12 (August, October, November): 112-116, 273-276, 379-382.
Robinson, Abraham
  1979   "The Metaphysics of the Calculus." In *Nonstandard Analysis and Philosophy, Selected Papers of Abraham Robinson*, volume 2, edited by W. A. J. Luxemburg and S. Körner. New Haven: Yale University Press.
Roosevelt, Franklin D.
  1941   *The Public Papers and Addresses of Franklin D. Roosevelt. 1940 Volume: War — and Aid to Democracies.* New York: Macmillan.
  1950   *The Public Papers and Addresses of Franklin D. Roosevelt. 1941 Volume: The Call to Battle Stations.* New York: Harper & Brothers.
  1950a   *The Public Papers and Addresses of Franklin D. Roosevelt. 1943 Volume: The Tide Turns.* New York: Harper & Brothers.
  1950b   *The Public Papers and Addresses of Franklin D. Roosevelt. 1944-45 Volume: Victory and the Threshold of Peace.* New York: Harper & Brothers.
Rousseau, Jean-Jacques
  1964   *The First and Second Discourses.* Edited by Roger D. Masters. New York: St. Martin's Press.
  1978   *On the Social Contract.* Edited by Roger D. Masters. New York: St. Martin's Press.
RPCCL
  1945   *Report of the President's Committee on the Cost of Living, November 17, 1944.* [Washington]: Office of Economic Stabilization, U. S. Government Printing Office, 1945.
RRRLPW
  1947   *RAMP's: the Recovery and Repatriation of Liberated Prisoners of War.* Frankfurt-am-Main: United States Army, Office of the Chief Historian, European Command.
RSRI
  1865   *Records of the State of Rhode Island and Providence Plantations in New England.* Volume 10. Edited by John Russell Bartlett. Providence: Providence Press.
Ruse, Michael
  2003   *Darwin and Design: Does Evolution Have a Purpose?* Cambridge: Harvard University Press.
Rush, Benjamin
  1773   *An Address to the Inhabitants of the British Settlements in America Upon Slave-Keeping.* Philadelphia: John Dunlop.
  1786   *An Oration Delivered Before the American Philosophical Society, Held in Philadelphia on the 27th of February, 1786; Containing An Enquiry into the INFLUENCE of PHYSICAL CAUSES upon the MORAL FACULTY.* Philadelphia:

Charles Cist.

1786a   *A Plan for the Establishment of Public Schools and the Diffusion of Knowledge in Pennsylvania; To Which Are Added Thoughts Upon the Mode of Education, Proper in a Republic. Addressed to the legislature and citizens of the state.* Philadelphia: Thomas Dobson.

1787   *Thoughts Upon Female Education, Accommodated to the Present State of Society, Manners, and Government, in the United States of America.* Philadelphia: Prichard & Hall.

1789   "Account of a Wonderful Talent for Arithmetical Calculations in an African Slave, living in Virginia." *The New-Hampshire Spy* (February 3): 120.

1948   *The Autobiography of Benjamin Rush: His "Travels Through Life" together with his Commonplace Book for 1789-1813.* Edited by George W. Corner. Princeton: Princeton University Press.

1951   *Letters of Benjamin Rush.* Edited by L. H. Butterfield. 2 volumes. Princeton: Princeton University Press.

Rushton, Edward

1797   *Expostulatory Letter to George Washington of Mount Vernon in Virginia on His Continuing to Be a Holder of Slaves.* Liverpool: [No publisher given.].

Ruskin, John

1903-12   *The Works of John Ruskin.* Edited by E. T. Cook and Alexander Wedderburn. 24 volumes. London: George Allen.

Russell, Bertrand

1937   *A Critical Exposition of the Philosophy of Leibniz.* London: George Allen & Unwin, Ltd.

1957   *Mysticism and Logic.* Garden City: Doubleday & Co.

1973   *Essays in Analysis.* Edited by Douglas Lackey. New York: George Braziller.

Russell, John H.

1913   *The Free Negro in Virginia, 1619-1865.* Baltimore: Johns Hopkins Press.

Rutherford, Samuel

1644   *Lex, Rex: The Law and The Prince.* London: John Field.

Saari, Donald G. and Jill Van Newenhizen

1988   "The Problem of Indeterminacy in Approval, Multiple, and Truncated Voting Systems." *Public Choice* 59: 101-120.

1988a   "Is Approval Voting an 'Unmitigated Evil'?: A Response to Brams, Fishburn, and Merrill." *Public Choice* 59: 133-147.

Saint-Just, [Louis Antoine Léon de]

1984   *Oeuvres Complétes.* Edited by Michéle Duval. Paris: Gérald Lebovici.

Samuelson, Paul

1966-86   *The Collected Scientific Papers of Paul A. Samuelson.* 5 volumes. Cambridge: MIT Press.

Sanders, James D., Mark A. Sauter, and R. Cork Kirkwood

1992   *Soldiers of Misfortune: Washington's Secret Betrayal of American POWs in the Soviet Union.* Washington, D.C.: National Press Books.

Sandler, S. Gerald.

1960   "Lockean Ideas in Thomas Jefferson's 'Bill for Establishing Religious Freedom.'" *Journal of the History of Ideas* 21 (January-March): 110-116.

Sandoz, Ellis

1993   (editor) *The Roots of Liberty: Magna Carta, Ancient Constitution, and the Anglo-American Tradition of Rule of Law.* Columbia, Missouri: University of Missouri Press.

Santayana, George

1954   *The Life of Reason, or the Phases of Human Progress.* One-volume edition. New York: Charles Scribner's Sons.

Schiller, Friedrich

1982   *On the Aesthetic Education of Man.* Edited by Elizabeth M. Wilkinson and L. A. Willoughby. Oxford: Clarendon Press.

Schmidt, Fredrika Teute and Barbara Ripel Wilhelm
1973 "Early Proslavery Petitions in Virginia." *William and Mary Quarterly*, Third Series 30 (January): 133-146.

Schopenhauer, Arthur
1948-50 *The World as Will and Idea*. 3 volumes. London: Routledge & Kegan Paul.
1999 *Prize Essay on the Freedom of the Will*. Edited by Günter Zöller. Cambridge: Cambridge University Press.

Schröder, Hannelore
1997 "Kant's Patriarchal Order." In *Feminist Interpretations of Immanuel Kant*, edited by Robin May Schott, 275-96. University Park, Pennsylvania: Pennsylvania University Press.

Schrödinger, Erwin
1996 *Nature and the Greeks* and *Science and Humanism*. Cambridge: Cambridge University Press.

Schuh, Fred.
1968 *The Master Book of Mathematical Recreations*. Edited by T. H. O'Beirne. New York: Dover Publications.

Schutz, John A. and Douglass Adair
1966 *The Spur of Fame: Dialogues of John Adams and Benjamin Rush, 1805-1813*. San Marino, California: The Huntington Library.

Schweninger, Loren
1998 *Race, Slavery, and Free Blacks: Petitions to Southern Legislatures, 1777-1867*. Bethesda, Maryland: University Publications of America.

Seabrook, John
2007 "Fragmentary Knowledge: The Mystery of the Antikythera Mechanism." *The New Yorker* (May 14): 94-102.

Sen, Amartya
1987 "Social Choice." In *The New Palgrave: a Dictionary of Economics*, 4 volumes, edited by John Eatwell, Murry Milgate, and Peter Newman, 4: 382-93. London: Macmillan.

Seneca
1970-75 *Moral Essays*. Translated by John W. Basore. 3 volumes. Cambridge: Harvard University Press.
1989-96 *Epistles*. Translated by Richard M. Gummere. 3 volumes. Cambridge: Harvard University Press.

Shelley, Percy Bysshe
1891 *A Defense of Poetry*. Edited by Albert S. Cook. Boston: Ginn & Co.

Shostakovich, Dmitri
1979 *Testimony: the Memoirs of Dmitri Shostakovich*. Edited by Solomon Volkof. New York: Harper & Row.

Shute, Daniel
1767 *A Sermon Preached to the Ancient and Honorable Artillery Company in Boston, New-England, June 1, 1767. Being the Anniversary of the Election of Officers*. Boston: Edes and Gill.
1768 *A Sermon Preached Before His Excellency Francis Bernard, Esq.; Governor, His Honor Thomas Hutchinson, Esq.; The Honorable His Majesty's Council, and the Honorable House of Representatives, of the Province of Massachusetts-Bay in New-England, May 25th. 1768. Being the Aniversary for the Election of His Majesty's Council for Said Province*. Boston: Richard Draper.

Sidney, Algernon
1990 *Discourses Concerning Government*. Edited by Thomas G. West. Indianapolis, Indiana: Liberty Classics.

Smith, Adam
1981 *An Inquiry into the Nature and Causes of the Wealth of Nations*. 2 volumes. Edited by R. H. Campbell and A. S. Skinner. Indianapolis: Liberty Classics.
1982 *The Theory of Moral Sentiments*. Edited by D. D. Raphael and A. L. Macfie. Indianapolis: Liberty Classics.

Smith, Paul
1976-81   (editor) *Letters of Delegates to Congress: 1774-1789, May 16 - August 15, 1776.* 7 volumes. Washington: Library of Congress.
Smith, Samuel Stanhope
1810   *An Essay on the Causes of the Variety of Complexion and Figure in the Human Species.* Second edition. New-Brunswick: J. Simpson and Co. .
Smith, William
1755   *A Sermon, Preached in Christ-Church, Philadelphia; Before the Provincial Grand Master, and General Communication of Free and Accepted Masons.* Philadelphia: B. Franklin and D. Hall.
Solomonoff, Ray J.
1964   "A Formal Theory of Inductive Inference. Part I." *Information and Control* 7 (September): 1-22.
Solzhenitsyn, Aleksandr I.
1974   *The Gulag Archipelago, 1918-1956, An Experiment in Literary Investigation, I-II.* New York: Harper and Row.
Sophocles
1886   *The Plays of Sophocles.* Translated by Thomas Francklin. London: George Routledge and Sons.
1994   *I, Ajax, Electra, Oedipus Tyrannus* Edited by Hugh Lloyd-Jones. Cambridge: Harvard University Press.
SOUTH
2000   "South: One State Isn't So Solid, and It Creates a Cliffhanger." *New York Times* (November 9): B15.
Spooner, Lysander
1860   *The Unconstitutionality of Slavery.* Enlarged Edition. Boston: Bela Marsh.
Stanton, Elizabeth Cady, Susan B. Anthony, and Matilda Joslyn Gage
1899   *History of Woman Suffrage.* 3 volumes. Rochester: Charles Mann.
Stanton, Lucia C.
1993   " 'Those Who Labor For My Happiness': Thomas Jefferson and His Slaves." In *Jeffersonian Legacies*, edited by Peter S. Onuf, 147-180. Charlottesville: University Press of Virginia.
Stedman, John Gabriel
1988   *Narrative of a Five Years Expedition Against the Revolted Negroes of Surinam.* Edited by Richard Price and Sally Price. Baltimore: Johns Hopkins University Press.
Stephens, Alexander H.
1886   *Alexander H. Stephens, in Public and Private. With Letters and Speeches, Before, During , and Since the War.* Edited by Henry Cleveland. Philadelphia: National Publishing Company.
Stern, Nancy
1981   *From ENIAC to UNIVAC: An Appraisal of the Eckert-Mauchly Computers.* Bedford, Massachusetts: Digital Press.
Stern, Philip M.
1973   *The Rape of the Taxpayer.* New York: Random House.
Sterne, Laurence
1927   *The Sermons of Mr Yorick.* Volume I. Oxford: Basil Blackwell.
Stettinius, Edward R. , Jr.
1949   *Roosevelt and the Russians: The Yalta Conference.* Edited by Walter Johnson. Garden City: Doubleday.
Stiefel, Tina
1977   "The Heresy of Science: A Twelfth-Century Conceptual Revolution." *Isis* 243 (July 1977): 346-62.
Stiles, Ezra
1783   *The United States Elevated to Glory and Honor.* New Haven: Thomas & Samuel Green.
Stockdale, James Bond
1995   *Thoughts of a Philosophical Fighter Pilot.* Stanford: Hoover Institution Press.

Strabo
1917   *The Geography of Strabo*. Edited by Horace Leonard Jones. 8 volumes. New York: G. P. Putnam's Sons.

Suber, Peter
1990   *The Paradox of Self-Amendment: A Study of Logic, Law, Omnipotence, and Change*. New York: Peter Lang.

Suetonius
1944   *Suetonius*. Translated by J. C. Rolfe. 2 volumes. Cambridge: Harvard University Press.

Sutcliff, Robert
1812   *Travels in Some Parts of North America, in the Years 1804, 1805, & 1806*. Philadelphia: B. & T. Kite.

Swade, Doron D.
1993   "Redeeming Charles Babbage's Mechanical Computer." *Scientific American* 268 (1993): 86-91.

Tacitus, Cornelius
1969-92 *Tacitus in Five Volumes*. 5 volumes Cambridge: Harvard University Press.

TAP
1791   *The American Preacher*. Edited by David Austin. Volume 3. Elizabeth-Town, New Jersey: Shepard Kollock.

Tarski, Alfred
1949   "On Essential Undecidability." Abstract. *Journal of Symbolic Logic* 14 (March): 75-6.

TCSPP
1948   "Truman Calls Stalin Politburo Prisoner." *New York Times* (June 11): 1.

Tertullian
1842   *Tertullian*. Translated by C. Dodgson. Volume 1: *Apologetic and Practical Treatises*. Oxford: John Henry Parker.
1972   *Adversus Marcionem*. Edited by Ernest Evans. 2 volumes. Oxford: Clarendon Press.

Thacher, Samuel
1796   *An Oration, Pronounced July 4, 1796, at the Request of the Inhabitants of the Town of Concord, in Commemoration of the Twentieth Anniversary of American Independence*. Boston: Samuel Hall.

Thomsen, Dietrick
1981   "Mathematical Physical Birthday Party." *Science News* 119 (June 20): 397-98.

Thorpe, Francis Newton
1909   *The Federal and State Constitutions, Colonial Charters, and Other Organic Laws of the States, Territories, and Colonies, Now or Heretofore Forming the United States of America*. 7 volumes. Washington: Government Printing Office.

Thucydides
1928-33 *History of the Peloponnesian War*. Translated by Charles Foster Smith. 4 volumes. London: William Heineman.

Tickle, Sally [pseudonym]
1773   "Mr. Holt." *The New-York Journal;or, The General Advertiser* 1568 (January 21): 836

Tiffany, Joel
1849   *A Treatise on the Unconstitutionality of American Slavery: Together with the Powers and Duties of the Federal Government, In Relation to that Subject*. Cleveland, Ohio: J. Calyer.

Tindal, Matthew
1697   *An Essay Concerning the Power of the Magistrate, and the Rights of Mankind in Matters of Religion*. London: Andrew Bell.

TJG
1794   *The Trial of Joseph Gerrald, Delegate from the London Corresponding Society, to the British Convention*. New York: Samuel Campbell.

Todhunter, I. (Issac).
1865   *History of the Mathematical Theory of Probabilities from the Time of Pascal to that of Laplace.* London: Macmillan.
Tolstoy, Leo
1964   *The Death of Ivan Illych and Other Stories.* New York: New American Library.
Tolstoy, Nikolai
1977   *The Secret Betrayal.* New York: Charles Scribner's Sons.
1982   *Stalin's Secret War.* New York: Holt, Rinehart & Winston.

Torrey, Jesse
1817   *A Portraiture of Domestic Slavery in the United States.* Philadelphia: [No publisher given.].
Trenchard, John and Thomas Gordon
1995   *Cato's Letters or Essays on Liberty, Civil and Religious, and Other Important Subjects.* Edited by Ronald Hamowy. 2 volumes. Indianapolis, Indiana: Liberty Fund.

Truman, Harry
1964   *Public Papers of the Presidents of the United States: Harry S. Truman.* Washington: United States Government Printing Office.
Trumbull, John
1841   *Autobiography, Reminiscences and Letters of John Trumbull, from 1756 to 1841.* New Haven: B. L. Hamlen.
Tucker, John
1771   *A Sermon Preached at Cambridge, Before His Excellency Thomas Hutchinson, Esq; Governor: His Honor Andrew Oliver, Esq; Lieutenant-Governor, The Honorable His Majesty's Council, and the Honorable House of Representatives of the Province of the Massachusetts-Bay in New-England, May 29th, 1771. Being the Anniversary for the Election of His Majesty's Council for said Province.* Boston: Richard Draper.
Tucker, St. George
1796   *A Dissertation on Slavery with a Proposal for the Gradual Abolition of It, in the State of Virginia.* Philadelphia: Mathew Carey.
Tullock, Gordon
1979   "Public Choice in Practice." In *Collective Decision Making: Applications from Public Choice Theory,* edited by Clifford S Russell, 27-45. Baltimore: John Hopkins University Press.
Turgot, Anne-Robert-Jacques
1895   *The Life and Writings of Turgot, Comptroller-General of France, 1774-6.* Edited by W. Walter Stephens. London: Longmans, Green, & Co. .
Turner, Charles
1773   *A Sermon Preached Before His Excellency Thomas Hutchinson, Esq.; Governor; The Honorable His Majesty's Council, and the Honorable House of Representatives of the Province of the Massachusetts-Bay in New-England, May 26th. 1773. Being the Anniversary of the Election of His Majesty's Council for said Province.* Boston: Richard Draper.
1972   *Adversus Marcionem.* Books 1 to 3. Edited by Ernest Evans. Oxford: Clarendon Press.
Tyldesley, Joyce
1996   *Hatchepsut: The Female Pharaoh.* London: Viking.
Tyler, Moses Coit
1887   *Patrick Henry.* Boston: Houghton, Mifflin.
VGPI
1790   "Constitution of The Virginia Society." *The Virginia Gazette and Petersburg Intelligencer* 3 (July 8): Insert. [Copy from The Virginia Historical Society.]
Villaseñor, Victor
1977   *Jury: the People vs Juan Corona.* Boston: Little, Brown.

Virginia Committee of Correspondence
1905   "[Letter to the Agent. Discussion of a Stamp Act.]" *Virginia Historical Magazine of History and Biography* 12 (June): 8-13.
Voltaire
1733   *Letters Concerning the English Nation.* Translated by John Lockman. London: C. Davis and A. Lyon.
von Ahn, Luis
2006   "Games With A Purpose." *IEEE Computer Magazine* (June): 96-98.
von Neuman, John
1959   "On the Theory of Games of Strategy." In *Contributions to the Theory of Games,* volume 4, edited by A.W. Tucker and R.D. Luce, 13-42. Princeton: Princeton University Press.
von Neuman, John and Oskar Morgenstern
1967   *Theory of Games and Economic Behavior.* New York: John Wiley & Sons.
VPFITB
1772   *The Votes and Proceedings of the Freeholders and Other Inhabitants of the Town of Boston.* Boston: Edes and Gill, and T. and J. Fleet.
VPHR
1777   *Votes and Proceedings of the House of Representatives of the Province of Pennsylvania.* Volume 6. Philadelphia: Henry Miller.
Wade, Nicholas
2000   "Genetic Code of Human Life is Cracked by Scientists." *New York Times* (June 27): A1, A21.
Walker, David
2000   *David Walker's Appeal to the Coloured Citizens of the World.* Edited by Peter P. Hinks. University Park, Pennsylvania: Pennsylvania State University Press.
Washington, George
1783   *A Circular Letter, from His Excellency George Washington.* Philadelphia: Robert Smith.
1791   "By the President of the United States of America. A Proclamation." *The Burlington Advertiser* L (February 8): 1.
1931-44 *The Writings of George Washington.* Edited by John C. Fitzpatrick. 39 volumes. Washington: United States Government Printing Office.
1976-79 *The Diaries of George Washington.* Edited by Donald Jackson. 6 volumes. Charlottesville: University Press of Virginia.
1985-2008 *The Papers of George Washington. Revolutionary War Series.* Edited by Philander D. Chase. Charlottesville: University Press of Virginia.
1987-2007 *The Papers of George Washington. Presidential series.* Edited by Dorothy Twohig. 13 volumes. Charlottesville : University Press of Virginia.
1992-97 *The Papers of George Washington. Confederation Series.* Edited by W. W. Abbot and Dorothy Twohig. 6 volumes. Charlottesville: University Press of Virginia.
Webster, Noah
1785   *Sketches of American policy.* Hartford, [Connecticut]: Hudson and Goodwin.
1787   *An Examination into the Leading Principles of the Federal Constitution Proposed by the Late Convention held at Philadelphia.* Philadelphia: Prichard & Hall.
1790   *A Collection of Essays and Fugitiv Writings on Moral, Historical, Political and Literary Subjects.* Boston: I. Thomas and E. T. Andrews.
1793   *Effects of Slavery on Morals and Industry.* Hartford, Connecticut: Hudson and Goodwin.
1802   *An Oration on the Anniversary of the Declaration of Independence.* New Haven: William W. Morse.
1820   *A Plea for a Miserable World: 1. An Address, Delivered at the Laying of the Corner Stone of the Building Now Erecting for the Charity Institution in Amherst, Massachusetts, August 9, 1820.* Boston: Ezra Lincoln.

1843　　　*A Collection of Papers on Political, Literary, and Moral Subjects*. New York: Webster & Clark.

Weinberg, Steven
1977　　　*The First Three Minutes: a Modern View of the Origin of the Universe*. New York: Basic Books.

West, Benjamin
1963　　　*Life in the South, 1778-1779: The Letters of Benjamin West*. Edited by James S. Schoff. Ann Arbor, Michigan: William Clements Library.

West, Samuel
1776　　　*A Sermon Preached Before the Honorable Council, and the Honorable House of Representatives, of the Colony of the Massachusetts-Bay, in New-England. May 29th, 1776*. Boston: John Gill.

Weyl, Hermann
1932　　　*The Open World: Three Lectures on the Metaphysical Implications of Science*. New Haven: Yale University Press.

Wheatley, Phillis
1989　　　*The Poems of Phillis Wheatley*. Edited by Julian D. Mason, Jr. Chapel Hill: University of North Carolina Press.

White, Michael and John Gribbin
1994　　　*Einstein: A Life in Science*. New York: Dutton.

Whiting, William
1788　　　*An Address to the Inhabitants of the County of Berkshire. Respecting their Present Opposition to Civil Government*. Hartford: Watson and Goodwin.

Whitman, Walt
1963-4　　*Prose Works of 1892*. Edited by Floyd Stovall. 2 volumes. [New York]: New York University Press.

Whitrow, Gerald J.
1967　　　(editor) *Einstein: The Man and His Achievement*. New York: Dover Publications.

Wiecek, William M.
1975　　　"*Somerset*: Lord Mansfield and the Legitimacy of Slavery in the Anglo-American World." *University of Chicago Law Review* 42: 86-146.

Wigner, Eugene P.
1960　　　"The Unreasonable Effectiveness of Mathematics in the Natural Sciences." *Communications on Pure and Applied Mathematics* (February 1960): 1-14.
1967　　　*Symmetries and Reflections: Scientific Essays of Eugene P. Wigner*. Bloomington: Indiana University Press.

Williams, Roger
1867　　　*The Bloudy Tenent of Persecution*. Edited by Samuel L. Caldwell. In *Publications of the Narragansett Club*, First Series, Volume 3. Providence, Rhode Island: Narragansett Club.

Williams, Samuel
1775　　　*A Discourse on the Love of Country; Delivered in a Day of Thanksgiving, December 15, 1774*. Salem, New-England: Samuel and Ebenezer Hall.

Wilson, Arthur, M.
1972　　　*Diderot*. New York: Oxford University Press.

Wilson, James
2007　　　*Collected Works of James Wilson*. Edited by Kermit L. Hall and Mark David Hall. 2 volumes. Indianapolis, Indiana: Liberty Fund.

Winthrop, James
1795　　　*A Systematic Arrangement of Several Scripture Prophecies Relating to Antichrist; With Their Application to the Course of History*. Boston: Thomas Hall.

Wirt, William
1847　　　*Sketches of the Life and Character of Patrick Henry*. Revised edition. Ithaca, New York: Mack, Andrews & Co.

Wise, John
1717   *A Vindication of the Government of New-England Churches*. Boston: J. Allen.
Witherspoon, John
1802   *The Works of the Rev. John Witherspoon*. Second Edition. Philadelphia: William W. Woodward.
Woods, Leonard
1796   *Envy Wishes, then Believes. An Oration, Delivered at Commencement, Harvard University, Cambridge, July 20th, 1796*. Leominster, Massachusetts: Charles Prentiss.
Wolff, Geoffrey
1971   Review of *Bury My Heart at Wounded Knee* by Dee Brown. *Newsweek* 77 (February 1): 69.

Wolff, Robert Paul
1970   *In Defense of Anarchism*. New York: Harper & Row.
Wollaston, William
1725   *The Religion of Nature Delineated*. London: S. Palmer.
Woolf, Harry
1980   (editor) *Some Strangeness in the Proportion: a Centennial Symposium to Celebrate the Achievements of Albert Einstein*. Reading, Massachusetts: Addison-Wesley.
Wortman, Tunis
1800   *A Treatise, Concerning Political Enquiry, and the Liberty of the Press*. New York: George Forman.
Wright, Wilber and Orville Wright
2001   *The Papers of Wilbur and Orville Wright*. 2 volumes. Edited by Marvin W. McFarland. New York: McGraw-Hill.
WS
1787   [No title]. *The Worcester Magazine* (October 1787): 56-7.
WuDunn, Sheryl
1993   "Chinese Buy American Dream by the Inch." *New York Times* (January 29): 1, 6.
W. W.
1753   "An Essay on Happiness." *The Boston Post-Boy* (July 23): 1.
X [pseudonym]
1919   "Science: Einstein's Theory of Gravitation." *The Athenaeum* (November 14): 1189-90.
Xenophon
1995   *Oeconomicus: A Social and Historical Commentary*. Oxford: Clarendon Press.
2001   *Xenophon: The Education of Cyrus*. Edited and translated by Wayne Ambler. Ithaca: Cornell University Press.
Yeats, William Butler
1989   *The Poems* (Revised). Edited by Richard J. Finneran. New York: Macmillan.
Yeomanry of Massachusetts, The
1788   "To the Publick." *The Massachusetts Gazette* (January 25): 4
Zwelling, Shomer S.
1986   "Robert Carter's Journey: From Colonial Patriarch to New Nation Mystic." *American Quarterly* 38 (Fall): 613-36.

Acknowledgements

I work alone and do my own research. Nevertheless, during the years I was writing this book I was aided by many people, and I am in their debt. My first debt is to my teachers, especially Donald Richmond, Lawrence Beals, and John William Miller of Williams College, and to Gregory Vlastos, Peter Hempel, and Walter Kaufmann of Princeton University. These men exhibited great diversity but I feel I learned something important from each of them. I also learned an immense amount from various contemporary scholars and have acknowledged those debts in the references. I am aware that there are many, many other writers who could have been mentioned because they influenced me in a minor way, or because their articles or books are very relevant to the topics in this work. I suspect that some readers will take it to be a sign of incompetence or ingratitude that I have not mentioned them. However, I thought there were already too many references and I didn't want to make a bad situation worse by citing the works of scholars which, however relevant, did not influence me in any substantial way. Further, to cite these scholars might obligate me to criticize their claims where they differ from mine. With regard to them, I agree with Democritus: "It is better to examine one's own faults than those of others"(Freeman 1966 100). When I did so, I discovered I had to correct hundreds of errors, thoughtless assertions, and inappropriate expressions contained in earlier drafts of this book. I am solely responsible for the many that surely remain. In any case, I make no great claims of originality, In this book, I believe there are only a few ideas expressed that others haven't expressed before, and I may be wrong about those few. If there be any originality here, it is in the organization of ideas already known, and in the arrangement and context of a large number of quotations, many of which are not found in any other book (known to me) on the American revolution.

For their comments, criticisms, and help on part or all of the text I want to thank John Alcorn, Myron Anderson, Douglas Blackmon, Miller Brown, Harold Byrdy, Steve Courtney, Pete Daniel, David DeLong, Karen DeLong, Shirley DeLong, Grace Einsel, Karl Fleischmann, Laura Foley, John Gettier, Roger Hanlon, Anne Hillman, Drew Hyland, Richard Lee, Anthony Macro, Philip Meguire, Christopher Nadon, Peter Skagestad, Ronald Spencer, Grayson Taylor, and Maurice Wade. In addition, I profited from the criticisms of Charles Griswold on the subject of Jefferson and slavery. (For Griswold's views, see his thoughtful paper "Rights and Wrongs: Jefferson, Slavery, and Philosophical Quandaries"(1991).) I was also helped, particularly with regard to my account of Jefferson, by the criticisms of Bill Puka, who used a draft of this book in a course at Rensselaer Polytechnic Institute in the Fall of 2003. I am indebted to David Mauro and especially Ralph Walde for their insights and computer results concerning Condorcet's Jury theorem. I want to thank Miller Brown and Ronald Spencer for their encouragement early on, and especially John Alcorn for many helpful conversations and much encouragement toward the project's end.

My research burden was lightened considerably by help from the Trinity College library staff, all of whom were unfailingly supportive; in particular, I would like to thank Alice Angelo, Gwendolynne Arthur, Sally Dickinson, George Graf, Katherine Hart, Doris Kammradt, Janice Lambert, Lee McCallum, Linda McKinney, Alesandra Schmidt, Laura Searles, Nancy Smith, and Rebecca Wondriska. Patricia Bunker and Mary Curry were especially helpful in finding obscure sources. Much of my work was done using Trinity's magnificent collection of Americana in the Watkinson Library. There Jeffrey Kaimowitz, Peter Knapp, and Margaret Sax were very generous with their time and expertise.

Finally, I am grateful to Trinity College for the support it provided at various times throughout the years I worked on this book. In addition, it was indirectly through Trinity that I received funds coming from the Mellon, Dana, and Sloan Foundations, to whom I am likewise appreciative.

Index

Abbot, Abiel 9

Abbot, Robert 444-445

abolitionism 13, 56, 64, 66, 68-70, 78,
87, 89-91, 93, 95-96, 101-102, 124,
128, 130, 140-142, 204, 325, 330, 449,
497

Adair, Douglass 29, 293, 367, 426, 483

Adams, Abigail 1, 48, 52, 92, 220, 338,
369, 515

Adams, John 1, 24-29, 31, 39-40, 44,
47-48, 52, 59-60, 65, 67, 81, 89,
96-97, 99, 101, 120, 122, 134, 142,
146, 156, 159, 161-163, 177, 187-188,
192, 194, 205, 208, 211, 216, 220,
224-226, 233, 235, 239, 251-252, 280,
283, 289, 291, 293-294, 298, 301-302,
304-305, 312, 316, 319-320, 322, 326,
330, 360-362, 365-368, 372, 390-396,
399, 405, 410, 412-414, 426, 428, 439-
440, 448, 450-451, 462, 466-467, 469,
471, 481-483, 491, 495-496, 499-501,
504-506, 510, 513, 515-516, 519, 522

Adams, Samuel 15, 44, 109, 131, 208,
211, 216, 504

Addison, Joseph 426

Aeschines 193

Aeschylus 262, 345, 423

Aesthetic Amendment 484, 486

aesthetics / aestheticism 171, 191, 259,
272, 291, 377-382, 385-386, 389, 391-
392, 397-398, 400-406, 415, 417, 419,
422, 435-436, 440, 447, 453, 469, 484,
486

Africa / Africans 31, 51-57, 63, 70, 75,
78, 81, 83, 95-96, 102, 123, 137, 140,
322, 442

Agency for Public Choice 162, 164,
166, 168, 180, 218, 231, 274

Agrippa (pseudonym) 149

Aiken, Howard 173

Alcidamas 12

Aldridge, A. Owens 31

Alembert, Jean Le Ron d' 302, 329, 418

alienation 14-15, 131, 188, 194, 282,
320, 402, 425-426

Alison, Hugh 328

Allen, Carlos 122

Allen, Ethan 389

Allen, John 52, 156

American perfectionist democracy 4,
162, 171, 187, 194, 199, 224, 232-233,
250, 265, 282, 306, 314, 316, 347,
358, 449, 453, 479-480, 498, 500, 507,
518

American revolution 3, 1-5, 8, 26, 29,
32, 49, 51, 69, 88, 92, 104-105,
130-131, 134, 138, 140, 143, 152, 175,
188, 192, 195, 204, 208, 215-217,
219-220, 225-226, 228, 232, 236, 263,
270, 279, 285-286, 288, 303, 305, 315,
323, 328, 336, 341, 369, 371-372,
375-376, 383, 392-393, 397, 399, 401,
404, 416, 421-423, 426, 428, 430, 433,
440, 455, 459, 462-464, 466, 471, 486,
489, 496, 504, 508, 513, 515-522

Ames, Fisher 399

Ames, Nathaniel 515

Anthony, Susan 364

antislavery/ idea, movement, society
64, 73, 79, 101, 126, 128, 130, 132,
134, 139-143, 145, 327

approval voting 215, 528

Aquinas, Thomas 30

Arendt, Hannah 414

Aristotle 12, 20, 23, 25-27, 30, 36, 38,
59, 72, 89, 156-157, 164, 168, 172,
187, 191, 197, 245, 282-283, 285, 305,
311, 317, 335, 338, 350, 355, 376,
381-382, 392, 398, 404, 407, 409, 411,
415, 420, 423-424, 428-429, 439, 442,

462, 489, 491, 504, 521

Arrow/ Kenneth, theorem 172-173

Ash, John 13,

Atkin, Edmond 373

Aubrey, John 221

Aurelius, Marcus 190, 510

Auschwitz 289, 470-471

Backus, Isaac 37

Bacon, Francis 24, 62, 174, 185, 189, 198, 237-238, 244, 298, 328, 335, 339, 368, 381-382, 409, 419, 432, 448, 518

Bacon, Roger 244

Bailey, Nathan 13

Baldwin, Simeon 56

Banneker, Benjamin 73-74, 78-79, 87, 90, 104

Barlow, Joel 78-79, 142, 235, 270, 327, 479, 485

Barnett, Randy 146

Barron vs Baltimore 146

Barrow, David 122

Bartram, John 21

Bartram, William 373

Bayle, Pierre 30, 302

Bazile, Leon 92

beauty / beautiful 3, 8, 52, 73, 177, 193, 211-212, 224, 259, 275, 282, 313, 354, 367, 377-382, 384-389, 391-393, 399-406, 409, 412-413, 415, 417-418, 421-422, 426, 429, 436, 439-440, 446-447, 450, 454, 473, 487-488, 496

bend-over-backwards honesty 344-345, 477-479

Benezet, Anthony 51

Bentham, Jeremy 173-174

Bentley, Richard 391-392

Bentley, William 25

Berend, Daniel 196

Berenson, Bernard 314

Bethell, Nicholas 109-110, 112

Beveridge, Albert 373

Bible/Biblical 9-10, 12-13, 15-16, 18-19, 26-31, 41, 144, 158, 245, 288, 299, 361, 381-2, 389, 393, 397, 409, 431-434, 436. 464, 467-468, 477, 485, 488

bill of rights 1, 58, 95, 98, 117, 123, 125-129, 132, 139-140, 142, 144-150, 153, 158, 174, 181, 204, 207, 219, 231-232, 360, 371, 453, 483, 493, 495, 502-503, 522

Blackmon, Douglas 90-91, 331

blacks 14, 47-48, 50-51, 53-55, 58, 64-81, 83--92, 94, 96--104, 110, 122-124, 126-127, 131, 135, 137, 142-143, 156, 192, 205, 211, 221, 258, 315, 322, 324-325, 360, 364, 372, 401, 415-416, 472-473, 476, 486, 516

Blackstone, William 37, 133, 136, 365

Bland, Richard 109

Bloomfield, Moses 98, 138

Blumenbach, Johann 79

Bolingbroke, Henry 30, 394, 496

Born, Max 434

Bostonian (pseudonym) 316

Brahe, Tycho 211, 405

Brams, Steven 215

Branagan, Thomas 70, 79

Brissot de Warville, Jaques-Pierre 55, 67-68, 70, 95, 129

Broch, Hermann 412

Browne, Thomas 465

Bruce, Neely 503

Bruce, William 88

Brumbaugh, Robert 406

Bruns, Roger 57

Brutus (pseudonym) 14, 39, 148

Buchanan, George 57, 79, 81

Buhrman, Parker 106

Burke, Edmund 293, 365, 425

Burlamaqui, Jean-Jacques 30

Bush, Vannevar 173

Butler, Joseph 59-60, 329, 353

Butterfield, Fox 356

Butterfield, Lyman 1, 52, 220, 319, 369, 515, 519

Byrnes, Daniel 52

Byrnes, James 107, 112, 118

Caesar, Augustus 8, 133, 233, 393

Caesar, Julius 220

Calaprice, Alice 398

Calhoun John 89

Calvin, John 9, 29

capitalism 278-280

Cappon, Lester 25, 27, 44, 82, 97, 134, 161, 225, 293-294, 316, 326, 330, 385, 391, 414, 426, 462, 465, 491

Caspar, Max 388

Catholic/ Catholics/ Church 139, 293, 302, 394,

Chaitin, Gregory 297

Chamberlain, Mellen 31

Charette, François 406

Chase, Frederick 209

Chauncy, Charles 190

Chomsky, Noam 430

Christ 139, 302, 393, 466, 513

Christian 29, 51, 53, 59, 68-69, 72-74, 86, 139, 293, 383, 393, 395, 442, 454-456, 466-467

Christianity 8, 27, 29, 41, 54, 63, 85, 139, 293, 338, 393, 395, 431, 455-456, 466, 469, 470, 488, 513, 540

Churchill, Winston 108, 113, 117, 502

Cicero 26, 30, 46, 109, 136, 158, 220, 301, 374, 381, 385, 388, 407, 410-411, 462, 506

Civil war 71, 87, 90, 93, 97, 130, 141, 206, 331

Clark, Ronald 452-3

Clavelin, Maurice 245

Clinton, Bill 164

Clinton, George 131, 330, 370, 482

Clinton, Hillary 164

Coffin, Joshua 156

Coffin, William 106-107

Cohen, William 69

Coke, Edward 30, 132-133, 190, 448

Coleman, Thomas 36-37

Coles, Edward 96, 124, 129

Collingwood, Robin 328, 348, 418, 459

Collins, Francis 465

Colman, Benjamin 52

Columbus, Christopher 48, 518

Commager, Henry 91, 548

common law 4, 133, 190, 354

common reason of society/ the people 4, 161-162, 166, 181, 186, 188, 190, 198, 212, 232, 264, 278, 284, 325, 329, 344, 354, 402, 405, 415, 417, 438, 449, 488, 495, 499-500, 518

Condorcet, Marquis de 70, 78, 196, 302, 473, 508

Condorcet Jury Theorem 196, 198, 224

Conrad, Clay 192, 530

considered judgments 160, 163-167, 170, 183, 185, 207, 209, 213, 215, 219, 224, 230, 232, 258, 274, 279, 281-282, 286, 320, 332, 350, 357-358, 360, 383, 415, 492, 509, 511

constitutional convention 122, 125, 159, 174, 183, 209, 232, 302, 425, 490, 492-493, 499, 502, 506, 513

Constitution of the U.S. 1, 16, 32, 48, 55 58-59, 63, 65, 91, 95, 102, 113, 121, 123-130, 132-135, 137-155, 158, 163, 173, 204, 206-210, 219-220, 226, 228, 231, 252, 289, 291, 302, 304, 317, 327, 331, 360, 370-371, 394, 399-400, 423, 425, 439, 453, 471-472, 481-484, 488-490, 492, 494, 496, 500-501, 506, 508, 513, 515, 522-523

Constitutional Court 490-492, 497

Cooke, Samuel 11, 15, 483

Cooper, David 54, 64, 72, 126

Cooper, John 126

Cooper, Samuel 9

Copernicus, Nicolaus 21, 386, 389, 404, 426-427, 429, 431, 440, 442, 453

Coram, Robert 373

corruption of consciousness 328, 330, 346

cosmopolitan/ cosmopolitanism 455, 462, 494, 506-507

Count, Earl 472

Countryman, A (pseudonym) 55, 148

Coxe, Tench 482

Craig, Edward 222

Crawford, Charles 134

Crèvecoeur 100, 373, 521

Crick, Francis 377

Culbert, David 110

Cumings, Henry 328

D***, F***, H*** (pseudonym) 23, 132

Dallas, A. J. 121, 192, 235, 283, 288, 495

Dallin, David 117

Dana, James 55

Daniel, Pete 90-91, 331

Darwall, Stephen 60

Darwin, Charles 177, 380, 385, 405, 416, 427-428, 436, 438-439, 463-464, 469

Darwinian evolution/ nihilism/ scientism/doubt 271, 300, 431, 436, 452, 467

Dauben, Joseph 387

Davies, Samuel 37

Davis, David 101

Davison, R. R. 107

Day, Thomas 83, 330

Deane, Silas 488

Declaration of Independence 1, 8, 13, 16-17, 19, 22, 29-30, 32, 35, 38, 45-51, 53-58, 69-69, 71-73, 77, 80, 88-89, 91, 95-96, 98-99, 104-105, 117-118, 121-122, 128, 131, 133, 136, 138-139, 142-145, 147, 150-152, 158, 173, 204-205, 207, 209, 218-219, 221, 279, 282, 295, 299, 360, 364-366, 372, 385, 391, 399, 401-402, 420-421, 46, 470, 483, 489, 494, 503-504, 508, 510, 516, 521-522

deliberate sense 4, 144, 158-161, 163, 170, 172-173, 175, 179-180, 189, 205-206, 217, 231-232, 259, 269-270, 282, 286, 298, 332, 337, 340-341, 345, 353, 356, 359, 363, 371, 392, 401, 406, 415, 437, 439, 463, 483-484, 486, 518, 522

deliberator science 202, 512

deliberator software 199, 201, 498

deliberators, personal 332-339, 341-345, 355

deliberators, private 332, 466-467, 495

deliberators, public 332, 356, 363, 490, 499

DeLong, Howard 173, 297, 459, 461

democracy 8, 4, 22, 24, 56, 157-158, 161-162, 164, 166, 168, 171-173, 180-181, 185, 187, 189, 193-195, 199, 202, 207, 211-212, 223-224, 232-233, 239-241, 250, 253, 260, 262, 265, 268, 275, 279, 282, 292, 306, 314, 316-317, 331, 345, 347, 358, 360, 366, 380, 391, 403, 423-424, 441, 443, 449-450, 453, 455, 463, 480-483, 487-488, 491-492, 498, 500-502, 507-508, 511-512, 516, 518

democrat 1922, 196, 497

democratic excellence 175, 498, 502

democratic wealth 282-286, 361

Demosthenes 60, 235, 351, 361, 363, 481

Descartes, René 291-292, 412, 452

Dexter, Andrew 424

Dickinson, John 15, 136, 290, 504, 507

Dijksterhuis 388

Diogenes Laertius 25, 506

Dipple, Horst 507

Dirac, P, A, M, 377, 385, 405, 436, 438, 453-454

Donne, John 432-434

Dougall, Richardson 227, 512-513

Douglas, Stephen 87

Douglas, William 209

Douglass, Friederick 104, 127, 129, 326

Drake Stillman 449, 533

Dred Scott 57, 99

Dunn, Susan 145

Dwight, Jasper (pseudonym for William Duane) 63

Dwight, Theodore 38

Dyke, Daniell 60

Echeverria, Durand 508

Eden, Anthony 108

Edmonds, John 431

Edwards, Jonathan 91

Eid, Leroy 373

Einstein/ Einsteinian 279, 314, 377-379, 383-385, 387, 389, 393, 396, 398, 400, 403-405, 411-413, 418, 421, 425, 434, 436-439, 452-453, 465, 467, 469, 479

Einzig,Paul 261

Eisenhower, Dwight 108, 115-118, 327

Eisenstein, Lewis 484

Eisenstein, Sergi 326

Eleusis 444-449, 451-453

Elihu (pseudonym) 302

Eliot. Andrew 52, 218

Eliot, Jared 28

Elkis, Lois 371

Ellicott, Andrew 74, 78-79

Elliot, Jonathan 4, 11, 58, 147, 150, 160, 192, 504

Elliott, Mark 109, 111, 113

Ellis, Havelock 460

Ellis, Joseph 66, 375

Emerson, Ralph 426

Emmons, Nathanael 21, 389

engineering/ engineer 181, 198, 201, 214, 263, 311, 403, 406, 408-409, 415, 417, 445, 469, 476, 479, 496, 503

ENIAC 173-174, 205, 498, 512

Epictetus 322, 327, 337-338, 506

Epstein, Julius 109, 112-113

Eratosthenes 12

ergonomic government/ civilization 187, 194, 270, 375, 415, 455, 486, 514

Ernst, Robert 87, 398

ethical positioning systems 343

Euclid 78, 221, 365, 379, 400, 403, 417-419, 442, 450, 469

Euripides 12, 345, 363, 423

Evans, Emory 324

evolution 177-179, 195, 201, 228, 300-301, 305, 416, 428, 431, 436, 464, 467, 492

fame 38, 74, 87, 95, 98, 211-212, 218, 296, 367-370, 400, 403, 406, 408, 425-426, 429, 491

Farr, James 31

Farrand, Max 40, 84, 96, 122, 148, 159, 164, 183, 302, 361, 365, 374, 400, 422, 425, 481, 507, 513

Farrar, Cynthia 20

Farrington, Benjamin 174

Federal Farmer (pseudonym) 148, 150, 159, 219

Federal Reserve 241, 243-244, 247, 250-255, 258-260, 264

Federalist 20, 35, 47, 125, 127-128, 131, 134, 147, 151, 154, 207, 275, 483

Festival America 316-322, 325-326, 330, 340-341, 344-346, 354, 370-372, 441, 503-504, 509

Festival Earth 511

Feuer, Lewis 412

Feynman, Richard 320, 344, 415, 477, 486

Fifth Amendment 123, 125, 251-252,

275

Filmer, Robert 140

Finkelman, Paul 65, 69, 86

First Amendment 132, 135, 224, 259

Fishburn, Peter 219

Fitzgerald C. P. 247

Flavell, John 24, 37, 319

Fletcher, Elijah 81

Flournoy, H.W. 152

Floyd, Marcus 113, 115, 117

Fobes, Peres 399

Forney, John 430

Fosset, Joseph 86

Foster, Augustus 90

Founders 2-4, 20, 23, 25, 41, 43-45, 48-49, 58, 61, 85, 97, 103-104, 111, 121, 129, 142-144, 158-159, 164, 175, 187, 204, 258, 280, 301, 305, 311, 314, 325, 332, 360-361, 363, 365, 368-369, 393, 400-401, 410, 415, 423, 440, 454, 481, 483, 487-488, 495, 507, 513, 515, 517

Fourth Amendment 145-146

fractal 348, 392, 416, 437, 498

Franklin, Benjamin 20, 24, 44, 70, 73, 85, 109, 127, 131, 139, 142, 211, 227, 252-253, 302, 312, 337-338, 355, 362-363, 373-374, 395, 410-411, 425, 429, 453, 489, 499, 505, 514, 520

Freeman, Kathleen 12, 361, 423, 467, 506

Freeth, Tony 406

French Revolution 2, 65

Freud, Sigmund 427, 457-461

fugitive slave law 64, 94, 102, 107, 113, 127

Fuller, Thomas 70

Gage, Matilda 364

Gale, Benjamin 121

Gales 28, 51, 56, 123, 127, 138

Galileo 21, 189, 237, 245, 254-255, 278-279, 302, 314, 379, 382, 387-388,

390, 393, 404, 435, 437, 442, 449, 453, 464-465, 467

Gardner, Martin 172, 444-445

Gay, Ebenezer 18, 28, 413

George III 66, 68-69, 88, 95

George Stibitz 173

Gillard, John 65

Glanz, James 177

Gödel, Kurt 297, 379, 386, 393, 396, 400, 461, 469

Goethe, Johann 426

Gooch, William 323

Goodell, William 141

Gordon, Thomas 30, 496

Gordon, William 53, 68

Gordon-Reed, Annette 81

Gorenstein, Daniel 487

Graham, Ronald 294

Grant, Anne 373

Great Seal of the United States 512-513

Greeks 8, 19, 22-23, 26-27, 60, 244, 293, 313, 317, 338, 345, 363, 370, 381-382, 386, 406-409, 415, 431, 481-482, 506, 514

Greenleaf, Richard 156

Grew, Joseph 114

Gribbin, John 412

Grigsby, Hugh 59

Griswold vs Connecticut 206

Grofman, Bernard 196

Grotius, Hugo 14, 30, 133, 302

Guthrie, W. K. C. 386

Hall, Aaron 520

Hall, Francis 77

Hallowell, A. Irving 373

Hamilton, Alexander 15, 19-21, 40, 97, 123, 131, 146-147, 153-154, 159, 165, 187, 192, 207, 211, 217-218, 227, 251, 253, 268, 275, 277, 281, 284-285, 289, 361, 364-365, 367-369, 391, 405, 425, 453, 472, 474, 481, 483, 507

Hammond, Isaac 54

Hammurabi 170, 271, 503

Hancock, John 48, 133, 218

Hansen, Morgans 481

Haraszti, Zoltán 394

Hardy, Godfrey 304-305, 378, 539

Harrington, James 11, 30-31, 44, 138, 158-159, 163, 193, 362, 393, 401, 451, 483, 491

Harrington, R. Ward 455

Hart, Levi 52, 64

Hartley, Thomas 147, 208

Hegel, Georg 173-174, 415

Heisenberg, Elizabeth 378

Heisenberg, Werner 378

Hempel, Carl 255

Hendrick, Caesar 156

Henig, William 99

Henry, Patrick 58-59, 62, 132, 208, 373

Hermite, Charles 386, 393, 396

Herodotus 345, 350, 370, 407, 428

Hewatt, Alexander 82

Hichborn, Benjamin 285

Hippel, Theodore Gottlieb von 473

Hippocrates 342

Hitchcock, Enos 202, 521

Hitchcock, Gad 9, 29, 39, 226, 328, 483

Hitler, Adolf 2, 90, 105, 108, 117, 222, 277, 312, 314, 326, 400-401, 423, 472, 474, 478

Hoare, Prince 139-140

Hobbes, Thomas 14, 30, 34, 83, 135, 193-195, 208, 221, 239, 429, 439

Hobson, John 311

Hochhuth, Rolf 101

Hoffman, Banesh 412

Hoffman, Paul 329

Hofstadter, Douglas 438, 459

Holton, Gerald 388, 439, 465

Homer 7, 326, 407

honest economy 243-244, 248, 260-261, 266, 271, 276, 357

Hopkins, Samuel (1693-1755) 475

Hopkins, Samuel (1721-1803) 37, 55

Horne, Alistair 115

Hosack, David 515

Höss, Rudolf 470-471

Howard, Simeon 226, 306, 515

Hubbard, Jame 82-85, 87, 94, 325

human flourishing 23-25, 46, 85, 153, 162, 179, 224-225, 289, 310, 312, 314, 320, 338-340, 350, 355, 401, 414, 420, 429.-430, 439, 454, 463, 504, 508, 514, 518

humanities 310, 317-318, 322, 422, 478

Hume, David 15, 24, 30, 37, 64, 85, 165, 226, 253, 276, 285, 292, 303, 365, 367-369, 385, 443, 497

Humphrey, Edward 70

Hutcheson, Francis 16, 30, 33, 85

Hutchinson, Thomas 53

Hyperides 481

hypocrisy 48, 58-59, 62, 104, 121, 129, 140, 142, 226, 484

Imlay, Gilbert 74, 79

individual happiness 195, 332, 339

Infeld, Leopold 383

informed values 160, 163, 170, 180, 183, 190, 193, 195, 211, 213, 215, 217-219, 230, 232, 271, 274-275, 332, 350, 356, 358, 375, 383, 402-405, 415, 440, 446, 453, 492

Inge, Francis 90

Intelligence, distributive 201, 231

Isocrates 23, 224, 227, 363, 471, 491, 513

Jackson, Luther 99

Jackson, Robert 108, 152

James I 9

Jauch, J.M. 438

Jay, John 1, 7, 21, 73, 121-122, 131, 165, 192, 424, 441, 495, 507, 512, 515

Jefferson, Thomas 1-2, 4, 7, 9, 12-13,

15, 18, 22, 24-25, 27, 32, 35-38, 41, 43, 47, 62, 68-99, 101-102, 104, 109-110, 112, 122, 128-129, 131, 134-135, 138-139, 142-143, 146-147, 151, 154, 156, 161-162, 166, 175, 181-182, 185, 187-188, 190, 192, 195-196, 202-206, 208-209, 211, 218, 221-222, 226-227, 232, 235-236, 243, 262-263, 273, 277-278, 280, 283, 285, 287, 292-293, 302, 311-316, 323-327, 333, 352, 354, 360, 362, 365-366, 371-375, 383, 385, 391-393, 395-396, 399-401, 405, 410, 414-417, 421-422, 428, 441, 443, 448-450, 452, 455, 462, 466-467, 473-474, 482-483, 485, 487, 491, 496-497, 500, 503, 505, 507, 511, 516-520

Jespersen, Otto 320

Jesus 7-8, 18, 27, 41, 59, 139, 343, 393, 395, 397, 409, 456-457, 466-467, 488, 496

Jeter, Mildred 91

Jews 9, 10-11, 18, 76, 101, 106, 109, 113, 134-135, 139, 393-395, 401, 442, 455, 468, 470-471, 474

Jim Crow 122, 260, 331

Jobs, Steven 211

Johnson, Samuel 37, 60, 112

Johnson, William 192-193

Johnston, James 28, 55, 57, 100

Jones, Ernest 427, 457, 460

Judaism 8, 393, 431, 468-469, 488

Judson, Horace 377-378

justice, distributive 348, 352, 356-358, 375

Kames, Lord 30, 425

Kant, Immanuel 296, 419, 469-477

Kaplan, Sidney 74, 156

Kasparov, Garry 335, 509

Kaufmann, Walter 396

Kelso, William 85

Kemeys, John 75

Kennedy, John 499

Kenrick, William 13

Kepler, Johannes 21, 211-212, 254-255, 314, 379, 384-390, 393, 396, 400, 403-405, 417, 421, 429, 435-437, 439, 442, 452-453, 465, 467, 483

Ketcham, Ralph 96, 124

Keynes, John 277

King, Martin 104

King, Rodney 184

Kirkwood, R. Cork 113

Kleene, Stephen 297, 304-305, 461

Klinghoffer, Judith 371

Koestler, Arthur 388

Kolyma 289

Koppes, Clayton 110

Koyre, Alexander 388

Kudirka, Simas 118-119

Kuran, Timur 176

Kurtz, Paul 396-397

La Boétie, Estienne de 253

La Rochefoucauld, François, duc de, 74, 129

La Rochefoucauld-Liancourt, François-Alexandre-Frédéric, duc de 74

Lafayette, Marquis de 65

Land, Edwin 211

Langdon, Langdon 10, 17

Lee, Arthur 51

Lee, Richard 35

Lee, Robert 98

Lee, Thomas 49

Leibniz, Gottfried 181, 301, 329, 438, 512

Leighton, Robert 486

Leland, John 143, 302, 394-395, 455-456

Leonardo, da Vinci 244, 409, 428

Lessing, Gotthold 287

Levy, Stephen 195, 252

liberal arts 259, 308-312, 321-324, 327-328, 330, 333, 335, 337-338,

340-341, 343-344, 393, 405, 411, 415, 479, 495

libertarianism 46, 279

Liles, George 465

Lincoln, Abraham 25, 71, 87, 126, 182, 226, 282, 367, 398, 430, 450, 481, 521-522

Linn, William 74

Lipit Ishtar 170

Livy 393

Locke, John 8, 7, 14, 17-18, 20, 30-32, 34-44, 46, 68, 76, 109, 132, 135-136, 140, 159, 175, 195, 203, 209, 218, 227, 245, 287-290, 302, 305, 309-312, 315, 319, 327, 337, 339-340, 363, 366, 372, 374, 391, 393, 405, 409-410, 422, 435, 440-441, 448, 451-453, 455, 464, 471, 500, 514, 521

Loewen, James 320

Logan, George 382

Long, Edward 75

Lorentz, H. A. 385

Lorenz, Eward 428

Louden, Robert, 472

Loving, Richard 91

Lublin, Joanne 349

Luther, Martin 9, 29, 292-293, 394

Lycophron 12

Lysias 19

MacDonogh, George 117

Machiavelli, Niccolò 17, 30, 44, 157, 368, 496

MacMaster, Richard 51

Macmillan, Harold 108, 114

Madison, James 4, 15, 18, 21, 26, 35, 39-40, 43-44, 46-47, 86, 88, 97-99, 101, 121, 124-131, 134, 139, 142, 144-145, 147, 149-151, 158-159, 161, 164-165, 183, 195-196, 203-205, 211, 219-222, 228, 236, 263-264, 269, 277, 280, 283-284, 289-290, 306, 315, 324-325, 327, 361, 363, 365, 367, 370,

392, 395, 399, 401-402, 405, 410, 414, 416, 420-421, 428, 441, 448, 462, 471, 481, 483, 489-493, 498, 502, 507, 511, 516

Maidment, K. J. 481

Mandelbrot, Benoit 348-349, 392, 400, 419

Mandeville, Bernard 37, 289-290

Mann, Charles 414

Manuel, Frank 389

Mao, Zedong 279, 312, 423

Marchant, Jo 406

Marcus Aurelius 190

Marshall, George , 131, 143, 373

Marshall, John 112-114, 118

Martin, Luther 121-122

Martin, Mike 60

Marx, Karl 2, 41, 279, 400, 457-461, 478

Mason, George 13, 26, 33-34, 37, 49, 67, 84, 139, 160, 290, 361, 441, 456, 471, 496, 503

Mason, John 221

mathematical logic 161, 174, 304, 310, 399, 459, 479

mathematics 3-4, 22, 48, 90, 179, 196-197, 214, 224, 244-247, 263, 297-298, 304, 308, 310, 344, 377-379, 386-387, 393, 396, 400, 403, 405, 409-410, 414-415, 418, 420, 436-437, 440-442, 444-445, 447, 453-456, 461, 467-469, 486-487, 503, 517

Matthewson, Tim 69

Maxwell, C, Mervyn 394

Maxwell, James 465

Mayer, Lewis B. 484-485

Mayhew, Jonathan 389, 411, 47

McGuire, James 8, 494

McLaughlin, Brian 60

McLaughlin, Kathleen 107

McNarney, Joseph 115

Meade, Robert 58

Medawar, Peter 431
Mellen, John 299, 328, 413
Melville, Herman 424
Merrill, Samuel 215
metajuries 167-169, 181-182, 213, 228, 491
metaphysics/ metaphysical 8, 291, 386-387, 418-422, 423, 435, 438-442, 443-444, 449-52, 454, 459, 463-464, 494
Methodists 54
M'Henry, James 70
Mill, John 287, 309, 478
Miller, Helen 50
Miller, John 102
Milton, John 30, 133, 203, 326, 463, 471, 500
Minsky, Marvin 314
monarch/ monarchy 10, 40, 134, 195, 316, 345, 453, 471-473, 475, 481
monopoly 112, 253, 264, 273, 275, 510
Montesquieu, Baron de 14, 18, 30, 51, 173, 187, 365, 483, 496
Moore, Clement 74
Moore, George 53
Moore, Jason 109, 117
Moore, Wayne 248
moral courage 65, 76, 98, 129, 291, 309, 315-316, 326, 345
moral cowardice 68, 94, 142, 330
moral freedom 29, 39, 195, 327-330, 412, 492
moral geometry 416
moral prosperity 263, 402-403, 522
Morgan, Richard 508
Morgenstern, Oskar 240, 301, 303
Morison, Samuel 91
Morris, Gouverneur 15, 127, 131-132, 365, 367, 373, 425, 505-507, 515
Morris, Robert 63, 66
Morton, Louis 99

Mott, Lucretia 364
mulattos 12, 50, 72, 80, 323-324
Murray, Judith 367, 369
Musonius Rufus, Caius 81
Nash, Gary 65
natural rights 14, 17, 43, 49, 52, 55, 67, 83, 86, 96, 98, 109, 122, 127, 136, 147, 149, 152, 205, 208, 283, 363-364, 394, 450, 475
Nature's God 14, 17, 49, 88, 91, 94, 122, 139-140, 209, 299, 385, 436, 439, 465-46, 470, 494
negroes 31, 70, 49-51, 55, 63-65, 69-75, 78, 81-82, 85, 88-90, 92, 97-98 100, 102, 112, 121, 124, 127, 131-132, 142, 156, 205, 324, 472, 481, 519, 527-528, 531-533, 533, 535, 537, 541, 547, 550, 554, 556
Nelson, Harry 408
Nelson, William 98
Nelson, William Edward 156
Newbeck, Phyl 92
Newton/ Newtonian 4, 21, 79-80, 175, 254-255, 301, 379, 384-385, 388-389, 391-393, 396, 400, 403, 405, 419, 429, 435-437, 439, 442, 447-448, 452-453, 465, 467, 483, 502, 534, 546, 549, 557
Nicolaevsky, Boris 117
Nietzsche, Fredrich 111, 286, 423, 427, 492
Niles, Hezekiah 21, 411, 521
Niles, Nathaniel 10, 52
Ninth Amendment 133, 146, 150-155, 206-210, 231, 281, 300, 370, 462, 495, 498
Nips, Jack (pseudonym) 302
Noah 16
Noah, Mordecai 395
Noble, Oliver 9
Noonan, John 143
Notes on the State of Virginia 73-75, 77, 79-80, 91, 135

Nuremberg 108, 114, 152, 472

Ohanian, Hans 384

Oldschool, Oliver 75

Onishi, Norimitsu 321

orangutan 74-76, 431, 479

Othello 54

Otis, James 51, 136, 364, 504

Owen, Guillermo 196

Page, John 138

Paige, Lucius 550

Paine, Thomas 11, 21, 23, 31, 46, 49, 52, 59, 86, 110, 162, 225, 277, 282, 362, 369, 374, 389, 394, 424, 472-473, 489-490, 493, 504-505, 514, 519

Palmer, Elihu 336, 513

Panofsky, Erwin 387

Parker, Issac 398

Parker, Jonathan 56

Paroush, Jocob 196

Parrish, John 141, 513

Parsons, Theophilus 17, 24, 192, 226, 366

Pascal, Blaise 329, 428

Patterson, Bennett 146

Patterson, Richard 227, 512-513

Patterson, Samuel 67

Pauli, Wolfgang 388

Payson, Phillips 4, 306, 328

Pennington, James 86

Penrose, Roger 378

Penzias, Arno 435, 437

perfecting the pursuit of happiness 195, 263, 283, 315, 337, 358, 501, 503

perfectionist respect 385-386, 388-390, 397, 402, 404, 406, 413, 417, 421-422, 431, 433

Perot, Ross 164

Perry, William 13, 94

Peterson, Christopher 311

Philadelphia freedom 24, 345

Phocion (pseudonym) 482

Piattelli-Palmarini, Massimo 222

Pico della Mirandola, Giovanni 288

Pinkney, William 56

Planck, Max 411

Plato 2, 7, 12, 20, 26-27, 30, 162, 168, 173, 183, 189, 252, 286, 296, 314, 319, 333, 378, 388, 400, 407, 409, 411, 423, 431, 439, 464, 502

Pleasants, Robert 63, 68, 129

Pliny [the Younger] 367

Plutarch 30, 224, 350, 407-408, 411

Poincaré, Henri 130, 378

Pol Pot 312

Polybius 30, 312, 393

Pope, Alexander 235

Porter, David 71

posterity 8, 47, 49-50, 53-54, 57, 80, 95, 98, 121, 128, 132, 141, 276, 278, 367, 369-370, 397, 477, 494, 507, 511, 515, 522

Preamble to the U. S. Constitution 121, 132, 138, 494-495, 503

prescriptive metaphysics 419-420

Price, Richard 59, 513

Priestley, Joseph 399, 508

Pritchard, James 494

property 33, 36, 41-44, 49-50, 53, 55, 58, 63, 71, 74, 80, 85, 99, 119, 123, 125-126, 128-130, 140, 145-146, 155, 171, 196, 203, 219, 236, 251, 260, 262-263, 266, 268-269, 272, 275, 281-285, 295, 303-304, 348, 350, 360-366, 369, 371-372, 374, 426, 461, 493

property in men 125, 128, 130, 140, 281, 284

proslavery interpretation of the Constitution 130, 141, 143, 145, 327

Protagoras 20

Protestant/ protestantism 8, 10, 27, 29, 139, 293-294, 393

public happiness 25, 40, 44, 159, 162, 164, 169, 176-179, 191, 195, 197-198,

201, 210, 215, 218, 224-225, 228, 250,
262-263, 270, 274, 284-285, 288,
290-291, 308-309, 317, 327, 339-340,
344, 351, 353, 356, 358, 368, 370,
380, 398, 422, 429, 439, 449, 473,
479, 490, 492, 501-502, 511, 514
Publius (pseudonym) 134, 361,
Pufendorf, Samuel 30, 360
pursuit of happiness 1, 23-26, 32,
36-40, 44, 47, 50, 53, 55, 57, 59-60,
78, 116, 134, 142, 180, 201, 206, 230,
236, 278, 283, 297, 301, 315, 319,
322, 327, 334, 336-337, 343, 350-351,
355, 358, 365, 376, 391, 403, 414-415,
423, 430, 446, 493, 501, 503-504, 521
Pythagoras/ Pythagorean 3, 221, 244-
245, 314, 320, 386, 404, 442
Quakers 64, 66-67,, 72, 127, 142, 349
racism/ racist 76, 80, 83, 90, 92, 104,
122, 142-143, 184, 221, 315, 318-319,
327, 416, 472-473
radioactive money 255
Ramachandran, V. S. 372
Ramsay, David 5, 11, 21, 46, 73, 217,
220, 479, 489, 505, 507, 515, 520
Randolph, Beverly 101
Randolph, Edmund 123-124, 148
Randolph, Richard 88
random money 254-255, 260
rational money 247-250, 255, 257,
264, 286
Rauschning, Hermann 90
Ravitch, Diane 320
Raynal, Abbé 508
Reese, Thomas 27, 40, 503
Reid, Constance 384
Reid, Thomas 20, 268
representative democracy 212, 331, 482
republic 10, 12, 27, 122, 124, 134,
137, 141-142, 145, 226, 235, 251-252,
270, 283, 330, 371, 479, 482, 497, 501
republican 4, 10-11, 17, 22, 24, 27-30,

41, 63, 95, 102, 122-124, 126-130,
134-135, 137-146, 148, 159, 167,
172-174, 183, 185, 196, 227, 284-285,
289-290, 316, 319, 326-327, 343, 355,
369, 371-372, 374, 383, 389-390, 392,
399, 414, 422, 425, 434, 441-442, 449,
482-483, 497, 507, 512
responsible decisions 160, 163,
182-183, 224, 308, 323
retributive justice 348, 352-355, 357-
358
Rice, David 57, 69, 80
Riefenstahl, Leni 326
Robinson, Abraham 418, 503
Roe v. Wade 209
Roosevelt, Franklin 108-110, 112-114,
117-118, 277, 327
Rorty, Amélie 60
Rousseau, Jean-Jacques 173, 188
Ruse, Michael 553
Rush, Benjamin 29, 51, 70-72, 79, 85,
94, 131, 137, 140, 220, 289, 308, 358,
383, 394, 411, 413-414, 462, 473,
520-521
Rushton, Edward 63, 74
Ruskin, John 235
Russell, Bertrand 397, 413, 444, 512
Russell, John 99
Rutherford, Samuel 30
Rutledge, John 96
Saari, Donald 215
Saint-Just, Louis Antoine Léon de 145
St. Paul 8-9, 21, 28-29, 466
Sally Tickle (pseudonym) 366, 369
Samuelson, Paul 172
Sanders, James 113
Sandler, S. Gerald 36
Sandoz, Ellis 364
Sands, Mathew 486
Santayana, George 415
Sarsfield, Count 516
Sauter, Mark 113

Schiller, Friedrich 379, 392

Schmidt, Fredrika 28

Schmohl, Johann 507

Schopenhauer, Arthur 411-412, 427

Schröder, Hannelore 473

Schrödinger, Erwin 333

Schuh, Fred 329

Schutz, John 293, 483

Schweninger, Loren 57

Seabrook, John 406, 555

self-belittlement 426-434

self-deceit 60, 65-66, 76, 83, 87,
93-94, 113, 128-129, 140, 142, 162,
221-222, 224, 292, 326

self-deception 60-64, 67, 73, 76, 81,
90, 103, 125, 128, 187, 191, 227, 270,
327, 345, 484

self-reference 442, 459, 576

Seligman, Martin 311

Sen, Amartya 172

Seneca 338, 364, 381, 506

sexism 320-321, 416

Shakespeare, William 94, 305, 321,
423, 428-429

Sharp, Granville 140

Shelley, Percy 313

Shostakovich, Dmitri 314

Shulgi 170

Shute, Daniel 10, 416

Sidney, Algernon 11, 30-31, 138, 483,
496

slave revolts 46-47, 69, 89, 486

slave trade 64, 66, 91, 97, 123, 127,
143

slavery 12, 14, 27-28, 31, 46-47,
50-58, 61, 63-64, 66-69, 74-75, 78,
80-99, 101-104, 111, 115, 119,
122-124, 126-145, 156, 171, 173, 181,
204-206, 221, 226, 237, 260, 280, 289,
291, 315, 322, 325-326, 328, 330-331,
340, 406-407, 423, 468, 484, 487, 506,
516, 519

slaves to themselves 125, 290, 328,
346

Smith, Adam 60, 224, 263, 289, 353,
375, 506

Smith, Paul 49

Smith, Samuel 75, 79

Smith, William 41

social justice 348-351, 358, 392

socialism 278-280

Socrates 7, 20, 60, 162, 165, 284, 286,
333, 342, 407

Solomonoff, Ray 447

Solzhenitsyn, Aleksandr 117, 315, 325

Sophocles 136, 350, 423

soul-searching 20, 113, 162, 180. 194,
203, 206, 220, 225, 233, 310, 319,
326, 341, 345-346, 441, 450, 466, 479,
496, 499, 501, 507

Soviet refugees 105, 110, 113, 117,
192, 227, 315, 340

Soviet Union 105-108, 111, 113,
115-117, 192, 312, 353

Spencer, Joel 294

spirit of 1776 1, 3-4, 30, 73, 118, 121,
130, 143-146, 188, 209, 270, 303, 329,
383, 404, 440, 471, 480, 487, 496,
500, 502, 514, 517-518, 520-521

Spooner, Lysander 141

Stalin, Joseph 105, 107-114, 117-119,
279, 312, 314, 326, 423, 478, 527

Stanton, Elizabeth 364

Stanton, Lucia 74

state of nature 32, 41, 50, 208-209,
289, 364, 373-374

Stedman, John 79

Steele, Richard 426

Stephens, Alexander 89

Stern, Nancy 173

Stern, Philip 484

Sterne, Lawrence 37, 60, 87

Stettinius, Edward 114, 118

Stibitz, George 173

Stiefel, Tina 409
Stiles, Esra 131, 398
Stockdale, Jim 337-338
Stowe, Harriot 315, 325
Strabo 12, 393
Suber, Peter 459
subhonest economy 262, 329
Suetonius 233
Sullivan, James 122, 372
Supreme Court 11, 92, 130, 141, 143,
146, 152, 154, 156, 206, 208, 214,
441, 490, 498
Sutcliff, Robert 47, 100
Swade, Doron 202
Tacitus 140, 370, 477, 483
Taney, Roger 57-58, 142
Tarski, Alfred 461
Tenth Amendment 150, 152, 206-207,
510
Tertullian 383, 464
Thacher, Samuel 5
The Deputy 101
Thomsen, Dietrick 377
Thorpe, Francis 14, 46, 140, 496
Thucydides 157, 191, 223, 285, 338,
356, 361-362
Tiffany, Joel 141
Tindal, Matthew 33
Todhunter, I. 329
Tolstoy, Leo 103, 339
Tolstoy, Nikolai 108-109, 112
Torrey, Jesse 123-124
totalitarianism/ totalitarian 2, 46-47,
116, 230, 277-278, 471-473, 476, 478
Trenchard, John 30, 496
Truman 107-108, 112, 118, 327
Trumbull, John 374
Tucker John 9, 64
Tullock, Gordon 173
Turgot, Anne-Robert-Jacques 508
Turner, Charles 9, 28
Turner, Nat 47

Twelve Angry Men 197
Tyldesley, Joyce 370
Tyler, Moses 59
unalienable/ rights/ duties/ arbitrariness
13-16, 22, 25, 32, 53-55, 78, 97, 114,
118, 122, 131, 133-134, 138-139, 151,
171, 203, 216, 278, 297, 323, 370, 494
United States 9, 32, 38, 43, 46, 63, 69,
91-93, 95, 106-108, 110-119, 121,
123-124, 127, 132-133, 140-141, 144,
150, 206-207, 225-226, 231, 235, 250,
256, 278, 306, 322, 331, 363, 371-372,
393-394, 411, 443, 466, 471, 482, 490,
494, 505, 507-515, 520-521
United States v. Darby 206
Ur-Nammu 170
Van Newenhizen, Jill 215
Vanderbilt, William 253
Villaseñor, Victor 323
Virginia Committee of Correspondence
135
Virginia Declaration of Rights 13, 26,
37, 49, 139, 290, 456, 496
Voltaire, François Marie Arouet de 79,
394, 448
von Ahn, Luis 449
von Neuman, John 303
voting paradox 169
Walker, David 90-91, 104
wards 161, 175, 181, 185, 205, 208,
232, 262, 383, 449, 518, 520
Washington D. C./ Federal City 66, 73,
80, 97, 102, 114, 123-124, 130, 142
Washington, George 13, 21, 36, 47, 62-
69, 79, 81, 93-94, 96, 98-99, 101-102,
104-105, 113, 129, 141-143, 146-147,
165, 186-187, 209, 211, 325, 327, 336,
370, 374-375, 393-394, 396-399,
410-411, 413-414, 422, 424, 442, 505,
507, 513, 516, 522
Webster, Noah 1-2, 40, 50, 131, 147,
153-154, 311, 362, 399, 410, 482, 504,

519, 521
Weinberg, Steven 427
West, Benjamin 99
West, Samuel 9, 35, 226, 328
Weyl, Hermann 386, 396, 436, 438
Wheatley, Phillis 79
White, Michael 412
whites 47-51, 54, 57, 69-70, 72-75, 79, 81, 89, 90, 92-93, 96, 99-103, 122, 124-125, 131, 135, 137, 140, 142, 144, 152, 192, 203, 205, 211, 324, 360, 372-373, 413, 415
Whiting, William 14
Whitman, Walt 440
Whitrow, Gerald 378
Wiecek, William 130
Wigner, Eugene 436, 438, 446
Williams, Roger 17, 30
Williams, Samuel 29, 413
Wilson, Arthur 508
Wilson, James 4, 7, 11, 21, 23, 32, 38-39, 41, 44, 46-47, 95, 109, 121, 147, 150, 162, 164-165, 188, 192, 195, 199, 207, 211, 220-221, 226, 231, 235, 283, 287-288, 333, 340, 353, 367, 374, 391-392, 400-401, 405, 413, 435, 437, 439, 448, 453, 462-463, 471, 479, 482-483, 489, 491-492, 496, 500-501, 503-504, 506-508, 514, 520-521
Wilson, Robert 435, 437
Winthrop, James 482
Wirt, William 373
Wise, John 17, 25
Witherspoon, John 426
Wolff, Geoffrey 318
Wolff, Robert 172
Wollaston, William 37
Wood, James 101
Woods, Leonard 285
Woolf, Harry 412, 446
Wortman, Tunis 280
Wright, Martha 364

Wright, Orville 175
Wright, Wilber 175
WuDunn, Sheryl 349
X (pseudonym) 385
Xenophon 337-338, 407
Yalta 105, 113-115
Yeats, William 426
Yeomanry of Massachusetts 63
Zwelling, Shomer 99